Readings in Arkansas Politics and Government

2ND EDITION

EDITED BY

KIM U. HOFFMAN
JANINE A. PARRY
CATHERINE C. REESE

The University of Arkansas Press
Fayetteville
2019

ISBN: 978-1-68226-123-1
eISBN: 978-1-61075-682-2

DOI: https://doi.org/10.34053/parry2019.riapag2

23 22 21 20 19   5 4 3 2 1

Designed by Liz Lester

♾ The paper used in this publication meets the minimum
requirements of the American National Standard for
Permanence of Paper for Printed Library Materials Z39.48–1984.

Library of Congress Control Number: 2019947839

Supported in part by

UNIVERSITY OF ARKANSAS

DIANE D. BLAIR CENTER
of Southern Politics & Society

For our colleagues, with gratitude;
and for our families, with love.

CONTENTS

PART III
Public Policy Conflicts
in Arkansas Politics and Government

ACKNOWLEDGMENTS

Every book is the product of the work of many more people than those whose names appear on the cover. In the case of this edited volume, the number of people deserving of thanks is likely in the hundreds. In the interest of space, we first extend our gratitude to the writers and scholars who, together with their heirs and publishers, have made such a fine collection of work available to us. Their contributions (as well as the dozens more we could have included) have proven invaluable to our own understanding of, and appreciation for, Arkansas politics and government. We suspect that our students and the many political hobbyists populating the state, will be equally grateful to have this collection for their backpacks and bookshelves.

Particularly deserving of our thanks are Lauren Husband and Meredith Paige Brady with the political science department at the University of Arkansas, as well as David Scott Cunningham, Jenny Vos, and Molly Rector at the UA Press for their patient, capable assistance. Finally, we thank our families for their patience, as well as their encouragement and understanding.

INTRODUCTION

The editors of this new edition are long-time teachers, scholars, and followers of state government and politics. Our collective passion for Arkansas politics and government made choosing the most interesting and significant topics for this book a truly gratifying endeavor. We hope this edited work will be used by students in the classroom and others who want to know more about Arkansas politics, political actors, and policies, both past and present. Since the first edition some ten years ago, there have been significant political changes in Arkansas. Once a Democratic stronghold, Arkansas state government today is squarely in the hands of the Republican Party. Most astonishingly, this total change in party dominance occurred over a short period of time. This recent political transformation was part of the motivation to revise the first edition.

This collection draws upon the efforts of historians, lawyers, journalists, public administrators, and political scientists in order to paint a rich picture of Arkansas politics and governance from varying viewpoints and perspectives. This new edition would not be possible if it were not for the efforts of others—both past and present—to write scholarly accounts of Arkansas politics and government. Our selections are drawn from the *Arkansas Historical Quarterly* at the University of Arkansas; the *Midsouth Political Science Review*, a journal of the Arkansas Political Science Association and other scholarly journals from that field; law reviews; and books. All of our selections have been subject to peer review at some level; indeed, most have been published previously in blind-peer-reviewed academic journals.

The book is divided into three sections. The first section examines the state's historical foundations and political context with a particular focus on several conflicts central to the state's development: racial tensions, rigid social values, and political corruption. This section also looks at past political patterns and behaviors in the Arkansas electorate as well as analyzing the significant, recent transformation in Arkansas's political landscape.

The second section investigates the structure and operation of Arkansas's policymaking institutions, including chapters on the impact of term limits in the state legislature; changes to the Arkansas court system and a discussion of judicial selection methods; an analysis of the strength of political party organizations in the state; and a description of the many unique aspects of the budget process in Arkansas. This section further examines several of the most influential political figures of the twentieth century, including governors Faubus, Rockefeller, Bumpers, Pryor, and Clinton.

The final section emphasizes several key policy issues and their implementation in Arkansas, including racial integration, gender equality, the struggle to improve public education, obstacles encountered in a recent round of "welfare reform," and the impact of alcohol prohibition policies on public safety in Arkansas counties.

For the editors, selecting these chapters for the new edition was a labor of love; we had the good fortune to read many excellent pieces. Considered independently, each of the twenty-one chapters is noteworthy and thought-provoking. Taken together, the collection lays a firm foundation for a real understanding of Arkansas government and politics, past and present. We hope readers of this new edition come away with a deeper appreciation for what has changed in Arkansas politics since the mid-twentieth century as well as what has not; for the things we assume "everyone knows" and yet perhaps many do not; and for what is predictable about Arkansas politics and what, wonderfully, is not. Ultimately, we hope all—but most especially our students—will come away with a better understanding of the state in which they reside and a willingness to participate in, even to shape, Arkansas's political future.

I

Foundations and Context in Arkansas Politics and Government

CHAPTER I

The Antievolution Law

Church and State in Arkansas

CAL LEDBETTER JR.

One of the state's most respected intellectuals and political activists, Cal Ledbetter provides us with an account of a policy dispute that stretches back nearly a century. Although both the study and the specific policy details are dated, the issues raised are as salient today as they ever were in that Arkansas lawmakers continue to find themselves at frequent odds with national laws and rulings. The particular issue addressed here is the constitutionality of the state's anti-evolution law, approved by the voters as Initiated Act No. 1 in 1928, a measure that outlawed the teaching in any Arkansas public school or public institution of higher learning of the theory that "mankind ascended or descended from a lower order of animal." The issue returned as a high-profile controversy almost forty years after its enactment when the law was successfully challenged in the courts on the grounds that it violated the Establishment Clause of the 1st Amendment to the US Constitution [Epperson v. Arkansas (1968)]. Interestingly, Epperson did not settle the conflict in Arkansas over the teaching of Darwin's theory, as the legislature passed, and Gov. Frank White signed into law, another "monkey law" only months after Professor Ledbetter's study was first published. That law also was struck down by the federal courts [McLean v. Arkansas (1982)].

Some three years before the United States Supreme Court struck down the Arkansas Antievolution Law as unconstitutional,[1] Harry Pearson, a reporter for the Pine Bluff *Commercial*, had this to say about that particular law:

Originally published in *Arkansas Historical Quarterly* 38 (Winter 1979): 299–327. Reprinted with permission. DOI: https://doi.org/10.34053/parry2019.riapag2.1

> There is a law in Arkansas that forbids the teaching of the theory
> of evolution in the public schools. It is an unenforceable law; it is a
> disregarded law, but its very existence in the Arkansas statute books
> is a symbol. To the fundamentalist it is a symbol that the state
> tacitly endorses his concept of religion. To the liberal it is a symbol
> of darkness and witches and monkey trials. To the professional
> educator . . . it is an affront to the principle of academic freedom.[2]

The anti-evolution law in Arkansas has managed to generate intense emotions long after the passing of the historical period that prompted its adoption. In 1959, a state representative from Pulaski County, at the request of
a young high school student, introduced a bill to repeal the antievolution
law.[3] The bill was withdrawn three days later[4] after unexpected opposition
developed, and the sponsor of the repealing legislation stated that "It now
appears to me that the Majority of the people of my county do not wish to
grant the academic freedom these young people requested."[5] On June 28,
1966, sixteen hundred people attended a meeting in Little Rock that lasted
three and a half hours and featured a general debate on the subject of evolution.[6] One reason for this article is to explore the causes and consequences
of these still-strong feelings produced by a law passed a half century ago.

It is also interesting to look at Arkansas as a case study of the only state
to pass an anti-evolution law by popular vote. This action came at a time
when the national movement to embody anti-evolution sentiment in law
had probably peaked. Nevertheless, when an initiated act is passed that can
only be changed by a two-thirds vote of the legislature,[7] it poses serious
problems in strategy for those who may wish to challenge the protection
that a popularly-passed law can give to theological position. Commenting
on this problem, John T. Scopes, an expert in these matters, said that once
such a law gets on the books it is next to impossible to change because "no
politician is going to go out on a limb and try to repeal it."[8] The question
of what strategy was pursued to get the law removed from the books, and
why, will be another focus of the article.

Although the United States Supreme Court decision striking down the
Arkansas Antievolution law was unanimous, there were three concurring
opinions. Some members of the United States Supreme Court also seemed
quite critical of the Arkansas Supreme Court for not disposing of the case
adequately, and, consequently, forcing the nation's highest court to choose
between the conflicting legal values of a state's power over curriculum and
an individual's right to freedom of speech and ideas and the guarantee that

church and state be kept separate. The legal questions raised by this case will be also explored.

It is hoped, too, that a study of the Arkansas Antievolution Law can produce insights into the strongly-held values that led to its passage, the problems faced in the implementation and repeal of such a law, and the legal consequences that arise when church and state are mixed.

Background

By the beginning of the twentieth century, urbanism, industrialization, and expanding education had begun to threaten the traditional values of rural and small town America. Many thought that traditional religious values were especially jeopardized by social gospelism, scholarly Biblical criticism, and the spread of the teaching of evolution through the nation's colleges. To counter these new trends, supporters of social and religious orthodoxy presented their views in a set of twelve pamphlets published during 1909–1912 and entitled *The Fundamentals: A Testimony to Truth*; hence the name "fundamentalists."[9]

To compensate for the ground lost in the colleges and to prevent the spread of the teaching of evolution to the more numerous students in high schools, state legislatures were approached by fundamentalists in the South and Middle West to outlaw the teaching of evolution in state-supported schools. A contributing factor to the urgency of this move was the realization that the number of high schools in the country had doubled between 1897 and 1912 and that a high school diploma was now becoming a prerequisite for success in life.[10]

Evolution seemed to incorporate all the evils, real or imaginary, against which the defenders of the social and religious status quo were battling. It threatened their religious viewpoint because one tenet of fundamentalism was an infallible Bible, literally interpreted,[11] and the logical corollary of that belief is that if any portion of the Bible is not literally true, none of it may be true. The teaching of evolution in the public schools undermined the values of their children, and hence, put the family as an institution in danger. Evolution was identified with science, science was identified with materialism, and materialism was seen as eating away the moral fabric of society, particularly in the 1920s.[12] To the fundamentalists, evolution became the hated symbol of all that was threatening in a modern and increasingly urban society, and their efforts to turn back the tide in the 1920s were focused on such projects as banning the teaching of evolution in the public schools, preserving prohibition, defeating Al Smith in 1928, and supporting William Jennings Bryan in his struggle to preserve traditional values in the Scopes trial and elsewhere. Perhaps the menace of evolution to the fundamentalists is best described by Bryan who said in 1924 that "All the ills from which America suffers can be traced back to the teaching of evolution. It would be better to destroy every other book ever written, and just save the first three verses of Genesis."[13]

William Jennings Bryan was the charismatic leader around whom the anti-evolution movement coalesced and it was not until he "entered the conflict in 1920 that the movement became one of national importance."[14] Support for the movement was strong in the Middle West, and, at least for a time, it probably also had "the active support and sympathy of the overwhelming majority of the Southern people."[15] One goal of the movement was to use this popular support to pressure state legislatures into passing anti-evolution laws and into becoming major instruments in the revolt against modernity.

Many different techniques were used to ban the teaching of evolution in the public schools from 1920 to about 1926. Three states (Arkansas, Mississippi, and Tennessee) passed specific statutes to accomplish this, either by action of the legislature or vote of the people.[16]

The Florida legislature by joint resolution condemned the teaching of evolution in the public schools and, in Oklahoma, the textbook law was amended to outlaw the teaching of evolution.[17]

In North Carolina and Texas, state boards with educational responsibilities banned textbooks that made reference to evolution.[18] The same result was accomplished by Louisiana by order of the state superintendent of education.[19] Nationwide, in the eight-year period from 1921 to 1929, thirty-seven anti-evolution bills, resolutions, and riders were introduced in twenty state legislatures.[20] In addition, "Informal restrictions through the censorship of textbooks by superintendents of education, local school boards, etc., were widely applied."[21]

The anti-evolution movement, despite its initial successes in the South from 1920 to 1925, experienced near disaster in July 1925. The unfavorable publicity that came from the Scopes trial that began on July 13, 1925, and the death of William Jennings Bryan two weeks later were two events that had a crippling effect on fundamentalism and the anti-evolution movement. The loss of Bryan was especially devastating not only because of his eloquence and charisma but also because he was the most important national figure associated with the anti-evolution cause. The necessity of defeating Al Smith in 1928 also diverted time and effort from the anti-evolution cause. By 1930, even though religious orthodoxy remained, the kind of fundamentalism that held anti-evolution as its central component had collapsed as an organized movement.[22] This made the Arkansas experience even more interesting since it came at a time when the anti-evolution movement was in decline.

The 1927 Legislative Attempt

As early as 1924 the Arkansas State Baptist Convention had officially gone on record as totally rejecting the theory of evolution.[23] By spring 1926, petitions began to circulate in several communities requesting that legislators enact a bill similar to the Tennessee Antievolution Law,[24] and by summer 1926 it was fairly clear that a bill would be introduced in the 1927 session.[25] The two individuals most identified with the bill to be proposed were State Representative Astor L. Rotenberry of Pulaski County and the Reverend Ben M. Bogard, pastor of the Antioch Missionary Baptist Church in Little Rock and chairman of the Antievolution Committee of the Arkansas Association of Missionary Baptist Churches, a group that had officially separated from the Arkansas State Baptist Convention in 1902 but still shared with the convention a common opposition to evolution.[26] Another strong supporter of an anti-evolution bill was the Reverend James Seth Compere, editor of the *Baptist Advance,* the official publication of the Arkansas Baptist State Convention. Compere not only contributed editorials to the cause but was instrumental in drafting and passing resolutions against evolution at Baptist state conventions from 1924 to 1927.

On December 19, 1926, Representative Rotenberry released his bill to the newspapers and asked for public comment on its provisions. The proposed bill did not contain references to the Biblical story in Genesis, but it did make it unlawful for the theory of evolution to be taught in the public schools or for a teacher or textbook commissioner to use or adopt any textbook that teaches that mankind descended from a lower species of animal. Penalty provisions included a fine not to exceed $1,000 and revocation of the license to teach.[27] Before the legislative session began, letters to the editor in the *Arkansas Gazette* dealing with the proposed new law developed both sides of the issue. Those favoring the proposed bill advanced the arguments that people who pay taxes to the public schools need to have a voice in what is taught there and that evolutionists may teach their doctrine but not in the public schools. Opponents stressed the difficulty of legislating against theories or doctrines, and one letter writer who opposed the Rotenberry bill hoped that Arkansas would not become "the laughing stock of the educated world by passing such a law."[28] Ministers were also divided in their comments. Dr. Hay Watson Smith, minister of the Second Presbyterian Church in Little Rock, quoted the scientist Luther Burbank to the effect that "Those who would legislate against the teaching of evolution should also legislate against gravity, electricity, and the unreasonable velocity of light"[29] while Calvin B. Waller, pastor of Little Rock's Second Baptist Church, said "There is no common ground of compromise between evolution and the Bible."[30]

On January 12, 1927, Representative Thomas P. Atkins of Prairie County introduced an anti-evolution bill (House Bill No. 4) on the first day of the 1927 session of the Arkansas legislature.[31] The Rotenberry bill was introduced the very next day, January 13, and became House Bill No. 34.[32] The major difference between the two bills was that the Atkins bill prohibited the teaching of any theory that conflicted with the Biblical story of creation[33] while the Rotenberry bill prohibited only the teaching that men descended from a lower order of animals.[34] At any rate, Atkins became a co-sponsor, along with four others, of the Rotenberry bill and apparently decided not to actively push his bill. The Rotenberry measure was referred to the House Education Committee on January 13, 1927.[35]

A hearing on the bill was set for the night of January 28, 1927, to begin at 7:30. The *Arkansas Democrat* was not pleased with what was about to take place and reported:

> Arkansas will take the stage in the "monkey business" entertainment that has been going the rounds in various states, Friday night when the house committee on education will hold a public hearing on Representative Rotenberry's antievolution measure. The meeting will be held in the house chamber at the state capitol, and the curtain will be raised promptly at 7:30 o'clock. There will be no preliminaries or orchestral numbers, the whole program being devoted to the drama itself.[36]

On the night of the hearing, the house galleries were packed and the meeting continued until 11:00. Eleven people testified for and against, with the proponents being led by the Reverend Ben M. Bogard and the major opponent being Hay Watson Smith, the Presbyterian minister. The committee adjourned without taking any action, but the chairman announced that it would meet again.[37] Another public meeting was scheduled for February 2, 1927, but interest was apparently waning. The crowd was not nearly as big, and only four of the thirteen committee members were present when the hearings opened, and one of these left before the hearings were finished.[38] Fourteen people testified, equally split between those for and against, and at the conclusion of the meeting, the chairman announced that no more open hearings would be held but that the committee would meet at a later date and prepare its report.[39]

Perhaps anticipating that the committee vote would be negative, Bogard had a circular placed on every legislator's desk on February 2, 1927. It began with the phrase "Fair Warning" and ended with the admonition that if the Rotenberry bill does not become law "the war has just started. We shall appeal to the people to make it an issue in every county for the next two years."[40] The circular was signed by Bogard as chairman of the Antievolution Committee of the Arkansas Association of Missionary Baptist Churches. The house responded by passing a resolution by a vote of forty-three to thirty-four stating that "We do condemn such methods endeavoring to coerce the passage of any bill whether we are for or against the proposed measure."[41] Bogard's reaction to the resolution was to thank the house members for the free publicity given to the anti-evolution law and to repeat his warning.[42]

The House Education Committee gave a "do not pass" recommendation to the Rotenberry bill on February 3, 1927.[43] Only seven of the thirteen members of the committee attended the meeting at which the vote was taken, and six of the seven who attended voted "no" and one voted "yes." The lone dissenter at the committee meeting was later joined by a second member who was not at the meeting in a minority report recommending that HB No. 34 "do not pass."[44] After an unsuccessful attempt by opponents to amend the bill to prohibit any library supported with tax funds to have on its shelves any books "relating to biology, anthropology or genetics, or any other phase of evolution,"[45] The measure was first made a special order of business on Monday, February 7, 1927.[46] A motion to table was defeated by a vote of thirty-eight in favor and fifty-three against, and the bill was then made a special order of business on Wednesday, February 9, 1927, at 2:00 p.m.[47]

Some confusion still lingers as to the outcome of the vote on that Wednesday afternoon in February 1927. Debate lasted about three hours with Representative Harney M. McGehee from Crawford County arguing for the bill because "the legislature is the guardian of the state's children and has a right to say what shall be taught in the public schools"[48] and Representative H. Jordan Monk of Jefferson County arguing against the measure because "the bill strikes at the heart of freedom of thought and speech."[49] Although the first roll call seemed to indicate that the bill had been defeated by one vote, some quick maneuvering switched two no votes, those of Arthur J. Jones of Pulaski County and W. E. Spencer of Drew County, to the affirmative column so that the final official total showed that the bill passed by a vote of fifty-one to forty-six with three absent and not voting.[50]

The bill went to the senate in the late afternoon of February 9, 1927, and as soon as the bill was read a second time there on February 10, it was tabled by an overwhelming voice vote.[51] The entire process took less than fifteen minutes.[52] On February 15, 1927, an attempt was made in the senate to take the measure from the table, but after it was discovered that the bill had been returned to the house, another motion was made to return the bill so that the senate could still take some action on it. This attempt was probably an effort to put senators on record one way or another, and the final test came on a motion to table the motion to return the bill from the house. The motion to table carried by a vote of seventeen for, fourteen against, and four absent and not voting.[53] Opponents of the bill voted to table, while proponents voted not to table, and the result was the final defeat of the Rotenberry bill.

The *Arkansas Democrat* was pleased with the outcome and declared that the senators who had voted against the anti-evolution bill deserved to be placed on an honor roll for political courage and commended the senate itself for deciding that "the province of the legislature is not to settle debates over theology."[54] Representative Rotenberry was not so pleased with the performance of the senate and recommended that the initiative now be used so that the issue could be settled by popular vote. He felt that the senate had not responded to the popular will and that the use of the initiative would give the people an "opportunity of bringing into being an antievolution law with teeth in it."[55] Ben Bogard was equally unhappy with the results and he quickly incorporated an organization called the American Antievolution Association with himself as president. One purpose of the organization was to get enough signatures so that an initiated anti-evolution measure could be put on the ballot in November 1928.[56]

The 1928 Campaign

Securing the number of names to place an initiated act on the ballot in November 1928 was not really a difficult problem, given the high emotional content of such an issue and the low number of names required. An initiated act required signatures equaling only 8 percent of the votes cast for governor in the last preceding general election.[57] Since general elections in Arkansas in the 1920s for the office of governor seldom involved any real Republican challenge to the Democratic nominee, the turnout was minimal, and in the general election of 1926, only 111,656 people voted for the office of governor.[58] This meant that fewer than 9,000 legal voters could place an initiated act on the ballot. Representative Rotenberry, Bogard, and Dr. John F. Hammett, president of the Arkansas Antievolution League, were the chief sponsors of the initiated act. The provisions were almost identical to the Rotenberry bill.[59] The proposed initiated act outlawed in any college or public school, financed in whole or in part with state or local taxes, the teaching of "the theory or doctrine that mankind ascended or descended from a lower order of animal."[60] It was also made illegal for teachers or textbook commissioners to select textbooks that taught the prohibited theory to be used in any state institution. Teachers or textbook commissioners violating the law were guilty of misdemeanors and, upon conviction, had to vacate their positions and were subject to fines not to exceed $500.

In May 1927, Reverend Ben Bogard began sending out letters with petitions enclosed[61] and by November 1927, he announced that petitions were being circulated over the state and that the required percentage nearly had been achieved.[62] Bogard and Rotenberry stumped the state to secure petitions and support for the proposed initiated act. The Reverend James Seth Compere, editor of the *Baptist Advance,* gave both his editorial endorsement and his personal support to the movement. Compere, at the time, was a powerful figure at Baptist state conventions and his stand with Bogard and Rotenberry gave significant assistance to the campaign for an initiated act. In May 1928, the *New York Times* reported that the Arkansas Antievolution League claimed to have 4,000 more names than required.[63] On June 6, 1928, petitions with more than 19,000 names were filed in the secretary of state's office.[64] This was more than sufficient and the anti-evolution measure appeared on the November 1928 general election ballot as Initiated Act No. 1.

The opponents of Initiated Act No. 1 formed a statewide Committee Against Act No. 1 with Charles T. Coleman, a Little Rock attorney and judge, as chairman. The college establishment of the day was well represented on the committee and its membership included many prominent academic figures such as Charles H. Brough, former governor and president of Central Baptist College at Conway; John C. Futrall, president of the University of Arkansas; John Hugh Reynolds, president of Hendrix College at Conway; Virgil Jones, dean of the College of Arts and Sciences at the University of Arkansas, and Dr. Frank Vinsonhaler, dean of the Arkansas Medical School at Little Rock. Other members included John Netherland Heiskell, editor of the *Arkansas Gazette,* and the Reverend Hay Watson Smith, minister of the Second Presbyterian Church in Little Rock. The Committee Against Act No. 1 took out a series of newspaper advertisements beginning on October 7, 1928, and ending on November 6, 1928. The advertisements stressed the general acceptance of evolution in the scientific and intellectual communities, and the idea that evolution and religious faith were not incompatible. Above all, they pleaded with the voters to avoid making Arkansas look ridiculous and to protect "our schools from foolish and futile legislation and the good name of our state from ridicule."[65]

The idea that evolution was atheistic was a theme stressed by the supporters of Initiated Act No. 1 and was an argument that the opponents of Initiated Act. No. 1 sought to counter in their advertisements. The opponents were sorely distressed by the arrival in the state of Charles Smith of New York, who was president of the American Association for the Advancement of Atheism. Smith, a native of Sebastian County, had returned to Arkansas during the first week of October 1928 to campaign against the initiated act.[66] A flamboyant individual who did identify evolution with atheism, Smith set up an atheist headquarters in Little Rock as part of his campaign. He was arrested and fined for breach of the peace, then went to jail rather than pay the fine, and while in jail went on a hunger strike to protest his own arrest and the proposed anti-evolution act. He was finally released from jail, but opponents of the initiated act devoted much of the space in their advertisements attempting to avoid any identification with the out-of-state atheist and his campaign.

Other support for the opponents of the anti-evolution act came from both Little Rock newspapers. The *Arkansas Democrat* editorialized on October 28, 1928, about the unfairness of applying the proposed law only to state-supported institutions, pointing out that it would have no effect on private schools. The *Arkansas Gazette* deplored the tendency to equate evolution with atheism and urged its readers not to "make Arkansas the Monkey State."[67] The University of Arkansas, which would be directly affected by the law, probably took the leading role in the fight against it with President Futrall, Dean Jones, and Dean Vinsonhaler all actively involved. The faculty members at Fayetteville also participated individually through the American Association of University Professors.[68] Ironically enough, the University of Arkansas was attempting to secure a chapter of Phi Beta Kappa at this time.[69]

The supporters of the anti-evolution act had overwhelming support both from official Baptist groups, and undoubtedly from rank-and-file Baptists in the state. In fact, popular support was so strong that occasional tirades by Bogard to the effect that the move to teach evolution had been brought about by the John D. Rockefeller Foundation "which has been controlled by skeptics and infidels and atheists"[70] did not seem to matter. The proponents of Initiated Act No. 1 spent very little money on newspaper advertising and had only one advertisement in the *Arkansas Gazette,* headed simply "The Bible or Atheism, which?" The advertisement stressed the theme that atheism equals evolution and stated that "All atheists favor evolution. If you agree with atheism, vote against Act No. 1. If you agree with the Bible, vote for Act No. 1."[71] The piece concluded: "The *Gazette* said Russian Bolshevists laughed at Tennessee. True, and that sort will laugh at Arkansas. Who cares? Vote FOR ACT NO.1."[72]

In the 1928 November general election, Initiated Act No. 1 carried by a vote of 108,991 to 63,406.[73] The margin of approval was 63 percent, and the anti-evolution act lost in only five counties. Although the measure lost in Pulaski County by a vote of 5,374 in favor and 7,662 against, it carried four other urban counties (Jefferson, Garland, Sebastian, and Washington) by a substantial margin. The vote was 11,324 to 7,025.[74] Even though opposition to the act was led by the University of Arkansas, the *Arkansas Gazette* reported that the act "obtained a majority in the ward where the university is located."[75] For the rest of the nation, reactions to the victory of the anti-evolution act ranged from outrage to acceptance. "For the first time in the history of the world the teaching of a scientific theory has been made a statutory offense by a vote of the people," declared Maynard Shipley in *Current History.*[76] But the New York *World* voiced approval: "Foolish as a referendum on such a subject may appear, the ultimate right of the taxpayers to say what shall be taught in their schools cannot be denied unless we are able to repudiate Democracy."[77]

Shortly after the victory of the anti-evolution act, J. P. Womack, state superintendent of public instruction, said that he thought the law would have no effect on the public schools since no state-approved textbooks in the public schools contained any reference to Darwin's theory.[78] Later, however, Womack wrote a letter to county and city school superintendents notifying them that the State Department of Education approval had been withdrawn from *World Book Encyclopedia,* pending a court decision, because it contained statements that might be in violation of the new law. He also said that the act raised questions concerning dictionaries, encyclopedias, and other reference works and that the word "teach" in the law needed to be clarified as well as the word "textbook."[79]

The issue raised by Womack had bothered others also, and there was speculation in the *Arkansas Gazette*[80] that a group of lawyers, businessmen, and physicians might bring suit to determine not only the constitutionality of Initiated Act No. 1 but whether it prohibited mentioning and explaining the theory of evolution so long as it was not taught as fact or truth. Just at this point, Ben Bogard, in his capacity as president of the American Antievolution Association, wrote a letter to the *Arkansas Gazette* stating that "the law does not prohibit teaching what evolution is, so that students may know what it is. . . . To tell a student what a theory is vastly different from telling him that the theory is true."[81] Although this obviously was not the final legal judgment in the matter, this opinion from Bogard that evolution can be mentioned or explained so long as it is not taught as fact seemed to dampen the enthusiasm for a lawsuit. This interpretation that the law did not prohibit mentioning or explaining the theory of evolution came to be accepted by those who had to enforce the law, and was one of the important factors that blunted intellectual anger and allowed the anti-evolution act to stay in place for forty years.

1928–1968

There were other historical factors that helped to leave the antievolution law untouched for forty years. Major historical events during this period, such as the depression, World War II, and the changing international situation after World War II diverted energy and attention elsewhere. The unofficial policy that no one would be bothered so long as he or she did not teach evolution as truth amounted almost to a "no enforcement" policy. As a columnist for the *Arkansas Democrat* noted in 1966: "The law had been dormant and all but forgotten for years, literally repealed from neglect,"[82] particularly since there had never been any prosecutions under the act. This failure to enforce kept dissatisfaction at tolerable levels. There was also the difficulty of finding a teacher plaintiff for a lawsuit since a teacher's time, money, and even job could all be involved. The requirement that an initiated act can be changed only by a two-thirds vote of the legislature gave strong protection to the anti-evolution act, and two legislative attempts, one in 1937[83] and one in 1959,[84] failed before even coming to a vote. Al these factors assisted in keeping the anti-evolution act on the statute books.

A more serious legislative attempt was made in 1965. Even though the outcome was the same as previous attempts, this effort in 1965 seemed to act as a catalyst. Representative Nathan Schoenfeld of Garland County introduced House Bill No. 275[85] which would have repealed Initiated Act No. 1 of 1928. Schoenfeld said the 1928 act was "blatantly wrong"[86] and the *Arkansas Gazette* editorialized the Schoenfeld's bill was a means of "rectifying the ancient error."[87] Although Schoenfeld had not contacted any of the education groups that might have been interested in repeal before introducing his bill,[88] the Arkansas Education Association (AEA), the Arkansas School Boards Association, and the Arkansas Congress of Parents and Teachers decided to support his bill.[89] Forrest Rozzell, executive secretary of the AEA, drafted a statement on behalf of these three groups for Schoenfeld's use in case his bill came to a vote. The bill was never voted on, but it apparently stimulated the thinking of those most interested in repealing the anti-evolution law.

According to Forrest Rozzell,[90] the unsuccessful 1965 attempt convinced him that any legislative approach to repeal could not succeed and that the judicial route must be pursued. Newspaper discussion of the Schoenfeld bill and its lack of success had aroused many to write and say that the anti-evolution act should be enforced, and had also left some doubt in the minds of teachers as to whether the law was still a dead letter. The public debate aroused by the Schoenfeld bill convinced Rozzell that the issue of the anti-evolution act had to be resolved finally, and strengthened his resolve to go to court. He consulted Eugene R. Warren, attorney for the AEA, and they made plans to bring a suit.[91]

The first move in the new campaign to repeal the 1928 law was a "personal position" statement issued by Rozzell at a news conference on September 14, 1965. His statement was very similar to the one that had been made available to Representative Schoenfeld, stressing that religious beliefs should not be coerced by the state and that an understanding of the environment in which people live is necessary for survival.[92] It recommended, of course, that the law be repealed. Reaction was favorable from State Commissioner of Education Arch Ford who said that "the law was a dead issue and there was no reason for keeping it on the statute books."[93]

The Arkansas Gazette commended Rozzell for tackling the 1928 law and commented further that "The reason that Mr. Rozzell is a state resource of first importance is that once he has set his mind on this kind of problem, he is likely to peel it like an onion."[94] Governor Orval Faubus was less complimentary, feeling that the law should not be repealed but should be kept "as a safeguard to keep way out teachers in line."[95] Public debate on the issue had begun, and the foundation was being laid for a lawsuit.

The strategy pursued by Rozzell and Warren was to keep the legal case as local as possible. This meant finding a plaintiff who had roots in Arkansas, finding an Arkansas group and an Arkansas attorney to undertake the financing and trial of the case, and keeping national groups that might be interested in the case for reasons of ideology or political belief out of the case as sponsors. The AEA agreed to sponsor the case,[96] and its attorney, Warren, agreed to try the case charging only for his expenses.[97] National groups such as the National Education Association and the American Civil Liberties Union were not allowed to join the suit as sponsors because of the emphasis on local origination. Costs of the suit paid by the AEA amounted to only $2,500.[98]

The most crucial matter, however, was a plaintiff who had an impeccable Arkansas background. The person finally chosen met that requirement and also had many other attributes that helped the case greatly. Susan Epperson was in her second year of teaching biology at Central High School in Little Rock when she was approached about being the plaintiff in the case. She was contacted first by Virginia Minor, a fellow teacher at Central High School, who was also president of the Little Rock chapter of the American Association of University Women, a group that had supported the Schoenfeld bill in 1965.[99] Epperson was then interviewed by Rozzell and Warren[100] and agreed to become the plaintiff. She was a native of Clarksville, Arkansas, who had graduated from the College of the Ozarks, a Presbyterian school in Clarksville where her father was a professor of biology. She was married to an Air Force officer who was stationed at the Little Rock Air Base. She was also a religious person who saw no conflict between her religious beliefs and evolution; although in the classroom she taught evolution only as theory and not as fact.[101] For those interested in overturning the anti-evolution act, Mrs. Epperson was a dream come true.

In November 1965, a "John Doe" complaint was sent by Eugene Warren to Floyd Parsons, superintendent of the Little Rock Public Schools, indicating generally what kind of legal issues would be raised in the forthcoming lawsuit. This was designed to alert the Little Rock school system since the members of the Little Rock School Board and Superintendent Parsons would technically be defendants in the case. One December 6, 1965, a suit was filed in Pulaski County Chancery Court by Susan Epperson seeking a declaratory judgment that the Arkansas Antievolution Law (Initiated Act No. 1 of 1928) was unconstitutional. It was a civil suit, to be heard in chancery court without a jury. Mrs. Epperson said at the time the suit was filed that if she obeyed the law she would neglect "the obligations of a responsible teacher of biology. This is the sure path to the perpetration of ignorance, prejudice, and bigotry."[102] In March 1966, Hubert H. Blanchard, associate executive secretary of the AEA, entered the case on behalf of his two sons who were both attending the North Little Rock Public Schools at the time.[103] This was done to show that damage was occurring to students as well as teachers because of the Arkansas act.

Under Arkansas law, the attorney general of the state is involved whenever the validity of Arkansas law is challenged. The attorney general at that time, Bruce Bennett, was eager to get involved and showed signs initially of wanting to turn the case into a second Scopes trial. Bennett quickly began lining up witnesses to attack the validity of the evolution theory and wrote Judge Murray O. Reed, the chancellor in the Epperson case, that "Mrs. Epperson was the only person since the law was approved to 'clamor' in favor of teaching that man evolved from monkeys, apes, sharks, porpoises, seaweed, or any other form of animal or vegetable."[104] In a pre-trial hearing before Judge Reed, Warren accused Bennett of trying to make a joke of the case and encouraging the "carnival atmosphere or the buffoonery that went on in Tennessee to go on in Arkansas."[105] Judge Reed, at this time, saw the case as primarily a question of law in which private beliefs about evolution were not relevant. Bennett argued that Mrs. Epperson wanted to "advance an atheistic doctrine."[106]

As time went on and the date of the trial approached, Bennett seemed to alternate between saying that the main issue in the case was simply the legal question of whether Mrs. Epperson's freedom of speech outweighs the people's right to prescribe the subjects to be taught in school,[107] and, on the other hand, attacking the theory of evolution as an atheistic doctrine whose validity had great bearing on the case. Apparently irritated by a letter sent to him by the Executive Committee on Christian Education of the Arkansas Presbyterian Church that commended Mrs. Epperson for bringing the suit and expressed deep concern about Bennett using the case for political propaganda and "giving Arkansas an undeserved reputation for backwardness,"[108] he said that he planned to offer in evidence the views of fourteen scholars on the validity of Darwin's theory. He also warned that if the anti-evolution act was ruled unconstitutional, the public schools would be thrown open to the "haranguing [sic] of every soap box orator with a crackpot theory of evolution" even extending to the "'God is dead' theory, or the theory that man came from a gorilla."[109]

The trial of the case before Judge Reed was scheduled for April 1, 1966. On the day before the trial, Karr Shannon, a columnist for the *Arkansas Democrat,* was not encouraged about the prospects saying that: "The monkey trial to open in Judge Murray O. Reed's court tomorrow will not only be a waste of the taxpayer's money but will net Arkansas a slush of adverse publicity that may require decades for recovery."[110] The results were otherwise, as Judge Reed ruled that the question of whether evolution is true or false was not before the court and sustained more than fifty objections by Warren that blocked Bennett's efforts to question the validity of the evolution theory.[111] The trial took only two hours and twenty minutes, and the only witnesses to appear were Epperson and Blanchard for the plaintiff and four school superintendents for the defendants who testified that the 1928 law did not have any adverse effect on their schools.[112] Warren argued for the plaintiff that the law infringed freedom of speech, violated the separation of church and state, and was vague and indefinite. Bennett argued for the defendants (the Little Rock School Board members and the superintendent) that the state as Mrs. Epperson's employer was entitled to tell her what she could teach while on duty in the public schools.

At the conclusion of the trial, Judge Reed announced that he would render no decision for at least a month and gave the attorneys thirty days to file briefs. Although the courtroom was packed during the trial, with about one hundred people crowded into a room that seated fifty comfortably,[113] the consensus seemed to be that the trial was dignified, decorum was maintained, and the carnival atmosphere of the Scopes trial never materialized.[114]

On May 27, 1966, Judge Reed issued a nine-page memorandum opinion holding that Initiated Act No. I of 1928 was unconstitutional because it violated the constitutionally protected right of free speech and tended to "hinder the quest for knowledge, restrict the freedom to learn, and restrain the freedom to teach."[115] He further stated that the issue presented was whether or not Initiated Act No. I of 1928 conflicts with freedom of speech and expression and not whether the theory of evolution was true or false.[116] Judge Reed also distinguished the Scopes case[117] saying that later decisions of the United States Supreme Court had made the ruling in that case obsolete.[118] Notice of appeal by the state was given on June 21, 1966.

Briefs in the case were filed before the Arkansas Supreme Court on October 7 and October 21, 1966. Warren's brief on behalf of Susan Epperson concentrated on five major points. The first point argued was that school teachers are entitled to all the guarantees of both the state and federal constitutions. At the time the Scopes case was decided, the Tennessee court had held that the state, when dealing with its own employees and their conditions of employment, is not hampered by the "due process" constitutional guarantees of either the state or federal constitutions.[119] The argument of the brief for the appellee (Epperson) was that United States Supreme Court decisions since the Scopes case had greatly modified the decision of the Tennessee Supreme Court in 1927. A second argument was that the anti-evolution law violated the "free speech" guarantees of both the federal and Arkansas constitutions. The third point raised was that the law violated the "equal protection" clause of the Fourteenth Amendment to the United States Constitution, since it only applied to public schools and did not include private schools. The fourth point related to the third and raised the question of violation of the "due process" clause of the Fourteenth Amendment to the United States Constitution. This argument was that since Initiated Act No. 1 of 1928 imposed criminal penalties, its language had to be definite, certain, and clearly understood, but such was not the case because of ambiguity surrounding such words in the antievolution act as "to teach" and "textbooks." The fifth argument was that the law violated the religious freedom guarantees of both the Arkansas and United States Constitutions, in that the state cannot prohibit the teaching of a theory in order to assist religion.

The brief for the state of Arkansas, the appellant in the case, was filed by Attorney General Bennett and Fletcher Jackson, an assistant attorney general. The argument for the state was briefly that the act in question was constitutional since it was "a reasonable regulation of the conduct of a public employee, a school teacher, and a reasonable regulation of the curriculum in the public schools."[120] Since the state provided part of the money for local school districts, it had some authority to control curriculum and to determine what subjects should be taught. Initiated Act No. 1 of 1928 became part of the contract that Mrs. Epperson signed and under which she worked since one provision in her contract was that "Both parties hereto agree that this contract shall be construed in accordance with all applicable laws and regulations governing the employment, compensation, and conduct of teachers."[121] The concluding argument for the state pointed out that freedom of speech is not absolute, particularly when it is curtailed on the basis of the employer-employee relationship. Examples were given of the Hatch Act and certain state laws prohibiting state employees, including college staff and faculty, from running for political office. The argument was that laws like the Hatch Act and the anti-evolution act were valid even though they interfere to some extent with freedom of speech.

On June 5, 1967, the Arkansas Supreme Court upheld the constitution-ality of Initiated Act No. 1 of 1928 with one judge (Lyle Brown) dissenting and one judge (Paul Ward) concurring.[122] In a one paragraph decision, the court said:

> Upon the principal issue, that of constitutionality, the court holds that Initiated Measure No. 1 of 1928 is a valid exercise of the state's power to specify the curriculum in its public schools. The court expresses no opinion on the question whether the Act prohibits any explanation of the theory of evolution or merely prohibits teaching that the theory is true; the answer not being necessary to a decision in the case, and the issue not having been raised.[123]

Judge Ward concurred in the decision because he agreed with the first sentence in the opinion but thought that the second sentence cast some doubt on the clear meaning of the first sentence. A petition for rehearing was denied by the Arkansas Supreme Court on July 26, 1967.

Epperson v. Arkansas

Once the decision of the Arkansas Supreme Court was made, there was no doubt that the case would be appealed to the United States Supreme Court.[124] The Supreme Court agreed to hear the case March 4, 1968,[125] and oral arguments were held on October 16, 1968. By the time for oral argu-ments, friend-of-the-court briefs had been filed on behalf of Susan Epperson, now the appellant in the case, by the National Education Association, the National Science Teachers Association, the American Civil Liberties Union, and the American Jewish Congress.[126] According to Eugene Warren, still the attorney for Mrs. Epperson, the written briefs which he and the attorney for the state of Arkansas submitted to the United States Supreme Court were very similar to the ones submitted to the Arkansas Supreme Court earlier.

In the time period between the decision of the Arkansas Supreme Court and oral arguments before the United States Supreme Court, a new attorney general, Joe Purcell, had been elected in Arkansas, and he did not seem to have the same degree of enthusiasm for this case as his predecessor. Oral arguments in the case and the brief for the appellee, now the state of Arkansas, were handled by Don Langston of the attorney general's office. Langston stressed that the case had gone to trial under a previous admin-istration, and, according to a *New York Times* report, he also made it clear that he was defending the case for the state of Arkansas only because state law required it.[127] Langston did concede during the questioning before the court that in his opinion, Initiated Act No. 1 made it a crime not only to teach that the theory of evolution is valid but even to inform students that such a theory existed, saying that "if Mrs. Epperson were to tell her students that there is a Darwin's theory of evolution, then I think she would be liable for prosecution."[128] This turned out to be a very damaging admission for the state's case.

The oral arguments took only thirty-five minutes mainly because Langston did not use all the time allotted to him.[129] Warren and Langston were the only two attorneys involved in the oral arguments, and at the conclusion of the arguments, Warren felt that the judges were favorably inclined, with the exception of Justice Hugo Black who had been the most critical.[130] Justice Thurgood Marshall seemed amazed by the brief decision by the Arkansas Supreme Court and suggested facetiously that the United States Supreme Court should write a one-sentence opinion and upstage the Arkansas Supreme Court.[131] Another reporter concluded that the judges, by their questioning, were trying to find as narrow a ground as possible for their decision.[132]

On November 12, 1968, the United States Supreme Court struck down Initiated Act No. 1 as unconstitutional because it violated the separation of church and state provision of the First Amendment.[133] Justice Abe Fortas wrote the majority opinion and there were three concurring opinions written by Justices Hugo Black, John M. Harlan, and Potter Stewart.

Although Justice Fortas sounded a note of restraint at the beginning of his opinion by cautioning that "Judicial interposition in the operation of the public school system of the Nation raises problems requiring care and restraint,"[134] nevertheless, he said that when basic constitutional values are involved, there can be court intervention. In the present case, the opinion concurred, there is a narrower issue of violation of the "establishment" clause of the First Amendment on which the decision can be based. The anti-evolution act unconstitutionally aided religion because it prevented teachers "from discussing the theory of evolution because it is contrary to the belief of some that the Book of Genesis must be the exclusive source of doctrine as to the origin of man."[135] The state's right to determine curriculum for the public schools does not include the power to prohibit "the teaching of a scientific theory or doctrine where that prohibition is based upon reasons that violate the First Amendment."[136] Justice Fortas concluded the opinion of the court by stating that the Arkansas law attempted "to blot out a particular theory because of its supposed conflict with the Biblical account, literally read. Plainly, the law is contrary to the mandate of the First, and in violation of the Fourteenth, Amendment to the Constitution."[137]

Justice Black concurred in the decision reached but had grave reservations about the whole matter. He questioned whether an actual "case or controversy" was involved since no attempt to prosecute under the antievolution act had ever been attempted and the theory of evolution was presumably taught openly without punishment in the public schools. He was upset by the "pallid, unenthusiastic, even apologetic defense of the Act"[138] presented by the state of Arkansas. He was worried about federal intrusion into state power to determine curriculum and had grave doubts that "'academic freedom' permits a teacher to breach his contractual agreement to teach only the subjects designated by the school authorities who hired him."[139]

He preferred to rest his own concurrence on the vagueness of the Arkansas statute since it was unclear whether the statute allows discussion so long as it is not contended that the theory is true, or whether it precludes even a mention of Darwin's theory. Black felt that "the statute is too vague for us to strike it down on any grounds but that: vagueness."[140]

Justice Harlan concurred with the majority on the ground that the "establishment" clause had been violated. However, he wished to disassociate himself from the language of the majority opinion discussing the extent to which freedom of speech guarantees apply to school teachers since it was not necessary to the decision in the case. He also was very critical of the Arkansas Supreme Court, saying that he found it "deplorable that this case should have come to us with such an opaque opinion by the State's highest court"[141] and that the Arkansas Supreme Court's handling of the case "savors of a studied effort to avoid coming to grips with this anachronistic statute and to 'pass the buck' to this Court."[142] Justice Stewart's concurrence followed Justice Black's line of reasoning that the Arkansas law was so vague as to be unconstitutional.[143]

There were several themes that seemed to recur throughout the Epperson decision in both the majority and the concurring opinions. One theme was that of restraint, a reluctance to get involved in the sensitive area of the power of a state over curriculum and the related area of the extent of a teacher's free speech guarantees when they clash with the state's power over curriculum. The result was that these areas were touched on only so far as was absolutely necessary to decide the Epperson case. In fact, the decision was narrowed to a "separation of church and state" question which is much easier to decide and which sets a precedent fairly narrow in scope.

Another theme found in both the majority and concurring opinions about which the court was not so reluctant was its general dissatisfaction with the Arkansas Supreme Court and the way it had decided the Epperson case. These criticisms ranged from subtleness in the case of Fortas to bluntness in the cases of Harlan and Black where such language as a "studied attempt to pass the buck" is used. This also probably reflected the Court's reluctance to intrude into the area of curriculum and their resentment at being compelled to decide a case which forced them into this area. The justices undoubtedly felt that the case should have been decided in a more thorough and complete manner by the Arkansas Supreme Court in the first place.

Reaction to the decision of the Supreme Court ranged from favorable on the part of Mrs. Epperson, who said that Arkansas schoolteachers could now "teach the full subject of biology with an open and clear conscience,"[144] to unfavorable from the Reverend M. L. Moser, Jr., pastor of the Central Baptist Church in Little Rock, who said that now "someone who believes in the creation should also be present when evolution is taught."[145] Forrest Rozzell was pleased because the decision had been based on the "establishment" clause that killed the issue once and for all rather than the "vagueness" objection favored by Black and Stewart that might have left the issue still dangling.[146] The *Arkansas Gazette* commended Mrs. Epperson again for her efforts "to remove from the books an obstacle to quality education that was rooted in ignorance and perpetrated through 40 years of legislative indifference."[147] Perhaps the most memorable quotation of all came from John T. Scopes, the defendant in that famous trial in Tennessee in 1925, who was now sixty-eight years old and living in retirement in Shreveport, Louisiana. Scopes said that he was pleased with the decision in the Epperson case but that "The fight will still go on with other actors and other plays. You don't protect any of your individual liberties by lying down and going to sleep."[148]

CHAPTER 2

Low Villains and Wickedness in High Places

Race and Class in the Elaine Race Riots

JEANNIE M. WHAYNE

In the fall of 1919, the small Phillips County town of Elaine, Arkansas, became the scene of one of the most violent racial conflicts the country had (yet) experienced. Not surprisingly, the Elaine race riot/massacre has generated numerous scholarly efforts over the years and continues to interest researchers, and trouble citizens, to this day. Noting that the written descriptions of the event have produced wildly contradictory accounts of the underlying causes, failing to generate even a "common narrative" surrounding the violent outbreak, historian Jeannie Whayne does not offer here her own account of the disturbance. Rather, she critiques several of the most high profile accounts, finds some merely inadequate and others downright misleading, and argues that each of these flawed narratives is a product of the historical context within which it was written. Whayne argues that the key to understanding what happened in Elaine is to place the event in proper historical context. This context must include the pressures generated by the expanding plantation system in the delta counties during the preceding years; the changed attitudes and aspirations of returning black and white WWI veterans; and class conflict within the white community, i.e., planters versus landless whites.

Perhaps no event in the history of the Arkansas delta has received as much attention and been the subject of more speculation than the Elaine Race Riot of 1919. Historians, struggling with a mass of rich but contradictory

Originally published in *Arkansas Historical Quarterly* 58
(Autumn 1999): 285–313. Reprinted with permission.
DOI: https://doi.org/10.34053/parry2019.riapag2.2

and even tainted evidence, have failed to arrive at a common narrative of events. One noted account amounts to little more than propaganda for the planter elite of Phillips County, while another, a contemporary essay written by a future black leader, focused on exposing the evils of the plantation system.[1] As varied as their interpretations have been, however, virtually all share a common shortcoming. The only exception is to be found in a novel based on the Elaine riot by an Arkansas protégé of Norman Mailer—and that book failed to find an American publisher.[2]

Competing interpretations of the riot emerged almost as soon as it had ended. Walter White, assistant secretary—and, later, executive secretary—of the NAACP, visited Phillips County incognito in mid-October 1919 in order to secure material for an article he later published in the *Nation*. White's interest in the riot almost cost him his life. An African American who, with his blue eyes and blond hair, passed for white, he barely escaped a lynch mob that had discovered his true identity.[3] White took exception to the official version of the riot embraced by white officials and published in Arkansas newspapers. This version insisted blacks intended to murder certain white planters and take their lands. Whites, it was said, had discovered the plot accidentally after two deputies whose car had broken down were fired upon by blacks attending a meeting of a sharecroppers' union at Hoop Spur church outside Elaine. Walter White countered that African Americans had organized the Progressive Farmers and Household Union of America to sue planters for a fair settlement of their crops; that whites had fired into the church at Hoop Spur in order to disrupt a meeting of the union, and that blacks had returned fire only in self-defense.[4]

However the incident really began, one deputized white official, W. A. Adkins, lay dead and another, Charles Pratt, was seriously wounded. Several days of brutal violence ensued. A posse was quickly raised and rushed to the scene. White men from other parts of Arkansas, as well as from Mississippi and Tennessee, joined in the hunt for the alleged "insurrectionists," some of whom fought back. Local white leaders wired Governor Charles Brough asking for federal troops from Camp Pike to restore law and order. Colonel Isaac C. Jenks commanded the 583 soldiers who were dispatched early in the morning of October 2 and were accompanied by Brough. Immediately upon his arrival, Jenks disarmed all blacks as well as white civilians and set about quelling the violence. Martial law was declared, and federal troops patrolled the streets of Elaine and Helena and scoured the countryside. By the time order was restored two days later, five whites and at least twenty-five blacks lay dead. Several hundred blacks were incarcerated in Elaine and

Helena. When the Phillips County Grand Jury convened on October 27, 1919, over one hundred were still being held. In subsequent trials twelve were sentenced to death for first degree murder and another sixty-seven to prison terms. The white community celebrated the trials and convictions as evidence of the rule of law over mob violence.[5]

Most of the facts in the official version of the riot were disputed not only by Walter White but by lawyers who appealed the convictions of the twelve black men sentenced to death. Yet the official version showed some staying power. One account written forty years after the riot essentially reiterated it. In 1961 J. W. Butts and Dorothy James published "The Underlying Causes of the Elaine Riot of 1919," in *Arkansas History Quarterly*, arguing that a few disgruntled and misled African Americans hatched a plot to murder white planters and take their lands, that this "insurrection" was discovered before the conspirators could bring their plans to fruition, and that the white community responded reasonably given the situation. Butts and James, who relied largely on interviews with white Phillips County residents and references to reports of unidentified "negro detectives" from Chicago, took pains to establish that the black sharecroppers of Phillips County, rather than being exploited, were actually "rather prosperous" and contented with their situation. The trouble was caused by an outside agitator and confidence man, Robert L. Hill of Winchester, Arkansas, who founded the Progressive Farmers and Household Union of America strictly for the purpose of "making easy money" from the members through an assortment of "schemes." Although Hill escaped prosecution, the other guilty parties, a few disgruntled and misguided souls, according to Butts and James, secured fair trials and were subsequently convicted.[6]

Butts and James were writing specifically to counter an article, "The Elaine Race Riots of 1919," by O. A. Rogers, Jr., which had appeared in the *Arkansas Historical Quarterly* less than a year earlier. The first of the modern accounts to appear in print, Rogers' introduction promised to place the Elaine Race Riot within the context of the 1919 "Red Summer" of racial and union violence. He failed, however, to develop that theme. Instead, in addition to a brief overview of the riot, his article focused attention on the exploitation of African Americans on Phillips County plantations as the basic reason for the creation of the Progressive Farmers and Household Union of America.[7] As such, it was a credible extension of Walter White's argument, and it stood in direct contrast to the planter perspective supported by Butts and James.

These two schools of thought, the planter vs. the black perspective, were elaborated upon in two books published in 1970 and 1988, respectively. The first, *Union, Reaction, and Riot: A Biography of a Rural Race Riot*, by B. Boren McCool referred to both the essays written in 1960 as "propaganda," and began with a lengthy discussion of social and economic conditions in Phillips County. While he took issue with Butts and James in the matter of whether blacks were being economically exploited in the sharecropping system and dismissed the notion of an insurrectionary plot, he largely accepted their general narrative of events as they developed after the incident at Hoop Spur Church. In doing so, McCool failed to consider crucial evidence undermining that narrative. Perhaps because he drew heavily upon a collection of documents held by J.W. Butts, his rendering of the violence tended to affirm the planter perspective.[8] The other full length study of the riot, Richard C. Cortner's *A Mob Intent on Death*, returned to the themes pursued by White and Rogers, but had as its ultimate goal an explication of the appeals arising out of the convictions. A scholar interested in the legal significance of one of the cases, Cortner drew heavily upon Arthur I. Waskow's account in *From Race Riot to Sit-In*, published in 1966. Though Waskow devoted only fifty-three pages to the Elaine Race Riot, his deeply researched and cogently argued account stands as the best counter to the planter perspective and is a useful vehicle for addressing the main issues raised by Butts and James.

Was the Progressive Farmers and Household Union of America intent upon murdering unsuspecting planters, or did it merely intend to file lawsuits against planters believed guilty of cheating the union's black members—as Waskow, following White—believed? Most of the Phillips County white population certainly believed that a black insurrection was at hand, and the *Helena World* employed language that echoed the hysteria that surrounded rumors of imminent slave rebellions in the antebellum South. White women and children were dispatched in a special train to the safety of Helena; others were gathered in buildings heavily guarded by white men. Even some local whites sympathetic to blacks were scared. The family of musician Levon Helm believed the "rumor that all the white farmers and their families were going to be murdered by the rioters." Helm's father and grandfather armed themselves and prepared to defend their homes, but "the riot never did come down the road."[9]

As all the facts came to light in the months and years following the riot, the existence of an insurrection plot grew less plausible. While some blacks had clearly fought back, there was little evidence of African Americans hunting down white targets or assaulting white institutions—as insurrectionists would presumably do. Even James E. Miller, the attorney who led the successful prosecution of the Elaine blacks, indicated in an interview in 1976 that events in Phillips County "had every appearance of [a black insurrection] until you got in and went to the bottom of it." He believed that the planters were determined to crush the union, and that the death of W. A. Adkins outside the church gave them the excuse to do so. "When that boy was killed they decided to crush it." Although Miller continued to believe that the convicted blacks had committed murder, he said "I'm awful glad the court reversed" the convictions. "While they were guilty all right, technically, but hell if there was a provocation, they had a provocation."[10]

Other prominent white Arkansans, certainly not beholden to the NAACP perspective, also came to repudiate the insurrection theory. David Yancey Thomas, a professor of history and political science at the University of Arkansas and the first editor of the *Arkansas Historical Quarterly,* after a lengthy correspondence with a variety of individuals connected to both sides, eventually rejected the story that the events in Elaine were an insurrection. At first, Thomas had stopped short of rendering such an opinion. Immediately following the riot, he corresponded with several individuals in an effort to discover the facts behind the alleged insurrection. At the time of one of these queries Thomas was representing the University of Arkansas at a meeting of the University Race Commission in Tuskegee, Alabama. Although, as Arthur Waskow suggests in his book, Thomas may have had doubts about the official version as early as February 1920, he only repudiated it publicly some ten years later with the publication of his *Arkansas and Its People.* In that book he remarked that the insurrection plot idea "was later shown to be incorrect" and that the report that it was an insurrection "only aggravated the situation."[11] This judgment—rendered in a well-known history text—makes the Butts and James article all the more curious. In spite of the doubt cast on the insurrection theory by a prominent Arkansas historian, they relied on suspect contemporary newspaper accounts, confessions of blacks and the testimony of witnesses that had been shown—decades before Butts and James wrote—to have been coerced or falsified, and the unsubstantiated testimony of individuals interviewed forty years after the events.[12]

Waskow, on the other hand, judiciously dismissed the newspaper accounts as hysterical, repudiated the coerced confessions, and relied heavily on the affidavits of two white witnesses who had recanted the testimony they had given at the time of the trial and told a version of events that supported the black perspective. The testimony of both T. K. Jones and

H. F. Smiddy was offered in support of the appeals of six of the black men convicted and sentenced to death. Jones and Smiddy lived in Helena at the time of the riot and were "co-workers of the first man killed at Hoop Spur," W. A. Adkins.[13] According to Jones, a party of white men fired upon the church with the express purpose of breaking up the union meeting, and, according to Smiddy, the black trustee accompanying Adkins and Charles Pratt told him the next day that the white men had fired first.[14] In direct contradiction to the story broadcast by the newspapers and authorities at the time and later repeated by Butts and James, Smiddy further testified that the literature found in the church contained "nothing to indicate a criminal or unlawful purpose on the part of the organization."[15] Both men witnessed and participated in the torture applied to secure damning testimony from blacks taken into custody, and both men described whites systematically hunting down and shooting blacks, armed or unarmed. So "out of control" was one group that Smiddy suggested at least one of the white casualties was at the hands of "a member of our own posse."[16]

John E. Miller, the prosecuting attorney in Helena, later supported this view of the source of the bloodshed. The Mississippians who joined the posse, he said, "came over with blood in their eye."[17] Certainly a letter in the Brough Papers (cited but misread by McCool) suggests that whites were the ones on the rampage and that some local authorities likely did little to restrain them. Harry Anderson of Bon Air Coal and Iron Corporation in Nashville, Tennessee, wrote Governor Brough that he had lived in Phillips County twenty years earlier, described himself as a "rough rider" there, and indicated that "knowing Frank Kitchens [Phillips County sheriff] and his crowd as well as I do, I am quite sure your action was the direct cause of saving a great number of lives—both white and black down there. Nothing would have suited Frank better than to have been given free hand to hunt 'Mr. nigger' in his lair and in-as-much as the negroes seem to have been well prepared, I am of a firm belief that your action nipped a small war in its bud."[18]

Given the apparent murderous intent of the white posse, it is little wonder that some blacks resisted. That they were armed at all was not evidence of the existence of an insurrectionary plot, but rather emblematic of a rural culture dependent in part on hunting for subsistence. For Waskow—as for other partisans of the "black" perspective—their resistance suggests not rebellion but a determination to defend themselves in the face of a hostile force of whites.[19]

This hostile white mob, though, warrants closer scrutiny than it has

received. As varied as they are, all historical accounts take for granted
something that very much needs to be explained. Few have noted that
the white assault represented a phenomenon rare in the delta outside of
periodic lynchings: an alliance of white planters and working-class whites
against black sharecroppers. Even prosecutor Miller believed that planters
played a role in the violence—at the very least by using the shoot-out at
Hoop Spur as an excuse to destroy a union that had been worrying them
for some time.[20] But the posses clearly included more humble whites—
clerks, veterans, tenant farmers, lumbermen, railroad workers—with few
ties to the planter class. With the exception of the Arkansas novelist Francis
Irby Gwaltney, though, those who have written about the events at Elaine
have tended to view the white community within Phillips County as one
monolithic whole.[21] Some have recognized divisions within the black community, divisions briefly overcome in the aftermath of the riot, but no
one has grasped the class conflict within the white community, a conflict
only temporarily surmounted in the brutal suppression of the Progressive
Farmers and Household Union of America.[22]

Behind this conflict was an expansion of the plantation system in
Phillips County between 1880 and 1920, an expansion challenged by a violent campaign on the part of landless whites. Phillips County had long
been dominated by the plantation, but as the lumber industry boomed in
the last decades of the nineteenth century, land was being reclaimed, and
many new immigrants to the Arkansas delta, both black and white, looked
for opportunity there. While the number of acres in cotton increased from
42,654 in 1880 to 92,944 in 1920, though, the percentage of farm owners
decreased from 70.3 percent in 1880 to 18.8 in 1920.[23] Lumbering operations
were bringing new land into production in the southern portion of the
county—that area rocked by violence during the riot—but draining and
developing cleared land was expensive, and even those who could afford
to engage in such an enterprise usually did so through borrowing large
sums of money.[24] Expense doubtlessly undermined many whites' efforts to
secure land—as did the decline after 1910 in the amount of land coming
into cultivation. Frustrated in their ambitions to own land, many whites
found that neither could they rent it. Black sharecroppers rather than white
owners or tenants cultivated the vast majority of acres in Phillips County
because planters preferred black to white labor; the former was cheaper and,
given legalized disfranchisement and segregation, blacks were regarded as
more tractable. The result was growing animosity on the part of landless
whites toward those who controlled most of the land, the planters. In the

mid-1890s, landless whites who had pinned their hopes on the "agricultural ladder"—by which they could work their way up from the ranks of tenancy to proprietorship—struck at the planter class by terrorizing sharecroppers who had secured places on Phillips County plantations. Just as planters viewed blacks as more tractable, working-class whites recognized blacks were an easier, intermediary target through which they could more safely strike at planters.

In February 1898 at Connell's Point, less than ten miles north of Elaine, "a gang of irresponsible [white] men" began to terrorize "the defenseless negroes of that vicinity until they have actually succeeded in driving the majority of them out of the neighborhood. They [the whites] profess to be actuated by a desire to rent land at reasonable prices, and say they cannot do so because the negroes will take it at the prevailing prices." Planters were eager to protect their cheap labor supply, but, according to the *Helena World*, "when a gang of hoodlums circle[s] around the back end of large plantations at the hour of midnight and fire into negro cabins and then disappear, it is difficult to swear who did the nefarious work." Four men arrested in early February had been "discharged for lack of sufficient evidence to hold them." The alleged whitecappers were accused not only of terrorizing black share-croppers, but also of destroying the property of plantation owners. One of the discharged men, Jones Strawn, had lost his tenancy on a plantation which subsequently witnessed depredations against its black sharecroppers and suffered the burning of 5,000 pounds of seed cotton. The *Helena World* declared itself "morally sure" that Strawn, along with the other arrested whites, were guilty. In another incident a year earlier, the barn of another planter "was burned, resulting in the loss of two fine mules, wagons, tools, feed, a new buggy, etc." By February 1898 the situation had become so unstable that the *World* editor, a reliable spokesman for the planter perspec-tive, was moved to suggest that "if a few of [the white nightriders] were shot to death when they are out marauding, it would have a wholesome effect," and that "if they are caught while at their unlawful work, they should be shot down like dogs, for the man who would burn his neighbor's barn and substance is worse than an assassin."[25]

Such violence was not confined to Phillips County. Rather it accom-panied the expansion of the plantation in all parts of the Arkansas delta. Whitecappers struck in Cross and Poinsett Counties in 1902, in Crittenden County in 1904, and periodically plagued Mississippi County from 1908 to 1921. Two cases involving nightriders in Cross and Poinsett Counties were well publicized in Phillips County in 1903 and 1904 because they were tried in federal court in Helena. In the Cross County case, planters hired white detectives to track down nightriders who were attempting to drive blacks from plantations. The fifteen men arrested in Poinsett County were charged with attempting to drive African American workers away from a sawmill. Although no convictions were secured in the first case, three men were convicted in the Poinsett County case. When the Supreme Court overturned the convictions in 1905, planters were again left without adequate protection against such white marauders and successfully pressed the state to pass a nightriding law in 1909. Although the law provided local authorities with a new weapon, it by no means ended nightriding activities, and planters continued to complain about such depredations.[26]

Nightriding persisted because white men looking for the main chance in the Arkansas delta continued to be doomed to disappointment. An examination of the manuscript census of population for the three Phillips County townships (Tappan, Mooney, and Searcy) where most of the fighting occurred in 1919 is quite revealing.[27] Although the number of white farmers in these townships increased from 36 in 1900 to 155 in 1920, those owning farms dropped from 60 percent to 19.1 percent. The number of black farmers meanwhile increased from 289 in 1900 to 1,132, with only 92 (8.4 percent) owning farms. White farmers were greatly outnumbered by African Americans, and they were less likely than ever to own the farms they operated. The ground was shifting beneath them, and the plantation was advancing on all fronts. The majority of these farmers, both white and black, were not native to Arkansas, had lived only a few years in these townships, and likely knew very little about one another. Only 23.9 percent of the white farmers had been born in Arkansas. Most of the rest hailed from Mississippi (32.3 percent) and Tennessee (11.0 percent). Only 7.1 percent came from outside the South. As for black farmers, 25.2 percent were native to Arkansas, with 39.9 percent from Mississippi and 14.8 percent from Louisiana. Only .7 percent were non-southern. These statistics had changed very little from 1900, but, interestingly enough, less than 10 percent of the whites or blacks listed in these townships in 1900 remained in 1920. This was a community in turmoil.[28]

This turmoil and the diminishing opportunities available to many whites may have intensified that community's hostility not only toward black croppers and tenants but also toward African Americans in general—such that by 1919 accomplished blacks of the professional classes could likewise be targets of an enraged white mob. One of the most controversial aspects of the Elaine riot involved the deaths of Dr. D. A. E. Johnston, a wealthy black dentist and druggist from Helena, and his three brothers. Two of his brothers lived with him and ran an automobile business, a third, Dr. L. H. Johnston, was a physician from Oklahoma who had the misfortune to be visiting at the time of the riot. According to the official version, the heavily armed Johnston brothers were "driving in a car south of Elaine" on October 2 when warned of the trouble there. They boarded a train for Helena, but when that train stopped at Elaine, the four Johnstons were arrested. They were placed in a car with Orley R. Lilly, who intended to take them to Helena, with several deputies following in a separate car. On the way to Helena, Dr. D. A. E. Johnston was alleged to have grabbed Lilly's gun from his holster and shot and killed him. The whites in the other car then opened fire and killed all four Johnstons.[29]

But even Bessie Ferguson, who wrote a thesis on the riot generally sympathetic to the planter perspective, rejected that version of the Johnstons' deaths.[30] Her rendering more nearly resembles that of Ida B. Wells-Barnett, the black crusader against lynching who investigated the Elaine Riot in 1920 and offered a more chilling account of the incident. According to Wells-Barnett, the four Johnstons were returning from a successful hunt for game—which explains the guns—when they were warned of the trouble in Elaine, turned back, and boarded a train at Ratio. Taken off the train at Elaine, the Johnstons were bound with ropes and placed in the car with Lilly. As the car pulled away, the white mob opened fire, killing everyone in the car, including Lilly.[31] The newspapers reported the official version, however, and even implicated Dr. D. A. E. Johnston in the insurrection plot. According to the *Arkansas Gazette*, "a dozen high-powered rifles and hundreds of rounds of ammunition were confiscated" from his dental office after the incident.[32] This report both supported the contention that there had been insurrection plans and further legitimized the killing of the Johnstons. Because there was no coroner's inquest, neither the high-powered rifles nor any other evidence of the Johnstons' purported involvement in the plot was ever produced, however.[33]

The attempt to justify the deaths of the Johnstons by implicating them in an insurrection plot is simply ludicrous. The social distance between wealthy blacks and poor sharecroppers was just too great.[34] Elite black men like the Johnstons were more likely to found benevolent organizations and engage in charitable activities than to lead a rebellion of black sharecroppers. Though the Johnstons' deaths must have stunned the rest of Helena's black upper class—which included one of the most prominent black Baptists in the country, Dr. E. C. Morris—elite blacks seem not to have been cowed by those deaths. Morris, who was pastor of the Centennial Baptist Church in Helena and the founder of both Arkansas Baptist College and the National Baptist Convention, apparently "lost the confidence" of the local white community when he refused to participate in the interrogation of the black defendants. The Committee of Seven, made up of prominent Phillips County white citizens, including Sheriff Kitchens, "tried to prevail upon various of the negro leaders to question the prisoners here, to read over the written evidence, and to verify the data collected by our committee, but in no single instance were we successful."[35] Dr. Morris probably understood that he would be party to a whitewash or risk retaliation if he differed with the white investigators. Other black leaders in Helena also refused to participate in what they likely regarded as a kangaroo court and likewise suffered the "loss of confidence" of the white community.[36] In correspondence with the NAACP, Morris went so far as to straightforwardly repudiate the white version of events. Although black leaders throughout the Arkansas delta denounced violence and reassured whites that they did not support union activities, Helena's black elite subsequently contributed to the defense fund established by the NAACP through Scipio Jones, a black attorney in Little Rock who helped represent the black defendants in their appeals.[37]

A rare instance of whites transcending class differences in order to crush a black union had, it seems, led to an instance of blacks transcending their own class differences. When called upon to aid the white community in railroading black sharecroppers, local black leaders indulged in an uncommon display of race consciousness trumping class consciousness. The potential for this may well have made the continuing violence increasingly worrisome to the white elite. The greater solidarity among different classes in the African American community that the killing of black professionals might forge could not have been understood as serving the interests of white planters.[38]

That the circle of violence had widened to include not only the black union members who clearly threatened planter interests but also some of the most accomplished blacks in Helena puts the telegraph to Governor Brough requesting aid in a different light.[39] Although the Johnstons were not to die until October 2, the situation in Phillips County was already deteriorating rapidly when the first telegraph was dispatched to Brough the day before. Officials in Elaine wired the governor at noon on October 1 that they were "having race riots here in Elaine and need some soldiers at once. Several white men and Negroes killed last night and this morning."[40] Subsequent urgent messages from Helena followed up on that initial request for troops with one indicating "one hundred and seventy-five negro prisoners are expected to arrive at any moment among white men." As Arthur Waskow suggests, "it is not clear . . . whether the local authorities hoped that the troops would help in tracking down Negro 'insurgents,' or would protect the prisoners from white lynch mobs, or both."[41] The fact that Col. Jenks ordered that white civilians as well as all blacks be disarmed is suggestive. Waskow indicates that Jenks was too easily convinced by local authorities that a black insurrection was taking place, but the colonel did establish as one objective "preventing lynchings of Negro prisoners" and of O. S. Bratton, the only white man held in jail in connection with the riot.[42]

With the possible exception of Waskow, historians have assumed that white leaders in Phillips County required federal troops to subdue the black population, either because they were engaging in an insurrection or at least fighting back against whites. Harry Anderson's letter to Governor Brough suggests another possibility. In congratulating Brough for taking "prompt measures," Anderson expressed his conviction that the governor's actions had prevented the loss of black as well as white lives.[43] Furthermore, the messages to Brough implying a fear that the jailed African Americans might be lynched suggest that some planters may well have been as concerned with protecting their labor force from whites run amuck as with protecting themselves from blacks run amuck. Planters had been very much interested in the suppression of the union, and that interest could for a time make common cause with the grudges and fears that working-class whites harbored toward African Americans. But planters may have become alarmed as the violence escalated. Certainly in the weeks after peace was restored, it became clear that the mob had done its work too thoroughly, at least as far as planter interests were concerned. An unknown number of blacks had fled the area, and planters in Phillips County complained about the cotton going unpicked in the fields. They had been so successful in supplanting white with black labor that they had few options open once their black labor force was dispersed. In the townships where most of the violence occurred, black sharecroppers outnumbered white plantation laborers by 1,003 to 123, and the whites who had swarmed into Arkansas to put down the so-called insurrection apparently had no interest in remaining behind to labor on plantations.[44] Accordingly, some planters felt compelled to post bond for blacks jailed in the aftermath of the riot.[45] What common purpose whites found in the initial suppression of the black union apparently faded quickly.

The defection of Smiddy and Jones serves as another example of the fragility of the alliance that planters and working class whites had forged in the interest of suppressing the union. Both men were employed as special agents for the Missouri-Pacific Railroad at the time of the incident and Jones supervised Smiddy and Adkins, the white man killed at the Hoop Spur church.[46] By their own admission they were very much involved in the events that transpired during the riot, but, later gave affidavits that discredited the "official" narrative of events. Afterward they received threats from Phillips County whites and were branded as "low villains" by Justice James McReynolds, a Tennessean on the US Supreme Court.[47] The alliance between planters and men such as Smiddy and Jones was tenuous at best and did not survive those few horrifying days in early October 1919, largely because it was at odds with more than two decades of tension existing between planters and working-class whites.

In addition to recognizing how divisions within the white community complicated events, understanding what happened at Elaine very much depends on a closer examination of the relationship between planters and their sharecroppers than is to be found in much of the existing literature. Butts and James portray that relationship as non-exploitative. Virtually every other historian suggests otherwise, yet neither side examines that relationship as it existed in the Arkansas delta in detail. McCool relies on data largely drawn from the printed census, while Rogers, Waskow, and Cortner merely assume exploitation within Phillips County. The fact is that planters sometimes acted as the protectors of African Americans against whitecappers, but their actions in suppressing the union in 1919 were not out of character. Their prime concern had always been to maintain a reliable supply of labor, and some of them had used every means at their disposal to hold black workers in place. At the same time that federal judge Jacob Trieber was convicting whitecappers in 1904 in Helena, a federal investigation of peonage resulted in several arrests and some convictions of planters in nearby Ashley County. U. S. Bratton, the attorney who was later engaged by the Progressive Farmers and Household Union of America to file suits for fair settlement, was an assistant US attorney investigating peonage in Arkansas in 1905. In July of that year, writing to the US attorney in Texas concerning a case that crossed state lines, he declared, "We have had a number of peonage cases in this State recently."[48]

Many years later, Bratton would have cause to recall this investigation into peonage. In answer to a letter from David Y. Thomas, who in 1921 was still attempting to uncover the facts behind the Elaine riot, Bratton indicated that he had learned when he was an assistant US attorney that "large plantation owners were practicing what is known as 'peonage,' and which is nothing more than slavery."[49] Bratton claimed to have secured "convictions or had pleas of guilty entered," on peonage charges, but peonage was difficult to prove, and Arkansas law, similar to laws passed in other southern states, armed planters with potent weapons. Vagrancy laws provided for the arrest of apparently unemployed blacks who could be put to work on plantations in the locale where they were apprehended. Other laws established the planter's lien as superior to that of any other creditor and prohibited a sharecropper owing a debt from leaving the employ of a planter. John Miller, the man who prosecuted the Elaine cases, conceded that conditions in Phillips County "came as near a feudal state as ever existed."[50]

Clearly, Butts and James's apparent endorsement of the notion that sharecroppers' circumstances were satisfactory cannot be sustained. Debt was an endemic problem. The authors of one study of Arkansas plantations reported that "those workers who approach full share cropper status have little capital of their own upon which to draw for living expenses from the time the crop is started until the cotton is sold in the fall. As a matter of necessity, therefore, the plantation operators must furnish either money or supplies while they are engaged in making the crop."[51] John Miller indicated "never was a bigger fraud on any set of people then was perpetrated on those sharecroppers [in Phillips County]. The deducts, as they call it . . . they [the planters] got all the money and everything else, they sold the crop." According to Miller, "there isn't any question but the sharecroppers were being defrauded."[52]

It was at crop settlement time that problems sometimes surfaced. Many planters did not furnish a written accounting to sharecroppers even though far many more could read by the turn of the century than was true at the time of emancipation. There was plenty of room for misunderstanding and for outright fraud on the part of planters. Southern planters did not extend credit interest-free, and some historians have concluded that the interest charged sometimes amounted to over 40 percent.[53] Bessie Ferguson showed that interest rates were that high in Phillips County, listing figures from the firm of Dowdy and Longnecker of Elaine. Like many merchants, Dowdy and Longnecker had one price for cash and another for credit, and their interest rates hovered around 50 percent. For example, a cash customer paid $1.00 for twenty-four pounds of low grade flour. A credit customer paid $1.50. Some items carried even higher interest. A pair of work shoes cost $2.50 if a customer paid cash and $4.00 if the transaction involved credit.[54] A planter having an arrangement with such a merchant would pass the cost of the credit along to his sharecroppers and sometimes add a carrying charge. As Henry Lee, an African American immigrant to the Arkansas delta put it, sharecroppers traditionally "got figured clean out" by planters at settlement time.[55] The Department of Agriculture reported in a 1901 study that those sharecroppers who succeeded in "getting out of debt at the end of the crop year" became indebted "again almost immediately" because they would have to pay for the coming year's "meat, meal, tobacco, molasses and other things necessary."[56]

U. S. Bratton described how black sharecroppers, aware that he was prosecuting peonage cases, "came by the droves to my office telling their stories as to how they were being robbed by the landlords, who took their crops at their own prices, charged whatever they saw fit for the supplies furnished, and as a final consummation of the whole thing, refused to make any kind of settlement with them whatever, the end being that they received a statement, written upon blank tablet paper as a rule, showing 'balance due' in a lump sum."[57] Bratton also illustrated how a sharecropper's obligations could travel from one plantation to another, thus perpetuating the vicious cycle of debt. He said "that the planters refused to consider making any arrangements with one of these people who happen to live upon an adjoining farm, without first ascertaining how much the balance due is claimed to be. If the planter is willing to pay the balance due, or in other words buy him at that price, then he is at liberty to take him; but the custom is so well established that it is not proper to take one with a balance due unpaid, that this is rarely done."[58]

Whatever Butts and James's sources may have told them, other Phillips County whites were not necessarily under any illusions about the circumstances of local sharecroppers in the years immediately preceding the Elaine riot. Charges of mistreatment of black sharecroppers in Phillips County surfaced in 1916 in an unlikely place. According to the *Helena World*, the Reverend Burke Culpepper, a white preacher holding a revival over several days in Helena, at one point "took up another line of spiritual wickedness in high places in this community, in the unfair treatment of labor, especially colored farm labor, on the part of those whose positions as financial and social leaders should make them above such practices." In a rare admission for the generally pro-planter *Helena World*, the editor remarked that "the evangelist evidently knows that some large fortunes in Helena have been founded on unfair and unrighteous treatment of negro farmers."[59]

Whether or not union organizers were engaged in a money-making scheme, they had clear grievances to build on. The organization of the sharecroppers' union in Phillips County did not, furthermore, represent the first instance of black resistance to this state of affairs, yet few who have written on the Elaine Race Riot have grasped that fact. Waskow came closest to appreciating that longstanding tensions existed between planters and their black sharecroppers and that the Elaine Race Riot was one manifestation of a long struggle over settlement of the crop. His evidence, however, does not include specific examples of earlier resistance in Phillips County. O. A. Rogers went so far as to suggest that until the formation of the Progressive Farmers and Household Union, the blacks of Phillips County were simply "illiterate and docile tenant farmers and laborers."[60] In fact, 73.3 percent of the adult black men in the townships where most of the violence occurred in 1919 reported in the 1920 census that they could read.[61] If not necessarily illiterate, neither were these men always docile.

Long before the Elaine Race Riot, some Phillips County African American sharecroppers became frustrated enough to confront planters at settlement time. The results were usually disastrous. For example, in October 1898, Charles Munn, an African American tenant in Phillips County, confronted the planter he sharecropped for, Frank DuBarry. He "went over to Mr. Frank's house and axed him ef he had looked at his book to see how much he owed me. He said no and took and lit it and cussed me and told me to get outer his house unless I wanted him to kill me. Then I hit him." Munn confessed to burning DuBarry's house to the ground while DuBarry lay unconscious within it. Munn was arrested, convicted, and executed.[62] Another conflict involving a planter and black sharecropper was reported in the *Helena World* the same day as the Munn/DuBarry affair, but according to the planter it involved a quarrel brought on when the planter demanded that his sharecropper haul his cotton to the gin before an expected rain began. "The negro demurred, and finally told Mr. Ferrell he would haul the cotton when he d— pleased to do so. This brought on a quarrel and the negro finally became so infuriated at what he considered an invasion of his personal rights that he ran to one of his cotton baskets and got out a butcher knife and made for Ferrell. The latter ran back a few steps until he could get his pistol from his pocket when he fired, the ball entering the left side just below the heart." There were no witnesses to the incident, and Ferrell was not charged with any crime in the "unfortunate affair."[63]

Tensions persisted throughout the Arkansas delta well into the twentieth century. By 1916 a federal study of plantation conditions in Arkansas was warning that "as a result both of the evils inherent in the tenant system and of the occasional oppression by landlords, a state of acute unrest is developing among the tenants and there are clear indications of the beginning of organized resistance which may result in civil disturbances of a serious character."[64]

The existence of tensions severe enough to warrant fears of serious civil disturbances prior to World War I suggests that some historians may be attributing too much to the experience of that war and the postwar "Red Summer" in attempting to explain the emergence of the Progressive Farmers and Household Union of America and the Elaine Race Riot. To be sure, the form that longstanding discontent took was influenced by the war and its aftermath. Black veterans and civilians were conditioned by black participation in World War I, and their horizons had been expanded. Participation in the war also influenced the white response. The American Legion, an organization founded by returning veterans, played an instrumental role in fashioning that response, issuing a call to arms and generally massing white veterans in the offensive against black sharecroppers. But the Legion could no more control the wild and undisciplined white mob that descended upon Phillips County than could the planters who must have been, once the initial scare was past, aghast at their behavior. Nevertheless, planters publicly closed ranks, asking for troops—troops who disarmed white civilians as well as blacks—and then touted an official version of the riot that concealed what really transpired. Such a version served to obscure the abuses of the sharecropping system and to restore the delicately balanced white class structure, dominated at the top by planters.

Just as the official version of events was concocted within a certain historical context, its adoption by Butts and James forty years later cannot be divorced from events taking place in the late 1950s and early 1960s. Butts and James were writing just three years after the Central High crisis and in the midst of a swelling civil rights movement. The Arkansas delta soon became the center of a voting rights campaign by the Student Nonviolent Coordinating Committee, and, again, the white community there felt besieged. It is only within this context that Butts and James's wildly contradictory portrait of Robert Hill, the union organizer described as a con man and troublemaker, can be understood. He is seemingly presented as a forerunner of the Civil Rights Era's "outside agitators," come—in the minds of many white southerners—to muddy the "peaceful relations between the races."[65] Hill was an ambiguous figure whose motivations troubled even sympathetic historians and whose demeanor, behavior, and origins disquieted class-sensitive NAACP officials. Yet the convoluted scenario created by Butts and James is implausible at best. They would have it that Hill created the union simply as a money-making scheme. Yet at the same time, they argue he forged an insurrectionary force and hatched a plot to murder planters. Complicating these two obviously contradictory lines of thinking, Butts and James insisted that Phillips County sharecroppers were neither exploited nor unhappy. Their explanation of why Phillips County blacks joined the union rests on the condescending assumption that they were ignorant and easily duped by a smooth talking black con man. Butts and James, furthermore, failed to note that, on the morning of the Hoop Spur incident, Robert Hill, unaware of the violent turn of events at the church, was meeting O. S. Bratton, son of attorney U. S. Bratton, at the railroad station in McGehee, Arkansas. Hill had earlier approached the senior Bratton to represent union members in the suits they planned to file, and the younger Bratton was on his way to Phillips County to secure information. Butts and James never explained why a con man would hire an attorney, especially one with U. S. Bratton's credentials, to represent the individuals the alleged con man was swindling.[66]

In portraying black southerners bestirring themselves at long last to resist their oppression, O. A. Rogers, Jr., president of Arkansas Baptist College, a black institution in Little Rock, was likely influenced in his own way by the momentous events swirling around him. He discovered all too quickly that there were some in the Phillips County white community who still held to the traditional narrative of events. Rogers was acquainted with novelist Francis Irby Gwaltney who claimed in a letter to his literary agent to have helped him research his essay, and Gwaltney was to discover that even a fictionalized account of the riot would receive a cool reception in certain quarters.[67] The reaction of American publishers to Gwaltney's novel about Elaine, *The Quicksand Years*, suggests that they too found the topic problematic for reasons other than the book's literary quality. If Butts and James refused to acknowledge that the planters had brought events upon themselves, those more sympathetic to civil rights had little reason at this point to dwell on the legitimacy of black armed response. One publisher thought the premise was too farfetched, and another described the story as "too unreal."[68] Gwaltney was forced to go to a London publisher, and the book came out to some very good reviews in the summer of 1965.[69] By that time, the events it described may have seemed not "unreal" but all too real. In October 1965, just two months after the Watts riot rocked Los Angeles, Gwaltney's Hollywood agent reported on his failed efforts to sell producers on the idea of a movie based on the Elaine Race Riot. "I realize you really did not expect any other reaction," the agent wrote, but "without exception" the response from producers was "that the material is beautifully written, but quite impossible to do as a motion picture in this town at this time."[70]

Arthur Waskow, publishing a year after Gwaltney's Hollywood rejection, was seeking to understand governmental attempts to control individual and group violence, and thus was more consciously viewing the Elaine Race Riot from the perspective of the 1960s. B. Boren McCool, writing four years later, had witnessed more urban rioting and the assassination of Martin Luther King, Jr. These developments perhaps led McCool to recognize a greater degree of militancy on the part of Phillips County African Americans in 1919, which stands in contrast to Rogers, who saw them as simply defending themselves from white attacks.

What this suggests, in fact, is that history is constantly being rewritten and reinterpreted, and that no historian, including the one writing this essay, can escape the influence of the environment in which he or she lives and writes, no matter how much one strives for objectivity. The Elaine Race Riot reminds us that violence has been a part of almost every age, including our own. This violence can be triggered by a complex of social, economic, ethnic, racial, psychological, and other factors. Behind the events in Elaine is a "white" story as well as a "black" story, and understanding what motivated groups of landless whites to rampage against blacks at the beginning of the twentieth century may be crucial to understanding why minorities continue to be the targets of racial violence at the end of the twentieth century—and not simply in Arkansas or Jasper, Texas, but in Howard Beach, New York, and Chicago, Illinois.

CHAPTER 3

A Place at the Table

Hot Springs and the GI Revolt

PATSY HAWTHORN RAMSEY

Most readers will be at least broadly familiar with Arkansas's storied history of political corruption. Garland County—Hot Springs, in particular—was the home of an especially blatant example of crooked politics well into the 20th century. Relying largely upon the manipulation of poll tax receipts as a way of engineering election outcomes and protecting the lucrative gambling industry, the political machine of Hot Springs Mayor Leo P. McLaughlin finally was defeated in 1946 by a group of returning World War II veterans and their allies. In this selection, the author details the backgrounds, motivations, and career paths of Sid McMath, Q. Byrum Hurst, I. G. Brown and other members of the "GI Revolt." While Ramsey paints a more complicated picture of the men and the movement than past accounts, she concludes that their legacy was indeed one of cleaner elections, if not a Hot Springs free of gaming interests.

On June 14, 1946, the *Arkansas Gazette* reported that a retired marine, Lt. Col. Sid McMath, and a group of his fellow World War II veterans were staging a "GI Revolt" in Garland County. They intended to oust the entrenched political machine of Hot Springs mayor Leo P. McLaughlin, who was identified as the kingpin of a corrupt and illegal gambling industry in the spa city.[1] Subsequent newspaper articles and historical narratives continued to use the term "revolt" to describe the entrance of World War II veterans into Arkansas politics, citing McMath and the Garland County GIs as the pioneers and the most conspicuous examples of this phenomenon.

Originally published in *Arkansas Historical Quarterly* 59
(Winter 2000): 407–28. Reprinted with permission.
DOI: https://doi.org/10.34053/parry2019.riapag2.3

Encouraged by the rhetoric of the GIs themselves, writers have repeated the story that the GIs, having so recently fought totalitarianism abroad, were eager to make Arkansas safe for democracy by bringing fair and honest government to their own communities.[2] A number of accounts do acknowledge that a more complex mixture of idealism and ambition went into the revolt, but few have taken a very close look at the personalities and backgrounds of the men involved.[3]

The war-hero imagery that the veterans themselves indulged in obscures what appears to have been profound differences within the Garland County group that fought the McLaughlin machine. Although some of them were war heroes, others were not even veterans. Some among the GIs wanted to rid Hot Springs of illegal gambling while others supported it. Some of the candidates may have decided to seek office because of their war experiences, but at least two of them were pursuing longstanding dreams of holding public office. And while some invited themselves to the table, others took a place already set for them. Still, whatever their motives or background may have been, the GIs possessed a common interest in securing honest elections in Garland County in 1946. Accomplishing that would earn them a place in Arkansas history.

Garland County was certainly a community in need of political change. For as long as most citizens could remember, political and economic power had been concentrated in the hands of Hot Springs mayor Leo P. McLaughlin's political machine, which protected and was supported by an illegal but open casino gambling industry.[4] While many local citizens did not necessarily object to gambling, which provided jobs in a rather underdeveloped area, they were dissatisfied with the attendant corruption in their local government and their limited access to the political process.

The little resort's gambling history reached as far back as the late 1800s. After several interruptions, legal pari-mutuel betting on horse races became a permanent fixture in 1934. Fashionable casinos and back street dives openly offered illegal gambling both to high rollers and penny-ante players.[5] Places such as the Belvedere Club and the Tower Club on the edge of the city and the chic Southern Club on Central Avenue catered to casino gambling as well as bookmaking. Slot machines were stuck in back rooms of small cafes and taverns, out of the way, but certainly not hidden. There was no need to hide the gambling devices because local officials, including those in law enforcement, accepted illegal gaming as part of the heritage of Hot Springs, and state officials often pretended to be completely unaware of it. Occasionally, in response to social reformers or political pressure, the gambling halls were raided and closed briefly. They never remained so for long.[6]

Since his election as mayor in 1927, McLaughlin and cohorts such as Circuit Judge Earl Witt and Municipal Judge Vernal Ledgerwood had operated a tightly controlled political machine that directed city and county politics and regulated the illegal gambling industry.[7] Many people thought Ledgerwood actually ran the machine while McLaughlin was merely its figurehead. Street talk sometimes credited unknown gangsters or underworld gambling figures with calling the shots for the whole operation. Yet, despite the presence of such figures as Owney Madden in Hot Springs, no one has offered proof of such control.[8] Regardless of who the real decision-maker was in the political machine, Leo Patrick McLaughlin enjoyed being its titular head. Flamboyant in dress and personality, the mayor, wearing a signature red carnation on his lapel, often drove down Central Avenue in his viceroy showbuggy drawn by matching horses named Scotch and Soda.[9]

The machine more than merely tolerated illegal gambling. By what Jim Lester terms a "gentlemen's agreement," entertainment businesses that wished to avoid problems with local law enforcement paid regular "fines," essentially semi-monthly fees, with a portion going to the city and part going to McLaughlin's group. Former bookmakers testified in the 1947 bribery trial of Hot Springs city attorney Jay Rowland that they had paid regular "fees" to Rowland or to the secretary of former mayor McLaughlin.[10] In return for the fees, McLaughlin allowed these establishments to operate without fear of police raids or other legal interference. McLaughlin openly promoted Hot Springs as a vacation spot for people interested in gambling.

Of course, McLaughlin could not provide such protection to the gambling industry without completely controlling local government. The machine hand-picked candidates for political offices. Persons seeking office knew they had little chance of winning without the blessing of "the Administration," as the machine was often called.[11] In turn, the machine made sure its candidates were elected. Its means of control was fraudulent manipulation of the poll tax, Arkansas's unofficial means of voter registration. Everyone desiring to vote, except citizens in military service, had to pay the tax. By Arkansas law, a person could pay eligible voters' tax by proxy. Law required that the tax receipts be turned over to the prospective voters within five days of purchase.[12] Liquor stores and other small businesses sometimes bought blocks of receipts, handing them over to customers as they came in to shop. In a small city where not everyone had regular transportation to the courthouse such a practice was a convenience, a kind deed, and a means of garnering business and political loyalty. But with no voter registration nor identity verification system in place, abuse of the system was inevitable. The Hot Springs machine routinely purchased large blocks of poll tax receipts and found voters to redeem them for ballots on election day. For the unscrupulous politician, it was not a large step from having poll tax receipts on hand for potential voters to signing up people who should be voting but were not. Apparently for many politicians, moving on to signing authorizations for deceased or absent voters was not so large a step either. To carry out the scheme, the county clerk, collector, and election officials had to be involved in the plan, choosing not to check the legitimacy of poll tax receipts in the hands of their political friends. Clearly, many local citizens also knew the truth but chose either to ignore it or to participate in its effacement.[13]

The McLaughlin regime met its first real political challenge with McMath's decision to run for prosecuting attorney in 1946. McMath later said that he had two motives in seeking office that year. His ambition since youth had been to hold public office, possibly that of governor, and he was ready to pursue that goal at this point in his life. But he also wanted to rid Hot Springs of the corrosive gambling industry. As a young man, McMath had spent many hours listening to former circuit judge C. T. Cotham talk about his own frustration at being unable to stem the corruption that accompanied open gaming in the city. McMath vowed to himself that one day he would do what Judge Cotham had been unable to do.[14] To carry out that goal, McMath called upon his fellow veterans and former classmates to join him on his self-appointed mission. Some of those who joined him shared his disgust with gambling. Others simply shared McMath's ambition for office. Either way, accomplishing their purposes necessitated the toppling of the McLaughlin machine.

In the winter of 1945 McMath met with a group of veteran friends at the Elks Lodge in Hot Springs to discuss his hopes of winning office and reforming local politics. His goal, he told them, was to establish honest government in their city and county. McMath convinced the men that together they could secure county and city offices and eliminate the McLaughlin machine.[15] Adopting the name "Government Improvement League," which was aptly, and perhaps opportunistically, shortened to GI League, the men began working toward their goal of winning the Democratic preferential primaries to be held that July. By the end of April, they had chosen their slots and announced their candidacies.

The GI League consisted of approximately twenty to thirty men. Most of them were, indeed, returned veterans. Of those who filed for county positions in the Democratic preferential primary, only Leonard Ellis, a longtime friend of McMath and candidate for circuit and chancery clerk, was not a veteran. Two other notable non-veterans in the group, Scott Wood and William Bouic, both local attorneys, worked on the campaigns but were not candidates.[16] Those in the group who had served in the war were not necessarily typical of the state's veteran population, however. Four of the veteran candidates were practicing attorneys: McMath, Clyde Brown, David Whittington, and Q. Byrum Hurst. A number of prominent members of the group who were not candidates were likewise attorneys, including Julian Glover and Richard Hobbs, who helped with legal work for the group.[17]

McMath filed to run for prosecuting attorney for the eighteenth judicial circuit, composed of Garland and Montgomery Counties. His opponent was incumbent Curtis Ridgeway, a McLaughlin insider. Because of its power to bring criminal cases to court, control of the prosecutor's office was essential to political reform. McMath's law partner, Clyde H. Brown, ran for the other key county position, circuit judge of the eighteenth circuit, against incumbent Earl Witt, an integral part of the McLaughlin machine.[18] I. G. Brown (no relation to Clyde) opposed incumbent sheriff Marion Anderson. J. O. Campbell drew no opposition for tax collector in the primary but expected an independent opponent in the general election, Filmore Bledsoe, a McLaughlin supporter.[19] GI attorney Q. Byrum Hurst ran for county judge against long-time incumbent Elza Housley. W. J. Wilkins opposed the machine's county treasurer, Henry Murphy. Veteran Ray Owen, owner of Hot Springs Credit Bureau, ran for tax collector against Mack Wilson. In the state senate race, local attorney and veteran David B. Whittington challenged Ernest Maner, who had served six terms in the state legislature. Nonveteran Ellis challenged John Jones for the position of circuit and chancery clerk that Jones had held since 1912, and E. M. Houpt (Hurst's uncle) ran for county clerk against fifteen-year incumbent Roy Raef.[20] The smallest race on the ticket was for the position of constable within the city of Hot Springs. Veteran Tommy Freeman, ex-Navy petty officer and former welterweight boxing champion of the world, ran for that position.[21]

Not all politically active veterans enlisted in the GI League. The Garland County sheriff's race drew another war veteran candidate, Charles "Stuffy" Dugan, who campaigned in decided opposition to the GI group. Dugan, twenty-five and a highly decorated flyer, was a student at Henderson State College during the campaign season.[22] His rather limited campaigning appeared to center around accusations that Hurst and GI attorney Scott

Wood had engineered the GI effort in order to continue their own control of the gambling industry.[23] That belief was apparently not shared by a large number of other people. No other person knowledgeable about the era has suggested that Hurst was anything more than one of the followers of the group.

In spite of considerable talk about McLaughlin not being the real head of the machine and the fact that the mayor's office was not on the July ballot, he was the main target of the GI campaign. According to McMath, the GIs felt that if they could expose McLaughlin, the rest of the machine would fall with him. Other than eliminating that machine, these ambitious young men, ranging in age from mid-twenties to mid-thirties, had no real political agenda nor a cohesive political philosophy.[24] Some of the men opposed illegal gambling, but some of them, notably Hurst and I. G. Brown, openly supported gambling because of its strong positive impact on Hot Springs's economy.[25] Accordingly, the GI campaign focused on political corruption and said next to nothing about gambling—as inextricably linked as the two phenomena were.

As real as the problem of corruption was, some GIs seem to have been driven chiefly by a sense that it was time to resume career trajectories that prior political interest, family connections, and professional background had charted but the war had delayed. Hurst, for example, had dreamed of holding public office since his youth. The son of a well-known Church of God minister who was active in local politics and the real estate market, Hurst spent many evenings at county Democratic Party meetings listening to men talk politics. Hurst entered the army in 1943, serving as a counselor to men preparing for discharge but not participating in any overseas military action.[26] The GI movement presented a golden opportunity for Hurst to enter the political fray with group support and the prestige of wartime military service on his resume.

By Hurst's own account, some of the incumbents were "good men" who were challenged chiefly because he and other veterans wanted their positions. He remembered Curtis Ridgeway, the circuit judge who used his court to protect machine members, as a "dear man," and not part of the McLaughlin machine (McMath disagreed, insisting that Ridgeway was definitely a McLaughlin man who assisted in the maintenance of corrupt government).[27] Former sheriff Mack Wilson and former county judge Elza T. Housley, whom Hurst put out of office, were likewise not corrupt, he said, but instead were honorable men who tried to steer clear of the taint of McLaughlin. When asked why he worked so hard to win the office from Housley, Hurst laughed and replied, "I wanted his job."[28] Some of the support the GIs received also apparently partook of this "outs vs. ins" spirit. Without naming names, McMath recalled in a 1996 interview that he had received contributions in 1946 from "people who were mad at the Administration because they were not part of it."[29]

Furthermore, the distinct battle lines drawn between the GIs and the McLaughlin group obscured the personal and family connections that existed between the veterans and the old regime. Most of the veterans had grown up in Garland County and had family on both sides of the gambling issue. Some had family members who worked in some aspect of the gaining industry or for the local government. Circuit judge candidate Clyde Brown was married to the daughter of Sam Watt, former owner of the Belvedere Club, the most elegant of the gambling establishments.[30] Brown's father was Hot Springs assistant fire chief, Captain Riley Brown, a McLaughlin appointee. Captain Brown expected to lose his job after the election and had considered retiring before the election, but McLaughlin chose to be magnanimous, letting him know that he would not be fired because he was a good man and could not help what his son was doing.[31]

Whatever their backgrounds or reasons for participating in the revolt, the GIs needed to prove to voters that the McLaughlin regime was indeed corrupt. They knew that they could not possibly win if machine candidates continued the unscrupulous practice of ballot box stuffing by means of illegal poll tax receipts. They set about looking for evidence of poll tax fraud. Knowing that a challenge under state election laws would be heard in Circuit Judge Earl Witt's court, a court under the control of the McLaughlin machine, they found a candidate for the local congressional seat so that they could mount a challenge under federal election laws. Patrick Mullins of Dumas agreed to be a write-in candidate against unopposed incumbent W. R. Norrell in the August preferential primary. They began preparations to challenge the validity of one-third of Garland County's poll tax receipts in federal court.[32]

Meanwhile, the official campaign opened on July 4, 1946, with the equivalent of a twenty-one gun salute. Using a World War II propaganda technique, I. G. Brown flew over the small community of Lonsdale, a few miles east of Hot Springs, dropping campaign leaflets inviting people to attend the GIs' first rally, to be held that night at the Colony House in Lonsdale. Presumably, they bypassed Hot Springs for their opening night in order to avoid problems with McLaughlin. Before an audience of the loyal and the curious, the handsome and eloquent McMath promised voters that his group would clean up the corruption that kept good citizens from enjoying democracy as it should be. To the more than 800 persons there, he vowed to "protect you against the violation of your civil rights; I will champion the rights of the people against all opponents—yes, against his majesty Der Fuehrer of Hot Springs."[33] On stage with him, the line-up of exuberant and sincere young candidates in their military uniforms seemed to present a picture of America at its best.

As members of the audience left the rally to drive away in their automobiles and pickup trucks, they were reminded of the sinister forces the GIs were fighting. While people were inside listening to speeches someone had sneaked into the parking lot and salted it with roofing tacks.[34] In her memoir of growing up in Hot Springs, author Shirley Abbott related her father's assertion that "Leo's boys"—in plainclothes rather than policemen's uniforms—had scattered the tacks.[35] People certainly assumed McLaughlin was responsible. The young veterans who had so enthusiastically promised to respond to the needs of their community had their first opportunity to do so right then. They ended their evening changing flat tires for their audience.

While the candidates were busy pursuing votes, other GI League members worked to gather evidence of fraudulent use of poll tax receipts. Five candidates for office (Leonard Ellis, Tommy Freeman, I. G. Brown, Egbert M. Houpt, and Patrick Mullins) and three taxpayers (Brad O. Smith, Jr., John T. Kilgore, and Oliver Livingston) filed suit in US District Court complaining that nineteen individuals had made block purchases of poll tax receipts, then forged ineligible or fictitious names on them for the purpose of "stuffing" the ballot boxes of Garland County. Tax Collector Mack Wilson and County Clerk Roy C. Raef were also named in the suit because of their roles in poll tax sales. So were three Garland County election commissioners accused of knowingly certifying the illegal poll tax receipts. Defendants alleged to have purchased blocks of receipts included black ward boss Will Page, casino operator Jack McJunkin, Walter Weldon, Mrs. Fannie McLaughlin, A. J. Karston, Erb Wheatley, Elmer Walters, George Young, Arthur Young, Ben Rogers, George Pakis, R. Manning, Charles Dieckriede, Mike Baucher, H. A. Bledsoe, Charles Appleton, Ross B. Adams, Bill Abbott, and Frank Grant.[36]

Three days before the trial began, a man robbed GI campaign workers Oliver Livingston and Earl Fulton of a briefcase containing depositions of persons who said their names had been used on receipts without their permission. The pair identified McLaughlin's special deputy assessor Ed

Spears as the person who held them at gunpoint and took the briefcase.[37] GI leaders promptly paid a visit to the mayor's office, demanding the return of their briefcase. Two hours later, the case was returned, contents intact. McLaughlin knew that keeping the case would not stop the GIs but apparently wished to use their information against them. Several individuals whose depositions were in the case would appear in court three days later as witnesses for the defense. Ed Spears later admitted to, and was convicted of, stealing the briefcase.[38]

The poll tax fraud trial opened July 8 in Judge John E. Miller's federal court. Presenting the contents of the rescued briefcase as evidence, the plaintiffs charged that 3,825 poll tax receipts issued to the defendants were illegitimate. Some of the signatures were of persons who were deceased or had moved from Garland County years before, others belonged to persons who swore that their names had been forged.[39]

Even after getting the briefcase evidence to court, the GI attorneys had to fight to prove it credible. The defense produced several witnesses whose signed affidavits were in the case but who suddenly "remembered" on the witness stand that they had authorized purchase of their poll taxes. Club operator and defendant Jack McJunkin admitted, however, that he had personally signed more than 200 authorizations, which had been purchased in a block. Other defendants admitted making similar purchases and signing them, using ineligible and unauthorized names. Garland County collector Mack Wilson testified during the trial that he had issued many illegal poll tax receipts in his years in office but defended himself by insisting that such practices were common all over the state.[40]

The largest block of poll tax receipts in contention was held by Will Page, a black ward boss and gambling house operator who had 1,483 receipts issued over a period from May 29 to August 24, 1945. They were numbered in a way designed to impede detection. Anne McMath and J. O. Campbell discovered a pattern of skips while working through the night to decipher the code of receipt entries. When Campbell testified in court, the defense attorneys did not even cross-examine him; they knew they had lost.[41] Handwriting expert W. H. Quakenbush of the Kansas Bureau of Investigation had already testified that "an overwhelming majority of the signatures of authorizations held by Will Page were signed in the same writing." He gave the same testimony about names on the McJunkin list, a fact to which McJunkin readily admitted. The evidence against Page turned the case in the GIs' favor. On July 11, Judge Miller canceled 1,607 Garland

County poll tax receipts, 776 of those held by Will Page and 831 of those obtained by other followers of McLaughlin.[42] The first battle had been won. The veterans were closer to an honest election.

In an attempt to further curb the power of McLaughlin, GIs immediately filed another suit, this time in circuit court, to remove Mayor McLaughlin as chairman of the Garland County Democratic Central Committee. With McMath and Clyde Brown acting as their attorneys, the GI plaintiffs contended that officeholders or candidates could not be members of the central committee. Citing section 19 of the Arkansas Democratic Party rules, McLaughlin responded that he was not an elected member of the committee. Instead, he had been appointed and, though chairman, did not have voting privileges.[43] In a rather heated exchange with GI attorney David Whittington, the mayor drew a laugh from the audience when he told Whittington, "If you're questioning our legal methods I'll remind you that for years one of our best legal advisors was your daddy."[44] The late George Whittington had indeed been an attorney for and supporter of Leo McLaughlin. Not surprisingly, the GIs' claim was denied by Circuit Judge Earl Witt, a principal in the machine, and the mayor continued as chairman of the Garland County Democratic Central Committee.[45]

The three weeks between the poll tax trial and the Democratic primary saw local opinion sharply divided and tensions reaching the boiling point. Supporters of both sides were reported to be carrying weapons. Members of labor unions and the "entertainment industry" supported McLaughlin, but the GIs appeared to have captured the popular imagination. At a final rally the night before the election a crowd of nearly 6,000 listened to the veterans promise clean government. At a rally for the incumbents held at the city auditorium only a few hundred people showed up to hear members of the old regime plead to be returned to office. Neither side knew for sure what to expect the next day.[46]

Voters going to the polls on July 30 for the Democratic preferential primary saw a sight they had not seen in a long time, if ever, in Garland County. Poll watchers for both sets of candidates were carefully monitoring the proceedings. Supporters of the veterans used home movie cameras to record citizens going into the voting stations. When Mayor McLaughlin tried to enter the sixth ward polling station (not his voting place) a poll watcher stopped him and informed him that he could not proceed. When the mayor protested that as chairman of the Democratic Central Committee he had a right to enter the polling place, the poll watcher still refused. McLaughlin was so "flabbergasted" that he shook the man's hand twice before he hurriedly left the room.[47] Hot Springs native James Holt remembers that his father and other GI workers stationed themselves in buildings adjacent to the polling places, armed with shotguns to make sure no one tampered with the ballot boxes. McLaughlin forces took the same precaution.[48]

Yet, in spite of the GIs' vigilance, what had probably been the most honest election in Garland County in years did not overturn the McLaughlin regime. Only the charismatic McMath defeated an "Administration" incumbent, unseating Curtis Ridgeway with a vote of 3,900 to 3,375. Veteran J. O. Campbell was unopposed in his bid for tax assessor after incumbent Roy Gillenwater resigned from office and left town. Votes from Montgomery County, the other part of the local judicial district, probably secured McMath's victory.[49] Clyde Brown came within 300 votes of upsetting incumbent circuit judge Earl Witt, mostly through the support of Montgomery County voters. Brown's loss probably reflected the fact that Witt was viewed by the public as a much more honorable man than McLaughlin or Ridgeway. The candidates who depended upon votes exclusively from Garland County lost by larger margins.[50]

Charges of election fraud emerged immediately. Poll tax receipts that had been canceled by Judge Miller in the July federal court decision were used for voting in two black wards that went heavily for the incumbents. The margins in these two wards brought the defeat of circuit judge candidate Clyde Brown and I. G. Brown, candidate for sheriff. GIs claimed that they had film of black voters going into the polls with receipts to which pink slips had been attached instructing them how to mark their ballots. The veterans announced plans to contest the election in court. In turn, "Administration" candidates accused the GI camp of intimidating legitimate voters, keeping some from the polls.[51] Their threats to have ballot boxes impounded amounted to little, however, since they had won most of the elections.

Following the primary, McMath declared in a public statement that he would continue the fight to clean up Garland County and Hot Springs government. "The war for free government has just begun," he said.[52] The GIs' plan now called for the defeated veterans to enter the general election race as independent candidates. The move would allow opponents in later campaigns to question these men's loyalty to the Democratic Party, but running as independent candidates seemed a more fruitful option than filing a lawsuit contesting the vote. Judge Miller's federal court would not have jurisdiction over an election that did not involve any federal offices, so this time the case would have to be heard in circuit court. The veterans, however, did announce plans to ask the Arkansas Supreme Court to remove McLaughlin as chairman of the county Democratic committee. For its part, the McLaughlin camp threatened to enter an independent candidate against McMath, but he ended up being unopposed in the November general election, except for the token write-in candidacy of Jay Rowland, the "Administration's" city attorney.[53]

The general election of November 5, 1946, put Garland County GI candidates in all county offices and in the circuit judge and prosecuting attorney positions. In a solidly Democratic state and county, all county and circuit judicial officers were elected as independents. Voters apparently saw the single win in the primary election as a signal that new leadership was possible in their counties. A record 16,000 voters cast ballots that day. Clyde Brown's 200 vote loss changed to victory by a 2,008 vote margin in the circuit judge's race. I. G. Brown won the sheriff's position from incumbent Marion Anderson. Q. Byrum Hurst beat Elza T. Housley to become county judge. Ray Owen won as tax collector, and E. M. Houpt secured the county clerk position. Leonard Ellis beat John E. Jones for circuit clerk. Only two veterans failed in their races. Attorney David Whittington lost his bid for state senator to the twelve-year incumbent, Ernest Maner, and Tommy Freeman lost his race for constable, presumably because his contest was restricted to city voters, among whom McLaughlin was stronger.[54]

In a radio address following the election, Municipal Judge Vern Ledgerwood admitted that the McLaughlin regime had come to an end.[55] The implicit message was that without the support of the circuit judge and prosecuting attorney the machine would be unable to manipulate the court system. Without the cooperation of the county tax assessor, clerk, and collector they would have no control over the electoral process. For his part, McMath proclaimed that the era of machine politics was over in Garland County and Hot Springs. Responding to speculation that the young veterans might become the next machine, McMath stated, "There's a difference between an organization and a machine. Yesterday's election was proof that the residents of this county will not bow to another machine in the next 20 years."[56]

On November 7, the *Arkansas Gazette* reported the GIs' "course for the future." It included defeat of Mayor McLaughlin in the 1947 municipal elections, grand jury investigation of multiple unspecified charges against McLaughlin, and a straw vote after the city election to ascertain citizen support of open gambling.[57] Such a vote would have no legal standing because all gambling except restricted pari-mutuel betting at Oaklawn Park was illegal by state law. But the GI campaign had been quite cautious with respect to the gambling issue, and some of the veterans seem to have been eager at this point to assure their constituents that they were not opposed to it.

It turned out that the transfer of power from the McLaughlin machine to the GI forces would be completed even before the municipal elections of 1947. Knowing their regime had ended, Vern Ledgerwood announced he would not seek reelection.[58] McLaughlin attempted another campaign for mayor but saw his political support shrivel up along with the gambling industry. GI Earl Ricks, part owner of Ricks-Clinton Buick dealership, quickly announced his candidacy for the mayoralty. Following the seating of a special grand jury to investigate his administration, McLaughlin publicly admitted that he had allowed illegal gambling and withdrew from the race. Voters elected Ricks that spring in a landslide vote, along with a new slate of aldermen.[59]

In March the grand jury returned thirty-two indictments against McLaughlin. It also indicted his secretary, Hazel Marsh, for perjury and his brother, George McLaughlin, for wrongfully receiving public funds.[60] McLaughlin's city attorney, Jay Rowland, was charged with bribery in multiple gambling cases. Former circuit judge Earl Witt and former municipal judge Vern Ledgerwood, rumored "brain" of the old machine, escaped any indictments and retired to their respective private law practices. Witt died of throat cancer a short time later.[61]

In Rowland's bribery trial, October 10, 1947, Prosecuting Attorney McMath focused on the corruption associated with gambling. He called six former operators of gambling establishments to the stand to give testimony about their payments to the city for operating privileges. Otis McGraw, former operator of the Southern Book Club and the Ohio Club, admitted that he paid Rowland a retainer of $50 each month for very little legal work. A. J. Karsten, of the White Front Club, testified that he also paid $50 per month to the city attorney during 1946. He delivered the payments to McLaughlin's secretary, in the mayor's office. Karsten and McGraw stated that when their businesses were raided by state police in previous years Rowland represented them in circuit court, and arranged for the return to them of 50 percent of the cash seized in the raids. Rowland retained the other half for the "Administration." City Clerk Emmett Jackson stated from the witness stand that local gamblers contributed $60,757.25 in monthly fees during 1945 and 1946 for licenses to operate. Each gaming establishment paid $131.30 a month, with $100 going to the city and $25 going to the city attorney. Jackson had no explanation for where the remainder went.[62] The

$50 retainer to Rowland paid by some gamblers was apparently a separate payment from the "licensing fee" paid to the city.

Rowland's first trial ended in deadlock, but Judge Maupin Cummings granted McMath's immediate request for a new trial, which brought a conviction. The attorney was sentenced to a year in state prison and a fine of $750.[63] Ultimately, Rowland would be the only "Administration" defendant to receive jail time.

McLaughlin's attorneys requested and were granted a change of venue for his trial on charges of malfeasance of office and bribery. The trial was moved to Mount Ida, the seat of Montgomery County, which had furnished majorities to McMath and Circuit Judge Brown. Yet, on November 19, 1947, McLaughlin was acquitted of the malfeasance charges, which centered around his brother George being on the city payroll without actually engaging in any work. One year later, Circuit Judge Cummings declared a mistrial when a second jury deadlocked in their deliberations on the bribery charges. Prosecutor McMath immediately dropped all charges against the former mayor.[64]

In *The Bookmaker's Daughter*, Shirley Abbott recalled a conversation with Earl Witt in which he claimed to have engineered McLaughlin's acquittal. After the jury was chosen, Witt said, he sent some cattle buyers to visit each juror's farm, with offers to buy cattle at more than twice the market price, in cash. The trial was not mentioned, and no promises were asked for or offered. "You'd be surprised at what a little money can do," Abbott remembered Witt saying.[65]

In the jury's defense, however, it might be noted that the evidence to convict on the malfeasance charge was scanty. George McLaughlin's own trial had ended in a hung jury. Witnesses had testified that George McLaughlin showed up in municipal court every day, although he engaged in no courtroom activities other than "standing there." Mayor McLaughlin stated that his brother had been hired as an "undercover" agent to keep track of gamblers and gangsters visiting the city. When giving instructions to the jury, the judge admonished members that they could not convict a man for not earning his paycheck but only for getting a fraudulent salary.[66]

Despite losing his battle to convict McLaughlin, Sid McMath was able to use the trials as a stage for his next political venture. He appointed Julian Glover and Richard Hobbs as deputy prosecuting attorneys to handle the eighteenth circuit's caseload and hit the road making public appearances in as many Arkansas towns as he could. Leaning upon his name recognition and prestige among veterans, McMath invited GI political organizations that had sprung up in other counties—including Yell, Crittenden, Jefferson, Cleveland, and Montgomery—to join the Young Democrats of Arkansas, of which he was president, in taking their revolt to the state level. He had not announced for governor, but that was not far away.

Even with only one local political campaign in his portfolio, McMath had enough political savvy to know that he needed more than just GI identification and support to get elected. Campaigning on promises of better roads and education, McMath courted traditional Democrats with a tone of moderate conservatism and built support by welding together coalitions of regionally powerful political leaders.[67] His strategies were effective, and, after a tough gubernatorial race, McMath went to the governor's office, where he served two terms (1949–1953). Leaving hometown ties behind, the new governor distanced himself from his former political allies and avoided entanglement in the controversies over gambling and corruption that still swirled around Garland County politics. The state police under McMath staged a few raids on Hot Springs gambling establishments, but those raids made little difference in the amount or types of gambling taking place.

Of the other original GI candidates, Leonard Ellis, Ray Owen, and Q. Byrum Hurst enjoyed lengthy careers in politics. J. O. Campbell served three terms as tax assessor and I. G. Brown two terms as sheriff before they each moved on to other interests. W. J. Wilkins left the treasurer's office after two terms.[68] Clyde Brown spent one lackluster year as circuit judge, then returned to private law practice. He had a reputation as a heavy drinker who "lived off his wife's money." His wife had received a substantial inheritance from her father, gambling club owner Sam Watt.[69]

The GIs of Garland County achieved their primary goal—securing honest elections that displaced the McLaughlin machine. Balloting on November 2, 1946, was probably the cleanest in many years—and the most honest for some years to come, if some poll watchers are to be believed. After the GI victory, the machine quickly withered. For some among the GI group, that was enough. But those among them interested in more enduring political reform and, especially, those interested in doing away with illegal gambling would find their ambitions frustrated.

The men who had campaigned against the corruption of the McLaughlin machine would have some problems keeping their own political organization clean. Honest elections did not guarantee honest or good government. Some of the GIs tried to perform the jobs to which they were elected honorably and efficiently. Others took the opportunity to build political power and reap economic rewards through public office. After serving at least six terms as tax collector, Ray Owen was convicted of poll tax fraud and sentenced to prison.[70] Leonard Ellis, a supporter of open gambling from the start, moved in 1955 from the circuit clerk's office to that of sheriff, where he stayed for many years. By reputation, Ellis was "Dane's man," meaning he received election support from Dane Harris, a prominent gambler and casino owner in Hot Springs, in return for political favors.[71] In 1959, Harris and Owney Madden opened the Vapors, a sophisticated supper club and casino that presented Las Vegas quality entertainment and casino gambling without interference from law enforcement. The club operated openly as a premier illegal gambling spot until 1967, when newly elected Republican governor Winthrop Rockefeller carried through with a promise to shut down illegal gambling in Hot Springs.

Near the end of his single term as county judge, Q. Byrum Hurst, elected as a GI in 1946, sold the county road equipment and pocketed the proceeds. A grand jury indicted him on a charge of malfeasance of office, and several taxpayers filed suits against him in an effort to recover the $7,950 that he received and some of the equipment.[72] He returned at least part of the money and avoided a jail term. Hurst then ran for prosecuting attorney the following spring and narrowly lost the Democratic nomination in a run-off with his GI colleague Julian Glover. Interestingly, Hurst's strongest show of support came from Hot Springs's second ward, where more than a thousand illegal poll tax receipts had been disqualified in 1946, thanks to the GI effort. In that ward, Hurst received 1,103 votes, Glover 214 votes, and a third candidate 127 votes.[73] The voters, or at least the ballot boxes, of Garland and Montgomery Counties did not hold Hurst's transgressions against him for long. A short time later he ran for state senator of that district, won, and served in that position for many years. While he was senator, he also faced more criminal charges, this time of federal income tax evasion. Hurst won acquittal on those charges when several Hot Springs businessmen, including gambler-gangster Owney Madden, testified that the income in question came from substantial loans they had made to Hurst over a period of years, rather than from payment for professional services. In his last trip to federal court, Hurst was not so fortunate. After he retired from the state senate in the late 1970s he was convicted of misuse of bank funds in a savings and loan scandal and was sentenced to time in a federal penitentiary.[74]

Though some among the GI group, such as McMath, seemed genuinely to oppose illegal gambling, the impact of their clean sweep of county government on gaming seems to have been only temporary. Shortly after the 1946 election the gambling houses quietly closed their doors and ceased operation. The GIs did not ask them to leave or threaten them, but, stripped of the friendly protection of Earl Witt and Vern Ledgerwood, casino operators must have been unsure of their future in Hot Springs. Not knowing who controlled the police, or if anyone did, gamblers kept under cover. Some of the gambling houses would open again in the spring, but only secretively and irregularly. In separate interviews, people who were involved in Hot Springs public life assert that the only gambling in town in the late 1940s was hidden. One of the most prominent casino operators of the 1950s referred to the gambling of 1947–1950 as "sneak gambling," in which people surreptitiously placed bets and played the horses in garages and back rooms. The casinos had closed, though "people knew where to find [gambling] if they wanted it."[75]

In early 1948, the Garland County grand jury issued a statement insisting that laws prohibiting illegal gambling be enforced and praising the men who assumed office after January 1, 1947, for "the courageous, efficient, and honest efforts they have made and are making to enforce the ordinances of Hot Springs."[76] The city jail docket for 1946–1947 suggests that arrests for gambling decreased in 1947. In November 1946, twenty men were arrested for gambling, with fines of $50 noted by the names of twelve of them. Only the first six of those men, arrested November 2, paid their fines. In December, thirteen people were arrested for gambling, with fines of $50 or $100 each, though none of these fines were paid. On February 3, 1947, thirteen men (no repeats from those of the previous year) were arrested, with fine of $10, not paid. No other gambling arrests were recorded until June, with one, and July, with four arrests. These June and July arrests also ended in fines of $10, none paid, and the cases were dismissed. City policeman Captain Young signed the book in 1946 as the arresting officer in all the arrests for that year. "Sheriff's office" was the entry for arresting officer in all of the 1947 cases.[77]

It might be that, rather than illegal gaming being in decline, law enforcement personnel were just not pursuing gamblers. But it appears that by the beginning of 1948 the future of gaming was sufficiently uncertain that the divisions over gambling that had always existed within the GI group became public. On January 16, 1948, the *Arkansas Gazette* reported that a new political party, the Business Man's party, had formed in Hot Springs to work for election of "candidates who will serve Hot Springs rather than themselves." Referring to the new party as "Another chapter . . . in the bitter fight that has been going on for more than a year to restore commercial gambling to Hot Springs," the article detailed the growing conflict between Prosecutor

McMath and Business Man's Party leaders, including County Judge Hurst and Tax Collector Ray Owen, both former GI group members.[78]

Whatever decline had occurred in the immediate aftermath of the GI Revolt, open commercial gambling had returned to Hot Springs by 1951 with the re-opening of the Southern Club casino, one of the oldest and most prominent of the McLaughlin-era establishments. Soon other gambling houses sprang up, and Hot Springs was on its way to re-establishing its reputation as an entertainment resort. The Belvedere, the Southern, the Ohio, Stute's, and other clubs opened under slightly different rules from those of McLaughlin's day. The highly structured system of "licensing" used earlier gave way to a less organized system of individualized bribery, payoffs, and officials looking the other way.[79] After his election as governor in 1956, Orval Faubus sent a message that he would not interfere with the city's local affairs. City leaders again imposed a system of fines on gambling establishments and prosperity reigned for another decade.[80] Sheriff Leonard Ellis, Tax Collector Ray Owen, and State Senator Hurst were the only GIs still holding local office by 1956. All were both supporters and beneficiaries of the gambling industry.[81]

The men of 1946 rode onto the field of Arkansas politics upon white chargers of honor and justice and free elections. But if they used their war hero image to generate political support, they were simply employing a campaign strategy that had been effective since the days of George Washington. American voters have a long tradition of expecting war heroes to be good political leaders, and World War II's victory over totalitarianism made heroes of many young men. If ambition, even opportunism, intertwined with idealism in some or most of them, they were not so very different from many politicians nor, indeed, from some of American history's greatest statesmen. And if some seem to have betrayed the group's principles, one should remember the distinctive environment in which they operated. When asked if any of the GI politicians ever compromised their integrity, Q. Byrum Hurst responded, "Yes, some of us did. The people demanded it."[82] The people of Garland County had voted to clean up local politics, but many among them supported—perhaps even depended upon—the illegal gambling industry, which could hardly exist if every politician did his duty honestly and well.

CHAPTER 4

The Arkansas Electorate

JIM RANCHINO

In 1968 Arkansas voters simultaneously returned an anti-Vietnam Democrat to the US Senate, installed their first post-Reconstruction Republican in the governor's mansion, and cast their electoral college votes for the segregationist nominee of the American Independent Party. It was this "schizophrenic" election that led Jim Ranchino to write Faubus to Bumpers: Arkansas Votes, 1960–1970, *the larger work of which this selection is a part. Arkansas's unpredictable political preferences are a subject about which many have speculated but few have studied. Here, Ranchino makes two important contributions to the study of Arkansas politics. First, he offers some of the earliest survey-based research on the Arkansas electorate, concluding that "Mr. Average Voter" of the mid-20th century was—above all things—a moderate, and a Democrat. Second, he uses county-level election registration and turnout data to highlight the regional influences that remain important in the state's politics.*

The elections of 1968 focused national attention on voting habits in Arkansas. Added to Winthrop Rockefeller's victory in the race for governor was the state's plurality for presidential candidate George Wallace, and a resounding majority for Senator J. William Fulbright. This combination of a Republican with massive black support, an American Independent with an anti-black following, and a dovish Democrat made for a strange victory party in the New South.

Some accused Arkansas of going to the polls blindfolded; others were less kind and described the response as political schizophrenia. At least three scholars of national reputation took one look at the precinct returns in the official records of the secretary of state's office in Little Rock, and walked

---

Originally published in *Faubus to Bumpers: Arkansas Votes, 1960–1970* (Arkadelphia, AR: Action Research, Inc., 1972). Reprinted with permission. DOI: https://doi.org/10.34053/parry2019.riapag2.4

away with a dull headache and an unbelieving shake of the head. The results simply made no sense.

Whatever triggered such a curious set of voting results may never by fully known (I am not at all convinced that we will ever completely know why people vote for certain candidates and reject others). However, there are some known factors about the Arkansas electorate in the 1960s that are worth discussing, and when combined with a detailed breakdown of major state elections, some distinctive clues as to what happened do appear.

Who is the Arkansas Voter?[1]

If you had to describe the "average" Arkansas voter in detail, the voter who actually participates regularly in the democratic process (which is only about 32 percent of those of voting age), it would go something like this.

That voter is a white, male, Baptist, about forty-nine years of age, who stopped his formal education after graduation from high school, holds down a white collar job in an office, or a blue collar job at a minor supervisory position, has an income of $6,500 a year, and lives in either the northwestern part of Camden, or in eastern Jacksonville.

He considers himself a Democrat, and usually votes for the party's nominees, although his party loyalties are less then deep, especially at the national level. He has, on occasion, voted for a Republican in state races, especially when he examines the qualities of the candidates, and prides himself in knowing that the party does not control his vote. After all, he does appreciate that "different" kind of candidate who is an individual , not a fanatical party man.

He is not extremely concerned with who wins an election, but says he does have an average to strong concern. His participation in politics is primarily that of a spectator. Every two years, he simply watches a little closer. If he has bought tickets to a banquet or breakfast to help finance a campaign efforts, he does not attend the meeting. He has never written a letter to a public official and does not actually believe it would have much effect anyway.

On the race issue, he considers himself a mild integrationist, although he is not quite sure of the exact implications of that stand. It does mean that he has moved into a little better white neighborhood in the last ten years and does not care for blacks to move into that area.

Most of his information about a candidate comes from what he sees on the television screen, although a bit here and a bit there are picked up by headline browsing the newspapers. He does little or no research into the candidate and the issues, and frankly admits that television images influence his final decision on how to vote. Besides, daily living, the family, sports, the church, the job and the needed money, are all a great deal more important than politics and much easier to understand. So goes Mr. Average Voter in Arkansas.

This brief picture of an average voter has its flaws, as all average descriptions do. It does not allow for the individual nuances, the personal prejudices, and the many motives that make all voters separate and definable entities. Nor does it give much credit to the impact of issues on the voting public. But it does present some revealing faces of the Arkansas electorate that deserve discussion.

There has been much talk in the last four or five years about the "independence" of Arkansas voters. Some estimates have been published that as high as sixty percent of the voters are independent. The term "independent" is somewhat misleading, for while it may imply that the individual will make up his own mind about candidates, it does not mean a sharp divorce from party identification or preference.

When asked, "Generally speaking, what do you usually think of yourself politically regardless of how you vote?," those surveyed responded in the following way:

> 8% strong Republican
> 9% not very strong Republican
> 24% Independent
> 31% Not very strong Democrat
> 28% Strong Democrat

The Democratic Party of Arkansas still maintains a majority identification in the state. Almost sixty percent consider themselves Democrats, regardless of that meaning or the way they vote. Identifiable Republicans number less than two-out-of-ten, and those willing to admit no party label were slightly less than one-out-of-four. In everyday terms these percentages proclaim clearly that if a Republican wins a state-wide race, Democrats elect him by providing the essential majority.

It is also worth considering the response to this question: "Have you always voted for the same party, mostly for the same party, or equally divided your vote?"

21% Always the same party
57% Mostly for the same party
22% Equally for each party

A revealing eighty-six percent of those who admitted some party identification in the prior question answered this question "mostly for the same party." Arkansas is still influenced, but not dominated, by party loyalties and the discerning politician or politician-to-be should underscore that point.

The lack of active, concerned participation in the political arena by "average voters" is reflected in a series of responses: "Did you give any money, or buy any tickets to help a party or candidate pay campaign expenses in the past year?"

9% Yes
91% No

"How many letters have you written to public officials this year?"

78% None
15% 1 or 2
4% 3 or 4
3% 5 or more

"Did you go to any political meetings, rallies, or dinners, etc., this year?"

70% None
16% 1
11% 2 to 4
3% 5 or more

Apathy and lack of involvement in the political process is present in Arkansas as in the remainder of the nation. Overall, relatively few voters get involved in the action in a meaningful way; it is just not that important.

Television has replaced the political machine, the radio, and the newspapers in providing information and guidance to Arkansas voters. The influence of this electronic media is so overwhelming in a state-wide race that the wise politician of the future would do well to measure carefully his own expertise and talent in this element of the campaign. Too, it is the most expensive area of campaigning. "Of all the ways to gain information about a candidate or a campaign, which one would you say you got most information from?"

30% Newspapers
6% Radio

59% Television
5% Other

"Which of the following influences you most in your decision to vote?"

25% Newspapers
5% Radio
62% Television
8% Other

The racial issue, a crucial one for years in southern politics, and perhaps the real decisive force in defining a liberal, a moderate, and a conservative in Arkansas, seems to have been muffled across much of the state, at least in most areas. When asked to rate themselves on the issue of integration, the following breakdown resulted:

19% Strong segregationist
30% Mild segregationist
40% Mild integrationist
11% Strong integrationist

No majority for segregation was recorded, and a very slight majority gave integration the nod. Statistically there is no difference; politically, the moderate on the race issue is the man of the future in Arkansas. The extremists, on either side, are the losers. The blatant segregationist may still have his way in his own backyard, but the state-wide candidate who builds his campaign with racial overtones is now appealing to a distinct minority. Arkansas simply will not give a majority to an extremist on the issues of race. And that goes for all candidates on all issues says Mr. Average Voter.

Arkansas politicians, with as much expertise as is found in any part of this country, have practiced for years the art of clouding and confusing the voter on issues (it has always been much safer to give voters what they desire—no controversies). They have seldom taken a strong stand on a particular issue and when they did, defeat was usually around the corner. It can be safely argued that most voters simply do not care about issues, or at least do not understand them enough to make crucial electoral decisions. When asked, "When you cast your vote, what primarily determines your choice of the candidates?," the replies were revealing:

57% the candidate
14% the party of the candidate
26% the issues involved
3% not sure

Most voters discover that issues are often too difficult to define; at that point the voter's psyche responds to the one clear object he perceives—how a candidate looks, how he speaks and how he relates to the perceiver's experiences. Issues play a role in the final decision, but seldom dominate that decision. The Rockefeller-Fulbright-Wallace victory has to be understood, partly, in the candidate's image, rather than bed-rock issues.

On the basis of this assertion, some critics of the Arkansas electorate have argued for a cardinal principal: "Never underestimate the ignorance of the voter." What is defined as ignorance, however, is most always lack of discernment and comprehension of the issues. Arkansas voters are not ignorant of the differences in the images they receive from the candidates. It takes a good deal of sophistication to vote for candidates of different parties—split-ticket voting—and that is exactly what the state electorate has been consistently doing in the last decade. The candidates, furthermore, have had sharp differences in their political philosophies. "Ignorant" voters would have great difficulty establishing such a voting pattern.

Finally, even if the issues are confusing, they are important to Arkansas voters when they directly involve the voter. Economic and racial problems dominated Mr. Average Voter; education and crime rank just behind as important issues in the survey. Prison concerns, ranking very low on the scale, reflect the assumption that the less personal and less related the issue is, the lower the concern. But even at that Mr. Average Voter of Arkansas, with moderate concern, and moderate understanding, would prefer a moderate candidate with a moderate stance on the issues. No extremists, please!

Where the Votes Are

As in all parts of the United Sates, the majority of Arkansas voters live in a small area. The widely-dispersed rural vote which at one time dominated the selection of state officeholders, as well as the state legislature, is no more. The 1970 registration figures illustrate the growing concentration of potential voters. Only sixteen counties contain over fifty percent of the registered voters, and thirty counties have almost seventy percent of the vote (Table 1).

Some differences appear when ranking actual voter turn-out, but the concentrated strength still exists (Table 2). In the 1968 gubernatorial contest, the largest vote to ever be cast in Arkansas, totaled 615,595[2] and sixteen counties represented over half the vote. The wise politician who desires a state-wide office will spend his budget and time accordingly—where the votes are.

TABLE I.

Arkansas Counties by Number
of Registered Voters, June 1, 1971

COUNTIES	REGISTERED VOTERS	PERCENT OF STATE TOTAL	CUMULATIVE PERCENT
Pulaski	108,895	13.0	13.0
Jefferson	36,775	4.4	17.4
Sebastian	34,222	4.1	21.5
Washington	28,526	3.4	24.9
Garland	25,376	3.0	27.9
Craighead	21,344	2.5	30.4
Union	21,251	2.5	32.9
Mississippi	21,166	2.5	35.4
Benton	21,033	2.5	37.9
White	16,712	2.0	39.9
Crittenden	15,969	1.9	41.8
Ouachita	15,563	1.9	43.7
Saline	14,615	1.7	45.4
Faulkner	14,550	1.7	47.1
Phillips	14,456	1.7	48.8
St. Francis	13,591	1.6	50.4
Miller	13,563	1.6	52.0
Greene	12,507	1.5	53.5
Pope	12,169	1.4	54.9
Crawford	11,280	1.3	56.2
Lonoke	11,181	1.3	57.5
Independence	11,135	1.3	58.8
Hot Spring	10,771	1.3	60.1
Poinsett	10,758	1.3	61.4
Ashley	10,505	1.3	62.7
Columbia	10,215	1.2	63.9
Clay	9,948	1.2	65.1
Clark	9,938	1.2	66.3
Arkansas	9,592	1.1	67.4
Baxter	9,406	1.1	68.5
Hempstead	9,360	1.1	69.6

COUNTIES	REGISTERED VOTERS	PERCENT OF STATE TOTAL	CUMULATIVE PERCENT
Boone	9,320	1.1	70.7
Conway	9,050	1.1	71.8
Jackson	8,975	1.1	72.9
Lawrence	8,648	1.0	73.9
Logan	8,159	1.0	74.9
Chicot	7,661	.9	75.8
Desha	7,590	.9	76.7
Johnson	7,498	.9	77.6
Cross	7,431	.9	78.5
Lee	7,332	.9	79.4
Polk	7,077	.8	80.2
Monroe	7,045	.8	81.0
Drew	6,798	.8	81.8
Yell	6,792	.8	82.6
Franklin	6,434	.8	83.4
Carroll	6,355	.8	84.2
Madison	6,062	.7	84.9
Bradley	6,057	.7	85.6
Cleburne	5,871	.7	86.3
Randolph	5,800	.7	87.0
Howard	5,537	.7	87.7
Lincoln	5,355	.6	88.3
Van Buren	5,204	.6	88.9
Nevada	5,127	.6	89.5
Woodruff	5,066	.6	90.1
Grant	5,040	.6	90.7
Lafayette	5,022	.6	91.3
Dallas	4,840	.6	91.9
Prairie	4,836	.6	92.5
Searcy	4,791	.6	93.1
Sevier	4,761	.6	93.7
Sharp	4,558	.5	94.2
Scott	4,563	.5	94.7
Izard	4,497	.5	95.2

COUNTIES	REGISTERED VOTERS	PERCENT OF STATE TOTAL	CUMULATIVE PERCENT
Little River	4,376	.5	95.7
Pike	4,320	.5	96.2
Fulton	4,298	.5	96.7
Marion	4,262	.5	97.2
Stone	4,069	.5	97.7
Newton	3,927	.5	98.2
Montgomery	3,660	.4	98.6
Cleveland	3,340	.4	99.0
Perry	3,174	.4	99.4
Calhoun	3,026	.4	99.8
Total	839,976		

TABLE 2.

Arkansas Counties by Size of Votes Cast[a]

COUNTIES	VOTES CAST	PERCENT OF STATE TOTAL	CUMULATIVE PERCENT
Pulaski	78,192	12.7	12.7
Sebastian	26,930	4.4	17.1
Jefferson	23,785	3.9	21.0
Washington	21,824	3.5	24.5
Garland	20,167	3.3	27.8
Union	16,904	2.7	30.5
Benton	15,945	2.6	33.1
Craighead	15,556	2.5	35.6
Mississippi	15,245	2.5	38.1
White	12,187	2.0	40.1
Ouachita	11,860	1.9	42.0
Phillips	11,371	1.8	43.8
Saline	11,215	1.8	45.6
Faulkner	10,922	1.8	47.4
Crittenden	10,430	1.7	49.1
Miller	10,427	1.7	50.8

COUNTIES	VOTES CAST	PERCENT OF STATE TOTAL	CUMULATIVE PERCENT
St. Francis	8,792	1.4	52.2
Pope	8,621	1.4	53.6
Columbia	8,126	1.3	54.9
Hot Spring	8,027	1.3	56.2
Poinsett	8,003	1.3	57.5
Ashley	7,993	1.3	58.8
Greene	7,977	1.3	60.1
Independence	7,851	1.3	61.4
Lonoke	7,692	1.2	62.6
Arkansas	7,611	1.2	63.8
Boone	7,378	1.2	65.0
Hempstead	7,301	1.2	66.2
Clark	7,150	1.2	67.4
Crawford	7,110	1.2	68.6
Jackson	6,945	1.1	69.7
Baxter	6,895	1.1	70.8
Conway	6,534	1.1	71.9
Logan	6,496	1.1	73.0
Lawrence	6,208	1.0	74.0
Clay	6,201	1.0	75.0
Desha	5,757	.9	75.9
Cross	5,700	.9	76.8
Chicot	5,644	.9	77.7
Yell	5,214	.8	78.5
Johnson	5,174	.8	79.3
Polk	5,154	.8	80.1
Carroll	5,073	.8	80.9
Madison	4,991	.8	81.7
Monroe	4,818	.8	82.5
Lee	4,799	.8	83.3
Bradley	4,792	.8	84.1
Drew	4,769	.8	84.9

COUNTIES	VOTES CAST	PERCENT OF STATE TOTAL	CUMULATIVE PERCENT
Franklin	4,602	.7	85.6
Randolph	4,214	.7	86.3
Cleburne	4,131	.7	87.0
Howard	4,016	.7	87.7
Nevada	3,898	.6	88.3
Lincoln	3,834	.6	88.9
Sevier	3,752	.6	89.5
Grant	3,681	.6	90.1
Van Buren	3,674	.6	90.7
Lafayette	3,622	.6	91.3
Woodruff	3,621	.6	91.9
Dallas	3,568	.6	92.5
Prairie	3,553	.6	93.1
Sharp	3,476	.6	93.7
Searcy	3,407	.6	94.3
Scott	3,385	.6	94.9
Little River	3,324	.5	95.4
Pike	3,308	.5	95.9
Marion	3,281	.5	96.4
Fulton	3,227	.5	96.9
Izard	2,983	.5	97.4
Newton	2,945	.5	97.9
Stone	2,751	.4	98.3
Cleveland	2,694	.4	98.7
Montgomery	2,515	.4	99.1
Perry	2,288	.4	99.5
Calhoun	2,189	.4	99.9
Total	**615,595**		

[a] The figures are for the largest vote cast in the past ten years, the election for governor, 1968. The presidential figure would have been larger, except for the error in Jefferson County's reported results.

The Non-Voter in Arkansas

Arkansas, like so many of her southern sisters, has been plagued in the past by low voter participation in the electoral process. Disenfranchisement of blacks, lack of serious party competition, the dominance of the Democratic Primary, and the poll tax were some of the guarantees that only a small part of the voting-age population would go to the polls.

In the 1920s, only a fraction over twenty percent participated in state and national elections. In school board contests, the figure remains under twenty percent even today (in one year, only 174 ballots were cast in a North Little Rock city election, and 59 in Fayetteville).

With increased party competition at the end of the Faubus era, voter participation increased. Blacks registered in a massive Republican drive in the mid-1960s that added to the turn-out. The overall results indicated some increase at the polls from 1960 through 1970, although national levels of participation remained higher (Table 3).

Some Arkansas counties voted over eight-of-ten of those registered in 1970, a figure which parallels national efforts (Table 4). Other counties, including Pulaski, Garland, Ouachita, Miller, Mississippi, Union, Craighead, St. Francis, Phillips, and Crittenden, some of the larger counties in the state, had very poor participation. This raises a question whether or not urbanization, education, and a higher income are exclusive incentives for voting more. Good habits of regular voting are still a future goal for most Arkansans, and future politicians could reap a bonanza by spending more money and time on turning out the voting potential than competing for those who turn out regularly.

TABLE 3.

Voter Registration and Participation:
Arkansas and the Nation, 1960–1970

ARKANSAS	1960	1962	1964	1966	1968	1970
Voting-age Population	1,041,000	1,073,000	1,109,000	1,126,000	1,142,000	1,168,000
Registered Voters[a]	603,795	601,991	715,528	687,631	769,704	821,122
Votes Cast	428,509	308,092	592,050	563,527	615,595	609,198
Percent Voting of Voting Age	41.2	28.7	53.4	50.0	53.9	52.2
Percent of Registered Voters Voting	71.0	51.2	82.7	82.0	80.0	74.2
United States						
Voting-age Population	107,597,000		112,184,000		116,535,000	
Registered Voters[b]	79,000,000		82,000,000		90,000,000	
Votes Cast	68,838,219		70,644,510		73,211,562	
Percent Voting of Voting Age	64.0		63.0		62.8	
Percent of Registered Voters Voting[c]	87.1		86.2		81.3	

[a] Arkansas had no permanent voter registration law until after 1964. Figures for the preceding years are poll taxes paid.

[b] Some states require no registration at all and these figures are estimates.

[c] The advance statistics, available from the US Census Bureau, state that approximately 55 percent of the voting-age population participated in the 1970 elections. The figures indicate the usual massive drop of interest in voting in non-presidential years. Arkansas proved somewhat of an exception to this rule in 1970.

TABLE 4.

Voter Participation of Registered Voters by County, 1970

RANK	COUNTY	PERCENT-AGE	RANK	COUNTY	PERCENT-AGE
1	Baxter	89.4	39	Crawford	74.5
2	Lee	86.5	40	Woodruff	74.2
3	Johnson	85.7	41	Pulaski	74.0
4	Saline	82.0	42	Sevier	73.4
5	Searcy	81.6	43	Prairie	72.9
6	Van Buren	81.3	44	Yell	72.9
7	Newton	80.2	45	Garland	72.7
8	Washington	80.1	46	Little River	72.7
9	Logan	79.8	47	Ouachita	72.7
10	Pope	79.1	48	Sharp	72.7
11	Arkansas	78.9	49	Nevada	72.6
12	Faulkner	78.3	50	Mississippi	72.4
13	Scott	78.3	51	Union	72.4
14	Sebastian	78.2	52	Hempstead	72.2
15	Dallas	77.5	53	Ashley	72.1
16	Bradley	77.4	54	Cleburne	72.1
17	Cleveland	77.4	55	Randolph	71.5
18	White	77.4	56	Madison	70.8
19	Lonoke	77.2	57	Craighead	70.1
20	Boone	77.2	58	Lawrence	69.9
21	Jefferson	77.1	59	Pike	69.9
22	Benton	77.0	60	St. Francis	69.5
23	Conway	76.7	61	Montgomery	69.2
24	Independence	76.6	62	Phillips	69.0
25	Hot Spring	76.3	63	Cross	68.8
26	Howard	76.2	64	Miller	68.8
27	Franklin	76.0	65	Izard	68.7
28	Grant	76.0	66	Lafayette	68.4
29	Carroll	75.7	67	Drew	67.8
30	Lincoln	75.7	68	Crittenden	67.1

RANK	COUNTY	PERCENT-AGE	RANK	COUNTY	PERCENT-AGE
31	Marion	75.5	69	Jackson	67.0
32	Stone	75.2	70	Greene	65.8
33	Calhoun	75.1	71	Chicot	65.4
34	Desha	75.1	72	Poinsett	64.6
35	Columbia	75.0	73	Polk	64.3
36	Monroe	74.8	74	Clay	64.2
37	Perry	74.7	75	Fulton	61.2
38	Clark	74.5			

CHAPTER 5

Arkansas

Trump Is a Natural for the Natural State

JAY BARTH AND JANINE A. PARRY

While Arkansas's electoral college votes between 1960 and 2000 were awarded to Republicans five times, Democrats five times, and once to independent candidate George Wallace, the state's down ballot posts remained among the most thoroughly Democratic in the country through the turn of the century. Starting in 2008 however, a host of factors—including the total rejection of Democrat Barack Obama in 2008 and 2012, the influence of the Tea Party insurgency among Republicans and independents, and the explosion of outside money in the wake of multiple national court rulings—converged to turn the state's partisan landscape upside down. In this analysis, the authors draw upon pre-election surveys, news accounts, exit poll data, and county-level election results to chronicle and explain another double-digit blowout for the GOP. Once again, it was the state's white voters in "rural swing" counties who fueled Republican wins at every level.

While Arkansans have voted consistently for Republican presidents since 1980 (when Bill Clinton was not the Democratic nominee), those elections remained competitive until recently because of the continued strength of Democrats at the state level. The wholesale rejection in 2008 of Barack Obama by the state's white rural "swing" voters however ushered in a series of blowouts. That was the year Senator John McCain earned 59% of the state's vote, followed by Romney's 61% in 2012. In the latter contest, the Democratic incumbent, so popular nationally, won only a handful of

Originally published in *The Future Ain't What It Used to Be*, edited by Branwell DuBose Katepluck and Scott E. Buchanan (Fayetteville: University of Arkansas Press, 2018), 127–45. Reprinted with permission. DOI: https://doi.org/10.34053/parry2019.riapag2.5

counties in the Arkansas Delta plus urban Pulaski County (Little Rock). Most startling for the state's Democrats, Romney ran up his largest margins in the "rural swing" counties that historically have been so determinative.[1]

Beyond these suddenly decisive presidential contests in 2008 and 2012, a more fundamental realignment occurred in Arkansas during the Obama era. Indeed, no state political party in the modern era has experienced a more precipitous decline than Arkansas's Democrats during this period. Going into the 2010 election cycle, the Democratic Party of Arkansas controlled every statewide elected position, maintained solid majorities in both houses of the General Assembly and held five of six positions in the state congressional delegation. Just six years later, that balance of power has been upended with Republicans now boasting every statewide post and all members of the state's Washington, DC delegation. Republicans also achieved a supermajority in the state House as a result of the 2016 election (and two subsequent party switches by Democratic legislators). Donald Trump's extraordinary appeal in the rural quadrants of Arkansas—adding to the rejection of national Democrats associated with President Obama—helped propel Arkansas Republicans to these new heights.

Despite the absence of any real campaigning in the state and another easy win for the Republican nominee, Arkansas still played an outsized role in the 2016 election. Attacks on Trump's character, behavior and statements were the dominant theme of the Clinton campaign, but the key subtheme of Hillary Clinton's general election campaign was her lifetime of service. As many of the key moments in that career of service occurred during her nearly two decades in public life in Arkansas, Arkansas was featured prominently. Still, neither that fact—nor the fact that numerous Arkansans were central to the Clinton campaign, eager to return to a second Clinton Administration—mattered a lick as another national Democrat was demolished in this suddenly, and stunningly, red state.

The Primary Season

The ascendance of the GOP in the state's politics set the stage for the state to matter more than ever in the nomination battle on the Republican side. Consequently, during its 2015 session the General Assembly voted to move the state's traditional late May contest so the state could participate in the so-called "SEC Primary" scheduled for March 1. Initially, the state GOP's dream of candidate visits and campaign spending in the state was stymied because of Mike Huckabee's candidacy. When the former Arkansas governor announced another bid for president in May 2015 in his home town of Hope, most high-profile Arkansas Republican officeholders lined up behind him. The stances of these state GOP elites and Huckabee's having gained more than 60 percent of the Arkansas primary vote in his 2008 run for president limited other candidates' inroads into the state before the Iowa caucuses.[2]

Still, indicative of Huckabee's distance from Arkansas temporally (he left the governorship in 2007) and physically (he had relocated to Florida at the start of the decade), a handful of state legislators representative of the post-Huckabee wave of Republicanism in the state announced for other candidates.[3] Several of those candidates made brief stops in the state during 2015, including an appearance by Donald Trump as the keynoter at the state GOP's annual Reagan-(Winthrop) Rockefeller dinner in July. A ticket sale surge forced a change of venue for the Hot Springs event, and his hour long remarks included many of the phrasings that would become commonly known in the year and a half to follow. Specifically, he targeted Hillary Clinton for having "deserted Arkansas" and declared emphatically that the "last thing we need is another Bush."[4] By Arkansas's November 2015 filing deadline, thirteen GOP candidates had paid the $25,000 filing fee, to the benefit of the state GOP coffers.

Huckabee's departure from the race, following a miserable ninth-place showing in the Iowa caucuses he had won in 2008, opened the floodgates for the leading candidates to invest time and money in Arkansas.[5] Even before Huckabee's February exit, Trump had scheduled a rally at Little Rock's Barton Coliseum that took place two days after Iowa's event. Approximately 6,000 Trump acolytes, spectacle seekers, and scattered protestors turned out for what was a classic Trump rally in style and content.[6] (Paula Jones, who accused Bill Clinton of sexual harassment, was photographed greeting Trump at the rally; she would return to the story in the fall campaign.[7]) In the lead-up to the March 1 primary, Trump was joined by Texas Senator Ted Cruz and Florida Senator Marco Rubio in contesting the state vigorously. Throughout the second half of February, each made appearances in Little Rock and/or in northwest Arkansas.

The three candidates represented the three major branches of the contemporary Arkansas GOP.[8] Rubio received the endorsements of most high-ranking state elected officials—including Governor Asa Hutchinson and the leaders of both the state House and state Senate—and others in the state GOP establishment. Cruz, on the other hand, was the candidate arguably the best fit for the mix of Tea Party adherents and evangelicals who had fueled the GOP rise in the Obama era; many of those activists came on board for Cruz. Finally, while receiving little warmth from party elites of any stripe (indeed, Governor Hutchinson became a harsh critic of Trump, saying his "words are frightening" in a national interview just before the "SEC Primary"), Trump showed the same ability he had shown in other states to bring into the GOP primary disaffected independents who rarely participated in primaries.[9]

The geographical patterns of the votes received across the state by Rubio, Cruz, and Trump on March 1 illustrate these factional divides. Rubio only won two counties—Pulaski and Benton—but this success in the two largest (and the two wealthiest) counties in the state equated to nearly a quarter of the overall primary vote (24.8%). Cruz showed success in the suburban counties around Little Rock and the handful of exurban counties across the state along with those counties closest to the Texas border to gain him just over 30 percent of the electorate.

Yet it was Trump's success across the entire state, particularly in rural counties where voters had shied away from GOP primary participation before his arrival on the scene, which won the day. In 2008, the most recent, comparable primary, just under 230,000 voters participated in the Republican selection process (fueled of course by Huckabee's candidacy that year) (see Table 1). In 2016, 410,920 voters took part in the GOP primary with a disproportionate amount of that increase coming outside of the traditional GOP enclaves of Northwest Arkansas and the Little Rock metropolitan area. A good example is Polk County, a rural county on the western border of the state. There, a 148% increase in turnout from 2008 to 2016 emerged (nearly double the already impressive statewide increase), and Trump earned over 40% of those votes. Ironically, considering his origins in an America so culturally disconnected from rural Arkansas, it was grass-roots strength in these isolated counties that pushed Donald Trump to a first-place finish on March 1's primary with just under one-third of the vote.

The results from the primary vote showed a dramatic reversal from one recent pattern in Arkansas elections: the decline in primary voting in general in the state.[11] At the same time, the results showed a further acceleration of a second trend: the relative growth in participation in the GOP primary as compared to the Democratic primary. The decidedly less vibrant battle in Arkansas between Clinton and Vermont Senator Bernie Sanders helped promote this decrease in Democratic primary participation.

In her 2008 nomination contest with Barack Obama, Clinton won over 70% of the vote in the Arkansas primary, her strongest performance anywhere in the country. Her history in the state along with that recent

TABLE I.

Primary Voter Turnout in Arkansas
in Presidential Election Years, 1976–2016

YEAR	DEMOCRATIC PRIMARY	REPUBLICAN PRIMARY
1976	525,968	22,797
1980	415,406	8,177
1984	492,321	19,040
1988	497,506	68,305
1992	502,130	52,297
1996	300,389	42,814
2000	246,900	44,573
2004	256,848	38,363
2008[10]	315,322	229,665
2012	162,647	152,360
2016	221,020	410,920

Source: Arkansas Secretary of State

success limited any real Arkansas contest between her and Bernie Sanders. Clinton came to the state to headline the state's Jefferson-Jackson Dinner in the summer of 2015 addressing 2000 attendees and helping sustain the budget of the state party. Even then, her strongest supporters were conscious of the general election challenges in the state. Out of office only six months, former Governor Mike Beebe, the last of Arkansas's high-profile Democrats for the foreseeable future, said "it'll be an uphill battle" for Clinton to win its electoral votes.[12] She followed up with a September 2015 visit that combined a public audience at Philander Smith University—an HBCU in Little Rock—with a $2700 per person fundraiser. Before a thousand supporters at Philander Smith, Clinton recounted her time in Arkansas and reiterated her commitment to the state, saying, "I can tell you this: When I'm president, Arkansas will be on my mind every single day."[13] In addition, while no formal Clinton campaign operation established itself in the state, there was a rebirth of the Arkansas Travelers program that sent Arkansans to other key states at their own expense to tout their friend's attributes, as had been the case in 1992 for her husband and for her own 2008 candidacy.

Sanders himself never made an appearance in the state, ceding it to

Clinton entirely. (Maryland Governor Martin O'Malley did campaign for a state Senate candidate in 2014 and returned to hold an event with only 20 people at Philander Smith University, the Arkansas Democratic Black Caucus Christmas Gala, and a fundraiser for his presidential campaign in early December 2015.)[14] The Sanders camp did open two offices (an official office in Little Rock and a volunteer-run office in Fayetteville), had six paid staffers in the state ahead of March 1, and had a social media-based presence in the state.

The absence of an energetic approach by either Democrat led to a predictable result. Clinton won two-thirds of the votes in the Arkansas primary. Although not as strong a position for Clinton as in other southern states with larger African-American populations, she took seventy-three of the state's seventy-five counties. Still, the real challenge for Clinton was obvious to anyone watching: while she remained strong with the Democratic stalwarts, the majority of the long-blue state had turned ruby-red.

The General Election Campaign

Because the outcome in Arkansas was never in any real doubt, general election action there also was limited. That said, the state was front and center for much of the fall campaign as the Clinton campaign emphasized her work on children's issues while in the state as evidence of her commitment to public service. On the other hand, particularly while under attack for his own treatment of women, Donald Trump brought to the forefront a different side of Clinton's Arkansas years: the allegedly abusive treatment of several Arkansas women by Bill Clinton—and by his wife.

Only two campaign appearances by candidates or spouses occurred in Arkansas during the general election campaign—both on the Democratic side. After Clinton had the nomination in hand, former President Bill Clinton followed his wife's lead from the prior year in headlining the Democratic Party of Arkansas's Jefferson-Jackson Dinner (the last to bear that name).[15] There, he gave a meandering speech in which he insisted it was necessary for the Democratic Party to contrast itself with Republicans on bread-and-butter economic issues, both to gain votes and to live up to the core values of the party. As Clinton summed up his argument: "We've got to do a better job of explaining to people that we're in it for them and that anybody that spends all their time trying to keep you mad at somebody else is not really your friend. . . . They want your vote, not a better life for you."[16] Following Clinton's November 8th defeat, many cited the absence of a clear economic argument from her campaign as a reason for her weakness in the upper Midwest and in Coal Country. [17] Democratic Vice Presidential Candidate Tim Kaine appeared briefly in Little Rock in late August, stopping by to open officially the Clinton Little Rock headquarters en route to a fundraiser. At headquarters, Kaine expressed his typical optimism in touting his running mate's chances in Arkansas, saying: "This is a state where person-to-person contact matters and people know Hillary Clinton."[18]

While she never made a stop in the state during 2016 as the general election date approached, Arkansas remained omnipresent in Hillary Clinton's campaign. The 2016 Democratic National Convention was a celebration of her lifetime of service, and much of it focused on her time as Arkansas's first lady. In recounting "the best darn change-maker I ever met in my entire life," Bill Clinton recounted in great detail Hillary's work in the state—from organizations she founded to programs she brought to the state to her work in reforming the state's educational system.[19] To provide handy visuals to accompany these remembrances of her Arkansas years, the Arkansas delegation was front and center at the DNC and Saline County teacher Dustin Parsons appeared as a speaker on the stage to highlight the impact of the educational reforms in Arkansas.[20]

The campaign's focus on her Arkansas years did not stop at the convention. Her fall advertising push used Arkansas examples to demonstrate her lifetime of dedication to children and family issues, and Clinton herself made overt references to her Arkansas experience in the final presidential debate both in expressing her understanding of American gun culture and in contrasting herself with Trump. "In the 1980s, I was working to reform the schools in Arkansas," she said. "He was borrowing $14 million from his father to start his businesses."[21]

While the Clinton campaign's version of her time in Arkansas emphasized her work and accomplishments, her opponents focused on a different version of those years. In the lead-up to the second debate with Trump that occurred just after Trump's infamous "Access Hollywood" videotape came to light, the Republican nominee brought forward two women from the Clinton years in Arkansas—Paula Jones and Juanita Broaddrick—who renewed their allegations of sexual abuse by Bill Clinton (and, in the case of Broaddrick, a heavy-handed effort by Hillary Clinton to maintain her silence) and a rape victim whose rapist was represented by Hillary Clinton as a court-appointed defense attorney. The woman, Kathy Shelton, said, "At 12 years old, Hillary put me through something you would never put a 12-year old through . . . Now she's laughing on tape saying she knows they [carried out the rape]."[22] Whether Clinton had indeed laughed at the rape victim received some attention in the state with Roy Reed, the longtime journalist who had conducted the interview in question over three decades earlier, characterizing the laugh as one of exasperation with the unprofessional actions of local law enforcement, and not targeted at the victim.[23]

Despite their coolness to Trump during the primary campaign, Arkansas's GOP leaders and activists united behind him once it became clear Trump would be the GOP nominee. Their loyalty (at least compared to others in the party from across the nation) was rewarded with a series of appearances by Arkansas elected officials at the Republican National Convention in July. Former Governor Huckabee, Governor Hutchinson, US Senator Tom Cotton, and Attorney General Leslie Rutledge all took the stage to tout Trump. Rutledge ripped Clinton, saying, "Sometimes Hillary Clinton speaks with a New York accent. Sometimes an Arkansas accent. But, y'all, this is what a real Arkansas woman sounds like."[24] As the fall campaign continued, Rutledge would become a regular media surrogate for the Trump campaign.

In addition to the Clintons themselves, a number of Arkansans also were deeply involved in the Clinton campaign. Particularly prominent in this group were Adrienne Elrod, director of strategic communications for Clinton after beginning the campaign cycle at Correct the Record (a super PAC built to respond rapidly to attacks on Clinton); Craig Smith, who headed up the Ready for Hillary super PAC that preceded her candidacy and was in a leadership role on the Clinton Florida campaign down the stretch run; and Greg Hale, the campaign's director of production.[25] Working collaboratively with the Clinton campaign, the volunteer Arkansas Travelers were active throughout the campaign often visiting smaller towns in parts of swing states similar to Arkansas in terms of their cultural conservatism. The Travelers' primary task was to engage in direct voter contact through door-to-door interactions and phone calls to tell of their longstanding personal connection with Clinton.[26]

Similarly, Clinton's deep connections in Arkansas with individuals used to giving political money to Democrats paid off as she received campaign donations from Arkansans totaling $2.4 million. This swamped Trump's take in the state as he gained just over $800,000 to his campaign across the year.[27] However, that advantage to Clinton was countered by one donation to the Trump super PAC—a $2 million donation by Little Rock's Ronald Cameron, owner of the Mountaire Corp. (the nation's sixth-largest poultry company), who had been the major super PAC backer of Mike Huckabee during his failed campaign.[28] While the Trump campaign showed little formal organization in the state, the enthusiasm for his candidacy showed itself in *ad hoc* pro-Trump billboards and farm implements painted with "Trump for President" in fields across the state. It was those actions rather than the actions by political professionals that showed the depth of the Trump movement in Arkansas.

The Outcome

The fact that Arkansas again cast its six Electoral College votes for the Republican nominee in 2016 surprised no one. Statewide polls stretching back into 2015 had revealed a double-digit lead for the generic Republican (against a generic Democrat and against Clinton specifically), and from September of 2016 forward, the average projected margin of victory among all polls exceeded 20 points, approaching the actual margin of 23.7 (see Table 2). Indeed, Trump's vote share was higher in only eight other states. These included many of Arkansas's low-density and/or southern peers, including Wyoming and West Virginia (68%), Kentucky (66%), Oklahoma (65%), North Dakota (63%), Alabama and South Dakota (62%) and Tennessee (61%).[29] It is particularly telling to examine the Republican vote share in 2016 as compared with 2012. Although both the final vote share and the statewide margin of victory for Republicans (exactly) matched that of 2012, Donald Trump increased his party's share in the state's most rural US House

TABLE 2.

Selected Polls in Arkansas, Presidential Race 2016

POLL AND POLLING DATES	TRUMP	CLINTON	SPREAD
The Arkansas Poll (University of Arkansas) 10/18–10/25	58	31	27 points
Talk Business/Hendrix College Poll, 10/21	56	33	23 points
Talk Business Poll/Hendrix College Poll, 9/15–9/17	55	34	21 points
Emerson, 9/9–9/13	57	29	28 points
Talk Business Poll/Hendrix College Poll, 6/21	47 ·	36	11 points

Source: Arkansas Poll results available at https://goo.gl/uXInjm. Talk Business/Hendrix College Poll results available at https://goo.gl/Qw9q6N. More polling results available from RealClearPolitics at https://goo.gl/1oyYJK.

districts (the first and the fourth) while incurring modest losses compared to Mitt Romney in the state's urban areas (the second and third).[30] The complete results of the presidential and congressional elections are in Table 3.

The explanation for this dueling force lies in a fact noted above: that statewide elections in Arkansas are decided by a large collection of "rural swing counties" identified by political scientist Diane Blair in the 1980s.[31] Most of these counties—disproportionally white and rural— have been experiencing population stagnation, if not decline, for decades. They cut a diagonal swath from the southwest to the northeast and long have demonstrated a propensity to "swing" between Republican candidates and Democratic candidates, depending on the central issues—economic or cultural. For three consecutive election cycles—in presidential politics—we have watched these counties swing emphatically Republican. In 2008 and 2012 in particular, we argued that it was voters in these counties who felt most culturally disconnected from Barack Obama.[32] Table 4 provides evidence of still another burst—indeed, a larger one—of GOP support in these communities. While the statewide average for Trump was 60.6 percent in both 2012 and 2016, the rural swing counties that gave him 65.7 percent in 2012 gave him 69.0 percent in 2016, a gap of more than eight points from the statewide average. Conversely, counties with bigger (and more diverse populations) showed less enthusiasm for Trump than they had for Romney. The former's vote share, for example, declined about 6 points in Benton and Washington Counties, and nearly 5 points in Pulaski.

Social/Demographic Factors

Of course, regional differences alone do not explain Arkansas's third, consecutive presidential rout. Hampered again by the reduction of state-level exit polling to just twenty-eight states [33] exclusive of Arkansas, we turn to an examination of the University of Arkansas's annual pre-election Arkansas Poll presented in Table 5[34] Overall, the GOP candidate of 2016 maintained (or saw only small downturns) in support from members of nearly every demographic category, while significantly improving vote share among the young, the poor, and—in keeping with nationwide patterns—white women.

The multiethnic coalition that brought President Obama to power nationally is not of sufficient size to wield influence in Arkansas's statewide elections. Black voters, the largest state's largest minority group, compose only about 10 percent of the electorate (and just under 16 percent of the population), and the Latino presence remains small. The 60-percent-plus

TABLE 3.

Results of the 2016 Arkansas Presidential and Congressional Elections

CANDIDATE (PARTY)	VOTE PERCENTAGE (2012 PARTY VOTE)	VOTE TOTAL (2012 PARTY VOTE)
President		
Donald Trump/Mike Pence (REP)	60.6 (60.6)	684, 872 (647,744)
Hillary Clinton/Tim Kaine (DEM)	33.7 (36.9)	380,494 (394,409)
Gary Johnson/Bill Weld (LIB)	2.6 (1.5)	29,829 (16,276)
Evan McMullin/Nathan Johnson (BFA)	1.2 (n/a)	13,255 (n/a)
Jill Stein/Ajamu Baraka (GRN)	0.8 (0.9)	9,473 (9,305)
US Senate		
John Boozman (REP)*	59.8 (44.1⁺)	661,984 (458,036⁺)
Conner Eldridge (DEM)	36.2 (55.9⁺)	400,602 (580,973⁺)
Frank Gilbert (LIB)	4.0 (n/a)	43,866 (n/a)
US House of Representatives		
FIRST DISTRICT		
Rick Crawford (REP)*	76.3 (56.2)	183,866 (138,800)
(no candidate) (DEM)	n/a (39.1)	n/a (96,601)
Mark West (LIB)	23.7 (2.6)	57,181 (6,427)
SECOND DISTRICT		
French Hill (REP)*	58.3 (55.2)	176,472 (158,175)
Dianne Curry (DEM)	36.8 (39.5)	111,347 (113,156)
Chris Hayes (LIB)	4. 7 (2.3)	14,342 (6,701)
THIRD DISTRICT		
Steve Womack (REP)*	77.3 (75.9)	217, 192 (186,467)
Steve Isaacson (LIB)	22.7 (8.1)	63, 715 (19,875)
FOURTH DISTRICT		
Bruce Westerman (REP)*	74.9 (59.5)	182,885 (154,149)
(no candidate) (DEM)	n/a (36.7)	n/a (95,013)
Kerry Hicks (LIB)	25.1 (1.9)	61,274 (4,984)

Key: * denotes incumbent, ⁺ denotes totals for 2004, the last time Arkansas hosted a competitive US Senate race in the same year as the presidential contest.
Source: Arkansas Secretary of State. Finally, at the state legislative level, Republicans swept almost all contested races, moving them close to supermajority status (75%) in each house of the General Assembly. A series of party switches in the state House following the election allowed Republicans to surge above that threshold going into the 2017 legislative session, sealing the GOP's unprecedented dominance of state government.

TABLE 4.

Republican Vote in Arkansas (%), 2008, 2012 and 2016 by County

COUNTY	2008	2012	2016	CHANGE 16–12 % PTS	CHANGE 12–08 % PTS	CHANGE 16–08 % PTS	2010 % BLACK
Arkansas	60.0	60.0	61.6	1.6	0.0	1.6	24.5
Ashley	62.3	61.4	66.0	4.6	-0.9	4.6	27.8
Baxter	64.3	70.8	74.3	3.5	6.5	3.5	0.3
Benton	67.2	69.0	62.9	-6.1	1.8	-6.1	1.1
Boone	68.3	72.5	75.9	3.4	4.2	3.4	0.3
Bradley	56.1	58.4	59.2	0.8	2.3	0.8	28.2
Calhoun	**65.9**	**67.1**	**68.6**	**1.5**	**1.2**	**1.5**	**23.2**
Carroll	57.5	60.2	63.1	2.9	2.7	2.9	0.3
Chicot	40.3	38.3	41.1	2.8	-2.0	2.8	53.9
Clark	50.7	51.7	51.7	0	1.0	0	22.3
Clay	**55.0**	**63.1**	**63.0**	**-0.1**	**8.1**	**-0.1**	**0.3**
Cleburne	70.2	74.6	78.3	3.7	4.4	3.7	0.5
Cleveland	**69.9**	**70.8**	**73.4**	**2.6**	**0.9**	**2.6**	**13.5**
Columbia	61.1	61.2	61.4	0.2	0.2	0.2	36.6
Conway	**57.6**	**58.4**	**61.2**	**2.8**	**0.8**	**2.8**	**12.5**
Craighead	61.0	64.2	64.4	0.2	3.2	0.2	9.7
Crawford	71.5	73.6	74.3	0.7	2.1	0.7	1.1
Crittenden	41.9	41.9	43.7	1.8	0.0	1.8	49.4
Cross	61.6	63.9	66.7	2.8	2.3	2.8	23.4
Dallas	**53.0**	**54.0**	**54.4**	**0.4**	**1.0**	**0.4**	**40.7**
Desha	43.3	42.9	45.0	2.1	-0.4	2.1	46.8
Drew	58.4	58.6	60.2	1.6	0.2	1.6	27.5
Faulkner	62.9	64.5	61.8	-2.7	2.6	-2.7	9.3
Franklin	68.1	70.8	74.4	3.6	2.7	3.6	0.7
Fulton	57.8	65.2	72.7	7.5	7.4	7.5	0.3
Garland	61.2	63.9	64.0	0.1	2.7	0.1	7.9
Grant	**73.9**	**74.5**	**74.7**	**0.2**	**0.6**	**0.2**	**3.1**
Greene	**63.0**	**65.9**	**73.5**	**7.6**	**2.9**	**7.6**	**0.3**
Hempstead	58.1	61.9	62.5	0.6	3.8	0.6	29.1
Hot Spring	**60.3**	**63.0**	**68.5**	**5.5**	**2.7**	**5.5**	**10.2**

COUNTY	2008	2012	2016	CHANGE 16–12 % PTS	CHANGE 12–08 % PTS	CHANGE 16–08 % PTS	2010 % BLACK
Howard	**61.1**	**64.8**	**67.5**	**2.7**	**3.7**	**2.7**	**20.7**
Independence	**67.1**	**70.4**	**73.0**	**2.6**	**3.3**	**2.6**	**2.1**
Izard	**61.2**	**67.7**	**74.2**	**6.5**	**6.5**	**6.5**	**1.5**
Jackson	**55.9**	**57.5**	**63.3**	**5.8**	**1.6**	**5.8**	**19.4**
Jefferson	36.0	34.8	35.7	0.9	-1.2	0.9	51.9
Johnson	**60.1**	**62.5**	**66.8**	**4.3**	**2.4**	**4.3**	**1.8**
Lafayette	**58.1**	**58.5**	**61.5**	**3**	**0.4**	**3**	**36.1**
Lawrence	**57.6**	**63.8**	**71.5**	**7.7**	**6.2**	**7.7**	**0.7**
Lee	38.7	37.4	40.7	3.3	-1.3	3.3	57.2
Lincoln	57.1	59.0	64.2	5.2	1.9	5.2	32.9
Little River	63.0	67.0	68.3	1.3	4.0	1.3	21.2
Logan	67.7	69.3	72.5	3.2	1.6	3.2	1.3
Lonoke	72.7	74.2	73.7	-0.5	1.5	-0.5	6.5
Madison	62.8	64.9	72.0	7.1	2.1	7.1	0.2
Marion	63.2	67.7	74.9	7.2	4.5	7.2	0.3
Miller	65.8	69.3	70.2	0.9	3.5	0.9	23.4
Mississippi	49.9	49.4	53.4	4	-0.5	4	34.1
Monroe	50.9	49.1	50.4	1.3	-1.8	1.3	39.3
Montgomery	**65.3**	**69.9**	**74.1**	**4.2**	**4.6**	**4.2**	**0.6**
Nevada	56.7	59.0	61.7	2.7	2.3	2.7	32.7
Newton	67.0	68.5	76.6	8.1	1.5	8.1	0.2
Ouachita	**53.9**	**53.5**	**53.9**	**0.4**	**-0.4**	**0.4**	**40.2**
Perry	**64.2**	**65.5**	**69.9**	**4.4**	**1.3**	**4.4**	**2.0**
Phillips	34.5	32.8	35.2	2.4	-1.7	2.4	61.4
Pike	**68.8**	**75.2**	**79.1**	**3.9**	**6.4**	**3.9**	**3.9**
Poinsett	**61.8**	**65.8**	**59.1**	**-6.7**	**4.0**	**-6.7**	**7.4**
Polk	71.3	77.0	80.4	3.4	5.7	3.4	0.3
Pope	70.9	72.2	72.1	-0.1	1.3	-0.1	3.0
Prairie	**65.8**	**68.6**	**72.8**	**4.2**	**2.8**	**4.2**	**14.5**
Pulaski	43.5	43.3	38.4	-4.9	-0.2	-4.9	34.0

COUNTY	2008	2012	2016	CHANGE 16–12 % PTS	CHANGE 12–08 % PTS	CHANGE 16–08 % PTS	2010 % BLACK
Randolph	**57.2**	**62.1**	**70.7**	**8.6**	**4.9**	**8.6**	**1.2**
Saline	69.4	70.0	68.2	-1.8	0.6	-1.8	50.5
Scott	**69.9**	**72.3**	**78.3**	**6**	**2.4**	**6**	**3.2**
Searcy	70.9	73.1	79.3	6.2	2.2	6.2	0.5
Sebastian	66.3	67.3	65.2	-2.1	1.0	-2.1	0.2
Sevier	68.3	72.4	71.8	-0.6	3.9	-0.6	6.3
Sharp	62.5	67.6	74.6	7	5.1	7	4.4
St. Francis	41.7	40.3	43.0	2.7	-1.4	2.7	0.9
Stone	**66.4**	**70.5**	**73.3**	**2.8**	**4.1**	**2.8**	**0.3**
Union	62.2	62.3	62.1	-0.2	0.1	-0.2	33.0
Van Buren	63.8	67.9	75.6	7.7	4.1	7.7	0.5
Washington	55.5	56.3	50.8	-5.5	0.8	-5.5	2.7
White	**72.2**	**75.5**	**75.3**	**-0.2**	**3.3**	**-0.2**	**4.0**
Woodruff	43.7	49.9	52.4	2.5	6.2	2.5	28.7
Yell	**63.1**	**67.7**	**71.6**	**3.9**	**4.6**	**3.9**	**1.5**
Avg. (all counties)	60.1	62.6	64.8	2.4	2.3	4.7	na
Avg. (RSC)	**62.6**	**65.7**	**69.0**	**3.3**	**3.1**	**6.3**	**na**
Statewide Vote	58.7	60.6	60.6	0.0	-1.9	1.9	na

Key: Bolded counties denote Blair (1988)'s "rural swing counties." RSC = Rural Swing Counties
Source: Data compiled by the authors from the official website of the Arkansas Secretary of State at https://goo.gl/9FP9O5. See also US Census Bureau's American FactFinder at https://goo.gl/lzIVZU.

support awarded to Trump by the whites who dominate the state's demographic landscape consequently wins the day. The patterns again proved equally predictable with respect to income and age with Clinton trailing Trump in nearly every category, with the exception of the very poor.

Sex/Gender: The election of 2016 nationwide put a spotlight on the strong support of white females for the GOP candidate. This was strongly evident in Arkansas, with more than two-thirds of those voters selecting

TABLE 5.

Poll Results of Arkansas Voters, 2016 (in percent)

CHARACTERISTIC	TRUMP	CLINTON	GOP '12
Party Identification			
Democrat	10	89	13
Republican	94	4	96
Independent	62	29	67
Most Important Problem*			
The economy	65	31	65
Education	46	48	40
Healthcare	54	41	47
Crime	51	47	n/a
Taxes	72	28	57
Politicians	67	28	n/a
White Evangelical/Born Again?			
Yes	65	32	65
No	48	48	55
Sex			
Male	60	33	71
Female	59	39	59
White Males	64	29	71
White Females	67	31	62
Racial/Ethnic Identity			
White	65	30	66
Black	4	96	3
Age			
18–29	56	28	44
30–44	61	37	61
45–64	60	34	61
65 or older	60	38	60

CHARACTERISTIC	TRUMP	CLINTON	GOP '12
Income			
Under $7,500	45	48	28
$7,501-$15,000	56	41	42
$15,001-$25,000	60	38	57
$25,001-$35,000	55	39	56
$35,001-$50,000	67	30	65
$50,001-$75,000	52	42	65
$75,001-$100,000	60	32	58
$100,001+	72	26	77
Size of Community			
Urban	42	54	57
Suburban	66	26	63
Small town	65	31	58
Rural	67	30	61
Vote Medical Marijuana			
Yes	52	45	50
No	67	27	77

*The Arkansas Poll allows respondents to direct the "most important problem"
categories, so comparability is lost year-over-year on some issues.
Source: The Arkansas Poll, 2016, accessed electronically on 8 Nov 2016,
https://goo.gl/DzpIrN.*Ethnicity, Income, and Age*.

Trump, (barely) outpacing his support among white males. This marked
a reversal of 2012 with respect to the state's gender gap, which usually is at
or approaching the gap recorded nationally. For example, in 2012 Arkansas
males (all ethnicities) compared to Arkansas females (all ethnicities) preferred Romney over Obama by 12 points. In 2016, the gender gap collapsed.

Other Social/Demographic Factors: Support for Trump was robust among
the three-quarters of Arkansans who consider themselves "born again" or
evangelical Christians; as in 2012, nearly two-thirds of this group reported
support for the Republican candidate. With respect to educational attainment, although not all analyses are shown in the interest of space, Trump
earned strong support among likely voters at nearly every level. His support
fell considerably as attainment rose (from, for example, 66 percent among

those with "some college" to 50 percent of those with a graduate degree), but his support still outpaced Clinton's. The marriage gap remained significant in Arkansas as elsewhere, with two-thirds of married respondents preferring the Republican candidate, as compared with just 40 percent of singles.

Political Factors

Partisanship: Arkansas voters in just three election cycles (2010, 2012, and 2014) appear finally to have experienced the partisan realignment most of their southern peers experienced decades earlier. As in 2012 however, the shift remains subtle at the individual level. In the last decade, the proportion of Arkansas Poll respondents identifying as either generically Democrat or generically Republican has not much changed save a modest, but relatively steady, contraction in the size of the former. The more important change has been among the state's always-robust proportion of self-identified "independents" who in 2010 took a hard right turn and have not looked back.[35] This has bearing on the party identification data featured in Table 5. As in 2012, Arkansas's partisans voted for their party's nominee at rates consistent with those seen nationwide. Partisan defectors, even in an unusual election cycle, were few.

Issues: With respect to specific issues, the economy once again proved to be the "most pressing issue or problem in Arkansas today" among Arkansas Poll respondents, and Trump earned the strong support of this group. The former first lady who spearheaded significant education reform in the state in the 1980s was the choice only among those for whom education was of greatest significance.

Turnout: Turnout among registered Arkansas voters statewide was about as predicted at 64.7 percent (see Table 6). The distribution of this participation however merits attention. About half of the state's total population (see Table 7) remains concentrated in just ten counties. As in elections past, turnout and vote preference varied in these ten. The booming suburban communities of Saline and Benton Counties, for example, not only exceeded the statewide turnout average by six and three percentage points (respectively), but again posted healthier-than-average margins for the Republican nominee. (Indeed, the Saline County vote spread was 69–25; in high-growth White County, it was 75–19.) Heavily African American Jefferson County, in contrast, again threw its still-substantial weight to the Democrats, but suffered a post-Obama decline in turnout, rendering its preferences irrelevant in Arkansas's rising Republican tide.

TABLE 6.

General Election Voter Turnout in Arkansas, 1972–2016

YEAR	PERCENT TURNOUT (REGISTERED VOTERS)
1972	69 (g)
1976	71 (g)
1980	77 (g)
1984	76 (g)
1988	69 (p)
1992	72 (p)
1996	65 (p)
2000	59 (p)
2004	64 (p)
2008	65 (p)
2012	67 (p)
2016	65 (p)

Key: Voter turnout figures are based on gubernatorial voting (g) or presidential voting (p) depending on the highest turnout race of the year. After shifting from two- to four-year terms in 1986, Arkansas gubernatorial elections are no longer held in presidential years.

Source: Data compiled from the official website of the Arkansas Secretary of State and from various volumes of *America Votes* (Congressional Quarterly: Washington, DC).

Other Election Races

Down the ballot, this increasingly baked-in Republicanism was shown in two ways: the absence of high-quality Democratic challengers to engage in contests with Republican incumbents and in the strong support in the handful of elections that were contested. The highest profile of those races was Senator John Boozman's reelection to his second term in the US Senate. Former federal prosecutor Conner Eldridge, in his first race for elective office, was never able to gain traction against Boozman, aside from national attention that came from his cutting-edge attack on Boozman in May 2016 for his support of Trump. In a web ad that received national play, the Eldridge campaign strung together a litany of Trump's crude comments

TABLE 7.

Registered Voter Turnout and Presidential Vote in the 10 Most Populous Arkansas Counties, 2016

COUNTY AND POPULATION 2010 (2000)	PERCENT POP. CHANGE 2000–2010 (1990–2000)	2016 TURNOUT % (2012)	VOTE %	
			REPUBLICAN (2012)	DEMOCRAT (2012)
Pulaski 373,911 (361,474)	3.4 (3.4)	65.5 (67.5)	38.3 (43.3)	56.1 (54.8)
Benton 203,107 (153,406)	50.0 (57.3)	67.8 (68.7)	62.9 (69.0)	28.9 (28.6)
Washington 191,292 (157,715)	21.3 (39.1)	64.0 (66.2)	50.7 (56.3)	40.8 (40.1)
Sebastian 121,766 (115,071)	5.8 (15.5)	60.9 (63.8)	65.3 (67.3)	27.6 (30.2)
Faulkner 104,865 (86,014)	21.9 (43.3)	64.2 (61.8)	61.8 (64.5)	30.8 (32.9)
Garland 96,371 (88,068)	9.4 (20.0)	63.1 (65.5)	63.9 (63.9)	30.2 (33.9)
Saline 96,212 (83,529)	15.5 (30.1)	70.5 (71.3)	68.8 (70.0)	25.4 (27.3)
Craighead 91,552 (82,148)	11.4 (19.1)	60.4 (57.0)	64.4 (64.2)	29.6 (33.2)
Jefferson 78,986 (84,278)	-6.3 (-1.4)	61.5 (69.0)	35.7 (34.8)	60.9 (63.8)
White 73,441 (67,410)	8.9 (22.6)	65.7 (56.8)	75.3 (75.5)	18.5 (21.7)

Source: Data compiled from the US Bureau of the Census and the official website of the Arkansas Secretary of State.

regarding women and charged Boozman with standing idly by in allowing the "sexual harasser" to become his party's standard bearer.[36] Following the release of the "Access Hollywood" tape in the fall, Eldridge returned to this line of attack but was never able to establish his own identity in the race against the mild-mannered—and still relatively unknown—senior senator.

In three of the state's four Congressional districts, Arkansas Democrats were unable to even field an opponent to GOP incumbents (a breathtaking reversal of events in 2008), leaving only Libertarian candidates to contest the races. Dianne Curry did carry the Democrat banner in the state's Second Congressional District, but was swamped in the suburban counties around Little Rock, winning only a slight majority in Pulaski County—home of both herself and incumbent French Hill (see Table 3).

Still, as is normal, Arkansas's voters again showed contradictory behavior as they voted on a medical marijuana amendment to the state's constitution (a competing initiated act was struck from the ballot only weeks before the election by the state Supreme Court). While voting for a host of socially conservative candidates at every level of government, voters solidly supported legalization of the medical use for marijuana. Voters in counties where Trump did worst in the state—those with higher percentages of nonwhite voters and those with higher levels of well-educated voters—were strongest in their support of the measure, but—as shown in Table 5—even a slight majority of Trump voters in the state supported allowing individuals with a series of medical conditions access to regulated marijuana.

Conclusion

The 2016 election—a Republican rout up and down the ballot—sealed the tomb of a southern Democratic Party that until 2010 had managed not only to remain competitive but indeed to dominate state elections. Once the rural swing counties veered right, and stayed there in 2010, 2012 and 2014, Arkansas Democrats found themselves where their Republican counterparts had spent more than a century: so much maligned they could not even field high-quality candidates to contest most races. Although a handful of Democratic Pollyannas, mostly from outside the state, speculated that the national Democrats' nomination of a (quasi) hometown girl would put the state's Electoral College votes back up for grabs, it did not come to pass. Instead, the Republican standard-bearer—Donald Trump—stimulated another large increase in Republican primary participation and then played a central role in maintaining the rightward tilt of the state's large proportion of independents. Outside of a smattering of local races in a handful of urban and/or diverse counties, Arkansas Democrats are in for some lean years.

II

Institutions and Actors
in Arkansas Politics and Government

CHAPTER 6

"The Great Negro State of the Country"?

Black Legislators in Arkansas, 1973–2000

JANINE A. PARRY AND WILLIAM H. MILLER

*Scholars have paid little attention to African American political par-
ticipation at the state level. Here, Parry and Miller provide an introduction to black legislative activity in the state of Arkansas with a
focus on descriptive and substantive representation issues. Specifically,
the article investigates the presence and role of black Arkansans in the
state's General Assembly from the 1960s to the turn of the century, assessing their acquisition of legislative seats, their ascendancy to committee
and chamber leadership positions, and—especially—their attempts to
present an influential voting bloc. The authors conclude that although
African American legislators in Arkansas are disadvantaged by their
small numbers, they have found ways to exercise power, including playing the "spoiler" in close votes, sensitizing the white majority to African
American concerns, and crafting strategic alliances with institutional
leaders and/or occupying such posts themselves. While this remains true
on some issues, black influence was diluted further by the surge of
Republican victories that wholly remade the state's longstanding partisan landscape between 2010 and 2014.*

Scholarship on African American political participation—like research on
political participation generally—has focused largely on the national-level
preferences of citizens and policy makers.[1] Considerably less attention has
been paid to such dynamics in the American states.[2] Here we provide an
introduction to black legislative activity in the state of Arkansas with an

Originally published in *Journal of Black Studies* 36
(July 2006): 833–72. Reprinted with permission.
DOI: https://doi.org/10.34053/parry2019.riapag2.6

eye on descriptive and substantive representation issues. Specifically, we investigate the presence and role of black Arkansans in the state's General Assembly in the post-1960s era of civil rights reforms, assessing their acquisition of legislative seats, their ascendancy to committee and chamber leadership positions, and—especially—their attempt to present an influential voting bloc.

Central to our examination is the context within which the state's black legislators operate. On one hand, scholars of Arkansas's political history have long argued that the 1957 events surrounding Little Rock's Central High School—events that came to stand for the South's stubborn insistence on the preservation of segregation—belie a history of relative racial toleration in the state. In the late 1800s, for example, a bishop in the African Methodist Episcopal Church declared that Arkansas was "destined to be the great Negro state of the Country" and that "the Colored people have a better start there than in any other state in the Union".[3] Indeed, half a century later some of the earliest and most peaceful experiments with school integration occurred in Arkansas, most just a few years before the Little Rock crisis. Key (1949) presented evidence that white Arkansans also were less stalwartly obstructionist about voting practices at mid-century than their peers in other states. Yet Arkansas is a state of the Old Confederacy. As such it "manifested all the major symbols of southern segregation and white supremacy" including Jim Crow laws, inferior public services for its black citizens, a white primary and other restrictions on political activity, and lynchings.[4] Compound these considerations with the fact that the state maintains a relatively low statewide African American population—pre- and post–Civil War—and the prospects for black legislative success become even cloudier.

Research Design

As this primarily is a descriptive project, our first step was to document every African American elected to the Arkansas state legislature after Reconstruction. Similar to other southern states, the first 20th-century Arkansas elections that included substantial African American participation did not occur until after the civil rights movement and accompanying political reforms of the 1960s. This opened the way for greater participation in the last twenty-five years of the century. We compiled data on African American legislators for each chamber independently, taking note of the party (all were Democrats, other than the two house terms served by

Christene Brownlee, a Republican), sex, committee assignments, leadership posts, and years of service of each member.

Our second step involved looking for patterns in the legislators' voting behavior. Using two chief criteria, we selected twenty-seven policy proposals of the tens of thousands considered by both chambers during the period in question. Our first criterion was that the proposal had to have been sub-jected to significant news coverage, a quality we determined by examining the pages of the two newspapers with statewide circulation (though the *Arkansas Gazette* was folded into the *Arkansas Democrat* in 1991). Because Arkansas remains one of only a handful of states to depend on biennial legislative meetings, we focused on articles appearing in the week before and after the official adjournment dates in each odd-numbered year.[5] The "session wrap-up" articles produced by the state's journalists with regularity were particularly helpful.[6] Our second criterion was to try to represent as many policy areas as possible, some of general interest to all policy makers, and some likely to be of greater interest to African Americans. These areas were education; crime, health, and abortion; race and/or ethnicity; eco-nomic development; and government reform.

Descriptive Representation in Arkansas

Integration of Arkansas's legislative chambers arrived with little fanfare in 1972 when a handful of the eleven African Americans who had appeared on the general election ballot were elected to office. Only the four Democrats prevailed—all against black, Republican opponents—supplying African American representation in the Arkansas General Assembly for the first time since 1893, and making Arkansas the last southern state to elect a black legislator.[7] Among the four was Dr. Jerry Jewell, a Little Rock dentist and past president of the Arkansas chapter of the National Association for the Advancement of Colored People (NAACP), who was elected to serve in the state senate (and would serve as its sole African American member for more than twenty years). Jewell, who also was the first African American to serve on the Little Rock Civil Service Commission, won the post by defeating businessman Sam Sparks who had run unsuccessfully for a senate seat just two years earlier.[8] Entering the state house were Richard Mays, a partner in the state's first multiethnic law firm and a former prosecuting attorney; Dr. William Townsend, an optometrist and veteran civil rights activist[9]; and Professor Henry Wilkins III, a political science professor at the University of Arkansas at Pine Bluff (the state's Historically Black College) who had been the only African American member of the state's 1969 constitutional convention. Mays and Townsend were elected to serve the multimember and majority Black 3rd District of eastern and central Little Rock, whereas Wilkins scraped out a narrow victory to represent the northern region of Pine Bluff, a city just southeast of the capital with a large African American population.[10]

The proportion of African American members in the Arkansas General Assembly held fast at just 3% of each chamber (1 of 35 in the senate and 3 of 100 in the house) through the 1970s, rendering the prospect of future diversification less than promising. One long-time political observer and pollster, Jim Ranchino, observed in 1977 that if "you want to run for office in the state and lose, then simply be a woman, a Black, a Jew, or a Republican—in that order."[11] Indeed by 1989, the percentage of African American house members had inched up to just 5% as Senator Jewell continued to be the only African American member of the senate. Growth was accelerated, however, by a court ruling later the same year declaring that past legislative redistricting plans (a process completed in Arkansas by the governor, the secretary of state, and the attorney general sitting together as the Board of Apportionment) had violated the national Voting Rights Act.[12] The remedy ordered was the creation of black-majority legislative districts, a directive the board met by creating—and maintaining despite further court challenge—thirteen such house districts and three such senate districts.[13] The action was smaller in scale than many black activists preferred but spurred a new wave of African American representation in Arkansas politics nonetheless.[14]

The resulting forward thrust of African Americans being elected to the state legislature was marked (see Tables 1 and 2). Specifically, the 1990 election brought the number of black representatives to nine as two additional African American members joined Dr. Jewell in the senate. Two years later, the house proportion grew to 10%, and house and senate held steady at 10% and 9%, respectively, until the 1998 election when the house increased by still two more African American members, though the senate dropped back by one member. Given his extended term of service, it is worth noting that Jewell was not among the state senators around to usher in a new century. An African American opponent (Rep. Bill Walker) defeated him in the primary election of 1994. After a bitter battle, the twenty-two-year veteran legislator confided "It was hell being here . . . alone".[15] Heading into the 2000 election cycle, then, the number of African Americans in the Arkansas General Assembly stood at 2 senators and 12 representatives, a grand total of 14—or 10.4%—of 135 state legislators. This was an improvement but still

TABLE I:

African American Legislators
in the Arkansas House of Representatives

1981–1982	1983–1984	1985–1986	1987–1988	1989–1990
Brown	Brown	Brown	Brown	Brown
Richardson	Richardson	Hunter	Townsend	McGee
Townsend	Townsend	Townsend	Wm. Walker	Townsend
Wilkins, III	Wilkins, III	Wilkins, III	Wilkins, III	Wm. Walker
				Wilkins, III
4 members	4 members	4 members	4 members	5 members
4% of House	4% of House	4% of House	4% of House	5% of House

1991–1992	1993–1994	1995–1996	1997–1998	1999–2000
Brown	Bennett	Bennett	Bennett	Booker
Brownlee	Brown	Booker	Booker	Eason
McGee	Brownlee	Brown	Brown	Harris
Roberts	McGee	Harris	Harris	Johnson
Smith	Roberts	McGee	McGee	Jones
Townsend	Smith	Roberts	Roberts	Lewellen
Wm. Walker	Townsend	Smith	Smith	Steele
Wilkins, III	Wm. Walker	Townsend	W. Walker	Thomas
Wilson	J. Wilkins	J. Wilkins	J. Wilkins	W. Walker
	Wilson	Wilson	Wilson	White
				Wilkins, IV
				Willis
9 members	10 members	10 members	10 members	12 members
9% of House	10% of House	10% of House	10% of House	12% of House

Note: The last two rows indicate the total number of African Americans in the state house, and their percent of the total chamber membership of 100 members. The complete names of African American members in the 20th century are: M. Dee Bennett, Michael D. Booker, Irma Hunter Brown, Christene Brownlee (the sole African American Republican legislator during the period under study), John Eason, Joe Harris, Jr., Clarence Hunter, Calvin Johnson, Steve Jones, John Lewellen, Ben McGee, Richard L. Mays, Grover C. Richardson, Jacqueline Roberts, Judy Seriale Smith, Tracy Steele, Lindbergh Thomas, William Townsend, William Walker, Wilma Walker, Robert White, Henry Wilkins, III, Henry "Hank" Wilkins, IV, Josetta E. Wilkins, Arnett Willis, and Jimmie L. Wilson. Of these twenty-six total individuals, six (23%) are female.

Source: Various legislative guides, Arkansas History Commission; photograph collection, Arkansas Black History Advisory Committee.

TABLE 2:
African American Legislators in the Arkansas Senate

1981–1982	1983–1984	1985–1986	1987–1988	1989–1990
Jewell	Jewell	Jewell	Jewell	Jewell
1 member	1 member	1 member	1 member	1 member
3% of Senate	3% of Senate	3% of Senate	3% of Senate	3% of Senate

1991–1992	1993–1994	1995–1996	1997–1998	1999–2000
Edwards Jewell Lewellen	Edwards Jewell Lewellen	Edwards Lewellen Wm. Walker	Edwards Lewellen Wm. Walker	Edwards Wm. Walker
3 members	3 members	3 members	3 members	2 members
9% of Senate	9% of Senate	9% of Senate	9% of Senate	6% of Senate

Note: The last two rows indicate the total number of African Americans in the state senate, and their percent of the total chamber membership of thirty-five members. The complete names of African American members in the 20th century are: Jean C. Edwards, Jerry D. Jewell, Roy C. "Bill" Lewellen, and William L. "Bill" Walker.
Source: Various legislative guides, Arkansas History Commission; photograph collection, Arkansas Black History Advisory Committee.

fell short of the approximately 16% of the state's population composed of African Americans.

The General Assembly's small number of black members did not easily acquire leadership positions once elected. Ethnicity, however, was not the major obstacle. Until the implementation of term limits in 1998, Arkansas manifested a low legislative turnover rate compared to other states. According to the National Conference of State Legislatures, for example, whereas the average turnover nationally among state senators between 1987 and 1997 was 72%, Arkansas's was just 57%, making it the fourth most stable in membership. As leadership opportunities for newcomers were unlikely in such a context, the early African American members of the General Assembly generally were appointed as rank-and-file members mainly of the Education, Legislative Affairs, and Judiciary Committees. Yet by 1979, Representative Townsend and Senator Jewell had been elevated to committee vice chairs; and by the mid-1980s, Jewell was chairing the Senate Committee on Agriculture and Economic Development.

The 1990s found additional African Americans serving as committee vice chairs, including the elevation of Rep. Irma Hunter Brown (D-Little Rock), the first African American woman to serve in the Arkansas General Assembly, to second in command on the House Revenue and Taxation Committee.[16] Of perhaps greater significance, at least symbolically, was Senator Jewell's election as the president pro tempore of the senate in 1993, a post tradition- ally held by the member with the most seniority who has not previously served in the position.[17] Representative Townsend was elevated to chair of the House Aging and Legislative Affairs Committee in the same year and continued in that post through the 1995 session. In the last half of the decade, Sens. Jean Edwards (D-Sherrill) and Roy C. "Bill" Lewellen (D-Marianna) chaired the upper chamber's committees on city, county, and local affairs and aging and legislative affairs, respectively, and Reps. Ben McGee (D-Marion) and Joe Harris, Jr. (D-Osceola) each served a term heading up the House's Public Transportation Committee. A timeline of African American commit- tee chairs in both chambers is presented in Tables 3 and 4.

Although it had existed as an unofficial network for many years, the Arkansas Legislative Black Caucus was officially incorporated in 1989. Instrumental to its establishment was Rep. Henry Wilkins III.[18] The cau- cus's official mission

> is to provide a major forum primarily for African American state
> legislators interested in improving the quality of life for African
> American and other disadvantaged people in Arkansas; to provide
> an organizational framework for the passage of legislation; to over-
> see a more beneficial operation of state agencies; and to provide an
> additional channel for constituent input.[19]

In keeping with a key tenet of the organization's objectives, caucus members formulated an official list of shared legislative priorities for the 2001 legislative session. Increased teacher salaries and other investments in education topped the list.[20] Further signs of the unit's greater "institu- tionalization" are found in the weekly meetings held by the caucus, regular gatherings in the "off season," and sustained collaborations with an orga- nization of significantly wider membership (i.e., not simply current state legislators), the Democratic Black Caucus.[21] The latter is an official auxiliary organization of the Democratic Party of Arkansas.[22] Such developments no doubt play a role in Haynie's (2001) report that the Arkansas legislature has experienced a dramatic increase in the political incorporation of African Americans in recent years.[23]

TABLE 3:

African American Committee Chairs
in the Arkansas House of Representatives

1981–1982	1983–1984	1985–1986	1987–1988	1989–1990
None	None	None	None	None
0 chairs of 16 total committees	0 chairs of 17 total committees	0 chairs of 17 total committees	0 chairs of 16 total committees	0 chairs of 18 total committees
0% of total	0% of total	0% of total	0% of total	0% of total

1991–1992	1993–1994	1995–1996	1997–1998	1999–2000
None	Townsend— Aging and Legislative Affairs	Townsend— Aging and Legislative Affairs	McGee— Public Transportation	Harris— Public Transportation
0 chairs of 18 total committees	1 chair of 18 total committees	1 chair of 18 total committees	1 chair of 17 total committees	1 chair of 17 total committees
0% of total	6% of total	6% of total	6% of total	6% of total

Note: The last three rows indicate the total number of African American committee chairs, the total number of committees in the state house (including select committees), and the percent of committees chaired by African Americans.
Source: **Arkansas Legislative Digest**, Arkansas General Assembly.

Of course, the caucus has not been free of criticism. When a prominent civil rights lawyer entered the race for state senator in 2002 against Caucus Chair Representative Tracy Steele, he sharply criticized the caucus for failing to "raise issues and make advocacy" on behalf of the state's African American population. Caucus members responded by pointing to recent policy successes including changes to the state's plans for a large tobacco settlement and setting aside a day to honor a prominent civil rights activist.[24] Additional evidence of the caucus's growing significance in the Arkansas political environment lies in the fact that the support of its members was actively courted by US Senate candidates in a close election in 2002.[25]

TABLE 4:

African American Committee Chairs in the Arkansas Senate

1981–1982	1983–1984	1985–1986	1987–1988	1989–1990
None	Jewell— Agriculture and Economic Developm't	Jewell— Agriculture and Economic Developm't	Jewell— Agriculture and Economic Developm't	Jewell— Agriculture and Economic Developm't
0 chairs of 18 total committees	1 chair of 17 total committees	1 chair of 17 total committees	1 chair of 17 total committees	1 chair of 18 total committees
0% of total	6% of total	6% of total	6% of total	6% of total

1991–1992	1993–1994	1995–1996	1997–1998	1999–2000
Jewell—Joint, Retirement and Social Security	Jewell— Education	Lewellen— Aging and Legislative Affairs	Edwards— City, County, and Local Affairs	Edwards— City, County, and Local Affairs
	Jewell—also President Pro Tempore			
1 chair of 19 total committees	1 chair of 19 total committees	1 chair of 19 total committees	1 chair of 18 total committees	1 chair of 17 total committees
5% of total	5% of total	5% of total	6% of total	6% of total

Note: The last three rows indicate the total number of African American committee chairs, the total number of committees (including select committees) in the state senate, and the percent of committees chaired by African Americans. Source: ***Arkansas Legislative Digest***, Arkansas General Assembly.

Substantive Representation in Arkansas

Although widely examined to answer innumerable questions in the political science literature, roll call votes possess many obvious limitations. The two most significant we encountered were (a) the overwhelming propensity of legislators to vote with unanimity by the time measures come to a floor vote and (b) the tendency of members to be absent or to vote "present" when a consensus emerges on a controversial issue and they find themselves on the

losing side of that consensus. Future research stands to fill in the gaps left
by such practices. Still, several patterns emerged and we discuss them below.

Tables 5 through 9 provide a summary of twenty-seven roll call votes
on key pieces of Arkansas legislation between 1973 and 1999. The tables
are divided by the issue areas noted earlier: education; crime, health, and
abortion; race and/or ethnicity; economic development; and government
reform. What is perhaps most striking about the data, at first glance, is the
degree of relative consensus in the African American vote across time and
issue area. Black delegates diverged from one another on thirteen measures
(or 48% of the time), and five of these were inter-chamber-only disputes
in which intra-chamber voting was unanimous among African Americans.
Although not insubstantial, such cumulative discord is far less than the
twenty-one measures (or 78% of the time) in which white Democrats cast
ballots in opposition to other white Democrats. Also worth noting is that
disagreement among African American legislators increased as their numbers increased; 62% of the measures in which a split is evident, for example,
occurred during the last ten years of the study (1989 to 1999).

We turn now to a more in-depth look at the five issue areas in our
analysis. With regard first to the seven education measures examined in
Table 5, the 1983 Teacher Testing Bill represents well the intense debate
surrounding the state's most significant education reforms to date, as well as
the multifaceted position of the state's black leadership on education matters. A special session was called in the fall of that year to address a public
education system widely considered to be in crisis. A 1978 study on school
finance commissioned by the legislature had concluded, for example, that
"the average child in Arkansas would be much better off attending the public schools of almost any other state in the country."[26] Buoyed by this report,
by an ad hoc Education Standards Committee (chaired by Hillary Clinton),
and by a state supreme court decision declaring the state's school funding
system unconstitutionally inequitable (*Dupree v. Alma School District*, 1983),
Governor Clinton pitched a wide-ranging package of reforms to the special
session.[27] These proposals included raising teacher salaries, establishing a
more rigorous core curriculum, mandating smaller class sizes, implementing
a longer school day and a longer school year, elevating standards for high
school graduation, and requiring kindergarten statewide.[28] Three major
varieties of tax increases served as the companion bills to fund such reforms;
only one of them—the first one-cent hike in the state sales tax in more than
twenty years—eventually passed. In exchange, the governor promised, and
delivered, a comprehensive battery of teacher testing.[29]

TABLE 5:

Roll Call Votes in the Arkansas General Assembly on Education Issues

	HOUSE OF REPRESENTATIVES			SENATE		
	BLACK DEMS	WHITE DEMS	REPUB-LICANS	BLACK DEMS	WHITE DEMS	REPUB-LICANS
1973 Free Kindergarten Measure						
For	100%	69%	—	100%	100%	100%
Against	0	31	—	0	0	0
N= Total Voting Members	(3)	(89)	(0)	(1)	(25)	(1)
1977 School Funding Formula						
For	100%	22%	100%	100%	100%	100%
Against	0	88	0	0	0	0
N= Total Voting Members	(3)	(88)	(4)	(1)	(33)	(1)
1979 Aid to Schools						
For	100%	78%	50%	100%	76%	—
Against	0	22	50	0	24	—
N= Total Voting Members	(3)	(83)	(6)	(1)	(34)	(0)
1983 Teacher Testing						
For	0%	74%	67%	0%	65%	33%
Against	100	26	33	100	35	67
N= Total Voting Members	(4)	(76)	(6)	(1)	(31)	(3)
1985 Home Schooling						
For	100%	97%	100%	0%	72%	100%
Against	0	3	0	100	28	0
N= Total Voting Members	(2)	(71)	(9)	(1)	(29)	(4)
1989 School Choice						
For	50%	53%	82%	0%	52%	50%
Against	50	47	18	100	48	50
N= Total Voting Members	(4)	(80)	(11)	(1)	(29)	(4)
1991 School Choice						
For	17%	89%	100%	0%	56%	75%
Against	83%	11	0	100%	44	25
N= Total Voting Members	(6)	(79)	(7)	(3)	(16)	(4)

Note: In the Senate vote on the 1989 School Choice Bill, the tie-breaking vote in favor of the measure's passage was cast by Lt. Gov. Winston Bryant, a white Democrat. One of the House Republicans voting on the 1991 School Choice Bill was an African American. Source: House and Senate journals of the Arkansas General Assembly, 1973–1991 volumes, Secretary of State's Office.

Although broadly supportive of improved public education in Arkansas, members of the Arkansas Black Caucus criticized many of the reforms, especially teacher testing. In a meeting with the caucus in early October, Clinton told the members that the onetime "inventory" of all presently certified teachers would "go a long way to restoring public confidence in what . . . is still the most important profession in our country."[30] The governor further explained to the members that although he recognized that "there are people who have been victimized by institutional racism and institutional limitations in the past," he rejected "the notion that any group of people . . . have any inherent, God-imbedded limitation."[31] He concluded that "given the proper opportunity, everybody can pass this test and can prove that our people are just as capable as any people in the country."[32] Caucus members were unpacified, however, and closed the meeting with votes to oppose the examination requirement for current teachers as well as to oppose the sales tax increase unless exemptions for food and utilities were made.[33] They later made good on these resolutions with a unanimous—if futile, in light of the white majority's support for the measure—no vote on teacher testing during the session.

Also of particular interest among the education measures examined was the 1989 School Choice Bill, the only education issue to evoke yes and no votes (and one nonvote) among the African Americans in the Arkansas legislature. (This division was particularly significant because the measure passed only narrowly in both chambers.) The precise cause of the divide among the Black Caucus on the measure remains unclear; however, an interview with former Rep. Ben McGee, who was in his first term that session and voted yes, revealed several related possibilities. The first was that rural legislators—black and white—were not particularly concerned with parents in their communities pulling kids out of one school to the perceived detriment of another. In most cases, McGee noted, there was not another school for many miles, so school choice "wasn't really feasible" in his district. Combine this practical reality with the fact that rural legislators often were frustrated with the cost of desegregation efforts in the central Arkansas region, and the protest of Little Rock public school advocates failed to resonate with McGee. "I was not a fan of the Little Rock district," he admitted, voting for the School Choice Act, and against the preferences of many of his urban, black colleagues, was not particularly troubling. Representative Brown confirmed this analysis, identifying the divide as largely "a geographic thing," a consequence of the fact that legislators—black or white—often strive to serve the interests of constituents with markedly different demographics.[34]

With regard to the no votes, a successful effort to expand the School Choice Act two years later is further revealing. An element of Governor Clinton's legislative package for the 1991 session, HB 1449 promoted expansion of school choice and was raised amid concerns that it would enlarge, rather than diminish, racial and ethnic segregation in Arkansas schools.[35] Many urban, black legislators were especially vocal against its passage, citing the risk of "white flight."[36] "I am unalterably opposed to this legislation because it is not progressive" noted Senator Jewell at the time.[37] "It provides an opportunity for discrimination against white kids and black kids."[38] McGee countered in an interview that most of the whites likely to flee from an integrated public school system "had already bought a house at Cabot," a small, homogenously white town Northeast of Little Rock that experienced explosive growth in the 1980s.[39]

On crime, health, and abortion issues, the African American senate delegation experienced one break in their ranks while members of the house were consistently unified (Table 6). Of the four (of six) measures in this category on which black legislators split (either between or within chambers), a 1991 conflict over the availability of contraceptives in school-based health clinics and the adoption in 1995 of a "Two Strikes" criminal justice reform measure merit further investigation. Specifically, the former was a provision imbedded in the state health department's budget that erupted in the final days of the 1991 session. Several house members—including Gus Wingfield (D-Delight) and John Miller (D-Melbourne), both white—supported amending the budget to prevent the purchase and/or distribution of condoms in school-based health clinics, a restriction the senate refused to support.[40] Although a compromise eventually emerged (the language forbade the use of only state funds for condom purchase and distribution, leaving school nurses free to use federal funds for such purposes), only six black house members (including Rep. Christene Brownlee, the sponsor of a controversial antiabortion measure in the same session) voted for it (three others abstained), and one of the three African American senators voted against it.[41]

Such division was surprising. After all, the state's black political leadership had been among the strongest supporters of sex education throughout the 1980s, and the measure's most vocal proponent was Dr. Jocelyn Elders, an African American female and director of the State Health Department.[42] Recalling the conflict in an interview, Dr. Elders explained the divide as a consequence of some members "voting their minister." African American legislators would not have wanted to vote "against her," she said; however,

Table 6:

Roll Call Votes in the Arkansas General Assembly on Crime, Health, and Abortion Issues

	HOUSE OF REPRESENTATIVE			SENATE		
	BLACK DEMS	WHITE DEMS	REPUB-LICANS	BLACK DEMS	WHITE DEMS	REPUB-LICANS
1983 Loosened Parole						
For	0%	100%	100%	100%	100%	100%
Against	100	0	0	0	0	0
N= Total Voting Members	(2)	(64)	(6)	(1)	(20)	(3)
1985 Restricted Abortion						
For	100%	100%	100%	0%	96%	100%
Against	0	0	0	100	4	0
N= Total Voting Members	(3)	(81)	(8)	(1)	(28)	(4)
1985 Indigent Health Care						
For	100%	93%	33%	100%	100%	100%
Against	0	7	67	0	0	0
N= Total Voting Members	(4)	(72)	(6)	(1)	(30)	(4)
1991 Birth Control Clinics						
For	100%	86%	100%	67%	85%	100%
Against	0	14	0	33	15	0
N= Total Voting Members	(5)	(79)	(8)	(3)	(27)	(4)
1995 Two Strikes						
For	0%	91%	100%	100%	100%	100%
Against	100	9	0	0	0	0
N= Total Voting Members	(7)	(74)	(12)	(3)	(24)	(7)
1995 Drive-By Shooting						
For	100%	100%	100%	100%	100%	100%
Against	0	0	0	0	0	0
N= Total Voting Members	(6)	(75)	(10)	(3)	(24)	(7)

Note: One of the House Republicans voting on the 1991 Birth Control Clinics Bill was an African American.
Source: House and Senate journals of the Arkansas General Assembly, 1983–1995 volumes, Secretary of State's Office.

they did not want to vote "against the church," either. Abstention on the controversial vote was the sensible solution.[43]

Positions virtually flipped on the 1995 criminal punishment reform measure that established a minimum prison sentence of forty years for people convicted of more than one violent crime. Backed by Dem. Gov. Jim Guy Tucker, the measure received support from all three African American senators; however, the seven voting house members broke with 91% of their white, Democratic colleagues to vote against it (three other black representatives abstained).

McGee could not recall, in a 2002 interview, exactly why he was among the abstainers but suggested his vote had been tied to some other piece of legislation. "People don't pass legislation . . . because it's good policy," he said. Often, they take a position based instead on the fact that somebody will owe them later, or as a show of support for a particular individual.[44] The measure's chief sponsor, Rep. Lisa Ferrell, a white Democrat from Little Rock, confirmed McGee's recollection. Specifically, she remembered that Sen. Bill Walker, a member of the Black Caucus in his first term in the upper chamber, had introduced another criminal justice reform measure during the same session, one that required persons convicted of serious crimes to serve at least 70% of the time sentenced. "Some of the sentiment in the Caucus," she said, was "'we've got to support Bill Walker,' so we can't support the other bill." Noting that she did not feel the bills were mutually exclusive, she also characterized the split as "not at all rancorous."[45] Ferrell (2002) added that there likely was a more substantive consideration driving the Black Caucus's opposition: concern about the disparate impact of a two strikes law on African American males. Although Ferrell disputed that hers was the "harsher" measure of the two bills, she acknowledged that its effect on black men was a clear worry among many caucus members. This response is not surprising in light of a special session on Governor Tucker's anticrime package the previous summer, a session that had produced several measures that allegedly "targeted young Blacks" and had generated considerable concern among the Assembly's African American membership.[46] Representative Brown attributed her no vote to exactly this context. "No one condoned criminal activity by anyone—Black or White," she said. However, many of the "tough on crime measures," often used, in her view, to justify ballooning corrections budgets, seemed to be aimed at young African Americans, particularly those who were economically disadvantaged and lacked access to good legal representation.[47]

Our efforts uncovered only three overtly race-relevant issues that made it to a vote of the full assembly and received notable publicity in the period under study (Table 7). The first two measures passed with unanimous African American support. The establishment of a Human Resources (or Civil Rights) Commission had been a failed administration measure of Dem. Gov. David Pryor previously but was shepherded to passage by African American lawmakers in the 1977 session: Rep. Henry Wilkins and Sen. Jerry Jewell. During the days just prior to adjournment, three white senators spoke in opposition to the commission's establishment, all going to some length to deny that their opposition had anything to do with race. Ultimately, it was adopted by the chamber, 18–5, with twelve senators not voting.[48]

A 1989 vote to approve a $118 million settlement over the Little Rock school desegregation conflict—a measure Representative McGee, the first black house member from the Arkansas Delta since Reconstruction, called "an opportunity (finally) to put '57 behind us"—proved even more contentious in the chambers, though not among the African American membership.[49] The matter stemmed from a federal court order mandating that the state help finance desegregation efforts in Little Rock's three major school districts because the state had facilitated the segregation of Pulaski County schools. The state's financial portion concentrated mainly on magnet schools and remedial programs.[50] Although several white legislators balked at the steady increase of the settlement total during the session, the final vote demonstrated the eagerness of the entire Assembly to put thirty years of school-related racial strife to rest.

The third overtly race-relevant measure—the Civil Rights Act of 1993—caused considerable strife among the state's African American lawmakers. The breach centered on how much to compromise in Arkansas's struggle to leave Alabama as the only state to lack an antidiscrimination statute. Sen. Bill Lewellen's bill emerged early as the most stringent of the measures introduced in the 1993 session. The two primary bills circulated in the House, by Rep. Bill Walker and by Rep. Bob Fairchild (a white Democrat from the northwest corner of the state), lacked the Lewellen bill's public accommodation protection for gays and lesbians and its hate crimes provision. Both House measures also mandated that only businesses of fifteen or more employees would be subject to the law, rather than Lewellen's nine. With such differences still intact, all three proposals had cleared either the House or the Senate by the end of February, clearing the path for an inter-chamber battle of epic proportions.[51]

Senator Lewellen's bill received a cold reception indeed in the house. It was immediately referred, for example, to the Public Health Committee,

TABLE 7:

Roll Call Votes in the Arkansas General Assembly on Race/Ethnicity Issues

	HOUSE OF REPRESENTATIVE			SENATE		
	BLACK DEMS	WHITE DEMS	REPUB- LICANS	BLACK DEMS	WHITE DEMS	REPUB- LICANS
1977 Human Resources Comm.						
For	100%	100%	100%	100%	76%	100%
Against	0	0	0	0	24	0
N= Total Voting Members	(3)	(79)	(4)	(1)	(21)	(1)
1989 Desegregation Settlement						
For	100%	95%	90%	100%	97%	50%
Against	0	5	10	0	3	50
N= Total Voting Members	(5)	(73)	(10)	(1)	(30)	(2)
1993 Civil Rights Act						
For	100%	98%	100%	0%	100%	75%
Against	0	2	0	100	0	25
N= Total Voting Members	(7)	(66)	(8)	(3)	(27)	(4)

Note: One of the House Republicans voting on the 1993 Civil Rights Act was an African American.
Source: House and Senate journals of the Arkansas General Assembly, 1977–1993 volumes, Secretary of State's Office.

on which Walker and Fairchild sat, rather than to the more hospitable Judiciary.[52] Furthermore, though Dem. Gov. Jim Guy Tucker endorsed Lewellen's proposal early in the session, by late March he was actively lobbying senators to accept one of the house measures. The ensuing debate was exceptionally rancorous, with Walker and Lewellen repeatedly blocking consideration of the other's bills in their respective chambers. Members of the Black Caucus suggested—anonymously—that the standoff was a personal dispute between Walker and Lewellen. The charge was denied by both as Lewellen assured reporters that the "Black Caucus itself is making moves to compromise the two bills."[53] Ultimately, however, printed news accounts placed the credit—or blame—for crafting a deal with Governor Tucker. In the closing days of the session, Tucker pushed the Walker bill through the senate, leading Rep. Jimmie Wilson, a Lewellen ally, to lash out at the governor and fellow caucus members. The governor, he said, led Rep. Walker "down the primrose path to sponsor and encourage passage (of) legislation that would be the infamy of all African Americans. . . . I would hate for any African-American across this nation to read our so-called civil rights law and think that was the best people of color in this state could propose."[54]

Despite the opposition of all three African American senators and abstentions by Representative Wilson and one other African American member, the measure was adopted by a wide margin in both chambers.[55]

Arkansas's black legislators also experienced considerable conflict on four of the six economic development measures analyzed (Table 8). The 1983 adoption of Gov. Bill Clinton's enterprise zones sparked opposition from two African American house members; another abstained while Senator Jewell joined three fourths of his white colleagues in approving it. Jewell likely was persuaded, as was Benjamin Hooks, executive director of the Arkansas NAACP, by the argument that the plan's tax breaks and other incentives might address depressing employment figures among African Americans.[56] Representatives Brown and Richardson, together with *Gazette* columnist Ernie Dumas, seem to have reasoned instead that tax breaks for corporations were unlikely to improve the structural unemployment problems plaguing the state's poor. "Education and a stronger economy," Dumas argued, "will put more Blacks to work than tax subsidies."[57] Brown (2002) added that she was dubious about who such business incentives actually would reach. "Many of the folks that truly needed to be targeted," she said, "would not have received those breaks."[58] In particular, she recalled that the definition of *minority* was being expanded at that time to include women. "Otherwise-majority businesses," she said, were putting women up front on their applications because they could then qualify for the enterprise zone incentives. The result, in her view, was great risk that the benefits would not go to people who were genuinely economically disadvantaged.[59]

A 1987 one-quarter-cent sales tax increase produced similar division, though in that case most black legislators joined a large majority of their white counterparts in defeating Clinton's plan for raising additional revenue for education and other social programs. News accounts of the marathon battle over the measure noted much concern with the impact of an increased sales tax on "Blacks and poor Whites."[60] Reacting to Governor Clinton's speech to the full legislature on the matter, however, Senator Jewell advocated the additional revenue generation as a "way to take care of our children."[61] "Their needs are the increased funding of the schools, more efficient operation of the schools, [and] qualified teachers," he said.[62]

TABLE 8:

Roll Call Votes in the Arkansas General Assembly on Economic Development Issues

	HOUSE OF REPRESENTATIVE			SENATE		
	BLACK DEMS	WHITE DEMS	REPUB-LICANS	BLACK DEMS	WHITE DEMS	REPUB-LICANS
1973 Tax Exemption for Poor						
For	100%	96%	—	100%	100%	100%
Against	0	4	—	0	0	0
N= Total Voting Members	(3)	(81)	(0)	(1)	(31)	(1)
1977 Minimum Wage Increase						
For	100%	100%	100%	100%	100%	100%
Against	0	0	0	0	0	0
N= Total Voting Members	(2)	(82)	(3)	(1)	(28)	(1)
1983 Enterprise Zones						
For	33%	65%	67%	100%	73%	50%
Against	67	35	33	0	27	50
N= Total Voting Members	(3)	(84)	(6)	(1)	(26)	(2)
1987 ¼ Cent Sales Tax Increase						
For	25%	27%	11%	100%	61%	0%
Against	75	73	89	0	39	100
N= Total Voting Members	(4)	(85)	(9)	(1)	(28)	(4)
1995 Five Cent Gas Tax Increase						
For	80%	79%	25%	33%	64%	100%
Against	20	21	75	67%	36	0
N= Total Voting Members	(10)	(76)	(12)	(3)	(25)	(7)
1995 Bonds for Roads						
For	100%	87%	42%	33%	68%	43%
Against	0	13	58	67	32	57
N= Total Voting Members	(8)	(75)	(12)	(3)	(25)	(7)

Source: House and Senate journals of the Arkansas General Assembly, 1973–1995 volumes, Secretary of State's Office.

Similar arguments accompanied the two 1995 measures. The five-cent increase in the diesel gasoline tax and the bond package were key components of Governor Tucker's large-scale road construction plan. The governor insisted that transportation upgrades were essential to economic development. Despite general support for the improvement of Arkansas highways, some Republican and African American lawmakers were concerned about a tax increase and the state's debt load. Bill Walker, the House member who had authored the winning civil rights bill two years earlier and had defeated Jerry Jewell for a state senate seat in 1994, was a leading opponent of the roads plan, voting against both measures.[63] Despite eventual adoption by the legislature, voters resoundingly rejected the package in a special election the following year.

Finally, just one of the five government reform measures we identified appears to have been a matter of significant dispute, among African Americans or white legislators (Table 9). Similar to most such efforts in southern states, the 1991 congressional redistricting plan for Arkansas's four US House seats raised questions about the historic disenfranchisement of the black population and appropriate remedies at the congressional-district level. Rep. Ben McGee (D-Marion) put forward a plan that would have put 87% of the state's African American residents into one district (the 4th), resulting in a district with a 42% minority population. The vast majority of the Black Caucus supported the idea, as did the state Republican Party; however, it found little support elsewhere in the legislature.[64] Although these rather strange political bedfellows presented several versions of this "Black influence district" concept during the course of the 1991 session, white Democrats preferred a plan that would bring little change to the lines drawn ten years earlier.

Racial rhetoric was central to the debate. Republicans and Black Democrats charged that the state Democratic Party historically had "fractured" the bulk of Arkansas's African American population among three different districts (the 1st, the 2nd, and the 4th) and, thus, diluted their voting strength.[65] "They put enough Blacks in those districts . . . by running fingers of them" into the delta and through the black neighborhoods of Little Rock, asserted former Representative McGee, "so a White male who says he's a Democrat could get elected."[66] Such Democrats, in McGee's view, then pay only "lip service" to their black, delta constituents to avoid alienating the conservative, white voters who compose the rest of the district. White Democrats parried that consolidating the African American vote in the way McGee proposed actually would reduce overall black political

TABLE 9:

Roll Call Votes in the Arkansas General Assembly on Government Reform Issues

	HOUSE OF REPRESENTATIVE			SENATE		
	BLACK DEMS	WHITE DEMS	REPUB- LICANS	BLACK DEMS	WHITE DEMS	REPUB- LICANS
1977 Freedom of Information Act Expansion						
For	100%	100%	—	100%	100%	100%
Against	0	0	—	0	0	0
N= Total Voting Members	(1)	(71)	(0)	(1)	(28)	(1)
1987 Move Primary/Super Tues.						
For	100%	99%	100%	100%	96%	100%
Against	0	1	0	0	4	0
N= Total Voting Members	(4)	(79)	(7)	(1)	(26)	(4)
1991 Congressional Redistricting						
For	20%	92%	71%	0%	96%	100%
Against	80	8	29	100	4	0
N= Total Voting Members	(5)	(72)	(7)	(2)	(27)	(4)
1995 Ethics Violations Fines						
For	100%	100%	100%	100%	100%	100%
Against	0	0	0	0	0	0
N= Total Voting Members	(10)	(76)	(12)	(3)	(25)	(7)
1995 Motor Voter						
For	100%	100%	100%	100%	100%	100%
Against	0	0	0	0	0	0
N= Total Voting Members	(10)	(73)	(12)	(3)	(25)	(7)

Note: The one African American House Republican voting on the 1991 Congressional Redistricting plan joined the one white House Republican in opposing the plan, while five white House Republicans favored it.
Source: House and Senate journals of the Arkansas General Assembly, 1977–1995 volumes, Secretary of State's Office.

influence in Arkansas's congressional delegation. They added that the Black Caucus–Republican alliance was disingenuous, charging that Republicans simply desired to unseat Democratic congressional incumbents "and to create an apartheid Black district under the guise of being great friends of Blacks."[67] A conference committee in late March brought victory to the white Democrats in the form of the status quo, majority-backed bill, a plan that shuffled only six counties among the state's four congressional districts. The only no votes on the committee came from its three black members— Representative McGee and Senators Jewell and Lewellen.[68] It is important to note, not only did all but one member of the Black Caucus later vote against the redistricting plan upon final roll call in their respective chambers (though five abstained) but also all except Representative Wilkins (who was ill with cancer and missed most of the 1991 legislative session) participated as plaintiffs or interveners in a subsequent lawsuit filed by the state Republican Party.[69] The US Supreme Court, however, rejected the challenge.

It is interesting to add that a similar conflict, and alliance between some Black Caucus members and the state Republican Party, emerged with the 2001 redistricting effort at the state legislative level. Rep. Gov. Mike Huckabee (who is white) put forward a redistricting plan that would have increased the number of majority-black districts in Arkansas to fifteen in the house and five in the senate, figures not far off from the NAACP's goals of seventeen and six, respectively. White Democrats Sharon Priest, secretary of state, and Mark Pryor, attorney general, preferred a plan that placed the number at thirteen in the house and four (up one) in the senate. Rep. Tracy Steele (D-North Little Rock), chair of the Black Caucus, supported the Democratic plan because "Huckabee wanted more Black-majority districts . . . [to] dilute Democratic voting strength in other districts."[70] Dale Charles, state NAACP president, countered that Steele, director of the state's Martin Luther King, Jr., Commission, was "the rabid mouth of racism for the Democratic Party."[71] The issue generated much controversy among African American political leaders and likely played a role in a three-way primary race among Steele, former Rep. Wilma Walker, and civil rights attorney John Walker for one of the majority-black Little Rock senate seats in May of 2002. Steele won with 56% of the vote, a victory pundits attributed to his "harmony-seeking demeanor."[72]

Conclusions and Implications

This preliminary effort to catalog and analyze the presence and behavior of African American legislators in the Arkansas General Assembly produced two key findings. First, the proportion of black state legislators increased steadily following the voting rights reforms of the 1960s. This process was accelerated, significantly, by the court-ordered, race-conscious legislative redistricting of the late 1980s. Still, although a state legislative membership that is 10% black (12% of the house and 6% of the senate) may be an improvement over thirty years ago, the goal of full descriptive representation for African Americans in the Arkansas legislative process has yet to be realized. Although it is true that most southern states long have had, and continue to maintain, African American populations of at least twice the size of Arkansas's, this is not ample justification for the state's still-low ratio of black legislators to black residents. If indeed Arkansas was "destined to be the great Negro state of the country" at the dawn of the past century, such promise remains unfulfilled with regard to their descriptive representation at the dawn of the next.

That promise remains unfulfilled in terms of substantive representation as well. Specifically, our second—and most important—finding is that African Americans in the Arkansas General Assembly have been unable to exercise consistent influence over policy outcomes. In part, this is because African Americans—like any demographic group—have not been wholly homogenous when it comes to policy preferences. (In fact, the greater the degree of chamber-wide contention over the policy questions included in this analysis, the greater the propensity of black legislators to take opposing positions among themselves.) However, as noted earlier in the chapter, African American members have voted together more often than not and have presented a unified front far more frequently than white Democrats.

The chief obstacle to black influence in Arkansas lies primarily in the small proportion of the total state legislative membership composed of African Americans. One senior member, a white Democrat who was influential throughout the 1980s and 1990s, indicated that the Arkansas Black Caucus was simply never big enough to "really kill anything." From time to time, he intimated, they wielded enough votes that the governor or the senior member shepherding a measure through the chamber would indeed need to court them on controversial issues. They did so, however, largely on an individual basis. This was because the Arkansas legislature was not traditionally a place in which members "caucused off"; efforts to do so were, in fact, seen as a bit of an "irritant" by senior members who, until the adoption of term limits in 1992, controlled the Arkansas legislative process.[73] The only measure on which the member could recall leverage exercised by black legislators as a group was on a redistricting plan for the state Court of Appeals debated through the mid- and late 1990s. Caucus members pressed for black-majority districts and although "they didn't get their way," the majority did have to postpone its actions.[74]

Interviews with African American leaders active during the period of investigation confirmed that black legislators in Arkansas have been too few in number and have not occupied the necessary leadership positions to wield much observable influence. Former state health director (and, later, US surgeon general) Dr. Elders (2002) noted, for example, that although most of the Black legislators "were very proud to be there . . . representing their constituents," few of them took positions not already congruent with the white majority's preferences. The fact that the assembly was controlled by "four old, White leaders, [who, if they] couldn't get it done, it wasn't going to get done," contributed to an inhospitable environment for the Black Caucus.[75] Former State Representative McGee echoed this sentiment, noting first that with just "13 Black folks in the house and 51 needed for passage, getting all the Black folks wasn't going to help you."[76] He also concurred that the lack of numbers was not the only—or even the most significant—part of the equation. Rather, a measure stood little chance during his term of service unless "kissed" by at least one of the senior members of the body. Among these was Lloyd George, a white Democrat from Danville, who, McGee reported, was ultimately responsible for the passage of the much-disputed 1993 Civil Rights Act. According to McGee, George agreed to cosponsor the measure by Rep. Bill Walker (after McGee delivered an unrelated favor and a promise that it would not apply to gays and lesbians). Suddenly, introduced and rejected at the committee level every session for many years, the Arkansas Civil Rights Act—with the George imprimatur—"flew through the house."[77]

Few in number and not counted among the "network of senior members," it is thus not surprising that in each of the eight times in which the majority of the Black Caucus split with the majority of white Democrats on the twenty-seven measures examined, they lost.[78] And, by at least one measure, the future does not look much more promising. The state's African American population is small, now less than 16%. Even if the proportion of black legislators grows to match that figure, it will still play only a minor role in the vast majority of roll call votes. Under such circumstances, perhaps the caucus's best hope is to pursue a three-pronged strategy. First, their current numbers allow them to play the spoiler on closely divided votes such as the appellate court dispute noted above, and—very nearly—the 1989 School Choice measure. Rep. Tracy Steele, the current chair of the Black Caucus (and the executive director of the Arkansas Martin Luther King, Jr. Commission), offered the state's recent debate over the use of its share of the national tobacco settlement money as an additional example. "Obviously [the black membership] is not enough to pass bills, but it is [now] enough to stop them on a close vote."[79] Dissatisfied with the insufficient level of attention paid to minority needs in the major tobacco settlement plan crafted in a special legislative session, they did just that in April of 2000.[80] Playing this card too often, of course, could turn their white peers off to future cooperation; however, Black Caucus members will be increasingly well positioned to successfully impede distasteful measures as the assembly's partisan balance becomes more evenly weighted between Democrats and Republicans.

African American legislators also can continue to play the "sensitizer" role identified by former Representative Brown. The election and service of people who long have been political minorities sensitizes "those who had not had to think about certain things before."[81] This idea was firmly reiterated by former representative and chair of the Women's Caucus Lisa Ferrell, a white Democrat. "It helps to have folks who bring other worlds to the table," she said. In her view, this is not to suggest that other legislators purposely ignore non-majority groups. Instead, it is "a question of educating [the white, male majority] about the needs of various populations."[82] The success of this role rests, in part, on the Black Caucus's ability to "galvanize community support for the issues . . . outside the halls of the Capitol."[83] An important tactic of the current caucus, in fact, is to appeal to their white colleagues for cooperation by reminding them of the proportion of minorities in their districts.

Finally, Arkansas's black legislators can look toward crafting strategic alliances[84] with the major players in the General Assembly, a strategy made easier and more difficult by the full implementation of term limits with the 2002 election cycle. Senior members similar to Reps. Lloyd George and John Miller have disappeared from the state's political landscape. Black legislators now must negotiate—for policy victories, committee assignments, and leadership posts—with white Democrats who have no more than four (in the House) or six (in the Senate) years of experience in the respective chambers. They also must negotiate with a white, Republican governor and a much-expanded Republican legislative delegation that has benefited from term limits and a population boom in the white, conservative, business mecca of northwest Arkansas.

Their success in such an environment will depend heavily on the elevation of African American members to legislative leadership posts, an area in which they had some success in recent sessions. African Americans have chaired the Public Health, Welfare, and Labor Committees in both chambers. Black Caucus members have served as vice chairs for the house Education and Management Committees as well, and Senator Bill Lewellen recently chaired the legislative caucus for the central Arkansas region.[85] If the state's African American legislators can aggressively retain and expand their influence in this manner, and continue to play the spoiler and education roles, the Arkansas political landscape stands—finally—to be significantly transformed.

CHAPTER 7

Term Limits in Arkansas

Opportunities and Consequences

ART ENGLISH

Unfazed by the warnings of the academic community that capping the number of terms elected officials can serve would have dire consequences for state government (e.g., would upset the balance of power between the legislative and executive branches and would increase the influence of special interests in the Capitol), Arkansas voters in 1992 approved, by a wide margin, a strict "Term Limits Amendment." In this brief study, veteran political scientist Art English takes stock of the changing demographics of the General Assembly—especially growing number of Republicans serving in both chambers—in the decade following. He concludes that Arkansas's limits resulted in increased opportunity for public service, producing a more diverse legislative body. But this came at the expense of the experienced leadership many view as essential to the operation of the legislative branch of government. This was one reason many efforts were made to repeal or extend term limits for years afterward, succeeding only when tucked discreetly into an "ethics, transparency, and accountability" amendment adopted in 2014. The tactic— which increased the maximum years of service in a single chamber to sixteen and was accompanied by another wave of legislative scandals in the years following—infuriated term limits supporters who retaliated with proposals to reinstate some of the strictest limits in the country, a policy seesaw ripe for future scholarly investigation.

In April 2003, the 84th Arkansas General Assembly, following one of its most hectic and disorderly sessions in the last twenty-five years, submitted

Originally published in *Spectrum: The Journal of State Government* 76 (Fall 2003): 30–33. Reprinted with permission. DOI: https://doi.org/10.34053/parry2019.riapag2.7

a constitutional amendment that would extend the potential for House and Senate service from six to twelve years and from eight to twelve years respectively. While the vote on the new term limits amendment will not take place until the November 2004 general election, the Assembly's action has added more fuel to the ongoing debate over the merits of term limits in Arkansas.

It is fair to say that the Arkansas General Assembly was not a likely candidate for term limits in the first place. Arkansas has a citizens' legislature that is required to meet only sixty days every odd numbered year. Arkansas legislators are not professional legislators. They are part-time, have other full-time vocations, and are not the beneficiaries of full time salary or extensive staff support. However, Arkansas during the last half of the 20th century has had a very senior legislature. Compared to most state legislatures its turnover rate has been low, seldom averaging over 15 percent from session to session. Senior legislators were especially dominant in the Senate where power coalesced around the floor leader, the pro tempore, and those senators who controlled the rules, budget and efficiency committees. In the House, power was somewhat more decentralized around the long serving senior committee chairs and the Speaker of the house as the institutional symbol and leader of that chamber.[1]

During the 1980s power became more fractured in the Senate as a new breed of legislator challenged the old bulls for control. In part, the number of senior legislators in the Arkansas General Assembly during this period may have provided fodder for the term limits movement that was aimed at professional-congressional types of legislators who were reelected year after year. With 59.9 percent of the voters supporting a term limits amendment in 1992, which also limited constitutional executive officers to no more than eight years in office, it could hardly be doubted how the electorate felt over a decade ago. Certainly the expectation among term limit supporters was to even out the playing field for challengers, stimulate more balanced party competition, generate new blood and ideas, eliminate complacent and unresponsive legislators, and produce a more efficient and effective legislative process. Opponents of term limits responded that there would be a loss of leadership and institutional memory, members would become less rather than more responsive, and the legislative process would become more subordinate to interest groups and the executive branch. Based on twenty-three interviews with legislators, legislative leaders, and prominent staff members,[2] coupled with observations of some fundamental legislative trends over the last two decades, this analysis is aimed at assessing some of the recent effects of term limits on the Arkansas General Assembly.

Sessions

One of the apparent effects since the introduction of term limits has been longer legislative sessions. Legislative sessions in Arkansas are constitutionally mandated for sixty days but they can be extended by a two-thirds vote of the legislature. Longer sessions have occurred prior to term limits however. In the 19th and early 20th centuries legislative sessions were commonly ninety days or more and that was certainly the case with the 84th Arkansas General Assembly, which had to confront not only severe revenue shortfalls but also the seemingly intractable problem of school consolidation. Nonetheless, the prior pattern before term limits was not characterized by long sessions. From 1953 to 1991—a total of twenty legislative sessions— only one exceeded ninety days with the average length of session 70.1 days. However, since term limits were implemented in 1992, four out of the six and three out of the last four sessions have lasted ninety days or over with an average session length of 88.3 days, eighteen legislative days longer than the average over the previous twenty sessions. One of the common themes of our interview data was that under term limits, members accelerated the introduction of legislation in the expectation that they would have less time to achieve its passage. Several of our respondents noted that you had to hit the ground running when your entire legislative life was limited to just 180 regular session days in the House and 240 in the Senate. Among the various impacts of term limits, this was one of its most unexpected consequences.

Bills

Bill and act totals reflected the more frenetic and heavier "lawmaking" pace the Arkansas General Assembly has worked under since the invocation of term limits. The first session under tern limits produced an increase of over 100 bills from the 78th Assembly, which suggested that perhaps some legislators were getting the quick start message and that less powerful committee chairpersons could not stop as many bills emerging from their committee. But it was not until the term limited members from 1993 began to get close to completing their terms and new members began to enter the House and Senate in 1999 and 2001 respectively that bill introductions began to increase at their most rapid rate. Two hundred more bills were introduced in the Senate in 1999 than the previous session and there were steady increases of almost 300 bills in each of the last two House sessions from the preceding sessions.[3] The increase in bill passage should also be noted, although the

TABLE 1.

Bills Introduced and Passed: 1981–2003

YEAR	SESSION	SENATE BILLS	HOUSE BILLS	TOTAL	ACTS
1981	73rd	629	1018	1647	994
1983	74th	572	1011	1583	937
1985	75th	705	1069	1774	1097
1987	76th	681	1079	1760	1072
1989	77th	618	958	1576	995
1991	78th	743	1125	1868	1246
1993	79th	837	1144	1981	1319
1995	80th	855	1168	2023	1358
1997	81st	756	1285	2041	1362
1999	82nd	967	1291	2258	1598
2001	83rd	988	1655	2643	1843
2003	84th	979	1906	2885	1816

Arkansas General Assembly has long had a high batting average passing bills. This characteristic of the state's political culture in combination with the more equitable distribution of power in the House because of term limits—as several of our respondents noted—is likely responsible for the increase in bill introductions and passage in the Arkansas General Assembly.

Demographic and Party Change

Proponents of term limits also anticipated fundamental changes in the demographic and partisan characteristics of the Arkansas General Assembly, a legislature that for virtually all of its history was overwhelmingly white, male, and Democratic. Some of these effects have taken place but not all of them can be attributed to term limits. The South has seen a rise of Republicans in state legislatures overall because of party realignment although it has proceeded at a slower pace in Arkansas. And legislative reapportionment, which has resulted in the drawing of more black majority districts, has had an effect on the larger number of minority legislators in the Arkansas General Assembly. The increased number of African-Americans, women, and Republicans in the Assembly is evident nonetheless and it appears that at least some of these increases can be attributed to the effects of term limits. In analyzing Table 2, the big jump in the number of females in

TABLE 2.

African-Americans and Women
in the Arkansas General Assembly: 1981–2003

	1981	1983	1985	1987	1989	1991	1993	1995	1997	1999	2001	2003
African Americans												
House	3	3	4	4	5	9	10	9	10	12	12	12
Senate	1	1	1	1	1	3	3	3	3	3	3	3
Total	4	4	5	5	6	12	13	12	13	15	15	15
Women												
House	4	6	9	8	7	8	12	16	22	20	14	15
Senate	1	1	1	1	2	1	1	1	1	0	4	7
Total	5	7	10	9	9	9	13	17	23	20	18	22

the 135-member body actually started to take place in the early 1990s when the number more than doubled those from the 1980s sessions culminating with the election of 22 women in 1997 and 20 in 1999 as term limits began to take effect for the 1993 members.

Term limits do not seem to have had a dramatic effect on the overall number of women in the legislature since, however, as other women elected in 1995 and 1997 have been term limited and in some cases have been replaced by male legislators. However, this analysis is a bit misleading in respect to the impact of term limits on women in the Assembly. The number of women in the Senate has increased dramatically from one, for most of the last twenty years, to four women in 2001 and seven in 2003. What is interesting about the larger number of women in the 2003 Senate is that five of them have served in the House, so the effect of term limits may be more subtle than direct. Now that there are open seats in the Senate because of term limits, more women with House experience are running for them. The number of African Americans in the Assembly however has remained flat since a doubling in their numbers took place in 1991. Term limits do not seem to have had an appreciable effect on the number of blacks in the Arkansas General Assembly and as term limited African Americans leave the legislature, there is no guarantee black legislators will replace them.[4]

Where term limits in Arkansas have had a significant effect—indeed the desired impact by many who supported it—is the much larger contingent of the minority party in the Arkansas legislature and the dramatic increase of new members—turnover in other words—from previous legislative sessions. While Republicans were gaining seats in the legislature before term limits, Table 3 documents that in 1999, when term limits first took effect, the number of Republicans increased in the Assembly by 50 percent from the previous legislature. If term limits were intended to help balance out the partisan playing field in one-party dominated legislatures, then it has helped move towards that goal in Arkansas. And while new, fresh ideas cannot be correlated with raw numbers, the increase in the number of new legislators in the Arkansas General Assembly has been extraordinary. In 1999, 61 new legislators were elected, forever transforming a senior dominated body. Consider, for example, that as recently as 1993 (the first Assembly to live under term limits) turnover was only about 9 percent. Since 1999, however, when turnover approached a remarkable 50 percent of the membership, better than a third of the Arkansas General Assembly has been new members.

Leadership Changes

Since the introduction of term limits, the changes that have taken place in the Arkansas General Assembly have been stunning. Once the territory of legislators in their sixties with twenty and even forty years of service, the Arkansas General Assembly has seen an influx of young legislative leaders with few legislative sessions under their belt. Since term limits legislators with only four years of experience have chaired standing committees in the House. The 2003 pro tem of the senate is only in his second term, when the usual number of years of experience for assuming that office has been sixteen to twenty years. The real and symbolic effects of term limits have been even more dramatic in the House. In 2001, the Speaker of the House assumed the office with just two completed terms and at the tender age of twenty-eight years, just half the average age of speakers of the last thirty years, almost all of whom have been in their fifties or sixties when they took office. The 1999 session speaker was only thirty-three when he was elected speaker. Interestingly both of these youthful leaders took early steps to combat the perceived problems of term limits. They instituted training sessions for new legislators well before the session started. They met frequently with new and veteran members to smooth the socialization process, and they worked closely with legislative staff to enhance communications, technology, and procedures so that new members could adapt to legislative life as quickly as possible. The trade-off then in Arkansas has been experience versus new members. Term limit supporters have argued that new members translate into new ideas and a more responsive legislature. Those opposed to term

TABLE 3.

Republican and New Member Representation: 1981–2003

	1981	1983	1985	1987	1989	1991	1993	1995	1997	1999	2001	2003
Republicans												
House	5	6	7	7	11	9	10	12	13	24	21	30
Senate	1	3	4	4	5	4	5	7	7	6	8	8
Total	6	9	11	11	16	13	15	19	20	30	29	38
New Members												
House	17	17	16	7	10	18	18	29	20	56	32	35
Senate	5	11	5	2	2	6	4	7	5	5	16	16
Total	22	28	21	9	12	24	22	36	25	61	48	51

limits point out that it is experience that is the stuff of effective lawmaking and representation.

Recruitment and Departure

Where have the new legislators been coming from? Where have the former legislators gone? These are important questions to ask because they help us assess whether the fundamental goals of term limits are being met. While this question cannot be fully answered because this is still an experiment in progress, the preliminary findings are nonetheless interesting and instructive.

Table 4 indicates that more new legislators seem to be coming at least with county legislative experience. County legislative districts in Arkansas are single member and county legislators serve part-time like their state legislative counterparts. The transition then to the state legislature these numbers suggest would seem to be a relatively natural one.[5] A glance at the overall experience levels in the state legislature however, especially since term limits, would show that a large number of new legislators come with local and county government experience. They are not just county legislators but also county judges, mayors, city directors, alderman, and school board members. What the term-limited legislatures do not lack is prior governmental experience. Indeed, one recent study found that forty legislators in the 1981 session had local government experience while sixty-six did in the

TABLE 4.

County Legislative Experience in the Assembly and Previous
House Experience in the Senate: 1985–2003

YEAR	1985	1987	1989	1991	1993	1995	1997	1999	2001	2003
County Legislative Experience	8	10	11	12	15	17	17	18	21	17
Senators with House Experience	9	8	8	6	7	9	8	8	21	29

2001 session.[6] If anything, term limits have opened up the Arkansas General Assembly to a host of local government officials who want to be legislators.

And what of the legislators who leave? Where do they go? As Table 4 indicates, many of them run successfully for the upper house. Twenty-nine of the 2003 members of the Senate have served in the House including the 1999 and 2001 speakers, while the average number of state senators with House experience from 1985 to 1997 was a mere eight.[7] Other legislators find it hard to give up public life and seek jobs in state government. Several resigned before their term was over—since they cannot come back—to take positions as lobbyists and in state government.

Others give up their House term before it ends to run for the Senate. Two long-term members of the Senate have actually come back to the house when their Senate terms ended. Three recent legislators (Tim Hutchinson, Vic Snyder, and Mike Ross) ran successfully for Congress while several others have tried the waters of federal elected service without success. Many state legislators who otherwise would have run for their legislative seats again have sought other public opportunities. Other legislators, however, without the right connections and timing, have seen their legislative and political careers end while they still believed they have much to contribute.

Discussion: Opportunities and Consequences

The 84th (2003–2004) regular legislative session was a frayed one. It was long and acrimonious for the most part. Some in and out of the legislature blamed term limits for its foibles. They argued that the new legislators did not know how to get along in the legislature and use its information sources. Some of our respondents added that the new legislators were not experienced enough to ask penetrating questions of the staff and executive agency heads. The press (while not supporting the extension of term limits) printed articles criticizing the more individualistic styles of the legislators who they said were more interested in pork for their districts and advancing their own electoral careers than the good of the state. In truth, much of the debate over the worth of term limits was obscured by the difficult issues the assembly was facing: consolidation, revenue shortfalls, and executive branch reorganization. Supporters of the legislature cited the large number of bills as an indication of the hard work that the new legislators were doing. Interestingly, some of our respondents suggested that the legislature was a kinder and gentler one for staff, that the new legislators were more respectful and courteous than the senior legislators of the past—and more reliant on them. Other respondents pointed to the deficit of lawyers left in the Senate after term limits—the Senate is known for its legal eagles that could rewrite or stop bad legislation before it became law. Overall more research will need to be done to assess whether term limits have produced positive benefits. More state analyses with more precise public policy linkages need to be looked at. For the present though it appears that the Arkansas General Assembly has accepted term limits as a part of its political system for many more years. The current constitutional amendment if approved by the people would not abolish term limits; it would only extend them to twelve years of possible service. In part the legislators that adopted this amendment seem to be saying that they can and will have to live with term limits. It has brought more people into legislative life that hopefully will have the energy and ideas to produce good public policy. While that important part of the term limits enigma remains to be more fully evaluated, it also seem fair to say that greater flexibility in term limits may be the best way to tandem experience and opportunity in Arkansas and the other state legislatures.

CHAPTER 8

Orval E. Faubus

Out of Socialism into Realism

ROY REED

Governor Orval E. Faubus was arguably the best loved, the most hated, and, according to Roy Reed at least, the most misunderstood public figure of twentieth century Arkansas. Influenced by the politics of his father, a former secretary of the Madison County Socialist Party, Faubus developed radical politics as a young man but evolved quickly into one of a long line of Arkansas "hill-country populists." In this classic essay, Reed focuses on the political beliefs of the six-term governor who, despite his socialist roots and his instrumental role in bringing New Deal-style liberalism to Arkansas, will be forever defined by his part in the Little Rock Crisis of 1957 and the southern resistance to attempts to force desegregation of public schools in the South.

Orval E. Faubus was reared a liberal. His father, Sam Faubus, was a Socialist who detested capitalism and bigotry with equal fervor. The son's critics, myself included, have accused him through the years of selling out the beliefs of his father on both race and economics. The story may be less straightforward than that.

Orval Faubus came to power in Arkansas after World War II when two things were happening:

First, the old populist revolt that had inflamed the hills for several generations was burning itself out.[1] The end of Faubus's own radicalism coincided almost perfectly with the decline of radicalism among his people not only in the Ozarks but right across the southern uplands. Prosperity, meager as it was, finally intruded into the hills and nudged out not only

Originally published in *Arkansas Historical Quarterly* 54
(Spring 1995): 13–29. Reprinted with permission.
DOI: https://doi.org/10.34053/parry2019.riapag2.8

the Socialists like his father but also the intellectually tamer populists who had used their hillcountry base to shower invective on the delta planters and their establishment cohorts in banking, business, and industry. Resentment slowly began to give way to the other side of the populist coin, hope. Hope and appetite and a vestigially populist belief still current: that our fellow hillbilly Sam Walton made it and, with a little luck, I can make it, too.

Second, a national phenomenon with farreaching consequences was coming to a head during the 1950s. The racial equilibrium of the South was being extraordinarily disturbed, not merely by local agitation but more importantly by external forces that eventually would sweep away the entire breastwork of white supremacist defenses. The liberal Faubus might have thrown in with the national mood, a growing impatience with southern heeldragging. Realistically, however, how much can he be blamed for choosing to be seen as defender of the local faith, no matter how little he shared that faith? What would have been the fate of a governor who chose the other side? Some of my heroes have argued that he could have exerted leadership for the rights of blacks and survived. Or that, at the least, he could have died an honorable political death.

Maybe so. But Orval Faubus had seen quite enough of honorable struggle for lost causes in his boyhood home. And there was something else. By the time he was grown, he had seen enough fear, loss, and death to last a lifetime.

Literally from the beginning, Orval Eugene Faubus's life was threatened. He weighed two-and-one-half pounds when he was born the night of January 7, 1910, and was so frail that the midwife expected him to die before morning. One night when he was a year old, he caught the croup and stopped breathing. His father rushed him outside into the cold air and plunged a finger into his throat to save his life. The toddler was just learning to talk when he wandered from the house and fell into a deep spring of water and somehow did not drown but climbed out just as his mother got there.

Danger continued to surround him as he grew and became part of the community. The year he was seven, one playmate died of diphtheria and another was crushed to death by a falling tree. During another year flux swept the community and killed two children in a neighboring family.

Life was not only perilous at Greasy Creek; it was also hard. Southern Madison County was like most of the Ozarks at that time. The residents scraped by. The towns had a small prosperity, but the countryside provided little more than subsistence. Rural people like the Faubuses raised almost all their food. Shoes and coats were practically luxuries because they had to be bought with cash, and cash was pitiably scarce. Even kerosene for the lamps was so dear that, after John D. Rockefeller cornered the market and raised the price, young Orval had to walk behind the wagon and carry the filled can the two miles from Combs to Greasy Creek, so as not to spill any—or so he recollected in 1964 when Rockefeller's grandson Winthrop tried to wrest the governorship of Arkansas from him.

Even granted that poverty and fear may be goads to ambition, it still seems extraordinary that a youngster could rise from such circumstances in such a place to be governor of his state, to keep the job longer than any other person, and to become a public figure known around the world.

Greasy Creek was, in every sense, the end of the road. Orval had to walk twelve miles to his first job across mountain trails; no roads went there from his home. Communication was primitive. News in Greasy Creek—that is, any report that reached beyond Madison County and the community grapevine—was limited to what certain elders deemed worth passing on from the occasional mail subscription to the *Kansas City Weekly Star* or the even rarer subscription to the *Arkansas Gazette* or the *Daily Oklahoman.* Politics was conducted almost entirely face-to-face, man-to-man, in a kind of slowmotion pulsation radiating from the county seat at Huntsville. Politics was also an important diversion, and there we have a clue to his escape and survival.

From his earliest years, young Orval carried a double burden of shyness and pride. He was not strong enough to excel in physical competition. He turned to the private world of words and found that he had a talent not only for language but also for retaining information. Through reading magazines and books, he learned of a world far different from the hillside farm of his father. He dreamed of entering that world.

There were two ways out for a young man of his background and temperament: teaching and politics. His mother and father together pushed the shy son toward the first. His father pushed him, perhaps unwittingly, toward the second.

John Samuel Faubus was anything but shy. He came from a large, loud, sometimes boisterous family of fifteen children, counting stepsiblings. He claimed to have a fourthgrade education, but that was a flexible interpretation of the record. He once confessed that he had attended only three or four months of school by age eleven and that he did not learn to write until he was twenty, about the time he married. But before the last of his seven children was born, Sam Faubus had become known as one of the best informed people in his part of Arkansas. The same year Orval was born,

Sam took the lead in one of the most baffling political movements in the history of the state. He and two friends signed up most of the voting-age population on Greasy Creek as members of the Socialist party.

Not that socialism itself was baffling, although many people do not appreciate how significant a hold it had on Arkansas at that time. The southwestern states of Oklahoma, Louisiana, Texas, and Arkansas provided a substantial vote for the Socialist party candidate for president, Eugene V. Debs, in the election of 1912. The mystery is how Marxian socialism penetrated to the fastnesses of Greasy Creek, twenty-five miles from the nearest county seat, seventy years before the first pavement would be laid on the one dirt road to the place. The best guess is that it was imported by a gentlemanly old bachelor from the North, probably from Illinois, one O. T. Green. After a sojourn in a boarding house at Combs, where his socialist views caused a few embarrassing arguments, Green settled on a small farm near Sam Faubus's place. He raised goats and peacocks, corresponded with Socialist acquaintances in other states, and befriended the young neighbor whose inquiring mind intrigued him.[2]

From whatever source, Socialist publications began to appear in the Faubus household.[3] And Sam, once convinced that the big corporations controlled the American economy and that capitalism was his enemy, became an outspoken advocate of the socialist system. He and his friend Arch Cornett, a teacher, wrote eloquent letters to the editor of the Huntsville newspaper denouncing the entrenched interests.[4] Their concern spread to political reform; Sam circulated petitions calling for woman's suffrage, old-age pensions, and abolition of the voterestricting poll tax.

In May 1910 Sam and his friends formally established the Mill Creek Local of the Socialist party. The charter from the state committee was addressed to "the comrades of Combs" and carried the names of ten men, four of them named Faubus. Whoever copied the names apparently inverted Sam's initials so that he is listed as S. J. Faubus. The post of secretary, carrying with it the responsibility of chief organizer, went to him. Arch Cornett, O. T. Green, and Sam Faubus became the most devoted members of the south Madison County local.[5]

As many as thirty people, including some from neighboring communities, might have been members of the Mill Creek Local at one time. The party had a majority of the adult residents of the Greasy Creek community. The local was large enough to provide the swing vote in district election contests between the Democrats and Republicans.[6] Madison County had at least two other thriving Socialist locals, one at Witter and the other at Kingston. Several other locals sprang up across the Ozarks.[7]

Sam and Arch joined other Socialists in opposing World War I. They almost went to prison for their troubles. Just before the war ended, the two men were arrested for distributing literature protesting the war. The charge was serious: violating the Alien and Sedition Act. Only the timely end of the war and the help of a good lawyer kept them out of the penitentiary. Sam has been referred to in recent years as an "oldtime mountain Socialist." The designation suggests that people like Sam Faubus were too innocent to fully understand the implications of socialism. The old man would be indignant at that condescension if he were alive. It is probably true that the Socialists of the Southwest were less rigorous in the faith than their comrades in the industrial East. But they were apparently earnest in their attempt to change capitalism in the United States. Their hatred of Wall Street and capitalism was as intense as that of their hero Debs and any of the eastern Marxists.

Sam's interest in public affairs rubbed off on his eldest child. Orval read the Socialist party literature that came to the house. He even joined his father on at least one occasion when the two of them debated the merits of socialism with a pair of teachers at nearby St. Paul.

In 1935, after he was married and had been teaching several years, Orval indulged in his most serious flirtation with the political left. He hitchhiked to Commonwealth College, a labor selfhelp school near Mena, with the intention of gaining there the college education that he had not been able to afford elsewhere. The college comprised Socialists, Communists, labor organizers of various persuasions, and a smattering of unaffiliated idealists. They apparently had in common a conviction that the American economic system, then in collapse, was basically flawed.

How long Faubus remained on the campus has been disputed, but he was there long enough to give a May Day speech and be elected president of the student body. He says he never formally enrolled, but simply took part in campus activities in what sounds like a walkon role. Whatever the case, there is little doubt that young Faubus about that time began to develop a streak of political realism that was largely missing in his father. He shook the dust of Commonwealth from his feet after a few weeks or at most a few months. Instead of turning him into a cryptoCommunist, as some of his later enemies put it about, the close encounter with Marxism seems to have left him eventually disenchanted. It might be argued that the Commonwealth experience, far from producing a Communist subversive, was actually the beginning of a slow swing to the right that would send him into the conservative orbit more than twenty years later.

Back at Greasy Creek, Sam continued to urge socialism on his son. But Orval understood early that if he wanted a future in politics, a minority party with a radical reputation was not the way to go. And he was definitely interested in a political career.

Luckily, he was offered an alternative by national developments. Franklin D. Roosevelt was elected president in 1932. The New Deal, with its extensive social programs, coopted some of the Socialist party's more appealing ideas. Orval became a New Dealer. Eventually, so did Sam.

Orval remained a Democrat, at least nominally, throughout his long career. He remained a liberal of declining intensity until his second term as governor.

Faubus entered public life just as his part of America, the South, was starting to revive after threequarters of a century of lassitude. In the language of economics, the South was entering the takeoff stage in 1940—just when young Faubus was proving himself in county politics and entering his own takeoff stage.[8] He had been elected circuit clerk of his county in 1938 and had hopes of moving up to county judge—or even higher, with a little luck. Along with his growing success in politics, it would be his fate to come to maturity while his region was seeing its first real love affair with capitalism. The affair would bring greater prosperity to more people than the South had ever seen. It would also bring the evils of makeitfast gogetterism: industrial pollution, runaway greed, corruption of institutions, and what is probably misnamed as conservatism in politics. As governor during the 1950s and 1960s, Faubus would preside over his state's immersion in all this, the good and the bad.

For starters, he plunged headily into the race for industrialization. He saw that the only way that backward Arkansas could ever catch up with the rest of the country was to build a base of industrial production to balance the state's traditional and always uncertain agricultural base. He induced the conscienceridden Baptist playboy Winthrop Rockefeller, who had fled to Arkansas to escape a disastrous marriage and his family's disapproval, to head up Arkansas's program for attracting industry. They made a good team, the compassionate capitalist and the Socialistreared hillbilly. Steadily, outofstate industry moved into the state and enriched its payroll. Faubus later estimated that 125,000 industrial jobs had been added during his twelveyear administration. The new industry also, in many cases, exploited the state's resources and fouled its air, water, and forests. Not much thought was given to regulation of industry in those days. A people who had never had any easy factory jobs—easy compared to subsistence farming—was not concerned with unfortunate consequences. Neither was the governor, except for a few notable instances when his Ozarks upbringing asserted itself, as it did, for example, when he threw in with the environmentalists and stopped the Corps of Engineers from damming the Buffalo River.

The business establishment of Little Rock was openly contemptuous of the country boy from Madison County when he first became governor. He swallowed his pride and set out to win them over. Within a year he had made peace with many of the capital's gogetters, including some who had held him up as a figure of amusement at posh cocktail parties. Even after he had made peace with them, many of the country club set continued for years to poke fun at his country speech and country ways.

Faubus never became a country clubber. He built his own set of affluent friends and associates. At the center of his set was another selfmade man, a country boy who took his own revenge against the city sophisticates by simply piling up a larger fortune than any of them had. W. R. (Witt) Stephens was already a behindthescenes power in Arkansas politics when Faubus became governor. He and Faubus quickly formed an alliance of mutual benefit.

For Stephens the alliance provided friendly, profitable treatment from state agencies and administration allies in every institution from banks to the state legislature to scores of courthouses and city halls across the state. Early in 1957, when the state Supreme Court struck down a lucrative pricing arrangement for Stephens's Arkansas Louisiana Gas Company—one that Faubus's complaisant Public Service Commission had approved—the legislature, equally complaisant, overruled the court and passed a law reinstalling the pricing arrangement. The entire exercise, from the court decision to the governor's signature on the new law, took only a week. Stephens got the same friendly reception when his various enterprises needed official help on other matters. For example, bonds for municipalities, school districts, and other public bodies were almost always handled through Stephens, Inc., or one of its allies.

For Faubus the alliance provided vital support during the increasingly expensive election campaigns that he was obliged to run. Stephens not only contributed heavily to Faubus's campaigns, but he also cajoled, conned, and armtwisted his many wealthy friends around the state and persuaded them to throw their collective weight behind Faubus. With the wealth of the Stephens combine behind him, Faubus became almost unbeatable. Faubus spread the benefits to his friends. An ally who headed the state Democratic Party became the lawyer for a large Stephens gas company in Fort Smith.[9] A number of Faubus administration officials, including members of the governor's staff, became owners of cheap ArkLa stock before the stock price, inspired by action of the Public Service Commission, increased substantially.[10]

Among the most reluctant power bases to come around to Faubus was the Arkansas Power and Light Company. AP and L had had its way with the state's politics for many years. Governor Francis A. Cherry had been the latest in a long series of public figures who had been in the utility's debt. He found the association so congenial that he raised no objection when AP and L, with customary arrogance but uncharacteristic ineptness, raised its electric rates during the 1954 election campaign. Faubus leapt on the issue. He had already come to the utility's attention as a gnatlike irritant several years earlier when he had had the gall to editorialize in his *Madison County Record* against the company and in favor of publicly owned electric cooperatives. Now that he was governor, Faubus knew that he could expect no favors from the power company.

The flexible Witt Stephens had become a Faubus man in a matter of hours after the voters turned out his man Cherry in the Democratic primary. The men who ran AP and L were more stiffnecked. It took a while for them to absorb the new reality. Within one eighteenmonth period during Faubus's first term, the Public Service Commission—not yet dominated by him, but certainly alert to his growing power—granted two rate increases to Stephens's gas company. One of those allowed Stephens to sharply boost his rates to AP and L for the gas used in power generation. The power company objected, to no avail. During the same eighteen months, AP and L applied to the PSC for two increases of its own. It was turned down each time. When the power company persisted and applied a third time, the commission finally allowed it a fraction of its requested increase—just enough, it turned out, to pay for the rise in its gas bill. Witt Stephens made no secret of his satisfaction at lining his pockets with money from his adversaries at AP and L.

It can be argued that Faubus, with Stephens providing the goad, broke the generationslong dominance of AP and L over the state of Arkansas. Once the men in charge there understood their new situation, they lined up behind the hillbilly governor. Years later, Faubus could speak of the men at AP and L with friendly warmth. They became good corporate citizens, he said, with no discernible trace of triumph in his face.

There were many others from the moneyed establishment whom he came to count as supporters and in some cases social friends. They included builders, developers, insurance and real estate executives, bond dealers, road builders, heavy machinery sellers, printing company owners, newspaper publishers, and highpowered lawyers. They also included a disproportionate share of the wealthy landowners of the plantation country. These last helped to push the socialistreared, egalitarian man from the hills in an unexpected direction on the most explosive domestic issue of the midtwentieth century.

Race had been the defining quality in southern politics from the beginning. A dominant consideration of the white leaders of the deep South had been to assure the subordination of the black population. The issue might lie dormant for long years, then erupt when something threatened the racial equilibrium. Much of the middle and upper South was not dominated directly by the race issue, but such was the political strength and determination of the lowcountry black belt—"a skeleton holding together the South," V. O. Key called it—that all of the region was in its grip.[11]

The populist revolt divided the hills from the black belt. The latter allied itself with the conservative business forces in the cities and towns to beat down the radicals flourishing in the hills. That schism continued into the twentieth century. Rebellion simmered in the uplands, but the lowlands seldom lost control of the state governments. Alabama might throw up a Hugo Black or a Jim Folsom, but the "big mules" of the cities and the planters of the black belt finally dominated. The same was true in Arkansas. The hills produced political figures of prominence—J. W. Fulbright, Brooks Hays, J. W. Trimble, Clyde Ellis, Sid McMath—but none of them succeeded without the support of the powerful forces of the delta and their business allies. Any who resisted those forces were punished.

Faubus was the latest in a line of hillcountry progressives. The delta landowners were suspicious of him. In the early 1950s few questioned their ability to punish their opponents at the state capital. And yet there were signs that Arkansas was beginning to turn away from the delta domination and toward a more racially neutral politics. Key, writing in the late 1940s, thought that Arkansas, along with Texas and Florida, seemed destined to develop a nonsouthern sort of politics, one no longer ruled by the negative influence of race.[12] On the other hand, there was no doubt that race still had the power to inflame large numbers of white voters, and not just in the lowlands. In Arkansas, Jim Johnson demonstrated as late as the gubernatorial campaign of 1956 that white feelings were still intense, especially in the wake of the 1954 Supreme Court decision requiring school desegregation. Indeed, it was Johnson's strong showing against him in 1956 that persuaded Faubus to pay more attention to the voice from the delta.

But if anyone had been listening for nuance and not simply volume in that voice, he might have detected a note of weakness and even desperation.

From the beginning it had been the white fear of being overrun by blacks that had inspired the success of the delta's political oppression. The term black belt referred to a swath of southern counties where African Americans had a majority of the population. Arkansas, admittedly one of the least "threatened" states, had fifteen counties with black majorities in 1900. That number declined steadily as the century wore on: eleven in 1920, then nine in 1940.[13] By 1950 the state had only six counties where blacks predominated.[14] Yet those six counties, relying on the racism of varying virulence to be found in Little Rock and elsewhere, effectively imposed their politics of race on the other sixty-nine counties. Looking back across these forty years, racial fear seems to have been given more authority than it deserved. Alongside the numerical decline in the black "threat," the state was becoming increasingly urban and presumably more politically sophisticated. It was also poised to industrialize and prosper. Altogether, Arkansas was just at the takeoff stage in both politics and economics and might have been expected finally to cast off the burden of racial politics. Thanks to a convergence of currents, national and local, it did not.

What happened is well known. The Little Rock School District was ready to desegregate its first public school in the fall of 1957. A few other Arkansas districts, bowing to the Supreme Court's Brown decision of 1954, had already taken that step, and Faubus had accepted their decisions. He balked at Little Rock. Saying he had reason to fear violence if the plan went forward, he ordered out the National Guard to block the nine black pupils assigned to Central High. President Dwight D. Eisenhower sent army troops to suppress segregationist mobs, protect the black youngsters, and enforce the authority of the federal courts that had ordered desegregation. The event dominated headlines for months, not only in Arkansas but around the world. Faubus, by forcing the federal government to intervene first in Little Rock and then in other places around the South, probably hastened the end of the southern resistance to black civil rights. His action also ensured him six twoyear terms as governor and earned him a reputation, fairly or not, as a sellout to the politics of fear that had been exploited long and effectively by the delta planters.

It might be argued that Orval Faubus captured the delta as certainly as the delta captured him; that the influence of the lowlands was on the wane, and that this canny hill man stepped in at the historically propitious moment and took over the whole state, the delta included. Not much stretch of his sympathies was required. He had always felt warmly toward the poor people of his own section. It was easy to include the poor white people of the delta, along with their betters, in his affections. That his sympathies were not expansive enough to include a public declaration of friendship for the poor black people of the delta might have seemed to him a small price to pay. In any event, a kind of regional harmony ensued that Arkansas had not seen since the swamps were slashed and burned and turned into plantations, to be worked and in a perverse way dominated by slaves and the fear they engendered. For the first time, lowlanders and hill people were not competing for control of the capital. They shared control of the governor's office and, through the harmony Faubus imposed, the legislature, as well.

The race issue, after its last sensational eruption in 1957, finally lost its grip on the Arkansas mind. With the election of Winthrop Rockefeller, the aberrant moderate Republican who succeeded Faubus, the black population pretty well ceased to exercise the power of fear that it had had on the state's politics throughout its history. Black voters achieved this paradoxic loss of control through the happy circumstance of becoming important in the state's electoral system. They had voted in some numbers for several years, but those in the delta had had no real choice on election day. Rockefeller brought blacks into the system in large numbers, voting more or less freely and in any case jubilantly, although there were those who claimed that the millionaire New Yorker voted his blacks as surely as any delta planter ever had. The difference was this: Rockefeller made it worthwhile financially, in some cases, to vote right; the old planter voting his field hands had made voting right a condition of employment.

Before Rockefeller, no statewide candidate who was perceived as soft on the Negro question could attain and hold office if any creditable opponent insisted on exploiting that softness. Since Rockefeller, no candidate has achieved any lasting success without the approval of black voters. Interestingly enough, that change began during the last years of Faubus's administration. He quietly achieved a rapprochement with many black leaders, including L. C. Bates, the husband of his old nemesis, Daisy Bates, who led the Arkansas branch of the National Association for the Advancement of Colored People. L. C. Bates frequently offered advice to Faubus during the mid1960s, and on at least one occasion, according to Faubus, urged him to run for reelection.[15] The Faubus administration also supported a reform of the voter registration laws that paved the way for relieving the delta planters of the burden of buying thousands of poll taxes and trucking all those black workers to the polls every election day.

Faubus accommodated to the prevailing political realities, as he saw them. He continued into old age to insist that he was a true liberal, meaning

a New Dealer. But he kept up a running flirtation with Republicans and con-
servatives during the decades following his tenure in office. He offered advice
to such Republicans as John Connally of Texas and Representative John Paul
Hammerschmidt of Arkansas.[16] He had friendly contacts with the Nixon
White House and expressed his gratification that Nixon had carried Arkansas
in 1972.[17] He was friendly with the conservative administration of Harding
College, a Searcy, Arkansas, institution connected to the Church of Christ.[18]
He was active in the presidential campaign of George C. Wallace in 1968.

Did Faubus betray his father's idealism when he abandoned the left
wing and opted for the more conservative mainstream? This is a more difficult question than it appears to be at a glance. Answering it requires going
beyond historical evidence and making a speculative leap of judgment. The
heart of the question is this: What kind of Socialist was Sam Faubus? Was he
a revolutionary Marxist who would have been at home in Eastern Europe?
Or was his socialism more American, that is, more diluted? Even some of
America's Socialists were fairly dedicated Marxists; was Sam one of those?
If Sam Faubus wanted to overthrow the American capitalist system and
install a governmentcontrolled economy, then how could he bear to see his
famous son become an established part of the system he hated? But if Sam
was actually a populist who liked to call himself a Socialist, then his son's
success would have pleased him.

While the more determined Socialists worked for a fundamental
change in the economic system, many populists merely raged against its
inequities. Remove whatever was causing them a momentary discontent—
unfair banking practices, railroad domination, trusts—and large numbers
of the populist farmers would subside and let capitalism go on its way.[19]

It is hard to know what to make of Sam's beliefs. They probably fell
somewhere between populist and socialist. On the one hand, he could write
with apparent earnestness, after Franklin D. Roosevelt became president,
"This country is owned and controlled by a few bankers and other capitalists
and the quicker Mr. Roosevelt takes over all industry the better it will be for
the country."[20] During the same season, his friend and fellow Socialist Arch
Cornett was denouncing private ownership by "the few" of mines, mills,
shops, storehouses, transportation lines, steamship lines, and electric light
and water systems.[21] Whether these Madison County Socialists seriously
advocated government ownership of those enterprises is not clear, but it
seems fair to infer that they did.

On the other hand, southwestern Socialists like these, while generally
more emotionally volatile than their comrades in other regions, tended to be

less intellectually doctrinaire.[22] At times, it appeared that they would have been satisfied with a throughgoing reform, rather than a radical rebuilding, of the economic and political system. They were a little like their hero Eugene V. Debs. He embraced socialism gradually, like a swimmer entering a springfed pool. Debs had begun as a Democrat and a craft unionist. Then he supported the Populist party in 1896 before joining Victor L. Berger to organize the Social Democratic party. That was the forerunner of the Socialist party, on whose platform he ran four times for president. The Socialists of Arkansas, Texas, Oklahoma, and Missouri idolized the fiery but undoctrinaire Debs.[23]

The platform of Arkansas's own Socialist party contained the usual railings against an unjust economic system, but it also carried a number of reform ideas that in time would be considered middleoftheroad. Socialists here opposed the death penalty and corruption in elections. They favored the initiative and referendum, woman's suffrage, and the graduated income tax.[24] Sam Faubus worked hard for those reforms. How hard he would have fought in an armed revolution to overthrow the government is anybody's guess. I think he would stopped far short of that. He was willing to go to prison for his beliefs when he agitated against World War I—and almost did—but I have trouble seeing him at the barricades trying to bring down the government of Calvin Coolidge. Once Roosevelt launched the New Deal, which ameliorated some of the discontents that Sam had suffered, he became a New Dealer. By the time of John F. Kennedy's presidency, he was an enthusiastic Democrat.

Orval became as devoted a New Dealer as his father. The New Deal may seem quaint to today's young liberals, but in its time it stirred fierce emotions. Those emotions had not subsided entirely by the time Orval Faubus became governor. He spent substantially of his political capital to move Arkansas along in its own version of the New Deal, a movement that had been pursued fitfully in the state during the previous twenty years. Faubus most notably stood up to powerful forces—including those of the delta—and pushed through the legislature a 50 percent increase in the sales tax to finance improved education and other state services. He brought more compassion to the state welfare system. He was generally friendly to labor. He spent state funds generously to improve the lot of the mentally ill and retarded. These and other accomplishments are what he had in mind when he described himself as a true liberal as opposed to the presentday liberal who is concerned—unduly, Faubus believed—with the rights of various cultural, racial, ethnic, and sexual minorities.

One final question remains: If Orval Faubus did not betray his father and the father's idealism, did he then betray his own class? Probably not. The populist, hillcountry class that he came from is always ready to forgive the person who escapes it. Far from seeing escape as betrayal of one's fellows, as it was and to some extent remains in the more classencrusted nations of Europe, rising from one's class is seen with approval in America. Shannon put it this way: "Americans have generally believed it easier and more desirable to rise *from* their class rather than *with* their class."[25] Orval Faubus escaped into the world he had dreamed of as a boy, a world of fame, power, and material comfort. He never came close to entering the traditional establishment, but there is no doubt that he learned to traffic with the capitalists and power brokers that his father had hated. It could be argued that far from betraying his class, he fulfilled its secret yearnings.

CHAPTER 9

Noblesse Oblige and Practical Politics

Winthrop Rockefeller and the Civil Rights Movement

CATHY KUNZINGER URWIN

As the first Republican to serve as governor of Arkansas since Reconstruction, a transplant from New York, and a member of one of the most prominent families in America, Winthrop Rockefeller has generated considerable attention from the scholarly community. In this essay, Cathy Urwin focuses on Rockefeller's attitudes toward race and his actions during the early years of the civil rights movement. Her assertion that Rockefeller's personal commitment to civil rights was long-standing and genuine is hardly controversial. The author then turns to Rockefeller's actions as governor, focusing on the goal of desegregating the state's public schools and busing as a public policy tool to aid in achieving that goal. On these issues, she considers Rockefeller's civil rights record "erratic." But she also argues that, in the Arkansas of the 1960s, his overall position on race relations was progressive, and that, in the words of a contemporary, Rockefeller made racial toleration "acceptable and respectable in Arkansas."

On Sunday April 7, 1968, Arkansas Governor Winthrop Rockefeller stood hand-in-hand with black leaders on the steps of the state capitol and sang "We Shall Overcome." Approximately three thousand people, two-thirds of whom were black, had gathered at this prayer service to remember Dr. Martin Luther King, Jr., slain three days earlier in Memphis. In his eulogy the governor asked the assembled crowd to "not forget that we are all creatures of God." Rockefeller was the only southern governor to publicly eulogize King in the days following the assassination.[1]

Originally published in *Arkansas Historical Quarterly* 54
(Spring 1995): 30–52. Reprinted with permission.
DOI: https://doi.org/10.34053/parry2019.riapag2.9

Winthrop Rockefeller was unique in Arkansas history. Elected in 1966 and reelected in 1968, he was the state's first Republican governor since Reconstruction. But it was in the field of civil rights that Rockefeller made one of his greatest contributions to the state's history. It was not political expediency that moved Rockefeller to adopt the cause of civil rights. In fact, he repeatedly downplayed his association with civil rights during his political career in Arkansas in order to avoid alienating the segregationist vote. Winthrop Rockefeller championed the cause of civil rights because he was raised to do so. Helping to advance African American rights, particularly in education, was a family tradition. John D. Rockefeller, Winthrop's grandfather, made his first gift to African American education in June 1882, when he gave $250 to the Atlanta Female Baptist Seminary, a school for black women. On Winthrop's paternal grandmother's side, the fight to uplift African Americans predated the Civil War. As a girl, Laura Spelman Rockefeller with her family helped runaway slaves as part of the Underground Railroad. Atlanta Female Baptist Seminary was renamed Spelman College in 1884 in honor of Laura's parents. John D. Rockefeller continued to give money and land to both Spelman College and its counterpart for men, Morehouse College.[2]

This family commitment to African American causes intensified in succeeding generations. Winthrop's father, John D. Rockefeller Jr., was one of the founders of the United Negro College Fund. The Rockefeller family became involved with the National Urban League in 1921. Winthrop joined the executive board in 1940 and in 1947 became chairman of the Urban League Service Fund's corporate division.[3] In 1952 he donated Standard Oil of California stock worth approximately one hundred thousand dollars for the purpose of purchasing a league headquarters building. Rockefeller's connection to the National Urban League, actively and financially, continued until his death.[4]

Rockefeller involved himself in other civil rights issues and organizations long before he ever thought of moving to Arkansas. In 1936, while learning the oil business in Texas, he tried unsuccessfully to establish a local community health organization that would be run by blacks for blacks. His interest had been aroused when his black maid suffered an appendicitis attack. Through a letter to his father, Rockefeller enlisted the aid of both the Rockefeller Foundation and the Rosenwald Foundation but ultimately failed because of disinterest on the part of the white trustees of the local black hospital.[5]

Rockefeller toured the United States for the secretary of war in 1946, surveying veterans' readjustment problems. James "Jimmy" Hudson, a black private detective from Harlem who had been working for Winthrop since 1937, accompanied him. At each stop on the tour, Hudson collected data on the problems faced by black veterans, and this information was incorporated into the final report. In the report Rockefeller stated that the black veteran faced great difficulty reverting to civilian life because "his color nullifies the fact that he is a veteran." The report asked the armed forces to help combat racial prejudice at home.[6]

Throughout the late 1940s and early 1950s, Rockefeller promoted the cause of fair employment practice legislation both in federal employment and in American industry. In a 1952 speech to the National Urban League Conference, he called fair employment practice legislation a "very useful tool" against discrimination. He called for an educational campaign to awaken people to the immorality and economic waste of racial discrimination.[7]

In 1953 Winthrop Rockefeller moved to Arkansas, and while he may have changed his state of residence, the causes and values he championed did not change. His move south was closely followed by the events that have been heralded as the start of the modern civil rights movement: the Supreme Court decision *Brown v. Board of Education* and the Montgomery, Alabama, bus boycott. Governor Orval Faubus appointed Rockefeller the first chairman of the Arkansas Industrial Development Commission (AIDC) in 1955, and the following year Rockefeller warned publicly that southern opposition to integration would have a negative effect on industrialization.[8] Those words would prove prophetic in 1957 when Little Rock became the site of one of the most significant desegregation cases of the modern era—the Central High Crisis. When Governor Faubus used the Arkansas National Guard to prevent the integration of Central High by nine African American students, he forced a very reluctant President Eisenhower to send the 101st Airborne Division to the school to protect the nine students. A month after the crisis began, Rockefeller issued a statement that the crisis was damaging industry. In fact, not one major firm moved to Little Rock in the three years following the crisis.[9]

The Central High Crisis gives a clear indication of how important segregation was to white voters in Arkansas. Orval Faubus got what he wanted out of the crisis—a third term as governor—making him the first to win a third term in fifty years. The voters of Little Rock closed the city's high schools for the entire 1958–1959 school year rather than continue integration. And seven-term Congressman Brooks Hays, who had tried unsuccessfully to reach a compromise between Eisenhower and Faubus, was defeated in his bid for reelection in 1958 by a segregationist write-in candidate who announced his campaign just one week before the election.[10] These lessons would not be lost on Rockefeller when he decided not long afterward to become actively involved in his adopted state's politics.

Nineteen-sixty-four was an important year in the history of American race relations. The twenty-fourth amendment to the United States Constitution was ratified, abolishing the poll tax. Three civil rights workers were murdered in Mississippi, and President Lyndon Johnson pressed the Civil Rights Act through Congress. In Arkansas Winthrop Rockefeller ran for the first time as a Republican candidate for governor.

Rockefeller did not win the 1964 election but garnered 43 percent of the vote against incumbent Orval Faubus. Race was an issue which Faubus used successfully against Rockefeller. Rockefeller's involvement with the National Urban League and his family's history of interracial philanthropy were well known. A pre-election poll showed that compared with the 49 percent of the voters statewide who felt that Faubus could do the best job of keeping racial peace in Arkansas, only 28 percent thought Rockefeller most likely to do so.[11] Rockefeller was very careful not to come out in favor of integration. The 1964 Arkansas Republican Party platform mentioned the illegality of separate schools, but called for correcting the inequality in funding for these separate schools which, "it is realistic to assume" would "exist for years to come." The only mention in the platform of civil rights was a statement that "human relations problems can best be solved on the local level and, in this area, the greatest permanent progress can be made through patient, good-faith, voluntary action rather than through violence, coercive legislation or court order."[12]

In part, the carefully worded appeal for voluntary gradualism in the 1964 Republican Party platform was political, but it must be noted that it also reflected Winthrop Rockefeller's own philosophy. Rockefeller opposed the 1964 Civil Rights Act on the grounds that it granted extraordinary powers to the executive branch of government.[13] He believed that in the long run, moral persuasion would be much more effective in bringing about racial equality. Rockefeller learned racial justice from his parents at least thirty years before the modern civil rights movement began. In the context of the 1960s, therefore, he was not a liberal. He did not believe in giving blacks any special favors to correct existing injustices but rather the opportunity and education to compete on an equal footing with whites.

Rockefeller ran for governor again in 1966, this time against "Justice

Jim" Johnson, a hard-core segregationist and one of the founders of Arkansas's white Citizens Council. Johnson did not back away from his segregationist views, but by 1966 most white Arkansans had accepted the existence of the civil rights movement and the futility of trying to stop it. Johnson's extremism was certainly a major factor in Rockefeller's victory. This was the first gubernatorial election under the new voter registration system, which eliminated block purchases of poll taxes, and approximately 90 percent of Arkansas's black voters cast their ballots for Rockefeller. But Rockefeller also defeated Johnson in about half of the state's rural counties, where segregationist support had traditionally been greatest.[14]

Rockefeller's years as governor, 1967–1971, coincided with vast changes in the direction, tone, and goals of the civil rights movement. Largely because of those changes, Rockefeller found greater success in working for and with the black community in Arkansas during his first term in office than he would find during his second. As governor, Rockefeller's main emphasis was on creating an equal playing field, to create an atmosphere in the state where blacks and whites would be considered solely on merit rather than race. This meant giving black Arkansans a voice in government by appointing them to state boards and commissions and hiring blacks for positions of power, not just the traditional custodial jobs.

High on the list of the new governor's priorities was the creation of a Human Resources Commission, the purpose of which would be to determine if the state was discriminating on the basis of race. Rockefeller attempted to have this commission created as an agency of the executive branch by the Sixty-sixth General Assembly in its regular 1967 session. The bill creating the commission passed the House, but was tabled by a voice vote in the Senate. When it was brought up in the Senate, one member inquired: "Isn't that that civil rights bill?"[15] Undeterred, Rockefeller created the Governor's Council on Human Resources by executive order in June 1967. The council first met that September; its goal was to upgrade "the employment opportunities available to our people, and make the best possible use of the state's human resources."[16] But, as John Ward, Rockefeller's public relations director and biographer noted, "the organization, for all its high purposes, never did much."[17] The council, created by executive order and not legislation, had no enforcement power; its purpose was to advise and recommend. By publicizing its goals, it could provide moral support and encouragement to those who already believed in its goals and advice to those with the power to change the status quo, but it could do little more.[18] In June 1968 Rockefeller appointed an African American, Ozell Sutton, executive director of the Governor's Council on Human Resources. Sutton, a native Arkansan, took a one-year leave of absence from his job with the US Justice Department to work for Rockefeller. Sutton tried unsuccessfully to obtain legislative authorization for the council. He also focused on improving relations between the police and the minority community through a suggested "Code of Conduct" sent to Arkansas chiefs of police and worked hard within the executive branch to increase minority appointments and state jobs.[19]

Rockefeller dramatically improved the number of blacks appointed to state boards and commissions. Prior to his election the only boards or commissions with any minority representation were those dealing with black institutions or those with federal financing where pressure from Washington made minority representation necessary.[20]

By far the most dramatic change came in Arkansas's draft boards. Rockefeller nominated Col. Willard A. Hawkins as state director of the Selective Service of Arkansas in January 1967. One of Colonel Hawkins's primary goals was to put minority representation on Arkansas's draft boards, which to that point had had none. Although the selective service was a federal agency, it was up to the governor and Hawkins to nominate members of the local draft boards and the two state appeals boards. Like the Hawkins appointment, those nominations would then be approved by the president. By October 1969 forty-eight African Americans and one Asian American were on local boards, and one African American sat on each of the two appeals boards. More than 85 percent of Arkansas's minority population was under the jurisdiction of local draft boards.[21] Integrating draft boards was relatively easy, since no one in Arkansas (i.e., the State Senate) had to approve the appointments aside from Hawkins and Rockefeller. However, there was opposition, much of which came from members of Arkansas's Republican Party. Their objections rested on their view of selective service board appointments as political patronage plums awarded at the discretion of the Republican Party county chairmen. In a long December 1968 letter to the executive director of the Arkansas Republican Party, Hawkins explained that while he was "most happy to receive any recommendations for appointments at any time from county chairmen or others in the county," he had other considerations and responsibilities. These included not only his and Rockefeller's commitment to integrating the draft boards, but also the reality of seeing that "the coming legislature work in harmony with the administration." In other words, the predominantly Democratic legislators needed to be consulted regarding appointments in their counties in exchange for their support for the governor's legislative program.[22] In spite of the political realities, the integration of Arkansas's draft boards was the most successful of Rockefeller's attempts to bring blacks into state government.

In November 1969 Rockefeller named William "Sonny" Walker head of the state Office of Economic Opportunity, making Walker the first black department head in Arkansas and the first black state OEO director in the South. Walker publicly admitted that it was "lonely" being the first and resigned after one year in office, citing other job offers as well as the refusal of the Legislative Council to increase his salary—a salary that was paid in federal funds and was the lowest in the region for a state OEO director. The council authorized a salary, also federally funded, $1,680 higher than Walker's for his assistant. Walker told the press that one legislator had remarked that "$15,000 was too much to pay a nigger."[23]

In terms of hiring blacks to fill white collar jobs in state government, Rockefeller was often criticized for not doing more. More than one year after assuming the governorship, Rockefeller publicly admitted that discrimination against blacks in state offices did exist. Although in 1968 blacks represented 21.9 percent of the population, they held less than 3 percent of the seventeen thousand available state jobs.[24] Rockefeller refused to order department heads to hire more blacks, relying instead on "persuasion and leadership."[25] Even Colonel Hawkins, with his impressive record of integrating draft boards, had no black employees in his office until January 1968.[26]

Rockefeller's refusal to impose hiring quotas on state department heads created a situation in which long-standing prejudices would often win out. Rockefeller's first director of the Office of Economic Opportunity, appointed in January 1967, was Glen Jermstad, an influential member of the state Republican Party. In August 1967 Jermstad fired a black employee of the agency, whose employment had preceded Rockefeller's election. An investigation by the regional Office of Economic Opportunity followed, revealing that the fired employee had a valid case in claiming discrimination. Though the black man told there was no place for him in the proposed reorganization of the office, as he lacked the "background or the qualifications," the white employee who was retained and given the job in the OEO's department of education had far fewer qualifications. The fired black employee had a college degree and twenty-five years teaching experience, while the white man had no degree and had been a grocer. In spite of attempts to involve Rockefeller, the case still had not been resolved in May 1968.[27]

The lack of blacks in state jobs was a major topic of a meeting between the governor and approximately thirty leaders of the African American community held on April 9, 1968, in the wake of Dr. Martin Luther King, Jr.'s death, as an attempt to prevent violent reaction to the assassination. At the meeting Rockefeller acknowledged that more needed to be done to improve the number of blacks hired by state agencies and promised to look into charges of discrimination by local state Employment Security Division offices but once again backed off from any promises to force state agencies to hire blacks.[28] During the 1968 campaign Rockefeller was criticized by Dr. Jerry Jewell, head of the Arkansas NAACP. Jewell told the *New York Times* that the black vote would not be a sure thing for Rockefeller, stating "He hasn't come out for the Negro. He could have done so much." Regarding the governor's black appointments, Jewell said "Sure it's a 'new thing,' but they're nothing but pets. We have more than our share of Toms."[29]

By 1969 the frequent pressures of black leadership had begun to pay off. The state revenue commissioner promised to fire any employee who discriminated in hiring practices and to adopt a system whereby all people would be notified of revenue office job openings rather than continue the practice of making appointments to these jobs based on political patronage.[30]

The middle to late 1960s saw an eruption of urban riots and violent protests across the nation as the civil rights movement turned its attention from legal segregation to economic discrimination, hopelessness, and despair. Though protests in Arkansas did not compare to the death and destruction of Watts or Detroit, the state saw its share of protests. As governor, Rockefeller usually found himself involved in these disturbances. Following the death of Martin Luther King, Jr., on April 4, 1968, riots flared up in 110 cities across the United States. Aside from a minor disturbance in Pine Bluff, Arkansas avoided the violence at that time, largely because of Rockefeller's own involvement in the memorial service at the state capitol. The service had been held at the suggestion of Rockefeller's wife, Jeannette Edris Rockefeller, following a request by black leaders for a marching permit. It is also important to note that while the service may have prevented violence, Rockefeller's presence created problems for him among some white Republicans.[31]

Little Rock did experience several days of violence in August 1968 after an eighteen-year-old black youth was killed by a white trusty at the Pulaski County Penal Farm. The trusty was charged with manslaughter. Rockefeller called out the National Guard and imposed a curfew on the county. The disturbances ended after a few days.[32]

The largest and most significant racial disturbances to take place during Rockefeller's governorship occurred not in Little Rock, but in Forrest City, a town approximately forty miles west of Memphis. Forrest City in 1969 had a population of fourteen thousand, 50 percent of whom were black. White intransigence to racial equality was especially strong in eastern Arkansas, a legacy of the plantation system. The black population of Forrest City itself had increased in recent years as mechanization forced tenant farmers into town in search of industrial jobs. In 1968 members of the John Birch Society gained control of the Forrest City school board, and in March the district fired, with no explanation, Rev. J. F. Cooley, a black, who had taught for eleven years at the city's all-black Lincoln Junior-Senior High. Reverend Mr. Cooley's problems seem to have stemmed from his activities in the civil rights movement. In December 1968 Cooley, along with Rev. Cato Brooks Jr., formed the Committee for Peaceful Coexistence with the purpose of better expressing black grievances to the white community. Cooley had also helped organize peaceful demonstrations and worked with young black males to prevent juvenile delinquency. In January the school board dismissed Cooley as black juvenile probation officer, a position he had held for eight years. After Cooley's March dismissal from his teaching position, junior high students vandalized Lincoln, breaking every window in the building, tearing down lockers and vending machines, and scattering debris in the halls. Cooley publicly condemned the riot, and Rockefeller called in the state police. Four youths were sentenced to juvenile training schools.[33]

The March incident was the beginning of a long year in Forrest City. In April the Committee for Peaceful Coexistence issued a list of ten grievances against the "community power structure," and asked for assistance from federal and state civil rights groups. The Forrest City mayor's reaction was that "They're just like all these groups. They can't come up with anything."[34] The mayor's response helps illustrate why change was so slow in coming to Forrest City; the white community refused to see that any inequities existed. A grand jury empanelled to investigate the Lincoln school riot failed "to conceive any justification for either the riot in March or a student walkout in April."[35]

Racial tension continued unabated throughout the summer, fed by the threat of a "poor people's march" from Forrest City to Little Rock. The march, scheduled for August 20–24, was meant to "dramatize outdated conditions black people are forced to live in throughout the state of Arkansas," according to its organizer, Reverend Mr. Brooks.[36] Rockefeller became directly involved, holding a meeting on August 6 with leaders from both sides of Forrest City's community. Rockefeller hoped to prevent the march by offering to travel to Forrest City with state department heads in an attempt to "find some solutions to problems that have been aggravating."[37]

The governor went to Forrest City as promised and also met twice with Brooks before the minister agreed on August 19 to postpone the march because the governor needed time to make good on his promises of change and because the level of racial tension and fear of the marchers on the part of whites "makes it dangerous at this time."[38] Rockefeller, prior to his August 19 meeting with Brooks, consulted with department heads as promised and issued a lengthy response to Brooks' complaints and requests. These complaints centered around the absence of equal opportunity and racial parity in both state services and jobs.[39]

Rockefeller had been under enormous pressure from various groups to see to it that the "poor people's march" did not take place—especially the state police, who feared outbreaks of violence along the marchers' route, and prominent Republicans, who had objected to Rockefeller's meeting with Brooks, preferring that the governor meet with Forrest City's "good Negroes," blacks the white community was willing to accept.[40] Despite the pressure and Rockefeller's apparent success on August 19, the march did take place as scheduled, but with different leadership. Renamed a "walk against fear," and beginning in West Memphis, it was led by Lance "Sweet Willie Wine" Watson, the leader of a militant Memphis group called the Invaders. Watson had been in Forrest City at the invitation of Brooks, helping to organize a summer boycott of white businesses by the town's black population. While Brooks had promised to arm his marchers only with prayer books, Watson told the press that he and his group would "survive and defend ourselves if necessary."[41] Rockefeller urged all Arkansans, black and white, to "completely ignore the marchers," and declared a state of emergency in Prairie County, where violent white reaction seemed most likely. The marchers were escorted by plainclothes state policemen, and although Watson had promised a marching force two hundred strong, only five people accompanied him. The march ended without incident in Little Rock on August 24.[42]

The march aggravated the racial climate in Forrest City, and several incidents in the week that followed made it much worse. After two white women were raped, allegedly by black youths, and several members of Watson's Invaders were arrested for beating, stabbing, and robbing a white grocery store clerk, a white protest erupted in violence. Between five hundred and one thousand whites gathered in front of City Hall, beating at least seven people, including Watson. Rockefeller declared a state of emergency and sent in the National Guard to prevent further violence. One white businessman told the *New York Times* that what the crowd wanted "is for the police to shoot some Negroes. And while they know that can't be, they do demand some show of force, and it's all very frustrating."[43] Not a single white was arrested as a result of the incident, but Watson was charged with and convicted of disorderly conduct. In September, following protests and boycotts by white students at the junior and senior high schools, the school board closed Forrest City's schools "indefinitely," but reopened them after four days.[44] Racial unrest and fear continued in Forrest City, Rockefeller having been unable to find a middle ground that would appease the many factions within the community. But a study of the unrest in Forrest City by a non-profit group called the Race Relations Information Center praised Rockefeller for "repeatedly putting himself on record in favor of equal opportunity and justice."[45]

Many of Forrest City's problems revolved around the schools. The 1954 *Brown v. Board of Education* decision declaring "separate but equal" schools unconstitutional had not ended segregation. Southern schools frequently adopted one of two methods to meet the letter of the law, while ignoring the spirit of it. One was gradualism, desegregating a few children at a time, as in the Little Rock Central High case of 1957. The other, and most common, was "freedom of choice" integration, as at Forrest City. Students, both white and black, were free to attend whatever school they wanted to. But few whites were likely to choose to attend an academically and physically inferior black school, while few blacks were willing to accept the social isolation and harassment that went with being one of the few to attend the white schools. In Forrest City the black schools were still all black in 1969, while the white schools were approximately 83 percent white.[46]

Rockefeller did not publicly condemn freedom of choice integration, in spite of the fact that it was an obvious attempt at avoidance. The governor was under tremendous pressure, even before his election, to allow school districts to maintain local control over desegregation. And Rockefeller himself had disagreed with the 1964 Civil Rights Act, considering it too vague, with too much power concentrated in the executive branch of the federal government.[47] During the 1966 gubernatorial election, Rockefeller's advisors urged him to support legal assistance for school districts fighting the federal government's guidelines for integration, either personally or as governor. Considering the nature of the statements being suggested, Rockefeller's public statement of August 30 was relatively mild. He expressed disapproval for the "Federal Guidelines as they exist today" but suggested that the remedy lie in electing to Congress "those candidates who will reflect the attitude of the people."[48]

In the May 1968 special session of the Arkansas General Assembly, Rockefeller supported a bill that would permit the state to help pay the legal costs of school districts fighting integration in the courts. The legal fund had first been established in 1959 but required reappropriation each legislative session. The regular session of the General Assembly in 1967 had passed Act 655, reimbursing up to 50 percent of the expenses incurred in 1965 and 1966. Almost all of the money went to the Little Rock law firm of Smith, Williams, Friday, and Bowen, which handled most of the desegregation lawsuits and drew up the new bill. This bill would extend payment through 1969. Two circumstances created a firestorm around the new bill: Rockefeller's sponsorship of the bill and the changes in many people's attitudes by 1968. The bill was defeated in the House. One state representative who spoke against the bill opposed it on the grounds that it financed resistance "to what now seems to be the law of the land."[49] Black leaders criticized Rockefeller for supporting the bill, and the *Arkansas Gazette* noted that support for the governor had weakened in the black community.[50]

Rockefeller regained some of that support the following year. Under the terms of the 1964 Civil Rights Act, dual school systems had to be merged or desegregated by September 1969 or lose federal funds. When it became apparent that President Nixon planned to relax the guidelines, Rockefeller sent him a telegram asking him to reconsider "because it breaks faith with the black community and compromises to a disturbing degree the position of those who have courageously gone ahead with objectivity and a sense of justice—if not always with enthusiasm—in the implementation of federal desegregation guidelines."[51]

The Nixon administration relaxed the guidelines by extending the deadline for those districts with "bona fide educational and administrative problems."[52] In April 1970 Rockefeller was notified that forty-nine Arkansas districts operated dual school systems and were not in compliance with the Civil Rights Act of 1964. As part of his continuing attempt to appease both sides of this passionate debate, Rockefeller asked the Justice Department to delay formal action in order to give the districts time to comply with the order voluntarily. The Justice Department's reply gave the Arkansas districts until September 1970 to achieve "full desegregation." The Justice Department also wrote to the Arkansas Board of Education as "the appropriate agency to be called upon to adjust the conditions of unlawful segregation and racial discrimination existing in the public school systems of Arkansas."[53] This was significant, because the state board of education had thus far adamantly refused to take an active role in achieving integrated schools. The board believed that "the right to require the interpretation of the court decision as applied to individual school districts cannot be questioned," and had consistently refused to advise school districts on matters of desegregation except upon request, claiming that "it is not our function or legal right to question the wisdom of legal decisions by local boards."[54] By the time school began in September 1970, all forty-nine districts were at least minimally desegregated, only three of them by court order.[55]

The most controversial aspect of desegregation was busing. The United States Supreme Court ruled in October 1969 in *Beatrice Alexander* et al., *ptrs. v. Holmes County (Mississippi) Board of Education* et al., that school districts must end segregation "at once." In December the court used this ruling to order six school districts in four states to desegregate by February 1, 1970.[56] These decisions increased pressure on politicians to take a stand on busing. In September 1969 the Southern Governors' Conference had passed a resolution calling for "restraint and good judgement" in the use of busing to desegregate. Rockefeller voted for the resolution after being the only abstention on a failed resolution that would have condemned busing.[57] But the October and December court rulings revived public fear of and opposition to busing. In January Rockefeller issued a statement regarding busing: "It should be used and used with discretion, but neither do I think we should blatantly disregard the usefulness of the bus in implementing the court orders and the law working toward sound integration." The *Arkansas Gazette* praised Rockefeller for not "joining in the hypocritical cry suddenly heard throughout the South after whole generations of whites and blacks alike were bused all over kingdom come to keep schools totally segregated."[58]

Rockefeller's courage and moderation regarding busing did not last long. Opposition to his statement was immediate and strong. State politicians, both Democrat and Republican, publicly disagreed with the governor. Rockefeller received petitions with the signatures of 4,495 people from one county disagreeing with his stand on busing and assuring him "that your statements will be publicized should you consider reelection."[59] A member of the governor's staff noted: "Politically, this misunderstanding seems to be costing a lot of votes."[60] Consequently, Rockefeller issued a new statement on February 21 to clarify what he called the "distortion" of his position:

> I endorse the position wholeheartedly which the Southern governors have taken on the resolution [of September 1969], and I want to make it perfectly clear that I have not recommended busing— and am not recommending it now.

. . . The decisions will be made in the local school districts, and the responsibility for carrying out those decisions also rests with each individual school board, working within the limitations of the law and the various court orders.[61]

Rockefeller had obviously backed down on the busing issue in an effort to avoid alienating conservative white voters. This was a deliberate political decision, as later recalled by Robert Faulkner, Rockefeller's executive secretary in 1970: "I was one of them that suggested, and it was strictly a political [move], that he modify, or 'fuzzy' if you will, his support of busing." In retrospect, Faulkner reflected "that may have been a mistake."[62] Rockefeller received criticism for his about-face, both from the press and civil rights groups. Even though Rockefeller's announcement that he would seek a third term as governor was still six weeks away, discussion of another campaign had been going on for months. If Rockefeller's Democratic opponent had been Orval Faubus as expected, the governor's backpedaling on busing might not have done as much damage. But when the Democratic candidate turned out to be a young liberal Democrat named Dale Bumpers, Rockefeller was in trouble. Faubus had accused Bumpers in the primary runoff of being pro-busing; nonetheless, Bumpers won an easy victory over Arkansas's symbol of white opposition to integration.[63]

Rockefeller lost decisively to Bumpers in the 1970 general election. The primary reason for Rockefeller's defeat was the return of white moderates to the Democratic fold.[64] But there was almost certainly a loss of support for Rockefeller among black voters. One survey showed that in Little Rock, Rockefeller received only 49 percent of the black vote in 1970, as compared with 81 percent in the 1966 election.[65]

Winthrop Rockefeller died February 22, 1973. At his memorial service on March 4 one of the eulogies was delivered by William "Sonny" Walker. Walker credited Rockefeller with treating black Arkansans as "full and equal partners to progress. . . . While Win Rockefeller helped free the black man from the oppression of Jim Crow, he helped free the white man from the prison of prejudice."[66]

Governor Rockefeller's record regarding civil rights was erratic. He promoted color blindness in state appointments and jobs but refused to require state agency heads to do the same. He applauded the spirit of the Civil Rights Act of 1964 but criticized its reliance on the executive branch of the federal government for implementation. He reversed his public support of busing in an obvious attempt to gain votes.

Rockefeller was not a liberal, but in Arkansas in the 1960s his actions in race relations were liberal. As a former Democratic legislator put it: "Probably his greatest accomplishment was to make racial toleration acceptable and respectable in Arkansas."[67] Considering the racial climate in the state during his term in office, Rockefeller showed great moral and political courage in his almost continual support of racial equality by example. When he stood on the steps of the state capitol and eulogized Martin Luther King, Jr., he did so at tremendous political risk. The same can be said of his handling of the disturbances at Forrest City. In September 1969 Rockefeller met with Arkansas's congressional delegation and briefed them on his efforts to ease racial tension in the state. Afterwards, Rockefeller told the press that the delegation had "pledged to support his efforts."[68] Three days later, the governor was forced to tell the press that his earlier statement was a "misunderstanding," that he had not asked for, nor had he received any support, "either direct or implied."[69] The retraction should not come as a surprise considering that Congress passed four major civil rights bills between 1957 and 1968, and all passed without a single vote from an Arkansas congressman or senator.[70] In the field of civil rights, Arkansas politicians, Democrat and Republican, liberal and conservative, were afraid of the political repercussions of endorsing civil rights actions or legislation. Rockefeller stands as a marked exception to that generalization.

There were concrete advances made as a result of Rockefeller's actions. In 1968 the US Department of Health, Education, and Welfare conducted a review of Arkansas's compliance with the 1964 Civil Rights Act in the area of state health and welfare services. Their report to the governor stated: "The review team was pleased with the evident progress in Arkansas in matters affecting compliance with Title VI of the Civil Rights Act. Overt, obvious forms of discrimination have almost disappeared. The attitude and desire of State people generally to achieve a nondiscriminatory treatment of people were gratifying."[71] Much of the progress made by Rockefeller was done despite attempts by other politicians, particularly state legislators, to stop it. Even before Rockefeller became governor, Arkansas and Mississippi were the only states in their region without state human relations commissions.[72] But the legislature refused to create one, so Rockefeller formed his own. In 1967 the legislature refused to consolidate the segregated state juvenile training schools despite the threatened loss of federal funds. So in 1968 the Juvenile Training School Board integrated the girls' schools without legislative authorization. The legislature protested, with one state senator remarking, "They're not going this fast in the public schools." But the schools remained integrated, without incident.[73]

Certainly Rockefeller could have done more to improve race relations in

Arkansas. But considering the political climate in Arkansas and Rockefeller's own aversion to both big government and affirmative action, he accomplished a great deal. And most importantly, he did make racial toleration "acceptable and respectable" in Arkansas. This was a tremendous legacy in and of itself. In 1987 Robert McCord wrote that Arkansans have "made much of the fact that Arkansas never experienced the violence that occurred in so many other American cities during the civil rights struggle. . . . The credit for this goes to Winthrop Rockefeller, who brought blacks into the mainstream of our society for the first time."[74] The credit rightly belongs primarily to those people who fought year in and year out to improve race relations and civil rights. What makes Winthrop Rockefeller so unique and so important is that he was the first major political figure in Arkansas to listen and try to help.

CHAPTER 10

The Big Three of Late Twentieth-Century Arkansas Politics

Dale Bumpers, Bill Clinton, and David Pryor

DIANE D. BLAIR

In this definitive essay about late 20th century Arkansas politics, Professor Blair profiles the political careers of three of its most prominent players: David Pryor, Dale Bumpers, and Bill Clinton: "The Big Three." Blair observes that the State of Arkansas was unique in the extent to which it resisted the "rising tide of southern Republicanism" that swept the American South in the 80s and 90s. The central argument of the essay is that Arkansas's long-lasting exceptionalism stemmed in large part from the collective impact of the Big Three on its politics. We know now, of course, that Arkansas remained stalwartly Democratic far longer than this essay might suggest, not fully changing its stripes until 2014.

The most publicized outcome of the 1994 national elections was the Republican Party's capture of both houses of the US Congress for the first time in forty years. A subsidiary, but no less consequential story, was evidence that the long-predicted realignment of the South, from its once solidly Democratic status to a partiality toward Republicans, had finally materialized. The southern preference for Republican presidential candidates, well-established by the 1980s, penetrated in 1994 to congressional choices as well, with Republicans capturing a majority of all southern seats in both the House and the Senate. Republicans also held a majority of southern governorships in the aftermath of 1994 contests, and for the first time since Reconstruction, control of some southern state legislative

Originally published in *Arkansas Historical Quarterly* 54
(Spring 1995): 53–79. Reprinted with permission.
DOI: https://doi.org/10.34053/parry2019.riapag2.10

chambers. As columnist David Broder observed, the Republicans "may have put the finishing touches on the 30-year-old effort to make the South their new foundation."[1]

Arkansas was not entirely immune to the rising tides of southern Republicanism. For the second time in a row its four seats in the US House of Representatives were split evenly between Republicans (Jay Dickey in the Fourth District, Tim Hutchinson in the Third) and Democrats (Blanche Lambert Lincoln in the First District, Ray Thornton in the Second). Republican Mike Huckabee, first elected lieutenant governor in a special 1993 election, was resoundingly reelected with a comfortable 59 percent majority. Republicans picked up two seats in the state Senate, two in the state House, and seventeen in assorted county contests. However, compared with what was happening elsewhere in the South, these were marginal rather than momentous gains. Arkansas remained firmly in Democratic hands.

Democratic Governor Jim Guy Tucker, despite a vigorous campaign attempting to discredit his fitness for office, carried all but two counties and was reelected with 60 percent of the vote. Since neither US Senate seat was at stake in 1994, those remained Democratic as well. Indeed, Arkansas is the only state never to have elected a Republican to the US Senate. Of the five other statewide elected positions (attorney general, secretary of state, auditor, treasurer, and land commissioner), all five were filled by Democrats, the latter two uncontested and the others being won by margins, respectively, of 80 percent, 53 percent, and 64 percent. Democrats also remained in firm control of both houses of the General Assembly with eighty-eight of one hundred House seats and twenty-eight of the thirty-five seats in the Senate. In other words, while Democratic majorities were being dramatically reduced or reversed elsewhere in the South, the traditional—some would say tyrannical—grip of the Democratic Party in Arkansas continued to diminish at incremental rather than torrential speed.

The reasons for Arkansas's ongoing resistance to Republicanism have been explored at length elsewhere, with particular emphasis on the state's long Democratic history combined with contemporary demographic characteristics.[2] These and other factors, such as the state's continuing failure to fund party primaries, undoubtedly have important explanatory value. Still, they do not quite suffice. Other southern states have at least some of the same components in their historical traditions, demographic profiles, and political structures, but they have moved much further down the path to realignment than has Arkansas.

What will be suggested here is that an additional factor may help to explain Arkansas's atypical ongoing attachment to Democrats, and that is the extraordinarily long run of three individuals who became the "Big Three" of late twentieth-century Arkansas politics: Dale Bumpers, David Pryor, and Bill Clinton. All three served as governor of Arkansas: Bumpers from 1971 to 1975, Pryor from 1975 to 1979, Clinton from 1979 to 1981 and again from 1983 through 1992. All three were elevated by the Arkansas electorate from the governorship to national office: Bumpers was elected to the Senate in 1974, Pryor to the Senate in 1978, and Clinton to the presidency of the United States in 1992.

None of the Big Three had a political career of absolutely unbroken success. Bumpers, in fact, lost his very first bid for office, a try for the Democratic nomination for state representative in 1962. Pryor's unsuccessful 1972 attempt to capture the Democratic nomination for the Senate away from venerable incumbent John L. McClellan failed so narrowly (Pryor got 48 percent in a runoff) that his political viability was sustained rather than terminated. Similarly, Bill Clinton's 48 percent loss to incumbent Third District Congressman John Paul Hammerschmidt was perceived as an amazing accomplishment for a twenty-seven-year-old law professor with no office-holding experience, and actually advanced rather than arrested Clinton's future political career. Governor Bill Clinton's 1980 loss to challenger Frank White, however, was a crushing defeat and one of the biggest upsets in Arkansas political history.

The Big Three, then, had their stumbles, but their setbacks were far outnumbered by their successes. A brief summary of their political careers and major accomplishments provides important context to the larger thesis here: In providing attractive models of progressive public service and thereby perpetuating their own tenure in public office, the Big Three did much to sustain and prolong the popularity and dominance of the Democratic Party in Arkansas.

First on the political scene was David Pryor. Born and raised in Camden, Pryor's initial venture into politics began when he was elected to the state legislature in 1960 while he was still in law school. He was reelected in 1962 and 1964. When longtime Congressman Oren Harris resigned in 1966 to become a federal judge, thirty-two-year-old Pryor defeated four Democrats and one Republican to win the Fourth Congressional District seat, to which he was reelected without opposition in 1968 and 1970. With a seat on the powerful Appropriations Committee and reams of favorable publicity from his exposés of abuses of the elderly in nursing homes, Pryor could easily have extended his stay in the House. He chose instead to challenge Senator

John L. McClellan in the 1972 Democratic primary. He lost by a narrow margin. In 1974, however, he successfully sought the governorship, first defeating six-time governor Orval Faubus in the Democratic Primary, (by a 51 percent margin, thus avoiding a runoff), then Republican Ken Coon (by 66 percent) in the general election.

Pryor served four undramatic but accomplished years as governor. In his first term he continued his longstanding, unsuccessful battle for thoroughgoing reform of Arkansas's 1874 Constitution, and saw to the establishment of the Department of Local Services, the Department of Natural and Cultural Heritage, a statewide energy conservation plan, and an overseas office (in Belgium) of the Arkansas Industrial Development Commission. Presenting a tightly budgeted but forward-looking record to the electorate, Pryor carried all seventy-five counties and 59 percent of the electorate in his reelection bid in 1976. In Pryor's second term, the legislature did not enact his proposed Arkansas Plan, designed to shift taxing powers and responsibilities from the state to the local level, and lawmakers repealed his anti-litter tax shortly after its adoption. However, Pryor's gubernatorial appointments were widely applauded, especially his breakthrough appointments of blacks and women.[3] It was a fiscally prudent, scandal-free gubernatorial record which Pryor presented to the electorate in 1978 when he faced and defeated two attractive opponents (US Representatives Jim Guy Tucker and Ray Thornton) for the Democratic nomination for the Senate.

There he joined Dale Bumpers, who in 1974 had parlayed an extraordinarily successful two terms as governor into a decisive primary victory over thirty-year incumbent J. W. Fulbright for the Democratic nomination to the Senate. Fulbright's towering national and international reputation and years of attentive service to Arkansas might have made him invincible to ordinary challengers. Bumpers, however, had swiftly moved from obscurity to legendary status as a giant-killer.

After nearly twenty successful years practicing law and doing good (teaching Sunday school, serving as city attorney and as school board and chamber of commerce president) in Charleston, Bumpers in 1970 announced what at first seemed a quixotic quest for the Democratic gubernatorial nomination. Three prominent Democrats (former Governor Orval Faubus, Attorney General Joe Purcell, and Arkansas House Speaker Hayes McClerkin) were joined by five unknowns (with whom Bumpers was classified) in a very crowded contest. Surprising the Democratic establishment with a second-place finish in the Democratic preferential primary, Bumpers next dispatched the once-invincible Faubus with a healthy 59 percent victory, and then, against one of the most expensive campaigns in Arkansas's history, defeated incumbent Governor Winthrop Rockefeller with 62 percent of the vote. Bumpers' attractive personality, masterful use of television, and untainted record struck all the right chords with the Arkansas electorate, grown weary of Rockefeller's gridlock with the legislature yet wary of a return to the Faubus era.

Bumpers' two terms as governor were equally marked by success. In four years he extensively reorganized the executive branch of state government, modernized the budgetary process, and effectively depoliticized the state's personnel system. He persuaded the necessary three-fourths of the state legislature to make the state's income tax both more progressive and more productive, then used the increased revenues for a variety of essential state services such as state-supported kindergartens for preschoolers, free textbooks for high school students, improved social services for elderly, handicapped, and mentally retarded citizens, and an expanded state park system for all. Despite extensive changes and hefty tax increases, neither usually associated with political popularity in Arkansas, Bumpers' gubernatorial performance earned him easy reelection in 1972 (by 67 percent in the Democratic primary, 75 percent in the general election) and an astonishing 90 percent approval rating at the end of his second term.[4]

Once in the Senate, both Bumpers and Pryor continued to serve in distinctive and distinguished ways. Bumpers promoted health programs for the poor, aid for rural development, arms control, deficit reduction, and reform of oil and gas drilling rights on federal lands. He opposed deregulation of oil and natural gas prices, attempted to block expensive defense and science projects such as the Star Wars initiative and the Supercollider, and repeatedly attempted reform of the 1872 Mining Act so as to require payment of royalties for mining on federal lands. Pryor continued his attention to the elderly by chairing the Special Committee on Aging and crusading against excessive prices on pharmaceuticals. He won passage of a Taxpayer Bill of Rights, guarded the interests of Arkansas agriculture, attacked government waste, exposed and limited excessive payments to private defense "consultants," and instituted reforms of inefficient Senate scheduling and procedures.[5]

Both senators also earned considerable national attention and acclaim. Bumpers was deemed one of the ten best senators by the national press and seriously mentioned as a likely presidential candidate for both the 1980 and 1984 contests, with columnist Mary McGrory describing him as the "Senate's premier orator" and Sen. Paul Simon expressing the opinion that he "would have more support in the U.S. Senate than any other candidate."[6]

Pryor was elevated by his colleagues in 1989 to the third highest position in the majority leadership ranks, secretary of the Democratic Conference.

Despite repeated attempts by election opponents to characterize Arkansas's senators as too liberal and too leftist for their constituent's tastes, their records were apparently highly acceptable to the electorate: Bumpers was reelected by 59 percent in 1980, 62 percent in 1986 and 69 percent in 1992; Pryor was reelected by 57 percent in 1984 and in 1990 became the first US Senator since 1976 to escape opposition in both the primary and the general election. In 1993 the senators were joined in Washington, D.C., by another Arkansas political phenomenon, President Bill Clinton.

Born in Hope, raised in Hot Springs, educated at Georgetown University, Oxford University, and the Yale University School of Law, Clinton returned to Arkansas in 1973 with a faculty position at the University of Arkansas Law School in Fayetteville. His 1974 attempt to unseat Third District Congressman John Paul Hammerschmidt failed. However, in 1976 Clinton defeated (by 56 percent in the Democratic primary) a former secretary of state and a deputy attorney general to become an active and visible attorney general. In 1978 he overwhelmed opponents in both the Democratic primary and the general election to become, at age thirty-two, the second-youngest governor in Arkansas history.

Clinton's first regular session was action-packed and highly success-ful as he proposed and persuaded the lawmakers to enact an ambitious and wide-ranging legislative package initiating new programs in economic development, education, conservation, health, and roads. National news magazines hailed him as a "rising star" and his fellow Democratic governors elected him to chair the Democratic Governors Association. However, the major mechanism for financing the road-building program (hefty increases in vehicle registration and license fees) proved highly unpopular, especially in rural areas, and Clinton's popularity further declined when Arkansas was selected by President Carter as a resettlement site for thousands of Freedom Flotilla Cuban refugees. These and other circumstances led in 1980 to Clinton's narrow but stunning defeat by Frank White, a businessman and former Arkansas Industrial Development Commission Director. Clinton became only the second twentieth-century Arkansas governor to be denied his bid for a second, sometimes called courtesy, two-year term, and the youngest ex-governor in Arkansas (and American) history.[7]

In 1982, however, having apologized to the Arkansas electorate for past "errors" (especially the car tag increases and some controversial commuta-tions) and perceived insensitivity, Clinton fought a vigorous, closely contested, ultimately successful (and in Arkansas unprecedented) campaign to recapture the governorship. Against both primary and general election competition he was reelected governor in 1984, again in 1986 (to Arkansas's first twentieth-century four-year term), and again in 1990, becoming only the second governor in Arkansas history (the first was Faubus) to win more than three terms.

Clinton not only re-established his credentials with the Arkansas electorate, but was increasingly turned to by his fellow governors to be their spokesmen and leader. He was elected chair of the National Governors' Association in 1986, chair of the Education Commission of the States in 1987, and chair of the Democratic Governors' Association in 1988. He led the governors' attempts to restructure national welfare laws in 1988 (securing approval of the Family Support Act of 1988), and, as co-chair of the President's Education Summit in 1989, played a critical role in drafting the National Education Goals. In 1987 a survey of practitioners and observers of state politics conducted by *U.S. News and World Report* found Clinton to be one of the nation's six best governors, citing particularly his "striking accomplishments" in education in a state lacking prosperity and his reputation as "probably the best-liked chief executive among his peers."[8] In 1991 a poll of all the nation's governors by *Newsweek* ranked Clinton "the most effective" governor in the country.[9]

In October 1991 Clinton declared his candidacy for the Democratic nomination for president. Clinton's record as governor came under exhaustive scrutiny during both the Democratic nomination battle and the three-way general election contest between incumbent Republican George Bush, independent billionaire businessman Ross Perot, and Democratic nominee Clinton, with Bush and Perot competing by campaign's end as to who could portray Arkansas in the most unflattering light. Opponents charged that despite 128 tax and fee increases during Clinton's governorship, Arkansas still ranked last or next to last in family median income and average weekly wages, in literacy rates, teacher pay, infant health, and environmental quality. In the third and final presidential debate, Bush said that what worried him most was for Clinton to "do to America what he did to Arkansas . . . We do not want to be the lowest of the low."[10]

The Clinton campaign issued data-filled documents arguing to the contrary: that Arkansas had the second lowest state and local tax burden in the country, with taxes as a percent of personal income actually lower than when Clinton took office; that by July 1992, due in part to Clinton's numerous economic development initiatives, the state ranked fifth nationally in job creation and ninth in wage and salary growth, with median income growing twice the nation's generally; that as a result of Clinton's education reforms, Arkansas had achieved the highest high-school graduation rate in the region, was sending 34 percent more students to college than it did ten years previously, and that Arkansas teachers received the highest percent salary increase in the country the preceding year; that Arkansas's infant mortality rate had declined 43 percent from 1978 to 1990 to virtual parity with the national average, while over 60 percent of the state's children were being served in free preschool programs resulting from Clinton initiatives; and that Arkansas, one of only eight states meeting all federal standards under the Clean Air Act, had developed some of the most progressive water quality standards in the nation and was among the top ten states in wetlands protection and energy research.[11]

Perhaps most telling was the behavior of Arkansans themselves. They traveled by the hundreds with and for Clinton around the country, volunteered by the thousands at the campaign's national headquarters in Little Rock, dug deeply and contributed generously (Arkansas ranked first in per capita contributions in the 1992 presidential election campaign cycle), gave Clinton his single biggest majority (53.8 percent in a three person race) of any of the fifty states, and celebrated wildly with him on election night when he claimed victory and thanked the people of "this wonderful, small state" for their support.[12]

Returning now to the central assertion of this article, that in sustaining their own appeal to the Arkansas electorate the Big Three helped prolong the appeal of the Democratic label, the sheer numbers tell a significant part of the story. Between 1970 and 1994 this trio of Democrats presented themselves to statewide electorates thirty-six times, and won in thirty-four of those instances. The average percentage received in those thirty-six contests (which included several crowded Democratic primaries and two losses) was an impressive 59.5 percent. Looking only at those seventeen instances when Bumpers, Pryor, or Clinton faced a Republican opponent, the average percentage of the vote received was an astonishing 64.1 percent. If Clinton's 1976 attorney general win and Pryor's 1990 return to the Senate, both without Republican opposition are calculated in, the average winning margin over Republicans is an even higher 67.8 percent. From 1970 (Bumpers' first election to the governorship) to 1992 (Bumpers' fourth election to the Senate and Clinton's presidential victory) at least one and often two of these three familiar names were on the ballot every two years (except in 1988, when Clinton was in the middle of his first four-year term and neither Bumpers nor Pryor was up for reelection to the Senate).

Until Clinton's favorite-son candidacy brought Arkansas back to the Democratic column, Arkansas, like the rest of the once solidly Democratic South, had begun voting Republican in presidential contests. Unlike the rest of the South, however, as noted above, Arkansas Republicans had made little progress below the presidential level. What is being suggested here is that the cumulative draw of the Big Three at the top of the ticket sustained and strengthened the popularity of the Democratic label in Arkansas, thereby withstanding the general southern trend toward Republican realignment. But what were the particular characteristics of the Big Three which gave them such strong appeal to the Arkansas electorate? In the presence of many possible alternatives, why did Arkansans so repeatedly and decisively demonstrate their preference for Bumpers, Pryor, and Clinton? What did these men offer to the electorate in apparently greater measure than did their many opponents? Interestingly, while each of these men followed a very singular career path, the three also possess some striking similarities.

The ability of some people rather than others to elicit electoral support remains, perhaps fortunately, more mystery than science. Still, the most obvious and perhaps best explanation for the extraordinarily long run of the Big Three is that their accomplishments in office, briefly reviewed above, convinced the voters that these politicians were as interested as were their constituents in producing a better life for most Arkansans. Their devotion to public service seems self-evident. Why else would talented lawyers who could (and did) make much more money in the private sector seek an office, such as the governorship, which paid so little? (The Arkansas governorship paid ten thousand dollars annually until 1976. It was increased by constitutional amendment to thirty-five thousand dollars annually until raised by constitutional amendment in 1992, to sixty thousand dollars annually.) As governor, all three proposed ambitious initiatives for economic development, educational and health improvements, environmental protection, and government reform, and secured passage of well over three-fourths of their proposals.[13] Additionally, as they solidified and strengthened the reform style of state government begun in the Rockefeller years, all three ran scandal-free administrations. Good government producing a better Arkansas is a fairly obvious common key to the Big Three's electoral success.

In addition to policy responsiveness, successful politicians must also be able to connect with people, to provide some bonds of empathy and identification between the citizen and the office-holder. Bumpers, Pryor, and Clinton all possess the gift for connecting in abundance. Perhaps this partially reflects a common element in their backgrounds: all were born and raised in small towns where they attended the public schools. As many other eminent Arkansans can attest, such beginnings provide a superb training ground for future success. Small town life exposes one at an early age to the whole spectrum of human accomplishment and failure, the lives of the few who are affluent, the ways of the many who live carefully and modestly, and the needs of those who are still struggling to survive. Pryor, Clinton, and Bumpers were all deeply imprinted with and grounded in the particulars of ordinary, everyday life in Arkansas, and they clearly drew deeply upon this motherlode of observation and understanding to inform their subsequent political decisions.

All three were also raised in households where issues and ideas were discussed and where public service was presented as a desirable undertaking. In numerous public addresses Bumpers told audiences that he had been taught by his father that "public service was the noblest of all professions."[14] Pryor's father and his grandfather and great-grandfather on his mother's side all served as sheriff of Ouachita County, and Pryor often referred proudly to the fact that his mother, Susie, was the first Arkansas woman to seek an elective county office (circuit clerk in 1926). Clinton's mother, a hardworking nurse, still found time to debate ideas with her son and encouraged him to share her interest in public affairs.

Furthermore, all were raised in households that were unashamedly Democratic. This is unsurprising in a state where almost everyone, and certainly everyone who "did" politics, was a Democrat. Pryor recalls accompanying his father to the post office to collect the mail and, upon inquiring about the identity of someone across the room, being told: "You don't want to know him, son. He's a Republican."[15]

However, unlike many Arkansans who were Democrats purely by reflex and tradition, in these three instances there was a philosophical underpinning as well. Bumpers, for example, often recalled how his father had sent him and his brother to get a glimpse of Franklin D. Roosevelt when the president was making a whistle-stop appearance nearby. Bumpers never forgot what the New Deal and later governmental initiatives had meant to his family:

> Born poor, but to devout and loving parents, my father was a small-town merchant whose business was barely surviving when REA came to the rural southland. It enabled him to start selling electrical appliances to a new market. In a small town where we choked on dust in the summer and bogged down in mud in the winter, where sewage ran down the ditches from overflowing outhouses and a few septic tanks, it was a caring Government in the

30's that gave us loans and grants to pave our streets and build a waste treatment facility. And when I returned from three years in the Marine Corps following World War II, it was a thankful and magnanimous Government that allowed my brother and me to attend the best universities in this Nation on the GI Bill—without which I would not be standing here today. And when Betty and I returned to our little hometown to begin my law practice and small business, and raise our beautiful children, we raised them free of the fear of polio and other childhood diseases that had been conquered because of vaccines developed with Government grants.[16]

Clinton also "grew up in the legacy of Roosevelt, where people talked about what government could do for people. My grand-daddy ran a little country store and fed hungry people before the advent of food stamps. He thought he was going to Roosevelt when he died."[17] Pryor was also imbued with the "superior" traits of a Democratic Party which incorporated the best of the populist tradition. He ascribed the strength of that tradition in large part to Huey Long's whirlwind campaign through Arkansas in 1932 in which he successfully engineered Hattie Caraway's reelection to the Senate.[18] The governing philosophy all three men eventually brought to office might be called progressive populism—a willingness to use the power of government to counterweight the power and privileges of the economic elite, or in other words, a partiality toward those striving to climb the economic ladder rather than those who had already arrived at the top. This identification with the underdog, with its suspicion of concentrated wealth and the use of government to right the balance, is a powerful part of the Arkansas political tradition and one of the most recurrent themes in the rhetoric and careers of the Big Three.[19]

Clinton's first gubernatorial inaugural address in 1979 articulated themes which continued to characterize his political career and those of Pryor and Bumpers as well:

> For as long as I can remember, I have believed passionately in the cause of equal opportunity, and I will do all I can to advance it.
>
> For as long as I can remember, I have wished to ease the burdens of life for those who, through no fault of their own, are old or weak or needy, and I will try to help them.
>
> For as long as I can remember, I have been saddened by the sight of so many of our independent, industrious people working too hard for too little because of inadequate economic opportunities, and I will do what I can to enhance them.[20]

Clinton, Bumpers, and Pryor share not only a common political philosophy but uncommon political skills. By the late twentieth century, success in achieving and maintaining major political office in Arkansas depended partially on the same sophisticated, professional paraphernalia that had become the hallmark of politics everywhere: skilled pollsters, paid media consultants, computer-generated mailings, and phone banks. Bumpers, as noted above, was the first Arkansas gubernatorial candidate to demonstrate how one could use television to reach voters directly, over the heads of unfriendly local bosses and a hostile political establishment. By the time Clinton left the governorship he had demonstrated the effectiveness of the new high-tech politics in governance as well as campaigns: building public support for gubernatorial initiatives, advertising what had been accomplished at the end of a legislative session, and testing a variety of messages for making a program more acceptable and popular.

However, while all of the Big Three demonstrated their mastery of the new mass media politics, they also demonstrated their grasp of and incomparable proficiency at the personal, almost intimate aspect of Arkansas politics, which remains equally important to success. Pryor's remarks announcing his bid for reelection in 1990 simply but eloquently capture this familial flavor:

> It was . . . thirty years ago this month that I first asked the people of Ouachita County for one of the most precious possessions they owned . . . their vote. I wanted to be their State Representative.
>
> As spring came and summer engulfed, the election to that job became our life. Barbara and I divided up the neighborhoods, then the county, and together we literally went door to door and person to person. Even then, this type of "electioneering" was branded as "old-fashioned" and "out of step." But for us it became the rhythm and poetry of what America is all about. From the oil fields in the south to the Red Hills of Chidister and Reader and White Oak, we asked for every vote. On Friday and Saturday nights there were pie suppers and political speakings. On Sunday afternoon there was gospel singings and cake raffles.
>
> Dee, our oldest son, was just a baby. We carried him everywhere we went in a wicker basket. And we still have that wicker basket.
>
> . . . America is not about Presidents or Congress or Senators. It's not about statistics, policies, or programs, or even politicians like me. It's about neighbors, whether across the street or across the ocean. People who want to educate their children . . . people

who need health care . . . farmers who want a chance . . . elderly who crave dignity . . . taxpayers who deserve fairness . . . and people who want to be free. I want to help.[21]

All of the Big Three became personally acquainted with tens of thousands of their constituents and made them feel like part of an extended family—calling them by name, inquiring about their jobs and health and parents and children, offering hugs as well as handshakes. All graced the stage at hundreds of high school commencements (even the smallest of which, according to Bumpers, takes the same length of time as the largest, as the achievements of each and every graduate are recounted).[22] All made the constant round of civic club speeches and community festival appearances and groundbreaking ceremonies and political rallies. And they managed to do so with a good humor and grace and gusto suggesting that there was nothing else they would rather be doing.[23]

Furthermore, they frequently used these personal appearances to advance their programs and defend their records in language that Arkansans easily understood and appreciated and with a style that invited listeners' attention and admiration. As the author has observed elsewhere:

> Continuing longstanding southern and Arkansas traditions, the present "Big Three" of Arkansas politics . . . are all superb storytellers, who rarely use a prepared address, who quote easily and effectively from Scripture, and who can bring down the house with wry, self-deprecating humor. They have very different oratorical styles: Clinton lists debating points against invisible opponents; Pryor chats and charms; Bumpers educates and preaches. All however, quickly establish a strong rapport with the tens of thousands of Arkansans they encounter each year, thereby building powerful insulation against challengers' suggestions that they are "too intellectual" or "too liberal" or of dubious patriotism.[24]

It was, of course, more than well-liked programs and engaging styles which established and sustained the political lives of the Big Three. In building the large circles of friends, supporters, and contributors essential to sustained political success, they were able early in their careers to make excellent use of the gubernatorial appointment power.

Each Arkansas governor, it is estimated, makes approximately one thousand appointments a year to various boards and commissions. While some positions may seem obscure and unimportant, most are highly prized, as they afford opportunities to have some impact in a particular sphere of interest and carry a connotation of inside status.[25] Counting the combined gubernatorial years of the Big Three translates into a conservative estimate of ten thousand people who, by virtue of their appointments, felt some tie to their benefactors, some obligation to work for and contribute to their continued political success, and perhaps, some partisan loyalty.

All governors in all states have always used their appointive power to political advantage. However, one very distinctive aspect of the appointments made by the Big Three was its deliberate use to advance and empower two groups which had been traditionally excluded from Arkansas's political power structure—blacks and women. Governor Winthrop Rockefeller had made some significant breakthrough appointments of blacks to such boards as Correction, Pardons and Paroles, and Public Welfare. Bumpers, Pryor, and Clinton, however, took this practice to new levels and literally changed the face of Arkansas government.

Bumpers appointed a Governor's Commission on the Status of Women in 1971, which reported to him that only 10 percent of those serving on state boards and commissions were women, and most of those dealt with such traditionally women's areas as nursing, cosmetology, and the arts. By the time Bumpers left office, women filled many more appointive slots and did so on boards ranging from Correction to the Board of Higher Education. Pryor appointed additional scores of women, including appointments to such previous all-male bastions as the Highway Commission, the Industrial Development Commission, and the Arkansas Supreme Court. As for Clinton, women managed most of his campaigns; his longest tenured chief of staff (Betsey Wright) was a woman; and women served prominently in his cabinets including the directors of the Departments of Education, Health, Pollution Control and Ecology, Parks and Tourism, and Natural Heritage. Furthermore, all of the Big Three supported the proposed Equal Rights Amendment to the US Constitution.

Black voters have become an indispensable component of contemporary Democratic victories in Arkansas; but in the late 1960s, while Democrats (like Lyndon Johnson and Hubert Humphrey) were overwhelmingly favored for president, it was Republican Winthrop Rockefeller who arduously and successfully courted, nourished, and attracted black voters at the state level. A sizable and overwhelmingly Republican black vote was critical to Rockefeller's gubernatorial victories in 1966 and 1968 and loyally remained with him against Bumpers in 1970.[26]

By 1972, however, Bumpers had demonstrated—by refusing requests from white political leaders to shut down a controversial medical clinic in

Lee County—that he was not simply a nonsegregationist, but a sympathetic friend, and black voters returned their undivided strength to Bumpers and the Democrats.[27] Pryor, who as a young state representative had sided with the black delegates from Mississippi in a controversial seating dispute at the 1964 Democratic National Convention, was also perceived as a courageous friend. And Clinton, throughout his tenure, named blacks to his staff, to the most powerful and prestigious cabinet positions (Finance and Administration, Health and Human Services, and Development Finance Authority), and by the hundreds to state boards, commissions, and judicial posts. By the time the Big Three moved on to national office, there were few appointive positions left that had not been held by women and blacks. Those two groups had become powerful political forces in their own right.

Additionally, the Big Three attracted numerous young voters into their campaigns and causes, thereby socializing a new generation of activists into the ranks of the Democratic Party. As Blytheville native Greg Simon, who was an active teen Republican and now serves as chief domestic policy adviser to Vice President Al Gore, recently observed, "Rockefeller cleaned up the system so . . . you could elect honest Democrats. When you can elect Democrats like David Pryor and Dale Bumpers and Bill Clinton, why vote Republican?"[28]

Furthermore, both Bumpers and Pryor operated substantial internship programs in their Senate offices which by 1994 had involved well over seven hundred students.[29] Clinton's gubernatorial operations also utilized student interns, and his campaigns extensively employed hundreds of young people who thereby sharpened their own political skills and reconfirmed their loyalty to the Democratic Party. The Big Three's combination of personal charisma, political success, and programmatic appeal, especially Clinton's decade-long emphasis on education reform in Arkansas, made the Arkansas Democratic Party an attractive option for a young person wanting to be politically involved or considering a political future of his or her own. Whereas by the mid-1980s in some southern states the baton of youthful energy and future leadership seemed to have been passed to the growing ranks of the Republican Party, the Democratic Party still had the look and feel of a winner in Arkansas.

In states dominated by one political party, the dominant party is less an election machine than it is a holding company, a label, under which each candidate organizes his or her own personal coalition.[30] In Arkansas, where both parties as recently as 1985 were ranked among the organizationally weakest in the nation, serious candidates realize that the parties are supplements to rather than substitutes for the candidate's own campaign apparatus.[31] Nevertheless, all of the Big Three willingly and generously performed their assorted party chores (appealing for contributions to lesser-known candidates, drawing a crowd to county rallies, speaking at Jefferson-Jackson Day dinners), most of which were of much greater benefit to down-ticket candidates than to themselves. And whereas many Democratic candidates in other southern states by the mid-1980s were creating as much distance as possible between themselves and the party, the Big Three made no secret of their partisan affiliation. In the last weeks of the 1994 elections, both Pryor and Bumpers appeared and spoke at a Washington County fund-raising lunch for Third Congressional District Democratic candidate Berta Seitz. Pryor gave passionate praise to President Clinton's legislative achievements, as did Bumpers, who concluded: "I have never been more proud to be a Democrat."[32] It was a phrase rarely heard elsewhere in Dixie in 1994.

This episode exemplifies another trait of the Big Three which contributed to their prolonged success: an amazing ability, over more than two decades of high-powered politics, to, in most instances, work with and for rather than against each other. In the beginning there were occasional and understandable tensions between the principals and among their respective supporters. When Bill Clinton first burst onto the scene, all wondered who might next become victim to his clearly lofty ambitions. In fact, there were rumors (always unconfirmed) that Clinton's narrow margin of defeat in 1980 could have come from the Pryor camp's wanting to squelch young Clinton early before he decided to turn his attention to the seat held by Pryor in the Senate. Many Democrats worried about a possible Bumpers-Clinton contest in 1986 and were bemused when both were mentioned as presidential contestants in 1988. However, considering the agendas and aides and egos involved, what is truly extraordinary is the extent to which relations among the Big Three were not only harmonious and good-humored, but helpful.

When Bumpers announced that he would not be seeking the 1984 presidential nomination, he paid special tribute to the good counsel and supportiveness of Governor and Mrs. Clinton and especially that of Senator Pryor: "To say that David Pryor is a good friend and good colleague would be a gross understatement. He is both and more, and one of the great honors of my life is to serve in the Senate with him."[33] In Clinton's darkest moments in the early 1992 presidential primaries, Pryor appeared by Clinton's side in the snows of New Hampshire, joining him in the kind of personal contact politics they had perfected in Arkansas. By the time of the general election, Pryor had become one of the most frequent and effective surrogate speakers in the Clinton-Gore campaign arsenal and a vital bridge to congressional Democrats. When a lengthy article denigrating Clinton's record in Arkansas appeared in the July 31, 1994, *New York Times Magazine,* Pryor and Bumpers co-authored a vehement response in praise of Clinton's gubernatorial accomplishments.[34] It was Pryor who became known in 1993 as President Clinton's "Best Friend in Congress," but it was Bumpers who took to the Senate floor on October 8, 1994, and spoke at length to his colleagues about Clinton's "intelligence and straightforwardness," his "knowledge and understanding of the problems of this country," and Clinton's many legislative accomplishments.[35] While the Big Three did not always see eye to eye, they tended to downplay rather than publicize their differences. With a common philosophical base and passion for Arkansas, they worked closely enough together to reduce the likelihood of some outside challenger's penetrating the winner's circle.

If, as John Brummett has suggested, Arkansas voters by the mid-1960s favored candidates who "would be good ambassadors for the state and representatives of a more sophisticated, intelligent culture than the one people might know from Dogpatch cartoons or the Little Rock Central High School crisis," then the Big Three clearly fit the model. That they generally cooperated with and complimented each other rather than carving each other up added to their positive aura.[36]

There is an additional asset with which each of the Big Three is favored: a wife who departs from the traditional "smile rapturously and say nothing" model of political wives. For each of these politicians a participating wife proved to be a significant advantage. Betty Flanagan Bumpers, during her husband's tenure as governor, led a statewide effort to immunize "every child by two," a program so successful that it was later used by the Center for Disease Control as a national model for other states. In 1982, drawing on her success with the immunization effort, she founded Peace Links, a peace education group, which she nurtured to life in all fifty states and in other nations. Barbara Lunsford Pryor campaigned door-to-door, sometimes alone, sometimes by her husband's side, in all his early races. During the congressional and gubernatorial years, she was primarily occupied, between nearly constant campaigns, with raising their three young sons. As a Senate wife, however, she has been a major supporter of Arkansas artists and artisans, using both the Washington and Little Rock offices of Senator Pryor to display and promote their works.[37]

Now most famous is First Lady Hillary Rodham Clinton, who will be best remembered in Arkansas for the critical leadership she provided for the centerpiece of her husband's gubernatorial accomplishments—a significant revision and strengthening of Arkansas's public schools. She also, however, founded Arkansas Advocates for Children and Families, helped upgrade and expand Arkansas Children's Hospital, and initiated and chaired other community initiatives to improve the lives of children and women. That she also maintained a private law practice while simultaneously performing the traditional hostessing functions of a governor's spouse, raising a young child, and teaching a Sunday school class left an array of possible options from which future Arkansas first ladies will be more free to choose.[38]

In January 1988 a light airplane in which both Bumpers and Clinton were flying to the annual Gillett Coon Supper came close to disaster, a disaster which would have dramatically altered the last decade of Arkansas's twentieth century politics.[39] Even without such a cataclysm, however, by the last decade of the twentieth century it was clear that further changes were in process or on the horizon and that sooner rather than later a genuinely competitive Arkansas Republican party would emerge. Northwest Arkansas had become not only one of the fastest growing areas in the state and nation, but as a result of the combined impact of successful entrepreneurs, affluent retirees from northern states, and religious fundamentalists, a bastion of straight-ticket Republicanism. As those with the deepest devotion to the Democratic Party continued to be replaced by new generations not raised on tales of either the Civil War or the New Deal, Republican candidates all over the state became increasingly electable.

Term limits, strongly advocated by Republicans and adopted by Arkansas voters in 1992, not only guaranteed record numbers of open seats in the state legislature by 1996 (always a boon to the out party wishing to get in) but also insured that future elected executives, limited to two four-year terms, could never amass the political strength that Faubus and Clinton had. The October 1991 death of the *Arkansas Gazette,* which had editorially favored Democrats, and its replacement by the *Arkansas Democrat-Gazette,* meant, according to one longtime observer, "that the real winners of the vaunted newspaper war were the Republicans."[40] The first years of Clinton's presidential administration were both highly productive and highly problematic, bringing pain as well as pride to Arkansas, and whether either Bumpers or Pryor would seek additional Senate terms was uncertain. For nearly twenty-five years, however, Arkansas politics was dominated by three exceptional leaders, who had made many citizens proud to be Arkansans and also proud to be Democrats.

CHAPTER II

The Evolution of Judicial Selection in Arkansas

External and Internal Explanations of Change and Potential Future Directions

MARK NABORS AND J. R. BAXTER

Much scholarly debate has swirled around the question of judicial selection methods and their consequences, often pitting political science scholars against legal scholars. Considerably less attention has been given to the causes of these constitutional changes. Since statehood, Arkansas has experimented with nearly every major judicial selection method. While the state has yet to adopt a merit-based system, language in Amendment 80 of the Arkansas Constitution incentivizes the switch for the state's appellate courts. This essay investigates the causes of these changes. Does the variance throughout Arkansas's history simply point to external explanations, like policy diffusion and constitution sharing between peer states? Or might it be influenced by internal explanations, like retaliation against the judicial branch or a change of party control? The authors argue that the influence of internal forces is limited by external forces; that is, external forces limit the number of viable selection options while internal determinants play the determining role in the ultimate policy outcome. Thus, both external and internal explanations should be considered in examining how judicial selection may evolve in the future.[1]

Introduction

Judicial selection methods and their potential consequences in the states have been subject to considerable scholarly debate. Political science scholars

Originally published in *The Midsouth Political Science Review*, 17 (2016): 83–113. Reprinted with permission. DOI: https://doi.org/10.34053/parry2019.riapag2.11

have often been pitted against legal scholars in this foray. Political scientists generally point to the need for accountability and argue that judges are political actors in a political system. On the whole, then, these scholars advocate for electoral methods of selection or argue that selection methods have little consequence.[2] By contrast, legal scholars tend to prefer non-electoral methods of selection, like gubernatorial appointment or merit selection and retention. These scholars stress judicial independence, and are concerned with the effect of electing judges on the public's confidence in the legal system as a neutral and fair arbiter.[3]

While much scholarly attention has focused on the potential consequences of judicial selection methods, scant attention has been paid as to why states change their selection methods in the first place.[4] Are these changes primarily caused by external explanations like constitution sharing among peer states or policy diffusion? Or rather, are these changes primarily driven by internal explanations, like judicial scandals, policy retaliation against the judiciary, or a change in party control? This chapter seeks to answer these questions by investigating the causes of judicial selection changes in Arkansas from statehood to the present. As we will see, Arkansas has experimented quite extensively with selection mechanisms, and there is reason to believe that the state will continue this trend into the future.

The focus of this article is limited to Arkansas for a variety of reasons. First, causes of judicial selection in Arkansas have been neglected by scholarly study.[5] Thus, this article fills a critical gap in the Arkansas politics literature. Second, Arkansas is rich for a study of causes in judicial elections because it has experimented with every type of judicial selection method, with the exception of merit-based selection. Even so, Arkansas' constitution expressly authorizes the possibility of merit-based selection by the legislature referring the issue to a vote of the people. Moreover, Arkansas is in the midst of a movement to change judicial selection from nonpartisan election to merit-based selection with the governor and numerous members of the state legislature calling for this change.[6]

We will argue that both external and internal explanations for change are valid—that is, both have contributed to selection changes in the past. Thus, going forward, both explanations should be considered when assessing how judicial selection may evolve in the future. This article proceeds with a review of relevant literature, focusing on both external and internal explanations of policy change, and from this review, several propositions are drawn. We will then show how judicial selection has changed since statehood, focusing on selection methods in the 19th and 20th centuries.

Subsequent discussion will review the influences of these changes (and attempted reforms) over time. Finally, in conclusion, this article will consider how the future of judicial selection in Arkansas may take shape based on changes in the past.

Literature Review

While there is a paucity of scholarship on the causes of judicial selection changes, other research offers insight into explanations for change. Indeed, one of the richest sub-literatures in the subfield of state politics deals with explanations for policy variance between states.[7] Of course, judicial selection is just one example of vast differences in policy that can exist between states.[8] Table 1 shows the variety that exists today, and Table 2 shows the variety that has existed in Arkansas since statehood.

The first set of explanations for this variance focuses on external forces, or influences on policy from outside the state, as the main cause of policy variance. This review will look primarily at constitution sharing and policy diffusion between peer states. On the other hand, scholars have pointed to internal explanations, or influences on policy from within the state, in order to explain policy variance.[9] Here, this chapter will focus on some aspects of political culture, policy retaliation from the legislature and governor, party power, and lobbying efforts from organizations within the state—particularly, in this context, the Bar Association. Before moving on to these explanations, though, the only scholarship that reviews this question will be addressed.

Judicial Selection, Historical Theory, and Opportunity Costs

While scholars have given significant attention to the effects of one selection system over another, few have focused on why such changes occur in the first place. Indeed, many scholars point to the traditional narrative within the scholarship that retention methods are simply a function of time and historical preferences.[10] In this view, states simply respond to contemporary trends in judicial selection that are thought to produce a "better" judiciary. For example, states in the early Republic tended to choose legislative election because of the prevailing wisdom of the era that neither the governor nor the people should be given too much power. Later, as Jacksonian Democracy swept the nation, states opted for the more democratic approach of partisan election. And in the 20th century, states responded to the Progressive

TABLE 1:

Current Judicial Selection Methods in the United States, 2015

COURT LEVEL	PARTISAN ELECTION	NON-PARTISAN ELECTION	GUBERNATORIAL APPOINTMENT WITH CONFIRMATION*	LEGIS-LATIVE ELECTION	MERIT SELECTION**
Supreme Courts	**AL**, IL, **LA**, NM, PA, **TX**, WV	**AR**, **GA**, ID, KY, MI, MN, **MS**, MT, NV, **NC**, ND, OH, OR, WA, WI	CT, DE, HI, ME, MA, NH, NJ, NY, RI, VT	**SC**, **VA**	AK, AZ, CA, CO, **FL**, IN, IA, KS****, MD, MO, NE, OK, SD, **TN**, UT, WY
Appellate Courts	**AL**, IL, **LA**, NM, PA, **TX**	**AR**, **GA**, ID, KY, MI, MN, **MS**, **NC**, OH, OR, WA, WI	CT, DE, D.C., HI, MA, NY, ND, VT	**SC**, **VA**	AK, AZ, CA, CO, **FL**, IN, IA, KS****, MD, MO, NE, OK, **TN**, UT
Inferior Courts	**AL**, IL, IN, KS****, **LA**, MO, NM, NY, PA, **TN**, **TX**, WV	AZ**, **AR**, CA, **FL**, **GA**, ID, KY, MD, MI, MN, **MS**, MT, NV, **NC**, ND, OH, OK, OR, SD, WA, WI	CT, DE, D.C., HI, ME, MA, NH, NJ, RI, VT	**SC**, **VA**	AK, CO, IA, KS****, NE, UT, WY

Source: The American Judicature Society, http://www.judicialselection.us/judicial_selection/methods/selection_of_judges.cfm?state=.

States in **bold** type belonged to the Confederate States of America.

*In many states, the governor may only appoint candidates chosen by a nominating commission. Confirmation, if necessary, can be through the senate or an executive council.

**Appointment with retention elections.

***The general election for inferior court judges in AZ is nonpartisan, but primary elections are partisan.

****Kansas presents an unusual case. Appellate court judges are appointed by the governor from a nominating commission, confirmed by the senate, and retained by the people. Seventeen inferior court districts are selected via merit selection, while fourteen are selected via partisan election.

TABLE 2:

Judicial Selection Methods in Arkansas, 1836-Present

YEAR	SELECTION METHOD
1836	Election of all judges by the legislature.
1848	Supreme court justices elected by legislature; lower court judges elected by the people.
1861	Supreme court justices appointed by the governor and confirmed by the senate; lower court judges elected by the people.
1864	All judges elected by the people.
1868	Chief justice and lower court judges appointed by the governor and confirmed by senate; four associate justices elected by the people.
1874	All judges elected by the people.
1970*	Merit selection for appellate judges proposed in first draft; nonpartisan election of judges proposed in final draft.
1980*	Ballot question proposed to the people: nonpartisan election or merit selection?
2000	Judges elected in nonpartisan elections, per Amendment 80; the legislature can refer an amendment to switch to merit selection.

*Proposed constitutions failed to be ratified by the people.

movement and activists who sought to insulate the judiciary from popular opinion by bringing nonpartisan elections and merit selection

This historical theory has become the standard, textbook explanation for why states choose particular retention mechanisms over others—so much so that it is rarely questioned by scholars. However, research by Epstein, Knight, and Shvetsova critiques this conventional wisdom, and attempts to empirically assess the reasons for changing judicial selection systems. Indeed, to date, this study represents the only significant attempt at answering the research question posed in this article.[11] Specifically, they argue that the conventional wisdom fails to account for politics, a more accurate understanding of political motives, and lacks empirical support.

The major thrust of Epstein, Knight, and Shvetsova is the idea that the uncertainty of the political climate will affect judicial selection mechanisms.[12] To test this, the authors plot retention mechanisms on a scale of low opportunity cost to high opportunity cost. By opportunity cost, the authors mean "the political and other costs justices may incur when they act sincerely."[13] As we will see below, this theory reinforces others' insights in many ways. This is particularly true of Laura Langer's work, which posits that justices are careful about venturing into the particularly salient areas of policy due to the risk of retaliation from elected officials.[14] It also reinforces the idea that a change in dominant party control might precipitate change; specifically, the newly seated party in power may want to increase the opportunity costs for judges by making them more accountable to elected officials and/or to the people.

However, this theory warrants a couple of major cautions. First, while it does seem reasonable to suggest that the uncertainty of the political climate would influence selection choice, this theoretical framework necessarily presumes the presence of all selection options as viable alternatives at any point in time. But if one looks at Arkansas' 1836 statehood constitution, only two viable selection options existed—namely, legislative election and gubernatorial appointment.[15] Similarly, Arkansas' judicial reforms in 2000 did not consider the outdated legislative election method, or even gubernatorial appointment. Indeed, we know that a state in the late-20th century is more likely to choose merit selection or nonpartisan elections, regardless of the uncertainty of the political climate. Thus, this theory downplays significantly policy diffusion trends and the limits they impose on choice in order to effectively counter the historical theory of judicial selection. Furthermore, the authors' proposed mapping of opportunity costs seems rather subjective. Indeed, one could imagine that reappointment by government officials might be more costly in particular circumstances than nonpartisan reelection by the relatively uninformed electorate.[16] Given these significant cautions, then, we will look to other scholarship to formulate our hypotheses.

Policy Diffusion among the States: External Explanations

First, many scholars argue that external factors best explain policy variance among the states.[17] While these scholars do not totally discount intrastate explanations, they believe national and/or regional interactions are the primary drivers of policy change. These scholars have identified networks of policy diffusion among states and have empirically shown that states are influenced by the national government and their fellow states.

Perhaps at the most fundamental level, Alan Tarr shows that similarities between state constitutions are often the result of constitution sharing among peer states.[18] In particular, Tarr notes that borrowing from other states is common because states have similar problems and like to borrow solutions from one another.[19] Additionally, borrowing from other states can decrease the time and effort needed to draft a new governing document. States in the 18th and 19th centuries looked to other state constitutions when drafting their first constitutions or rewriting old ones. Likewise, after the Civil War, many southern states borrowed heavily from the constitutions of states in the Union. In fact, the bulk of constitutional revisions happened between 1861–1880.[20] And of course, as people migrated west, they took their constitutional frameworks and ideas about government along for the ride. Tarr sums this up nicely when he writes "[w]hether in new states or old, convention delegates during the nineteenth century relied heavily on compilations of existing state constitutions, which clarified the progress of constitutional thinking and provided models for emulation."[21]

This borrowing was not unique to the 18th and 19th centuries. Indeed, the trend of interstate borrowing continued into the twentieth century. Many states, for instance, created constitution revision commissions that were charged with regularly looking at the state's constitution and recommending changes. As part of their work, these commissions would monitor constitutional changes in other states. Additionally, interest and citizen groups have been active in ensuring certain provisions are inserted into the drafts of new constitutions. The Model State Constitution, created by the National Municipal League in 1921, promotes what it considers to be the ideal state government. These observations give us our first proposition:

P1: JUDICIAL SELECTION CHANGES ARE CAUSED BY CONSTITUTION SHARING AMONG PEER STATES.

Similarly, Virginia Gray and Jack Walker find a national system of emulation and competition across several policy domains.[22] Walker further identifies regional clusters of policy diffusion.[23] He develops a tree system of pioneer states and laggard states, and argues that newer networks have sped up diffusion within regional clusters. Similarly and more contemporarily, Michael Mintrom and Sandra Vergari look at policy networks and the influence of policy entrepreneurs.[24] They find that external networks increase the likelihood that a state will consider a policy from another state, but have no effect on adoption. Instead, the presence of a policy entrepreneur and internal networks are significant for policy adoption.

Finally, scholars have pointed to public opinion forces across states as influences on policy change and diffusion. Erikson, Wright, and McIver and other scholars argue that while party identification trends in states may change, citizen preferences in states remain stable over time.[25] Thus, any change, they argue, is best explained by national trends, and not intrastate trends. Much change surrounding judicial selection seems consistent with this theory. This leads us to our second proposition:

P2: JUDICIAL SELECTION CHANGES ARE CAUSED BY NATIONAL AND/OR REGIONAL PUBLIC OPINION TRENDS.

And while reliable polling data from the 19th century is not available, we will look to larger trends in democratic thinking among the American people, e.g., Jacksonian Democracy.

Of the State Itself: Internal Explanations

Other scholars have focused more on internal explanations, arguing that the primary drivers of policy variance are characteristics within the state.[26] There is, in fact, a long history of state politics scholars taking this approach. For instance, Daniel Elazar's political cultures can account for policy variance— and indeed, many scholars still use political culture as an independent variable when empirically investigating variance. Similarly, Lieske used US Census data to uncover differences in political cultures that could account for policy variance. While their approaches are more narrowly tailored, methodologically sophisticated, and issue-specific, contemporary scholars have also investigated policy variance using this concept.[27]

We expect that judicial selection mechanisms will reflect the state's political culture. This, of course, assumes that constitutional mechanisms reflect the people's desires. Furthermore, this assumes that the people— outside of the legal elite—care about how judges are selected. Finally, it seems that if this hypothesis were to be valid, selection mechanisms would be more static than volatile. Change to these mechanisms would be difficult, then, particularly if the changes ran counter to the dominant trends of the political culture of the state. But political culture can be an elusive and unwieldy concept, and therefore difficult to operationalize. Indeed, one could look to several factors when evaluating Arkansas' traditionalistic culture. In this paper, we are primarily interested in citizens' distrust of political elites. We posit that this populist outlook will constrain elite efforts to reform the judiciary:

P3: JUDICIAL SELECTION CHANGES ARE CONSTRAINED BY
A POPULIST DISTRUST OF POLITICAL AND LEGAL ELITES.

Additionally, scholars have looked at the impact of public opinion—an attitudinal explanation—on policy variance. Unfortunately, there is a severe lack of comparable survey data for all fifty states.[28] For that reason, state politics scholars have been forced to take innovative approaches to measuring public opinion, which has resulted in the formation of two camps. In contrast to Erikson, Wright, and McIver and other scholars, who were discussed in the previous section, Berry et al. argue that public opinion in the states changes over time.[29] Using their Citizen Ideology Index as an indirect measure of public opinion, they argue that citizen preferences fluctuate between conservative and liberal, e.g., in reaction to public policy or a particular event. They hold, then, that policy changes within states more often reflect changing opinions of the state's citizenry. Critics argue, however, that this index is not a measure of citizen preferences, but of elite opinion.[30] Even if this is the case, we still hold that Berry et al.'s index has value; given low participation rates in the states, an understanding of elite opinions is crucial. This seems to be especially true for judicial politics, which generally have even lower political participation.[31] Moreover, as our research will show, judicial politics seem to be a particularly salient concern for legal elites in Arkansas. More broadly speaking, while constitutional change has been fueled by public passions in the past (e.g., the Populist movement), it is unclear how much influence the mass public has.[32] Indeed, the latter half of the 20th century shows that constitutional changes are most often guided by professional or political elites. The fluctuation of elite opinion, then, may help explain the tremendous variance in judicial selection mechanisms since 1836.

In Arkansas, as in other states, the elite organization that would be particularly concerned with judicial selection mechanisms is the Bar Association. Indeed, this seems to be the sort of internal network that is crucial for the successful adoption of policy change.[33] The professionals that belong to the bar have a considerable stake in selection, both because they regularly interact and work with judges, and because they may have professional ambitions of becoming judges. Moreover, the degree of control sometimes given to the bar in the Missouri Plan—like appointment power, for instance—could be another reason these professionals and legal professional organizations (e.g., the Institute for the Advancement of the

Legal Profession) tend to support merit selection. This leads us to our fourth proposition:

P4: JUDICIAL SELECTION CHANGES ARE DRIVEN BY THE OPINIONS OF THE LEGAL COMMUNITY IN THE STATE.

In addition to the Bar Association, research from Langer shows that elites in government, i.e., elected state officials, can and do exert influence on the judiciary, often in response to decisions that adversely affect their policies.[34] In other words, the judicial branch is sometimes subjected to policy retaliation. While Langer does not discuss judicial selection mechanisms, changes in selection methods could be an example of this retaliation. A change to a gubernatorial appointment system, for example, gives both the governor and senate considerable power and influence over judges. The recent debate over judicial selection in Kansas illustrates this point well.[35]

P5: JUDICIAL SELECTION CHANGES ARE CAUSED BY POLICY RETALIATION FROM THE LEGISLATIVE AND/OR EXECUTIVE BRANCHES OF GOVERNMENT.

Similarly, a change in the dominant party of a state could precipitate policy change. For one, policy change could be the result of policy retaliation. In other words, the party may be punishing judges for ruling a particular way, as Langer suggests.[36] It could also be that parties have different beliefs about appropriate selection mechanisms. As we will see below, a change in the dominant party in Arkansas has contributed to judicial selection changes for both of these reasons.

P6: JUDICIAL SELECTION CHANGES ARE DUE TO A CHANGE WITH PARTY POWER SHIFTS.

We expect that both external and internal forces influence judicial selection changes in the state. Furthermore, the dominant influences of change may vary with time. In other words, the forces that were important in 1874 may not be as dominant in the 21st century. Our analysis of the foregoing propositions will be descriptive in nature. While an empirical analysis might lead to more definitive and generalizable conclusions, we are employing a descriptive analysis for a couple of obvious reasons. First, given that all of Arkansas' constitutions were written and ratified in the mid- to late-19th century, a descriptive approach is more appropriate. The data needed in an empirical design are largely unavailable. Secondly, these available data lend themselves to a descriptive approach. Most of our information will come from a review of historical events surrounding these changes, as well as any information that may be garnered from journals, convention records, and, in the case of 20th century changes, personal accounts. Finally, while Epstein, Knight, and Shvetsova do provide an empirical framework, the data needed to run the model are elusive.[37] While we can point to a general account of uncertainty in the state, we cannot point to the uncertainty felt by individual legal elites and lawmakers in many (if not most) cases. Indeed, the subjective nature of uncertainty makes a descriptive approach more acceptable in the absence of personal accounts.

The 19th Century: From Statehood to Redemption

The 19th century was one of great flux in constitutional governance for Arkansas. As Tarr notes, states experimented greatly with their constitutional designs in the 19th century, and Arkansas was not unusual in this regard.[38] Many states, like Arkansas, were admitted to the Union during the century; and southern states, like Arkansas, went through an extensive revision process before and after the Civil War. In total, the citizens of Arkansas wrote and ratified five different constitutions during this century. This section will outline the judicial selection mechanisms prescribed in each of the constitutions of the 19th century, beginning with the statehood Constitution of 1836. As we will see, mechanisms for selecting judges varied extensively, both in response to external trends and in response to internal state politics.

THE CONSTITUTION OF 1836

The general assembly shall, by joint vote of both houses, elect the judges of the supreme and circuit courts, a majority of the whole number in joint vote being necessary to a choice. The judges of the Supreme Court [. . .] shall hold their offices during the term of eight years from the date of their commissions. [. . .] The judges of the circuit court [. . .] shall be elected for the term of four years from the date of their commission . . .

Art. 6, Sec. 7.[39]

The first judicial selection mechanism the state employed was legislative election for all judges. For Supreme Court justices, legislative election would remain the selection method until the Civil War. The question raised here is why the state of Arkansas may have chosen legislative election over gubernatorial appointment, the only other method at the time.

The primary, if not only, answer for this method is constitution sharing. As noted above, constitution sharing was very common in the 19th century, particularly for statehood constitutions. Indeed, Cal Ledbetter shows that the Constitution of 1836 was hastily written and speedily adopted, and that it borrowed heavily from other states.[40] In fact, he notes that one could switch Arkansas' constitution with those of Mississippi, Tennessee, or Missouri, and not find any significant differences.[41] This is not to say, however, that Arkansas did not make an informed decision, but it should be taken as strong evidence that the state leadership simply borrowed other states' judicial selection mechanisms without much deliberation. This idea is even more compelling when one takes the strong desire for statehood into account; Arkansans' desire to join the Union was strong enough to buffet the objections of policymakers at the national level.[42] Thus, the Arkansan elites writing the constitution would have turned to other states for a model in order to avoid complications with congressional approval of the state constitution.

1848 AMENDMENT

That the qualified electors of each judicial circuit in the state of Arkansas shall elect their circuit judge.

1848 Amendment

In 1848, the people ratified the above referred amendment from the General Assembly. This amendment made circuit court judges—or all inferior court judges at the time—elected by the people, but still retained legislative election for Supreme Court justices. It seems peculiar that the legislature would voluntarily forfeit its power to appoint circuit judges. However, when this amendment is examined in context of broader trends, it is logical.

First, this amendment falls squarely within the era of Jacksonian Democracy, pointing to the influence of national or regional public opinion trends. The election of circuit judges, then, represents a return of power to the people from the state.[43] Given the widespread popularity of this line of thought among the American people and some elites, the diffusion of elected judges is understandable. And yet, in Arkansas this power sharing is moderated by the legislature retaining the power to appoint justices on the state's Supreme Court.

In addition to these national and regional public opinion trends, this change was spurred on by constitution sharing. Ledbetter notes that Mississippi was the first to elect its judges about a decade before in 1832.[44]

The diffusion of elected judges across states can be attributed to states adopting the new constitutional provisions of its peer states: "Between 1846 and 1912 every new state entering the Union embraced this scheme of selection [i.e., partisan election], as did most of the previously settled states."[45]

THE CONSTITUTION OF 1861

The judges of the supreme court shall be appointed by the governor, by and with the advice and consent of the senate. The judges of the supreme court [. . .] shall hold their offices during the term of eight years from the date of their commissions, and until their successors are appointed and qualified.

Art. 6, Sec. 7

The qualified voters of each judicial circuit in the state of Arkansas, shall elect their circuit judges. The judges of the circuit courts [. . .] shall be elected for the term of four years, from and after the dates of their commissions, and until their successors are elected and qualified—and all elections of circuit judges shall be held as is, or may be provided by law.

Art. 6, Sec. 8

One of the primary characteristics of the Constitution of 1836 is its longevity vis-à-vis the other constitutions of the 19th century.[46] By that measure, regardless of whether the constitution should be considered exceptional or ordinary the Constitution of 1836 can be hailed as a success.[47] For that reason, the Constitution of 1861 does not meddle too much with the previous constitution, but by and large just rewrites it to join the Confederate States of America.[48]

One exception to that rule is judicial selection. In 1861, circuit judges continue to be elected by the people; however, the selection for Supreme Court justices is changed from legislative election to gubernatorial appointment with senate confirmation. Two explanations for this change are constitution sharing and national or regional public opinion trends. While New York had been the first to adopt gubernatorial appointment to select Supreme Court justices in the 18th century, southern states were hesitant to join the movement.[49] A century later, however, Arkansas and much of the South—including the Confederate States' government—decided to adopt the change as legislative elections became an increasingly outdated mode to choose judges.

THE CONSTITUTION OF 1864

The qualified voters of this state shall elect the judges of the supreme court. The judges of the supreme court [. . .] shall hold their offices during the term of eight years from the date of their commissions, and until their successors are elected and qualified . . .

Art. 7, Sec. 7

The qualified voters of each judicial district shall elect a circuit judge. The judges of the circuit court [. . .] shall be elected for the term of four years from the date of their commissions, and shall serve until their successors are elected and qualified.

Art. 7, Sec. 8

With the end of the Civil War, states were required to rewrite their constitutions in order to be readmitted to the Union. Of course, a new constitution would be required in just four more years after the assassination of President Lincoln and the heightened demands from the Radical Republican Congress. Much has been written about this elsewhere, thus there is not a need to delve too deeply into it here.[50] However, we see distinct differences in judicial selection between 1864 and 1868.

An obvious influence on change is constitution sharing. Ledbetter notes that at this time, southern states were adopting much from the constitutions of their northern neighbors in order to decrease any complications in the re-admittance process.[51] We might also expect to see that a change in dominant party control would influence selection mechanisms; however, that does not seem to be the case here. Republicans would have preferred selection by appointment—as we will see in 1868. Instead, the more moderate voices in 1864 opted for partisan election for all judges. Interestingly, then, this may point to the influence of populist distrust of elites, particularly outside or Republican elites, and the people's preference for selecting their judicial actors. In fact, this explanation fits well here because most of the drafters of this constitution were Arkansans; only four delegates had been in the state fewer than five years.[52]

THE CONSTITUTION OF 1868

. . . The supreme court shall consist of one (1) chief justice, who shall be appointed by the governor, by and with the advice and consent of the senate, for the term of eight (8) years, and four associate justices,

*who shall be chosen by the qualified electors of the state at large for
the term of eight (8) years . . .*

Art. 7, Sec. 3

*. . . The judges of the inferior courts [. . .] shall be appointed by the
governor, by and with the advice and consent of the senate, for the
term of six (6) years, and until such time as the general assembly
may otherwise direct . . .*

Art. 7, Sec. 5

In contrast to the Constitution of 1864, we see a different approach to judicial selection that gives considerably more power to elected officials instead of the people of the state. This change is due to a change in decision-makers; Radical Republicans in Arkansas and Washington expected constitutional mechanisms that would protect recently emancipated citizens. In other words, the judiciary was insulated from the people and their opinions.

We can say, then, that the primary reason for the rather bizarre selection arrangement is a change in party power. Unlike in 1864 when a more moderate coalition drafted the state constitution, the constitution of 1868 was drafted and ratified by more radical Republicans within the state. These decision-makers wanted to ensure that black citizens would be protected under the state and federal constitutions, and that those protections would be duly enforced by the judiciary. This change, then, not only reflects the change in the party power structure in Arkansas, but also the national trends pushed by the Radical Republicans in Congress.

In addition to ensuring that newly emancipated citizens would be given justice, there was concern about judges discriminating against Republicans and those who had sympathized with the North. The convention record from 1868 confirms this.[53] The journal records that a letter by L. Lamborn was sent to the convention on the subject of the judiciary. Lamborn writes,

> [. . .] there has been no loyal judiciary tribunal since the war, and no Union man could obtain impartial justice; and I hope you will pardon my boldness in making one suggestion to your honorable body; that is, that the new constitution shall provide that judges shall be appointed by the Executive of the State.[54]

The delegates went on to debate the merits of the letter. The convention record reflects that several denounced the letter, including a Mr. Duvall who had originally come from Virginia, and Mr. Cypert and Mr. McCown who had originally come from Tennessee. By contrast, Mr. Dale, who had been born in Indiana, lent his support to the merits of the letter.

This change also represents retaliation by the legislative and executive branches against the judiciary. As Stafford notes, between 1864 and 1868, there were rival governments in Arkansas, including two rival supreme courts.[55] The government in 1868, then, was concentrating power in a single court, and by appointing most judges—including all inferior court judges—the state was ensuring maximum control over the judicial branch during Reconstruction.

However, the above explanations can hardly explain why the drafters chose to allow the associate justices to be elected while appointing the chief justice and all inferior court judges. Indeed, electing associate justices runs counter to the above explanations. We propose that there are two possible explanations. The first, and more cynical, is political corruption. One notable chief justice under the Constitution of 1868 was McClure, who was a key member of the 1868 convention and a close ally and friend to future governors Clayton and Brooks. It could be argued that McClure pushed for the chief justice to be appointed in order to secure his own political future. However, this explanation falls short because McClure was democratically elected to the post of associate justice before being appointed by Clayton to the position of chief justice. Perhaps the best explanation is this structure de facto gave the chief justice expansive powers and control over the Supreme Court. For example, in exploring his impeachment, Ewing shows that Chief Justice McClure possessed broad administrative powers in fact, whether or not those powers were justified by law.[56]

THE CONSTITUTION OF 1874

. . . The judges of the supreme court shall be elected by the qualified electors of the state, and shall hold their offices during the term of eight years from the date of their commission . . .

Art. 7, Sec. 6

The judges of the circuit courts shall be elected by the qualified electors of the several circuits, and shall hold their offices for the term of four years.

Art. 7, Sec. 17

After Reconstruction, Arkansas quickly initiated efforts to "redeem" its constitution and government. In most ways, therefore, the Constitution of 1874 is drastically different from previous constitutions. Other scholars have dealt extensively with these southern constitutions.[57] With respect to judicial selection in Arkansas, we see a change back to the popular election of all judges. With popularly elected judges, judicial enforcement of certain civil rights provisions would be more unlikely, which only serves to reinforce the policy reasons for which the Constitution of 1874 was drafted.

With these so-called redeemer constitutions, we see several external forces at play. For one, constitution sharing was common. This is not only true of peer states, but states were also adopting provisions from constitutions in the past. Thus, we see a return to partisan elections for judges and justices across the South. Additionally, we see regional public opinion trends influencing developments. Many southerners were anxious to return to an antebellum state of existence, and while that may not have been possible in fact, it could be simulated constitutionally. With popularly elected judges, a return to the antebellum South and its hierarchal structure would be possible.

Many internal forces influenced the constitutional changes as well, including the change of judicial selection mechanism. Indeed, in 1874, many of these internal forces exerted strong influence on changes. The most obvious is a change in the party power structure. Democrats once again had control of the General Assembly and dominated the constitutional convention. With this dominance, they had the ability to return to the popular election of judges. In addition, this return to popular election is a form of retaliation against the judiciary, particularly against those judges who had been appointed by Republican governors. The drafters knew that Republicans could not be elected in much of post-Reconstruction Arkansas. Indeed, after the so-called return to home rule, the chief justice and two associate justices of the Supreme Court were impeached and removed from office.[58] Finally, distrust of political elites exerted a strong influence. The right to select its judges was again being returned to the people, who on the whole distrusted the government.

Overall, then, we see that the above changes were influenced by both internal and external forces. As the state moved into the twentieth century, Arkansas would see a halt to the frequent constitutional rewrites. Instead, the 1874 constitution and its method for judicial selection would remain until Amendment 80 in 2000, despite numerous attempts by elites to reform the judiciary.

THE 20TH CENTURY: A CENTURY OF (ATTEMPTED) REFORMS

While constitution adoption would drop off after the 19th century, reformers continued to work to change public policy in the states through state constitutional amendments and/or constitutional conventions. Consistent with the general preferences of the legal field today, many reforms over the 20th century attempted to limit ballot-box influence on judicial behavior. For example, the 6th edition of the Model Constitution, published in 1968, pushes for appointment of judges by the governor or nomination commission. Progressive reformers also pushed with considerable success for nonpartisan elections of judges during the first part of the 20th century. Similarly, the change to merit selection, or the Missouri Plan, has been promoted by a host of legal interest groups to insulate judicial actors from the influence of popular elections. This promotion has continued into the 21st century by groups like the Institute for the Advancement of the Legal Profession and the O'Connor Judicial Selection Initiative. This section will map changes and attempted reforms to judicial selection in Arkansas during this century. As we will see, reformers consistently failed to change selection mechanisms until Amendment 80 in 2000.

1970 AND 1980 CONSTITUTIONAL CONVENTIONS

The Governor shall fill vacancies on the Supreme Court and Circuit Courts by selecting one of three persons nominated by the appropriate Nominating Commission. If the Governor fails to make the appointment within sixty days after the three names are submitted to him, the Chief Justice of the Supreme Court shall make the appointment from among the three nominees.

Recommended change by the Arkansas
Constitutional Revision Study Commission, 1968

The Supreme Court shall consist of a Chief Justice and six Associate Justices, each of whom shall be elected by a majority vote on a nonpartisan basis at a statewide general election for a term of eight years.

Art. 5, Sec. 2, Proposed Constitution of 1970

FOR Merit Selection by Appointment of Supreme Court Justices and Court of Appeals Judges
OR
FOR Non-partisan Election of Supreme Court Justices and Court of Appeals Judges

Ballot Form for Selection of Supreme Court
Justices and Court of Appeals Judges, Proposed
Constitution of 1980

Consistent with broader national trends toward rewriting and/or revising constitutions, constitutional conventions were held in Arkansas in 1970 and 1980. While the people approved these two conventions, they failed to ratify the resulting documents. It should also be noted that there were two other conventions during the century. However, we have not chosen to include them here for a couple of reasons. First, an earlier convention was ruled unconstitutional by the state Supreme Court because the people were not asked if there should be a convention. And in the 1990s, Governor Tucker's proposed changes failed to gain any popular support.

The first significant convention, then, was held in 1970. As mentioned in the literature review, the mid-20th century was a time of extensive constitutional revision and review.[59] Political and legal elites in Arkansas were similarly pushing for reforms, particularly reforms that dealt with the judicial article and included a switch in selection methods. In fact, in 1968, the Arkansas Constitutional Revision Study Commission issued a report that urged for, among other things, the adoption of merit selection for judges. The writers of the report go on to note that "[t]he popular election of judges is a highly controversial method for selection of the judiciary which has recently been abandoned in a number of other states. It should be restudied."[60] The study ultimately recommended a merit system for two reasons: first, they argued that voters without legal experience could not make informed decisions, and secondly, that running for election can create conflicts of interest.[61] The commission they proposed would have been made up of lawyers and non-lawyers. The commission would send three nominees to the governor, and the selected judge would be retained in periodic elections.

However, at the convention itself, the delegates instead chose to adopt nonpartisan elections for the proposed constitution. Granted, the adoption of this selection method is also consistent with national public opinion trends and constitution sharing, though it is worth noting that most other states using this method had adopted nonpartisan elections several decades earlier. In addition to recommending the use of nonpartisan elections, it is interesting to note that the proposed constitution also established a court of appeals.

Similarly, in 1980 there was much momentum for the adoption of merit selection in Arkansas. However, unlike in 1970, the delegates of the 1980 Constitutional Convention could not come to a clear consensus on retaining judicial elections or adopting merit selection. In fact, the convention ended up sending both proposals to the people for a vote, meaning one would vote for the new constitution and then vote for their judicial selection preference.[62] After the convention, there was what appeared to be considerable organization campaigning for the adoption of the merit selection process.[63] Raymond Abramson, an arch proponent of merit-based selection recorded that numerous delegates to the constitutional convention were in favor of merit based selection as well as Walter Hussman, the owner of the prominent Arkansas Democrat newspaper. But Abramson also noted that the campaign effort was a low budget, grassroots affair. However, due to the fact that the proposed constitution itself failed with the voters, merit-based selection was a nullity.

As in 1970, this momentum in 1980 for adoption of merit judicial selection fits squarely in line with the rest of the nation adopting merit-based selection, or national and regional public opinion trends and constitution sharing. Of the thirty-four states that adopted merit selection, all did so between 1940 and 1988, predominantly between 1970 and 1980.[64] Thus, Arkansas' effort correlates strongly with the rest of her sister states, suggesting external influences were at play during the 1980 constitutional convention. Furthermore, the legal community in the state was pushing for reforms to the judicial article, including to the method of selection. In fact, a ledger kept by Cal Ledbetter shows plainly that the delegates were especially interested in reforming the judicial article.[65] Indeed, based on Ledbetter's papers, it appears that the legal community was pushing harder for merit selection in 1980 than in 1970.

After 1980, the rest of the nation appears to have veered away from merit selection, which is consistent with Arkansas' trajectory. The last state to adopt a merit selection system by constitutional amendment was New Mexico in 1988, and New Mexico was far from a full-fledged Missouri plan system as it retained contested partisan elections following initial appointment.[66] As merit selection fell off nationally, it also fell off in Arkansas until quite recently.

The reasons for which the proposed constitutions were not ratified deserve some attention. The first reason we can point to is populist distrust of political elites. Time and again, the people were cautious to adopt these new constitutions with their sweeping reforms, even though they had approved the conventions. Furthermore, Arkansas was endeavoring to rewrite its constitutions at a time when national public opinion was manifesting severe distrust of government and public officials in the wake of the Vietnam War, Watergate, and other political scandals.

2000: AMENDMENT 80

Circuit Judges and District Judges shall be elected on a nonpartisan basis by a majority of qualified electors . . .

Amendment 80, Sec. 17 (A)

Supreme Court Justices and Court of Appeals Judges shall be elected on a nonpartisan basis by a majority of qualified electors voting for such office. Provided, however, the General Assembly may refer the issue of merit selection of members of the Supreme Court and the Court of Appeals to a vote of the people at any general election. If the voters approve a merit selection system, the General Assembly shall enact laws to create a judicial nominating commission for the purpose of nominating candidates for merit selection to the Supreme Court and Court of Appeals.

Amendment 80, Sec. 18 (A)

On the one hand, it might appear that the idea behind merit selection in Arkansas is alive and well. Amendment 80 to the Arkansas Constitution, which was adopted in 2000, allows for the legislature to refer the issue of merit selection of appellate judges to the voters at any general election. This is a significant retreat from offering merit selection on the ballot as was done in 1980. Moreover, the legislature has never referred the idea to the people, possibly due to other states overwhelmingly rejecting merit-based selection around this time.[67]

Amendment 80 abolished partisan judicial elections and switched the state to nonpartisan judicial elections. This was done about fifty years after the idea of switching to nonpartisan judicial elections was in its heyday.[68] When examined nationally, then, Arkansas is clearly a laggard state (see Walker 1969 for a discussion of leaders and laggards). However, when one looks at other states in the region, it is clear that Arkansas' selection method was the norm—or at the very least was not unusual (see Table 1). Even so, we can say that Arkansas was influenced by constitution sharing with other states, in regard to both judicial selection and other provisions.

One thing that Amendment 80 does demonstrate about judicial selection in Arkansas is that changes in the party power structure again had an influence on judicial selection. In 2000, Arkansas was starting to show signs that pointed to rising Republicanism in the state.[69] Consequently, then, the Republican establishment had an opportunity to shape judicial selection methods by exerting influence from its newfound position of power.

Moreover, the drafters of the amendment proposed this switch purely to gain the support of their new, Republican negotiating partner.[70] This demonstrates that Arkansas' change from partisan to nonpartisan judicial elections was the product of a massive adjustment in party dominance in Arkansas, which resembles selection changes in the late-19th century.

John Stroud also notes that the amendment had the backing of the legal community.[71] Certainly many on the bar would have supported the selection change, either to nonpartisan elections or merit selection. However, many on the bar supported the amendment primarily because it updated Arkansas' judicial branch. Chiefly, it did away with the antiquated bifurcation between courts of equity and courts of law.

2016: THE PRESENT

In Arkansas, it seems the past has been predictive of the future as the debate over judicial selection in Arkansas is not over. In recent news, a task force created by the Arkansas Bar Association has submitted a report to the Arkansas Bar's board of delegates backing a switch from judicial elections to merit-based selection for the Arkansas Supreme Court. The governor of Arkansas as well as members of the legislature have likewise endorsed such a proposition.[72] Indeed, the debate about spending in judicial campaigns is also heating up nationally as well.[73] While it is impossible to judge the importance of the events without the state adopting a formal change in judicial selection mechanisms, it can be noted that the political structure toward adopting a change seems to be rooted in internal forces, i.e., the bar and governor. The fact that Arkansas is pushing toward merit-based selection, something which no state has done since 1994, strongly demonstrates the role external forces are playing in the current political structure. Whether these internal forces will breed success, though, remains to be seen.

Discussion

As the above has shown, preferences concerning judicial selection have varied over time in Arkansas. And generally, these shifting preferences are consistent with trends in other states. In this way, Arkansas is not unusual or unique in its experience. Indeed, all judges in Arkansas are presently retained at the ballot box, and as Robert Williams notes, the vast majority of state judges will be on the ballot at some point in their careers.[74]

Based on the above, what can we say are the influences on changing judicial selection methods in Arkansas? We have identified six propositions from the literature that may explain judicial selection changes. These influences can be divided between external or internal influences—that is, influences from outside the state and influences from within the state. Table 3 presents these propositions, and plots which forces are in play with each change.

The table shows that changes have been influenced heavily by external forces, particularly constitution sharing between peer states and national or regional trends of public opinion. In fact, in all of the above cases there is evidence to suggest constitution sharing between peer states has always been a force in play. National or regional public opinion trends have influenced selection changes to a slightly lesser degree, but have still been a significant force.

By contrast, several internal forces have influenced changes at different times. These influences by and large appear to have been less consistent than the two external forces identified above. Instead, different forces have risen to a prominent position of influence depending on the year and the political climate within the state. In fact, this makes logical sense in the context of the earlier propositions drawn about internal influences. Changes in the party power structure, for example, are rather infrequent, and retaliation against

TABLE 3:

Influences on Selection Changes, 1836-Present

YEAR OF CHANGE	PROPOSITIONS					
	EXTERNAL INFLUENCES		INTERNAL INFLUENCES			
	Constitution Sharing	National/ Regional Trends	Distrust of Elites	Legal Community Opinion	Legislative/ Executive Retaliation	Party Power Change
1836	X					
1848	X	X				
1861	X	X				
1864	X		X			
1868	X	X			X	X
1874	X	X	X		X	X
1970*	X	X	X	X		
1980*	X	X	X	X		
2000	X			X		X

*Failed attempts at reform.

the judiciary from the other branches of government is dependent on the state of internal politics at a specific time. Furthermore, Table 3 suggests that internal forces have been more important post-Civil War, particularly in the 20th century. During this time, Arkansas has seen the influence of populist distrust on selection changes, and has also seen the increasing influence and professionalization of legal elites.

One may have expected that populist sentiments would have had more consistent influence. Instead, in this analysis we could only identify a few occasions where citizens' distrust of political and legal elites seemed to play a role: 1864, 1874, 1970, and 1980. In each of these cases, this force served as a conservative force by inhibiting change (as in 1970 and 1980) and by keeping more power in the hands of citizens who, on the whole, tend to distrust the government and prefer the traditional way of doing things.

Based on this analysis, what might we say about the influences on judicial selection changes overall? While we see that both external and internal forces have influenced selection processes, they do not seem to have had equal influence. Indeed, external trends have been more consistent across time. Moreover, it appears that while internal forces did play a role, external forces (namely, policy diffusion trends) narrowed the viable alternatives to a select few. Thus, we can say that the influence of internal forces was limited by external forces. Additionally, internal forces have served as a catalyst or an inhibitor for change. This is particularly true of citizens' populist distrust of political elites.

Conclusion: Beyond Amendment 80

This paper has mapped the changes to Arkansas' methods of judicial selection from 1836 to the present and has explored several propositions about the potential causes of those changes. We have argued that both external and internal forces have influenced judicial selection mechanisms, though they have done so unequally. Specifically, constitution sharing and national or regional trends in public opinion—or external forces—have limited the viable judicial selection options. Of course, the analysis here is limited in its conclusiveness and generalizability. Hopefully future scholarship on this question will take a more empirical approach that looks at the changes in several states over time.

In Arkansas and across the nation, we know that judicial selection reform is generating great discussion. This article can offer two insights to scholars, lawmakers, and citizens who are interested in judicial selection reform. First, with respect to the diffusion of merit selection across the states, Arkansas is playing the roles of both laggard and leader.[75] When considered nationally, Arkansas is without doubt a laggard state, despite efforts by legal elites throughout the 20th century to adopt the Missouri Plan. However, when one looks at Arkansas and a small group of her peer states that once belonged to the Confederacy (Alabama, Florida, Georgia, Louisiana, Mississippi, North Carolina, South Carolina, Tennessee, Texas, and Virginia), Arkansas could be considered an adoption leader. To date, only Florida and Tennessee have adopted merit selection for their supreme and appellate courts. Assuming merit selection is adopted in Arkansas and subsequently begins to diffuse to these other peer states, scholars should take a second look at traditional regional networks of diffusion.[76] And secondly, both proponents and opponents of selection changes should remain cognizant of the past effects of citizens' populist distrust of political and legal elites on judicial selection changes—or the lack thereof. If reform efforts in the 20th century are any guide, the people may be hesitant to adopt any system that is heavily controlled by legal and political elites.

CHAPTER 12

A Practitioner's Guide to Arkansas's New Judicial Article

LARRY BRADY AND J. D. GINGERICH

In introducing this selection in its original form, the editors of the University of Arkansas at Little Rock Law Review wrote "The passage of Amendment 80 on November 7, 2000, was a watershed event in the history of the Judicial Department of this state. Jurisdictional lines that previously forced cases to be divided artificially and litigated separately in different courts were eliminated. This fundamental change naturally brings with it a whole host of issues, both theoretical and practical, concerning the form and structure of our court system."[1] The fusion of the state's two trial-level courts was only one of several changes included in the voters' overhaul of the judicial article of the Arkansas Constitution; others included removing political party labels from judicial elections, lengthening the terms of office for prosecuting attorneys, and consolidating the many layers and kinds of local level courts. In this short essay on Arkansas's early efforts to implement Amendment 80, Brady and Gingerich illuminate the challenge of carrying the state's overhauled judicial branch into operation. Even today, stable funding for local-level "district" courts and further reform to judicial selection remain matters regularly discussed in Arkansas.

On November 7, 2000, members of the Arkansas bench and bar and other interested citizens completed an odyssey which had begun more than thirty years earlier to bring comprehensive change to the state's court system.[2] Similar efforts had been attempted but defeated by the voters or the Arkansas General Assembly in 1970,[3] 1980,[4] 1991,[5] and 1995.[6]

While the effort to study and draft the new proposal and secure its passage was the result of substantial contributions, both personal and financial,

Originally published in *University of Arkansas at Little Rock Law Review* 24 (2002): 715–26. Reprinted with permission.
DOI: https://doi.org/10.34053/parry2019.riapag2.12

by the Arkansas bench and bar, the ultimate passage of Amendment 80 by such a large majority of the voters came as a surprise to both the supporters and detractors of the amendment. Due to a history of so many failed attempts, the large number of other items that appeared on the election ballot,[7] and the tendency of Arkansas voters to defeat long and complicated ballot measures, most were surprised by the successful outcome.

One result of this tendency to expect that the amendment would be defeated was a failure to prepare for its success. Neither the Arkansas Bar Association and the Arkansas Judicial Council, the main supporters of the amendment, nor the Arkansas Supreme Court, the body primarily responsible for its implementation, performed any serious work to plan for or study the actions that would be necessary in the event of the amendment's passage. In light of what was, in retrospect, a very short period between passage and implementation,[8] this failure to plan for the next steps, while understandable, made the implementation process much more difficult.

Despite this lack of preparation, a considerable amount of work has been done to implement the changes. The Arkansas Supreme Court has promulgated a number of administrative orders and rule changes, and the Arkansas General Assembly has adopted a package of legislation. This article begins by explaining the process that the supreme court has established for the implementation of Amendment 80. Next, it describes the new trial court structure that Amendment 80 created. The new rules regarding court administration, pleading, and practice are covered next. Finally, the article notes some of the unresolved issues that the supreme court and the bar will face as implementation of Amendment 80 continues.

The Process and Timing of Implementation

When the voters approved Amendment 80, the Arkansas Supreme Court recognized that it had the primary responsibility to implement it.[9] Within three weeks following passage, the supreme court appointed a nine-member committee ("the Committee") to oversee the implementation process.[10] The Committee immediately held a series of meetings and began to adopt both a short-term and long-term strategy for Amendment 80's implementation. The Committee determined that, with Arkansas's biennial session of the general assembly beginning in less than one month, the consideration of necessary action by the legislative branch should be the first order of business. The Committee considered and ultimately endorsed a package of legislation that was proposed to the general assembly. The proposals that were ultimately signed into law included a clarification of the qualification of justices and judges,[11] the repeal of all statutes relating to the Court of Common Pleas,[12] a designation for election purposes of each of the divisions of trial courts,[13] an amendment to various provisions of the juvenile code,[14] and a comprehensive act setting out the process for nonpartisan judicial elections.[15]

While the general assembly was considering this legislation, the Committee continued to review action to be taken by the supreme court. The central recommendation concerned the structure of trial court administration and the management of cases, resulting in the supreme court's adoption of Administrative Order No. 14, issued on April 6, 2001.[16] The Court also received recommendations from its Committee on Civil Practice and Committee on Criminal Practice. As a result, the court revised each of its administrative orders that were affected by Amendment 80[17] and adopted amendments to the Rules of Civil Procedure and the Inferior Court Rules,[18] the Rules of Criminal Procedure,[19] the Rules of Appellate Procedure-Civil and the Rules of the Supreme Court,[20] and, most recently, a new rule to allow for the certification of questions of Arkansas law to the supreme court by any federal court of the United States.[21]

During the process of study and review by the Amendment 80 Committee, it became clear that the full implementation of Amendment 80 by the time of its effective date, July 1, 2001, was next to impossible. The Committee noted that county governments, which were responsible for funding most of the operations of Arkansas trial courts, operated on a calendar year budget. Computer software programs would need to be reprogrammed, printed docket books and other court forms would have to be revised, some modifications in physical facilities might be required, and judges, lawyers, and court personnel would have to be educated. As a result, the supreme court, based upon the recommendation of the Committee, established the first of two transition periods.

For the period July 1, 2001, through December 31, 2001, all judges are circuit judges and may hear any type of case, but during this period of transition, circuit judges shall continue to be assigned the types of cases each was being assigned prior to the effective date of Amendment 80 of the Arkansas Constitution.[22]

The result of the court's order was that, during the transition period from July 1, 2001, through December 31, 2001, the circuit court became the unified court of general jurisdiction. Chancery and probate courts ceased to exist.[23] As to the filing and management of cases, however, judges continued to hear the same type of cases they previously had heard.[24] The court's dockets remained in place, and the required cover sheets from pre-Amendment 80 days continued to be used. By June 1, 2001, judges in each of the judicial circuits submitted the plans for court administration for their circuits, as required by Administrative Order No. 14. On June 28, 2001, the supreme court adopted the plans. In its consideration and review of the plans, however, the court found that several practical issues and substantive public policy questions needed answers before a full implementation of Amendment 80 and its purpose was possible. As a result, the court established a second period of transition from January 1, 2002, until July 1, 2003, during which all of the provisions of Amendment 80 would be in force, but evaluation and refinement of the procedures could also take place.

In formulating their administrative plans, the judicial circuits have recognized that the Arkansas judiciary is in a transitional stage. We have considered this fact in passing judgment on their proposed plans. Identifying these practical problems at the front end will hopefully permit the general assembly, as well as county quorum courts, to work with us in formulating answers to these issues, including the appropriation of necessary funding. Thus, we believe that a realistic target date for completing implementation of the new unified court system should be July 1, 2003. On that date, we expect all circuit judges to be available to try all "justiciable matters."[25]

Trial Court Structure

With the passage of Amendment 80, Arkansas voters reduced the number of states with separate law and equity jurisdiction from four to three, and joined the majority of states that have each created a unified court of general jurisdiction.[26] As of July 1, 2001, all Arkansas courts became circuit courts and all chancery and circuit/chancery judges became circuit judges.[27] There is no longer a division between law and equity jurisdiction. A judge hearing a case has full authority to dispose of any and all issues in the case.

As of January 1, 2002, the supreme court also mandated the establishment of five subject matter divisions in each circuit court. They are criminal, civil, juvenile, probate, and domestic relations.[28] The court outlined the scope and purposes of these divisions as follows:

> A circuit judge shall at all times have the authority to hear all matters within the jurisdiction of the circuit court and has the affirmative duty to do so regardless of the designation of divisions. . . .

The designation of divisions is for the purpose of judicial administration and caseload management and is not for the purpose of
subject-matter jurisdiction. The creation of divisions shall in no
way limit the powers and duties of the judges as circuit judges.
Judges shall not be assigned exclusively to a particular division so
as to preclude them from hearing other cases which may come
before them.[29]

Court Administration

One of the major unanswered questions raised by Amendment 80's adoption is the nature and structure of the administration of the trial court.
Arkansas has little, if any, history of trial court administration. The lack of
state and local resources for personnel and a long tradition and expectation
by trial judges that they will operate their courts in an autonomous fashion
have created a wide variation in the level and nature of administration from
circuit to circuit. With the removal of chancery and probate courts and an
expansion of jurisdictional authority for all judges, a new system is required.
Who or what should determine the types of cases a particular judge will
hear? In multi-judge circuits, how are decisions made? Should the system
be uniform from circuit to circuit? The specific language of Amendment 80
did not answer these and many other questions.

Shortly after the approval of Amendment 80, the Director of the
Administrative Office of the Courts contacted the National Center for State
Courts for an evaluation of the amendment and a recommendation on the
issues that would need to be addressed for successful implementation. This
report identified the establishment of a plan for trial court administration
as the central issue for any successful implementation:

> The major issue will be creating an administrative structure. . . .
> The judicial article brings about organizational unification and
> some degree of administrative unification. The problem is that the
> Supreme Court cannot manage a statewide court system from Little
> Rock. The best the high court can do is set guidelines and policies.
> There has to be a local system of judicial administration or the
> reform will flounder. There is no unified court system in the United
> States without local administrative judges, and some of these judges
> are supported by court administrators. With two sets of elected
> clerks, the circuit courts will already have problems of administrative

cohesion, not to mention the consolidation of various courts that were formerly separate from one another. It is hard to envision how this can be done through en banc administration. . . . .[30]

The Amendment 80 Committee faced this issue early in its deliberations and received a significant amount of input from judges, clerks, and other court officials. It became clear to the Committee, as evidenced by its recommendation to the supreme court, that the role of the supreme court should not be one of becoming involved in the day-to-day affairs of the trial court administration; rather, the supreme court should establish a uniform set of overriding goals and principles which should form the basis of each circuit's administrative structure. In this way, each circuit takes into account significant local issues or customs. The procedure adopted by the supreme court to carry out this role was the creation of local administrative plans. Administrative Order No. 14 required each multi-judge judicial circuit to submit a plan for circuit court administration to the supreme court by June 1, 2001.[31] In the plan, the circuit judges were required to set out the process by which they will determine case management and administrative procedures. All of the judges must unanimously agree on the manner in which decisions will be reached under the plan, but the decision-making structure agreed upon does not require unanimity for subsequent decisions. For example, the judicial circuit could hold periodic meetings among the judges with a majority, super-majority, or unanimity being required to bind the circuit. Alternatively, an administrative judge or an administrative committee could be established. In other words, the supreme court did not require any particular decision-making structure, but only that the structure adopted at the local level be clear and in writing.[32]

The heart of the plan is a policy on case assignment and allocation. Administrative Order No. 14 requires the following:

> The plan shall describe the process for the assignment of cases and shall control the assignment and allocation of cases in the judicial circuit. In the absence of good cause to the contrary, the plan of assignment of cases shall assume (i) random selection of unrelated cases; (ii) a substantially equal apportionment of cases among the circuit judges of a judicial circuit; and (iii) all matters connected with a pending or supplemental proceeding will be heard by the judge to whom the matter was originally assigned.[33]

Pursuant to the requirements of Administrative Order No. 14, judges in twenty-one judicial circuits submitted their proposed administrative plans to the court. Four judicial circuits were single-judge circuits, and did not have to submit a plan.[34] Three judicial circuits could not agree on a plan to submit.[35] The plans submitted offered a wide range of methods of case administration and case distribution. In some cases, a new position as administrative judge was designated. In others, a system of rotation between divisions was established. These variations were, to some extent, a result of the very different circumstances that existed from circuit to circuit.

On June 28, 2001, the supreme court issued a per curiam order in which it announced its decision on each plan.[36] Sixteen of the twenty-one submitted plans were approved, although the court required two of these circuits to provide clarification on or before August 15, 2001.[37] Five plans were rejected, primarily for their continuation of the distinction between law and equity cases in their case assignment plan.[38] These circuits were ordered to submit amended plans to the court on or before August 15, 2001. Each of these circuits ultimately had its plans approved. In the three circuits where no agreement was reached and no plan was submitted, the supreme court developed a plan for each circuit and appointed an administrative judge to implement the plan.

Because the administrative plans set out the types of cases that each judge will hear and the method for case allocation and management within each circuit, these are important documents that any practicing attorney should review. The plans must be filed in the office of each circuit clerk; copies are available through the Arkansas Judiciary Web site.[39]

Pleading and Practice

Effective July 1, 2001, all pleadings filed in the circuit courts should be styled "In the Circuit Court of County." The pleading should be so styled even if it is the continuation of a matter that had previously been filed in a chancery or probate court.[40] As of January 1, 2002, when a case is filed, it will be assigned to one of the five subject matter divisions of circuit court: criminal, civil, probate, domestic relations or juvenile. Pursuant to Administrative Order No. 8, a cover sheet must accompany all initial filings. There is a separate cover sheet for each of the divisions. Because of the expanded jurisdiction of the circuit court, it is possible that there could be issues in a pleading that would allow it to be filed in more than one division. In this case, the administrative order provides: "If a complaint asserts multiple claims which involve different subject matter divisions of the circuit court, the cover sheet for that division which is most definitive of the nature of the case should be selected and completed."[41] To commence an action, the attorney or pro se litigant filing the initial pleading is responsible for the completion of the filing information on the appropriate cover sheet. The court clerk cannot accept the pleading unless the reporting form accompanies it.[42]

Cover sheets take on a greater importance in the Amendment 80 environment. Because there are no longer separate chancery and probate courts through which to filter cases, all cases are filed in circuit court. In order for the clerk to understand the type of case and to properly assign the case to the appropriate judge, the clerk will have to rely on the information contained in the cover sheets.[43]

When a case is filed, it will be docketed pursuant to Administrative Order No. 2. Cases shall be assigned the letter prefix corresponding to that docket and a number in the order of filing. Beginning with the first case filed each year, cases shall be numbered consecutively in each docket category with the four digits of the current year followed by a hyphen and the number assigned to the case beginning with the number "1." For example: criminal CR2002–1, civil CV2002–1, probate PR2002–1, domestic relations DR2002–1, juvenile JV2002–1.[44]

Circuit clerks then assign the cases to particular circuit judges based upon the provision of the circuit's administrative plan. One complicating factor in the process of filing cases has to do with "where" the pleading is to be filed, that is, which clerk is responsible for receiving and filing the court record. Arkansas's circuit and county clerks are constitutional officers,[45] but Amendment 80 did not amend or repeal any of the constitutional language regarding clerks. The role of each clerk is, at best, unclear after Amendment 80's abolishment of probate court, which had been the responsibility of the county clerk.[46] The supreme court received a recommendation from its Committee on Civil Practice that the circuit clerk be designated as the sole clerk for all circuit court matters, eliminating any role for the probate clerk. The Supreme Court Committee on Amendment 80 also debated this issue. As this discussion took place, the Association of County Clerks pursued legislation before the 2001 General Assembly, which eventually enacted Act 997 of 2001.[47] The act provides that if the supreme court creates a probate division, then the county clerk will continue to serve as the clerk for the probate division. The act designates the county clerk as the ex officio clerk of the probate division of circuit court. When the supreme court eventually adopted the probate division as one of the five divisions of circuit court in Administrative Order No. 14, this statutory role for the county clerk became effective. However, because the five subject matter divisions did not go into effect until January, 2002, a gap existed in the statutory responsibility of county clerks. A transitional provision added to Rule 3 of the Arkansas Rules of Civil Procedure remedied this gap. This provision states that for the period of July 1, 2001, through December 31, 2001, probate matters shall continue to be filed with the same clerk for such matters as were filed prior to July 1, 2001.[48] Administrative Order No. 8 now incorporates this notion:

> Court Clerk means the elected circuit clerk . . . except in the event probate matters are required by law to be filed in the office of the county clerk, then the term clerk shall also include the county clerk for this limited purpose.[49]

Unfinished Business

Much has been accomplished in the sixteen months since passage of Amendment 80, but the implementation of Amendment 80 is an evolving process. Decisions that have been made may need to be reconsidered,[50] and questions that have not yet been asked will need to be answered. Some issues can be resolved by legislation or court rule while others will be decided in the context of appellate court decisions. Issues that are currently on the table include the implementation by January 1, 2005, of the new district court system,[51] and the appointment of masters, referees, and magistrates.[52]

Some of the more vexing of the unresolved issues are those which were raised by the supreme court in its June 28, 2001, per curiam order.[53] One question that confronted the court in weighing the merits of the various plans was how a judge's experience and specialization should be balanced with the potential for burnout as a factor in the assignment and allocation of cases.[54] Another issue was the matter of juvenile proceedings and whether they should be treated differently from other cases. The court took note of the "state apparatus" related to these proceedings, "such as the prosecutors, public defenders, probation officers, DHS attorneys and caseworkers, attorneys ad litem, CASA volunteers, intake officers, and so forth."[55]

Is it necessary or desirable to keep these types of cases segregated in order for the system to operate efficiently? If so, should there be a regular rotation system whereby a circuit judge may be assigned to the juvenile or criminal division of circuit court for a specified period of time, at the end of which he or she would be assigned to other cases?[56]

The court also expressed concern over the practical issues related to facilities, staff, and education.

Even if all the theoretical questions were answered, we could not immediately implement the necessary changes because of time and financial constraints. We must allow time for incumbent and newly-elected circuit judges to participate in judicial education programs to train them in areas of the law with which they are not as familiar since all such judges must become available to try any type of case.[57]

These issues remain unresolved, but will have to be addressed very soon to allow the 2003 General Assembly to enact necessary legislation and to meet the court's directive for full implementation of Amendment 80 by 2003.

Conclusion

With the adoption of Amendment 80, the Arkansas judicial system has experienced comprehensive and fundamental change. While many of the basic structural issues were made clear by the language of the amendment, numerous other important issues were not. The supreme court and its committees and the members of the circuit court bench have accomplished an extraordinary amount during a short period of time. It is incumbent upon the bench and bar, however, to become familiar with both the changes that have been wrought and the issues that have yet to be addressed in order to successfully implement Arkansas's new judicial article.

CHAPTER 13

The Natural State in a Time of Change

A Survey-Based Analysis of State Party Organizations in Arkansas, 1999–2013

JOHN C. DAVIS

Arkansas' political environment has undergone considerable change over the last several election cycles, from one of Democratic Party dominance to one of Republican Party dominance. In 2019, Arkansas is now represented by Republicans in all six congressional offices, both state legislative chambers, and all state constitutional offices. In contrast, as recently as 2008, Democrats held five of six congressional seats, all seven state constitutional offices, and super majorities in the state legislature. This study compares survey data from a 1999 study to a 2013 examination of state party organizations to evaluate the changes that have taken place with regard to the operations and organizational strength of both state parties in a time of political change in the Natural State. The analysis reveals that changes undergone over this period by both state organizations resulted in stronger, more capable political parties. The author concludes with an explanation for the increased organizational strength exhibited by today's state parties in Arkansas: increased electoral competition.

Introduction

In 1999, Aldrich, Gomez, and Griffin conducted the "State Party Organizations Study."[1] This survey assessed the role of state party organizations in an increasingly candidate-centered environment. More recently, in 2013, Davis and Kurlowski sought to update and build upon this previous work to evaluate the changes that have taken place with regard to the

Originally published in *The Midsouth Political Science Review* 15, no. 2 (2014): 81–102. Reprinted with permission.
DOI: https://doi.org/10.34053/parry2019.riapag2.13

operations and organizational strength of state parties.[2] By comparing the results of these two surveys, this paper analyzes the Arkansas Democratic and Republican state party organizations over a period of significant change, from 1999 to 2013. The electoral success enjoyed by Arkansas Republicans over the last few election cycles is nothing less than historic. In addition to holding five of the six federal offices—as of 2014—Arkansas has a Republican majority in both state legislative chambers for the first time since Reconstruction. While it is beyond the scope of one paper to attempt to explain the Republican Party's recent electoral success, the question of whether or not the state party organizations have changed during this pivotal time is a puzzle worthy of consideration.

In addition to evaluating the changes these two state party organizations have undergone since the late 20th century to today, this paper addresses the organizational strength of these parties with a particular focus into their institutional characteristics, degree of coordination with their respective national committees, roles in campaign issue development, candidate recruitment, and candidate support. The more recently collected data used in this paper are derived from an ongoing survey concerning the organizational characteristics of state political parties.[3] Respondents from this most recent survey include the Democratic Party of Arkansas and the Republican Party of Arkansas. In order to assess the changes undergone in these two state party organizations, I report the survey results of each and compare the findings with those of Aldrich, Gomez, and Griffin.[4] Additionally, I use Dulio and Garrett's party organization strength index which enables me to assess the extent to which changes among these two party organizations have occurred since the late 1990s.[5]

Following my analyses of these two party organizations, I conclude that—according to the conventional measures of state party organizational strength—both parties have become stronger organizations over the last fifteen years. Finally, I offer an explanation for the increased organizational strength exhibited by both parties today: increased electoral competition in Arkansas. Consistent with existing literature, political developments have increased interparty competition in the state and pushed both state parties' organizations to enhance their abilities to support and assist their respective candidates.

State Party Organizations

Anthony Downs described a political party as a group of individuals seeking control of government collectively.[6] In order to achieve these ends, political parties—seeking strength in numbers and the advantages of pooled resources—form party organizations. James Q. Wilson contended that political party organizations in the United States were decentralized, since most elected offices and political resources are found at the local and state-levels.[7] Additionally, Wilson suggested governmental reforms of the 20th century had reduced the benefits such organizations had once offered in the form of patronage. This—along with a growing middle class—had resulted in weaker state and local level organizations. At the time, Wilson's assessment was a common one among the discipline as political scientists continued to observe lower voter turnout, increased ticket-splitting, and a decline in self-reported partisan identification among the public in the 1970s.[8] These factors led many to suggest that American party organizations were waning in strength. However, John Bibby in 1979 found evidence suggesting that the national organizations for the Democratic and Republican parties had actually strengthened over this time.[9] Likewise, other scholars provided evidence to the contrary at the state and local levels.[10] Around this same time, Xandra Kayden and Eddie Mahe Jr. proposed that a growing reliance upon professional staff—among state and national party organizations—and the rise of political action committees had strengthened state party organizations.[11] Overall, scholarship in the 1970s and 1980s showed that states' party organizations' strength—measured most often by operating budget, number of paid staff, and institutional capacity—had become stronger as they adapted to their changing environments.

Specifically, Cotter et al.'s *Party Organizations in American Politics* provided evidence to suggest state party organizations had become stronger in the 1960s and 1970s—directly refuting the conventional wisdom of the day.[12] In addition, their survey-based effort to describe and assess the bureaucratic characteristics of state party organizations became the method of choice for ensuing studies on the topic. In 1999, Aldrich and his colleagues' examination of state party organizations allowed for cross-sectional comparisons with Cotter et al.'s study and have served as a model for the most recent survey effort by which this paper's data are collected.[13]

1999 STATE PARTY ORGANIZATION SURVEY

In 1999, Aldrich, Gomez, and Griffin facilitated a survey-based study of state party organizations.[14] Reaching out to all one hundred major state party organizations, the study boasted a 64% response rate. Survey questionnaires were mailed specifically to state party chairs. Aldrich and his colleagues' effort was a useful update to Cotter et al.'s work and accounted for the condition of state party organizations leading up to the 21st century.[15]

Unlike the data collected by Cotter and his colleagues, this survey's state-identifiable results are publicly available.[16] The 1999 study reported data which had been collected over the course of several years.

2013 STATE PARTY ORGANIZATION SURVEY

In late 2013, Davis and Kurlowski began distributing an updated state organizational survey in order to assess changes which had taken place over the nearly fifteen years since the effort by Aldrich, Gomez, and Griffin.[17] Unlike the earlier study, the questions for this survey were not directed to any one staff member of the state party organization—enabling state chairpersons, executive directors, or anyone else knowledgeable and authorized to participate in the survey.[18] While some of the surveys were conducted over the phone, the majority of responses were completed online using Qualtrics. It is important to note that despite the differences in survey delivery systems, the question wording was identical. The Republican Party of Arkansas' survey was conducted over the phone while the Arkansas Democratic Party's was online. As was agreed before the administering of each survey, the names and positions of the individuals who participated remain anonymous. The survey codebook is provided in Appendix 1.

Institutional Characteristics

Existing literature on state parties examine their institutional characteristics as a means to more fully understand the day to day operations and assess organizational strength. Additionally, these details might also offer insight into the priorities and purpose of these institutions. The following reports the findings from the 2013 survey, and assesses the changes in the institutional characteristics of Arkansas' state party organizations.

The respondent for the Democratic Party of Arkansas reported that the organization's chairperson serves at a full-time capacity, but does not receive a salary. Earlier, in the Aldrich, Gomez, and Griffin study, the position was reported to have been a part-time position.[19] In 2013, the chair position remained term-limited. Regarding office staff, the party currently maintains a public relations director and a full-time executive director. As of 2013, the Democratic Party of Arkansas reported employing a field staff, conducting direct mail fund-raising, operating "get out the vote" (GOTV) programs, and conducting public opinion surveys all in the last year. In terms of party contributions to different campaigns for state and congressional office, the party reported giving to all levels except local positions—consistent with the party's reported contribution behavior in 1999.

Another aspect of the survey which addresses the institutional characteristics of the state party office is the staff and budget differential between
election years and non-election years. During election years, the Democratic
Party of Arkansas reported in 2013 an estimated budget of $3.5 million and
a staff of seventy-three employees (seventy full-time, three part-time). In a
year which no regular elections are held, the party cuts back significantly
with a budget estimation of $750,000 and a staff of six. The scaling down
during non-election years is consistent with the average calculated from all
respondents for the 2013 survey.

The Democratic Party of Arkansas reported one of the highest numbers
of election-year staff of any participating state party organization in the
Davis and Kurlowski survey.[20] The discrepancy in election year funding
and staffing to that of non-election years offers insight into the priorities
and purpose of the organization and is worth closer investigation. The
dramatic increase in reported election year staff is—in part—explained by
the Democratic Party of Arkansas' use of a coordinated campaign. The
Democratic Party's respondent offered the following regarding the coordinated campaign,

> The Party operates a coordinated campaign in election year [sic]
> which campaigns buy into [sic] but it's normally not included in the
> campaign budget. They raise money for the coordinated campaign
> and then gain the benefits of a strong coordinated campaign.[21]

This coordinated effort between the party organization and its candidates explains the high number of election year staff reported in the
2013 survey (seventy-three total)—as these individuals serve to assist those
Democratic candidates who invest in the coordinated campaign. In addition, the fact that candidates reportedly "buy into" the coordinated campaign suggests their own investments into the program provide a portion of
support required for such an increase in election year staff.

Table 1 provides a comparison of the party's institutional characteristics
between the findings of the 2013 Davis and Kurlowski survey and the 1999
Aldrich, Gomez, and Griffin study.[22] In the earlier survey, the party reported
that it did not employ research staff or a public relations director. Apart
from the growth in staff over the last several years, the organization's budget
has also increased—a prerequisite for the dramatic increase in the number of
overall election-year staff. While a modest increase in reported non-election
year budget is reported between the two studies (just short of $700,000 in
1999—adjusting for inflation—to $750,000 in 2013), the party's election
year budget has dramatically increased from nearly $2.1 million—adjusted

for inflation—reported in 1999 to $3.5 million in 2013. The party now reports employing research staff and a public relations director—increasing its level of organizational sophistication. Additionally, the increased budget and staff during election years suggests strong electioneering efforts on behalf of the state party organization.

A representative for the Republican Party of Arkansas also provided information regarding the party's institutional characteristics, allowing for a comparison of the party today to the organization at the time of the Aldrich, Gomez, and Griffin study.[23]

The chair of the Republican Party of Arkansas is a paid, term limited, and full-time position. Unlike the Democratic Party's chair, who does not receive a salary, the Republican state organization most recently reported paying the chairperson between $50,000 and $75,000 annually. This is a change from what the organization reported in 1999. At the time of the Aldrich, Gomez, and Griffin study, the survey participant selected the answer option reading, "State party considered job part-time but it is actually full time."[24] At that time, the Republican Party chairperson did not receive a salary.

In 2013, the Republican Party of Arkansas reported that it contributes to all levels of state office and US Congress, but does not contribute to local races—a change from the organization's reported actions in 1999. The extent of involvement in contributing to different levels of office is of interest particularly given the changing nature of campaign contributions in American politics over the last several decades. Between the end of the "soft money" era and the proliferation of advocacy group spending, one might expect state party organization involvement in financial contributions to have changed since the 1990s.

Much like the Democratic organization, the Republican Party hired additional specialized staff since the earlier survey. In 2013, the party reported having a public relations director. A comparison of the party's reported election year budget to non-election year budget is not possible as the non-election amount was not reported. The reported non-election year budget in 1999 was $500,000 or—accounting for inflation—$699,150.66 at the time of the 2013 survey. Accounting for inflation, the reported election year budget appears to have increased only modestly from $2,097,451.98 in 1999 to approximately $2.2 million in 2013. The numbers of overall election year and non-election year staff did not change over this time period. Unlike the Democratic Party, the Republican Party did not report a change in the overall number of staff from election to non-election years. Table 2 provides

Democratic Party of Arkansas Institutional Characteristics

INSTITUTIONAL CHARACTERISTICS	DAVIS & KURLOWSKI (2013)	ALDRICH, GOMEZ, & GRIFFIN (1999)
Chair Position Full-time	Yes	No
Chair Position Term-Limited	Yes	—
State Party Chair Salaried	No	No
Annual Salary	—	—
Contributed to Governor	Yes	Yes
Contributed to Other Constitutional Offices	Yes	Yes
Contributed to Congressional Offices	Yes	Yes
Contributed to State Senator	Yes	Yes
Contribute to State Legislator	Yes	Yes
Contributed to County or Local Offices	No	No
Held Fund-raising Event	Yes	Yes
Direct Mail Fund-raising Program	Yes	Yes
Employed Research Staff	Yes	No
Employed Public Relations Dir.	Yes	No
Employed Full-time Executive Dir.	Yes	Yes
Employed Field Staff	Yes	Yes
Employed Comptroller/Bookkeeper	Yes	Yes
Conducted Campaign Seminars	Yes	Yes
Recruited Full Slate of Candidates	Yes	Yes
Publish Newspaper/Newsletter/Magazine	Yes	Yes
Operated Voter Registration Programs	Yes	No
Conducted Public Opinion Surveys	Yes	Yes
Typical Election Year Budget	$3.5 million	$2,097,451.98*
Typical Election Year Full-time Staff	70	8
Typical Election Year Part-time Staff	3	4
Typical Non-Election Year Budget	$750K	$699,150.66**
Typical Non-Election Year Full-time Staff	5	4
Typical Non-Election Year Part-time Staff	1	0

* In 1999, the Democratic Party of Arkansas' reported an election-year budget of $1.5 million. The amount presented in Table 1 adjusts for inflation (USD 2013).
**In 1999, the Democratic Party of Arkansas' reported a non-election year budget of $500,000. The amount presented in Table 1 adjusts for inflation (USD 2013).

TABLE 2:

Republican Party of Arkansas Institutional Characteristics

INSTITUTIONAL CHARACTERISTICS	DAVIS & KURLOWSKI (2013)	ALDRICH, GOMEZ, & GRIFFIN (1999)
Chair Position Full-time	Yes	No
Chair Position Term-Limited	Yes	—
State Party Chair Salaried	Yes	No
Annual Salary	$50K-75K	—
Contributed to Governor	Yes	Yes
Contributed to Other Constitutional Offices	Yes	Yes
Contributed to Congressional Offices	Yes	Yes
Contributed to State Senator	Yes	Yes
Contribute to State Legislator	Yes	Yes
Contributed to County or Local Offices	No	Yes
Held Fund-raising Event	Yes	Yes
Direct Mail Fund-raising Program	Yes	Yes
Employed Research Staff	No	Yes
Employed Public Relations Dir.	Yes	No
Employed Full-time Executive Dir.	Yes	Yes
Employed Field Staff	Yes	Yes
Employed Comptroller/Bookkeeper	No	Yes
Conducted Campaign Seminars	Yes	Yes
Recruited Full Slate of Candidates	Yes	Yes
Publish Newspaper/Newsletter/Magazine	Yes	Yes
Operated Voter Registration Programs	Yes	No
Conducted Public Opinion Surveys	Yes	Yes
Typical Election Year Budget	$2.2 million	$2,097,451.98*
Typical Election Year Full-time Staff	8	5
Typical Election Year Part-time Staff	0	3
Typical Non-Election Year Budget	—	$699,150.66**
Typical Non-Election Year Full-time Staff	4	3
Typical Non-Election Year Part-time Staff	0	1

* In 1999 the Republican Party of Arkansas reported an election-year budget of $1.5 million. The amount presented in Table 2 adjusts for inflation (USD 2013).
** In 1999, the Republican Party of Arkansas reported a non-election year budget of $500,000. The amount presented in Table 2 adjusts for inflation (USD 2013).

a comparison of the Republican Party's institutional characteristics between the findings of the 2013 and 1999 studies.

Both party organizations have changed somewhat with regard to institutional characteristics since the late 1990s. The Democratic Party of Arkansas reports a significantly larger election year budget and election year staff between the two surveys. The dramatic increases in election-year budget and staff is likely explained by the party's unique coordinated campaign effort whereby candidates reported "buy into" the effort in order to benefit from the sources of the party organization. While the survey data provide little insight into the direct relationship of budgetary capability and staffing, the increase in election-year staff reported by the Democratic Party strongly suggests a large portion of the organization's increased budget has funded the coordinated campaign effort. The Republican Party of Arkansas reports only slight changes in the number of staff and even less in regard to budget, but boasts a full-time, salaried chair and other traits of increased institutional sophistication including the addition of a public relations director. Overall, a comparison of institutional characteristics suggests each state organization is stronger today than they were at the end of the 20th century. The organization that has undergone the most change in regards to these measures is the Democratic Party of Arkansas.

Candidate Recruitment

Given that parties seek to gain control of government by winning elections, recruiting candidates for office is a natural role of any state party organization. While the literature on the topic continues to enhance our knowledge of alternative origins of candidate recruitment—such as groups of citizens and political elites and state legislative leaders, previous studies surveying those within party organizations report active involvement in recruiting.[25] However, the issue might suffer from response bias—as studies asking candidates to report the nature and extent to which state parties actively recruit individuals have called parties' involvement into question. Kazee and Thornberry raise doubts that state parties play particularly active roles in recruiting candidates for Congress, specifically.[26] Additional evidence of limited state party recruitment for seats in the US House, specifically, is found in Thomas Kazee's edited volume.[27] Thus, it is possible state party organizations overstate their involvement in recruiting efforts. With this caveat, I will report results from both state party organizations from the 2013 survey concerning candidate recruitment and compare them to the reported levels of involvement from the 1999 study (Table 3 and 4). Each survey respondent was prompted with the following question, "Please describe the level of involvement of the state party in recruiting candidates for the following offices as Active, Limited, or Not Involved."

In 1999, the Democratic Party of Arkansas reported active involvement in recruiting at all levels of government except for local and county offices. In 2013, the party's survey participant reported limited party involvement in recruiting for governor, and US Senate and active recruitment efforts for local and county offices. Why the change? It appears the party focused its attention on recruiting for offices highest on the ballot in 1999, but has since shifted the organization's attention more toward recruiting and culti-vating political talent at the local level. Term limits—enacted in the state in 1992—began to impact the Arkansas House and Senate in 1998 and 2000, respectively, and have likely directed more attention to recruiting state leg-islators over the last fifteen years.[28]

While the survey results from the state Democratic organization suggest a shift in recruiting efforts, the Republican Party of Arkansas, as reported in 2013, claims the same levels of involvement in candidate recruitment reported in the earlier Aldrich, Gomez, and Griffin study.[29] As it did before, the Republican Party reports active involvement at the gubernatorial level, other state constitutional offices, as well as all legislative levels, and reports limited involvement at the local and county level.

TABLE 3:
Democratic Party of Arkansas Involvement in Candidate Recruitment

CANDIDATE RECRUITMENT	DAVIS AND KURLOWSKI (2013)	ALDRICH, GOMEZ, AND GRIFFIN (1999)
Governor	Limited	Active
Other State Constitutional Offices	Active	Active
US House	Active	Active
US Senate	Limited	Active
State Legislator	Active	Active
Local and County Offices	Active	Limited

TABLE 4:
Republican Party of Arkansas Involvement
in Candidate Recruitment

CANDIDATE RECRUITMENT	DAVIS AND KURLOWSKI (2013)	ALDRICH, GOMEZ, AND GRIFFIN (1999)
Governor	Active	Active
Other State Constitutional Offices	Active	Active
US House	Active	Active
US Senate	Active	Active
State Legislator	Active	Active
Local and County Offices	Limited	Limited

Campaign Issue Development

One question asked by Aldrich and his colleagues in 1999 was, "During your tenure as state party chair, has the state party organization developed campaign issues or has this normally been left to the candidates?" This question was asked again by Davis and Kurlowski without specifically addressing the respective state party organization's chair.[30] In both surveys, the Democratic Party of Arkansas reported to jointly develop campaigns issues with candidates. The Republican state party organization reportedly left the development of campaign issues to their candidates in in 1999, but reported being jointly involved with the process in 2013.

Candidate Support

In addition to institutional characteristics, previous literature suggests the level of support a party organization provides its candidates is a function of its organizational strength.[31] Aldrich, Gomez, and Griffin asked party chairpersons to report whether or not they performed several electioneering and party-building activities with county party organizations.[32] However, Davis and Kurlowski sought to learn the extent of coordination between the state organization and its candidates.[33] Therefore, the 2013 survey question regarding candidate support read, "Has the state party organization participated in any of the following activities with candidates?" The difference in word usage from "county party organizations" to "candidates" could potentially produce different survey responses.

The results are presented for comparison in Table 5. Overall, both party organizations indicate providing more candidate support today than they did in 1999. The Democratic Party of Arkansas reported coordinating joint fund-raising, GOTV efforts, and voter registration drives with its candidates.[34] The Arkansas Republican Party reportedly carries out all four types of candidate support—as indicated in the 2013 survey.

TABLE 5:

Comparison of Reported Candidate/County Committee Support Activities

CANDIDATE SUPPORT	DAVIS AND KURLOWSKI (2013)		ALDRICH, GOMEZ, AND GRIFFIN (1999)	
	DEMOCRATIC PARTY OF AR	REPUBLICAN PARTY OF AR	DEMOCRATIC PARTY OF AR	REPUBLICAN PARTY OF AR
Shared Mailing Lists	No	Yes	Yes*	Yes*
Joint Fund-raising	Yes	Yes	No*	No*
Participated in GOTV	Yes	Yes	Yes*	Yes*
Voter Reg. Drives	Yes	Yes	No*	No*

Note: * indicates Aldrich et al. survey response to question regarding support offered to county committees

Coordination with National Committee

Many scholars reported increased collaboration between the two national parties and their respective state organizations.[35] Cotter et al. provided convincing cross-sectional evidence of state-national party integration.[36] However, the topic is complicated by interparty differences between Democratic and Republican committees. William Crotty asserts that—with regard to party rules concerning delegate selection—the Democratic Party reforms in the 1970s empowered the Democratic National Committee while diminishing the autonomy of the party's state organizations.[37] However, Longley warns against overstating the party centralization thesis.[38] Citing disputes related to national convention delegate selection, Gary Wekkin proposes these changes in the Democratic Party power structure created a "two-way street" conceptualized within Deil Wright's framework of inter-governmental relations.[39] Regarding the Republican Party, Bibby observes:

> Unlike the Democratic National Committee, which has asserted control over the presidential nominating process, the RNC has achieved increased power and an enlarged role in the political system by performing or supplementing the campaign functions previously thought to be the exclusive domain of state party or candidate organizations.[40]

Aldrich and his colleagues asked the state chairpersons how often they dealt with their respective National Committees on the following issues: federal appointments, speakers, assisting state candidates, fund-raising, national convention activities, and implementing national committee programs.[41] This same question was asked more broadly by Davis and Kurlowski and Table 6 and Table 7 report these surveys' results regarding this line of questioning for the Democratic Party of Arkansas and Republican Party of Arkansas, respectively.[42] While both surveys neglect the issue of organizational interactions concerning presidential nominations, specifically, much can be assessed from the data available.

The Democratic Party of Arkansas—in both surveys—reports regular coordination with the Democratic National Committee (DNC). The results of the 2013 survey suggest the existence of a lasting, integrated partnership between the state party organization and the DNC. With exception to federal appointments and patronage and the implementation of national committee programs, the state party reported to regularly coordinate with the DNC.

The earlier Aldrich, Gomez, and Griffin data report the Republican Party of Arkansas never coordinated with the Republican National Committee (RNC) regarding federal appointments.[43] While the party reported to regularly reach out to the RNC to gain assistance for state candidates and general fund-raising, the state party only occasionally worked with the organization to obtain political speakers, assist in the implementation of RNC committee programs, and coordinate national convention activities.

Overall, the state party's responses to the same questions posed in 2013 suggests increased levels of coordination. Most recently, the Republican Party of Arkansas reported to occasionally coordinate with the RNC concerning federal appointments and patronage and fund-raising. Additionally, the state organization now reports regularly working with the RNC to obtain speakers (at the time of the interview, the survey respondent volunteered that the

TABLE 6:
Democratic Party of Arkansas' Coordination
with the National Committee

COORDINATION WITH NATIONAL COMMITTEE	DAVIS AND KURLOWSKI (2013)	ALDRICH, GOMEZ, AND GRIFFIN (1999)
Federal Appointments	Never	Occasionally
Speakers	Regularly	Regularly
Assisting State Candidates	Regularly	Occasionally
Fund-raising	Regularly	Regularly
National Convention	Regularly	Regularly
Implementing Nat'l Cmte. Programs	Occasionally	Regularly

TABLE 7:
Republican Party of Arkansas' Coordination
with the National Committee

COORDINATION WITH NATIONAL COMMITTEE	DAVIS AND KURLOWSKI (2013)	ALDRICH, GOMEZ, AND GRIFFIN (1999)
Federal Appointments	Occasionally	Never
Speakers	Regularly	Occasionally
Assisting State Candidates	Regularly	Regularly
Fund-raising	Occasionally	Regularly
National Convention	Regularly	Occasionally
Implementing Nat'l Cmte. Programs	Regularly	Occasionally

state party was hosting Sen. Rand Paul of Kentucky), assist state candidates, implement RNC programs, and participate in national convention activities. In short, a comparison of these two surveys suggests an increased interdependence between the RNC and the state party organization—circumstantial evidence in support of Bibby's earlier conclusion.[44]

Party Organization Strength

Existing literature on party organizations assesses strength based largely on the institution's characteristics and ability to provide resources to their candidates. It is believed that stronger state party organizations possess the institutional capacities to attain their electoral ends. Using the Aldrich, Gomez, and Griffin survey data, Dulio and Garrett created an index of state party organizational strength.[45] In their study, responses from what I have categorized as institutional characteristics, candidate recruitment, and candidate support were each given a value of 0 or 1, where the combined minimum score of overall organizational strength was 0 out of 15 and a maximum score was 15 out of 15. Based on the Aldrich, Gomez, and Griffin survey data, the Democratic Party of Arkansas scored a 9 out of 15 and the Republican Party of Arkansas scored a 10 out of 15 when surveyed in 1999.[46]

Using the 2013 survey data and assessing the two state party organizations on the same criteria as Dulio and Garrett, the Democratic Party of Arkansas scores 13 out of 15 and the Republican Party of Arkansas scores 15 out of 15.[47] A simple quantification, Dulio and Garrett's index allows me to compare the organizational strength of these two parties in two points in time.[48] The results provide further evidence that both state parties are stronger organizations today than they were at the close of the 20th century.

Conclusion

Much can be gleaned by comparing the data from these two state party organization surveys. A great deal has changed in Arkansas' political landscape since the Aldrich, Gomez, and Griffin study.[49] The Republican Party of Arkansas has enjoyed unprecedented success in the state over the last few elections. As recently as 2008, the party had difficulty convincing viable candidates to challenge incumbent congressional Democrats. As of fall 2014, five of the state's six congressional seats are held by Republicans. Similar success has also been enjoyed at the state legislative level. The goal of this paper has been to address what, if any, changes have occurred to the state's party organizations over this time.

The survey analysis I have presented leads me to conclude that the Democratic Party of Arkansas and Republican Party of Arkansas have each strengthened in terms of staffing, budget size—to varying degrees, and organizational sophistication. The Democratic Party's reported increase in election year budget and overall election year staff is the most noteworthy change between the Aldrich, Gomez, and Griffin and Davis and Kurlowski surveys.[50] The increase appears to be explained by the organization's utilization of a coordinated campaign effort whereby candidates collaborate in order to collectively benefit from the resources of the party. I can also report that both parties appear to have increased their means of candidate support. While some may see the Democratic Party of Arkansas' self-reported decrease in candidate recruitment at the gubernatorial, and US Senate levels as evidence of lost influence in the political processes of state politics, I believe it is more likely the case that term limits—which were applied to state legislators in the late 1990s—have prompted more focus on recruitment for these impacted positions. Despite term limits taking effect, the Republican state organization reports being actively involved in all levels of candidate recruitment with the exception of local and county offices. Of course, as previously stated, findings regarding party organization involvement in recruiting need to be presented with caution, as previous studies on candidate recruitment suggest the possibility of response bias.

Can the electoral gains by Republicans, resulting in increased two-party competition, indirectly explain the increased party organizational strength exhibited by both state party organizations? It is easy to assume the Arkansas Republican Party's state organization has gained in its ability to assist its candidates for office over the last fifteen years. It is perhaps more difficult to accept the idea that the Democratic Party of Arkansas has also improved in terms of organizational strength over the same time period, given the same recent political developments in the state. However, Dwaine Marvick once wrote, "In any electoral democracy, there are reasons why rival party organizations in the same locality will look somewhat alike. There are functional grounds for expecting considerable performance symmetry."[51] Since the Aldrich, Gomez, and Griffin survey, the Democratic Party has not only increased its election-year budget, but dramatically retooled its electioneering efforts which have resulted in a significantly larger number of election year staff via the coordinated campaign.[52] This paper provides an additional case in support for previous studies which have reported a positive relationship between state two-party electoral competition and organizational sophistication.[53]

The Republican Party's recent state-level electoral gains have increased interparty competition in Arkansas. Austin Ranney wrote that southern states, such as Arkansas, in the middle 20th century, possessed moderate to weak party systems.[54] This lack of party strength in the region is attributed to the long-term Democratic Party domination in southern states. V.O. Key writes that the region was almost entirely Democratic and, despite strong interparty factions, southern states were dominated by Democratic politics.[55] This one-party domination led to unorganized Democratic Party and non-existent Republican Party structures until the 1960s.[56] Over the last three decades, several southern states have experienced increased two-party competition. Sarah Morehouse and Malcolm Jewell contend this increase has resulted in more disciplined and capable parties.[57] This paper is not intended as an empirical test of the relationship between organizational strength and intraparty competition. However, the reported changes undergone by Arkansas' Democratic and Republican state party organizations over the last fifteen years provide circumstantial evidence supporting previous studies on this relationship—particularly among other southern states.

Appendix 1: Survey Codebook

1. State of respondent

2. Party of respondent
   0=Democratic; 1=Republican

3. Is the job of State Party Chair a full or part time position?
   0=Part-time; 1=State party considers job part-time but is actually full-time; 2=Full-time

4. Is the job of State Party Chair a term limited position?
   0=No; 1=Yes

5. Is the job of State Party Chair Salaried?
   0=No; 1=Yes

6. What is the annual salary?
   0=Below $10,000; 1=$10,000–$20,000; 2=$20,000–$30,000;
   3=$30,000–$40,000; 4=$40,0000–$50,000;
   5=$50,000–$75,000; 6=$75,000–$100,000; 7=Above $100,000

7. Does the State Party currently make contributions to the campaigns of any of the following candidates:
   a. Governor—0=No; 1=Yes
   b. State Constitutional Offices—0=No; 1=Yes
   c. US House—0=No; 1=Yes
   d. US Senate—0=No; 1=Yes
   e. State Legislature—0=No; 1=Yes
   f. County or Local Offices—0=No; 1=Yes

8. What percent of the campaign budget of these offices comes from party funds in the typical election?
   a. Governor:
   b. State Constitutional Offices:
   c. US House:
   d. US Senate:
   e. State Legislature:
   f. County or Local Offices:

9. Which of the following items describe the State Party organization during recent years?
   a. Held at least one major fundraising event per year—0=No; 1=Yes
   b. Operated a direct mail fundraising program— 0=No; 1=Yes
   c. Employed research staff at headquarters—0=No; 1=Yes
   d. Employed a PR director—0=No; 1=Yes
   e. Employed Executive Director—0=No; 1=Yes
   f. Is the job of Executive Director full-time or part-time?— 0=Part-time; 1=Full-time
   g. Employed a field staff—0=No; 1=Yes
   h. Employed a Comptroller or Bookkeeper—0=No; 1=Yes
   i. Conducted campaign seminars for candidates and managers—0=No; 1=Yes
   j. Sought to recruit a full slate of candidates at the State, Congressional, and Courthouse Levels—0=No; 1=Yes
   k. Published a Party newsletter or magazine— 0=No; 1=Yes
   l. Operated Voter ID programs—0=No; 1=Yes
   m. Conducted or Commissioned public opinion surveys— 0=No; 1=Yes

10. During a typical election year and non-election year, please estimate the size (number of individuals) of the state party headquarters and the typical state party budget (in dollars).
    a. Election year full-time staff:
    b. Election year part-time staff:
    c. Election year budget:

    d. Non-election year full-time staff:

    e. Non-election year part-time staff:

    f. Non-election year part-time budget:

11. Which of the following best describes the party rule or practice of pre-primary endorsements currently?

    1=Pre-primary endorsements required by law;

    2=Pre-primary endorsements required by party rules;

    3=Pre-primary endorsements allowed by law;

    4=Pre-primary endorsements allowed by party rules;

    5=We do not make pre-primary endorsements but they are
allowed by rule or law;

    6=Pre-primary endorsements are not allowed by party rule;

    7=Pre-primary endorsements are not allowed by law

12. In an average election year, in how many races does the party
usually endorse a candidate?

1=0–25%; 2=25–50%; 3=50–75%; 4=75–100%

13. Could you please elaborate more on why the party does not
make pre-primary endorsements?

14. Have there been discussions within the party regarding
changing party rules or attempting to change state law regarding pre-primary endorsement rules?

15. Does the state regularly, occasionally, or never collaborate
with the National Committee on the following types of State
Party matters?

    a. Federal Appointments and Patronage—0=Never;
1=Occasionally; 2=Regularly

    b. Speakers—0=Never; 1=Occasionally; 2=Regularly

    c. Gaining Assistance for State Candidates—0=Never;
1=Occasionally; 2=Regularly

    d. Fund-raising—0=Never; 1=Occasionally; 2=Regularly

    e. National Convention Activities—0=Never; 1=Occasionally;
2=Regularly

f. Implementing National Committee Programs—o=Never;
    1=Occasionally; 2=Regularly

16. Has the State Party Organization developed campaign issues
    or has this normally been left to the candidates?
    o=Party develops issues; 1=Left to candidates;
    2=Joint party-candidate activity;
    3=Party and candidates operate separately

17. I will now read a list of offices. Please describe the level of
    involvement of the state party in recruiting candidates for the
    following offices as Active, Limited, or Not Involved.
    a. Governor—o=Not involved; 1=Limited; 2=Active
    b. Other State Constitutional Offices—o=Not involved;
        1=Limited; 2=Active
    c. US House—o=Not involved; 1=Limited; 2=Active
    d. US Senate—o=Not involved; 1=Limited; 2=Active
    e. State Legislature—o=Not involved; 1=Limited; 2=Active
    f. County and Local Offices—o=Not involved; 1=Limited;
        2=Active

18. Has the State Party Organization participated in any of the
    following activities with candidate?
    a. Shared mailing lists of contributors or party members—
        o=No; 1=Yes
    b. Conducted joint fundraising—o=No; 1=Yes
    c. Participated in get out the vote drives—o=No; 1=Yes
    d. Participated in registration drives—o=No; 1=Yes
    e. Other joint activities:

19. Do you have any other insights into the operation of your
    state party that you would like to share with us at this time?
    Also, if you would like to elaborate on any of your previous
    answers, feel free to leave those comments below.

CHAPTER 14

The Arkansas State Budget Process

A Unique and Reliable Approach

KIM U. HOFFMAN AND CATHERINE C. REESE

The budget process in the State of Arkansas is quite unusual, and little has been written about it. This essay discusses that process, including budgetary actors, their roles and responsibilities, key deadlines and outcomes, and more. The most distinctive aspect of the Arkansas budget process is the Revenue Stabilization Law. Prior research suggests that the main function of the Revenue Stabilization Law is to maintain the status quo and ensure that the state budget does not fall into deficit. Also, due to the state's ability to largely ride out national-level economic storms, some analysts have characterized the state's budgetary process as enviable.

Introduction

The budget decision is one of the most important policy decisions made by governors and state legislatures. Public budgets have many goals such as promoting the control and accountability of public funds, planning for the present and future, and enhancing the economy. Ultimately, creating the budget means setting priorities that represent the values of a state. Today, state budget decisions occur in an environment of conflict and uncertainty due to fiscal stress, political and ideological differences, institutional battles among the branches, the impact of federal government decisions, legal requirements, and public expectations for efficient and effective government operations. Public budgeting, unlike private sector budgeting, is more open and transparent. Public budgets are subject to intense public and media scrutiny and must adhere to the democratic process with participation from

DOI: https://doi.org/10.34053/parry2019.riapag2.14

many budget actors. Therefore, the process of making decisions regarding how public funding is obtained and allocated is the embodiment of politics, or who gets what, when, and how.[1] As Aaron Wildavsky stated in his seminal work on the politics of budgeting, "in the most integral sense the budget lies at the heart of the political process."[2]

In this challenging and uncertain environment, governors and legislatures spend a great deal of time on the budget decision. Most states now meet annually to make the budget decision, although that was not always the case. The long-term trend among all state governments has been to move from biennial budgets to annual budgets.[3] For many states, the transition to annual budget review grew out of the legislative reform movement of the 1960s and 1970s. Reformers argued that the increasing complexity of state government necessitated the shift from biennial sessions to annual sessions and with annual sessions came annual budgeting in many states. At the same time, many states that opted for annual budgeting had to address revenue volatility due to the growth in federal grant programs and an increase in state dependence on the less-stable income and sales taxes.[4] Today, some thirty state governments meet annually to make decisions regarding the state budget while twenty states make budgetary decisions biennially or every two years.[5] Arkansas recently changed from biennial budget review to annual budget review due to a legislatively-referred constitutional amendment that Arkansas voters approved in November of 2008.

The budget process in all fifty states follows four basic stages: budget preparation and submission, legislative review and approval, budget implementation, and budget audit and evaluation. However, within these stages there can be quite the variation in timelines, deadlines, key budget actor powers and responsibilities, organizational structures, budget procedures, budget format, and other budget processes.[6] The most important political difference among states is the balance between legislative and executive authority in creating the budget.[7] In several ways, the Arkansas budget process is unique from that of other states, as will be discussed. This chapter focuses on the first two stages: budget preparation and submission and legislative review and approval.

Public budgeting is central to the operation of government, yet it is quite complex and most citizens know very little about how the budget decision is made, where revenues come from, and how they are allocated. This chapter seeks to explain Arkansas budgeting in a way that makes it less confusing and daunting. This chapter will also explain the Arkansas state budget process and in so doing, will discuss state government revenues and expenditures, examine the roles and responsibilities of key budget actors in the creation of the operating budget, and identify the unique aspects of the Arkansas budget process.

Arkansas Revenues and Expenditures

First, Arkansas determines the amount of gross general revenue received by the state from fees and taxes levied on the general population of Arkansas. Gross general revenue is basically a financial figure involving everything coming into the state general fund from state own-source revenues. Net general revenue is the amount available for distribution after deducting allocations for such items as constitutional officer salaries, debt service on college savings bonds, rainy day amounts, educational excellence trust fund amounts, and income tax refunds (a total of $1,337,800 in 2019). Net general revenue is then distributed to state agencies and institutions of higher education.

Figure 1 shows the estimated gross general revenue for fiscal year 2019 at $6,942.0 million. The majority of state own-source gross revenue comes from the state income tax (56.3%), followed by the sales tax (35.8%), and the luxury tax (4.8%).[8] The income tax is levied on individual gross wages, less various deductions and exemptions, somewhat similar to the way the federal income tax is levied. The sales and use tax, at this point in time, largely exempts groceries but taxes other consumer sales at the retail level. Luxury tax revenues in Arkansas are levied on alcoholic beverages, tobacco, horse and dog racing, and electronic games of skill. Insurance revenue consists of taxes on insurance premiums, license fees, and insurance-related business fees.[9]

In addition to state own-source revenues that are placed in the general fund, the state collects special revenues (taxes or fees earmarked for a particular state agency and/or program), federal funds from various grants-in-aid, trust funds such as for retirement systems, and cash funds (primarily from institutions of higher education in the form of tuition and fees). Receipts from all sources for the state of Arkansas for Fiscal Year 2017–2018 totaled $22,109,027,049. Expenditures from all sources for the state of Arkansas for Fiscal Year 2017–2018 totaled $25,518,064,063.[10]

Figure 2 shows the estimated total general revenue available for distribution for fiscal year 2019 at $5,604.2 million. The largest expenditure category from the general revenue fund is for public schools at 39.2%, followed by health and human services at 31.1%. Higher education represents 13.3% of the budget, followed by general government at 11.2% of the total. General government includes state functions such as corrections, parks and tourism,

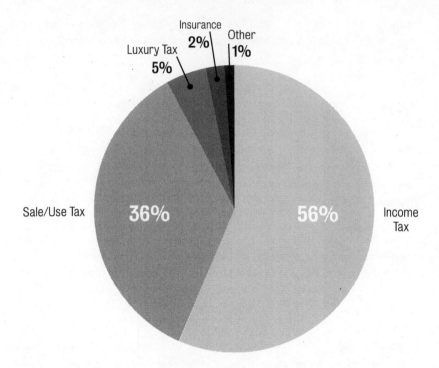

FIGURE I: Arkansas Gross General Revenue by Source – FY 2019 $6,942.0 Million. Source: State of Arkansas Revenue Flowchart, Fiscal Year 2019, available from the Department of Finance and Administration at https://www.dfa.arkansas.gov/images/uploads/budgetOffice/fy19_gr_flowchart.pdf

and economic development. For the 2019 fiscal year, the government of the State of Arkansas estimates a $64 million surplus for the state budget. Figure 2 indicates that well over half of the state general revenue budget is allocated for education (K-12, Arkansas Department of Education, and institutions of higher education).

The Arkansas Budget Process

There are several key actors involved in the Arkansas budget process. Executive branch actors include the governor and staff, budget analysts and revenue officials from the Arkansas Department of Finance and Administration, and state agencies. The current governor is a Republican and the state has operated under unified government since 2015. As is common in most states, the governor plays an important role in budget creation

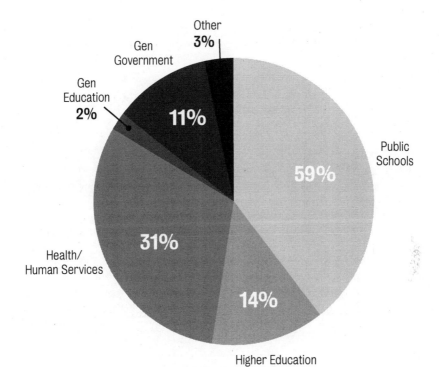

Figure 2: Total General Revenue Available for Distribution by Area of Major Expenditure, FY 2019 $5,604.2 Million.
Source: State of Arkansas Revenue Flowchart, Fiscal Year 2019, available from the Department of Finance and Administration at https://www.dfa.arkansas.gov/images/uploads/budgetOffice/fy19_gr_flowchart.pdf

by setting priorities for the state. The governor has assistance from individuals in the governor's office as well as budget analysts and economists in the Office of Budget and the Office of Economic Analysis and Tax Research within the Arkansas Department of Finance and Administration. These professionals advise on budgetary matters, assist state agencies in budget request preparation, project state revenues and other economic trends, and monitor state agency budgets throughout the year.

The legislature's role in the budget process is twofold: 1) oversight and review of the governor's budget and 2) passing appropriation bills to give state agencies and institutions of higher education the authority to spend. These activities occur in a term-limited environment where most legislators have full-time employment outside of the legislature. The legislature consists of two chambers: one hundred representatives and thirty-five senators. The Republican Party became the majority party in 2013 after a long period of party control by the Democrats.[11] Legislators are assisted by legislative analysts, operating in a nonpartisan staff organization, who provide fiscal information, draft the appropriation bills, and staff the Joint Budget Committee and its subcommittees.

State agencies play a role at the beginning and end of the process by evaluating their funding needs and submitting budget requests to the governor at the beginning of the process. After budgetary decisions are made by the governor and legislators, the state agencies prepare their annual operating budgets and implement the programs and services that have been funded.

CAPITAL PROJECTS BUDGET

Unlike the federal government, states create two budgets: the operating budget and the capital projects budget. The operating budget provides funding for the day-to-day expenses of state agencies and institutions of higher education. The capital projects budget provides funding for major maintenance and construction of state agency facilities and buildings. A capital project could be a new roof for a state facility, the renovation of a state park visitor center, or a new science building on a college campus. In Arkansas, capital projects are funded from interest earnings, recovered fund balances from some state agencies, and other funds designated for capital improvements. Agencies and institutions prepare capital requests using uniform submission forms provided by the Office of Budget within the Arkansas Department of Finance and Administration. These capital requests are considered and approved by the legislature during the regular legislative session. In most cases, there are more capital improvement needs than funding, therefore, not all capital project requests from state agencies and institutions are funded. Although capital budgets are worthy of a separate discussion, we will focus for the remainder of the chapter on the operating budget.[12]

OPERATING BUDGET

The state operating budget is written for a fixed period of time called a fiscal year, which is any consecutive twelve-month period that a state uses to plan state spending. Arkansas is similar to most states in that the fiscal year is July 1 to June 30. Up until 2009, the 1874 Constitution of the State of Arkansas restricted the Arkansas legislature to biennial legislative sessions (referred to as regular sessions) whereby all 135 state legislators met in session once every two years to discuss both substantive and fiscal matters. Budgetary decisions were made by the governor and legislature once every two years and appropriations (the authority for state agencies to spend money) were effective for two years.

In 2008, Arkansans passed Amendment 86 to the state constitution. This amendment continued the process of holding regular sessions, added a fiscal session, and prohibited appropriations for more than one year.[13] Today, regular sessions are held in odd-numbered years for a constitutionally-mandated sixty days to deal with both substantive and fiscal legislation. Constitutional language provides the state legislature with the ability to extend the regular session beyond the sixty-day limit. The state legislature has routinely extended the session, with the average session ranging from eighty-five to eighty-nine days.[14] Fiscal sessions are held in even-numbered years for thirty days, with a provision to extend up to fifteen days. With the addition of a fiscal session, Amendment 86 requires the Arkansas governor and legislature to make budgetary decisions annually instead of biennially.

Legislators and others who supported Amendment 86 argued that annual budgetary review would allow the legislature to better check the powers of the governor, deal with necessary budget revisions due to economic changes, increase the accuracy of revenue forecasts, and increase the budgetary knowledge of term-limited legislators.[15] However, some legislators, powerful interest groups, and the statewide newspaper opposed the amendment for increasing the opportunity for more government spending, creating professional politicians out of part-time legislators, and reducing the amount of time spent with constituents.[16]

In November of 2008, much to the surprise of many legislators and political observers, Arkansans approved Amendment 86 by a margin of 69.4% to 30.5%.[17] After the passage of the amendment, the Joint Budget Committee (the committee responsible for authorizing state spending) began discussing the procedural changes necessary for annual budgetary review. By August of 2009, the Joint Budget Committee had adopted procedures and a timeline for the review of agency budgets during the first fiscal session held in 2010.[18] The following sections explain the operating budget process in both the regular session and fiscal session by discussing the primary roles for the governor and state agencies in budget preparation and submission and the role of the legislature in the review and approval of the governor's budget recommendations.

Budget Preparation and Submission—Regular Session

The regular session budget process in Arkansas begins in late spring, some thirteen to fourteen months before the beginning of the fiscal year (July 1). As with most states, the governor starts the process by preparing the official revenue forecast and sending budget instructions and policy preferences to each state agency, board, and commission.[19] See Figure 3 for the budget calendar.

In Arkansas, the executive branch has the statutory authority to provide the official revenue forecast. The forecast is prepared by professionals in the Office of Economic Analysis and Tax Research within the Arkansas Department of Finance and Administration. The governor of Arkansas also has the statutory authority to revise the forecast, if needed.[20] Nationally, thirty states use some type of formal group to project revenues that could include several state agencies, legislators, and outside individuals such as academics. The remaining twenty states, including Arkansas, generally rely on professionals within the state budget or revenue office.[21]

The Arkansas governor outlines his/her policy preferences to state agencies in a letter that accompanies the budget request instructions. Budget analysts from the Department of Finance and Administration—Office of Budget assist many state agencies in developing the budget requests.[22] Although Amendment 86 requires annual budget review by the governor and legislature in a fiscal session, this amendment did not change the budget request process for state agencies. Prior to Amendment 86, state agencies submitted an annual budget request for each of the two years of the biennium. This practice did not change after the passage of the amendment. The biennial budget format is still in use and the fiscal session simply provides an additional opportunity for the legislature to review the budget requests for the second year of the biennium and pass appropriation bills for the upcoming fiscal year.

Budget requests for state agencies, boards, and commissions are uniform with agencies submitting the same information in the same format.[23] This information includes a brief agency history, organization chart, employment summary report, agency commentary explaining requests, and appropriation summaries.[24] Agencies submit their budget requests in July.[25]

After submission of the requests, executive budget hearings begin in the late summer and continue through the early fall where the executive committee reviews the agency budget requests. This committee is made up of officials from the Department of Finance and Administration, directors and

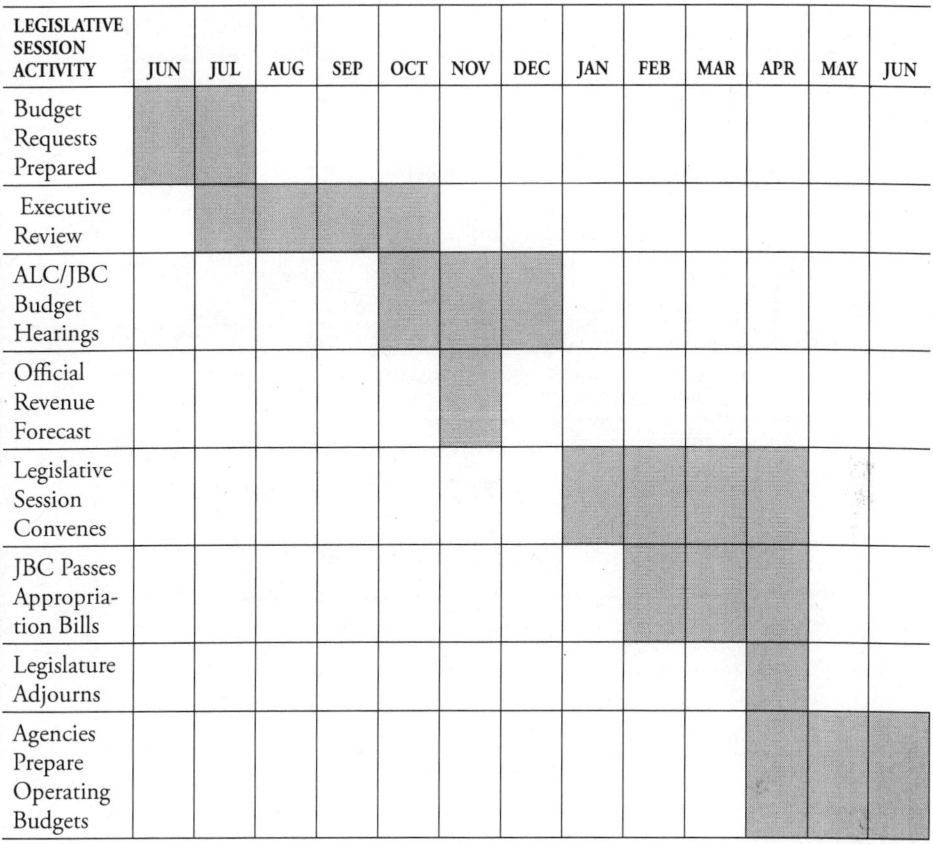

LEGISLATIVE SESSION ACTIVITY	JUN	JUL	AUG	SEP	OCT	NOV	DEC	JAN	FEB	MAR	APR	MAY	JUN
Budget Requests Prepared	░	░											
Executive Review		░	░	░									
ALC/JBC Budget Hearings					░	░							
Official Revenue Forecast						░							
Legislative Session Convenes								░	░				
JBC Passes Appropriation Bills									░	░			
Legislature Adjourns											░		
Agencies Prepare Operating Budgets											░	░	░

FIGURE 3. Arkansas Budget Calendar-Regular Session (Odd Years)

analysts from the Office of Budget, and a representative from the governor's office. The executive committee makes recommendations on the requests for each of the two years of the biennium. Both executive recommendations and agency budget requests are transmitted to the legislature in the fall via budget manuals. These manuals include most of the information identified above in addition to the governor's recommendation and agency requests. The governor is mandated by law to submit the official revenue forecast and a balanced budget to the legislature and this typically occurs in November prior to the regular session.[26] Arkansas is one of only four states where the legislature receives the governor's budget in November. The remaining state legislatures receive the gubernatorial budget later in the budget process.[27]

When presenting the budget to the legislature, the governor has the responsibility to identify new sources of revenue or revenue reductions in order to meet his/her budget recommendations.

Budget Preparation and Submission—Fiscal Session

Budget preparation and submission prior to the fiscal session is a more abbreviated process than that for the regular session based on rules adopted for the fiscal session by the Arkansas Legislative Council.[28] Only the budget requests of the state's largest six agencies are submitted and reviewed. These Big-6 agencies include the departments of Correction, Community Correction, Education/Public School Fund, Health, Human Services, and the institutions of higher education. These agencies and institutions prepare and submit budget requests to the governor from October—November. The executive committee reviews the requests from late November—December. The budget requests are essentially the same requests submitted to the governor prior to the regular session. The fiscal session provides the governor and executive budget staff a second look at those requests. The governor has an opportunity to make revisions if necessary; if not, the governor's recommendation does not change from the recommendation made prior to the regular session. As required by law, the governor must submit a revenue forecast in December prior to the pre-fiscal session legislative budget hearings. As is the case prior to the regular session, the governor must also submit a balanced budget to the legislature before the fiscal session.

Legislative Review and Approval—Regular Session

During the regular session budget process, the Arkansas legislature reviews the governor's recommendations and agency budget requests prior to the beginning of the legislative session in January via two legislative committees meeting jointly, the Arkansas Legislative Council (ALC) and the Joint Budget Committee (JBC). The ALC is a joint committee responsible for making decisions for the legislature during the interim (when the legislature is not in session), while the JBC reviews and passes appropriation bills during the session. Unlike the executive budget hearings described above, the pre-regular session budget hearings are open to the media and the public.

Collectively, these two joint committees comprise 83 of the 135 or 61% of the members of the state legislature.[29] Therefore, a majority of legislators

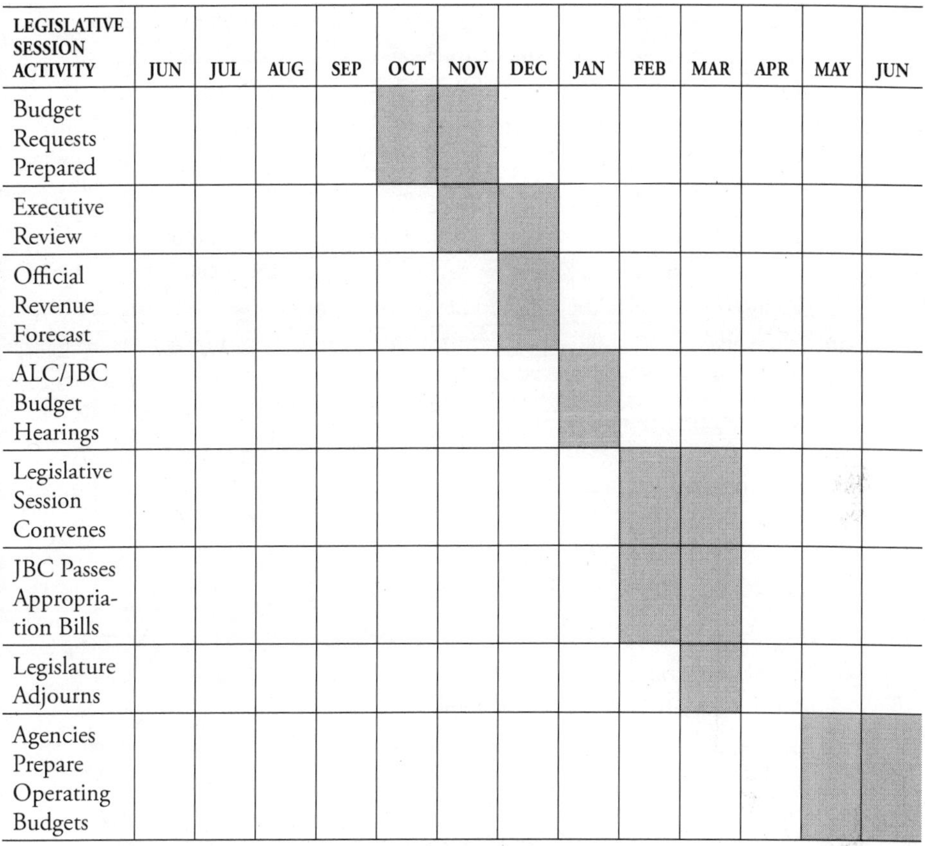

LEGISLATIVE SESSION ACTIVITY	JUN	JUL	AUG	SEP	OCT	NOV	DEC	JAN	FEB	MAR	APR	MAY	JUN
Budget Requests Prepared					▓	▓							
Executive Review						▓	▓						
Official Revenue Forecast							▓						
ALC/JBC Budget Hearings								▓					
Legislative Session Convenes									▓	▓			
JBC Passes Appropria-tion Bills									▓				
Legislature Adjourns										▓			
Agencies Prepare Operating Budgets												▓	▓

FIGURE 4. Arkansas Budget Calendar-Fiscal Session (Even Years)

have the opportunity to review the state budget prior to the regular session. Legislative budget hearings run for about two months beginning in October and ending in late November or the first two weeks in December.[30] These pre-regular session legislative budget hearings allow the Arkansas legislature the opportunity to review executive recommendations and agency requests well before the regular session begins. Legislatures in most states have far less time to consider the budget; because the governor submits the budget later in the process in most states.[31] Because of this enhanced role for the Arkansas legislature in budgetary review before the regular session, the legislature is said to have shared budgetary responsibility with the governor as opposed to the full gubernatorial responsibility as is found in twenty-seven states.[32]

During the budget hearings, legislative fiscal analysts present a summary of each state agency's budget request and the corresponding executive recommendation. Each state agency head is available to appear before the committee and respond to questions if asked by the legislators.[33]

Both the ALC and the JBC make decisions on the amount to appropriate and legislative fiscal analysts draft the appropriation bills based on ALC/JBC recommendations. An appropriation is the authority to spend money. Appropriations are control mechanisms; no state agency, board, commission or institution of higher education can spend money without one and only the legislative branch can appropriate. Therefore, appropriations act as a check on the executive branch. When the regular session begins in January, appropriation bills are introduced as Joint Budget Committee bills and referred to the JBC for a final review and passage before being sent to the full House and Senate for approval.

Legislative Review and Approval—Fiscal Session

During the fiscal session, limited budget hearings are held two to three weeks before the beginning of the fiscal session in January. Budgets are only presented for the "Big 6" agencies: Public School Fund, Department of Correction, Department of Community Correction, Department of Human Services, Department of Health, and institutions of higher education.

Agencies, other than the "Big 6," have their appropriation bills pre-filed based on legislative recommendations from the previously held pre-regular session budget hearings, unless the governor presents a change to the legislature during pre-fiscal session budget hearings.[34] Non-"Big 6" agency budgets can be included in the budget hearings if approved by the Arkansas Legislative Council (ALC) prior to the start of hearings.[35]

Pre-fiscal session budget hearings are not only more limited in scope than those held prior to the regular session, but also the ALC does not participate. Only the JBC reviews the "Big 6" budget requests and executive recommendations, and then directs legislative fiscal staff to draft appropriation bills. The non-"Big 6," appropriation bills are drafted based upon recommendations made during the regular session budget hearings. Therefore, budget recommendations for most agencies continue to be presented to the legislature on a biennial basis. However, the budgets for the "Big 6" encompass over 90% of the state general revenue budget.[36] Therefore, it makes sense for the legislature to limit annual review to these agencies.

APPROPRIATIONS PROCESS

The Joint Budget Committee's role during both the regular session and fiscal session is to provide a second review of appropriation bills approved during pre-session budget hearings. In addition, the JBC reviews and approves member-sponsored appropriation bills, acts as an appeals mechanism for state agencies if they did not get what they wanted in pre-session budget hearings, and responds to changes that the governor would like to make to his recommendations.

Arkansas has quirky constitutional language that requires all appropriation bills to be of a single subject.[37] In practice, this means that each state agency, board, commission, and public, state-supported institution of higher education must have a separate appropriation bill for operating expenses. In addition, there are other kinds of appropriations such as supplementals (providing additional authority to spend for the current year), capital projects (major construction projects or major maintenance), and reappropriations (re-authorizing an appropriation for an ongoing construction project). Further, individual members of the legislature can sponsor appropriation bills for specific state agency activities. Therefore, several hundred appropriation bills are introduced, debated, and enacted each year. For the last four regular sessions (2011, 2013, 2015, and 2017), 596, 751, 674, and 349 appropriation bills were introduced, respectively. Likewise, for the last four fiscal sessions (2010, 2012, 2014, and 2016), 303, 296, 306, and 278 appropriation bills were introduced, respectively.[38] The large number of bills in Arkansas is highly unusual; most states enact significantly fewer appropriation bills.[39] In Arkansas, legislative fiscal staff are responsible for drafting all appropriation bills. In slightly over half of the states (twenty-eight), the executive branch is responsible for drafting appropriation bills; in thirteen states, appropriation committee staff have bill drafting duties; and fifteen states (including Arkansas) rely on fiscal staff in a nonpartisan fiscal office to draft the bills.[40]

Another constitutional constraint is the vote requirement for passing appropriation bills. A supermajority vote (3/4) is needed to pass all appropriation bills.[41] Arkansas is only one of three states with a supermajority vote requirement.[42] For most of Arkansas's modern history, the supermajority vote requirement was not an impediment to passing bills due to the dominant Democratic majority in both chambers. However, beginning in 2012 and for a short period of time afterwards, the chambers were closely divided between Republicans and Democrats. There were some appropriation battles between the parties where several votes had to be taken in order to obtain the supermajority vote requirement. Today, the Republican Party is firmly in power and these battles are less likely to occur in the future if the Republicans maintain their majority status. However, the supermajority vote requirement was tested in 2013 and 2014 when blocs of Republicans in both chambers attempted, unsuccessfully, to oppose the implementation of health insurance for the poor under the federal Patient Protection Affordable Care Act (Obamacare). In 2014, multiple roll call votes over several days were needed to reach the seventy-five-vote requirement in the House of Representatives for the appropriation bill.[43]

Another interesting aspect of the appropriations process is the fact that each appropriation bill is arbitrarily assigned as either a House bill or Senate bill. Unlike at the federal level, where both the House and Senate chambers draft separate appropriation bills, the Arkansas legislature drafts a single appropriation bill that goes to one chamber for debate and vote and then it is sent to the other chamber for debate and vote. Arkansas is one of only ten states where bills are divided between chambers.[44]

After an appropriation bill has passed both chambers, the bill is sent to the governor for approval. The Arkansas governor has several options: sign the bill into law, veto the entire bill, or line-item veto the bill. If the governor vetoes an appropriation bill, the legislature can override with a simple majority rather than a supermajority vote as is required in most states.[45] Furthermore, Arkansas is one of forty-three states that allows the governor to line-item veto proposed expenditures.[46] The line-item veto is the power for a governor to strike particular lines in a budget bill, without rejecting the entire bill. Prior research shows that governors in the state of Arkansas have used the line-item veto relatively few times and for low amounts of money.[47] This is likely due to the interaction of the line-item veto power with the extremely high number of appropriation bills passed each year in Arkansas (the highest in the nation). Basically, if the legislature passes several hundred—rather than the norm of one—appropriation bills per year, then there is not much use for a line-item veto. A governor could just as easily veto a whole (small) bill as he/she could veto a major appropriation. Overall, states that pass large numbers of appropriation bills are less likely to use the line-item veto.[48]

Appropriations in Arkansas are funded by various revenue sources, including general revenues, special revenues, federal funds, and general improvement funds for capital projects. After the legislature appropriates funds for state agencies and institutions of higher education, general revenue must be allocated to those entities. The process of allocation is the Revenue Stabilization Act and the annual amendment to that act.

Revenue Stabilization Act

What truly makes the state of Arkansas unique is the use of its Arkansas Revenue Stabilization Act (ARSA), which is the state's process for allocating general revenue. In contrast to most other states in the US, an appropriation act pertaining to a particular department, agency, or program in Arkansas simply authorizes a state agency to spend money on a theoretical basis; it does not allocate actual funds. In Arkansas, the mechanism for allocating general revenues is an annual legislative amendment to the ARSA.

The ARSA was passed in 1945 following the gubernatorial election of conservative Democratic businessman Ben T. Laney in 1944; Laney ran on a platform that emphasized changing the "inflexibility and insufficiency in state finances."[49] This inflexibility was a result of most revenues being earmarked for specific purposes at that time. Therefore, neither the governor nor legislature had the discretion to use state revenues based on agency needs and/or statewide priorities. Further, the ARSA is supposed to ensure that the state will not run a budget deficit.[50] In essence, the ARSA serves to stabilize the budget by acting the same as a rainy day fund in most other states.[51] It also reduces funding instability for those programs that relied on one source of earmarked funds because those funds could be negatively impacted by changing economic conditions.[52] Overall, the law "minimizes the impact of any decline in revenue" over the fiscal year.[53]

The way the law works is that each year the legislature, in consultation with the governor, establishes a dollar amount of funding for each of the general revenue funds, and the agencies and institutions are assigned an A, B, or C funding category where funds are allocated (if available), according to priority.[54] The total dollar amount of funding is based on general revenue estimates for the upcoming fiscal year. The funding level in category "A" is of the highest priority and will almost certainly be funded as it comprises continuing programs, including anything considered to be essential, such as education, corrections, and medical assistance. The items marked "B" will probably be funded, and generally are comprised of a cost-of-living-adjustments for various programs in category A, as well as critical new programs. The items marked "C" may be funded, but they are termed a "wish list," and their actual funding depends on economic performance. Generally, category C items will most likely not be funded, unless revenues come in better than projected. Although the legislature determines the dollar amount of funding for each state agency fund and category, the governor and his/her agency directors determine the programs and the programmatic priorities within those funds.[55] It is important to note that the number of priority categories can change from year to year based upon the maximum amount of general revenue for that year; sometimes there are more than three categories.[56] After the legislature makes the funding decisions, an amendment to the ARSA is drafted reflecting the funding that each state agency gets in each of the categories. This amendment must be passed by both chambers and signed by the governor during each regular session and fiscal session.

The Department of Finance and Administration monitors general revenue during the year and implements the law. In good economic times, agencies may be authorized to spend 100% of their funding in each category. In other words, categories A, B, and C, are fully funded. In bad economic times, the Department of Finance and Administration allows agencies to only spend some portion of their funding. For example, agencies may not be allowed to spend any money in category C and only 75% of funds in category B. During the Great Recession, Arkansas reduced spending on category A programs only once in fiscal year 2010 and these cuts were rather small compared to other states.[57]

In Arkansas, when revenues fall, budget cuts are made automatically without the type of political conflict that often occurs in other states. ARSA prevents big budget battles between the legislature and governor as well as the need to hold a special session to deal with budget cuts as is often the case in other states. In summary, the ARSA not only allocates general revenue to state agencies and institutions of higher education, but also acts as a deficit reduction tool in periods where revenues are coming in below projections. The ARSA serves overall to "maintain the status quo" in the state budgetary process, or in other words it keeps things like they already are.[58]

Summary of budget process

A 2011 *Stateline* article described the Arkansas budget process as the "envy of other states for years."[59] Some of the unique features of the process that might be the envy of the other states would include the Revenue Stabilization Law, which ensures that the people of the state do not have to be concerned with the effects of the ups and downs of revenue collection and/or the national economy. In addition to this unique method of revenue allocation and deficit reduction, the Arkansas legislature conducts pre-session budget hearings, which may serve to minimize political conflict over dollars once the session starts. Also, the state legislature receives both executive recommendations and agency budget requests earlier than most states, providing an information advantage to the Arkansas legislature. Further, eight state legislatures never even receive agency budget requests.[60] Also, as previously mentioned, the number of appropriation bills passed is the greatest in the nation, as most states only pass 1–6 per year (the norm is one single bill). Relatedly, since the single-subject rule is applied to all appropriation bills in Arkansas, a bill goes through each chamber alone, with no companion bills (with the possible exception of special sessions). Finally, in Arkansas the legislature can override a gubernatorial veto by a simple majority, where forty-one states require a supermajority vote to override the governor on a veto.[61] These budget process oddities make the Arkansas budget process quite unique from the rest of the states.

Overall, then, the legislature is fairly dominant over the budgetary process, at least on paper. However, the governor generally seems to get what he (or, possibly in the future, she) wants. The governor's ability to start the budget process enables budget prioritization early on. Additionally, the Arkansas legislature has an increased opportunity, compared to many other state legislatures, to review those gubernatorial priorities via the budget hearings held before the regular and fiscal sessions. While the legislature may not significantly alter the governor's budget recommendations, it certainly has the opportunity to do so.

Future Challenges and Issues

Central issues that we predict will continue to be important to the Arkansas state budgetary process include (1) the potential for future fiscal challenges due to recent and further proposed income tax cuts, (2) the effects of legislative term limits, which necessarily include lack of budgetary knowledge among state legislators and (3) proposals to repeal language in the state constitution requiring a fiscal session.[62]

INCOME TAX CUTS

Arkansas has become quite aggressive in cutting income taxes in the last several regular sessions. In 2013, the legislature reduced the capital gains tax. In 2015, Governor Asa Hutchinson signed another income tax cut bill focusing on the middle class since the capital gains cut benefitted primarily wealthy Arkansans. In 2017, the governor and legislature cut income taxes again, this time for low-income Arkansans (for those with income below $21,000), since they did not benefit from the 2015 cuts.[63] In 2019, the governor asked the legislature to cut income taxes again, this time for those wealthy Arkansans in the highest tax bracket.[64] While the state's economy continues to be strong with historically low levels of unemployment only time will tell if the state can weather an economic downturn in the future with fewer available resources.[65]

TERM LIMITS

Arkansas is one of fifteen states with legislative term limits; and prior to 2014, Arkansas had the most stringent term limits in the country.[66] Until 2014, house members could serve six years in office and senators could serve eight years in office.[67] Term limits precipitated much change in the legislature including rule changes in both chambers to allow legislators to assume leadership roles more quickly. Also, enhanced orientation sessions covering the state budget process and state finances were instituted by legislative fiscal staff. In 2014, the citizens of Arkansas increased the number of years that an individual could serve in the legislature up to a total of sixteen years, thus significantly extending the time of office for many legislators.[68]

One of the primary arguments for the addition of a fiscal session was the need for inexperienced, term-limited legislators to have an additional opportunity to review the state budget during a fiscal session. As noted previously, there is a tremendous amount of budget information submitted to the legislature. While the number of years a member may serve in the legislature has increased, the sheer amount of budget data along with the increasing complexity of state government make budgetary review a challenge for many Arkansas legislators. Some may argue that Arkansas legislators today have less institutional knowledge than their predecessors of several decades ago due to term limits. Others, however, may argue that the current, more expansive term limits reduce the need for additional budget review via a fiscal session.

PROPOSALS TO END FISCAL SESSION

The 2019 legislative session brings two legislative proposals to end the fiscal session from those who are the detractors of a fiscal session. Each bill abolishes the fiscal session and stipulates that appropriation bills are to be valid for two years, as opposed to the current one-year limit. Both bills are proposed constitutional amendments and must pass both chambers of the legislature in order to be sent to the people for approval. If Arkansans approve one of the proposed constitutional amendments in November of 2020, the budget process will revert back to biennial legislative sessions and biennial budget review.

Conclusion

Overall, the Arkansas budget process serves to preserve the economic status quo. The process is an excellent shield against national economic downturns and has been described as the envy of other states. The lack of volatility in the budgetary process, while enviable on many fronts, may not be a model for states that are considering widespread public policy changes. While the legislature has significant opportunities to review executive recommendations and agency budget requests via pre-session budget hearings, state budget priorities are largely set by the governor and routinely approved by the legislature, so the pecking order is the same as in many states. But, the opportunities that the legislature has along with the atypical budgetary process in the state makes Arkansas unique.

III

Public Policy Conflicts
in Arkansas Politics and Government

CHAPTER 15

"Dedicated People"

Little Rock Central High School's Teachers during the Integration Crisis of 1957–1958

GRAEME COPE

The Central High Crisis of 1957–1958 in Little Rock, Arkansas has received much attention from historians and other scholars. Most studies focus on broader issues such as judicial decision making, the role of Governor Faubus, and racial politics in Little Rock. Few historians have analyzed what happened inside Central High School when nine black students enrolled for the first time. For those scholars who have studied actions inside the high school, administrative decisions and responses have been the focus. In this chapter, Graeme Cope focuses on a group surprisingly ignored by historians: the teachers. The analysis reveals that teachers had little preparation for integration and were discouraged from discussing the subject with fellow teachers or others outside of the school. Cope finds that despite these obstacles and the fact that Central High teachers had differences in personal opinion regarding integration, most teachers performed their duties in a professional, dedicated manner; carried on as normally as possible; held their students' welfare as the primary concern; and provided students with high quality instruction within the halls of Central High School.

Despite their importance to the outcome of Little Rock Central High's first year of integration, September 1957 to May 1958, the school's teachers have received surprisingly little attention from historians.[1] Indeed, even Karen Anderson's recently published major study of the events of 1957–1959, while providing the most comprehensive review of school discipline cur-

Originally published in *The Arkansas Historical Quarterly* 70 (Spring 2011): 16–44. Reprinted with permission. DOI: https://doi.org/10.34053/parry2019.riapag2.15

rently available, concentrates on administrative responses to class, gender, and race-based nastiness. Anderson neither explains nor supplies evidence for a passing observation that "most teachers behaved professionally in a tense situation."[2] A chapter in a dissertation argues (also on the basis of administrative actions rather than classroom practice) that Central's faculty "dealt apathetically with the crisis of desegregation" despite an intention to maintain "some semblance of an ordinary educational environment." But, otherwise, Sondra Gordy's investigations of how teachers kept themselves engaged while the city's high schools were closed throughout the 1958–1959 school year are as yet the only specific studies of those who had to bear the immediate practical consequences of judicial decisions over which they had had little or no influence.[3]

Granting the inherently slippery nature of so much data derived from polarized opinion and perception, an examination of how Central's teachers responded to the presence of nine black students in their previously all-white institution suggests that, while educators were clearly divided on the subject of integration in the abstract, they were, on the whole and notwithstanding an untold number of barbs, jibes, and selective inattention to race-based classroom disorder, more likely to treat their black pupils as learners than as lepers. "As public school teachers and administrators," girls' vice-principal Elizabeth Huckaby declared, "we felt that education was our major responsibility and integration a secondary problem in the social revolution of our times." "My immediate goal," she continued, "was having the black children in school as just ordinary children."[4]

Investigating issues related to Central's faculty during what industrial arts teacher Paul Magro described as the "trying days" of 1957–1958 is, however, no easy task.[5] Until recently, few teachers or their pupils of either color have spoken freely on the public record about their racial views, let alone about what transpired in the relative privacy of their classroom kingdoms.[6] We have known, for instance, from accounts such as Huckaby's *Crisis at Central High* and Melba Pattillo Beals' *Warriors Don't Cry*, a great deal about the ongoing harassment the nine endured in common spaces, such as stairwells, corridors, restrooms, the cafeteria, and playing fields, but much less about what went on in situations where closer supervision meant there were potentially fewer opportunities for anonymous encounters to pass unnoticed or be excused as accidents or fair tackles.[7]

Because teachers were actively discouraged from airing their views to third parties, including their students and, most especially, the press, references to particular educators and specific classroom interactions during the first year of integration are not only scarce but also generally masked if the tenor of a remark was critical and the identity of its subject likely to become a matter of public knowledge. Elizabeth Huckaby's published memoir is accordingly somewhat less candid than her diary. Whereas, for instance, the latter identifies English educator Mildred Stalnaker as the source of a racially charged query about the whereabouts of the nine during an examination period in May 1958, the former simply describes the inquisitor as "one of the unsympathetic teachers."[8] And while it is possible to use school records to identify Thelma Mothershed's snide homeroom teacher and to pick up from a passing Huckaby remark that Margaret Dewberry was in all probability the source of Melba Pattillo's angst in English, the nine generally remain coy about those staffers who made no secret of their racial predilections, preferring, like Terrence Roberts, to use phrases such as "the tall, thin, severe-faced teacher" or, like Melba Pattillo, to refer only to "the teacher," often without any indication of her subject.[9] On the other hand, the rare faculty members prepared to talk on the record only did so on condition of anonymity. Typically, we do not know the name of the female instructor who defied pressure, if not orders, to tell the *Arkansas Gazette*'s Charles Allbright that she and her class "discussed every angle there was" or of the lady who informed her students that "if they did not approve of integration the only way to combat it was through the law and not in mob action."[10]

Most of what can be learned about teachers' attitudes to integration and their responses as blacks entered their classrooms comes not so much from contemporary references as from materials unavailable to the public during the crisis. Typically, newshounds were kept away from the school, or if they, like the *New York Times*' Gertrude Samuels, were granted access to its corridors, promptly ordered off the premises when they tried to wheedle information about teacher attitudes to integration from female staffers enjoying a cigarette in the ladies' restroom.[11] Few, if any, other correspondents were able to replicate a young *Arkansas Democrat* journalist's ability to pass herself off as a student and learn that teachers were barred from discussing "the integration problem" in class.[12] The likes of John Chancellor, on-the-spot NBC bureau chief, might have enjoyed the confidence of an inside informer named Ira Lipman, a senior who worked evenings at the *Arkansas Gazette* and was acquainted with one of the nine (Ernest Green). But if Lipman told his minder anything about staff attitudes and behavior, it did not enter the public arena.[13] Nor do we have any idea about the content of the "hot tips" an unnamed male teacher fed a local television cameraman.[14] All too often news from inside the school reached the public through the tainted "pipelines" some of the leading segregationist students—most notably Sammie Dean Parker and her confreres—established between themselves, the media, and the governor's mansion.[15] In effect, as Margaret Jackson, the president of the segregationist Mothers' League, found when she wanted to know whether vice-principal Huckaby was "for the Negroes," there was a "tight censorship at Central High School." The National Association for the Advancement of Colored People maintained "a protective curtain" around the nine, and its state president, Daisy Bates, remained chary of revealing details from the "careful notes" she took at their daily debriefings in her basement.[16]

In any event, Central's educators were constrained from speaking freely, if not by their principal's repeated insistence on neutrality, then (more likely) by the presence of an overbearing school superintendent, Virgil Blossom, who, with the exception of a few isolated and over general remarks from unnamed teaching staff, was virtually the sole source of published comment on the internal operations of the school throughout 1957–1958.[17] Instead of the usual monthly academic staff gatherings, there was only one in the first third of the year and even then "every effort was made by the administration to keep the problem of desegregation from reaching open discussion."[18] "Central High School subalterns and teachers," boys' vice-principal Jay Powell noted, "were understanding instructions to make nothing public without 'clearing' it through the principal or through the superintendent," both of whom, as the *Arkansas Democrat* found, "shy away from any discussion of integrated classes." "We were advised," recalled biology staffer Howard Bell, "almost daily throughout the school year to be quiet on the integration controversy as a policy, leaving its solution to the community. As a group we followed our instructions like good soldiers whether we agreed with them or not."[19]

Moreover, as several faculty told the *Arkansas Gazette*, "the less said the better," lest, like Minnijean Brown's sympathetic English teacher Susie West (who was verbally abused and had rocks thrown through her windows), they too were forced to confront the ugly reality of retribution from those in the community hostile to integration.[20] "Faculty members," the Arkansas Council on Human Relations' Nat Griswold wrote the Southern Regional Council's Harold Fleming in November 1957, "are intimidated . . . to the point they do not openly espouse desegregation or befriend the Negro students."[21] Revealing a stance on the issue of the day not only threatened to undermine professional effectiveness but also jeopardized collegiality. With math instructor William Ivy on the one side reckoning most of his colleagues felt integration was a mistake and vice-principal Huckaby on the other claiming a majority were "morally and philosophically committed to the fact that desegregation was right and desirable," Central's teaching staff was clearly divided on the subject and naturally reluctant to canvass racial issues even among themselves.[22] Indeed, as counselor Shirley Stancil, herself sensitive to the extent of not being seen with copies of "a certain newspaper" that might upset some of her more conservative colleagues, remembered, she "never heard any loud disagreeable confrontations." "It was never discussed at school," math and photography educator William Lincoln recalled, "black-white issues of any kind, really." For the sake of overall morale, Howard Bell noted, "We just deliberately avoided anything that had to do with the situation."[23]

Mistrust and suspicion also discouraged open discussion. "The teachers at the school," William Ivy also told an inquirer, "are afraid to talk to each other about the integration problem here at the school. We don't know who we are talking to. They may run to Blossom or the school board and the result would be that we could be fired for expressing our opinion on this matter. We are the most close-mouthed bunch you ever saw." "It is my opinion," added chemistry's Govie Griffin, "that teachers are hesitant to make any statement regarding integration because they do not know if they can trust each other."[24]

Any examination of Central's teachers is also hostage to narratives structured according to the great literary tradition of adversity overcome.[25] There must be heroes and villains to enliven the story. And while there can be no doubting the core truths of the struggles outlined, the very nature of the beast tends to emphasize the negatives over the positives. Willfulness and slights might sometimes be assumed where none were intended. Melba Pattillo's painful diary-based recollections are not demeaned by reminding ourselves that a young woman could misread the words and actions of adults just as readily as those adults could misinterpret hers. Of course, the accounts of vice-principals and teachers should be subject to no less scrutiny than those of Carlotta Walls and Terrence Roberts. Although they are not so obviously examples of an established genre, they too have both their own professional and personal agendas to defend. Vice-principal Powell had, for instance, a passionate preoccupation with what he perceived to be "a gelatinous attitude of permissive negligence" practiced by his immediate superior. On the other hand, as Gordy discovered when she interviewed twenty teachers from the "Lost Year" almost four decades after the event, candor was still at a premium.[26]

Anecdotal evidence also presents its problems. All too often singular incidents are described without any indication of their typicality or a consideration of their consistency with other actions and statements by the same person. Several different sources from several different times leave no doubt that Margaret Reiman's initial solicitude for the nine (evident in her support for a welcoming program) was just one example of an ongoing commitment to fairness.[27] We have, on the other hand, no way of telling which of Melba Pattillo's two accounts of her first encounter with her English teacher is the more accurate. At the time and as a young woman, she told the *New York Times'* Benjamin Fine that no one listened to a particularly voluble and abusive boy and that the instructor ordered him to leave the room. When, however, she came to organize her memoirs as an adult with the notion of "warriors" firmly in mind, the teacher did nothing.[28]

Yet, if information about Central's inner operations during 1957–1958 is compromised by administrative censorship and prone to potentially ill-founded personal summations of other people's racial predilections, it does not, as vice-principal Powell reckoned, amount to "little more than hearsay, hogwash and palaver."[29] State police teacher investigation records and incidental references (such as Lola Dunnavant's diary-based musings from the perspective of Central's library), traditional media reports, student narratives from both sides of the racial divide, academic staff memoirs, and latter-day interviews by Sondra Gordy not only afford insight into teacher attitudes to integration as such but also data on the degree to which those attitudes were reflected in classroom practice.[30]

Surprisingly, Central's faculty was not given any formal preparation for integration. Indeed, some teachers apparently did not realize that integration (limited though it was to be) was to occur across the board rather than just in twelfth grade as they had expected. Nor were those instructors who were to have black children in their classes notified until four days before integration was to begin.[31] Superintendent Blossom took it upon himself to explain his plans to the community at large, but his round of more than two hundred presentations singularly failed to include those specifically concerned. Furthermore, offers of assistance from both students and teachers were firmly and repeatedly rejected, and nothing specific about imminent integration was mentioned either when a new track coach was being recruited or at the first academic staff meeting of the new school year.[32] As Colbert Cartwright, pastor of the Pulaski Heights Christian Church, noted, Blossom "did not think well" of a suggestion that he convene informal meetings of teachers to discuss potential difficulties arising from integration. "At no time," Cartwright continued, "has he sought to help teachers face their own prejudices or to provide them with guidance in dealing with problems of group dynamics." In the words of Episcopal bishop Robert Brown, "The many speeches and addresses that were made in Little Rock were made by way of explanation, not preparation. . . . Neither was it deemed necessary to define, discuss, or study the possible consequences of desegregation before the opening of school, and the teachers were not encouraged to make their suggestions for improving the plan."[33]

Central's principal was no more helpful. A much admired veteran with more than thirty years of service in the Little Rock school system but, according to his son, deferential by nature and, in any case, heavily over-shadowed by a superior intent on making his mark with the successful implementation of a plan that bore his name, Jess Matthews does not appear to have mentored his staff either before integration or after he first met his black pupils with "an acknowledging frown and nod."[34] Indeed, the omens had not been auspicious since the fall of 1955, when, at Blossom's insistence, he suspended the activities of the faculty's Guidance and Community Cooperation Committees he had initially encouraged. Nor, in the spring of 1957, did he take the opportunity to probe the impact of integration in Oklahoma City and returned to Little Rock with three pages of questions given him by his female vice-principal neither answered nor even asked.[35] When a proposed orientation for his new black pupils fell through, he simply "left it up to Mr. Blossom as to any other instructions to the colored students."[36] Personally ambivalent about desegregation and by many accounts the sort of man who liked to be liked, he was apparently not the type of administrator to take a divisive stand. Instead, he remained attached to what he reputedly called his "neutrality" and, seeing his black charges not so much in racial terms as just another inconvenience to the smooth operation of a well-oiled machine, did his best to carry on as if the 1957–1958 school year was no different from any other.[37] "Our job," according to his male deputy's summation of his principal's position, "is to run this school and educate the best way we can and make our own business and not get out on any limbs by getting into any arguments, because just as sure as we say anything somebody's going to twist it all around and saw that limb from under us. So I say we should just sit tight and be real professionals." "I don't think," he hinted to the same vice-principal on the subject of informing the military about racial incidents, "that you ought to, er, suggest things in these, er, little write-ups that, er, might uh, reflect on us."[38] Girls' vice-principal Huckaby was more circumspect but clearly implied that, however competent Matthews was as an administrator and spokesman for education, he was perhaps not at his best in challenging times.[39]

Central began the first of its two years in the spotlight with a faculty of ninety, seventeen of whom, including six novices, were new to the school and, in a practical sense, replacements for the twenty who had transferred to Hall High School, newly established in affluent northwestern Little Rock.[40] Privately, Huckaby surmised that "possibly a third" of Central's staff were "philosophically opposed to integration," a third "actively in favor of desegregation," and a third "without strong feelings either way."[41] She also told historian Sondra Gordy that "a few" staff, probably including a number of the fifteen folk who declined to sign contracts with the segregationist Little Rock Public School Corporation in September 1958, were "a little past" being mere moderates.[42]

While the exact proportions of faculty holding different positions on desegregation remains uncertain, a sample of those who have left some indication of their views suggests that the majority were, if not formally integrationists (which would have been unusual at the time), then at least people prepared to demonstrate by word or deed that they were willing to meet their legal and professional obligations to provide black students with the same opportunities as white. Forty-five of Central's ninety staff (50 percent) aside from clerical, nursery, and custodial workers can be identified as what might be called moderates and fifteen (16.7 percent) as clearly segregationist.[43] Another six staff (6.7 percent) have commented on various aspects of the "crisis" year or been commented on, but not in such a way as to allow them to be classified as either moderate or segregationist. In other words, three-quarters of sixty teaching staff with known attitudes accepted a black presence in Central, while a quarter preferred ongoing racial separation.

With just over half having masters degrees and an overall average service of 15.4 years (7.2 years at Central), the "moderates" were no classroom novices.[44] A majority (52.2 percent) were from the humane side of the curriculum: guidance, languages, the social sciences, and creative arts, with the largest single subject representation being from English (22.2 percent) (Table 1). Given that three-quarters of Central's instructors were female, it is not surprising that these forty-five individuals were overwhelmingly women (82.2 percent). On the other hand (and bearing in mind that the evidence might well be warped by Huckaby possibly being less familiar with the opinions of the male staffroom than with those of her female colleagues), it is certainly worth noting that identifiable women were more likely than men to have been in some way or other supportive of black pupils.[45] Married women were more inclined to acceptance than their unwed sisters.[46]

With the exception of guidance counselors (who were over-represented) and business studies teachers (who were under-represented), the proportion of staff in a given field who were publicly accepting of a black presence was broadly equivalent to the proportion of staff in that area among the faculty as a whole.[47] At the extremes, just over three-quarters of all counselors were at least formally accepting of blacks (77.8 percent) compared with one in seven of their commercial studies colleagues (14.3 percent).

While only six of the twenty staff less than thirty years old were initially in regular contact with the nine, all were moderates. Huckaby believed her younger staff in general were on "the positive side." Daisy Bates, mentor to the nine and a woman not known for gilding lilies, agreed. "Many of the teachers—particularly the young ones," she observed, "did everything in their power to protect the nine students. Some went out of their way to help the students catch up with work they had missed when they were barred from entering the school in the first weeks of term."[48] Interestingly, almost four-fifths of instructors with two years or less experience at Central were moderates, though few were as frank as Jo Ann Henry, a new math educator who made "no secret of being for integration."[49]

Like the rest of the teaching staff, the smaller overtly segregationist contingent was predominantly female (80.0 percent) and, with an average service of 20.9 years, even more highly experienced than their associates.[50] On average, segregationist staff had worked at Central more than twice as long as their moderate colleagues (15.6 years compared with 7.2 years). The median service of a conservative at Central was twelve years, that of a moderate only two. To judge from biographical data and photographs in Central's 1958 yearbook, all but two of these segregationists were much nearer to the end of their teaching careers than to the beginning and, in a sense, relics of the past. For, as William Lincoln reminisced: "When I went to work at Central, there was a core of teachers who had been there on that staff for more than twenty years . . . And some of them were what you might call Southern belles and Southern gentlemen and some of them were still there in [19]58 . . . Their attitude was still that they were Southern and they were not willing to accept integration, although they had black children in their classes."[51] Bearing in mind the limitations of a sample of only fifteen, they included no representatives from creative arts, physical education, or the trades. Although the proportion of math/science staff was

Moderates among Little Rock Central High School Staff, 1957–1958, by Subject Area[a]

SUBJECT AREA	NO. MODER-ATES	TOTAL STAFF IN AREA	MODERATES AS % STAFF IN AREA	% OF SCHOOL STAFF IN AREA	AREA STAFF AS % OF TOTAL MODERATES
Humanities	14.5	29.5	49.2	32.8	32.2
Math/Science	8.5	13.0	65.4	14.4	18.9
Creative Arts	5.5	9.5	57.9	10.6	12.2
Physical Education	6.0	9.5	63.2	10.6	13.3
Practical Training	4.0	11.5	34.8	12.8	8.9
Guidance	3.5	4.5	77.8	5.0	7.8
Administration	2.0	3.5	57.1	3.9	4.4
Business	1.0	7.0	14.3	7.8	2.2
Library	0.0	2.0	0.0	2.2	0.0
	45	90.0	-	100.1	99.9

a—Halves are accounted for by teachers working in two fields.
Principal sources: Elizabeth Huckaby, *Crisis at Central High: Little Rock, 1957–58* (Baton Rouge: Louisiana State University Press, 1980); *Arkansas Gazette*, May 10, 1959; Elizabeth Huckaby, "Schedule-September 1957," series 2, box 2, file 13, Huckaby Papers; "Teacher Directory," series 2, box 2, file 13, Huckaby Papers; *The Pix of 1958* (Little Rock: Central High School, 1958).

higher than that found in the faculty as such (21.4 percent compared with 14.4 percent), the most notable contingent comprised middle-aged women teaching the humanities, particularly English and history (42.9 percent). Segregationist women were slightly more likely to be single than their moderate colleagues.[52]

Pertinent though they are to establishing that a majority of the school's faculty seem not to have resisted change in the nature of their clientele, the numbers of moderates and traditionalists were not as important in determining how integration worked in practice as the twenty-three women and three men who first encountered the nine in the course of their daily duties.[53] Although student counselor Shirley Stancil later claimed that those slated to teach black students were specifically chosen because they "were kind and people who would support and protect them," Huckaby was clearly nearer the mark when she reported that they were picked "without favor or discrimination."[54] Indeed, their selection might in hindsight be seen as yet another one of the bungles that plagued the implementation of the Blossom Plan. They certainly represented a wide range of ages, experiences, and competencies.[55] But, perhaps reflecting an assumption that professionalism would trump prejudice, they also included a slightly disproportionate number of staunch segregationists. Representing a quarter of the total academic staff with known positions on integration (fifteen of sixty), segregationists accounted for nearly one-third of those allocated black students (32 percent) or, from a slightly different perspective, just over half of identifiable racial conservatives were assigned the nine (53.3 percent) but only a little over one-third of known moderates (35.6 percent).

Unlike moderates whose racial views commonly have to be inferred from behavior such as Dorothy Langgenhager's taking umbrage at a parent's suggestion that she turn a blind eye to a regular offender's attempts to push Gloria Ray down some stairs, segregationists usually spoke for themselves.[56] Taking the opportunity to snipe at Daisy Bates for allegedly exaggerating the intellectual prowess of the Nine, history and government teachers Emily Penton and Vivian Daniel were convinced that "the action of the US government in sending troops to CHS was illegal and unconstitutional." "We feel," they continued, that "General Walker's speech [to Central's students emphasizing the vital importance of conformity to the law as determined by the Supreme Court] was a browbeating speech and we were stunned. It was actually impossible to believe an American general was standing there talking to an American audience."[57] Not surprisingly, Daniel was thought of as a woman "very set in her ways," while Penton, who was regularly praised as an excellent teacher, was "very adamant about not believing in integration."[58]

Govey Griffin, a chemistry instructor and Minnijean Brown's homeroom teacher, was also "stunned" by the general's "brutal" talk. Praising a teacher willing to give the nine what she perceived to be their just desserts and firmly convinced that white students would never accept blacks who were undoubtedly (she believed) in Central for reasons other than to get an education, she subscribed to the notions that the nine's grades had been inflated and that they got away with indiscretions inexcusable had they been perpetrated by whites. With, from her perspective, tension abounding, school spirit ebbing, and her own classes a month behind schedule, she concluded, "It's just not like it used to be at all." In her opinion, the only solution for "the entire problem [was] to remove the nine Negroes."[59]

Another science staffer—and, according to counselor Shirley Stancil, "a rabid segregationist"—agreed. Complaining that a truly exceptional cohort of physics students "died" the minute Ernest Green appeared in his classroom, Everett Barnes confessed to finding the presence of troops in Central's corridors "very distasteful."[60]

William Ivy, on the other hand, claimed that he was not initially opposed to teaching black pupils but told state police officers interviewing him in January 1958 that "This has changed now due to the conditions which we have to teach under." He too took issue with the tone of Walker's address and resented the "pressure" and "upset" that followed.[61]

It was, however, one thing for conservative faculty to express opinions about integration, another to translate those views into intolerance in the classroom. For it does not necessarily follow that teachers' perspectives on racial issues at large influenced how they carried out their day-to-day responsibilities.[62] Journalism teacher and school newspaper sponsor Edna Middlebrook was, for instance, according to a pupil especially well placed to know, "definitely a daughter of the Confederacy" and made no secret of her "very strong segregation views."[63] Remembered by *Arkansas Gazette* reporter and one-time *Central High School Tiger* editor Jerry Dhonau for her refusal to publish a column advocating the naming of a sports facility after an African American, Middlebrook nevertheless believed that it was her duty to "develop in my students' ability to think right on controversial subjects." "I do not desire," she explained, "to tell them what to think but I want them to learn to evaluate both sides of any question." True to her principles, she left Jane Emery free to use her own words and ideas in editorializing for a measured and peaceful acceptance of the law at the height of the crisis in September 1957.[64]

Traditional southern manners might also have dictated that it was one thing to maintain discriminatory attitudes toward African Americans as a community but quite another to maltreat an individual young person known by name—provided, of course, that that young person kept her place. Nor should it be forgotten that, even in the more authoritarian classroom atmosphere of the 1950s, teaching was still an interactive process in which the demeanor of the learner might well disarm adult preconceptions about his or her race, gender, and class. Positive educational outcomes for an individual were indeed possible despite persistent underlying antipathy to the group to which he or she belonged. Besides, classroom decorum was also a function of a teacher's persona. Regardless of her views on race-mixing, a sloppy disciplinarian like Terrence Roberts' Spanish teacher, Carolyn Bell, a woman in the last months of her career whose body language alone betrayed her resentments, could be as worrisome for the Nine as English and history classes "taught by teachers who probably would have preferred that the whole desegregation experiment be abandoned and the sooner the better."[65] On the other hand, a staff member proud of Central's standing as a prestigious and supremely well-ordered machine, could easily have considered the presence of the Nine as not so much an affront to racial sensibilities as an obstacle to the impeccable operation of a hallowed institution. From such a perspective, the color of the newcomers was inherently less an issue than the potentially routine and reputation-trashing disruption that threatened to follow in their wake. The significant issue, however, was the extent to which all twenty-six educators chosen to receive black pupils—moderates and segregationists alike—responded to their situation.

Although the evidence is again skimpy and, in this case, less transparent than it appears, a combination of poor classroom management, racial conservatism, and strident student segregationists commonly spelled trouble. Given the charged situation in which both teachers and the nine found themselves, however, actions on both sides of the racial divide could easily be misconstrued, particularly if the pupil concerned was, like Minnijean Brown, a youngster with "a low boiling point" who, according to her speech teacher Micky McGalin, took "offense at the evidently accidental moving of a chair in her direction, which set her to crying, disconcerting the girl who had stumbled over it and was turning to say she was sorry."[66] A teacher preoccupied with managing a roomful of exuberant adolescents could easily miss an incident that its victim saw as a blatant affront and been unfairly resented as a result.[67] Even in the best-managed of classrooms there were always opportunities for mischief when a teacher's back was turned or when she was head-down at her desk.[68] Although the nine were clearly irked by instances of apparent unresponsiveness, missing a particular incident of harassment did not necessarily imply a general indifference to affliction or, worse, a calculated oversight.[69] Yet, as Terrence Roberts reports, sometimes it could: "Sitting in my English class that year," he writes, "was an ongoing exercise in stress management. . . . It was not at all unusual for things to be thrown at me during class sessions—and for the teacher to claim she had no knowledge of any of it. One day . . . several can openers, the kind with sharp points for puncturing cans, were thrown at me. I immediately took the openers to the teacher, who looked at me incredulously and said, 'I didn't see it. Did you bring those in?'"[70]

As time passed and teachers came to realize that recalcitrant students were unlikely to be as severely disciplined as they initially anticipated, they perhaps slipped, albeit reluctantly, into blinking at race-based incidents they would not previously have countenanced. Vice Principal Powell certainly thought so. Lax enforcement at the top only made the hard-core trouble-makers "more overt and arrogant towards officials while becoming more contemptuous of citizenship standards in general." "And the teachers," he continued at the height of a spate of disturbances in early 1958, "began changing their minds about vigilance. Fewer offenders were referred to the office or taken there by guards or others during the second semester because the routine had become to all practical purposes a waste of time." "'Why discipline a kid at all?' teachers asked among themselves. 'Even if he does get suspended, which isn't likely, he'll be back in a few days to cause more trouble.'"[71] They had a point. For, as principal Matthews himself confessed, "I just approach most any dealings I have with any youngster a little more carefully and particularly when we get anything that relates to integration . . . we don't bolt into anything quite so much."[72]

Although a senior's recollections of a French class including Minnijean Brown and one of her chief tormenters and taught, perhaps significantly, by a first-year female teacher undercuts the principal's rosy assertion that "the teachers never once lost control of their classes," there is, neverthe-less, more evidence of individual persecution than of widespread classroom disruption.[73] Even so tart a critic of his superior's apparent reluctance to deal more severely with persistent malcontents as vice-principal Powell still believed (or wanted to believe) that "Teachers also maintained firm control in their classrooms. At no time did any situation get out of hand."[74] The evidence does suggest that a majority of educators responded pragmatically to their unprecedented situation and simply resolved to apply themselves more rigorously than ever to the tasks in hand. Distributive education instructor Nyna Keeton asked rhetorically, "I'm one lone teacher with forty kids. What can I do? And so I decided the thing I could do that year was the most helpful to do the best job I'd ever done. And to keep my kids busy and to just be sure that I handled my end of the world."[75] As Jo Ann Henry reported, contrasting teaching spaces with hallways: "In the classroom we really did have class. It was not chaos inside that place as some people I am sure think it was."[76]

If only because their activities regularly involved bodily contact between students and equipment that could double as instruments of torture, physical education specialists were at risk of suffering worse press than their classroom colleagues. Regardless of the best intentions of even the most sympathetic instructors, gymnasiums, ball courts, playing fields, and their associated facilities were harder to police than confined spaces. They provided ample opportunities for furtive mischiefs that could be misconstrued as derelictions of duty if and when they were not acted upon by supervisors preoccupied by the excitement of a sporting triumph or momentarily out of a locker room.[77] Like the corridor jostling and silly traditions such as tossing girls' gym shoes out windows that passed without undue notice in "normal" times, on-field incidents and shower-room shenanigans could easily have gained an unwarranted and potentially reputation-damaging racial *frisson* when they involved a black student.[78] On the other hand, the very nature of his responsibilities gave a hostile coach more than ample opportunity to exercise prejudices indirectly by tolerating the race-based indiscretions of his more pugnacious pupils. Elizabeth Eckford, Daisy Bates discovered, left school early one day "after girls in her gym class had hit her repeatedly with basketballs and the teacher had made no attempt to stop them."[79] In Ernest Green's words, "The instructors just didn't want us there, and they didn't hide it a lot. . . . You got the feeling they deliberately put you with the most hostile kids."[80] Indeed, as one of the more aggressive segregationist students still remembered four decades after the event, when Jefferson Thomas was struck by a rock at softball practice, "the coach gathered the team around. He said, 'We're not going to tolerate that' [but] he said it with a smirk, telegraphing the message, 'I'm not really upset it happened.'"[81] By contrast, both Thomas and Terrence Roberts recalled other sports instructors who were much more evenhanded, if not totally protective.[82] Even Melba Pattillo Beals, generally no fan of her teachers, characterized her volleyball coach as "a no-nonsense person" who cautioned her other charges not to bother their new classmate and showed genuine compassion when she spied a coven of foul-mouthed harpies scaling a fence and surging across the playing fields to "Get the nigger."[83]

The vital importance of resolute leadership can hardly be better illustrated than by noticing the coach of Central's famed football team, the Tigers. Long remembered by one of his charges as an "excellent" instructor despite his reputation as a "tyrant" with a "legendary" temper and, perhaps not coincidentally, as a man who had had no qualms about allowing a black groundsman (Riley Johns) to become, in his own words, "unofficially more like one of the coaches," Wilson Matthews was not prepared to allow the arrival of the 101st Airborne to interfere with his single-minded determination to maintain his previous season's unbeaten run.[84] Marshalling his lettermen at the very start of the crisis in September 1957, he issued his ultimatum: "Don't look out the window and worry about what's going on outside. If I hear of any of you getting involved in any of this, you're finished with football. You'll answer to me."[85] Not all of Matthews' men remained above the fray, but the great majority did. As his champion halfback Bruce Fullerton recalled, "I guess I was just too busy with school and athletics to be aware of all that was going on."[86] It was the team that shadowed Superintendent Blossom's daughter Gail, a senior, and, in history class, sat protectively around Jefferson Thomas out of the standard alphabetical order.[87] It was Link, another football player, whose spontaneous offer of an automobile enabled Melba Pattillo to escape a segregationist posse and who kept her informed of impending attacks.[88] Indeed, whereas almost one-fifth (18.5 percent) of Central's male students were party to activities indicative of varying degrees of antipathy to integration, only two of thirty-two of the school's top-ranking football players (6.3 percent) were similarly inclined.[89] While hard-to-supervise showers and change rooms remained high on the list of places perilous for the nine, there is no indication that the perpetrators of afflictions such as towel-thrashings and hot water scaldings were top-level athletes.[90] Coaches were certainly seen enforcing law and order on the day the nine first entered school.[91]

Coach Matthews was not alone in taking a firm stand. Terrence Roberts' math teacher was equally firm and her class was a "haven" compared with English and history where unsympathetic staff somehow failed to see flying objects and took exception to his "whining." "Mrs. Helen Conrad," he recalls, "let it be known from the first day that I was in class that she would not tolerate any nonsense from anyone who opposed my presence. She was emphatic about it and the class responded accordingly."[92]

A review of the fortunes of another five of the nine confirms that Roberts' varied experience was not unusual, even in those cases, like Minnijean Brown's, where first impressions were uniformly grim. Comments from Melba Pattillo, Thelma Mothershed, Carlotta Walls, Ernest Green, and Minnijean Brown illustrate that the varying degrees to which teachers allowed prejudicial personal attitudes to sully professional standards of student management guaranteed that each of Central's black pioneers found comfort in some rooms but purgatory in others.

Though perhaps not the most outspoken of the nine—that honor belonged to Minnijean Brown—fifteen-year-old junior Melba Pattillo was, at least in vice-principal Huckaby's eyes, "anything but meek" and, like Minnijean, attracted more than her fair share of segregationist ire. Indeed, with the notable exception of her time in the diminutive Getha Pickens' shorthand group—"a kind of oasis in my life" that quickly became "horrible" when Pickens was away from school—she characterizes her classroom experience as "hell—a living hell."[93] "Teachers," she stated, "treated me badly."[94]

What seems to have peeved and frustrated Pattillo more than anything else was not so much her mentors' sins of commission as their perceived reluctance to act against persistently disruptive and even violent segregationist miscreants. Challenging administrators' assertion that teachers had not lost control of their classrooms, she diarised at the end of September, "Even inside the classroom where things should be safe and civilized, I am never able to be comfortable because the teachers are not in control." If, she reports, other students were not mouthing abuse, they were inventing all manner of mean tricks without reprimand and, perhaps even more reprehensibly, with the tacit or even active connivance of unspecified elders. From her perspective, there were just too many instructors like the female teacher who tolerated racially pejorative language and "remained passive when students threw things at me or dumped water on my head;" too many people like the member of the English department who, on the first full day of integration (September 25), established the tone for the following year by sneering, after a request for some consideration in the wake of a period of constant segregationist muttering, "I hope you don't think we're gonna browbeat our students to please you'all."[95]

Furthermore, Pattillo not only thought too many of her teachers were willing to turn a blind eye toward persecutions as cruel as any of those practiced in the halls and stairways but, with some support from Terrence Roberts and counselor Shirley Stancil, also believed that they actively discriminated against the nine when it came to grades. Her B and C assessments were not, she reasoned, a true reflection of the "very, very good student" she bravely assumed, despite her tribulations, she still was.[96] That Central might have had more exacting standards than her old school was not a consideration. Nor did she think of the unsettling consequences of changing subjects in the course of a semester regardless of the reasons for so doing.[97] Carlotta Walls, by contrast, encountered staff with a range of views on integration but did not seem to have sullied her splendid record and regularly made the honor roll, even after she had missed several weeks of class.[98]

Slight in stature and suffering the ongoing consequences of rheumatic fever, Thelma Mothershed did not attract nearly as much unwanted attention as Melba Pattillo and, perhaps because of her unthreatening presence, found "most of the faculty helpful."[99] Even so, there were exceptions. "My homeroom teacher," she told an interviewer some twenty years after the events of 1957, remembering such things as seating arrangements if nothing else, "was kind of strange. . . . So she did little strange subtle things—subtle as a ton of bricks."[100]

Although Carlotta Walls agreed with Pattillo that "class offered little solace," she too enjoyed respite in some classrooms. Contrasting biology instructor Howard Bell with his mother (who taught Spanish), Walls acknowledged the existence of "a small group" of teachers and students "who were at times openly kind, who seemed to look beyond skin color and see nine students eager to learn, eager to be part of a great academic institution." More specifically, she has written that Bell "kept an eye on me in class and kept the troublemakers at bay. He didn't single me out, but he called on me as regularly as he called on my classmates. He even encouraged me to participate in the science fair. He chose to see me." Walls' first impression of her geometry teacher was also favorable. Margaret Reiman, she remembered decades later, "was a strict disciplinarian who didn't tolerate any nonsense. Her stern voice and face set the tone. She would put up with no disruptions, she announced firmly. We had much work to do, and she moved quickly into the business of class."[101]

There is nothing on the record to indicate that Ernest Green, the only senior among the nine, was the victim of overt academic prejudice, at least in the one subject for which there is evidence. By his own admission, Green had problems with physics and "almost up to the last minute" was unsure about passing a subject vital to his graduation and important to his plans to become an electrical engineer. For various reasons ranging from youthfulness—at just sixteen he was younger than the average senior— to inadequate prior knowledge, mathematical deficiencies, and persecution, his grades were, as Elizabeth Huckaby recognized, "poor."[102] Nor, so long as his teacher Everett Barnes (whom he initially reckoned was "very nice") believed he was responsible for destroying the spirit of a potentially outstanding scholarship group, was he likely to have been a particularly welcome presence in the science laboratory. Even so, he successfully completed the course with, in his own terms, "a fairly decent" grade, despite his instructor's reservations about his native ability in the discipline and reputation (among all students) for being "very difficult at times."[103]

Although her mother, Imogene Brown, remembered that at least one faculty member had been prepared to lend her daughter a book, Minnijean

Brown herself was not forthcoming on her teachers for many years after she left Little Rock for the New Lincoln School in New York in February 1958.[104] Interviewed by historian Elizabeth Jacoway in September 2003, she recalled that, because she was a young woman unafraid to challenge authority, it was "no wonder they hated my guts." Indeed, it was only in glee club that Minnijean ever really felt part of Central. There, she reminisced (without remembering her teacher by name), Naomi Hancock was "wonderful—[and] acted as if there was nothing different about me at all. . . . There never seemed to be a minute where I was anything other than a member of the class. That's quiet courage . . . and that's where I felt the safest."[105]

In fact, as Elizabeth Huckaby found when she made inquiries, Minnijean's teachers were more sympathetic to her situation than she might have realized. Far from being offended by Minnijean's drawing attention to the deficiencies of a history textbook on the subject of slavery, Margaret Stewart was "distressed" by her relative lack of progress and, like English instructor Susie West, attributed her problems to poor application and/or youthful high spirits rather than to any supposed racial characteristics. Even Govie Griffin, Minnijean's homeroom teacher and no fan of integration, readily acknowledged the extent to which Minnijean gradually curbed the attention-seeking and readiness to take offence that had marred their early acquaintance. To William Lincoln, there was nothing "grossly wrong with what she did. She was just sticking up for herself."[106]

In short, while the nine undoubtedly experienced many instances of coldness, sharp language, and intemperate behavior from teachers unhappy with the arrival of black students in their classes, they were taught by a faculty that by and large had not needed to be reminded (by principal Matthews) to treat the nine with "good judgment and professional impartiality."[107] As a senior recalled of a class she shared with Elizabeth Eckford and an educator unsympathetic to the changes going on around her, "There was little interaction with other students in most of my classes. Desks were in straight lines, the teacher taught and we were there to learn."[108] Of course, there were always some prepared to turn a blind eye or excuse a knife-wielding boy at an assembly on the grounds that "These children have tolerated a lot of upheaval." There were certainly faculty like the one who "could twist her face into the most grotesque mask of hatred you could imagine" and ask Terrence Roberts, "Why do you want to go to *our* school, why don't you go back to your own school?"[109]But, by the same token, there were others of a similar persuasion who, like Ernest Green's physics master and several of Carlotta Walls' instructors, assessed their black pupils on their merits. Math

instructor William Ivy could regret the nine's presence and yet still invite
them to attend the twenty minutes of readings, prayers, and hymns that
made Carlotta Walls look on chapel as "my haven, the place where I found
the spiritual fuel I needed to get through each day."[110]

More generally, it seems that, despite clear differences of opinion on
desegregation in the abstract, Central's educators at large battled through
the 1957–1958 school year without unduly betraying their professionalism.
Indeed, as openly integrationist student adviser Shirley Stancil noted, even
the "few faculty members [who] strongly resented integration . . . as a
whole performed their duties over and above expectations" with the result
that "order in the classroom went quite well."[111] "Teachers," the *Arkansas
Democrat* reported, "purposely have poured on the work to occupy their
[students'] time and leisure" and, from their superintendent's not unbiased
perspective, "tried to do a good job regardless of their personal views on
integration."[112] As five Central and Hall alumni remembered in organizing
a petition in favor of teachers to be purged in May 1959, "regardless of their
personal opinions during the integration controversy . . . they have without
qualification or exception acted only with their students' welfare and interest as their primary concern."[113] They were the sorts who endeavored "to
keep things on an even keel" from the beginning of the crisis and, at least
according to boys' vice-principal Jay Powell, outdid the administration in
maintaining discipline, so that even a woman who wanted "to do everything
for segregation that [she] could" was still able to concede that "probably the
work was not as good as it might have been, but we really have a fine group
of classroom teachers here at Central and they went on with the work and,
as far as I could tell here in the library, the actual teaching and learning went
on a good deal as usual."[114] They were people who, like American history
teacher Margaret Stewart, quietly rearranged seating so that a boy with a
dubious reputation would not bother Gloria Ray. Micky McGalin presided
over a speech class so relaxed that Elizabeth Eckford was able to reduce
everyone to laughter by telling a gawping white boy to close his mouth.[115]

It was, as a normally acerbic vice-principal Powell noted, "just not
realistic" to deny that things were "pretty rough" during the first couple
of months of integration but thereafter Central's educational program
progressed at "about the same" level as it had done previously.[116] "We got
through it. We really did do it," Jo Ann Henry recalled with obvious pride.
"We taught school all year. We did graduate a class. And in spite of some
disruptions, eight out of nine of the black students finished the year."[117]
Significantly, Central's accreditation as a premier high school in the North

Central Association was apparently never in jeopardy that year.[118] With Daisy Bates telling the press at an otherwise particularly torrid time for the nine after the expulsion of Minnijean Brown that, "The Negroes were not bothered in the classrooms," it might even have been true, as an optimistic Elizabeth Huckaby reported (also in early 1958), that "the teachers most disturbed originally about integration were not so much so, now." Her male counterpart certainly noted that he had heard fewer negative things about the nine after October 1957.[119]

In effect, there is a case for perspective. While the arrival of a mere nine black students among nearly two thousand whites undoubtedly had a symbolic significance well beyond their number, less than one-third of Central's teachers regularly encountered members of the Little Rock Nine in their classrooms.[120] Committed, like their principal, to maintaining their school's illustrious reputation, a goodly number of teachers seem to have tried to carry on as normally as possible. "A. L. Lape, my band director," Woody Mann, a senior and the son of Little Rock's mayor commented, "absolutely refused to let members of his band get caught up in all of the disruption taking place around us . . . [and] Josephine Feiock, my English teacher, was convinced that her students were going to graduate from high school with the ability to both speak and write the King's English, or we would have to deal with her."[121] "Coach Matthews," the principal's son told a latter-day inquirer, "kept me busy with doing football. . . . We were in our own little thing. . . . I didn't lie around worrying about the integration of Central High or where I was going to be twenty years from now. I worried about making the football team, surviving the two-day practices in the heat."[122]

Given the number of individuals involved and the frisson of the peculiar situation in which they found themselves, some antipathies were no doubt inevitable, as Ernest Green found in dealing (ultimately successfully) with his physics teacher. When any one of the nine had the misfortune to be assigned a teacher or, more specifically, either a long-serving, middle-aged female humanities teacher or a coach unable to moderate personal racial feelings and unwilling to curb the verbal and physical excesses of their more belligerent segregationist charges, then Central had the potential to become, as Melba Pattillo Beals recalled, "a furnace."[123] Yet, while ignorance and folly in the choice of those who were to shatter precedent by teaching black pupils combined to threaten Elizabeth Huckaby's best intentions, there was always hope so long as the likes of Jefferson Thomas could be seen by a known segregationist as just another very courteous young man anxious to learn and keep up with his classmates.[124] The twenty-six souls assigned to

teach the nine certainly included "those who were segregationists at heart
as well as some avowed integrationists," but, as Huckaby anticipated before
the commencement of classes, "all were professionals and would teach
each youngster, no matter what his race."[125] Notwithstanding unconscio-
nable lapses, her expectations were, by and large, not misplaced. As coach
Gene Hall summed up the experience of 1957–1958, "The group of teachers
that were at Central High during those times were, I would call dedicated
people. This was the situation that they were in and they were going to try
to make it work to the best of their ability."[126]

CHAPTER 16

Going Off the Deep End

The Civil Rights Act of 1964 and the Desegregation of Little Rock's Public Swimming Pools

JOHN A. KIRK

Have you ever thought of going to a public swimming pool as a political statement? This article chronicles the struggle to desegregate Little Rock's public pools. Earlier in the nation's history, public swimming pools were visible embodiments of our political-racial relations. In 1964, a motel manager in St. Augustine, Florida infamously dumped acid into the pool's water in an effort to chase away the activists trying to integrate it. Under the US Civil Rights Act adopted that year, denying access to any public accommodation, including public swimming pools, to anyone based upon their race was illegal. Implementation of the act was challenged, however, in Little Rock and elsewhere, eventually giving rise to the proliferation of private swimming pools across the US.

On July 2, 1964, President Lyndon B. Johnson signed one of the twentieth century's landmark pieces of civil rights legislation into law. The Civil Rights Act of 1964 had a wide-ranging coverage that tackled discrimination in education, voting rights, and labor relations. Its most immediate impact, however, came in the abolition of segregation in "public accommodations." Following on courts' piecemeal dismantling of certain segregated facilities and the community campaigns by civil rights activists that had intensified in the decade before, the 1964 Civil Rights Act finally outlawed segregation in all public places. These included any facility that was "owned, operated, or managed by or on behalf of any state or subdivision thereof," as well as commercial concerns.[1] US Supreme Court rulings that followed in cases

Originally published in *Arkansas Historical Quarterly* 73, no. 2 (Summer 2014): 138–63. Reprinted with permission. DOI: https://doi.org/10.34053/parry2019.riapag2.16

such as Heart of Atlanta Motel v. United States and Katzenbach v. McClung
upheld the Civil Rights Act's contention that the US Constitution's commerce clause gave Congress power to forbid racial discrimination even in
privately run businesses.[2]

Unlike the Supreme Court's Brown v. Board of Education ruling ten
years earlier, the 1964 Civil Rights Act did not meet with a campaign of
massive resistance to its implementation.[3] Reflecting the impact of the civil
rights movement in changing attitudes toward Jim Crow, many not-yet
desegregated facilities quickly moved to comply with the new law. That still
left civil rights activists with the task of testing whether other facilities and
businesses that claimed to have desegregated would actually admit and serve
African American customers, as well as the task of exerting direct pressure
on those that continued to refuse to do so. Without African Americans
actually turning up to use those facilities, there was no way of knowing if
they had desegregated or not. This would be a painstaking endeavor, since it
meant coordinating attempts of volunteers to use every single public facility
or business in every single community across the South.[4]

Most revealing about the response to the 1964 Civil Rights Act was the
pattern of compliance and non-compliance that developed. There were few
cast-iron certainties about how any given community would react to the
desegregation of one set of facilities as opposed to another. In fact, it was
the wide variety and range of responses that was often striking. Nevertheless,
there were some broadly discernable tendencies. Firstly, it often proved easier to desegregate both publicly funded facilities and private businesses in
Upper South states than in Lower South states, where attitudes toward
segregation were more entrenched. Secondly, it often proved easier to desegregate facilities in urban areas than in rural areas. In rural areas, sentiment
against change appeared to be more inflexible, local officials and businesses
were more isolated and therefore more susceptible to community pressure to
resist change, and African American populations were smaller and had fewer
resources to challenge the status quo. By contrast, urban areas generally
offered a wider range of opinions among whites, including more support
for desegregation; they offered protection in numbers for officials and businesses; and they harbored a larger African American community with more
resources and support structures in place to challenge segregation. Thirdly,
the larger chains of eating and retail establishments were often easier to
desegregate than smaller independent businesses. Larger chains were generally more conscious of their national image and standing, they were less
susceptible to local actions such as white boycotts, and, if it came down to

it, they had the option of relocating elsewhere. Smaller business were often family concerns and more likely to be attuned with and sensitive to community sentiment, since they relied on local goodwill for their custom, and they were more vulnerable to retribution and loss of their smaller clientele if they violated local mores.[5]

Yet, while they were concentrated in cities and not subject to the whims of private owners, public swimming pools, as the interracial civil rights group the Arkansas Council on Human Relations (ACHR) predicted, would join small restaurants in proving "the most serious holdouts."[6] Anything that involved interracial bathing often provoked the most steadfast resistance to change. More than any other publicly sponsored facility, swimming pools brought African Americans and whites into close and intimate contact. The prospect of African American men and white women bathing together in states of undress stirred deep-seated white fears of miscegenation, as well as white anxieties about African American cleanliness and disease. In his fascinating study *Contested Waters: A Social History of Swimming Pools in America*, historian Jeff Wiltse focuses on pools in northern and midwestern cities, but there is much about that story that sheds light on the southern experience. Whereas southern public pools were segregated from the get-go under Jim Crow, northern public pools were generally integrated along racial lines, although segregated by sex, when they were first built in the late nineteenth century. It was only when men and women began to share swimming pools in the 1920s that racial segregation began to take a firm hold. After that, efforts to desegregate swimming pools across the country proved problematic. In 1954, in a Baltimore case upholding racial segregation in swimming pools after the Brown decision, Judge Rozel Thomsen ruled that pools were even "more sensitive than schools."[7]

This article examines the struggle to desegregate public swimming pools in Little Rock, Arkansas, between 1963 and 1965. Initial failed attempts to integrate the pools were made in June 1963, after the courts ruled many of the city's segregated facilities (but not specifically swimming pools) unconstitutional. Anticipating the passage of the 1964 Civil Rights Act, African Americans, in concert with the National Association for the Advancement of Colored People (NAACP), made renewed efforts in the summer of 1964 to use the city's pools. In response, Little Rock, like a number of other southern cities before it, closed all of its public swimming pools. The following year, again following practices in some other communities, the city board of directors unsuccessfully sought to sell its public pools in an apparent attempt to privatize them so that they could be reopened on a segregated basis.[8] When this failed amid growing community pressure to reopen the pools, even if on an integrated basis, and with all other alternatives seemingly exhausted, the city finally and reluctantly opened its pools to African American and white swimmers. Mirroring the situation nationwide, however, after desegregation public pool attendance in Little Rock plummeted. The city halted all new construction of public swimming pools in mixed-race areas of residence, and the existing pools that it owned were abandoned by whites in droves. Many of them headed to private neighborhood pools and/or their own backyard pools in the western suburbs of the city, leaving the public pools with an overwhelmingly African American clientele.

Today's resegregation of swimming pools, which places the city squarely in line with many other communities, seems a far cry from what might have been anticipated in the early postwar period when, not without some justification, Little Rock established a reputation as one of the South's most progressive cities in race relations. Daisy Bates, co-owner with her husband, L. C. Bates, of the leading African American newspaper in the state, the *Arkansas State Press*, and president of the NAACP Arkansas State Conference of Branches, noted that when the couple moved to Little Rock in 1941 race relations were, "calm and improving," with a "notable lack of tension."[9] As early as 1942, Little Rock appointed its first black police officers of the modern era after the shooting of an African American US Army sergeant in the downtown African American business district of West Ninth Street (they were restricted, however, to policing West Ninth and could not arrest whites). In the late 1940s and early 1950s, the city began a phased program of opening its all-white public library to African American patrons. In 1956, it desegregated buses without problem. African Americans began to gain limited access to a selected few of the city's segregated public parks, though only by pre-arrangement, in small numbers, and with certain restrictions in place, such as prohibiting use of the swimming pools or the golf course. The Little Rock Zoo began to admit African Americans, but only on Thursdays, and with use of the amusement park and picnic areas discouraged. Some businesses eased restrictions, too. Pfeiffer's, a downtown department store, built a segregated lunch counter to cater to African American clients that were previously refused service altogether. Downtown hotels began to relax their policy of segregation by allowing groups to hold interracial meetings at their facilities, but still seated African Americans and whites at different tables for lunch. By the early 1950s, hotels were accepting group bookings of visiting African American sports teams while still prohibiting individual African Americans from occupying rooms. The city's two white newspapers, the *Arkansas Gazette* and the *Arkansas Democrat*, changed their policy of denying courtesy titles of "Mr." and "Mrs." to African Americans by dropping "Mr." altogether except for members of the clergy (African American and white) and applying "Mrs." equally. The first press pictures of African Americans in white newspapers began to appear. The *Democrat* even hired Ozell Sutton, the first African American reporter to work for a white newspaper in Arkansas, to write a weekly column about news in the black community.[10]

The trauma of the Little Rock school crisis of 1957–1959 halted the city's postwar progress for several years.[11] When the student sit-in movement mushroomed across the South in early 1960 in an attempt to desegregate downtown lunch counters, Little Rock used high fines and stiff prison sentences to break the demonstrations.[12] In 1961, when Freedom Riders came to Little Rock looking to desegregate interstate bus terminals, the city dispatched them quickly on their way via a jail cell, although the terminals did desegregate later in the year after the Interstate Commerce Commission ordered them to do so.[13]

It was not until 1963, far behind many other Upper South cities, that Little Rock finally embarked upon a program of downtown desegregation. In March 1962, twenty-two members of a newly formed local civil rights organization, the Council on Community Affairs (COCA), filed suit in US District Court against the city board of directors for the desegregation of "public parks, recreational facilities, Joseph T. Robinson Auditorium and all other public facilities."[14] In October 1962, the Student Nonviolent Coordinating Committee (SNCC) sent white civil rights activist Bill Hansen to Little Rock, at the request of the ACHR, to kick-start student sit-ins again.[15]

The new wave of protests finally convinced downtown merchants and businessmen that they needed to act. In January 1963, a phased program of downtown desegregation began, starting with lunch counters. By the end of January, several major hotels, including the Marion, Grady Manning, Albert Pike, Lafayette, and Sam Peck, as well as several motels, including Downtowner, Holiday Inn, and Howard Johnson, and the Midway Bowling Alley, had desegregated. In February, federal judge J. Smith Henley ruled in favor of the COCA lawsuit. The ruling ordered an end to segregation in all publicly funded facilities. In June, the city's movie theatres and drive-ins, along with Robinson Auditorium, admitted African Americans on an equal basis for the first time. In October, most of the city's main restaurants had begun to serve African American customers. By the end of the year, all city parks, playgrounds, golf courses, the Little Rock Zoo, and the Arkansas Arts Center had desegregated. The African American magazine *Jet* quoted James Forman, national executive secretary of SNCC, as saying that Little Rock was "just about the most integrated [city] in the south."[16]

In fact, only one set of city-owned publicly funded facilities remained segregated after the passage of the 1964 Civil Rights Act: swimming pools. Little Rock's first public swimming pool had opened in the Pulaski Heights amusement area known as White City on June 16, 1922. The pool operated for seventeen seasons before closing in 1939, after the land was sold to developers to create a new subdivision in the city's first, fastest-growing, and all-white suburb.[17] After the closure of the White City Pool, which the Little Rock Recreation Commission had run since 1930, the commission proposed a city bond to fund a 45 percent share in a new pool at a cost of $47,000. The other 55 percent came from the federal New Deal agency the Works Projects Administration (WPA).[18] The WPA was instrumental in building many new swimming pools across the United States in the 1930s and early 1940s, in what Jeff Wiltse refers to as America's "swimming pool age."[19] In the August 1940 election, the bond issue won resoundingly by 2359 votes to 311, alongside a much larger bond for the expansion of Little Rock's Adams Field Airport.[20] By 1941, the J. Curran Conway Pool was completed in the Fair Park neighborhood, and on Friday, May 28, 1942, ahead of Memorial Day weekend, it opened for its first season. As with public swimming pools across the country at the time, it proved a wildly popular facility. Designed to accommodate 1800 bathers at a time, it was packed to capacity from the first day of opening.[21]

The opening of the new pool only served to highlight the lack of similar facilities for the city's African American population. Under the terms of the US Supreme Court's "separate but equal" doctrine established in its 1896 Plessy v. Ferguson decision, the Fourteenth Amendment's requirement for "equal protection under the law" could be fulfilled by "separate" public facilities for African Americans and whites so long as they were of an "equal" standard.[22] Clearly, Little Rock's provision of a whites-only pool without any similar facility for its African American population violated this requirement. Indeed, Little Rock did not provide any publicly funded recreation facilities for its black citizens.

Ever since the mid-1930s, the city had made faltering attempts to develop a public park for African Americans at a remote location near Granite Mountain, four-and-a-half miles from the closest area of black res-

"Scrappy" Moore, swimming teacher at the pool in Fair Park, donned a Confederate uniform for his clown show, June 22, 1952. Courtesy Butler Center for Arkansas Studies, Central Arkansas Library System and the ***Arkansas-Democrat Gazette***.

idence at Broadway and Roosevelt Streets. Finally, in 1949, the city passed a bond issue for the development of Gillam Park. Using the funds also to entice federal urban renewal money, the park project was swiftly completed. Among its facilities was Gillam Park Pool, which opened on Sunday, August 20, 1950. L. C. Bates was less than impressed. "We are a little puzzled over the dedication of a new pool exclusively for Negroes," ran the *Arkansas State Press* editorial. "We believe it came about twenty odd years too late for us to shout joy. In this day and time when the entire country is planning programs to stamp out segregation, it seems a little ironical that Little

Rock Negroes should be dedicating the outmoded principles." When young
Tommy Grigsby drowned in Gillam Park Pool in 1954, it illustrated the
shortcomings of facilities there: the pool was without sufficient lifeguards;
it lacked a respirator that might have saved the boy's life; and its remote
location meant that a doctor and rescue squad could not make it there in
time to resuscitate him. The *Arkansas State Press* lamented, "the whole affair
was a study in second class citizenship."[23] Terrance Roberts, one of the Little
Rock Nine that desegregated Central High School in 1957, remembers,

> When I was about ten years old, the City of Little Rock built a sep-
> arate park complete with swimming pool and skating rink for black
> people—black people were banned from swimming at Fair Park
> pool. Gillam Park, as the new park was known, was constructed on
> land in Granite Heights, an area in the southeastern part of Little
> Rock where black people were allowed to live. Another example
> of the failure of "separate but equal," Gillam Park bore faint if
> any, resemblance to Fair Park. Although I often went to Gillam
> Park, it was no real substitute for Fair Park. From the beginning,
> the facility was substandard and soon showed signs of disrepair.[24]

COCA had intentionally not specified swimming pools in its 1962
desegregation lawsuit. According to COCA attorney Wiley Branton, a
"gentleman's agreement" had been reached with Little Rock city attorney
Jack Kemp that swimming pools would be left out of the lawsuit so as
not to derail desegregation in other areas. There would be at least a one-
year moratorium on revisiting the issue of desegregating pools. Of course,
that "gentleman's agreement" was between attorneys, Branton noted, and
it could not be considered binding on his clients or any other individuals
in the African American community. And Judge Henley had not exempted
pools in banning segregation in public facilities. Dr. Jerry Jewell, president
of the Little Rock NAACP branch and one of the plaintiffs in the COCA
desegregation lawsuit, and L. C. Bates, now an Arkansas field secretary for
the NAACP (the *Arkansas State Press* collapsed following the school crisis),
along with four other African American men, tested Branton's theory on
June 27, 1963, when they showed up at 2:00 p.m. to swim in the J. Curran
Conway Pool. "We are still segregated here," pool manager Leroy Scott told
them, refusing them entry and pointing out, "You have a pool of your own
in Gillam Park that is just as nice as this one." Jewell replied that they were
taxpayers, and "we'd like to use this one." Scott responded, "We're not ready
for you yet at this pool." Bates interjected, "Let's go back to court." Jewell

later told the press that he would first confer with NAACP state president George Howard, Jr., a Pine Bluff attorney, before making his next move.[25]

However, nothing transpired as a result of this first effort to desegregate the public swimming pools. Almost another year passed before, with the passage of the 1964 Civil Rights Act imminent in Congress, pool desegregation was again revisited. At 1:00 p.m. on Wednesday, June 10, 1964, Jewell and Bates, along with attorney Delector Tiller and fifteen African American boys and girls aged between seven and nineteen years old, sought to join 1500 white swimmers in J. Curran Conway Pool. The group had alerted the Little Rock police and the local FBI ahead of time for protection should any trouble occur. Pool manager Leroy Scott met the group at the front steps of the pool and told them that they could not enter because the facility was operated on a segregated basis. Jewell told him that they simply wanted to exercise their "inherent right to use the public pool." Scott replied that the Gillam Park Pool was just as good, and that many other cities, including in the North, had tried unsuccessfully to integrate their pools and were losing money because of it. Insistent, Jewell told Scott that he hoped he would have the courage to let them pass and swim. Scott replied that, rather, he had enough courage to keep them out for their own protection. Jewell told Scott that they would seek relief through the courts if he refused to admit them. Scott allegedly said that if they did get an injunction, he hoped that Jewell would be among the first to enter, "because there was a 240 pound lifeguard who would take care of him."[26]

Barely five hours later, Little Rock city manager Ancil M. Douthit announced that J. Curran Conway Pool and Gillam Park Pool "would be closed or sold to private owners." Reading a statement prepared by the city board of directors, Douthit said, "The board of directors has instructed this office to proceed with plans as soon as possible to take swimming pools out of the city's recreational program. This obviously will mean either a sale to private enterprise or cessation of operations." Jewell said later that "The NAACP position is that all facilities should be open to all persons. This was another opportunity for Little Rock to take the lead and it didn't." Local African American attorney Harold B. Anderson added that he felt "sorry that the city fathers got hysterical but these things have been worked out in other cities and they can be worked out here. It is unfortunate to punish the children of this city by their preconceived notion as to what will occur if children of different races visit the different pools."[27] The following day, L. C. Bates told the city newspapers that the pool test was just the beginning in a new assault on segregated facilities ahead of the expected passage of the 1964 Civil Rights Act and that "We have directed all branches of the NAACP to get committees set up to approach the power structure in each community." Bates added, "The NAACP doesn't believe in demonstrating in the streets. We want to talk out the problems but we are not having any of just talking about it without action. . . . We are definitely going on with the pool project. One of our people was threatened with harm and we intend to see how far the city intends to go to refuse our rights."[28]

Jewell reported that the Little Rock police and the local FBI had again been placed on alert that a group of African American swimmers planned to seek entry to the pool the following Monday at 1:00 p.m. Jewell said that the most difficult thing about integrating the pool so far had been "explaining to my little boy Wednesday night why he could not go into the pool and swim, and I am sure there are many white parents who have the same problem of explaining to their children why they can't swim with colored children."[29]

On Friday, Jewell had a telephone conversation with Little Rock mayor Byron A. Morse. Morse told him that it was the city's "final decision" not to integrate swimming pools. He added that any attempt to revisit the pool "might result in physical harm to some persons" and that Jewell would be responsible if that happened. Jewell informed the mayor that it was not his duty, but the mayor's duty, the city manager's duty, and the Little Rock police's duty to maintain law and order. He added, "since the city [i]s trying to sell itself as a site for blue-chip industries its segregation policy at the pool [i]s not a good one," and pointed out, "Little Rock [i]s trying to sell a bill of goods in one area and another bill of goods in another area as far as minority groups [a]re concerned." Meanwhile, rumors began to circulate that the city would close the public pools on Sunday ahead of the next planned visit of prospective African American swimmers on Monday.[30]

As at other points in the civil rights struggle, some white clergymen spoke up. Rev. Sam J. Allen, executive secretary of the Arkansas Council of Churches, said, "Ministers and dedicated laymen of all churches and faiths should rise in protest against the intention of the City of Little Rock to close or sell the city swimming pools. In the first place, the city would be doing a grave injustice to the great number of taxpayers and property owners who cannot afford the luxury of a country club for swimming and who are no longer concerned about the presence of Negroes in public places." He continued, "Second only to a segregated church, a segregated swimming pool clearly demonstrates the presence of deep racial prejudice and hatred, which, according to most local and national church leaders, ministers and laymen, and Bible scholars, is a flagrant and willful violation of the Will of God and the spirit of Jesus Christ, who would not hesitate to associate with Negroes at any level of life." Dr. Erwin L. McDonald, president of the Greater Little Rock Ministerial Association, added that he felt denying African Americans access to city pools "is no more logical, democratic, or Christian than ruling out all except those who are blue-eyed or red-headed."[31]

On Sunday, Gov. Orval Faubus responded to Reverend Allen: "If he wants to swim with Negroes, let him go to the Negro swimming pool."[32] The same day, Allen's ministerial station wagon, parked outside of his home, had eggs thrown at the windshield.[33] In other developments, City Manager Douthit announced that the public pools would close at the end of business on Sunday ahead of the planned attempt to integrate them on Monday. Douthit noted that,

> This decision was not hastily made but was arrived at only after careful and thoughtful deliberation. In addition to the city's responsibilities in maintaining peace and order, which is the motivating factor in this decision, the finances of the city are not strong enough to permit continuing operation of the pools at a financial loss. Attendance in the last few days dropped from approximately 1,800 per day to 700 per day.

Jewell reported that the NAACP would now take the case to court and hoped "that God will somehow awaken these gentlemen to the wrongs they have done to all segments of the community."[34]

On Monday, both J. Curran Conway Pool and Gillam Park Pool were closed and drained. Douthit claimed that the city was "close to selling" them. He advised the roughly 300 season ticket holders that refunds would be available from the front desk of the pool between 9:30 a.m. and 6:00 p.m. on Tuesday and Wednesday. Since approximately one-fifth of the season had already elapsed, the city would give a four dollar refund on the five dollar season tickets.[35] An *Arkansas Gazette* survey discovered that there were thirty-one other pools inside the city limits and another eleven in Pulaski County outside of the city limits. All of these were privately owned, only a few were open to the general public, and none of them were open to African Americans.[36]

Pressure began to mount on the city from a number of sources to keep the pools open by integrating them. In no small part, the stigma of the city's closed high schools during the 1958–1959 school year, the last time that the city had shut down public facilities to avoid integration, remained a painful memory to many. A letter from the Catholic Interracial Council of Little Rock to Mayor Morse, signed by its chaplain, Rev. Walter B. Clancy, and its president, W. T. Kelly, read:

> Past experience has shown that the only sensible way to meet the challenge of our day is to face its issues squarely and find real solutions. . . . It is unthinkable that the city of Little Rock would not provide the opportunity for healthy recreation to those children in the city who cannot afford membership in private clubs. We challenge the view that this action of the city directors reflects the sentiments of those who actually use these public facilities. The Board should also face the fact that any financial loss that the pool has suffered could be a direct result of their own actions. Surely our elected representatives can find the courage to enter into conversation with the Negro leadership to find a moral and workable solution that will benefit all the children of our city. Atlanta did so without incident. Why not Little Rock?[37]

A written statement from the ACHR director Nat Griswold expressed similar sentiments.[38] Also because of the pool closures, the Red Cross announced that it would be forced to cancel its summer swimming classes for the city's children.[39]

The closing of the public pools became an issue in political campaigns, from the governor's race to the state house of representatives, and from Democrats to Republicans. Joe Hubbard of Russellville, a candidate for the Democratic nomination for governor, described himself as a "states rights Democrat" but believed that "too often individual responsibilities as American citizens have been obscured by a one-sided emphasis on a states rights position which shirks all responsibility for our national obligation." He decried the fact that the closing of the pools "indicates a deep seated fear that Little Rock citizens cannot meet changing times with calmness and good judgment," adding, "Our solutions must point to the future, not the past. It will hardly be possible for us to grasp the vision of Arkansas leadership in a new South if we spend our energy and best talent trying to preserve the old South."[40] Cecil H. Higgins of North Little Rock, a taxi driver and Republican candidate for Pulaski County Position 5 in the Arkansas House of Representatives, urged a ballot on the pool closings and insisted that 95 percent of the voters would vote for integration and to keep the pools open. "The South is dead," he proclaimed. "That question was settled when the Civil War ended."[41] In a KATV interview, Governor Faubus said that he did not think most African Americans in the city wanted integration and that the whole fuss was caused by a few "Negro radicals" in the NAACP.[42]

With the pools closed and the passage of the 1964 Civil Rights Act pending, the NAACP chose to switch its attention elsewhere for the time being. Jewell announced that the organization would now focus on employment issues and specifically on gaining African Americans jobs in the "lily-white" Little Rock Fire Department, on appointing more African American policemen than those currently restricted to patrolling West Ninth Street, and on attaining more African American front office jobs in city hall to "give the city a progressive image when out-of-state industries visit the city."[43]

The final passage of the 1964 Civil Rights Act, after prolonged filibustering in Congress, highlighted the divergent opinions on desegregation among leading politicians and civil rights leaders in Little Rock and in Arkansas. White views ranged from outright hostility to extreme caution. All of Arkansas's congressional delegation voted against the civil rights bill, and its senators, John McClellan and J. William Fulbright, actively participated in a filibuster against it.[44] Governor Faubus stormed, "We're no nearer a solution in race relations now than before. I agree with the ones who voted against it, that two or three of the provisions are unconstitutional, and with [Republican presidential candidate] Barry Goldwater's statement that it flies in the face of the Constitution." Later, he added, "When people who are supposed to be responsible yield to pressure and through fear vote against their own conscience, you have the beginning of a police state. Now we'll have another added expense to government in employment of hundreds of enforcement agencies and millions of dollars in court costs which the federal government under this bill has agreed to assume."[45] Faubus's Republican challenger in the upcoming 1964 gubernatorial election, Winthrop Rockefeller, was not as belligerent as his opponent but still expressed misgivings about the bill, saying:

> The civil rights bill is now law and we must accept that fact. Certainly the act should be tested to determine its constitutionality. After the act's full implications are known, we must keep our perspective in order to meet these problems of human relations. It is still my conviction . . . that we can make greater permanent progress by voluntary action through faith, integrity, understanding and goodwill.[46]

Arkansas attorney general Bruce Bennett said that he thought "the bill is more political in nature than anything ever proposed in Congress. It is

primarily designed to secure votes from a minority. Hurrah for the 27 senators who voted against it."[47] He went on to add, "I don't believe anyone
realizes how deep this thing is going to affect every facet of our lives."[48]
Bennett later advised the state to take a wait-and-see, stonewalling approach
to the legislation. Confessing that he had not yet actually read the law, he
described his "present attitude" toward it:

> The Civil Rights bill as amended, passed and signed into law has
> not been interpreted by the courts . . . there has been no appro-
> priation made for the administration of this act, and there are no
> employees of the federal government that are available for consul-
> tation as to the extent of the act and who it affects. In other words,
> there is not a single individual, from President Johnson on down,
> who can on this day give an authentic and authoritative interpre-
> tation of the Civil Rights Law. By no stretch of the imagination
> can the ordinary citizen be presumed to know what is in it at this
> time; nor, can he be presumed to know whether or not it affects
> his particular business.[49]

Even more critical than Bennett was Amis Guthridge, president of Little
Rock's Capital Citizens' Council, who raged,

> If the Southern senators really were wanting to stop this vicious
> alleged civil rights legislation they should have told that dirty
> Southern scalawag [President Lyndon B.] Johnson that they would
> not vote for any legislation which he proposed and with their com-
> mittee chairmanships, they could have stopped it. Our federal gov-
> ernment, including Congress, the executive and the judiciary, are
> dominated by an alien philosophy which we will not accept. As
> an attorney but first as an American citizen I will resist this illegal
> tyranny by any means necessary.[50]

He went on to say, "I am going to advise my clients to refuse to follow the
act because in my opinion in addition to its being unconstitutional it even
exceeds the legal aspects and is a violation of their God-given rights."[51]

Little Rock city officials such as Russell H. Matson, president of the
school board, and Mayor Byron R. Morse were far more muted in their
responses. Matson said, "A wait and see attitude is best, to see how it's
going to work, how it is going to be implemented and enforced." Morse
conceded, "I haven't read the civil rights bill and I simply don't know what
all it contains and what the ramifications are."[52]

Senator J. William Fulbright, who had filibustered against the bill, cautioned civil rights activists, "Now that the bill is law it is time for calmness, reflection and adjustment—particularly on the part of those who have fostered demonstrations against local ordinances and practices now superseded by this federal legislation." Only the second southern senator behind Louisiana's Senator Allen J. Ellender to back acceptance of the new legislation in public, Fulbright continued,

> For reasons lost in history the South has borne the brunt of the nation's racial anxieties and turmoil. Until very recently poor in resources and capital, the South—and particularly Arkansas—is developing its natural resources, improving its educational systems, attracting industry and beginning to gain a fairer share of the nation's prosperity. This trend must continue and we must not allow racial strife to slow this progress.[53]

The views of African American leaders in the state were quite different from those of most white leaders. George Howard, Jr., NAACP state president, said, "Certainly the passage of the civil rights bill by the Senate is a significant step forward in eliminating discrimination in this country. As America is the leading exponent of democracy, it allows us to live up to the reputation of the greatest country on earth for the rights of the individual."[54] L. C. Bates further noted that,

> Around the world, Little Rock and Arkansas, as a whole, are still a symbol of racial bigotry, though the state has spent thousands of dollars in taxpayers' money trying to blot out the racial image. . . . If our governor, county and city officials will accept the fact that the civil rights legislation is now the law of our land, [despite] the efforts of Arkansas' delegation to block it, and appeal to the people for strict enforcement, the NAACP will insure them full cooperation.[55]

Dr. William H. Townsend, president of COCA, declared, "It is a step forward and it is evidence of the rapidly growing awareness of the need of perfecting a democracy that will protect, give justice and equality of opportunity in education, employment, housing, transportation, recreation and all areas of human living. It is a challenge to men of good will." Ozell Sutton, associate director of the ACHR, expressed similar sentiments: "For the first time all national law stands squarely behind those who would extend justice, human rights and human dignity to all our citizens. Now that the legislative branch of our government has joined the executive and judicial branches in recognition of the inherent right and worth of every man regardless of race or creed, we must move swiftly to make these rights meaningful and fulfilling."[56] As well as optimism, there was prudent caution too, as Sutton went on to say, "I take this opportunity to warn those who worked so hard that they have won a scrimmage and not the war. This bill simply gives some modern weapons with which we must wage total war on segregation, discrimination and the resulting dehumanization they effect."[57] I. S. McClinton, president of the Arkansas Democratic Voters Association, reported that he was "elated over the passage of the bill. We have what we call a Christian democracy. It is the first time since the Proclamation of Emancipation that anything of this magnitude has been done for equal justice for all people."[58]

For civil rights leaders, the next task was, as Townsend put it, "to take a close-up inventory of exactly what progress has been made and where and then work on what is not in line with the new legislation." But there was no rush to test the new laws before this fact-finding process was complete. Both Ozell Sutton and SNCC's Bill Hansen confirmed that their organizations had no immediate plans to organize the testing of facilities or for demonstrations. As L. C. Bates elaborated, "We must first approach this in a manner where we can persuade business owners of establishments to want to do it instead of in an attempt of forcing them to do it. I have enough confidence in the Arkansas people to believe that the majority will go along with the new legislation if they are approached in a sane manner."[59]

As in many places across the South, responses to the 1964 Civil Rights Act were varied in Arkansas. A patchy pattern of compliance and non-compliance emerged in just the first week after the act was signed into law. In El Dorado, African Americans successfully desegregated the Sky View Drive-In Theater, but the owner of the Old Fashioned Dairy Diner locked up the store when attempts were made to gain service there. In Pine Bluff, a movie theater and four formerly whites-only restaurants desegregated, but an attempt by eight African American men to gain service at Lusby's Coffee Shop ended in a melee, and Ray Watson's Trucker's Inn refused African Americans service. In Forrest City, a theater, a restaurant, a bowling alley, and a skating rink desegregated peacefully, but attempts to desegregate Forrest Lanes bowling alley led to a truck being overturned. In Fort Smith, African Americans successfully ate at Broadway Restaurant and Dinty Moore's Restaurant but were refused service at City Barbecue.[60]

Though varied, the initial responses to the 1964 Civil Rights Act in

Arkansas did reveal that the issue of interracial bathing caused more difficulties than any other area. On Sunday, July 5, at Lake Texarkana, an attempt by African Americans to use the public beach there led to a confrontation with whites that ended in twenty-three African Americans being charged with inciting a race riot and one of them with attempted murder after one white man and five African Americans ended up with gunshot wounds.[61] On Monday, July 6, in Helena, two SNCC volunteers were taken into custody when they tried to use the public swimming pool. On Tuesday, July 7, Forrest City closed its public swimming pool when African Americans tried to enter. Pine Bluff closed all of its public swimming pools.[62]

The pool issue lay dormant in Little Rock, however, until mid-April 1965, as Memorial Day, and the beginning of the new swimming season, approached. At that time, it was revealed in the local press that the city's M. Eberts Post No. 1 of the American Legion was considering purchasing the J. Curran Conway and Gillam Park pools. The plan was to operate both pools on a private and segregated basis, with the Gillam Park Pool being turned over to an unnamed African American Legion Post to run. Clovis Copeland, Eberts' business manager, was the head of a three-man committee that also included Letcher L. Langford, a former city director, and Lawrence Fisher, Eberts' financial director. The committee reported that they had been in negotiation with "selected city officials" including City Manager Douthit and city directors Leo H. Griffin and Ray Winder about the purchase "for several months." The proposed purchase price was put at $60,000 for the J. Curran Conway Pool and $20,000 for the Gillam Park Pool. Eberts Post sent out 1551 ballots to members about the purchase of J. Curran Conway Pool, while omitting the plan to purchase the Gillam Park Pool. Copeland said that the J. Curran Conway Pool would be open to "members of the American Legion and its auxiliaries," a reported 60,000 people in Pulaski County. Intriguingly, the latest three-man committee meeting had taken place in the offices of Claude Carpenter, Jr., an Eberts board member, an attorney for the State Commerce Commission, and one of Governor Faubus's aides. Whether the link between the Eberts Post's actions and the governor's office was simply coincidental or otherwise was unclear. Asked if Eberts had any African American members, Copeland evasively replied that he "did not know whether the Eberts Post has any Negro members now but that it has had in the past and probably would again." Early reports indicated that members were voting five-to-one in favor of the purchase.[63]

However, the ruse to privatize the pools and reopen them on a segregated basis was scotched by a US District Court ruling handed down just as the Eberts Post votes for purchasing them were pouring in. On April 12, 1965, federal judge J. Smith Henley decided a case that involved efforts at the Arkansas State Capitol to privatize its basement cafeteria to avoid desegregation. Henley ruled that the move was unconstitutional on the grounds that the Fourteenth Amendment explicitly prohibited state and local government entities from practicing discrimination and that gestures at privatization did not free operations associated with them from this prohibition.[64] Following the logic of this ruling, L. C. Bates concluded, "If Eberts Post of the American Legion think they can purchase the swimming pools and operate them on a segregated basis without trouble they are badly mistaken," adding, "If the city directors think they can sell taxpayers' property to dodge the responsibility of operating within the framework of the law then their usefulness is outmoded."[65]

A few days after the cold reality of the court ruling set in and a day after Bates's comments, Eberts dropped its plans to buy the city's public pools. "Our intentions were simply to attempt to purchase the Curran Conway Memorial Swimming Pool in War Memorial Park to operate as a country club on a minor scale for post members and their families. We weren't thinking of segregation or anything else," claimed Eberts's post commander Harrison E. Long. He added, "We did not know we were getting into the field of politics—which we absolutely do not want to do. . . . If we went ahead with it now a lot of people would think we did it for segregation." The three-man committee released a statement that pointed out, "the American Legion and its charter approved by Congress prohibits discrimination because of race, creed or color." New mayor Harold E. Henson quickly backpedaled too, claiming that "the swimming pool issue came as a complete surprise" to him and that he had "never met Clovis Copeland."[66]

The issue went quiet for another month before a major push to reopen the city's pools on an integrated basis began. On May 18, seven hundred and fifty letters on ACHR letterhead went out to members of the Little Rock Council on Human Relations, the Greater Little Rock Conference on Religion and Race, and the Catholic Interracial Council. The letters contained a copy of a letter sent to Mayor Henson on May 12, copied to all city manager board members and the city attorney, Joseph C. Kemp. It also contained pre-printed and pre-addressed postcards to City Manager Ancil Douthit that called for the reopening of the city's pools. Members of the organizations were encouraged to sign and send the postcards in protest. The letter to the mayor, signed by W. T. Kelley, chair of the Committee on

Public Facilities of the Little Rock Council on Human Relations, and Rev.
Walter B. Clancy, president of the Arkansas Council on Human Relations,
contained six compelling reasons for the city to act:

1. The attitude of compliance that has been created by government action in the area of education could well be used to
   make this step forward in terms of community progress. The
   delay of another year would not only be more costly with reference to maintenance costs and repairs, but also will be very
   expensive in terms of good will in the community.
2. A recent telephone survey of the actual patrons of the pools
   indicated that over 70 per cent of the actual potential users of
   the pools would favor their opening on an integrated basis.
3. The Red Cross is restricted by its national policy to co-operate
   in offering its services only to facilities where discrimination is
   not practiced. The loss of our children of water safety training
   and protected swimming facilities will create a dangerous situation. If one child loses his life for want of these instruction
   [sic], it would be tragic. Can we afford to endanger the lives
   of our children for want of enough community effort to meet
   the problems that integrated swimming proposes?
4. With the hot days of summer approaching, the children of
   families who cannot afford private swimming facilities will
   be left to their own devices. Can we afford the possibility of
   increased vandalism and destruction of property?
5. Other communities around us such as Pine Bluff, Fort Smith
   and Fayetteville, to our best knowledge, have opened their
   facilities on an integrated basis.
6. Finally, if the pools are opened on an integrated basis, no one
   is forced to use them. If a parent objects to such a practice, he
   can merely not send his children to swim in such a situation.
   Why penalize all the parents for the feelings of a few?[67]

Amid this growing pressure, and with their available options running
out, some city authorities appeared to be changing their mind about segregated pools. The *Arkansas Democrat* reported that "off the record" many city
hall officials and some members of the city board were advocating that the
pools be quietly reopened on an integrated basis.[68] The first to go public was
City Director Victor Menefee who said, "if we're going to provide swimming facilities in Little Rock, we're going to open up on an integrated basis,
and I feel it's the responsibility of the municipality to provide swimming,

for many reasons—recreation, water safety. With the pools open, the people can decide whether or not they want to attend." Others were not so sure. City Director James F. Hewitt still opposed opening the pools, and City Director Leo H. Griffin said he was "undecided." The other three city directors and the mayor were tight-lipped on the matter.[69]

Ahead of the next scheduled city board meeting, SNCC collected 1300 signatures in a petition to desegregate city swimming pools, and Arkansas state project director James O. Jones urged "the Board to face up to this problem."[70] At the meeting on June 2, five city directors—William F. Steinkamp, Ray Winder, Vic Menefee, Martin Bochert, and James F. Hewitt (who now appeared to have had a change of heart)—met privately with Mayor Henson thirty minutes before going into full session (Leo H. Griffin was absent). At the board meeting, City Manager Douthit announced that the city's swimming pools would open on an integrated basis "as soon as . . . physically able." Rev. Sam Allen, who had requested to speak on behalf of opening the pools at the meeting, said afterwards, "I'm quite happy to hear the statement that the pools will be opened as soon as physically possible and it's my hope that it will not require a long time to get the pools in condition to use. We'll be following with interest the progress in getting the pools in shape to open." Douthit later said it would take about ten days to get the pools ready.[71]

On Monday, June 14, the Gillam Park Pool was the first to open in drizzling rain. Only a small group of African Americans and no whites used it. The only white person there was Julius Breckling, director of the Little Rock Parks and Recreation Department, who along with Marlin Friday, the African American coach-manager at Gillam Park, supervised the re-opening.[72] Meanwhile, engineers over at J. Conway Curran Pool battled with water pump and motor repairs, along with a cracked pipe.[73] Finally, toward the end of the week, City Manager Douthit was able to announce that the pool would open the following Monday. He added that a canvas covering would be placed around the pool's perimeter chain link fence to "cut off the view of idle spectators . . . [and] help prevent racial incidents."[74]

Business was slow when the pool reopened Monday morning at 10:00 a.m. Clyde H. Trickey, pool manager and math teacher at Little Rock's Hall High School, oversaw proceedings. About two dozen whites, mostly children accompanied by their mothers, were ready and waiting to swim. The first three African Americans to enter the pool arrived that afternoon at 1:30 p.m. About half an hour before closing, at 5:30 p.m., there had been 210 swimmers that day, 22 of them African Americans. Gillam Park Pool's numbers had increased slowly since it had opened the week previously, and a few whites had swum there. No incidents at either of the pools were reported.[75]

Near the end of the summer, reports indicated that use of the public pools had fallen by 50 percent.[76] That short-term trend was indicative of the much longer term trend in swimming pool use in Little Rock and the nation. The post-desegregation era in America has witnessed a dramatic decline in public pool construction and usage and a massive expansion of privately-operated and individually owned pools. As historian Jeff Wiltse notes, at first white Americans retreated to neighborhood pools owned by swimming clubs that were privately financed by residents. Many of these, in expanding white suburbs, were whites-only by virtue of their location. However, since they were privately owned, not technically businesses, and therefore not covered under the "public accommodations" clause of the 1964 Civil Rights Act, if African Americans did try to join, private membership restrictions could be, and were, used to prevent interracial swimming. Increasingly, Americans built pools at home and retreated still further into their backyards for recreation. At mid-century, only 2500 American families owned in-ground home swimming pools. By the end of the twentieth century, that number had skyrocketed to 4 million. To be sure, a number of factors drove this change. Rising levels of prosperity in postwar America and cheaper production techniques meant that more Americans could afford to own pools. The massive expansion of suburban America provided the space to build them in. Nevertheless, based on his extensive research into the phenomenon, Wiltse concludes that, "The underlying cause of the private pool boom, however, was middle-class Americans' desire to recreate within more socially selective communities. Private pools enabled Americans to exercise much greater control over whom they swam with than was possible at public pools. Joining a club ensured that other swimmers would be of the same social class and race."[77]

The impact of this shift in Little Rock is still palpable today. Despite the increase in the city's population by nearly 80 per cent between 1960 and 2010, the number of operating outdoor public swimming pools has stayed just the same.[78] J. Curran Conway Pool was closed for demolition in 1989 and replaced by a significantly smaller outdoor pool in 1992 as part of the new Jim Dailey Fitness and Aquatic Center, which also contains Little Rock's first and only indoor public swimming pool.[79] Indicative of the shift in pool culture, in 1952 it was reported that there were over 10,000 swimmers in just one week at J. Curran Conway Pool. Sixty years later, in 2012, the new pool reported less than that number for the entire three-month

A crowd of boys at Fair Park Pool in 1945. Courtesy Butler Center for Arkansas
Studies, Central Arkansas Library System.

summer season.[80] Gillam Park Pool closed in 2001 and has lain derelict
since. Only two new public swimming pools have been constructed since
1965, both, tellingly, in areas of high African American residence, which virtually guarantees predominantly African American usage. East Little Rock
Pool opened at the East Little Rock Community Complex in 1972. It closed
in 2002, and it too has lain derelict.[81] Southwest Community Center Pool
opened in 1998 and remains in operation.[82] The southwest Little Rock area
witnessed a dramatic shift in population in the period before the pool was
built, with 9000 whites leaving and 6200 nonwhites arriving in the decade
between 1982 and 1992. In the same decade, the population in the predominantly white far west of Little Rock, where the number of private pools has
proliferated, leapt from 14,874 to 25,930.[83]

    Approaching fifty years of public swimming pool desegregation, Little
Rock perfectly fits historian Kevin Kruse's description of similar processes in
Atlanta: "In the end, court-ordered desegregation of public spaces brought
about not actual racial integration, but instead a new division in which the

public world was increasingly abandoned to blacks and a new private one was created for whites."[84] Of course, such a description not only refers to the situation in swimming pools but to a range of other facilities too—most notably schools. Little Rock, as other cities, has seen desegregation efforts lead to white flight to private institutions and public schools become largely patronized by African American students. As an *Arkansas Democrat-Gazette* article in 2003 noted, "Little Rock has become a city of mostly black public schools and mostly white private schools."[85] The Civil Rights Act of 1964 made an integrated society a possibility, but that possibility, fifty years on, is still very far from being genuinely realized.

CHAPTER 17

A Crime Unfit to Be Named

Arkansas and Sodomy

W. BROCK THOMPSON

This essay is about three decades of cultural and legal change in the state (and nation) with respect to gays and lesbians, and sexual privacy. The events which most directly define this changing environment include: (1) The adoption of a new Arkansas Criminal Code by the state legislature in 1975 that decriminalized sodomy, a practice which had been outlawed in Arkansas since statehood (1836); (2) an act of fellatio on February 12, 1976, committed by two men being held in a Pulaski County "drunk tank"; (3) the signing of a bill by Governor David Pryor on March 28, 1977, recriminalizing sodomy in Arkansas; (4) the US Supreme Court decision in Bowers v. Hardwick (1986) upholding a Georgia law banning homosexual sodomy (and containing Chief Justice Burger's characterization of homosexual sodomy as "a crime not fit to be named"); (5) the Arkansas Supreme Court decision in Jegley v. Picado et. al.(2002) which declared the state's law against sodomy unconstitutional; and (6) the announcement by Attorney General Mark Pryor, son of the governor who had signed the anti-sodomy bill into law, that the state would not seek a review of the case by the US Supreme Court. The author weaves these events together and, in the process, tells a fascinating story of how changing national attitudes towards sexual freedoms eventually changed public policy in Arkansas.

The turbulent decade of the 1970s witnessed extraordinary and hotly-contested transformations in American attitudes toward sex and sexuality. The values of "free love" and tolerance that had sprouted during the 1960s

---

Originally published in *Arkansas Historical Quarterly* 61
(Autumn 2002): 255–71. Reprinted with permission.
DOI: https://doi.org/10.34053/parry2019.riapag2.17

began to take root in everyday life in the 1970s. The gay and lesbian movement, prospering from the successes of earlier protest movements, gained many legal victories across the nation. Queer visibility was on the rise.[1] In 1972, for instance, moviegoers were charmed by director Bob Fosse's *Cabaret*, one of the first American films that openly dealt with the homosexuality of its characters.[2] On December 15, 1973, the American Psychiatric Association unanimously approved a referendum removing homosexuality from its list of mental illnesses.[3] This development had a tremendous impact on the public perception of homosexuality, not to mention the self-esteem of gays and lesbians living in the United States. Yet a conservative element, personified by orange juice huckster Anita Bryant, soon unleashed a backlash that would wash over the state of Arkansas.

Early in 1977, the *Arkansas Gazette* reported that the Arkansas House of Representatives had "discovered sex" and "intends to do something about it."[4] During the first seven days of the session, legislators introduced four bills dealing with sexual conduct. Rep. Arlo Tyer of Pocahontas took credit for the first two bills: House Bill 237 sought to prohibit "R" and "X" rated movies within the state, and House Bill 238 would levy a tax of $1,500 on men and women who lived together without having married. This latter bill sought, according to the *Gazette*, to make the point that while "such cohabitation is now common in many communities," it was not to be condoned by the state. Besides paying the tax, the couple would also be required to undergo blood tests and obtain a permit from a chancery judge to continue cohabiting. The judge would only issue the "living together permit" if the couple were able to show "good cause."[5] The third bill, House Bill 191, introduced by Rep. Earl Jones of Texarkana, sought to censor sexually explicit material in the state. The "comprehensive obscenity bill" would outlaw books and magazines that had no redeeming social or artistic value. The fourth bill was written hastily in reaction to a development that disturbed Rep. Bill Stancil, a high school football coach from Fort Smith. Two men had been caught in a sexual act by a police officer but apparently had broken no law.[6]

On February 12, 1976, James Black (Sammy to his friends) began drinking early. After several complaints from neighbors, Little Rock police took him into custody for public drunkenness. They put Black in the "drunk tank" at 3:30 p.m. An hour later, Willie Henderson, who had been arrested for driving under the influence of alcohol, joined him. The two men were not alone. Besides the jailers who periodically patrolled the drunk tank and its surrounding cells, about fifteen other detainees waited to sober up. But these circumstances did not diminish Black and Henderson's attraction to one another. An hour after Willie Henderson arrived in the drunk tank, patrolman Hugh Gentry noticed the two men engaged in an act of fellatio.

As it turned out, the behavior of the two men was perfectly legal, or at least no longer illegal. At midnight on January 1, 1976, the Arkansas Criminal Code had changed. The new code held no statute making sodomy a crime. The two men could not be charged with sodomy, as they could have been before January 1. Nor could the men be prosecuted for indecency, which was defined under the new code as follows: "a person commits public sexual indecency if he engages in any of the following acts in a public place or public view: (a) an act of sexual intercourse; (b) an act of deviate sexual activity; or (c) an act of sexual contact."[7] On February 13, 1976, Municipal Judge Jack Holt, Sr., long known for his liberal views, ruled that the Little Rock city jail was not a public place. In an interview with *Arkansas Gazette* reporter George Bentley, Judge Holt remarked that "a public place is a place that the public has access to at any time, no matter who they are."[8] The judge continued, "in any criminal offense, if the statute says the person so charged must commit it in a public place, that will be my ruling, if the crime is sexual deviation or drunkenness, or no matter what it is." Judge Holt remarked that "if someone slipped a bottle of liquor to a prisoner and he got drunk, you couldn't charge him with public drunkenness."[9] Thus the two men could not be charged with any sex crime.

At the time, no one publicly took issue with this. However, many police officers privately expressed dissatisfaction with the judge's ruling, and Chief Deputy Prosecuting Attorney Wilbur C. "Dub" Bentley worried that the city jail would soon turn "into a gay bar."[10] The case went otherwise unnoticed for several weeks. Deputy Prosecuting Attorney Jack Magruder, who at the time handled the state of Arkansas's cases in municipal court, declined to report the ruling to his supervisors in the prosecutor's office. He said he tended "to agree with the decision."[11] Judge Holt had given Magruder the option of declining to prosecute the charges against the two men or having the judge dismiss the charges himself. Magruder opted not to prosecute.

Under the law, however, the state had one year to file charges against the two men. After a *Gazette* reporter brought the case to the public's attention, the state did refile—but with the same result. Circuit Judge William J. Kirby ruled that the city jail's drunk tank was indeed not a public place and dismissed the charges of "public sexual indecency" against Sammy Black and Willie Henderson. Arkansas's new criminal code defined "public place" as "a public or privately owned place to which the public or substantial numbers of the public have access." The new criminal code also defined "public view" as "observable or likely to be observed by a person in a public place."[12] Under the new criminal code, Kirby ruled, the two men committed no real crime.

Under the old criminal code, the two men could have been charged with sodomy, whether the act had been committed in a private or public space. The Arkansas sodomy statute that was repealed in 1976 had been on the books since Arkansas achieved statehood in 1836 and had been upheld by the Arkansas Supreme Court as recently as 1973.[13] The statute read: "*Sodomy* or *Buggery*. Every person convicted of sodomy, or buggery, shall be imprisoned in the penitentiary for a period not less than five years nor more than twenty-one years."[14] The statute was ambiguous in three respects. First, it did not define what exactly constituted "sodomy or buggery." It was unclear if the statute outlawed anal penetration, oral penetration, or both. Second, the statute made no distinction between public or private space. Third, the sodomy statute was not same-sex specific. Indeed, given the language of the statute, it was not sexually specific at all. It did not pertain specifically to either homosexual or heterosexual acts. Under the older statute, sodomy was a crime and sodomites were criminals, whatever their sexual orientation.

When the state's new criminal code was enacted, the sodomy law was not the only statute that was removed. Across the country, debates over state criminal code reformation had been going on for several years. It was clear to many that the American criminal justice system was dangerously haphazard. Many states' legal codes included antiquated laws written in the colonial period, they themselves vestiges of English common law. In response to this crisis, the American Law Institute completed the Model Penal Code, a guide to help states modernize their existing penal codes by removing old and unnecessary laws from the books. This independent group of judges, lawyers, and law professors sought to "modernize American law in almost all aspects."[15] Though the institute did not have any formal control over legislative decisions, its recommendations carried a great deal of weight. While only one state, Illinois, adopted the code as written, many states, including Arkansas, used it as a guide in reforming their criminal statutes.[16]

The state of Arkansas formed the Arkansas Criminal Code Revision Commission, consisting of lawyers, law professors, and law enforcers, as well as ministers and Catholic priests. The commission drafted the 1976 Arkansas Criminal Code for consideration by the state legislature. Practically every major offense underwent at least minor definitional revision. With respect to sex offenses, the Revision Commission decided that any sexual activity

committed by consenting adults in private would not be illegal. The code it
drafted borrowed directly from the Model Penal Code in forbidding sexual
activities with minors, in public spaces or in public view, or with non-
consenting parties. The new criminal code prompted little scrutiny. It easily
passed both houses of the Arkansas legislature and was signed by Gov. David
Pryor to go into effect January 1, 1976.[17]

A year later, Representative Stancil claimed he had been hoodwinked.
After learning that Sammy Black and Willie Henderson had technically
committed no crime, he had discovered to his amazement that he had voted
for this new criminal code that essentially legalized sodomy. He soon took
action to rectify the situation. In haste, he drafted House Bill 117, which
would define sodomy as any deviate sexual behavior and make it a class
C felony punishable by as many as ten years in prison.[18] The bill and its
author soon drew criticism from legislative colleagues. Rep. Art Givens of
Sherwood noted that the new criminal code had decriminalized sodomy
because it was a "victimless" crime. He argued before the House Judiciary
Committee that Stancil's bill would potentially make criminals out of
many husbands and wives in the state and warned that "everything except
what is done strictly for reproduction may be criminal in nature."[19] Givens
suggested that Stancil consult the Arkansas attorney general's office for its
opinion, but Stancil responded that he was not particularly interested in the
attorney general's opinion. Nevertheless, Stancil agreed to amend the bill
to define sodomy more precisely and to reduce the penalties with which it
could be punished. As amended, House Bill 117 made bestiality and sodomy
class D felonies, carrying prison terms of as long as five years, and defined
sodomy as an act between two members of the same sex.[20]

Deputy Prosecuting Attorney John W. Hall of Little Rock spoke against
the measure, saying that the state had no compelling interest in prosecuting
sex acts between consenting adults. Hall argued that any such law would
surely be struck down by the courts for violating the Arkansas constitution's guarantees of equal protection and the individual's right to privacy.
He noted that under the amended bill, a homosexual couple committing
a sexual act in the privacy of their own home could be found guilty of a
felony, while a heterosexual couple committing a sexual act in public would
only be guilty of public indecency, a misdemeanor.[21] Despite this plea, the
Judiciary Committee adopted the amended bill and sent it to the floor with
a "do pass" recommendation.[22]

Despite the debate over the bill in committee, it seemed that few legislators took it seriously. During the committee's proceedings, the room often

exploded with laughter. Committee vice chairman N. B. "Nap" Murphy of Hamburg, who was presiding, continually pleaded for dignity. The giggles continued and, at one point, the hilarity was so intense that the course of business became difficult to follow. Murphy, repeatedly striking his gavel, pleaded: "Gentlemen, I do not know what is going on at this time."[23]

Though the bill passed the House Judiciary Committee, it was clear that once it arrived on the House floor it would have to be amended even further. Hall's argument with respect to the disproportionate penalties applied to sodomy convinced many house members, despite their reckless discourse while the bill remained in committee. Stancil agreed to change the proposed statute to define sodomy as a misdemeanor rather than a felony. This would carry a maximum penalty of up to a year in prison and a $1,000 fine.[24]

When the bill came up for a vote on the floor of the Arkansas House of Representatives, Stancil feared that there still was a possibility of it being defeated. To convince his fellow lawmakers, he took to the floor and produced from his briefcase copies of both the King James Bible and the Arkansas Constitution. Stancil paced the floor of the House waving the two works and shouting: "One of these can be amended, but the other can't." The bill passed the Arkansas House of Representatives on a vote of 66 to 2.[25]

When the bill arrived on the floor of the Arkansas Senate, it was treated in the same manner as it had been in the House Judiciary Committee. The bill's sponsor, Sen. Milt Earnhart of Fort Smith remarked apologetically that he did not "have any live demonstrations" to accompany his explanation of the bill.[26] The Senate chamber erupted with laughter and applause. Earnhart added that the bill was "aimed at weirdos and queers who live in a fairyland world and are trying to wreck traditional family life."[27] The Senate, on a vote of 25 to 0, passed the bill.

Eleven days later, on Monday, March 28, 1977, representatives of the American Civil Liberties Union and the Quakers met with Gov. David Pryor's legal advisor, Larry Yancey, and urged the governor's office to reject the bill. Several gay and lesbian organizations, as well as the governor of California, Edmund G. Brown, Jr., telephoned Pryor's office to inquire after the bill.[28] Their efforts were unsuccessful. Pryor signed House Bill 117 into law that very afternoon. As enacted, the law declared that "A person commits sodomy if such performs an act of sexual gratification involving: (1) The penetration, however slight, of the anus or the mouth of an animal or a person by the penis of a person of the same sex or an animal; or (2) The penetration, however slight, of the vagina or anus of an animal or person by any body member of a person of the same sex or an animal." Sodomy was defined as a Class A misdemeanor, punishable by a jail term of up to one year and a fine of up to $1,000.[29]

"Every governor bows to political pressure," Yancey later explained, "and no one, including the governor, wanted a 'nay' vote on their record, especially when it came to sodomy."[30] Though many of them had made light of the bill, all but two legislators fell prey to the same pressures as Pryor. Yancey recalled that legislators would complain that "preachers back home" were giving them the "what for about sodomy."[31] A national backlash had come to Arkansas.

Earlier in the same month that the sodomy bill became law, the Arkansas House of Representatives considered House Bill 32. Introduced by Rep. Albert "Tom" Collier, the legislation applauded singer and Florida orange juice spokeswoman Anita Bryant for her opposition to equal housing and employment legislation for homosexuals in the Sunshine State. It drew the attention even of White House aides who, after receiving dozens of phone calls and letters from gays and lesbians, called Collier, according to his own account, to ask what the resolution had to say. Collier also noted that in response to his legislation, he received "a real nice letter" from Bryant thanking him and the Arkansas House of Representatives for the resolution. House Bill 32 easily cleared the Arkansas House of Representatives.[32]

The actions taken by Pryor and Collier earned the pair commendations from the Independence Baptist Association of Arkansas. In a letter to Pryor, the association, seeking to preserve "moral and spiritual purity" in the state, noted that they had passed a similar resolution commending Bryant for her adamant stand "against the immoral practices of homosexuality and similar activities." The letter encouraged both Pryor and Bryant to "uphold always the Biblical teachings concerning these immoral practices."[33]

At the same time the Arkansas legislature debated the sodomy law, Bryant had been making national headlines campaigning against gay rights. Bryant had long been a popular performer in the American South, making a name by singing at conventions and state fairs and wooing audiences with patriotic numbers such as the "Battle Hymn of the Republic" and "God Bless America." However, by 1977, the native of Barnsdall, Oklahoma, had become most recognizable as the spokeswoman for the Florida Citrus Commission. Most memorably, she appeared in television commercials singing: "Come to Florida sunshine tree! Florida sunshine naturally!"[34] At the prompting of the citrus commission, she had made Miami, Florida, her home. Once there, she became alarmed upon learning from her local pastor that the Dade County Metro Commission, the legislative body for the city of Miami, was planning to add "affectional or sexual preference" to the city's civil rights ordinance. Adding this phrase would essentially protect homosexuals from discrimination in housing, public accommodations, and employment. Enraged, Bryant determined to defeat the measure. However, time was short and Bryant and her allies were only able to sway a few votes on the commission before the proposal was passed on a vote of five to three. In response, Bryant created the "Save Our Children" campaign aimed at toppling the legislation. In the campaign's literature, Bryant stated: "I don't hate homosexuals! But as a mother, I must protect my children from their evil influence. . . . *They want to recruit your children and teach them the virtues of becoming a homosexual.*"[35] This rhetoric proved highly effective. Bryant convinced many voters in the Miami area that the law would allow homosexuals employed in the county's public schools to freely advertise their sexuality. Bryant and her "Save the Children" campaign pressed for a referendum to decide if the ordinance forbidding discrimination against lesbians and gays should be allowed to stand. She got it, and 70 percent of voters supported the ordinance's repeal in a special referendum on June 9, 1977. Bryant pledged to continue her crusade. "We will now carry our fight against similar laws throughout the nation that attempt to legitimize a lifestyle that is both perverse and dangerous to the sanctity of the family, dangerous to our children, dangerous to our freedom of religion and freedom of choice, dangerous to our survival as a nation."[36]

Though Arkansas, at the time, hardly boasted a gay community as sizable and conspicuous as that of Miami, certain changes in the traditional family were clearly taking place. In September 1977, the cover of the *Arkansas Times*, a popular alternative magazine, featured an article by Jim Ranchino entitled "The Arkansas of the '70s: The Good Ole Boy Ain't Whut He Used to Be." Ranchino, a native of Arkadelphia, noted that "pre-marital sex, the use of marijuana and unfaithfulness to marriage vows are becoming more the rule than the exception."[37] The departure from traditional institutions of marriage and family that the article broadcast was not altogether lost on Arkansans. In fact, many had been observing it with growing anxiety for some time, as evidenced by the host of bills dealing with sexual conduct and the pressure put on legislators by "preachers back home."[38]

The backlash in Arkansas was swift, and it seems that it only took that isolated incident in the Little Rock city jail to incite action from the legislature. Apparently few were willing to have a vote against an anti-sodomy ordinance on their legislative record. An episode in southeast Arkansas suggested that legislators may well have had to pay a price had they possessed the courage to take a stand against the homophobic tide swelled by Bryant. On January 5, 1978, the *Lincoln Ledger*, the principal newspaper for Lincoln County and Star City, Arkansas, published an editorial by Ross Dennis. It urged Bryant to "sit down and shut up," insisting that she had no right to save the world from what she considered to be sin. The editorial set off a small firestorm. The small paper and its editors were bombarded with phone calls and visits from local pastors, who threatened a boycott if the editorial was not retracted. In the next issue, the *Ledger's* general manager and owner, Thomas Roark, apologized, stating that he was "very wrong in letting this material be published." In the same issue, Dennis published "An Open Letter to the Readers," in which he apologized for having caused offense by his editorial. He explained that he chose Bryant simply "because she is such a controversial figure and I needed someone to point a finger at" and admitted that he "chose the wrong person for this part of the country." Despite his apology, Dennis was fired from the *Lincoln Ledger* one month later.[39]

Ironically, for all of her crusade's seeming efficacy, Bryant paid a high price for her outspokenness. Under pressure from a gay-organized boycott, she lost her lucrative orange juice contract. Bryant suddenly found it hard to find venues for her concerts. In its July 1977 issue, the *Ladies Home Journal* published the results of a survey that asked high school students to identify the man and woman who have "done the most damage to the world." The man ranking first was Adolf Hitler. The woman was Anita Bryant.[40]

By late the following year, Bryant could not even draw a crowd in Little Rock. Wearing a red and white dress with a long, flowing cape, and carrying a red velvet-covered Bible, Bryant arrived in the state capital on Saturday, October 21, 1978. After the state's recriminalization of sodomy and the House of Representatives' passage of a resolution applauding her, Bryant probably assumed Arkansas would welcome her. Bryant may have been surprised then to find only 300 in attendance for her performance at the 3,000 seat Robinson Center Auditorium. Despite the rather poor turnout, Bryant continued with the show, entertaining the faithful few with such songs as "How Great Thou Art," "God Bless America," and "This Is My Country."[41]

It might have seemed that Bryant's influence in Arkansas and across the nation was fading fast. Yet the die had been cast, and Arkansas's sodomy law and similar antigay laws remained in force. Perhaps lawmakers, unwilling to take a stand on the issue, thought they could simply wait for a court to declare the laws unconstitutional, sparing them legislative hardship and political complications. A court challenge did occur, but its outcome would be far different than many expected. The case would become one of the more notorious ever heard before the Supreme Court of the United States.

In the summer of 1982, twenty-nine-year-old Michael Hardwick was arrested in Atlanta, Georgia, by a policeman sent to his home after he failed to show up for a court appearance related to a charge of public drunkenness. After entering the home, the policeman observed Hardwick and another man engaged in oral sex. The officer arrested Hardwick for violating the state's 1816 statute that made oral and anal sex, on the part of either homosexuals or heterosexuals, punishable by a prison term of one to twenty years. An arrest in a private home for consensual fellatio among adults was an extraordinary event, and Hardwick's case would find its way to the US Supreme Court. Those looking to challenge the constitutionality of such sodomy statutes could hardly have imagined a better case. There were no other issues, such as the participation of minors, prostitution, or public indecency, that could obscure the fact that the state of Georgia presumed to regulate sexual behavior in the bedroom. Georgia attorney general Michael Bowers argued before the Supreme Court that "the most profound legislative finding that can be made is that homosexual sodomy is anathema to the basic units of our society: marriage and the family." Bowers concluded that the possible decriminalization of sodomy would demote "those sacred institutions to merely alternative lifestyles."[42]

The Supreme Court handed down the *Bowers v. Hardwick* decision on June 30, 1986. The next day the *Arkansas Democrat* ran a bold three-column headline: "High Court Upholds Georgia Sodomy Law." The *Democrat* reported that the ruling dealt only with homosexual sodomy, noting that by a five-to-four decision the court upheld the principle that "consenting adults have no constitutional rights to private homosexual conduct."[43] Associate Justice Byron R. White, writing for the majority, argued that the "issue presented is whether the Federal Constitution confers the fundamental right upon homosexuals to engage in sodomy and hence invalidates the laws of the many states that still make such conduct illegal and have done so for a very long time." After asserting that Hardwick was asking the Supreme Court to establish "a fundamental right to engage in homosexual sodomy," White declared, "This we are quite unwilling to do."[44]

Although White's opinion promoted the state's role as guardian of traditional morality, his argument dealt mainly with the question of privacy and the individual and was written in coldly objective prose. It was Chief Justice Warren Burger, writing a separate concurring opinion, who went further in condemning the crime of sodomy, and indeed homosexuality, on the grounds of religious ideology. Burger called sodomy an "infamous crime against nature," an offense of "deeper malignity" than rape, and a heinous act "the very mention of which is a disgrace to human nature." For Burger, sodomy was truly a "crime not fit to be named." Invalidating the Georgia statute would "cast aside millennia of moral teaching."[45]

Commentary soon followed the front-page article in the *Democrat*. The newspaper published an essay by the syndicated columnist William Raspberry that remarked that "you don't have to be gay or kinky to believe that the state has no business sticking its nose into private bedrooms."[46] The *Democrat* itself, however, was not as quick to disagree with the court. Eighteen days after the Supreme Court handed down the *Bowers v. Hardwick* decision, the newspaper offered a final opinion on the case. The editorial stated, "the court has made good public policy by flinching away from any declaration that a sick, socially valueless, widely outlawed minority practice merits constitutional protection as a social good." The *Democrat* went on to say that Arkansas should look to the Supreme Court's decision as a forerunner to overturning *Roe v. Wade*, the 1973 US Supreme Court decision that invalidated state laws prohibiting abortions.[47]

Clearly, the pendulum had swung to the right, given a push, perhaps, by the state of Arkansas. In the wake of the Stonewall riots in New York City in June 1969, a gay rights movement had formed and succeeded in promoting tolerance of homosexuality among millions of Americans.[48] Between 1971 and 1980, twenty-two states repealed their sodomy laws. Large cities such as Seattle and Detroit adopted legislation forbidding discrimination on the grounds of sexual orientation. But these gains would be short-lived in the midst of the backlash conjured up by Bryant in Miami. Arkansas would be the only state to first repeal its sodomy law and then reinstate it targeting only homosexual acts, but it was part of a larger pattern.[49] Many states, as well as a host of large urban areas across the nation, would soon use legal methods to crack down on nascent queer visibility. Cities such as St. Paul and Wichita saw civil rights ordinances that included protection for gays and lesbians struck down only months after they had been passed.[50] As the conservative 1980s replaced the tumultuous 1970s, and the religious right began to gain further strength, the American legal establishment now considered it a legal duty to regulate homosexual behavior.

Curiously, though, in the twenty-five years after its passage, defenders of the Arkansas sodomy law often emphasized not its putative benefits but the fact that it was rarely enforced and thus presumably did gay people no harm. No one had been convicted under the law for private, consensual acts.

Yet the rare instances in which sodomy arrests were made seem to have been peculiarly well-timed. During the legislative session of 1991, state senator Vic Snyder proposed legislation to remove the sodomy law from Arkansas's criminal code. Shortly after Snyder's bill was accorded a "do not pass" recommendation by the judiciary committee, Pulaski County sheriff's deputies arrested four men for sodomy at an Interstate 40 rest area near Morgan, only a few miles north of Little Rock. Another eleven men were charged with loitering for the purpose of committing a sexual act.[51] It might appear that authorities wanted to illustrate to the public that there was still a need for a state sodomy law.

Whether or not that was the case, sodomy laws—however irregularly they were enforced—remained the bedrock for discrimination against anyone in the homosexual minority.[52] First, and perhaps most clearly, there would always be the threat of criminal prosecutions looming over gays and lesbians as long as they were sexual beings. Second, such laws served to support a number of explicit legal disabilities. In addition to branding lesbians and gay men as criminals, sodomy laws have been used to deny employment, access to housing, child custody and visitation rights, and a host of other privileges and public benefits to gay applicants. At the University of Arkansas, Fayetteville, for example, in 1983 the student senate denied funding to a gay and lesbian student group seeking money for a series of films and lectures promoting tolerance of homosexuality. Although the gay and lesbian student group met all of the criteria for funding, the student senate insisted that they could not fund a program which promoted an illegal act.[53] The laws also served as a rationale against enacting local civil rights laws that would bar discrimination based on sexual orientation, and they supplied warrant for countless private discriminations, which lacked any explicit sanction in the law. As homosexuals had been defined as criminal and abnormal by the law, they might be treated as such by private individuals.

These were among the arguments made by seven gay and lesbian Arkansans who gathered in the rotunda of the state capitol building on Wednesday, January 28, 1998, to announce a lawsuit seeking to have the state's sodomy law declared to be in violation of the Arkansas Constitution. Though the plaintiffs acknowledged that there had not been a single instance of anyone being arrested for violating Arkansas's sodomy law in a private place, one of them, Vernon Stokay, argued that the law "is always an overriding threat. . . . You never know what kind of regime will come around. . . . It's always hanging over your head." The seven— Stokay, Elena Picado, Robin White, George Townsand, Charlotte Downey, Bryan Manire, and

Randy McCain, all residing in different locations throughout the state—
were backed by Little Rock attorney David Ivers and the Lambda Legal
Defense and Education Fund, a national gay rights organization. They
believed that any future efforts to topple the law through the state legislature would fail as had two subsequent attempts by Vic Snyder, in 1993
and 1995 (the bills died in committee). The challenge would have to come
through the courts.[54]

There followed four years of legal jousting, which saw the plaintiffs win
a ruling from Pulaski County circuit court judge David Bogard that the
law was unconstitutional. On July 5, 2002, the Arkansas Supreme Court,
in a five to two decision, affirmed Bogard's ruling. A sodomy law that had
been on the books for twentyfive years was declared unconstitutional. The
majority opinion, written by Associate Justice Annabelle Clinton Imber,
stated that Arkansas could not use its police powers to "enforce a majority
morality on persons whose conduct does not harm others." Citing Article
II of the state constitution—particularly its guarantees of life, liberty, the
pursuit of happiness, and the right of Arkansans to be secure in their persons
and homes against unreasonable searches and seizures—as well as numerous
laws passed by the state legislature indicating the value it placed on personal
privacy, Imber wrote, "it is clear to the court that Arkansas has a rich and
compelling tradition of protecting individual privacy and that a fundamental right to privacy is implicit in the Arkansas Constitution." This right
extended to "all private, consensual, noncommercial acts of sexual intimacy
between adults." The court also ruled that the 1977 sodomy law violated the
state constitution's guarantees of equal protection in that it criminalized
sexual acts between homosexuals that would be perfectly legal if engaged
in by heterosexuals.[55]

The Arkansas Supreme Court had thus found more expansive guar-
antees of liberty, privacy, and equality in the state's constitution than the
US Supreme Court had been willing to find in the federal constitution.
Shortly after the decision, one of the seven who had challenged the law,
Randy McCain, declared, "I'm proud of the Supreme Court. I've always
been proud to be an Arkansan, but I'm even more proud today."[56]

At the same time, Attorney General Mark Pryor, the son of the governor who had signed the sodomy bill into law, issued a statement from
his office that he would not seek a review of the case by the United States
Supreme Court. His spokesman noted simply: "The issue is settled."[57]

CHAPTER 18

Keeping Hope Alive

A Case Study of the Continuing Argument for Ratification of the ERA

LINDSLEY ARMSTRONG SMITH AND STEPHEN A. SMITH

The US Constitution was written to protect the rights and liberties of men. Consequently, the US Supreme Court did not apply even the Fourteen Amendment's equal protection clause to discrimination on the basis of sex until the 1970s. Even now, the national court does not use the same "strict" scrutiny test to examine differential treatment of men and women that it uses for persons of different ethnic or religious backgrounds. It is for this reason that suffragist Alice Paul proposed, and activists continue to demand, the addition of an Equal Rights Amendment. Although Congress adopted a resolution in 1972 and ratification by the necessary three-fourths of states seemed imminent, opposition mounted and the measure fell three states short. Equality activists regrouped in late 90s, and won ratification in two more states: Nevada (2017) and Illinois (2018). In this case study, we learn of such efforts here. Among the takeaways: Arkansas is a (relatively) good prospect for ratification; legislators respond to constituent contact more readily than to policy experts or statewide opinion polls; and the debate is not hopelessly "quixotic" if it engages the public in debates about constitutional equality.

The call for this special issue asserted that the Equal Rights Amendment (ERA) "ultimately failed to receive enough state ratifications before its deadline in 1982. Despite its repeated failure the ERA has served as a symbolic torch carried by generations of feminists fighting for women's rights."

Originally published in *Frontiers* 38 (2017): 173-207.
Reprinted with permission.
DOI: https://doi.org/10.34053/parry2019.riapag2.18

However, not everyone has conceded defeat in the effort to ratify the ERA, and we argue that a prognosis is more appropriate than a postmortem.

At the federal level, there seems to be some interest but little chance of success in reviving the prospects for the Equal Rights Amendment by extending the time to secure ratification by three more states. At the state level, however, there are continuing attempts to ratify the Equal Rights Amendment, the presumed 1982 deadline notwithstanding. In more than half of the states that have yet to ratify the amendment, it is a clear and continuing point of stasis in legislative battles that have persisted for more than a decade. Explicating the ways people continue to engage with the Equal Rights Amendment in academia, legal and political practice, and grassroots advocacy, we present a case study of the ongoing twenty-first-century effort to ratify the ERA in Arkansas.

The literature addressing the political and rhetorical dimensions of the unsuccessful ratification campaigns of the past is voluminous and insightful, although most of it is now three decades old and focuses on the broad national dialogue before 1982.[1] Among these are several studies that looked specifically at the efforts in Arkansas.[2] Valuable case studies exist of individual state efforts during the original ratification period, such as that of Illinois, by Jane Mansbridge.[3] Another addresses North Carolina, by Donald Mathews and Jane Dehart, but there is scant scholarly attention to any state ratification efforts after the extended 1982 statutory deadline.[4]

Attempts to ratify the ERA in Arkansas in the 1970s, well covered in previous studies, were vigorously contested but ultimately unsuccessful. We focus upon and examine the revived efforts to secure ratification between 2005 and 2013. We confirm much of the earlier research about the failure to ratify in the first period of 1973–81; however, the main contribution here is our analysis of the renewed and continuing effort to persuade Arkansas to ratify after the expiration of the purported deadline, embracing the "three-state strategy."[5]

The 1997 publication of an article in the *William and Mary Law School Journal on Women and the Law* made the argument that the ERA was still viable—the rationale being that Congress could legislatively adjust or repeal the existing ratification deadline, determine whether or not state ratifications after the expiration of a time limit in a proposing clause are valid, and promulgate the ERA after the thirty-eighth state ratifies.[6] Supporters of this three-state strategy also argued that the ratification deadline was only in a resolving clause and not in the amendment itself and that Congress, having already extended the ERA deadline once, had the power to do so again. The

Congressional Research Service analyzed this legal argument in 1996 and 2014, concluding that acceptance of the Madison Amendment does have implications for the premise that approval of the ERA by three more states could allow Congress to declare ratification accomplished.[7] While this is a plausible argument, not all legal scholars agree. Yet no court has directly addressed the issue.

Arkansas, of course, is not the only state in which ratification continues to be pursued. Missouri led the way with introduction of a resolution to ratify in 2000.[8] Eight of the fifteen non-ratifying states have seen efforts in the last few years. Resolutions were recently introduced in Florida (2015), Nevada (2015), North Carolina (2015), Arizona (2016), Illinois (2016), Missouri (2016), and Virginia (2016). The Virginia Senate approved ratification resolutions in 2011, 2012, 2014, 2015, and 2016. The Illinois Senate approved a ratification resolution in 2014, but the Illinois House has not approved ratification since 2003.[9]

Closely examining the ratification efforts in Arkansas during the last decade, we explicate the changing nature of the arguments and the political culture. Drawing on these data, we conclude that the emerging strategy to ratify the ERA was and is politically viable, regardless of the constitutional uncertainty, and we argue that the continuing effort to ratify sustains a valuable public forum, not otherwise available, for education and discussion of the fundamental fairness of constitutional equality for women.

The ongoing ratification effort in Arkansas is especially appropriate for illuminating the changing conversation about equal rights for women. Arkansas had been the twelfth state to ratify the Nineteenth Amendment in 1919, and in 1932 it became the first state to elect a woman to serve in the United States Senate, Senator Hattie Caraway, who had announced her support for the Equal Rights Amendment in 1943. In 1972 the Arkansas delegation was unanimous in supporting passage of the ERA, with Senator John McClellan (D) voting to report the measure out of the Judiciary Committee, and bipartisan support on the floor from Senator J. William Fulbright (D) and Representatives Bill Alexander (D-AR1), Wilbur Mills (D-AR2), John Paul Hammerschmidt (R-AR3), and David Pryor (D-AR4).

When the amendment was referred to the states, Arkansas women expected quick ratification; however, the Arkansas General Assembly considered but failed to ratify the ERA at its biennial sessions in 1973, 1975, 1977, and 1979. When the legislature failed to act in 1981, ERArkansas President Brownie Ledbetter reminded supporters that it "took 72 years for women to get the vote. It took 58 years to get the ERA passed in Congress. We've only been working for state ratification for nine years, and we can't give up now." Nonetheless, the battle for ratification ended when the national ratification deadline became effective in 1982.[10] The public conversation in Arkansas about equality for women under the Constitution practically vanished with the end of the public forum provided by the ratification campaign.

Yet examining the characteristics of the thirty-five ratifying and fifteen nonratifying states in 1980, Ernest Wohlenberg posited that "nonratifiers may be ranked according to their combined ranks on religious and polit-ical conservatism" and suggested "that Arizona, Virginia, Illinois, Nevada and Florida, in that order, seem to be most likely to ratify."[11] Arkansas was ranked as the sixth most likely to ratify the amendment.

Despite the expiration of the purported deadline for ratification being extended to 1982, Arkansas presents a unique and specific opportunity to examine the rhetorical contest for the ERA in the twenty-first century. After a dormancy of more than twenty-five years, the effort was renewed, and rat-ification resolutions were introduced and debated in the 2005, 2007, 2009, and 2013 biennial sessions of the Arkansas General Assembly.

The concept of the three-state strategy and its role in Arkansas's attempts to revive and pass the Equal Rights Amendment deserve serious attention, because this effort has been responsible for restoring the forum for a con-versation on the importance of equal rights for women in Arkansas and the other states that have yet to ratify. We address the experience in Arkansas since 2005 to illustrate that point and illuminate the ongoing argument. It is significant that the opposition has accepted the viability of the three-state strategy, and the renewed contest has centered on the import of ratification rather than its possibility. In 2013 the lead opponent of the ERA, Arkansas Family Council director Jerry Cox, testified before the Arkansas Senate State Agencies Committee that "there is no provision in the US Constitution for the expiration of a proposed amendment," and "there is a pretty good deal of evidence to say it is, it is, still in play."[12] And so it is.

One visible change in the political environment in the twenty-first cen-tury has been an increase in the number of women serving in the Arkansas General Assembly, which has changed the nature of debate and consider-ation on a number of issues.[13] Throughout the ratification efforts in the 1970s, there were never more than five women among the 135 members of the Arkansas Legislature. During the period of renewed efforts to ratify the Equal Rights Amendment, as many as 8 of the 35 senators (23 percent) were women, and the House saw representation of as high as 25 of the 100 members. One study noted the fact that "a female state senator introduced a resolution calling for Arkansas to ratify the equal rights amendment to the United States Constitution. In a way this is a good symbolic measure of the new found power of women in the current 2005 Assembly because that amendment never got out of committee when it was introduced in the 1970's and never in fact even had a vote in committee. That a female senator has the backbone to introduce this resolution again—with the expectation that it would get a vote—is a measure in our view of how far female representation has advanced in the Arkansas General Assembly."[14]

Berta Seitz, the leader of the 2005 ERArkansas campaign, contacted members of the House and Senate from her district and asked them to sponsor a resolution for ratification of the Equal Rights Amendment in the 2005 legislative session.[15] Senator Sue Madison (D-Fayetteville) and Representative Lindsley Smith (D-Fayetteville) agreed, and on March 7, Madison introduced Senate Joint Resolution 17 in the Senate with Smith as the House sponsor.[16]

When organizing the ERA ratification effort, Seitz sought a unique approach: to "fly under the radar" so that the anti-ERA movement would not realize what happened until it was too late.[17] Opposition activist and former Republican state senator Peggy Jeffries commented that it really was a "sleeper this time."[18] However, both legislative sponsors recognized that their move was as much a part of a new national conversation about the Equal Rights Amendment as it was an attempt to ratify it in Arkansas. Senator Madison noted, "There may or may not be support in other places, but I think it's something that's been coming for a long time here in Arkansas." Representative Smith said, "Things have changed a lot since the 1970s, and I think we've got a real good shot at passing this." Moreover, she added, "Everybody is going to be looking at Arkansas. It's all about respect for other people and fair treatment, and that's going to interest a lot of people."[19]

Senator Madison secured a Do Pass motion in the Senate State Agencies Committee on March 4 with no questions or discussion and with only two dissenting votes. "I'm just embarrassed that we haven't already done it," she said. "I mean, think about it. It's largely accepted as a matter of law, and yet it's not in our Constitution."[20] Senator Gilbert Baker (R-Conway), chair of the Republican Party of Arkansas and one of the two negative votes in committee, said afterward, "I thought the whole ERA-change-the-Constitution thing was done a long time ago," and he was surprised when it was brought up in committee. He said he could think of no example of women not having equal rights under existing statutes, and "to change the

Constitution for the sake of making a statement—we just don't need to go there." Betsy Hagan of Little Rock, who fought the amendment in the 1970s as a member of Family, Life, America, God (FLAG) and now president of the Eagle Forum of Arkansas, was "quite shocked" that Madison's resolution made it out of committee. "I think it's . . . unnecessary, because women already have everything they need."[21]

The opposition lobbying campaign began immediately after the media reports that the resolution had been favorably recommended by the Senate committee. New to the political environment were the widespread availability of the Internet and the proliferation of blogs on the World Wide Web, being used both for directly contacting legislators and for sharing talking points with the committed. The motivated opposition used these much more effectively than did supporters of the Equal Rights Amendment. Seitz said many who were for ratification just thought it was logical that it would pass with no problem and believed it unnecessary to show up to take a stand.

The postings on the Arkansas Watch blog by Pam Manard of Paragould and Debbie Pelley of Jonesboro captured the actions and arguments of the opposition. Manard noted, "Jerry Cox of Family Council reports that ERA supporters are working on legislators very hard and that this is proving to be a real hard battle. Some who had at first said that they would oppose it have since changed their minds as they have been bombarded with calls by its supporters." In response, she said, "We need every person possible to be contacted about this and ask them to contact legislators immediately and maybe keep contacting them until this battle is over. There are apparently only a few states that are needed from 20 plus years ago—to ratify this thing to add it to the US constitution. This is a very serious matter!"[22] Pelley reinforced the call to action for the opposition and activated the phone-tree and e-mail-tree network. "Please take action. Legislator e-mails are listed below. Send something even if you have to copy and paste this e-mail or parts of it jsut [sic] so they will get messages opposing it."[23]

While proponents were making rational arguments grounded on fairness and engaging in "rights talk," the rhetoric of the opposition was quite different. Pelley's representation of the resolution and the House sponsor reflect her approach. "Beware! HCR1023 the ERA Amendment and the Resolution by Rep. Smith and in the Senate by Senator Madison is purposely written in very simple language so as to deceive," she charged. "If the ERA Amendment becomes part of our US Constitution, it would trump every law any state has passed on homosexual marriage, homosexual adoption, and other laws the conservatives have worked so hard to get passed. . . . The sponsor of this ERA Amendment is Representative Smith, the legislator that sponsored the law to make sexual orientation a civil right. She is praised highly by Arkansans on a homosexual website as championing their cause."[24] Manard joined in suggesting, "This is a backdoor Civil Rights amendment for the Homosexual, Bi-sexual, Transgender, Transsexual, and amoral Heterosexual-Free Sex movement!"[25] Another opponent, "Mr. Toast," wrote on the same blog: "This is merely showboating for Sen. Sue Madison and Rep. Lindsley Smith (both of the same homosexual-infested area of the state). . . . The feminists and their cohorts (i.e., Ted Kennedy) keep bringing up legislation to enable its ratification, but I think it has been around long enough for most people in D.C. to have decided to stay away from it."[26]

The opposition fear appeals were directed to their base and toward timid legislators wanting to avoid retribution at the polls. Legislators were not voting against the ERA because they believed all the wild charges, said Berta Seitz. "They don't. But because of the political power, and they know how destructive the group that opposes it can be, and how vicious they can be politically, they are afraid to stand up to them."[27] Seitz mentioned that "one of the men who had voted it out of committee and was so proud he had voted it out of committee, was afraid to be seen talking to me in the hallway after they [opponents of the ERA] had paid him a visit."[28]

Senator Madison brought the ERA resolution to the Senate floor on April 5. It was the first time that ratification would be voted on in either chamber during the three decades since it had been referred to the states by Congress. The supporters made a solid but perhaps uninspiring case that the ERA is needed, because the Fourteenth Amendment's equal protection clause has never been interpreted to grant equal rights on the basis of sex in the same way that the Equal Rights Amendment would. The Fourteenth Amendment had been applied to sex discrimination only since 1971, and the Supreme Court's more recent decision regarding admission of women to Virginia Military Institute did not move beyond the traditional assumption that males hold rights and females must prove that they hold them. They said the ERA was necessary, because until we have it women will have to continue to fight long, expensive, and difficult political and judicial battles to ensure that their rights are constitutionally equal to the rights automatically granted to males on the basis of sex. And they argued that the ERA is needed because women need a constitutional protection against a rollback of the significant advances in women's rights over the past fifty years.[29]

The Senate vote was sixteen in favor, fifteen opposed, and four not voting. Needing eighteen votes to pass, the resolution failed. The Democrats held twenty-seven seats in the Senate, but only sixteen members voted for the ERA. Voting no were seven Democrats, including Barbara Horn, joining all eight Republicans, including Sharon Trusty and Ruth Whitaker. The failure to ratify was sealed by four Democratic Senators not voting. Republican discipline (0–8) was greater than that of the Democrats (16–11).

Somewhat more surprising was that the six women senators split (3–3) on the issue, although the most vocal opponents in the public discussion had been women who raised fears about the consequences of ratification.[30] Senator Madison later said, "I think the most depressing part about what happened in the Senate was there was a group of girls from the gifted and talented class in Southern Arkansas sitting in the VIP gallery, and when it failed they clapped and cheered."[31]

Defeat in the state Senate ended the legislative activity in Arkansas, but it was clear that the conversation would continue. In August former US Surgeon General Dr. Joycelyn Elders was the keynote speaker at the opening of an exhibit at the state capitol celebrating the eighty-fifth anniversary of the Nineteenth Amendment. She remarked that the Equal Rights Amendment should have been passed in the recent legislative session, and she urged women to continue to fight for women's rights, including passage of the ERA. Following the ceremony, Representative Lindsley Smith said she had talked with Senator Sue Madison and that the two lawmakers planned to introduce the ratification resolution again in the 2007 legislative session.[32]

During the 2006 election, ratification of the Equal Rights Amendment again became a campaign issue in Arkansas. Addressing the Arkansas Business and Professional Women's Conference, State Representative Rick Saunders (D-Hot Springs) received a standing ovation when he announced that he wanted to co-sponsor ratification of the ERA, because women have no constitutional guarantee of equality. Saunders acknowledged the 1982 ratification deadline, but he said, "It's important and people want it done. It's a good policy, but sometimes good policy is the hardest to sell. A lot of people don't want change. They are enjoying the status quo. But change is happening. I celebrate change." Until the legislature convened in January 2007, he said he planned to increase public awareness and build legislative support.[33]

The ERA was an issue in the governor's race as well. Republican nominee Asa Hutchinson said he was a strong supporter of equal rights for women, but he opposed the ERA because existing laws against sex discrimination in the workforce ensure equal treatment for women. Independent candidate Rod Bryan and Attorney General Mike Beebe, the Democratic nominee, both said they supported ratification of the ERA. Beebe said he backed the ERA because women entrepreneurs "are an economic engine not just for our state, but for our country. We want to ensure that they continue to be a viable and strong force for the economy. Women are providing a huge, huge economic benefit and leadership for our state." Karen Garcia, legislative chair of the Arkansas Business and Professional Women, said the group wanted the 2007 legislature to ratify the ERA, which was one of the reasons that the BPW endorsed Beebe.[34]

The Democrats emerged from the 2006 elections with all seven constitutional officers, five of the six members of the congressional delegation, and control of both houses of the General Assembly. Supporters of ratification were more hopeful when the 2007 legislative session opened in January, and they held a massive show of support at a rally in the rotunda of the state capitol on January 24, sponsored by the Business and Professional Women, ERArkansas, Arkansas Education Association, Arkansas Federation of Democratic Women, American Association of University Women, League of Women Voters, American Association of Retired Persons, and the National Association for the Advancement of Colored People. Garcia, one of the rally organizers, said many people had not been aware of the issue two years before but that women's groups had spent the last year educating the public, talking with legislators, and building support for ratification.[35] Now, she believed that Arkansas could be the first state to ratify the ERA in the twenty-first century.[36]

Secretary of State Charlie Daniels issued a proclamation designating Equal Rights Day in Arkansas, and the other six constitutional officers spoke in favor of ratification at the rally. Governor Mike Beebe told the assembled group of about two hundred supporters, "All of the arguments against this amendment existed and were used against allowing women the right to vote. We all know how ludicrous the arguments against women voting sound now, and the arguments against giving women equal rights will sound just as ludicrous when we pass them."[37] He added, "It's a matter of justice. It's a matter of equality. It's a matter of fairness."[38] Attorney General Dustin McDaniel called it "an injustice in this country that we have not amended our Constitution with the ERA."[39] Lieutenant Governor Bill Halter, who had supported the ERA in his recent election campaign, said, "We have the opportunity to enshrine in the Constitution the ideal of equal rights for men and women. . . . It's an important principle to support."[40] State Treasurer Martha Shoffner, State Auditor Jim Wood, and Land Commissioner Mark Wilcox also spoke in favor of ratification.

Representative Smith and Senator Madison again handled the ratification resolution. Madison marveled at the broad public and legislative support and contended, "Women deserve to be in our country's constitution to preserve our rights. If there are things we truly believe are important, they are in our constitution." Representative Smith filed House Joint Resolution 1002 that morning with 65 House co-sponsors and 11 Senate co-sponsors. "It's the right thing to do; it's a fit for Arkansas and good for the people of the nation," she said, emphasizing "that Arkansas needs to be on the right side of history."[41] Representative Kathy Webb (D-Little Rock) claimed that she had organized the last rally for the ERA in 1982 and said she was "so excited that this week I'm going to be able to vote on this."[42]

Ratification was not yet assured, however. Max Brantley, editor of the *Arkansas Times*, commended Governor Beebe's courage in supporting the ERA, noting that "most politicians in Arkansas, sad to say, are too cowardly to fight [the ERA's opponents]," whom he called a "very loud, noisy minority" who would oppose the ERA by claiming it promoted homosexual marriage.[43] "The ERA anti-family activists are at it again," charged Patrick Briney, president of the Arkansas Republican Assembly, warning that 4ERA, a "national, anti-family group has targeted Arkansas as part of its three state strategy." He articulated the Republicans' fears that ratification of the Equal Rights Amendment would: (1) "legalize the granting of marriage licenses to homosexuals and generally implement the gay rights and lesbian agenda," (2) "make abortion funding a new constitutional right," (3) "force the sex integration of fraternities, sororities, Boy Scouts, Girl Scouts, YMCA, YWCA, Boys State and Girls State conducted by the American Legion, and mother-daughter and father-son school events" and "put at risk the tax exemption of thousands of Catholic, Protestant, and Jewish schools all over the country," (4) undermine states' rights and "give Congress the power to legislate on all areas of law which include traditional differences of treatment on account of sex: marriage, property laws, divorce and alimony, child custody, adoptions, abortion, homosexual laws, sex crimes, private and public schools, prison regulations, and insurance," (5) "take away women's traditional exemption from military conscription and also from military combat duty," and (6) forfeit male veterans' preference rights.[44]

As predicted, Jerry Cox of the Arkansas Family Council warned that the ERA would "give the courts a huge hammer to destroy all state marriage amendments," and Anne Britton of the Washington County Republican Women protested, "Marriage is sacred and should remain one man, one woman. Any effort to dilute the sanctity of marriage is not upholding the views and values of everyday Arkansans."[45] Whether this would prove persuasive with legislators remained to be seen, but the general public appeared unmoved by such arguments. "Our elected officials have the opportunity to move our state forward and send a message to the rest of the nation, a message that we recognize and respect the foundational rights of all Americans," wrote Leo Hauser of Little Rock, urging the legislators to "support progress, not paranoia. Support passage of the Arkansas ERA resolution."[46]

The House State Agencies Committee considered the ERA on February 7, but the legislative drama began when House Minority Leader Eric Harris (R-Springdale) presented and passed an amendment to remove twenty of the House co-sponsors he had convinced to remove their names. Among those reneging on their commitment were eighteen House Democrats, including Representative Toni Bradford (D-Pine Bluff) and three members of the State Agencies Committee, Lance Reynolds (D-Quitman), Buddy Lovell (D-Marked Tree), and Clark Hall (D-Marvell). Explaining his removal as a sponsor, Representative Allen Maxwell (D-Monticello) said, "All the hullabaloo about this ERA thing, I don't necessarily buy it, and I felt comfortable about being a co-sponsor, but they (constituents) asked me to get off. So I felt like I needed to yield."[47]

Representative Steve Harrelson (D-Texarkana), a member of the House State Agencies Committee and one of the co-sponsors of HJR 1002, said before the meeting, "I've received several (read "hundreds") of e-mails from people telling me to read the bill very carefully, because it clearly opens the door to gay marriage and abortion on demand. I just don't see it." He shared a resolution of support from the General Board of the American Baptist Churches, and asked, "Am I to believe that these sneaky organizations seeking to implement gay marriage and abortion through this vote have snowed not only our Governor and all other constitutional officers into supporting this legislation but the legislatures of 35 other states, the United States Congress, and the American Baptist Churches Association? I'm not buying it. I'm proud to support equal rights to both genders, which is exactly the stated purpose— and only purpose—of this legislation."[48]

The committee took three hours of public comment on the resolution before a packed room. Representative Smith presented the resolution and called for its adoption, then witnesses spoke for and against the measure. Headlining the testimony for ratification was former US Senator and Governor David Pryor, who had voted for the Equal Rights Amendment in the US House of Representatives in 1972. Pryor told the committee, "Arkansas has a rare opportunity today to once again make a statement, and a strong statement, for the equality of women. It's our opportunity to say we want to make sure this is a part of the bedrock of our system of our beliefs and that women should be treated no differently than men." Former State Representative Joyce Elliott of Little Rock also make spirited remarks in support of the ERA, asking committee members, "What's the problem with your going home and saying to your children, your grandchildren and to every woman in this room, 'We respect you enough to put it on paper'?"[49]

The opposition was again led by Eagle Forum's Phyllis Schlafly, who called the ERA "a fraud" that would make abortion and sexual activity a constitutionally protected right, and she warned of the dire consequences that would result from equal rights—placing women soldiers in combat, striking down laws defining marriage as between a man and a woman, and forcing sexual integration of scouting organizations, college fraternities, and prisons.[50] Representatives of the National Right to Life Committee also lobbied hard against the measure.

When the roll was called, only ten of the fifteen Democrats on the committee voted for the Do Pass motion. Five Democratic representatives, including Pam Adcock (D-Little Rock) and two former co-sponsors who reneged on their promise of support, Lance Reynolds (D-Quitman) and Buddy Lovell (D-Marked Tree), joined all five Republican members in voting no. The motion failed on a 10–10 vote, needing eleven for approval and consideration by the full House.[51]

Editorial commentary, both before and after the committee vote, was divided. The *Northwest Arkansas Times*, published in the home districts of Senator Madison and Representative Smith, did not support ratification of the Equal Rights Amendment. In the editors' opinion, "it remains unclear just what Madison, Smith and all the rest expect to accomplish by gaining approval of this resolution. It's like treading water, which is to say, going nowhere. . . . We cannot condemn the conviction behind this effort; no, we applaud it. But time would be better spent proposing a new approach rather than clinging to a failed measure of the past."[52]

The *Arkansas Democrat-Gazette* gave considerable ink to arguing against the Equal Rights Amendment. In rewriting history, the editorial recounted the failure to ratify thirty years before and claimed, "Just in time, it was realized that this tricky little amendment might actually take away protections for women in the law. And could lead to other, unanticipated consequences. Like upsetting state laws protecting marriage and the family." In characterizing the present efforts, it proclaimed, "The good news is that . . . a committee of the Arkansas House refused to rubber-stamp this nice-sounding but mischievous constitutional amendment. The commit-tee is to be commended, and the rest of the Legislature reminded to look beyond nice-sounding labels."[53]

Arkansas Democrat-Gazette columnist Mike Masterson said he was "pleased" that the committee "failed to recommend passage" of the Equal Rights Amendment. "A significant number of Arkansans believes it's being pushed primarily as one approach for implementing publicly funded abor-tions and same-sex marriage, so my hat is off to those who stood strong in the breach to oppose House Joint Resolution 1002," he wrote summa-rizing Schlafly's testimony as a projection of his own views.[54] Certainly not all readers agreed. A letter from Jake Tidmore responded, "In Mike Masterson's recent bigoted, biblical babblings against homosexuals, your opinion page has sunk to a new low."[55] A more charitable response was a letter from Beatryce Lewis, who wrote, "Mike Masterson's recent column proved how little he knows about the Equal Rights Amendment." She coun-tered that the "only agenda proponents of the ERA have is that the Arkansas Legislature ratifies the amendment to protect the rights that women have gained. . . . Equality of women and men is a fundamental human right that should be codified in our Constitution. Thirty-five states have ratified the ERA. The women, and men, of Arkansas need to ask why our legislators are unwilling to protect women's rights with the same conviction as they protect men's rights."[56]

Representative Dan Greenberg (R-Little Rock), who voted against the ERA in committee and who happened to be the son of the editorial page editor, was given significant space for an op-ed column in the *Arkansas Democrat-Gazette*. He alleged that ERA supporters suggested ratification "is just a matter of public relations—a symbolic method of showing we care about equality of the sexes," and Greenberg responded that "using a consti-tutional amendment just to make a statement has dangerous consequences," such as "taxpayer-funded abortion, affirmative action, gay marriage," and other policies that "move us closer to judicial supremacy and farther away from self-government—all in the name of an equal rights amendment that accomplishes little or nothing for equal rights."[57]

The effort in Arkansas and the three-state strategy received national attention on National Public Radio, and the argument was resonating with Arkansas citizens, despite the tie vote in the House committee that blocked ratification.[58] University of Arkansas political science professor Janine Parry parried Representative Greenberg's column with one of her own. "This time, same-sex marriage, publicly-funded abortions, and the draft are the red herrings being exploited by opponents of equality," she said of the arguments by Schlafly and Greenberg. "Perhaps Arkansas won't be fooled twice. Why? Because this time around the opponents' mole-hill-based speculations about the impact of an equal rights amendment can be countered by a mountain of facts." After a point-by-point refutation of each item of the opposition's case, she urged, "Let's be persuaded by experience over speculation, by facts over hyperbole. Let's be the first state since 1977 to declare that our sons and daughters are equal in the eyes of the law, and that we support including that simple declaration in the US Constitution."[59]

James Gately of Rogers wrote to upbraid Benton County Republican Representatives Hardwick, Harris, and Pace, who voted against the Equal Rights Amendment in committee, asking, "How do I explain to my granddaughter that the principle of equality should not be guaranteed to her?" He bemoaned that "irrational fears are being spread that the ERA will become a vehicle to fund abortion and legalize same-sex marriage and that it was a federal power grab. Analysis would expose the examples the opposition use as exaggerated and flawed." Moreover, he declared, "Citizens deserve a debate and vote to expose this reactionary agenda of legislators using the propaganda tools of fear and exaggeration to deny women a guarantee of the basic constitutional principle of equality," closing with the declaration, "It is time for our legislators to support the ERA!"[60]

"We have another chance at getting this through our Legislature if good citizens contact their legislators and tell them to support the ERA," wrote Mara Jarrett of Heber Springs, a constituent of Representative Lance Reynolds, one of the Democrats on the committee who withdrew as a co-sponsor and voted no on the ERA. "It will be a real shame and embarrassment if Arkansas is among the few states not to ratify the ERA. In advanced and sophisticated societies, attitudes about 'keeping women in their place' are repulsively harmful and need to be put to rest forever," she said with a conviction not shared by her own legislator.[61]

Following the end of the 2007 legislative session, legislators reflected on the outcome of the ratification efforts. Representative Jim House (D-Fayetteville), one of the co-sponsors of the resolution, said some legislators were intimidated by "fear of the unknowns" and that the ERA "was defeated because the lobbyists asked 'whatif' questions."[62] Perhaps his colleagues were also asking "whatif" questions about their own reelection chances and were unable to judge public opinion outside the circle of proponents and opponents. Representative Smith acknowledged that despite its failure the ERA was "the most important issue she worked on during the session," but she thought "there was a lot of good education given to the legislature. It has garnered a lot of national interest."[63]

It does appear that the ERA campaign had been more successful in educating the public than the elected representatives. The Arkansas poll conducted in October 2007 found that 73 percent of the state's population favored the adoption of the Equal Rights Amendment to the US Constitution, while only 18 percent opposed it.[64] The *Morning News of Northwest Arkansas* observed, "That number surprised us, as it may have the members of the Arkansas General Assembly, who had an opportunity to help ratify the amendment in its last session but decided against it." Reflecting on the unsuccessful recent attempts to ratify the ERA, the editors said they "were pleasantly stunned to see that nearly three-quarters of Arkansans support the ERA." Of course, they conceded that Jerry Cox of the Arkansas Family Council would still make the same old arguments, which they said "seem somewhat silly in this day and age." The editors then concluded, "We have no idea whether the legal argument that says the ERA can still be ratified is valid, nor do we know what the ultimate impact of the amendment would be. . . . But we do know this: The language of the US Constitution specifically ensures rights to people regardless of creed, color or national origin. Common sense—not to mention a significant number of Arkansans—says that list should also include gender."[65]

During 2008 the possible ratification continued to be a part of the public political conversation. The Jonesboro chapter of the Arkansas Business and Professional Women joined the cause and became active in lobbying for equal rights and equal pay on the state level, including "working to ratify the Equal Rights Amendment that will make it easier to pass the equal pay issue with guaranteed constitutional rights." It was again an issue during the 2008 election campaign in some legislative races. Representative Jim House (D-Fayetteville) said during a debate that he considered his co-sponsorship of a bill in the previous session to ratify the federal Equal Rights Amendment to be one of his proudest legislative accomplishments, while his Republican opponent, Gene Long, stated his opposition to the measure.[66]

As the Arkansas General Assembly convened in January 2009, Fran Alexander of Fayetteville published a long and thoughtful opinion column in the *Northwest Arkansas Times* calling for Arkansas to ratify the Equal Rights Amendment. "Part of what is so hard about securing these tenuous gains is that about 70 percent of the nation thinks the ERA has already passed," she wrote. "Worse, those state legislatures still holding out on ratification, for 'women's own good,' keep responding to irrational fears of what all this equality will do to society, just as they did while fanning racial equality fears."[67]

On January 24 Senator Madison introduced SJR 12 with eighteen co-sponsors, and Representative Smith introduced HJR 1014 with forty-three co-sponsors. Although no Republican members were among the co-sponsors of either resolution, both introducers anticipated passage if they were able to get approval of a Do Pass motion in either the Senate or House State Agencies Committee. Jerry Cox, president of the Arkansas Family Council, emerged as the leading lobbyist against the ERA, sending an e-mail blast asking all allies to contact lawmakers and tell them to kill the proposal, because it would "make all state and federal laws gender neutral" and place Arkansas's constitutional amendment defining marriage as being only between a man and a woman in "serious jeopardy."[68]

Madison brought the Senate resolution for consideration in committee on March 4. The committee was composed of five Democrats and three Republicans, and she needed five votes for a Do Pass motion to pass. During the hearing, three women spoke against the ERA. Rose Mimms, executive director of Arkansas Right to Life, expressed concern that ratification would override all abortion laws; Martha Adcock, attorney for the Arkansas Family Council, spoke of ominous "unintended consequences"; and Marianne Linane of the Catholic Diocese of Little Rock warned about far-reaching consequences ranging from legalization of prostitution to the elimination of the words "husband" and "wife." Madison spoke for the ERA, as did law professor John DiPippa of the University of Arkansas, Little Rock, who addressed the imaginary legal consequences; Larry Delashmit, a Vietnam veteran and chair of the Washington County Democratic Committee, who said women deserved the rights they had defended; and Cory Sailor of the Arkansas National Guard, who also debunked the arguments about women in military combat.[69]

Senator Steve Bryles (D-Blytheville) said he supported the ERA for his daughters and the other women in his family. Equality for women has come a long way, he said, but not far enough. As for the opposition, he added, "It's amazing what fear does to all of us." He was joined by two other members who had not supported the ERA in the 2005 Senate floor vote, Randy Laverty (D-Jasper) and Ed Wilkinson (D-Greenwood), as well as Senator Steve Faris (D-Central). Senator Bobby Glover (D-Carlisle) joined the three Republicans opposing the ERA, resulting in a 4–4 vote, and the motion failed.[70]

Meanwhile, Representative Smith was working the House State

Agencies Committee, which had a 12–8 Democratic majority. All eight Republicans were opposed, including Donna Hutchinson (R-Bella Vista) and Mary Lou Slinkard (R-Gravette). Among the twelve Democrats, she could only count ten affirmative votes for the ERA, with Butch Wilkins (D-Bono) and Larry Cowling (D-Foreman) siding with the Republicans in opposition. Unable to gain another vote in support, the resolution was never considered in the House Committee. "It's pretty sad that anyone finds it a difficult vote to support equality for women," lamented Smith after the Arkansas legislature again failed to ratify. "I heard that so much. It's easier to vote against equality than to vote for it."[71]

The public conversation about the ERA continued with passion. The *Northwest Arkansas Times* said it was time to give up, "because time has literally run out on the idea."[72] Senator Madison and Representative Smith, it opined, do not "appear concerned with the fact that their constituents aren't really clamoring for state movement on the ERA proposal. Where are the protests? The marches? The letters to the editor? Despite a lack of any apparent groundswell, both legislators spent a good deal of time and political capital to make Arkansas the 36th state to support the ERA." However, that newspaper's editorial page editor thought otherwise. "Maybe I'm wrong, but I believe that all Americans—every single one of us—deserve the same right to pursue happiness in whatever form he or she chooses," wrote Scott Shackelford. "It does not seem unreasonable, to me, that female soldiers who bleed and die just like the men they serve with deserve to come home to a country that treats them less than equally in the eyes of the law. Adding a total of three sentences to the Constitution in an effort to guarantee fair treatment for our wives, our daughters, our mothers (and every other creature of the opposite sex among us) does not seem like it would be a most controversial thing." As to the viability of the strategy currently in play, he said, that "should a court someday rule that the modern ERA process is no longer applicable, Congress and the states can start all over again. And why not? This effort is too important to give up on simply because it seems like discrimination no longer exists, particularly when the case evidence would tend to suggest otherwise."[73]

Likewise, Brenda Blagg's column in the *Morning News of Northwest Arkansas* cried, "Never give up." Expressing wonder that the legislature had not yet ratified the ERA, she asked, "How can that concept really be so threatening as to cause the ERA to fail time and again in the Arkansas Legislature? The simple answer is that it is not all that threatening—except to those who cling to irrational arguments against the amendment, arguments that were made and rejected long ago in the 35 states that have ratified the change."[74]

Berta Seitz wrote to shame the legislators who refused to allow a floor vote on the ERA. "It is time for lawmakers to stand up and say that all Arkansas citizens are valued and are part of the team by voting to ratify the ERA. Women have worked, fought and died for this country and deserve to be part of the team with all of the rights and protections given in the US Constitution. It is simple justice," she said.[75]

Senator Madison had commitments from twenty-five senators to pass the resolution, but it was still lodged in the Senate State Agencies committee. Governor Beebe, a former state senator and a strong supporter of ratification, urged her to use a Senate Rule to extract the resolution and place it on the Senate calendar for a vote.[76] Madison was reluctant to do that.[77]

Ultimately, Madison moved to send the measure to an Interim Committee for further study, a tactic allowing it a dignified death. The epitaph for the ERA in the 2009 legislative session was pronounced by an editorial in the Benton Courier, which lamented that "the Legislature again refused to ratify the Equal Rights Amendment, keeping Arkansas as one of 15 states that have not done so since the deadline passed in 1982. Whether it would make a difference nationally is debatable, but it would at least have been a recognition of an important principle. We're probably going to have to have more women in the Legislature before the ERA ever gets an endorsement."[78]

For the first time in thirty years, the Democratic Party of Arkansas included a plank in its 2010 platform calling for ratification of the Equal Rights Amendment.[79] The provision had been pushed by the Arkansas Federation of Democratic Women, but neither their support nor the Democratic Party platform had any influence on the Democratic members of the 2011 Arkansas General Assembly. Senator Madison, sponsor of ratification resolutions in 2005, 2007, and 2009, did not introduce the measure in 2011, and Representative Smith had retired due to legislative term limits.

The Democratic legislative leadership showed no interest in continuing to make the argument for equal rights. Representative Kathy Webb (D-Little Rock), a former national officer of the National Organization of Women and vice chair of the House Democratic Caucus, said she "didn't think that was the best use of our time and energy." Senator Linda Chesterfield's (D-Little Rock) bill to revive the Commission on the Status of Women was also defeated in the House after opposition by Speaker Robert Moore (D-Arkansas City).[80] No support for the ERA was offered by any Republican member. Representative Andrea Lea (R-Russellville) said she would oppose the ERA, stating, "I've never understood why it was an important bill. I'm standing here in the halls of the Legislature, so obviously a woman can do just about anything she wants."[81]

Despite their disappointment, supporters resumed the campaign immediately after the legislature adjourned, scheduling a rally on the steps of the state capitol. House Majority Leader Johnnie Roebuck (D-Arkadelphia) expressed surprise and dismissed the event. "I would have thought that they would have done that early in January to try to build some momentum and some support," she said. Lindsley Smith replied that she was "saddened" that no one had introduced a resolution to initiate the public discussion and explained, "It's got to be dropped in the hopper so that it allows for the voice of the people. People were ready to speak on that."[82]

Sheryl Flanagin of Fort Smith said with some exasperation, "We are still waiting for the women of the United States to be included in our Constitution. . . . The ERArkansas Coalition, through rallies like the one Saturday at the Capitol, hopes to create awareness and have Arkansas become one of the remaining three states [to ratify]." She closed by making a personal argument: "My mother was born before women had the right to vote; my older daughter was born in 1972, the year Congress passed the ERA; my hope is my granddaughters will grow up in a country that finally recognizes the rights of all its citizens."[83]

The ERA Ratification Rally on May 7 drew an enthusiastic crowd and a diverse group of speakers for ratification as well as a letter of support from former president Bill Clinton, which said, "Ratification of the ERA is a thoroughly non-partisan issue, and if successful, it will benefit women and men alike. . . . You each bear witness to what may become a truly pivotal moment in Constitutional history, and I join you in hoping for a successful outcome."[84] As the 2012 primary elections approached, supporters received encouragement from legislative candidates such as Democrat David Whitaker, a House candidate of Fayetteville, who pledged his support for ratification of the ERA and urged the members of the Senior Democrats of Northwest Arkansas to demonstrate their support and bring the pressure of public opinion to the effort. "I would rather see it pass than see it be a symbolic defeat," Whitaker said.[85] Letters to the editor were an active forum and offered evidence on the nature of support and resistance. Linda Ferrell of Bella Vista wrote recounting the struggle for female suffrage and urging women to exercise the right to vote in the 2012 elections.[86] Demonstrating the scope of the opposition to women's rights, David Sumrell of Springdale responded, "The granting of the vote to women was the time women first began to get out of their places and out of their God-given roles as housewives and queens of their homes. . . . Rebellion to God first, and man second. And the spiritually discerning person can witness the madness of this country and how it started with the granting of the vote to females."[87]

There were numerous responses and refutations of Sumrell's letter, but Sherry Faubus of Springdale shifted the conversation back to the ERA. "I find it very ironic that many of my fellow Arkansans, male and female alike, are surprised by the opinions put forth by David Sumrell," she said. "We live in one of the 15 states yet to ratify the Equal Rights Amendment. In order for an amendment to become 'real,' it must be ratified. The ERA was passed by Congress in 1972 and has been ratified by 35 of the necessary 38 states. When three more states vote yes, it is possible that the ERA could become the 28th Amendment." Faubus then advised her readers, "Turn your outrage into action; contact your local representatives and senators. I urge also that you ask the candidates running for legislative office. Demand results. In the eyes of the law, we are not equal until ERA is ratified."[88]

A series of opinion pieces in the *Arkansas Democrat-Gazette* in 2012 continued the conversation about the desirability and viability of the Equal Rights Amendment. Bernadette Cahill recapped the relevant Arkansas history, addressed the legal objections, and concluded, "Arkansans have two ways to help lead the nation out of this impasse: to call on local representatives to ratify the ERA in this state, and to call on our congressional representatives to support these two measures in Congress in order to remove any objections to ratification, both here and elsewhere."[89] In response Rose Mimms of Arkansas Right to Life replied with an essay restating her allegations about the potential of the ERA to undermine state restrictions on abortion procedures and questioning the continuing efforts to ratify, asserting, "The ERA is dead. Let's bury it."[90]

A rebuttal from Lindsley Smith noted that Justice Antonin Scalia recently reminded the nation, "Certainly the Constitution does not require discrimination on the basis of sex. The only issue is whether it prohibits it. It doesn't. Nobody ever thought that that's what it meant. Nobody ever voted for that. If the current society wants to outlaw discrimination by sex, hey, we have things called legislatures, and they enact things called laws." Smith urged, "Let's not continue to wait on full equality for our daughters and granddaughters. . . . Let's stand on the right side of history and do our part as a state to help the nation assure that men and women share the same citizenship rights. . . . While the Legislature has not passed this, polls

in Arkansas have consistently shown Arkansans' support for the ERA. The
General Assembly should make Arkansas a ratifying state for the Equal
Rights Amendment in the 2013 legislative session. What rational reason is
there to deny it?"[91]

The Democratic Party of Arkansas in August 2012 again adopted a
platform calling on the Arkansas legislature to ratify the Equal Rights
Amendment.[92] The game was on, yet again.

After waiting for almost two months with no legislator introducing
a resolution to ratify the ERA in the 2013, Lindsley Smith and Berta Seitz
asked Senator Joyce Elliott (D-Little Rock) and Representative Warwick
Sabin (D-Little Rock) to sponsor the legislation. Each gladly agreed. SJR
19 was filed by Senator Elliott on March 13 and was referred to the Senate
State Agencies Committee.

On April 2 the Senate committee heard testimony for two hours before
a standing-room-only audience of about two hundred that was overwhelmingly supportive, many wearing buttons that said, "Trust Women." Senator
Elliott led the proponents, stating, "What we're asking for you to do today is
to join other states and say to our Congress and to the world that Arkansas
believes in the ERA for women."[93] Lindsley Smith discussed the need for
a constitutional amendment to clarify the weakness of current statutory
provisions against discrimination, arguing that all "Americans deserve strict
scrutiny before a government can discriminate against them on the basis
of their sex, a stricter standard of review that comes with placement of this
guarantee of equality in the U.S. Constitution."[94]

Larry DeLashmit of Fayetteville presented a stirring argument about
honoring the women who had served their nation in the armed forces,
which one newspaper columnist called the "most remarkable" of the proponents, explaining that "DeLashmit had me about ready to run through
a wall to cram into the U.S. Constitution an amendment for the unambig-
uous guarantee of equal rights for women who serve in combat and bleed
and lose limbs, and in memory of women who have died in combat serving
this country."

The opposition was again led by Jerry Cox of the Arkansas Family
Council, who acknowledged the viability of the ratification effort and again
speculated about the dangers of co-ed dormitories, the impact on fraternities and sororities, and other unimagined and unimaginable consequences.
The "unintended consequences" coded argument was also presented by former Republican state representative Dan Greenberg of Little Rock.[95]

Once again the Senate State Agencies Committee failed to approve a Do Pass motion, voting on party lines with a 5–3 Republican majority, including Senator Jane English (R-North Little Rock). "Yes, it all was futile to the extent that this Legislature is not going to ratify the ERA. But these fundamentalist preachers and coffee-shop blowhards now making our laws need to see that there is actual political resistance to their nonsense," said John Brummett, columnist for the *Arkansas Democrat-Gazette*. "They need to see women who aren't subservient. They need to see that there are determined women standing between them and the door of the committee room in which they vote for the latest anti-woman outrage." In assessing the meaning of the day, and perhaps its purpose, Brummett concluded, "In the end, of course, the ERA died in committee with majority Republicans voting no. But its spirit lived for a couple of hours inside a government room once used for justice. And that was a good thing—not futile, but an incremental triumph."[96]

Discussion

The ongoing rhetorical contest in Arkansas reveals the ways local advocates and opponents continue to engage with the Equal Rights Amendment in legislative testimony and grassroots advocacy. It also demonstrates that the hopes of women supporting the Equal Rights Amendment persist in the face of repeated failure of the majority of state legislators to confront or combat the fears of the opponents. Undaunted after the latest capitulation, Roselinda Johnson of Russellville asked, "What is opposition to the ERA really all about? It is a frantic attempt to block, and then reverse, one of the most extraordinary and mighty tides of change in all of human history; the emergence, at last, of the long-suppressed women, half of the human race, to full and equal participation in society and the shaping of a better future for all."[97]

"Why an explicit guarantee of women's equality was rejected as part of the constituting document of the United States is a good question, one it takes some courage to ask. The answers are bound to be as unnerving, challenging, even anguishing as they are crucial and urgent for law and politics," wrote Catherine MacKinnon in 1987, between the first and second wave of ratification attempts. "The ERA came to mean the equality of the sexes to those who sought it, to those who abhorred it, and to those who found saying it in law somewhat obvious if not yet redundant. It is hard for women to face the fact that we live in a country that rejects our equality."[98]

In many ways, the state's reasons for reluctance to support equality for women in the twenty-first century are following the same pattern as with reluctance to support racial equality in previous centuries.[99] Phyllis Schlafly's 2007 testimony predicted that the Equal Rights Amendment would upset the social order by requiring women to register for the draft, forcing them to serve in combat units, striking down state prohibitions on gay marriage, and mandating unisex bathrooms. It echoed the mantra of segregationists and was a replay of the fear appeals she had fanned successfully in leading the opposition three decades earlier.

Arkansas legislators opposing ratification also had expressed hostility to the possibility that women would be serving in combat. Senator Jack Critcher (D-Batesville) said he was thinking of his daughter when he voted against the ratification resolution in committee in 2005. "Would that mean she'd go to the front lines?" He said that women are treated differently from men in the military and that it should stay that way.[100] On the other hand, Cory Sailor of the Arkansas National Guard, testifying in favor of the Equal Rights Amendment in 2009, said there are no distinctions between the sexes on battlefields, and there is no discrimination regarding pay in the military. But in civilian life, women do not have the equal rights they fought to defend.[101]

Now, however, women are eligible for all combat jobs in every branch of the armed forces, without exceptions. Defense Secretary Ash Carter announced "that as long as they qualify and meet the standards, women will now be able to contribute to our mission in ways they could not before."[102] Likewise, the recurring refrain that the ERA would subject women to a non-existent draft might soon be irrelevant, as the Pentagon and Congress appear to be moving toward requiring women to register with the Selective Service System.[103] In June 2016 Arkansas Senators John Boozman and Tom Cotton voted with the majority to approve the National Defense Authorization Act (85–13), which includes a provision requiring women to register for the draft.[104]

One of the primary fear appeals repeated by Phyllis Schlafly and allied opponents is that the ERA would prohibit sex-segregated restrooms.[105] Related to that proposition, Patrick Briney and the Arkansas Republican Assembly protested that the ERA would force sex integration of fraternities, sororities, and various youth organizations and activities.[106] Although this is not directly addressed through legislation or constitutional interpretation, the US Department of Justice explained that under Title IX of the Education Amendments of 1972, schools receiving federal money may not discriminate based on a student's sex. That advisory memorandum explained that a school has an obligation to allow students "to participate in sex-segregated activities and access sex-segregated facilities consistent with their gender identity."[107] Such policies prohibiting discrimination on the basis of sex do not prohibit sex-segregated activities or facilities, the fear appeals of opponents notwithstanding.[108]

Arkansas voters had adopted a state constitutional amendment in 2004 banning both same-sex marriages and civil unions. In 2005 State Senator Jerry Taylor (D-Pine Bluff) worried that ratifying the ERA could legalize same-sex marriages, a claim that Schlafly would make in 2007 and opponents would continue to repeat through the March 2013 legislative hearing.[109] This was perhaps the most persuasive claim for legislators opposing ratification, because it was the only one supported by a majority of their constituents, but it is one that has now vanished as a compelling argument.

A survey of public opinion in Arkansas by Greenberg Quinlan Rosner Research and Target Point Consulting in June 2013 found that only 38 percent of voters supported marriage equality while 55 percent opposed it. Opposition was led largely by Republicans (80 percent) and by observant Christians (66 percent).[110] Since then, the US Supreme Court has declared Section 3 of the Defense of Marriage Act to be unconstitutional "as a deprivation of the liberty of the person protected by the Fifth Amendment"; an Arkansas trial court struck down the state's constitutional and legislative ban on same-sex marriage; a federal district court struck down Arkansas's ban on same-sex marriage; the US Supreme Court held that the Fourteenth Amendment requires a state to license a marriage between two people of the same sex and to recognize a marriage between two people of the same sex when their marriage was lawfully licensed and performed out-of-state; and the Arkansas Supreme Court consequently dismissed as moot the state attorney general's pending appeal of state court decisions overturning the ban.[111] Should a resolution to ratify the ERA in Arkansas or other states be introduced again, this discredited argument will be moot.

Regardless of success, the continuing efforts for ratification pay unique dividends in providing a public forum and shaping public opinion in the non-ratifying states. Public consensus regarding the need for improving women's status in society was appreciably enhanced by the years of debate during the initial period for ratification. This is substantiated both by the enactment of federal legislation removing statutory barriers to equal treatment and in shifting sentiment revealed by public opinion polling. Harris and Roper polls from 1970 through 1985 "show steadily growing support for strengthening the status of women. . . . At the beginning of the 1970s,

40 percent of women and 44 percent of men who responded approved the idea. Fifteen years later in 1985, 73 percent of women and 69 percent of men favored such changes."[112]

Opinion polling since 1972 had found a national majority supporting ratification of the ERA, reaching 63 percent in 1981.[113] And "its supporters included at least a plurality of people living in unratified states, housewives, conservatives and fundamentalists. Thus, the failure of the ERA cannot be attributed to public opposition. Instead, the amendment's failure must be attributed to systemic factors in the political processes of non-ratifying states which thwarted ratification and produced legislator indifference to popular sentiment."[114]

As the three-state strategy began to evolve, a July 2001 survey by Opinion Research Corporation found that 72 percent believed, incorrectly, that the Constitution already guaranteed equal rights and that 88 percent believed the Constitution should be amended to make it clear that men and women have equal rights.[115] By August 2012 a Public Policy Polling survey found overwhelming support for a constitutional guarantee of equal rights, 91 percent to 4 percent. Perhaps confirmation bias leads citizens to conflate their preferences with reality. Even in 2016, said Congresswoman Carolyn Maloney (D-NY12), "Many people today take for granted that equal rights between men and women are enshrined in the U.S. Constitution—and are shocked when they learn that they are not."[116]

Favorable public opinion, however, does not always result in legislative success. Mansbridge concluded that the failure to ratify in Illinois was a result of several factors. Some were structural, such as the requirement of an extraordinary majority rather than a simple majority of each chamber, and some were strategic, such as the exaggeration of benefits by the proponents and of harms by the opponents, costing both sides potential legislative allies. "The only way to have persuaded three more state legislatures to ratify the ERA would have been to insist—correctly—that it would have done relatively little in the short run, and to insist—equally strongly—on the importance of placing the principle in the Constitution to guide the Supreme Court in its long-term evolution of constitutional law." Then it could be claimed that the real victory was a "public statement of moral commitment."[117]

"Moreover, the ratification struggle had suggested to proponents that the more they could characterize the ERA as a matter of high principle—of equality and justice in the abstract—the better," said Serena Mayeri. While most of the public opinion polls found that an overwhelming majority of Americans supported equality in broad terms, legislative jousting indicated weaker support when opponents mischaracterized the ERA's projected effects.[118] Such a strategy proved to have a weakness as well. Many of the goals sought by the ERA proponents were being won under the Fourteenth Amendment, and ERA proponents found it increasingly difficult to claim that the ERA would have tangible benefits—but the opposition had no trouble in pointing out tangible "costs."[119] After exerting considerable time refuting the opposition charges, proponents were expected to build their case with "good reasons" for ratification, and generalizations of moral principles were found wanting. State Senator Baker expressed his opposition to ratification in 2005, because no one could point to a specific problem or an example where women have unequal rights. As noted earlier, he said he did not favor changing the Constitution purely to make a statement.[120]

During the Senate State Agencies Committee hearing in 2009, Senators Bobby Glover (D-Carlisle) and Bill Pritchard (R-Elkins) both brushed aside broad moral arguments for equality and demanded specific instances of discrimination and problems that would be solved. Kristina Croslin of Greenbrier, a supporter in the audience, reported, "I kept thinking, 'You are discriminating against me, against all women of this great state, by not voting yes for my equality rights.'"[121] At the 2013 hearing before the Senate State Agencies Committee, Marti McKown of Hot Springs, when asked why she thought it was still important to ratify the ERA, replied, "So I don't have to attend these committee meetings every two years and continue to ask for my rights as a woman."[122]

A careful empirical examination of state court decisions under state equal rights provisions concluded that ratification of the ERA would make a significant difference and "generate a nearly irreversible sea change in sex discrimination jurisprudence." Specifically, "If we believe that it is desirable for courts to produce a larger number of equality-oriented outcomes, then an ERA is neither an impediment nor a constitutional redundancy. Quite the opposite. . . . And the application of a higher standard of law, even after controlling for other relevant factors, increases the probability of a court reaching a disposition favorable to litigants alleging a violation of their rights."[123]

Adding the Equal Rights Amendment to the Constitution would be more than the symbolic gesture Senator Gilbert suggested. Relying on a temporally variable Fourteenth Amendment, depending on the composition of the Court, or on statutes subject to legislative mood, is no security for equal rights.[124] "You can have rights, and they can be taken away," said

Congresswoman Carolyn Maloney. "Women have made incredible progress in the past thirty-five years, but unfortunately judicial attitudes can shift, and Congress can repeal existing laws with a simple majority vote. In recent years, there have been efforts to roll back women's rights in education, health, employment, and even domestic violence. As the great suffragist and author of the ERA Alice Paul said: 'We shall not be safe until the principle of equal rights is written into the framework of our government.'"[125]

Paul's point was echoed by Senator Kaneaster Hodges (D-AR) in 1978 when he argued and voted for H.J. Res. 638, the Resolution Extending the Deadline for Ratification of the Proposed Equal Rights Amendment. In a floor speech entitled, "No One Truly Has Freedom Unless All Do," Senator Hodges, both an attorney and an ordained Methodist minister with a master's degree from the Perkins School of Theology of Southern Methodist University, refuted many of the opposition arguments that relied on biblical authority to oppose equality by citing Galatians 3:28—that "there is neither male nor female: for ye are all one in Christ Jesus."[126]

Conclusions

Whether ratification of the Equal Rights Amendment is a constitutional possibility, its force as an issue for public debate continues to provide an essential and affordable forum for supporters in the fifteen non-ratifying states. No court has yet ruled on the validity of the three-state strategy, and none will do so until at least one of the remaining states votes to ratify. Nonetheless, the continuing effort to ratify the ERA is taken seriously, and the viability argument is implicit in any official action and sometimes, as in Arkansas, explicitly conceded by the opposition.

While the ratification struggle in Arkansas has become more difficult with the shift to Republican majorities in both the state House and state Senate, it is not a strictly partisan issue. Democrats failed to ratify when they held majorities in both chambers for four decades between 1972 and 2012, even abandoning the issue in 2011 and directing members not to bring the ERA for consideration.

Another factor in the Arkansas effort to ratify is the gender composition of the membership elected to the Arkansas General Assembly. The number of women members dropped from a high of 31 in 2009 to only 23 of 135 in 2013. Yet an increase in the number of women elected to the legislature does not directly correlate with their support for the Equal Rights Amendment, as women of both parties have opposed ratification during the last decade.

When women legislators argue that the ERA is not needed, it undermines the force of citizens who think otherwise and leads male legislators to wonder "What Women Want."[127]

Contrary to Jane Mansbridge's suggestion that to renew the fight for ratification would yield few returns and might even be detrimental to the cause, the continuing ratification debates of the last decade might well have contributed to increased public support for equal rights and a constitutional amendment to assure them.[128] While many social and cultural forces have shaped the national conversation, the renewed efforts and legislative debates in non-ratifying states have clearly generated media attention and amplified public discourse. No other issue or opportunity has provided such a highly visible venue to raise and address the question of equality as a constitutional right in those states that failed to ratify the ERA.

What is obvious from the continuing but unsuccessful experience in Arkansas is that the unratified ERA presents an opportunity to educate and advocate for constitutional equality that otherwise would not be available. Following the 2013 loss, supporters "reported a sense of victory despite the ruling because they see a stronger, improved movement of progressive interest groups fighting together."[129]

Supporters will again promote equality and ratification of the ERA in Arkansas and elsewhere. The continuing debate provides an educational forum not otherwise available, and it continues to be a valuable vehicle for recruitment and organizing. Moreover, "the very enterprise of amendment advocacy" has also become an effective "weapon of political combat" to hold legislators accountable for their votes on women's issues and equality in general.[130] Perhaps ratification is a political windmill and the quest is quixotic; however the continued public tilting by a new generation of women demanding constitutional equality occupies the public sphere and keeps the issue alive in the twenty-first century. As Mansbridge admitted, "There are many reasons to propose an amendment to the U.S. Constitution. Actually having that amendment become law is only one of them."[131] Arkansas supporters of equality know that it is important to educate, articulate, and vindicate those rights in the highly visible forum that appears every two years. The arguments continue to be worth making, and the conversation is sure to continue in those fifteen states yet to ratify the Equal Rights Amendment.

CHAPTER 19

Effects of Prohibition in Arkansas Counties

PATRICK A. STEWART, CATHERINE C. REESE,
AND JEREMY BREWER

*Do you live in a dry county, and wonder why? Perhaps your neighbors
believe a dry county is safer? Although the number of "dry" counties
(under the strictest definition) has declined since this article was published, nearly half of Arkansas's counties still are not totally "wet," a
greater proportion than for any other state in the nation. Previous
research has suggested that alcohol availability affects the frequency of
alcohol-related crashes. This study examines county-level alcohol control policies on drug- and alcohol-related arrest rates and related incidents in Arkansas. The authors control for other county-level variables
such as the number of law enforcement officers, median income, and
population density, testing them against local prohibition policies. The
findings reveal the number of police officers per 1,000 residents to be
the most potent determinant of both adult and juvenile alcohol and
drug arrest rates. Controlling access to alcohol may even have counterintuitive effects on behavior.*

Americans have attempted to control the conditions under which we drink
alcohol for longer than the nation has existed. Early laws focused on restrict-
ing excessive consumption and it was not until the nineteenth century that
alcohol came to be viewed as a social evil.[1] The states began to prohibit the
use of alcohol actively then, with Minnesota adopting a law making alcohol
illegal in 1852. In general, the earliest to support the notion of prohibition
were the New England states, reflecting their puritanical culture. Congress
then famously enacted national Prohibition, which was later repealed and
was originally intended to be temporary anyway, in 1917.

Today there are over 3,000 counties in the United States; alcohol

Originally published in *Politics & Policy* 32 (December 2004):
595–613. Reprinted with permission.
DOI: https://doi.org/10.34053/parry2019.riapag2.19

control policies vary widely and are in their hands. Eighteen states directly own and control their package stores, while thirty-two issue licenses for private entities to sell alcohol.[2] States of either type can have dry counties, or counties where alcohol sales are prohibited, although the dry condition is more prevalent in the license states and today in general is more common in the Southeast. One scholar who reviewed state liquor licensing stated, "The choice of the dry option does not necessarily imply the absence of consumption nor the absence of liquor sales in the locality; instead, it implies liquor will be obtained from nearby wet localities or from the underground economy in the dry jurisdiction."[3]

In some counties in Arkansas, a resident of a dry county need not even resort to acquisition via an underground economy. Rather, one need only pay small annual dues to be a member of a club that has secured a liquor sales permit. Craighead County, Arkansas, for example, the home of Arkansas State University and the city of Jonesboro, with a population of 55,000, is nominally dry and has been ever since it was voted that way while the soldiers were away fighting in World War II. [4] Today the county is arguably the most populous dry county in the United States and has twelve such permitted private, alcohol-serving clubs.[5]

Past research implies that alcohol availability affects the frequency of alcohol-related crashes[6] and suggests a public safety basis for morality-based regulations. However, other studies provide evidence that such policies do not work and limit individual freedom based upon spurious understanding of policy outcomes.[7] Specifically, an Arkansas study relating arrest rates to alcohol availability on a county by county basis has been central to the rhetoric of alcohol sales opponents.[8]

Several studies have shown mixed results concerning the effectiveness of wet or dry policies on actual behavioral outcome measures, namely motor vehicle accidents. A study by Brown, Jewell, and Richer[9] shows wet counties as having 2.145 more fatal alcohol-related motor vehicle accidents than dry counties. Colon[10] finds that states with county-level prohibition have significantly higher motor vehicle fatality rates than states without. Likewise, a time-series analysis of seventeen recently wet and seventeen recently dry counties in Alabama, Georgia, Kentucky, and Mississippi, found traffic fatality rates were higher in wet counties.[11] However, Dull and Giacopassi, in their examination of Tennessee, found county-level alcohol policy had no significant effect on motor vehicle fatality crashes.[12] Likewise in Kentucky, Winn and Giacopassi found no significant differences in alcohol and non-alcohol related fatal motor vehicle accidents, although dry counties had significantly lower nonfatal and property damage accidents.[13]

This study takes a two-stage approach to examine the influence of county level policies concerning the sale of alcohol in Arkansas. First, we replicate and extend a study used to support the prohibition of the sale of alcohol based on arrest rates. Second, we replicate studies carried out in Kentucky and Tennessee to consider whether alcohol-prohibition policies have an effect on alcohol and drug related automobile crashes, an outcome measure that better reflects behavior. In both sections we use analysis of variance (ANOVA) to consider the effect of policy alone and multivariate ordinary least squares (OLS) regression analysis to test a more fully speci-fied model before drawing conclusions. We conclude by discussing policy options in light of the findings.

Alcohol Policy in Arkansas

In a study of great policy salience for Arkansans, Grossman examines adult and adolescent drug and alcohol arrests in Arkansas by comparing 43 dry with 32 wet counties in the state.[14] He reports that between 1992 and 1996 an average of 12.5 arrests for drunk driving per 1,000 people in wet counties took place compared to the rate of 8.7 arrests per 1,000 in dry counties. Grossman also finds an average of 32 arrests per 1,000 for adult alcohol and drug related crimes in wet counties, compared to the rate of 21 arrests per 1,000 in dry counties. He concludes that alcohol acts as a "gateway" sub-stance, leading to the use of other drugs, since there were 2.5 drug-related arrests per 1,000 juveniles in wet counties as compared to 1.7 arrests per 1,000 in dry counties. Overall, Grossman concludes that the ready availabil-ity of alcohol is a key factor in alcohol-and-drug-related crimes.

The importance of Grossman's research in determining county-level public policy in the state of Arkansas is indisputable. Specifically, propo-nents of alcohol control policy have made frequent and prominent use of his findings, pointing to his analysis to buttress morality-based arguments. For instance, prohibitionists state that having a wet county could lead to "a decline in morality, increased drunk driving and a decrease in family values" and could lead to higher rates of alcohol addiction.[15] These arguments are premised on Grossman's assertion that alcohol is a "gateway" to drug use which "establish(es) the condition for illegal drug use" and that limiting access to alcohol will prevent their use.[16] However, recent research suggests that drug and alcohol addiction is at least partially genetically predisposed.[17]

Multiple critiques may be applied to his methodology and corrections, suggesting the need for a more rigorous analysis. First, Grossman's distinc-tion between wet and dry counties is incomplete. While wet counties serve alcohol in restaurants, bars, and taverns, and sell it from package stores and other outlets, and dry counties prohibit its sale outright, there is an intermediate category of damp counties in which alcohol is served in private clubs to members who pay a fee for membership. Specifically, within Arkansas are thirty-two wet counties allowing alcohol sales, thirty-two damp counties only allowing the sale of alcohol within private clubs, and eleven dry counties not allowing any alcohol sales. We introduce this distinction in Table 1 to better capture the state of Arkansas' alcohol policy.

Second, Grossman's pooling of data from 1992–1996 artificially inflates the difference between counties, at least in the descriptive sense, and does not reflect changes that may have occurred within a county during that period of time. Namely, population size increases and decreases while its composition changes, police force size waxes and wanes, and enforcement emphases change. As a result, we replicate Grossman's study using the most recent data available—from 1997, and limit it to a cross-sectional analysis. Further, the reliance on descriptive statistics alone is misleading. Arrest rates alone do not tell us how much variance occurs and whether these differences are significant. In addition, Grossman combines some variables, such as adult alcohol and drug arrest rates, and ignores others, including juvenile drug and alcohol arrest rates. To correct for this we suggest a difference of means test to assess whether the differences between wet, damp, and dry counties are meaningful for all available alcohol and drug arrest rate data.

Finally, an emphasis on arrest rates alone to measure the negative outcomes of alcohol-related activity is not reliable. Arrests are affected by a number of variables, the key variable being the number of police officers available to arrest individuals. Deviant behavior committed in private is not reflected in official crime statistics until a person is arrested. We deal with this problem by testing a more fully specified model, taking into account this policy-related variable by including a measure of the police force within a county based on the number of police per 1,000 residents.

It seems unlikely that policy alone affects behavior, criminal or otherwise. Thus, we add variables to capture the effects of factors other than public policy that might affect behavior. Variables representing the demographics of a county include population density and median household income. We hypothesize that a more densely settled area will affect such dependent variables as crashes and injuries positively, so to speak, simply because there are more things to hit and more people to injure. Median household income is included as a control as well; perhaps wealthier counties support higher levels of public service, which in turn may lead to more arrests.

TABLE 1:

Wet, Damp, and Dry Counties in Arkansas (2004)

WET COUNTIES	DAMP COUNTIES	DRY COUNTIES
Arkansas*	Ashley	Clay*
Baxter	Benton	Crawford
Calhoun	Boone	Grant
Carroll	Bradley*	Lafayette
Chicot*	Clark	Lincoln*
Cleveland*	Cleburne	Madison
Conway	Columbia	Newton
Crittenden*	Craighead*	Perry
Cross*	Faulkner	Scott
Dallas	Fulton	Searcy
Desha*	Hempstead	Stone
Drew*	Hot Springs	
Franklin	Howard	
Garland	Independence*	
Greene*	Izard	
Jackson*	Johnson	
Jefferson*	Lawrence*	
Lee*	Little River	
Logan	Lonoke	
Miller	Marion	
Mississippi*	Montgomery	
Monroe*	Nevada	
Ouachita	Pike	
Phillips*	Polk	
Poinsett*	Pope	
Prairie*	Randolph*	
Pulaski	Saline	
St. Francis*	Sevier	
Sebastian	Sharp	
Union	Van Buren	
Washington	White*	
Woodruff*	Yell	

Note: *=Delta County

In addition, variables representing the geography of a county, which also may be expected to have an effect on outcome measures, include number of total square miles in a county, number of highway miles per square mile in a county, and whether the county is a delta county.[18] County size and the number of highway miles in a county are expected to have a positive impact on arrests and crashes because more automobile traffic will likely take place. Finally, the geographic significance of the delta is that due to its proximity to the Mississippi River, the land there is flat, while land in the rest of the state is often hilly or mountainous. Thus, we expect fewer crashes in delta counties. In order to assess the inclusion of these independent policy and control variables, we use a multivariate model of statistical analysis.[19]

Methodology

In this study we consider seventy-four of seventy-five Arkansas counties. We drop from our analysis Pulaski County, home to Little Rock and 350,418 residents because it is the only urban county in a predominantly rural state and it has had a skewing effect on data analysis. Data analyzed in this study were collected by the Institute for Economic Advancement at the University of Arkansas at Little Rock (UALR) and titled, "Risk Factors for Adolescent Drug and Alcohol Abuse in Arkansas."[20] These data were collected for use by the Arkansas Department of Health, Bureau of Alcohol and Drug Abuse Prevention and consider juveniles as those between the ages of ten and seventeen and adults as those who are older than eighteen years. Drug-related arrests for juveniles and adults are based on violations such as possession, sale, use, growing, and manufacturing of illegal drugs. Alcohol-related arrests are based on such violations as driving under the influence (DUI), liquor law violations, and public drunkenness. Population data were compiled by Demographic Research, Institute for Economic Advancement at UALR, and the number of police were compiled from data collected by the Arkansas Crime Information Center.[21]

Alcohol Policy and Arrest Rates

The first stage of analysis is a replication of Grossman's[22] study. Here we analyze arrest rates in the 74 rural counties of Arkansas. Data are transformed, in line with Grossman's study, to reflect arrests per 1,000 people, and in the case of juvenile arrests, per 1,000 of those aged 10–17. Departing from Grossman, we consider four variables: juvenile drug arrests, juvenile alcohol arrests, adult drug arrests, and adult alcohol arrests.

An analysis of descriptive statistics, illustrated in Figure 1, reveals that juvenile alcohol and drug arrest rates are significantly lower than adult alcohol arrests and slightly lower than adult drug arrest rates, as can be expected from a population that predominantly does not use intoxicants until the mid- or later-teenage years. However, the difference between mean county

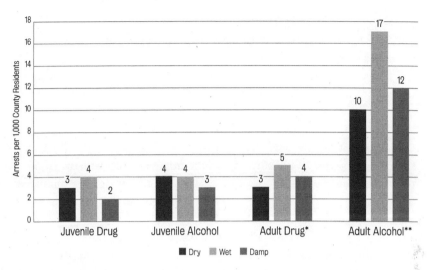

FIGURE I: Arrest Rates by Type in Damp, Dry, and Wet Arkansas Counties 1997
*Significant at .10
**Significant at .05
***Significant at .01

juvenile drug arrests and alcohol arrests per 1,000 people is slightly less than one; in comparison, the difference between mean adult drug and alcohol arrests shows that adults are arrested for alcohol nearly three and one-half times as often as for drugs. This suggests that juveniles may turn to drugs as intoxicants of choice due to relatively equal access to drugs compared to liquor, a factor that is not the case with the adult population.

The main question is whether alcohol related policy, in the form of wet damp-dry ordinances, affects arrest rates. As discussed earlier, in this analysis we attempt to improve on Grossman's work by discriminating among those counties not allowing alcohol to be sold in any manner, those counties allowing private clubs to sell alcohol on their premises, and those counties allowing the sale of alcohol from liquor stores and on the premises of clubs and restaurants.[23]

We use analysis of variance (ANOVA) to test for significant differences when comparing county data by the wet-dry-damp alcohol policies (see Figure I). Analyses of the outcome variables concerning arrest rates suggest that only differences in adult alcohol-$F = 8.006$, $p = .001$-and adult drug arrests, with $F = 2.988$ and $p = .057$, are significant. The wet-damp-dry policy distinction does not have an effect on juvenile alcohol arrests and juvenile drug arrests, $F = 1.669$ and $F = .653$ respectively, p-values not reaching significance for either. In this sense, we achieve only partial support for Grossman's research findings.[24]

However, one critique of Grossman's study is that arrests reflect enforcement activity, not the effectiveness of wet-damp-dry policy. In addition, other demographic variables are expected to play a role in arrests. To understand what determines arrest rates, a more fully specified model is run using OLS regression and the data are presented in Table 2. The policy variables of wet-damp-dry counties are entered here as dummy variables with dry counties as the reference variable. We also include the policy variable of number of police per 1,000 residents in a county, reflecting the enforcement and deterrent capacity of a county. Control variables representing the geography and demographics of a county parcel out other influences.

The variables of immediate interest, those regarding the limitation or prohibition of alcohol sales, do not have the effect anticipated by supporters of these policies when controlling for other pertinent variables. Specifically, wet and damp counties are not significantly different from dry counties when considering juvenile drug- or alcohol-related arrests. In fact, while the finding is not statistically significant, wet and damp counties are less likely to have juvenile drug and alcohol arrests than are dry counties. This suggests that in the absence of legally obtainable alcohol in a county, juveniles turn to breaking the law to use alcohol and drugs, a contradiction of the gateway hypothesis forwarded by Grossman's report.

Analysis of the other policy variable expected to have an effect on arrest rates, number of police per 1,000 residents, supports the contention that having more police leads to more arrests. For every added police officer per 1,000 residents, arrests of adults for alcohol-related reasons increase by nearly four and one-half per 1,000 residents and adult and juvenile drug arrests increase approximately by one. This suggests, rather obviously, that police are doing their job by arresting people who violate laws.

Other variables reaching significance are the number of highway miles per square mile in a county, population density, and median household income. Highway miles in a county contribute to juvenile alcohol arrests, likely due to the existence of a car culture in which young adults socialize, travel, and consume alcohol, not necessarily in that order. Median household income is predictive of juvenile drug arrests, although interestingly operating in the opposite direction than hypothesized; increased county affluence leads to higher levels of juvenile drug arrests. Finally, the density of a county's population leads to more adult drug arrests, possibly due to the existence of specific drug cultures not available in more sparsely populated counties.

TABLE 2.

Regression Predicting Arrest Rates by Type from Alcohol and Other Policy Variables in Arkansas in 1997

VARIABLES	JUVENILE ALCOHOL ARRESTS		JUVENILE DRUG ARRESTS	
	COEFFICIENT	STANDARD ERROR	COEFFICIENT	STANDARD ERROR
Constant	-1.040	3.671	-4.508*	2.271
Wet County	-0.954	1.472	-0.743	0.911
Damp County	-1.382	1.296	-1.270	0.802
Police per 1,000 Residents	1.280	0.826	1.164**	0.511
Total Square Miles	-0.004608	0.004	0.0005085	0.003
Highway Miles	0.02175**	0.011	0.006165	0.007
Population Density	-0.001195	0.010	-0.001624	0.006
Delta County	-1.197	1.025	-0.430	0.634
Median Household Income	0.0001503	0.000	0.0002175**	0.000
Adjusted R^2	0.046		0.208	
F-Statistic	1.448		3.435***	
	ADULT ALCOHOL ARRESTS		ADULT DRUG ARRESTS	
Constant	9.888	6.443	4.666**	2.347
Wet County	3.337	2.584	0.315	0.941
Damp County	0.851	2.274	0.215	0.828
Police per 1,000 Residents	4.438***	1.449	0.986*	0.528
Total Square Miles	-0.006957	0.007	-0.003301	0.003
Highway Miles	0.01431	0.019	-0.007537	0.007
Population Density	-0.002683	0.018	0.0003582**	0.007
Delta County	-1583	1.799	0.149	0.655
Median Household Income	-0.0002288	0.000	-0.0001264	0.000
Adjusted R^2	0.234		0.101	
F-Statistic	3.821***		2.041*	

*significant at .10   **significant at .05   *** significant at .01
Sources: Arkansas State University (1998), US Census Bureau (1990)

ALCOHOL POLICY, DRUNK DRIVING,
AND MOTOR VEHICLE ACCIDENTS

While arrest rates may provide important indicators of the effectiveness of alcohol policy enforcement, they do not consider actual outcomes. Tangible consequences—in other words, those having public safety implications and presenting a better assessment of the impact of alcohol policy—may be seen in the form of drunk driving arrests and alcohol and drug related automobile crashes. Specifically, proponents of damp and dry laws expect that limiting or prohibiting sales of alcohol will reduce consumption and thereby reduce negative outcomes such as drunk driving and motor vehicle accidents. As a result, we analyze five alcohol and drug related outcome measures per 1,000 county residents: drunk driving arrests, total crashes, property damage crashes, injury crashes, and traffic fatalities.

Drunk driving arrests are based upon violations for driving or operating any vehicle or common carrier while drunk or under the influence of alcohol or narcotics. Data from the Arkansas Department of Health are used here. Outcome variables that are not as likely to be affected by the number of officers include measures of alcohol and drug related accident rates and are taken from the Arkansas Highway and Transportation Department.[25] While some forms of accidents are likely to slip through the cracks, especially in rural counties where property damage may be less extensive and police presence not as large as in more urban areas, accidents leading to injury and death are more likely to be discovered. Therefore, motor vehicle accidents provide a reasonable behavioral measure of wet-damp-dry policy outcomes.

Univariate analysis of drunk driving arrests and the four automobile crash related variables initially suggests that arrests and all forms of crashes, with the exception of fatality crashes, are higher in wet than in damp counties, and higher in both wet and damp counties than in dry counties (see Figure 2). However, the difference in means among counties with wet-damp-dry alcohol control policies is statistically significant at the .01 level only for drunk driving arrests—$F = S.304$ and $p = .007$. Mean differences among counties are significant at the .10 level for traffic fatalities, $F = 2.762$ and $p = .07$, where more alcohol and drug related traffic fatalities occurred in dry than in wet or damp counties, and property damage accidents— $F = 3.009$ and $p = .056$— with fewer accidents in dry than wet or damp counties. Finally, the differences in means among wet, damp, and dry counties are not significant in either accidents where injuries occur, $F = .517$ and $p = ns$, or total accidents, $F = 1.659$ and $p = ns$.

Multivariate analysis using OLS regression provides a more finely

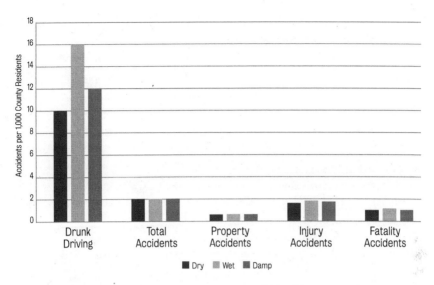

FIGURE 2 Accident Rates by Type in Damp, Dry, and Wet Counties in Arkansas, 1997.
*Significant at .10
**Significant at .05
***Significant at .01

honed analysis of the determinants of crashes. Specifically, we expect that in addition to the policy variables of alcohol availability and enforcement capability, variables concerning a county's geography and demography will have an effect on drunk driving arrests and motor vehicle accidents.

When considering the policy variables, we find, as was the case with arrest rates, that alcohol policy tends not to have a significant effect on either drunk driving arrests or automobile accidents, with the exception of property damage crashes, in which case slightly more accidents occurred in wet than dry counties, and accident fatalities, where residents of damp counties are less likely to suffer a fatal accident than those living in a dry county. The failure of these variables systematically to account for drunk driving arrests and accidents suggests that prohibition of alcohol sales within a county does not affect the ability of individuals to become intoxicated and to drive afterwards.

The only policy variable having a systematic predictive impact on drunk driving arrests and total crashes is the proportion of police in a county. As can be expected with drunk driving, the more police, the more arrests.

Specifically, for every additional police officer per 1,000 residents, an additional 1.7 drunk driving arrests are made. On the other hand, the finding that the more police officers there are per 1,000 citizens in a county, the more total alcohol and drug related property damage and total accidents occur, is a bit counterintuitive. This finding might indicate either a policy decision to deal with a perceived problem of drunk driving by employing more police, or it may imply that police are discovering more accidents.

Of the geographic and demographic variables, the delta dummy, geographic size and median household income significantly affect property damage and total accidents. Specifically, there is a greater likelihood of crashes outside the delta, which can be expected due to the delta's flat terrain and to the rest of the state being either hilly or mountainous. Geographically larger counties had more property damage crashes, potentially due to the need to travel greater distances. Median household income has a slight positive effect on property damage accidents, likely due to persons of higher income having more personal property that could potentially be damaged.

Discussion

Multivariate analysis of adult alcohol and adult drug arrest rates shows that crime control capacity in the form of the number of police per 1,000 residents is statistically significant and is the most powerful determinant of adult alcohol arrest rates. However, the policy variable concerning wet-damp dry counties, while operating in the expected direction, does not achieve statistical significance. Therefore, we can conclude that with adult arrest rate data, Grossman's assertions do not hold.

In addition, based on Grossman's "gateway" hypothesis, both juvenile drug and alcohol-based arrest rates should be highest in wet counties, then damp, and finally lowest in dry counties. When analyzed using multivariate OLS regression, juvenile alcohol and drug arrest rates are higher in dry than in either damp or wet counties, although the relationships are not statistically significant.

Univariate analysis of differences in drunk driving and accident rates based on county alcohol policy, with the exception of alcohol and drug related crash fatalities, suggests a distinct rank ordering on the basis of wet-dampdry alcohol policy applied in a county. However, only drunk driving arrests operate in the expected direction and reach statistical significance when using ANOVA.

When considering multivariate relationships for drunk driving arrests

TABLE 3:

Regression Predicting Accident Rates by Type
from Alcohol and Other Policy Variables in Arkansas in 1997

	DRUNK DRIVING ARRESTS		ALCOHOL/DRUG ACCIDENT FATALITIES		ALCOHOL/DRUG INJURY ACCIDENTS	
	COEFFICIENT	STANDARD ERROR	COEFFICIENT	STANDARD ERROR	COEFFICIENT	STANDARD ERROR
Constant	8.915***	3.236	0.292	0.136	0.02418	0.261
Wet County	1.101	1.298	-0.07338	0.055	0.008622	0.105
Damp County	0.213	1.142	-0.08171*	0.048	-0.004721	0.092
Police per 1,000 Residents	1.725**	0.728	-0.002895	0.031	0.06983	0.059
Total Square Miles	-0.003767	0.004	0.0001788	0.000	0.00007053	0.000
Highway Miles	0.005944	0.010	0.0001343	0.000	0.00004256	0.001
Population Density	0.003777	0.009	-0.00000721	0.000	0.0002907	0.001
Delta County	-0.412	0.903	-0.05154	0.038	-0.05120	0.073
Median House-hold Income	-0.0002639	0.000	-0.00001320	0.000	0.00001013	0.000
Adjusted R^2	0.167		0.065		0.002	
F-Statistic	2.853***		1.639		1.017	

	ALCOHOL/DRUG PROPERTY DAMAGE ACCIDENTS		ALCOHOL/DRUG TOTAL ACCIDENTS	
	COEFFICIENT	STANDARD ERROR	COEFFICIENT	STANDARD ERROR
Constant	-0.404**	0.182	-0.317	0.382
Wet County	0.124*	0.073	0.127	0.153
Damp County	0.06033	0.064	0.03716	0.135
Police per 1,000 Residents	0.07066*	0.041	0.147*	0.086
Total Square Miles	0.000447**	0.000	0.0005989	0.000
Highway Miles	-0.0004031	0.001	-0.0002661	0.001
Population Density	0.0002468	0.001	0.0003532	0.107
Delta County	-0.106**	0.051	-0.182*	0.000
Median House-hold Income	0.0001532*	0.000	-0.00002299	
Adjusted R^2	0.286		0.168	
F-Statistic	4.697***		2.874***	

*significant at .10   **significant at .05   *** significant at .01
Sources: Arkansas State University (1998), US Census Bureau (1990)

and total crashes, the policy variable of police per 1,000 residents in a county tends to be statistically significant. While we expected that having more police leads to more drunk driving arrests, the finding that the number of police per 1,000 residents either has no effect on accident rates, or is associated with an increase in them, suggests that such policies do not have an effect or are reactive. Additionally, and pertinent for our study, the wet damp-dry county policy distinction does not hold up well under further scrutiny in the multi-variate model. Significant findings in the expected direction occur only for comparison of wet and dry counties with property damage accidents, and counter-intuitively, with more drug and alcohol related fatality accidents in dry than damp counties. What does make a difference are geographical and cultural variables such as county size in total square miles, whether the county is located outside the delta, and median household income. In other words, alcohol and drug related accidents are most likely determined by the distance to be traveled and how many different objects will be likely hit, whether man-made or geographical.

Conclusions

By using more well-specified models than have been used in the past for the state of Arkansas, we can see that the results of this study have policy ramifications that may be generalizable beyond the individual state. This study demonstrates that county-level public policy regarding the availability of alcohol is a relatively insignificant determinant of such important outcomes as arrest and motor vehicle accident rates.

We find that juvenile drug and alcohol arrest rates are not significantly different in wet, dry, or damp counties. Our results correspond to prior research conducted by Winn and Giacopassi[26] and Dull and Giacopassi.[27] Our results refute Grossman's, on the whole, since the ready availability of alcohol has mainly an opposite, although not statistically significant, effect than that which his study purports.[28] Specifically, the "gateway" theory as related to alcohol is unsupported, as is his contention that arrest rates tell the whole story of the effects of public policy.

Overall, the number of police per 1,000 residents is a more potent determinant of both adult and juvenile alcohol and drug arrest rates than is local alcohol policy. Alcohol policy tends not to have a systematic, significant effect on drunk driving arrests or automobile accidents in Arkansas. In addition, enforcement capability as measured by the number of police per 1,000 residents is a more significant factor in explaining both property damage and total crashes than is local alcohol availability.

The counties in Arkansas, as well as those in other states, that propose that deterrent effects arise from their prohibitory alcohol policies, should reexamine the reasons underlying those policies. This study suggests that whether alcohol is legally available does not have as significant an effect on people's behavior as whether a local jurisdiction invests in an adequate police force. The findings of this study additionally imply that moralistic ideas about controlling access to alcohol may even have counterintuitive effects on individual-level behavior.

CHAPTER 20

Implementation of the Welfare-to-Work Program in Arkansas

The Importance of Inter-Agency Communication

CATHERINE C. REESE AND DAVID HARDING, JR.

How would you define "success" in a welfare reform policy? This article examines a snapshot of interagency communication in the early years of the implementation of the 2000 Arkansas Welfare-to-Work (WtW) program and considers its potential effects on the state's progress toward substantive welfare reform. Three key areas of successful program implementation are explored: case management, inter-agency communication, and goal congruence. Data for the evaluation were generated via surveys of agency personnel and program participants. The data reveal that interagency staff frequently disagree on responsibility for client assessment, that interagency staff do not always communicate effectively and seldom share data, and that staff from service providers and the Department of Human Services cite differing goals for the program all are charged with implementing. The authors reassess the adequacy of Arkansas' WtW program and suggest that in an era marked by systemic work-related program reform, it is imperative that administrative linkages between state labor-related agencies and personal welfare-related agencies operate effectively.

The passage of the Personal Responsibility and Work Opportunity Reconciliation Act (PRWORA) in 1996 signaled the fulfillment of President Clinton's pledge to "end welfare as we know it" and launched one of the largest social experiments in recent US history. The PRWORA, which became effective in Arkansas on May 1, 1998, replaced the old Aid to Families with

Originally published in *Politics & Policy* 35 (2007): 608–29.
Reprinted with permission.
DOI: https://doi.org/10.34053/parry2019.riapag2.20

Dependent Children (AFDC) program with a new, non-entitled status program called Temporary Assistance for Needy Families (TANF). The Arkansas version of TANF is Temporary Employment Assistance (TEA), and by most accounts, it has been approximately as successful as its counterparts in other states, even winning a major award from the federal Department of Health and Human Services (HHS) in November 2001, celebrating its success in moving welfare recipients off the rolls.[1]

The PRWORA was slated for review and renewal for several years, but was relegated to operating under a series of extensions until 2006. Debate in Congress surrounded virtually every aspect of the welfare law. As an indication of how contentious the renewal's passage was, the new law, which operates through 2010, was eventually bundled in with the budget reconciliation process and did not pass all on its own. During the years of dissensus over the act's renewal, discussion over whether the removal of participants from the "welfare rolls" is a sufficient measure of programmatic success ensued. Thus, as we head into an advanced era of welfare reform, it is a propitious time to suggest means of improvement for the central work-related programs associated with the law, hereafter referred to as Welfare-to-Work (WtW) programs. Further, such international actions as British Prime Minister Blair's stated goal of reducing poverty in his country by half may pressure the United States to expand its focus from the evaluation of program outcomes (e.g., reduced rolls) to broader social goals that may include the reduction of poverty.[2]

As a key aspect of welfare reform, WtW programs compelled the states to consider how they define a successful program. Do we measure success by how many people found jobs, found decent-paying jobs, or simply left the welfare rolls? Arkansas has struggled with its definitions and measures—as has every other state in a position of serving others as a laboratory for democracy. As such, the purpose of this paper is to review the kinds of progress and the problems that have surfaced in Arkansas' implementation of its WtW program while suggesting potential improvements to the processes involved in participant management. To address these issues it is necessary to review the "success" of Arkansas' WtW program and to briefly assess its successes and failures. This should not detract from the main focus of the paper, which is communication among relevant agencies. We feel that the patterns revealed may provide an impetus for improved policy implementation in the future. In conducting the survey research of (1) Department of Human Services (DHS) personnel, (2) Service Providers (mainly Employment Security Department [ESD]) designees, and (3) WtW program participants, in fall of 2000, several layers of descriptive statistics were generated and will be discussed in later stages of this paper.

The Welfare-to-Work Program and Administrative Structure

WtW is the program associated, as its name implies, with putting welfare/ TANF/TEA recipients to work. The philosophy is "work first," meaning that a work-related activity must be entered by a program participant prior to that participant becoming eligible for education or training benefits/ services. The aim of the program is thus to ensure employment first, with government-subsidized employment being a possible stepping-stone en route to the ultimate goal of unsubsidized employment at a self-supporting wage. The philosophy of the WtW program is in great contrast to the old AFDC program's employment philosophy, which was premised on the idea that education and training were needed first to then move program partic- ipants into work activities.

The WtW program, as conceived in Arkansas, is structurally complex. Two main state agencies are responsible for its implementation: the DHS is in charge of conducting initial client assessments, and the "service providers," under the direction of the ESD, are responsible for managing program par- ticipants throughout the employment process. There is a minimum of one DHS office for each of the state's seventy-five counties. These also administer the federal Food Stamp and Medicaid programs and are supervised by the state DHS offices in Little Rock. The service providers have main offices in each of ten federally designated regions in the state, and their work activities are generally overseen by the state ESD/Employment and Training Services (ETS) offices in Little Rock. However, service providers also fall under the advisory jurisdiction of federally required Local Workforce Investment Boards, which must be comprised of area business persons, representatives from the public and private sectors, and other interested individuals.

In addition, the state has sixty-six TEA Coalitions, which are primarily tasked with providing monetary assistance to help WtW and other (e.g., Workforce Investment Act [WIA]) program participants with obtaining transportation. Some TEA Coalitions have come under severe criticism in Arkansas for not spending their allotted funds, while others have been "out of money" now for over a year.[3] The job of the TEA Coalitions is to coor- dinate the provision of essential supportive services to program clients, and their main focus in Arkansas to date has been on providing transportation assistance (see Figure 1).

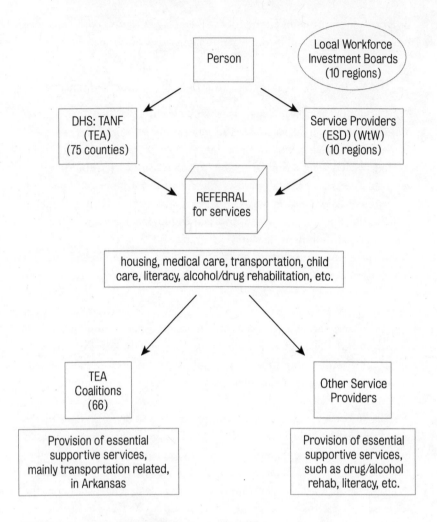

FIGURE I: The Welfare-to-Work Program in Arkansas.

The extant literature and press analysis of the work of the DHS or similarly named agencies of the states ignores the importance and impact of the other agencies and boards that are significant to the development and implementation of changes in WtW policy. In the state of Arkansas, if one were not a particular student of the implementation of WtW in Arkansas, one would be unaware that its implementation involved any state agency other than the DHS. For example, the federal Department of Health and Human Services (HHS) awarded the Arkansas DHS $2.8 million for its successes in the area of welfare reform in November 2001.[4] However, the main state department charged with implementing the WtW program in Arkansas is the ESD, which falls under the guidance of the federal Department of Labor (DOL). The DHS primarily refers "welfare" or TANF (TEA in Arkansas) participants to the ESD for case management but is not directly involved in job placement activities. Analysts often seem to assume structural simplicity, and in some cases, like in Arkansas, it does not exist (see Figure 1).

The work of Meyers, Riccucci, and Lurie compared three states: Georgia, Michigan, and Texas.[5] Georgia is neither structurally nor administratively complex. Specifically, in that state only one agency, the Department of Family and Children's Services (DFCS), controls all aspects of welfare services. Michigan is only structurally complex, while Texas is both structurally and administratively complex. In our assessment, Arkansas fits somewhere in between Michigan and Texas in its extreme structural complexity. Ramifications of the choice of a complex formal organizational structure for the delivery of TANF/WtW services, according to the authors, may include an uncoupling of policy and operational goals, diminished job satisfaction and employee productivity, and reduced public accountability.

Utilizing a complex program structure such as Arkansas' may not be the best way of implementing its WtW program for several reasons. Evidence from several case studies suggests that the structure of Arkansas' WtW program may not be the norm.[6] Some states that originally utilized complex administrative structures have now even abandoned them in favor of more streamlined approaches to policy implementation. For example, Mississippi started out with a complex structure somewhat analogous to that utilized in Arkansas, albeit with the addition of privatized case management and job placement functions.[7] Yet that structure was subsequently changed to one entirely directed and staffed by the state DHS, which is much more the nationwide norm. Keller and Morris conclude that problems in service coordination, goal definition, interagency communication, and, ultimately, public accountability led to the demise of the privatized, multiagency structure and to its replacement with a streamlined implementation workforce headed by a single agency.[8]

Keller and Morris suggest that several key aspects of programmatic organization are relevant to discussions on the matter.[9] First, shared case management among different departments or agencies may be difficult under a complex administrative structure. Second, interagency communication will likely be hindered, as compared with single-agency approaches. Third, shared ("congruent"), well-defined policy goals among different implementation actors or agencies are essential to programmatic success. This article focuses on these three aspects of program implementation when looking at several questions. How effective was Arkansas' initial implementation of its WtW program on each of these dimensions, given the structural and administrative complexity of the state's programmatic design? What can be gleaned from our surveys to help assess effectiveness along each of these lines? The literature suggests a theoretical framework that would have a state with a high level of administrative complexity, such as Arkansas, potentially not performing well on these key measures. While some authors have focused only on one of these aspects of the environment of welfare program implementation, we believe that they fit well together and wish to be the first to consider them under one umbrella.

CASE MANAGEMENT

Broadly defined, case management is "a collaborative process which assesses, plans, implements, coordinates, monitors and evaluates options and services to meet an individual's . . . needs through communication and available resources to promote quality cost-effective outcomes."[10] Moreover, case management is ideally both "holistic and client-centered, with mutual goals."[11] The precepts of the PRWORA, as well as its subsequent implementation by the states, indicate that such a holistic and client-oriented approach should be utilized in implementing TANF/WtW. The importance of the case management concept, more recently codified in the WIA specifically as the "one-stop" model of service delivery, implies that all relevant client-related agencies and programs communicate effectively, always keeping the program participant's needs at the forefront and easing application processes for program applicants. Thus, assessments of the needs of clients in terms of their employment barriers and resultant supportive service needs in areas such as transportation, child care, medical care, and drug/alcohol rehabilitation, along with the referral of these clients to programs that can help them meet these needs, are to be accomplished effectively with as little bureaucratic red tape as possible. The salience of effective case management, which has become a hallmark of social work professional practices in recent years, is a vital component of the achievement of programmatic results in terms of individual success in the implementation of state WtW programs. Some have questioned whether the pre-PRWORA caseworkers were even prepared to conduct the kind of case management required under the new law.

The welfare bureaucracy of the 1990s, as it is poised to implement welfare reform, is rife with deficiencies. The federal and state governments have jointly created depersonalized institutions fenced in by rules, and frequently preoccupied with error rates rather than human needs. The link between worker and client has been severed.[12]

As Riccucci and others stated, Congress "sent [a] signal [to change] . . . to a bureaucratic system that any consider incapable of dynamic change."[13] They also cite Bane and Ellwood's description of the old AFDC work environment as being comprised of an "eligibility compliance culture" obsessed with the accurate (error-free) determination of client eligibility rather than one that might encourage client self-sufficiency.[14]

INTERAGENCY COMMUNICATION

Many, if not most, public policies are implemented in multi-actor/ agency settings. Moreover, "if public programs are typically constructed in ways that do not neatly match agencies, administrative study is faced with profound questions about how people and resources can best be mobilized to accomplish public tasks."[15] That effective interagency communication is essential for programmatic success seems self-evident. Yet little literature to date explicates this concept as directly related to the implementation of such programs as TANF and WtW. This is partly because, as evidenced by case studies completed in the states of Mississippi and Georgia, in many states the entire TANF/WtW process, from initial client assessment, to referral for supportive services, to job placement, is directed by a single agency.[16] Thus, Condrey, Facer, and Hamilton note that communication among relevant TANF implementation actors is rated consistently high.[17] However, in Georgia all actors are members of the state DFCS. Specifically, communications among actors are rated as both relatively comprehensive and timely. Overall, the kinds of communication upon which a frontline caseworker relies may be seen as encompassing timely and accurate policy guidance, comparative programmatic data, and technical assistance.

One of the administrative effects of the "welfare devolution" under the PRWORA, which consists in giving policy and responsibility to the states by the federal government, is that the states have been given more flexibility than under the old AFDC program.[18] Policy analysts point to the states' experiments with devising benefit time limits, focusing on work, and enhancing supportive service assessment and referral processes as evidence of this new flexibility. Lens and Pollack, however, point out that the federal government not only defines exactly what an allowable "work activity" is, but also states exactly how long a TANF participant may be enrolled in that activity.[19] However, while many policy analysts describe the PRWORA law as granting great flexibility to state governments, the local officials and caseworkers who are actually doing the frontline work may be frustrated by the lack of policy and technical guidance to which they have become accustomed.

Part of this lack of guidance or administrative/technical support for WtW programs lies in the lack of state- or federal government-developed management information systems (MISs). For example, the study by Meyers, Riccucci, and Lurie notes that one thing that helps Georgia program administrators do a good job is that county personnel developed their own MIS for tracking case processes, progress, and outcomes.[20] In addition to having a structurally simple program run by one agency, this helps contribute to that state's achievement of its program goals.

GOAL CONGRUENCE

An effect of a fragmented TANF implementation structure in Mississippi led Keller and Morris to propose that different actors/agencies in the process held different goals regarding programmatic success.[21] Specifically, they noted that different actors/ agencies aspired to achieve goals that were only important for "their" component of the program. For instance, those contracted to provide job placement services might only be concerned with placing participants in jobs, but not with clients' overall success as individual TANF participants who would hopefully one day achieve a "living wage." Thus, the authors noted a preoccupation with job placement to the exclusion of consideration of work quality. DHS personnel might only be concerned with rendering initial client referrals to the TANF program, and not particularly interested in conducting participant follow-up beyond that initial activity. One might therefore see a focus by DHS workers on ensuring that the proper paperwork was completed for a program referral, rather than considering, again, overall participant success as defined under the PRWORA.

Further, congruence between formal policy goals and the day-to-day operational goals of caseworkers has been found to be highly significant not only for achieving overall programmatic success, but also for caseworker job satisfaction and morale. A fragmented policy implementation structure appears to contribute, overall, to a lack of goal congruence.[22]

The "Success" of the Welfare-to-Work Program

National data show that the PRWORA has been nominally successful; that is, welfare recipients have been removed from the states' rolls.[23] Some questions are evident regarding whether this movement has been because of the real progress of the individuals enrolled or because of the (then) performance of the national economy. When the economy slows, as it has of late, it is probable, if the doubters are correct, that welfare/TANF rolls will rise again.

The literature questions whether the removal of people from the welfare rolls does or should define the program's success. For example, Ewalt and Jennings state that "moving welfare clients off the rolls is only part of the story."[24] Further, they claim that "[a]s TANF is reauthorized, the critical question is whether reducing the welfare rolls enhances the well-being of former adult clients and their children."[25]

In addition, some of the literature notes—if at times obliquely, or in passing in a conclusion—that the real challenge of welfare reform is serving the remaining clients.[26] Specifically, the people who were easy to place are in jobs now. Those remaining on the rolls are harder to serve and face higher or greater barriers to employment. This phenomenon, sometimes called "creaming," refers to program participants who were easiest to place in jobs, being placed early in the program's life because of both their own suitability for employment as well as the superior performance of the national economy at that time. Rising to the top of the job placement list—like the choicest part of milk yields cream—these were the fortunate clients who were placed in jobs.

Data, Settings, and Measures

The main focus of the evaluation regarded state agencies' usage of information, the interaction of same agencies—primarily the state service providers and the state DHS—for the exchange of information, the availability of potential WtW employers by service providers, and the perceptions of WtW program participants. To adequately address each of the questions, we relied upon survey research to generate the most comprehensive picture of WtW programs and participants (see appendix). The surveys of employees and recipients allowed us to develop a snapshot of each of three areas under exploration: case management, interagency communication, and goal congruence. In addition to the original data collected via surveys, the findings have been supplemented by comprehensive case reviews conducted by Catherine C. Reese while in the process of monitoring federal case files over the course of two summers, newspaper articles, and informal discussions with policy actors across the state. To assess the effectiveness of Arkansas' WtW program, a total of 925 surveys were mailed in the fall of 2000 to the following groups: (1) 86 to DHS personnel; (2) 19 to WtW service providers; (3) 268 to WtW employers (not discussed here); and (4) 562 to WtW program participants. Overall response rates by group were 59.5 percent, 52.6 percent, 26.0 percent, and 21.4 percent, respectively, if the percent unopened and returned nondeliverable by the last group (128/ 558 = 22.9 percent) is discounted. The response rate is quite high, considering the nature of the survey and the socioeconomic status of the WtW participants. Survey respondents were, in all four cases, the entire universe of potential respondents in the state. State officials provided us with the lists of potential respondents from their database and questions were written based on a combination of the informational goals of state officials and the authors of this study. Percentage figures by response category are used throughout the discussion of the results.

Surveys of DHS and WtW service providers contained mostly closedended questions about their relationships and communication with other agencies, particularly with each other (see appendix). We also asked about their perceptions of responsibility for client assessment in a variety of areas (literacy, child care, transportation). We asked about workers' perceptions of the importance of various subgoals (alcohol/drug rehabilitation, child care, transportation) to the achievement of moving WtW clients into work. Finally, we asked both groups about the adequacy of their resources, including their use of the online database. The questions we wrote for these two state employee groups tapped our key concepts of case management, interagency communication, and goal congruence.

Surveys of WtW program participants included questions about their experience with the WtW program, what kinds of assistance they needed, whether they got it, and their evaluation of its quality. We also inquired about their job placement, including employment sector, starting wage, and working conditions. The questions we wrote for WtW program participants were designed to aid our evaluation of the performance or success of the program itself.

Findings and Discussion

Overall, the complexity of the structure of Arkansas' WtW program appears to affect case management, interagency communication, goal congruence, and even the overall success of the WtW program. That is, the two agencies primarily responsible for implementing WtW, DHS and ESD, do not share the same vision of their own responsibilities, the other's accuracy and timeliness of information, or the importance of various program subgoals to achieving work permanence. The findings regarding each of the three areas of exploration are discussed in further detail below.

CASE MANAGEMENT

According to the PRWORA's goals, participants or "cases" were to be proactively managed in perpetuity. WtW program participants were to be regularly contacted for progress updates. In fact, Arkansas service providers were entirely reluctant to close WtW cases for any reason— so much so that they left cases open for over a year when there was no way to contact the program participant. When we attempted to survey WtW program participants, 22.9 percent of all surveys were returned unopened/undelivered, indicating that current contact information is not regularly maintained for all participants.

Similarly, the ESD and the DHS disagreed as to which party was primarily responsible for conducting a wide variety of client assessments, including those for literacy, vocational rehabilitation, job skills, work experience, child care, transportation, medical care, and housing. For example, DHS officials were asked whether they, their local service provider (ESD), or another agency or party had primary responsibility for assessment and referral. DHS officials believed that they had total responsibility for TANF, work experience, child care, transportation, and medical care referrals, and 51 percent responsibility for literacy, 61 percent for vocational rehabilitation, 88 percent for job skills, and 80 percent of the responsibility for housing referrals. In contrast, ESD personnel believed that they had 90 percent of the responsibility for TANF referrals, 10 percent for literacy, 30 percent for vocational rehabilitation, 60 percent for job skills, 50 percent for work experience, 20 percent for child care, 20 percent for transportation, 10 percent for medical care, and 20 percent for housing assistance. Basically, in several areas, both of the main agencies responsible for implementing the WtW program indicate that they have the same responsibility for client referral, indicating a possible need to clarify responsibility between the departments.

INTERAGENCY COMMUNICATION

A major goal of the Arkansas WtW program under PRWORA was for proactive case management in the sense that excellent communication among all relevant parties was to be maintained in order to best serve program participants. Thus, when we were contracted to conduct an evaluation of the implementation of the state's WtW program, one of the primary foci of the evaluation was on interagency communication. Communication among the relevant parties (see Figure 1) was assessed via questions addressed to each party. For example, DHS officials rated communication between themselves and ESD/ETS (service providers) as the lowest among all possible communications, with a mean of 3.0 on a 5.0 scale, where higher numbers indicate a greater ability to provide accurate and timely information. From the ESD's perspective, communication between them and the DHS was rated at an average of 3.7. Neither number shows greatly trusted communication.

The two major parties differ on the use of the WtW database. Specifically, most DHS personnel are wholly unaware of its existence and so definitely do not utilize it. The few ESD officials who do use the database agree that it is not helpful, with two out of three personnel agreeing that it is "poor" in terms of usefulness. The database could be helpful in coordinating service provision, ascertaining statewide trends, and providing a means for cross-state programmatic comparison. As it is presently constructed, however, the information technology is fairly useless.

Finally, one might think that the increased state flexibility surmised by policy analysts might stimulate the states to develop their own policies for the WtW program. However, this is not the case in Arkansas. There has been no state policy manual for TEA caseworkers since the program's inception in 1998. In fact, anecdotal evidence obtained from informal interviews with policy actors across the state revealed that the requests of service providers for technical assistance and policy guidance/clarification were generally ignored by state ESD officials. Thus, the frontline workers responsible for the daily management of the WtW process either relied partially upon old AFDC policy, perused and interpreted the US DOL's implementation rules—which are, of course, not state specific—on their own, or in some cases, postponed action while awaiting the customary state-level guidance. Standards for federally required program monitoring were similarly conspicuously absent. We were charged with conducting the majority (seven out of ten Local Workforce Investment Areas) of the state's first policy monitoring for the TEA program in the summer of 2000. An initial monitoring instrument developed by ESD officials was supposed to be used in a joint WtW monitoring effort by the DHS and the ESD. Unsurprisingly, that plan of shared governance had to be scrapped because the two major departments could not agree on how to coordinate its use between themselves. Overall, the "welfare devolution" is apparently alive and well in Arkansas. In fact, a more specific form of the welfare devolution called "second-order devolution" is acting; this is when states devolve responsibility for public policy to local governments—particularly counties—after having been given that same responsibility by the federal government. Caseworkers in effect are simultaneously granted discretion in the form of a lack of technical/policy guidance from state officials, and reined in by it as well.

GOAL CONGRUENCE

ESD and DHS officials also differ regarding their perceptions of WtW program goals and the importance of several major subgoals such as child care, transportation, job placement, job retention, alcohol/drug rehab, medical care, on-the-job/work experience, literacy, housing, and work skills (see Table 1). Overall, mean ratings for these various subgoals differ fairly dramatically between the two primary agencies responsible for implementing the WtW program in Arkansas. In particular, DHS workers rate childcare and transportation as more important to achieving the end goals of WtW than either job placement or job retention. According to Meyers, Riccucci, and Lurie, a similar lack of goal congruence in other structurally complex states "can leave staff confused and demoralized."[27] They further suggest that goal congruence has a positive influence on staff commitment to achieving policy goals (like getting people into unsubsidized jobs). So, in a structurally complex work environment where the main two implementing agencies do not agree on what rank or importance operational goals have, it might be expected that the achievement of the overarching goal of unsubsidized gainful employment for program participants will be more complicated and difficult than it has to be.

The "Success" of the Welfare-to-Work Program in Arkansas?

When we were contracted to conduct policy monitoring for the TEA program in Arkansas in the summer of 2000, activity and progress was occurring for WtW program participants, as evidenced by documentation contained in the case files reviewed. However, when monitoring in the

TABLE 1:

Mean Ratings of Respondents on the Importance
of Subgoals to Achieving Overall WtW Program Goals*

WTW PROGRAM SUBGOAL	MEAN RATING BY DHS	MEAN RATING BY ESD
Child care	4.5/5.0	5.0/5.0
Transportation	4.5	4.8
Job placement	4.2	4.9
Job retention	4.1	4.8
Alcohol/drug rehab	4.1	4.1
Medical care	4.0	3.6
OJT/work experience	3.9	4.5
Literacy	3.9	4.2
Housing	3.9	4.1
Work skills	3.9	4.9
Subsidized employment	3.9	4.3

*Differences between the two groups are significance at the .05 level.
DHS, Department of Human Services; ESD, Employment Security
Department; WtW, welfare-to-work; OJT, On-the-Job Training

summer of 2001, case management and programmatic activity were conspicuously absent. Specifically, virtually no WtW program participants' files showed any activity since the previous program year. The lack of documentation reflected a real lack of programmatic activity; we were federal program monitors, our visits were scheduled, and local officials directed their caseworkers to have the files completely updated prior to our arrival. Furthermore, in any case when we could not locate documentation of any activity in case files, we asked the supervisor and caseworker about that in case they could provide it. WtW caseworkers revealed that there were no funds to conduct additional activities on many of the remaining cases. Also, in some instances, participants who had signed up for WtW had not returned to the office for further assistance and subsequently could not be located; in these cases, caseworkers were afraid to close the case files because they had never received direction on whether they were allowed to close case files from state ESD officials.

By available numerical standards, Arkansas' WtW program has been relatively successful. According to survey data, 72.8 percent of current/former program participants in Arkansas were placed in jobs, comparing favorably to the state's original goal of 68 percent. However, WtW program participants' evaluations of their pay paints a somewhat bleaker picture, with the most common average starting wage for an initial job falling between $5.00 and $5.99 per hour, or roughly the current US minimum wage of $5.15/hour (see Figures 2 and 3). Overall, though, the WtW program in Arkansas is attaining a level of initial success, as defined by the federal government, in that participants are "working first."

We raised several questions earlier about how WtW success should be measured and noted that one's definition drives the answer to the question of success. If we measure success by how many people found jobs, then Arkansas' program is successful. If we measure success by how many people have found or were placed in decent-paying jobs, then it becomes harder to argue that the state's program has been successful. Minimum-wage jobs

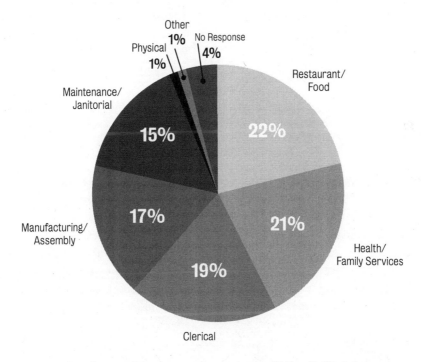

FIGURE 2: Distribution of Employment Sectors Among Welfare-To-Work Recipients In Arkansas, 2000

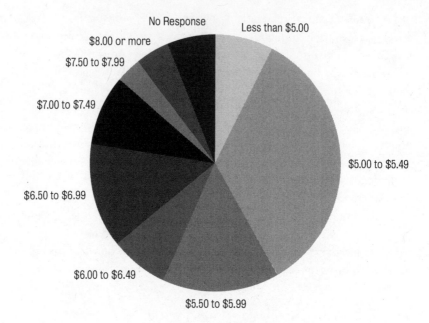

FIGURE 3: Distribution of Starting Wages Among Welfare-To-Work Recipients In Arkansas, 2000

fall under the 2000 federal poverty guidelines for every household size but a single one, and most poverty analysts agree that the methodology behind federal poverty guidelines is extremely outdated.[28] Popularly reported social experiments such as Barbara Ehrenreich's *Nickel and Dimed: On (Not) Getting By in America* reveal that many people simply cannot adequately subsist on these kinds of wages.[29]

As mentioned, there is a lack of programmatic activity for WtW in Arkansas during 2000–01 as the result of a pattern we previously referred to as "creaming." In other words, the easiest-to-place clients had been placed, just as they had in other states, yielding quick, high, politically popular reductions in the welfare rolls. The PRWORA is still in such a stage of infancy that the ability to serve these clients remains to be seen. As such, we feel that several recommendations are in order to further assess the success of WtW program implementation across the universe of states.

Conclusions

The major philosophical shift from the old AFDC to TANF under the PRWORA of 1996 involved a change in thinking from "education/training comes before work" to "work first" (education and training may come later). Now this new philosophy is even more important to understand because since the onset of the WIA of 1998, which became effective in 1999, the former Job Training Partnership Act is espousing the same, unproven philosophy.

An emphasis on the methods and quality of program administration is greatly needed. Regarding case management, we found that cases were not managed in the modern sense of the term; current contact information was not even kept for all clients. Further, DHS and ESD personnel disagreed on which entity was responsible for conducting client assessments for such areas as literacy, job skills, and childcare. The salience of case management to the effective implementation of WtW probably cannot be overstated. The idea of all relevant agencies communicating well and effectively, easing application processes for clients, and placing client interests first at all times is absolutely necessary for achieving program results. Programmatic activity is largely and conspicuously absent for the WtW participants who are more difficult to place, those facing significant barriers to employment. Regarding interagency communication, we found that communication between the two main agencies charged with the implementation of WtW—DHS and ESD—ranked their communication low on accuracy and timeliness. The two agencies also rated the WtW database as not very useful, and it was seldom used at all by DHS personnel. The two agencies could not even agree on a program-monitoring instrument when requested to do so by the federal government. The use of a well-developed MIS was a major factor cited by Meyers, Riccucci, and Lurie in their study of Georgia that affected the success of that state's WtW implementation.[30]

Regarding goal congruence, or lack thereof, the two agencies differ on their perceptions of WtW program subgoals like providing child care, transportation, and work skills. A lack of goal congruence by major implementing agencies or groups makes it more difficult to achieve program goals. A similar disagreement compelled Mississippi to streamline its WtW implementation structure.[31] As we enter the phase of administration where states try to serve the most difficult clients to place, those not exactly defined as the cream of the crop, all of these program elements are even more important.

Of course, while the complexity of administrative structure for the

WtW program in Arkansas makes effective interagency communication more difficult, it certainly does not make it impossible. Rogers-Dillon and Skrentny remarked regarding the pre-PRWORA implementation of WtW in Florida that "[t]he administrative details of [WtW] were not politically important."[32] We suggest that the administrative details of WtW are that much more important now as we enter the PRWORA's renewal phase. Increased attention to the state–local communication connection may enhance the achievement of overall policy goals. Specifically, more of a focus on administrative linkages will both help those on the frontlines of WtW policy implementation as they endeavor to focus on those clients who face the greatest obstacles to unsubsidized gainful employment.

Appendix: Key to acronyms used in this article

AFDC—Aid to Families with Dependent Children

CMSA—Case Management Society of America

DFCS—Department of Family and Children Services

DHS—Department of Human Services

DOL—Department of Labor

ESD—Employment Security Department

ETS—Employment and Training Services

HHS—Department of Health and Human Services

JTPA—Job Training Partnership Act

LWIA—Local Workforce Investment Areas

LWIB—Local Workforce Investment Boards

MIS—Management Information Systems

OJT—On-the-Job Training

PRWORA—Personal Responsibility and Work Opportunity Reconciliation Act

TANF—Temporary Assistance for Needy Families

TEA—Temporary Employment Assistance

WIA—Workforce Investment Act

WtW—Welfare-to-Work

GAO—General Accounting Office

CHAPTER 21

Making Progress?

Education Reform in Arkansas

GARY W. RITTER AND SARAH C. MCKENZIE

Because public schools long have been the chief priority of state govern-ments in the US, education nearly always tops the policy priority lists of both citizens and lawmakers. Here, Professors Ritter and McKenzie, both former school teachers who are now professors of education policy, recount Arkansas's efforts to improve the state's educational situation over the past two decades. In this essay, the authors discuss the Lake View litigation that in many served as the catalyst for reform, and describe recent changes in education policy related to curricular stan-dards, assessments, governance and structure of schools, and teacher recruitment and training.

Arkansas students have shown improvement since the 1990s. Nevertheless, like other rural southern states serving large numbers of low-income stu-dents, Arkansas continues to rank near the bottom on many of America's main indices of educational attainment: National Assessment scores, college entrance exam scores, and educational attainment. Arkansas ranked from 42nd to 45th in the nation on the most recent administrations of National Assessment exams, while the graduating class of 2018 placed Arkansas 41st among 50 states on the ACT college entrance exam. The most recent cen-sus data revealed that only 21.5 percent of the state's adults (age 25 and older) held bachelor's degrees or higher. Only West Virginia and Mississippi could claim a lower percentage. Although policymakers earnestly discuss the need to prepare all of our students for college and careers, four out of five Arkansas voters and taxpayers do not themselves possess college degrees. Many may not share the same sense of urgency about the priority that edu-cation should command. This creates one of the greatest challenges facing state leaders and policymakers.

DOI: https://doi.org/10.34053/parry2019.riapag2.21

TABLE 1:

How Does Arkansas Compare?

ADULT ATTAINMENT MEASURES	ARKANSAS	US	AR RANK (HIGH = 1)
% of population (age 25+) with high school diploma, 2012–2016	85.2%	87.0%	42 of 51
% of population (age 25+) with bachelor's degree, 2012–16	21.5%	30.3%	50 of 51
NAEP EXAMS, PERCENT (AT OR ABOVE) PROFICIENT			
Reading Grade 4, 2017	31%	35%	42 of 52
Reading Grade 8, 2017	29%	35%	43 of 52
Math Grade 4, 2017	33%	40%	44 of 52
Math Grade 8, 2017	25%	33%	45 of 52
Science Grade 4, 2015	33%	37%	38 of 46
Science Grade 8, 2015	28%	33%	38 of 46
HIGH SCHOOL OUTCOME MEASURES			
Graduation Rate, 2017	88%	85%	14 of 51
ACT Composite Score, 2018	19.4	20.8	41 of 51
COLLEGE ENROLLMENT RATE			
First Semester Expected: Class of 2016	56%	56%	

Sources: Census Data for the State of Arkansas, http://www.census.gov/. Retrieved February 2, 2019; National Assessment of Educational Progress, the Nation's Report Card. Reports available online at https://www.nations reportcard.gov/. Retrieved February 2, 2019; Adjusted Cohort Graduation Rate by State, 2016–17. Available online at http://nces.ed.gov/. Retrieved February 2, 2019; ACT Average Composite Scores by State, Graduating Class 2018. Available online at http://www.act.org/. Retrieved February 2, 2019.

Cries for reform should come as no surprise in light of such challenges; policymakers in Arkansas, as in many other states, have engaged in the work of educational improvement for decades. The current wave of school reform in Arkansas has been in the making since before 2000, when the state's *Lake View* litigation seemed to serve as a catalyst for change.

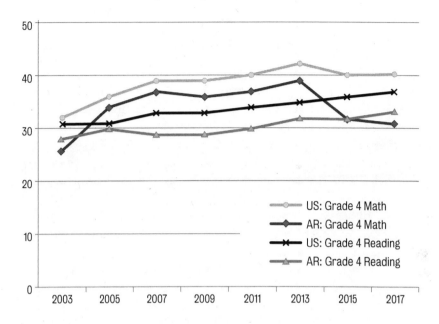

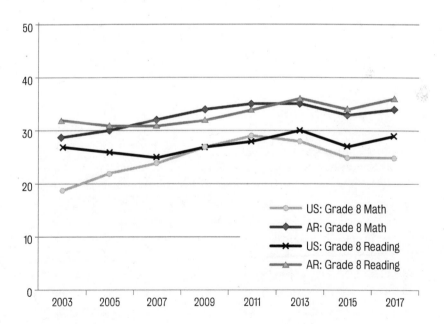

FIGURE 1: National Assessment of Educational Progress (NAEP), Percentage at or Above Proficient, Grades 4 and 8, Arkansas and the US 2003–2017
Source: National Assessment of Educational Progress, the Nation's Report Card.

Lake View: Catalyst for Reform

In Arkansas, as in more than forty other states, the school finance system has been challenged in court by disgruntled districts. Here as elsewhere, the plaintiffs have argued that the state has been remiss in its constitutional duty to provide an equitable and adequate system of public schooling to all students. In approximately half of these cases, including that in Arkansas, the courts have found in favor of the litigants and demanded changes in funding systems. Thus, Arkansas education policymakers now lead a school system that is under a state "constitutional mandate" to continue to support a school system that is equitably and adequately funded.

Some brief history: The series of lawsuits, appeals, and court orders known as "Lake View" began in 1992 when plaintiff districts sued over disparities in state funding. In 1994, a lower-court judge found the school funding system unconstitutionally inequitable.[1] After further turnings of the wheel, a definitive ruling came in 2001, when Chancery Court judge Collins Kilgore declared that Arkansas had failed to fulfill its constitutional obligation to provide a "general, suitable and efficient system of free public schools."[2] A November 2002 Supreme Court ruling substantially upheld the Kilgore ruling, made clear that the legislature bore fiduciary responsibility for public education, and gave lawmakers until January 1, 2004, to improve the system. The high court's indictment of the state's school funding system cited multiple shortcomings, including district-to-district disparities in teacher salaries, dramatic differences in the breadth and quality of curricula and the condition of school facilities, and starkly uneven per pupil expenditures.[3]

Importantly, Arkansas judges borrowed the definition of "efficiency" used by Kentucky's courts in the famous 1989 "Rose" school funding lawsuit, namely "substantial uniformity, substantial equality of financial resources and substantial equal educational opportunity for all students." Plainly, this demanded that policymakers contemplate far-reaching, system-wide changes in addition to greater and more equitably distributed resources.

Governor Mike Huckabee summoned lawmakers to action in his opening address before the 2003 legislative session. To his credit, the governor did not try to evade the judicial mandate or rail against the courts for usurping the prerogatives of the executive and legislative branches, as few suggested. Whatever he may have preferred, the handwriting was now clearly on the statehouse wall and the governor chose to commit himself to action.

In his "State of the State" address, Huckabee noted that many of his

FIGURE 2:

Arkansas School Finance Litigation Timeline

DATE	ACTION
1979	The Alma School District and ten other school districts file a lawsuit over the school-funding formula.
1983	The Arkansas Supreme Court strikes down the state's public school-funding formula, leading to a special legislative session later in the year.
1984	State raises sales tax by 1¢ to help fund public education.
1992	The Lake View School District in Phillips County sues the state over gross disparities in public school funding, including teacher salaries, school facilities, and curriculum.
1994	Pulaski County Chancellor Annabelle Clinton Imber finds in favor of Lake View, ruling Arkansas' education system violates equity provisions of the state constitution.
1995	Gov. Jim Guy Tucker signs a bill to create a school-funding system that sends money to districts equally on a per student basis.
1996	Voters approve Amendment 74 to the state constitution, mandating at least twenty-five mills of property tax in each school district for maintenance and operation.
1998	After amended complaints by Lake View, the state Supreme Court orders a new trial to determine if the state's reforms have met the requirements of the 1994 order.
September–October 2000	Pulaski County Chancellor Collins Kilgore conducts the Lake View trial. Thirty-six witnesses testified, and the court record totaled 20,878 pages.
2001	Kilgore declares the school-funding system to be not only unconstitutionally inequitable but also inadequate and orders the state to fund a preschool program.
2002	The state Supreme Court unanimously upholds most of Kilgore's ruling, noting that the state has the ultimate authority over schools. But it overrules Kilgore on preschool, saying there is no such constitutional mandate. The court gives the state until Jan. 1, 2004, to come up with a solution.
September 2003	Consultants issue school finance adequacy report, which calls for nearly $850 million in new spending.

DATE	ACTION
December 2003	The legislature convenes in special session called by Gov. Mike Huckabee to take up education reform after making little progress toward meeting the court's mandate during the 2003 regular session.
January 2004	The Lake View School District files a motion with the Supreme Court to hold the state in contempt for failing to comply with the Lake View ruling. The court decides to consider Lake View's motion, finds the state in "noncompliance," and retakes jurisdiction of the case. It decides to appoint two special court "masters" to evaluate actions of the legislature and Huckabee, later naming former justices Bradley Jesson and David Newbern as masters.
February 2004	The legislature wraps up the special session. It passes about $380 million a year in new taxes, a new funding formula which sends more money to districts with a higher percentage of low-income students, and consolidation of districts with fewer than 350 students. Huckabee calls legislative accomplishments "maximum taxes for minimum reform."
April 2004	Jesson and Newbern release their report calling many of the legislative acts "laudable" but adding that the state will likely continue to have inequities as along as districts are permitted to raise additional money locally.
May 2004	Huckabee's lawyer, Leon Holmes, urges the court to keep control over the case and order more school district consolidation. Attorney General Mike Beebe's office asks for the court to pull out of the case.
June 2004	The court removes itself from the case in a 4–3 decision, citing concerns over separation of powers. It complements the state's education-reform measures.
November 2004	After assessing nearly 6,000 school buildings in Arkansas, consultants find $2.3 billion in immediate needs. Legislators later debate this figure as unrealistic.
April 2005	The 2005 regular legislative session ends. Huckabee and lawmakers focus on increasing state aid to colleges and universities but delay increasing base funding for public schools. However, $104 million is set aside as a state aid to improve public school facilities and $35 million to subsidize teacher health insurance. On April 14, the day after the session ended, the Rogers School District files request for the Supreme Court to reopen the Lake View case, accusing the legislature of not adequately increasing school funding. Forty-six school districts join the Rogers district in asking the court to reopen the case. The number of districts eventually grows to forty-nine.

DATE	ACTION
May 2005	The Supreme Court hears oral arguments on whether to reopen the case.
June 2005	In a 4–3 decision, the Supreme Court agrees to reopen the case, reappointing Jesson and Newbern to take testimony on legislative actions. The court sets a deadline of Sept. 1, 2005, for the masters to complete a report.
August 2005	Court hears testimony. The deadline for the Special Masters' report is postponed to October 1, 2005.
September 2005	Legislature rehires consulting firm to conduct adequacy study.
October 2005	Special Masters release report finding that the 85th General Assembly did not adequately fund public schools or facilities improvements.
December 2005	In a 5–2 decision, the Supreme Court sides with the plaintiffs and retains jurisdiction of the case. The court concludes that the legislature failed to make education its top priority during the 2005 regular session and did not provide adequate funding for 2005–06 or 2006–07 because it made no effort to define an adequate level of funding. The court sets a deadline of Dec. 1, 2006 for the state to "correct constitutional deficiencies."
April 2006	The legislature meets in special session from April 3 through April 7 and passes education-related legislation that appropriates approximately $200 million to public schools for the 2005–06 school year and the 2006–07 school year. The legislation increases the per-student foundation funding level from $5,400 to $5,486 in 2005–06 and to $5,620 in 2006–07. The legislature also increases the minimum teacher salary for each year and appropriates an additional $50 million for school facilities.
December 2006	The Arkansas Supreme Court declines to end the case, arguing that it needs more information before it can say whether reforms approved by the legislature during the April 2006 special session had sufficiently addressed problems. In a 5–2 decision, the Court gives the state thirty days to demonstrate that it has complied with their order. The court also reappoints Special Masters to review the legislature's work.
January 2007	The Special Masters issue their report to the Arkansas Supreme Court.

DATE	ACTION
February 2007	The Arkansas General Assembly lays out its plan to uphold the mandates set for by the Special Masters, issuing two adequacy reports outlining its progress.
May 2007	In the 2007 session, the General Assembly made the following funding reforms: Per pupil foundation funding increased from the current level of $5,662 to $5,789 in 2009. Additional per pupil funding for students in "alternative learning environments" (such as special education programs) increased from $3,750 to $4,063. Funding for students in poverty increased depending on the concentration of impoverished students in a particular school district. The court also argued that teacher salaries had risen to an appropriate level when compared to neighboring states. The average Arkansas teacher earned $42,931 in 2006—which puts the state second among neighboring states, and ninth among all southern states.
May 2007	The Arkansas Supreme Court, acting on the recommendation of the reappointed Special Masters, unanimously declares that "our system of public school financing is now in constitutional compliance."

predecessors had made great pronouncements on education reform that had led to little. He quoted seven gubernatorial inaugural addresses since 1923, including Bill Clinton's 1983 exhortations, then drew this sharp conclusion:

> Every legislative session, every decade, every governor, every General Assembly gathers just as we have, and they talk about their constitutional responsibility to provide the kind of education that our Constitution says we must provide. And minor changes are made. And people go home having congratulated themselves for minor adjustments to a system that for 100 years at least every single governor and legislator has said is broken.[4]

The governor then called upon the legislature to "join me in not being another footnote in the pages of Arkansas history. . . . [W]e'll continue to lose until we finally . . . fulfill the constitutional mandate for an adequate, efficient, suitable, equitable education for every single boy and girl in this state."[5] As of today, it is not yet clear if the governor and the legislature succeeded in being more than just another "footnote."

The Legislative Response

The Arkansas legislature—which until 2010 met only every other year—had its first opportunity to respond to the Supreme Court's mandate when it convened for the 2003 session. Governor Huckabee opened with a proposal for far-reaching school consolidation, arguing that this would yield the efficiency necessary to comply with the court's ruling. However, the contentious debate over consolidation so divided the state's policymakers that, by the end of the 2003 regular session, the legislature had failed not only to resolve that issue but also to address the school funding challenges.

With the court deadline looming, Governor Huckabee convened a special session of the legislature on December 8, 2003, and laid four issues before it.

- restructure or consolidate smaller districts,
- increase school accountability for student performance,
- revise the existing school funding formula, and
- raise the revenue to pay for these reforms.

The central tenet of the *Lake View* ruling, he reminded the General Assembly, was equitable and adequate funding. All Arkansas districts, regardless of size, demographics or location, were obligated to provide equivalent and adequate educational opportunities, teacher salaries, and school facilities.

In response, lawmakers passed Act 59, which established that school funding would be determined by attendance during the previous year and provided both base funding for essential needs and supplemental resources for specialized needs. For 2004–2005, base funding was set at $5,400 per student, with districts to receive additional resources for various categories of disadvantaged students, including low-income students, English-language learners, and those in alternative secondary school programs. Moreover, districts were required to pay higher minimum base salaries of $27,500 for a new bachelor's degree holder and $31,625 for a new teacher holding a master's degree. As of the 2016–17 school year, the base level of funding per student stood at over $6,600, while the categorical funding set aside for disadvantaged students had also experienced similar increases over the decade following Act 59.

Overall, the implementation of Act 59 was projected to require $438 million more (though an outside study had concluded in 2003 that a fully adequate system would cost the state nearly twice that much). Overcoming its reluctance to raise taxes, the legislature devised a three-part package intended to raise at least $417 million more. The state sales tax rate of 5.125 percent was increased to 6.0 percent, some services were subjected to taxation for the first time, and the corporate franchise tax was increased.

The total state appropriation for elementary-secondary education in 2003–2004 had been $1.84 billion; thanks to the new tax dollars and other appropriations, the 2004–2005 budget was $2.29 billion. That represented an increased state commitment of more than 24 percent in a single year. After the conclusion of the special session in June 2004, the Supreme Court signaled its satisfaction by removing itself from a direct supervisory role, declaring the Lake View case closed, and turning matters over to the legislature.

The saga did not end there however. In the 2005 session, lawmakers devoted much attention (and some resources) to school facilities and teacher health insurance, but left the per-pupil foundation amount at $5,400 for the 2005–06 school year. This so angered some educators that forty-nine districts appealed to the Supreme Court to re-open the lawsuit.

On December 15, 2005, the court sided with these critics and, in a 5–2 decision, ruled that the legislature failed to make education spending its top priority in this year's regular session and under-funded school building repairs and construction. The court did not direct the legislature to appropriate a specific funding increase, but instead gave the state a December 1, 2006, deadline to "correct the constitutional deficiencies." The key points of the court's ruling were the following:

- The General Assembly could not have provided adequate funding for the 2005–2006 and 2006–2007 school years, because it made no effort to comply with Act 57 and to determine what adequate funding should be.
- Education needs were not funded first, as required by Act 108 of the Second Extraordinary Session of 2003. Rather, both foundation funding aid and categorical funding "were established based upon what funds were available—not by what was needed."
- Appropriations for the repair and construction of safe, dry, and healthy facilities were grossly under-funded and, thus, inadequate. The court observed that Immediate Repair Program funding equaled only one half ($20 million) of the

$40 million needed and only $120 million was appropriated for Priority One facilities, despite an estimated need of over $205 million.[6]

To address the December 2005 ruling, Arkansas lawmakers would need to meet in special session prior to the December 2006 deadline. The governor called the legislature into session in April 2006 after much behind-the-scenes legislative work to develop proposals with a good chance of satisfying the lawmakers. The special session moved quickly, beginning on April 3 and concluding April 7. The legislature passed education-related legislation which appropriated an additional $200 million to public schools for the 2005–06 school year and the 2006–07 school years. The per-student foundation funding level was increased from $5,400 to $5,486 in 2005–06 and to $5,620 in 2006–07. The legislation also increased the minimum teacher salary for each year and appropriated an additional $50 million for school facilities.

In December 2006 the Arkansas Supreme Court—in a 5–2 decision—declined to put an end to the *Lake View* case, arguing that the legislature had not provided enough information as to whether it had complied with the court's mandate. The court gave legislators thirty days to comply with its latest order. In addition, to oversee the General Assembly's reform efforts in the 2007 legislative session, the court re-nominated its Special Masters, a ruling which, predictably, stirred public outcry from policymakers. Governor Huckabee described the court as "out of control," and claimed that it was "usurping the constitutionally stated limitations and separations of powers."[7]

Despite this, the governor and the legislature expressed confidence that their actions effectively address the concerns of the court, confidence that—after an additional investment of $100 million by the Arkansas legislature in the spring of 2007—appears to have been merited. On May 31, 2007, a unanimous decision of the state supreme court officially closed the long-running *Lake View* case. While, predictably, legislators continue to debate and wrestle over education budgets each year, the work of school reform and improvement has moved forward without the involvement of the Supreme Court.

Nevertheless, many in the state still voice concern that school spending in Arkansas is low relative to that in other states. The Office for Education Policy at the University of Arkansas publishes regular reports on school spending in the state and the nation. The most recent report published in 2015, showed that the state was spending $9,618 in net current expenditures per pupil in 2011–12.[8] This figure was roughly one thousand dollars less than the national average and one thousand dollars more than the average of Arkansas's border states. When adjusted for differences in cost-of-living, the spending figure in Arkansas was over $10,500 and within $200 of the national average. Overall, these data indicate that school funding in Arkansas has improved in response to the *Lake View* case.

An even more important result of school spending reform in Arkansas has been the more equitable distribution of educational resources within the state. Thanks to the legislative initiatives throughout the *Lake View* case, Arkansas today boasts a school funding formula that is consistently identified as "progressive" by the series of "Funding Gaps" reports published by the Education Trust.[9] In the most recent report entitled "Funding Gaps: An Analysis of School Funding Equity Across the US and within Each State," Arkansas ranks in the top ten states in terms of progressivity of funding. This means that districts serving high percentages of students in poverty (and students of color) actually receive higher state and local revenues per pupil compared to districts serving lower percentages of those same students. This pattern of relatively progressive district funding has been evident in Arkansas since the initial *Lake View* ruling.

Of course, there is still much debate on whether districts serving students with the greatest need have access to compensatory resources that are substantial enough to level the playing field in terms of student outcomes. Indeed, troubling and persistent achievement gaps remain, so much work remains as policymakers continue to struggle with the question of how to best to deploy educational resources to ensure that all students in Arkansas actually learn more in the years to come. Meanwhile, the work of school reform marches on in numerous areas, three of which are considered next.

Recent Reforms

STANDARDS, ASSESSMENT, AND ACCOUNTABILITY

In the 1980s, as Americans focused on the message of *A Nation at Risk*, Arkansas awakened to the idea that it needed to strengthen its education system and boost its students' performance. The reform era opened with initiatives by then-Governor Bill Clinton (and first lady Hillary Rodham Clinton), including initial efforts to set standards, test teachers, and focus on school leadership.

Arkansas's first set of statewide curricular standards—called course content guides—were developed in the 1980s. In the early 1990s, the State

Board of Education gradually phased in a system of curricular frameworks. Assessments of student learning soon followed, when lawmakers passed the Arkansas Comprehensive Testing, Assessment and Accountability Program (ACTAAP) in 1999.[10] That law required that all public school students demonstrate proficiency in core academic subjects on standardized assessments aligned with the state standards.

In 2002, President George W. Bush signed into law the No Child Left Behind Act (NCLB), which required all states to administer annual assessments in reading and math to public school students.[11] States developed assessments aligned to their state curriculum standards, and determined the requirements for proficiency. Arkansas's assessments, named "Benchmarks" were given to all students in grades 3–8, in addition to students completing certain high school courses (algebra I, geometry, and junior English).

Arkansas's test results generated conversations about variation in the success of schools within Arkansas, but student performance was not comparable to any other state because, like Arkansas, each state had developed state-specific standards and assessments. In an effort to ensure some consistency in what students throughout the country were learning in school, state governors and commissioners of education came together to develop common educational standards that could be adopted by the states. When the Common Core Standards were released in 2010, forty-five states, including Arkansas, adopted them as state education standards.[12]

A backlash rose against the Common Core in Arkansas, as in many states throughout the nation. There were concerns of federal overreach into state control of educational standards, and that the new standards left teachers searching for instructional materials. Stories and pictures of "Common Core" math problems were prevalent on social media, and the new math standards became a focus for parents' complaints. In February 2015, newly-elected Governor Asa Hutchinson appointed a panel to study the Common Core and make recommendations. In the spring of 2015, Arkansas students were assessed using a new test. The PARCC exam, which was developed to measure the Common Core Standards and was being administered in a dozen states, took students about eight hours, and the results were bleak. Only 24% of Arkansas students met proficiency targets in math, down from 72% on the state-developed Benchmark assessments the year before, and literacy scores showed a similar decline. During the summer of 2015, the Governor's Common Core task force recommended that the state end the contract with PARCC and review and revise the Common Core standards.[13]

The Arkansas Department of Education reviewed the standards, made some revisions, and new "Arkansas Standards" were adopted the following year. A new assessment contract was entered into, and students throughout the state complete the ACT Aspire each spring. In 2018, the most recent year of data available, 47 and 44% of Arkansas students met readiness expectations in math and English language arts, respectively. Like the old Benchmark assessments, however, these scores cannot be compared with other states because Arkansas is currently the only state using only this assessment for statewide testing.

Perhaps the most significant change for Arkansas public schools occurred in September, 2017, when the state's Every Student Succeeds Act (ESSA) plan was approved by the federal government.[14] ESSA, an update to NCLB, allowed states to develop their own measures for school accountability. The new measures are aligned with the state's system of assigning A-F letter grades to schools, which is required under Act 696 of 2013.[15] Arkansas's measures of school performance include a weighted measure of student achievement that is more reflective of variations in school achievement than NCLB-era proficiency percentages, a growth measure that reflects how students at the school improved their scores over time, and for high schools, both four- and five-year graduation rates. In addition, indicators of school success are considered, such as school attendance, the number of students reading on grade level, meeting minimum ACT scores, and how many students are taking specific types of courses (e.g. Advanced Placement and computer science classes).

These specific courses included in the state's ESSA plan reflect investments that have been made on behalf of Arkansas students. Currently, all eleventh grade students are given the opportunity to take the ACT for free during the school day. Since 2003, Arkansas high schools have been required under to offer at least one Advanced Placement (AP) class in each of the four core content areas (Act 102).[16] Arkansas further supports students by covering the AP exam fees for all students. Governor Hutchinson led the effort to connect Arkansas' entire public school system to highly secure, all-fiber high-speed broadband internet, and signed Act 1280 of 2013 to require all high school students to take one digital learning class before graduation. [17] Computer science is one of Governor Hutchinson's highest priorities, and Act 187 of 2015 requires that every public high school in Arkansas offer at least one computer science course.[18]

As of 2019, Arkansas boasts more rigorous standards and assessments, accountability focused on student growth, heightened visibility of computer science, and statewide college entrance exam. Educational leaders in the state are hopeful that these initiatives will improve educational outcomes for Arkansas students.

SCHOOL CONSOLIDATION AND SCHOOL CHOICE

Two topics that dominated the discussion in Arkansas in the past two decades were the structure and the governance of school systems. First, immediately in the wake of the *Lake View* ruling, Governor Huckabee led the drive to consolidate tiny rural districts in the name of "efficiency." Two months after the Supreme Court handed down its November 2002 indictment of the state's schools, the governor opened the 2003 session with a proposal for far-reaching school consolidation. His initial shot across the bow was a bold proposal to consolidate any school district with fewer than 1,500 students; this ultimately unrealistic proposition would have reduced the number of districts from 310 to 116. Eventually, after much debate and consternation, a compromise bar was set at a minimum enrollment of 350 students district-wide during the special legislative session of 2003–04. While Huckabee maintained this was too low, he allowed the measure to become law without his signature. As a result of the law, the number of school districts in Arkansas decreased by 252 as of August 2005. For the most part, legislative interest in consolidating small districts has waned over time, perhaps because there is little evidence that school district consolidations bore the cost savings that proponents had anticipated.

Around that time, interest in open enrollment public charter schools was on the rise. Legislators tinkered with the Arkansas charter school law in 2005 by doubling the cap on open-enrollment charters to twenty-five statewide and raise the maximum term for charter authorization from three to five years; this number has since been increased again. In 2005, there were only seven open enrollment charter schools enrolling a total of 1,135 students across the state. As of the 2018–19 school year, that number has grown to twenty-five open enrollment charter schools, some with multiple campuses, enrolling a total of 17,985 students, representing 3.8% of all public school students in the state of Arkansas. The impact of charter schools is most prevalent in Pulaski County, home to fifteen of those charter schools and 11,844 of the charter students and nearly all of the accompanying public debate. There is not space here to delve into this complicated issue, but we have considered the relationship between public charter schools and traditional public schools in Little Rock in a series of Arkansas Education Reports on the website of the Office for Education Policy.[19]

TEACHERS

Teachers and teacher recruitment in Arkansas made national headlines in the 1980s. In an attempt to ensure the quality of teachers in Arkansas classrooms, then-Governor Bill Clinton pushed through an education reform plan in 1983 and famously appointed his wife, Hillary Rodham Clinton, to lead the effort. It included raises for teachers, new taxes to pay for them, and mandatory competency tests for both new and working teachers. When the teachers were finally required to sit for the National Teachers Examination two years later, reports emerged that more than one-third of the teachers in parts of the state failed to earn a passing score. Because of the potential political fallout, as many tell the story, the cutoff score was quietly lowered so that fewer than ten percent actually failed—and many of those teachers retained their jobs after re-taking the exam.[20] In the end, the plan generated a great deal of controversy but not much change in the state's teaching workforce.

Today, Arkansas trains, recruits, and pays its teachers in much the same way as most other states. Most teachers in the state emerge from the seventeen accredited institutions of teacher training.

While many have voiced concern over a teaching shortage in Arkansas, the problem is perhaps better described as a distribution problem. In other words, teachers are concentrated in some areas and subjects, while there remains a dearth of teachers in low-income, high-minority schools and in certain fields, such as math and science. A recent Office for Education Policy survey of Arkansas school districts showed, for example, that each teaching opening in the northwest region of the state drew an average of ten applications while each opening in the southeast, or delta, region drew only one applicant.[21] Similarly, districts in the highest poverty areas received only three applications for each opening while the wealthiest districts received nine applications per opening. Our survey showed that that, on average, administrators face little difficulty finding qualified elementary school teachers but find it very difficult to track down qualified math or science teachers.

Faced with such distribution challenges, the Arkansas Department of Education (ADE) has had to allow more teachers to teach out-of-field. In the 2018–19 school year, the department received out-of-field waiver requests from 826 teachers in 188 districts. Other than simply waiving requirements, how else have Arkansas policymakers dealt with these challenges? As mentioned earlier, the court-mandated strategy has been to simply increase minimum teacher salaries so that compensation in Arkansas remains competitive with surrounding states to stave off the possibility of Arkansas teachers defecting across the border for better pay. Currently in 2018–19, the minimum starting salary for teachers across the state is $31,800. Even so, 86% of school districts pay above and even well above this minimum level.

Of course, there are many innovative strategies for attracting and retaining good teachers that are policy options, such as alternative certification or merit pay for teachers in areas of great need. The state does offer an alternative licensure program: the Arkansas Professional Pathway to Educator Licensure (APPEL), through which bachelor's degree holders can work toward a teaching license while employed as classroom teachers. The program extends over a two-year period and involves assessment, teaching, and portfolio development, as well as summer and weekend instructional modules. There are approximately 30,000 teachers in Arkansas schools; currently, there were 350 participants in APPEL program.

Two other alternative certification programs recruit and support teachers specifically for districts serving low-income students. The first, the national Teach for America Program, has been placing teachers in Arkansas schools for more than a decade. Teach for America teachers make a two-year commitment to work in their placement schools, although some stay beyond the commitment period. Since 2013, the Arkansas Teacher Corps, headquartered at the University of Arkansas—Fayetteville, has followed suit by recruiting and placing approximately twenty-five new teachers each year into economically disadvantaged schools in the southern and eastern parts of the state. These teachers make a three-year commitment to their placement schools, and then receive full certification upon completing their commitment. The evidence thus far suggests that these alternatively trained teachers perform as well or better than other teachers teaching similar subjects in the same schools.

Finally, one last policy aimed at teacher quality involves National Board Certification (NBC). According to the National Board for Professional Teaching Standards, the voluntary and time-consuming process for teachers certifies that they "have developed and demonstrated the advanced knowledge, skills, and practices required of an outstanding educator." Since the late 1990s, Arkansas policymakers have incentivized participation in this process by covering all fees for teachers and even paying annual bonuses for NBC teachers of $5,000. Today, there are nearly 3,000 NBC teachers in Arkansas, representing roughly 7% of the teaching workforce. Recent legislative action from 2017 has increased the level of annual NBC bonuses for teachers in high poverty schools and decreased the bonus for those working in higher-income schools.[22]

Conclusion

Observers of school reform in Arkansas encounter few dull days. Despite the many ups and downs, there is good reason for optimism. In reaction to the Supreme Court's mandate to mend an unconstitutional funding system, Arkansas policymakers took a proactive stance. While those in other states have dug in their heels and resisted court-mandated reform, Arkansas leaders seized the opportunity to enact broad changes.

After the legislative session responding to the *Lake View* ruling ending in 2004, Arkansas students attended much more generously-funded schools. The state boosted K-12 education spending by almost 30 percent and, on average, schools had an additional $1,000 per pupil in state dollars. After further iterations and activity related to *Lake View* in legislative sessions, both regular sessions and special session, the total of funding increases that followed the last round of the *Lake View* litigation exceeded $900 million. Analyses of school district funding figures conducted by us at the Office for Education Policy in Arkansas and by researchers outside of Arkansas (such as the Education Trust), have continually shown that these increases have been substantially targeted to students in disadvantaged districts. The school funding system in Arkansas continues to be ranked in the top ten across the nation in terms of across-district equity in education spending.

Arkansas has made a good faith effort to revitalize its elementary-secondary education system by providing needed resources and encouraging efficiencies and reforms in several areas. A continuing challenge is determining how to best use the resources so all schools provide students what they need to be successful later in life.

NOTES

CHAPTER 1

1. *Epperson v. Arkansas,* 393 U. S. 97, 89 Sup. Ct. 266 (1968)

2. Pine Bluff (AR) *Commercial,* September 2, 1965, 8.

3. Little Rock *Arkansas Gazette,* February 13, 1959, 1B.

4. Little Rock *Arkansas Gazette,* February 17, 1959, 1A.

5. Little Rock *Arkansas Gazette,* February 17, 1959, 1A.

6. Little Rock *Arkansas Gazette,* June 28,1966, 1A.

7. Arkansas Constitution (1874), Amendment 7 (1920).

8. *Arkansas Gazette,* September 22, 1965, 18B. The Scopes quoted is the Scopes of the famous Dayton, Tennessee, "monkey trial."

9. Gail Kennedy, ed., *Evolution and Religion: The Conflict Between Science and Theology in Modern America,* in Problems in American Civilization Series (Boston: D.C. Heath and Company, 1957), viii.

10. Richard Hofstadter, *Anti-Intellectualism in American Life* (New York: Vintage Books, 1964), 126.

11. George Brown Tindall, *The Emergence of the New South, 1913–1945* (Baton Rouge, LA: LSU Press, 1967), 200.

12. Kennedy, ed., *Evolution and Religion,* ix.

13. Hofstadter, *Anti-Intellectualism in American Life,* 125.

14. Kennedy, ed., *Evolution and Religion,* viii.

15. W. J. Cash, *The Mind of the South* (New York: Vintage Books, 1941), 337–38.

16. Francis Butler Simkins, *A History of the South* (New York: Random House, 1956), 417.

17. Simkins, *A History of the South,* 417.

18. Maynard Shipley, "The Forward March of the Anti-Evolutionists," *Current History* 29 (January 1929): 579–80.

19. Tindall, *Emergence of the New South,* 206.

20. R. Halliburton, Jr., "The Adoption of the Arkansas Anti-Evolution Law," *Arkansas Historical Quarterly* 23 (Autumn 1964): 272–73.

21. Kennedy, ed., *Evolution and Religion,* ix.

22. Simkins, *History of the South,* 418.

23. William Foy Lisenby, "Brough, Baptists, and Bombast: The Election of 1928," *Arkansas Historical Quarterly* 32 (Summer 1973): 127.

24. *Arkansas Gazette,* April 24, 1966, 1E.

25. Halliburton, "The Adoption of the Arkansas Anti-Evolution Law," 273.

26. *Arkansas Gazette,* November 11, 1927, 18.

27. *Arkansas Gazette,* December 19, 1926, 28.

28. *Arkansas Gazette.,* January 9, 1927, 24.

29. *Arkansas Gazette,* January 9, 1927, 19. Hay Watson Smith outraged some fundamentalist Presbyterians by his outspoken opposition to any attempt to outlaw the teaching of evolution, and they brought formal charges of heresy against him.

He was finally cleared of these charges in 1934 after a series of hearings before various Presbyterian courts. See Leo Thomas Sweeney, "The Anti-Evolution Movement in Arkansas" (unpublished M.A. thesis, University of Arkansas, 1966), 119–21.

30. *Arkansas Gazette*, January 10, 1927, 7.

31. *Arkansas House Journal*, 1927, 60.

32. *Arkansas House Journal*, 1927, 68–69

33. The Tennessee anti-evolution statute that resulted in the Scopes trial was worded similarly.

34. Little Rock *Arkansas Democrat*, January 29, 1927, 3.

35. *Arkansas House Journal*, 1927, 82.

36. *Arkansas Democrat*, January 27, 1927, 1.

37. *Arkansas Gazette*, January 29, 1927, 1. For a more detailed account of the hearing, see Sweeney, "The Anti-Evolution Movement in Arkansas," 51–54.

38. *Arkansas Gazette*, February 3, 1927, 1.

39. *Arkansas Gazette*, February 3, 1927, 1.

40. *Arkansas Gazette*, February 3, 1927, 3

41. *Arkansas Gazette*, February 3, 1927, 14

42. *Arkansas Gazette*, February 3, 1927, 14

43. *Arkansas House Journal*, 1927, 263.

44. *Arkansas Gazette*, February 4, 1927, 3.

45. *Arkansas House Journal*, 1927, 272.

46. *Arkansas House Journal*, 1927, 292

47. *Arkansas House Journal*, 1927,, 293

48. *Arkansas Gazette*, February 10, 1927, 5.

49. *Arkansas Gazette*, February 10, 1927, 5.

50. *Arkansas House Journal*, 1927, 324.

51. *Arkansas Democrat*, February 10, 1927, 1.

52. *Arkansas Gazette*, February 11, 1927, 1.

53. *Arkansas Senate Journal*, 1927, 351.

54. *Arkansas Democrat*, February 11, 1927, 14.

55. Maynard Shipley, "A Fear of the Monkey War," *Independent* 119 (October 1927): 327.

56. Shipley, "A Fear of the Monkey War," 327.

57. Arkansas Constitution (1874) Amendment 7 (1920).

58. Arkansas Secretary of State, *Historical Report*, 1958, 194.

59. *Arkansas Democrat*, May 6, 1928, .

60. *Arkansas Acts*, 1929, Initiated Act No. 1, Section 1. Sections 1 and 2 of the act are as follows:

> Section 1. That it shall be unlawful for any teacher or other instructor in any University, College, Normal, Public School, or other institution of the State, which is supported in whole or in part from public funds derived by State and local taxation to teach the theory or doctrine that mankind ascended or descended from a lower order of animals and also it shall be unlawful for any teacher, textbook commission, or other authority exercising the power to select textbooks for above mentioned educational institutions to adopt or use in any such institution a textbook that teaches the doctrine or theory that mankind descended or ascended from a lower order of animals.

Section 2. Be it further enacted that any teacher or other instructor or textbook commissioner who is found guilty of violation of this Act by teaching the theory or doctrine mentioned in Section 1 hereof, or by using or adopting any such textbooks in any such educational institution shall be guilty of a misdemeanor and upon conviction shall be fined not exceeding five hundred dollars ($500.00); and upon conviction shall vacate the position thus held in any educational institutions of the character above mentioned or any commission of which he may be a member.

61. *Arkansas Gazette*, April 24, 1966, 1E.

62. *Arkansas Gazette*, November 11, 1927, 18.

63. *New York Times,* May 6, 1928, Sec. III, 2.

64. *Arkansas Gazette*, April 24, 1966, 1E.

65. *Arkansas Democrat,* October 14, 1928, 8.

66. *Arkansas Gazette,* October 17, 1928, 1.

67. *Arkansas Gazette,* November 3, 1928, 6.

68. Ralph W. Widener, Jr., "Charles Hillman Brough," *Arkansas Historical Quarterly,* 34 (Summer 1975): 113.

69. Ralph W. Widener, Jr., "Charles Hillman Brough," 114

70. *Arkansas Gazette*, October 31, 1928, 19.

71. *Arkansas Gazette*, November 4, 1928, 4.

72. *Arkansas Gazette*, November 4, 1928, 4.

73. *Arkansas Acts,* 1929, 1519.

74. Election Return Abstracts, on file, Arkansas Secretary of State's Office.

75. *Arkansas Gazette,* November 9, 1929, 1.

76. Maynard Shipley, "The Forward March of the Anti-Evolutionists," *Current History* 29 (January 1929): 578.

77. As quoted in the *Literary Digest,* December 1, 1928, 28.

78. *Arkansas Gazette,* November 9, 1928, 1.

79. *Arkansas Democrat,* November 11, 1928, 1.

80. *Arkansas Gazette,* November 9, 1928, 1.

81. *Arkansas Gazette*, November 21, 1928, 8.

82. *Arkansas Democrat,* March 31, 1966, 10.

83. *Arkansas House Journal,* 1937, 859.

84. See introduction to this article. For a more extensive treatment of the 1937 and 1959 legislative attempts, see Sweeney, "The Anti-Evolution Movement in Arkansas," 123–24.

85. *Arkansas Daily Legislative Digest,* 1965, 88.

86. *Arkansas Gazette,* February 2, 1965, 1B.

87. *Arkansas Gazette,* February 3, 1965, 6A.

88. Interview with Forrest Rozzell, executive secretary of the Arkansas Education Association until 1976, Little Rock, Arkansas, June 15, 1978. There were also two other interviews, one on June 21 and the other on June 22.

89. Interview with Hubert Blanchard, associate executive secretary of the Arkansas Education Association during the Epperson case, Little Rock, Arkansas, June 20, 1978.

90. Rozzell interview.

91. Rozzell interview.

92. *Arkansas Democrat,* September 4, 1965, 3

93. *Arkansas Gazette,* September 8, 1965, 1A.

94. *Arkansas Gazette,* September 7, 1965, 6A.

95. *Arkansas Democrat,* September 11, 1965, 3.

96. *Arkansas Gazette,* December 7, 1965, 1A.

97. Interview with Eugene Warren, attorney for the Arkansas Education Association, Little Rock, Arkansas, June 16, 1978.

98. Rozzell interview.

99. Rozzell interview.

100. Warren interview.

101. *Arkansas Democrat,* December 7, 1965, 2.

102. *Arkansas Democrat,* December 7, 1965, 2.

103. Blanchard interview.

104. *Arkansas Gazette,* March 18, 1966, 2A.

105. *Arkansas Gazette.,* March 19,1966, 5A.

106. *Arkansas Gazette.,* March 19,1966, 5A.

107. See *Arkansas Gazette,* March 25, 29A; March 30, 8A; and March 31, 1966, 8A; and the *Arkansas Democrat,* March 24, 1966, 2.

108. *Arkansas Gazette,* March 29, 1966, 1B.

109. *Arkansas Democrat,* March 27, 1966, 13A.

110. *Arkansas Democrat,* March 31, 1966, 10.

111. Warren interview.

112. *Arkansas Gazette,* April 2, 1966, 1A, 2A.

113. *Arkansas Democrat,* May 28, 1966, 2.

114. Rozzell interview; *Arkansas Democrat,* April 2, 1966, 2; *Arkansas Gazette,* April 3, 1966, 2E.

115. *Epperson v. McDonald,* No. 131575 (Pulaski Chancery Court, First Div., May 27, 1966), 7.

116. *Epperson v. McDonald,* No. 131575, 5.

117. *Scopes v. State of Tennessee,* 154 Tenn. 105, 298 S.W. 363 (1927). In this case, the Tennessee Evolution Law was held to be constitutional, but the fine levied upon Scopes was held not to be within the power of the court, and his conviction was reversed on this ground.

118. *Epperson v. McDonald,* No. 131575, 6.

119. *Scopes v. State of Tennessee,* 154 Tenn. 105, 298 S.W. 363 (1927).

120. *State v. Epperson,* 242 Ark. 922, 416 S.W. 2nd 322 (1967). Appellant's brief in this case (No. 4127), 3.

121. *State v. Epperson,* 242 Ark. 922, 416 S.W. 2nd 322 (1967). Appellant's brief in this case (No. 4127), 81

122. *State v. Epperson,* 242 Ark. 922, 416 S.W. 2nd 322 (1967).

123. *State v. Epperson,* 242 Ark. 922, 416 S.W. 2nd 322 (1967).

124. Rozzell and Warren interviews.

125. *Arkansas Gazette,* March 5, 1968, 1B.

126. *Arkansas Gazette,* October 17, 1968, 1A.

127. *New York Times,* October 17, 1968, 49.

128. *New York Times,* October 17, 1968, 49

129. Warren interview.

130. Warren interview.

131. *New York Times,* October 17, 1968, 49.

132. *Arkansas Democrat,* October 17, 1968, 3A.

133. *Epperson v. Arkansas,* 393 U.S. 97 (1968).

134. *Epperson v. Arkansas,* 393 U.S. 97 (1968), 104.

135. *Epperson v. Arkansas,* 393 U.S. 97 (1968), 107.

136. *Epperson v. Arkansas,* 393 U.S. 97 (1968), 107.

137. *Epperson v. Arkansas,* 393 U.S. 97 (1968), 109.

138. *Epperson v. Arkansas,* 393 U.S. 97 (1968), 109.

139. *Epperson v. Arkansas,* 393 U.S. 97 (1968), 114.

140. *Epperson v. Arkansas,* 393 U.S. 97 (1968), 112.

141. *Epperson v. Arkansas,* 393 U.S. 97 (1968), 114.

142. *Epperson v. Arkansas,* 393 U.S. 97 (1968), 115.

143. *Epperson v. Arkansas,* 393 U.S. 97 (1968), 116.

144. *Arkansas Gazette,* November 13, 1968, 1A.

145. *Arkansas Gazette,* November 13, 1968, 1A.

146. Rozzell interview.

147. *Arkansas Gazette,* November 14, 1968, 6A.

148. *Arkansas Gazette,* November 13, 1968, 1A.

CHAPTER 2

1. For the pro-planter perspective, see J. W. Butts and Dorothy James, "The Underlying Causes of the Elaine Riot of 1919," *Arkansas Historical Quarterly* 20 (Spring 1961): 95–104. For a black perspective, see Walter White, "'Massacring Whites' in Arkansas," *The Nation,* December 6, 1919, 715–16. Other important accounts include Arthur I. Waskow, *From Race Riot to Sit-In, 1919 and the 1960s: A Study in the Connections between Conflict and Violence* (Garden City, NY: Doubleday & Company, 1966); O. A. Rogers, Jr., "The Elaine Race Riots of 1919," *Arkansas Historical Quarterly* 19 (Summer 1960): 142–50; B. Boren McCool, *Union, Reaction, and Riot: A Biography of a Race Riot* (Memphis: Bureau of Social Research, Division of Urban and Regional Studies, Memphis State University, June 1970), 23–52; Richard C. Cortner, *A Mob Intent on Death: The NAACP and the Arkansas Riot Cases* (Middletown, CT: Wesleyan University Press, 1988); Nan Elizabeth Woodruff, "African American Struggles for Citizenship in the Arkansas and Mississippi Deltas in the Age of Jim Crow," *Radical History Review* 55 (1993): 33–51; and Carl H. Moneyhon, *Arkansas and the New South: 1874–1929* (Fayetteville: University of Arkansas Press, 1997), 107–8.

2. Francis I. Gwaltney, *The Quicksand Years* (London: Seker & Warburg, 1965).

3. Waskow, *From Race Riot to Sit-In,* 143–44; Cortner, *Mob Intent on Death,* 25–26.

4. White, "'Massacring Whites in Arkansas,'" 715–16.

5. McCool, *Union, Reaction, and Riot,* 23–52. There is considerable controversy over the number of blacks killed, with some contemporaries and historians concluding that hundreds may have died. In an eccentric book L. S. Dunaway argued 856 blacks were killed. Dunaway, *What a Preacher Saw Through a Key-Hole in Arkansas* (Little Rock: Parke-Harper Publishing Company, 1925), 102.

6. Butts and James, "The Underlying Causes," 95–104. The mysterious black detectives from Chicago allegedly reported that certain planters were slated to be killed. Sebastian Straub, a prominent merchant in Helena who had many plantation

accounts, was said to have hired at least one of these detectives. His son, Charles W. Straub, was interviewed by Butts and James in October 1960, and claimed to have been with his father when he met with the black detective prior to the riot and claimed to have seen the detective's report. These reports, however, were never entered as evidence and their existence cannot be confirmed. If they did exist, the reports would raise interesting questions about the activities and motivations of these black detectives and their willingness to play to the fears of white leaders in Phillips County. Ibid., 97–98. See also Cortner, *Mob Intent on Death*, 7.

7. Rogers, "The Elaine Race Riots," 142–47.

8. McCool seems also to have based his narrative of the riot on trial testimony later shown to be unreliable.

9. Levon Helm with Stephen Davis, *This Wheel's on Fire: Levon Helm and the Story of the Band* (New York: William Morrow and Company, 1993), 15. The Helms were farm renters. Helm indicates that his maternal grandfather Wheeler Wilson, who alternated between the life of a logger and a farmer, was opposed to Ku Klux Klan activity, and Helm credits him (and his mother) with "saving me from having to wear that whole damn load of racism that a lot of people had to carry." Ibid., 17.

10. John Elvis Miller, interview by Walter Brown, Bruce Parnham, and Samuel A. Sizer, Fort Smith, Arkansas, March 18, 1976, transcript pp. 16, 21, MC 279, Special Collections Division, University of Arkansas Libraries, Fayetteville.

11. For Thomas's efforts to investigate the causes of the riot, see A. C. Miller [a prominent Methodist preacher and editor and manager of the *Arkansas Methodist*] to D. Y. Thomas, December 23, 1919; a letter dated January 1, 1920 from D. Y. Thomas with a marginal note saying "copy of a letter sent to two people at Helena," which asks for information; E. M. Allen [a prominent Helena businessman, on "Business Men's League" stationery] to Thomas, January 4, 1920; Greenfield Quarles [a Helena attorney] to Thomas, January 5, 1920; U. S. Bratton to Thomas, March 1, 1920; Bratton to Thomas, September 15, 1921; Letter to Editor of the *New York Times,* "About Race Troubles in Arkansas," February 9, 1920. All in David Y. Thomas Papers, Series 1, Box 1, Folder 2, Special Collections Division, University of Arkansas Libraries, Fayetteville. For his book, see D. Y. Thomas, *Arkansas and Its People: A History, 1541–1930* (New York: The American Historical Society, Inc., 1930), 1:294.

12. Butts and James, "The Underlying Causes," 97. On the unreliability of the evidence presented against the Elaine defendants, see Cortner, *Mob Intent on Death*, 123–25.

13. The Smitty and Jones affidavits are themselves problematic, however. As Cortner reveals, the NAACP knew these witnesses were vulnerable, partly because both men took money from the NAACP and from Scipio Jones, the black attorney from Arkansas who assisted in the appeals, and partly because they were both afraid to return to the state if a new trial were ordered. Although the funds extended to them were not in return for their testimony, but rather in recognition of the fact that they could not find work and support their families because they had recanted, the "appearance" of collusion could have materially damaged the case. Despite threats of violence and loss of income, the two men persisted in their revised stories, and, as Waskow suggests, there is more reason to believe them than to suspect them. Waskow, *From Race Riot to Sit-In*, 125–26, 134; Cortner, *Mob Intent on Death*, 167–72.

14. Waskow, *From Race Riot to Sit-In*, 125–26.

15. Cited in *Moore v. Dempsey*, Brief for the Appellants, 12.

16. Cited in *Moore v. Dempsey*, Brief for the Appellants, 12.

17. Miller interview, 15.

18. McCool read the letter to suggest that whites had long "feared a Negro rebellion," and entirely neglected the more direct evidence it contained of a white impulse to attack the black community; McCool, *Union, Reaction, and Riot*, 20; Harry Anderson to C.H. Brough, October 7, 1919, Charles Brough Collection, Series 1, Box 4, Folder 55, Item 87, Special Collections Division, University of Arkansas Libraries, Fayetteville. Sheriff Kitchens was incapacitated by illness at the time of the shootings at the Hoop Spur Church, and Sebastian Straub was acting as sheriff in his place. Kitchens became involved in the events as they unfolded, however, and became a member of the Committee of Seven, made up of prominent white Helena men who investigated the causes of the riot. For the Committee of Seven, see Greenfield Quarles to D. Y. Thomas, January 5, 1920, Thomas Papers; McCool, *Union, Reaction, and Riot*, 22; Cortner, *Mob Intent on Death*, 13.

19. Waskow, *From Race Riot to Sit In*, 128–29.

20. Waskow, *From Race Riot to Sit In*, 125. Butts and James find planters alarmed about the union long before the riot. Butts and James, "The Elaine Riot," 97–98. See also McCool, "Union, Reaction, and Riot," 20, 22.

. 21. Gwaltney's portrait of a divided white community, however, did not move much beyond familiar literary representations of Snopes-like crackers and Compson-esque patricians. Gwaltney, *The Quicksand Years*.

22. For a study that recognizes divisions within the black community, see Cortner, *Mob Intent on Death*. To suggest an unusual unity within the white community is by no means to suggest unanimity. There were a number of examples of Phillips County whites warning or otherwise protecting blacks during the riots.

23. For figures on 1880 cotton production, see *Report of the Productions of Agriculture, Tenth Census* (Washington, DC: GPO, 1883), XIII, 214. For figures on 1920 cotton production, see *Fourteenth Census of the United States, 1920, Agriculture*, Vol. VI, Part 2, Table 4, 580 (Washington, DC: GPO, 1922); For figures on percentage of farm owners in 1880, see *Miscellaneous Documents of the House of Representatives* (Washington D.C.: GPO, 1896), Table 94, 248. For figures on percentage of farm owners in 1920, see *Fourteenth Census, Agriculture*, Vol. IV, Table 1, 565.

24. Bessie Ferguson, "The Elaine Race Riot" (Master's thesis, George Peabody College for Teachers, 1927), 22.

25. *Helena World*, February 23, 1898.

26. For a lengthier discussion of the Cross and Poinsett County cases, see Jeannie Whayne, *A New Plantation South: Land, Labor, and Federal Favor in Twentieth-Century Arkansas* (Charlottesville: University Press of Virginia, 1996), 47–54. For whitecapping elsewhere, see, for example, William F. Holmes, "Moonshiners and Whitecaps in Alabama, 1893," *Alabama Review* 34 (January 1981): 31–49; idem, "Moonshining and Collective Violence: Georgia, 1889–1895," *Journal of American History* 67 (December 1980): 588–611; idem, "Whitecapping: Agrarian Violence in Mississippi, 1902–1906", *Journal of Southern History* 35 (1969): 165–85; idem, "Whitecapping in Georgia: Carroll and Houston Counties, 1893," *Georgia Historical Quarterly* 64 (1980): 388–404; idem, "Whitecapping in Mississippi: Agrarian Violence in the Populist Era," *Mid-America* 55 (1973): 134–48.

27. In 1900 these were Mooney and Searcy townships. Between 1910 and 1920, Tappan township was carved out of both. Elaine was within Tappan township.

Manuscript Census of Population, Phillips County, AR, 1900 and 1920. For a note on the creation of Tappan township, see *Fourteenth Census of the United States Taken in the Year 1920, Volume I* (Washington, DC: GPO, 1921), 849.

28. Race relations, it should be noted, remained extraordinarily complicated in these turbulent delta communities. Whites and blacks, particularly single males, might interact with one another in honkytonks at the same time as nightriders were attacking black sharecroppers. See Whayne, *A New Plantation South*, 27–28.

29. This version of events is reported in McCool, *Union, Reaction, and Riot*, 31. McCool is quoting a private interview J. W. Butts had with J. M. Countiss in October 1960.

30. Ferguson, "The Elaine Race Riot," 55. Although Ferguson reported that Dr. Johnston's reputation was not spotless—he was said to have been charged with breaking the prohibition statutes and with "other minor offenses"—she concluded that "if only one made the attempt [to escape] it was surely cowardice to kill three other persons who were bound and possessed no means of defense." On Johnston's police record, Ferguson cites "the records of the police court," in the text, but she does not footnote that cite. In fact, druggists in those years often sold liquor, so there may be some truth to her assertion. As to Ferguson's overall study of the Elaine Race Riot, it is a curious document that reveals some understanding of the economic exploitation visited upon black people, but betrays the author's prejudices in declaring that Robert Hill "simply played upon the ignorance and superstition of a child like race." Ibid., 38.

31. Ferguson, "Elaine Race Riot," 54; Ida B. Wells-Barnett, *The Arkansas Race Riot*, (Chicago: Hume Job Print, 1920), 25. Black oral tradition in Phillips County supports the notion that the Johnstons had innocently been out hunting. See C. Calvin Smith, "Serving the Poorest of the Poor: Black Medical Practitioners in the Arkansas Delta, 1880–1960," *Arkansas Historical Quarterly* 57 (Autumn 1998): 302.

32. Arkansas Gazette, October 4, 1919, as quoted in Cortner, *Mob Intent on Death*, 9.

33. Nor was any cache of guns offered in evidence against the twelve black men convicted of murder, though they were similarly reported in the newspapers to have had a stockpile of arms. Miller interview, 22.

34. For a view critical of the black middle class and its failure to address the problems of poor blacks, see Fon Gordon, *Caste and Class: The Black Experience in Arkansas, 1880–1920* (Athens: University of Georgia Press, 1995). For more sympathetic views, see John William Graves, *Town and Country: Race Relations in an Urban-Rural Context, Arkansas, 1865–1905* (Fayetteville: University of Arkansas Press, 1990); Tom Dillard, "Scipio A. Jones," *Arkansas Historical Quarterly* 31 (Autumn 1972): 201–19; idem, "Golden Prospects and Fraternal Amenities: Mifflin W. Gibbs's Arkansas Years," *Arkansas Historical Quarterly* 35 (Winter 1976): 307–33; idem, "To the Back of the Elephant: Racial Conflict in the Arkansas Republican Party," *Arkansas Historical Quarterly* 33 (Spring 1974): 3–15.

35. E. M. Allen to D. Y. Thomas, January 4, 1920, Thomas Papers.

36. E. M. Allen to D. Y. Thomas, January 21, 1920; and E. M. Allen to D. Y. Thomas, January 4, 1920, Thomas Papers, Series 1, Box 1, Folder 2. In the January 21, 1920 letter, Allen indicated that Morris had been involved in organizing a cooks' union of Negro women "to demand that their mistresses use the title of Miss or Mrs. in addressing them." This seems a highly unlikely venture for the distinguished Dr. Morris. A. C. Miller, a white preacher, claimed that Morris had "somewhat discredited

himself by clamoring for repeal of separate coach law." A. C. Miller to D. Y. Thomas, December 23, 1919, Thomas Papers. For biographical information on Morris, see Jack Salzman, David Lionel Smith, and Cornel West, *Encyclopedia of African-American Culture and History* (New York: MacMillian, 1996), 1885–86. See also *The Booker T. Washington Papers*, Volume 7, (Urbana: University of Illinois Press, 1972), 387.

37. See Morris quoted in Waskow, *From Race Riot to Sit-In*, 146. On black assurances to the white community, see Cortner, *Mob Intent on Death*, 45–46.

38. Solidarity within the black community might also have been enhanced in these years by the progress of the "lily white" faction in the state Republican Party. The "lily whites" shunned cross-racial alliances even with elite blacks, further diminishing the latter's opportunities to make common cause with those outside the African American community. See Dillard, "Back of the Elephant;" idem, "Scipio Jones."

39. Brough's actions and official position on the riot, which was that it was an insurrection and that whites acted reasonably in the face of the threat, have been the subject of some controversy. As his biographer, Foy Lisenby, suggests, this posture was in keeping with his white supremacist ideology but "one might have expected a more empirical attitude from a former professor who had chaired the University Commission on Race Questions." Brough had been on the faculty at the University of Arkansas prior to his election as Governor. Foy Lisenby, *Charles Hillman Brough: A Biography* (Fayetteville: University of Arkansas Press, 1996), 48, 115.

40. McCool, *Union, Reaction, and Riot*, 27–28

41. Waskow, *From Race Riot to Sit-In*, 129.

42. Waskow, *From Race Riot to Sit In*, 130–31. O. S. Bratton, son of U. S. Bratton, the lawyer retained by the Progressive Farmers Union to sue unscrupulous planters, was arrested while on his way to interview union members interested in the litigation.

43. Anderson to Brough, October 7, 1919, Brough Papers.

44. Manuscript Census of Population, Mooney, Searcy and Tappan townships, Phillips County, 1920.

45. As Nan Woodruff suggests, this indebted those blacks to the planters who had paid their bond and thus tied them ever more firmly to the plantation system. Woodruff, "African American Struggles," 42.

46. Bessie Ferguson has it that Jones was a deputy sheriff. It may be that he was both a deputy sheriff and a special agent for the railroad. Ferguson, "The Elaine Race Riot," 46.

47. *Moore v. Dempsey*, 261 U.S. 86 (1923), 546. McReynolds used this language in his dissent from the Court's ruling overturning the convictions of six of the black defendants. Interestingly, Butts and James quote McReynolds without indicating that his was the one dissenting opinion on the court.

48. Bratton, referring to the case at hand, hoped to see the party "landed in the penitentiary, where he belongs." The accused lived in Wilmot, Arkansas and was later convicted in Texas. U. S. Bratton to Henry Terrell, US Attorney, San Antonio, Texas, July 5, 1905, Justice Department Papers, Record Group 60, National Archives and Records Administration, Washington, DC.

49. Bratton to Thomas, Sept. 15, 1921, Thomas Papers.

50. Miller interview, 11. See *Arkansas Code of 1987*, annotated, for a description of laws establishing the landlord's lien on the crop (1868); and the superiority of the landlord's lien (1876, 1878, and 1881), 216–24.

51. Glen T. Barton and J. G. McNealy, "Recent Changes in Farm Labor

Organization in Three Arkansas Plantation Counties," Preliminary Report, University of Arkansas College of Agriculture, Agricultural Experiment Station, Fayetteville, Arkansas, September 1939, 32, Special Collections Division, University of Arkansas Libraries, Fayetteville.

52. Miller interview, 11, 21.

53. US Department of Agriculture, "Farm Tenancy in Arkansas," Bureau of Agricultural Economics in cooperation with the Arkansas Agricultural Experiment Station, (Washington, DC, 1941), 11. Economic historians Roger Ransom and Richard Sutch concluded that credit arrangements were such that the interest rates charged by merchants "ranged from 40 to 70 percent" for the South as whole. Planters who did not themselves have commissaries made agreements with merchants to supply their sharecroppers. Roger L. Ransom and Richard Sutch, *One Kind of Freedom: The Economic Consequences of Emancipation* (New York: Cambridge University Press, 1977), 130.

54. Ferguson, "The Elaine Race Riot," 17.

55. George P. Rawick, *The American Slave: A Composite Autobiography* (Westport, CT: Greenwood Publishing, 1972), Vol. 9, pt. 4, 248.

56. US Industrial Commission, *Industrial Commission Report on Agriculture and Agricultural Labor* (Washington, DC: GPO, 1901), xviii.

57. Bratton to D. Y. Thomas, September 15, 1921, Thomas Papers.

58. Bratton to D. Y. Thomas. See, more generally, Pete Daniel, *Shadow of Slavery: Peonage in the South, 1901–1969* (Urbana: University of Illinois Press, 1972).

59. *Helena World*, July 21, 1916, cited in Susan E. C. Huntsman, "Race Relations in Phillips County, 1895–1920" (Unpublished honor's thesis, University of Arkansas, Fayetteville, 1996), 16.

60. Rogers, "The Elaine Race Riots," 144.

61. The black literacy rate had been 64.6% in 1900. The white rate was far higher—91.9% in 1900 and 94.7% in 1920. Manuscript Census of Population, Searcy and Mooney townships, Philips County, 1900; Searcy, Mooney, and Tappan townships, Phillips County, 1920.

62. *Helena World*, October 12, 1898, cited in Huntsman, "Race Relations in Phillips County," 11–12.

63. *Helena World*, October 12, 1898, cited in Huntsman, "Race Relations in Phillips County,", 13–14. For disputes between tenants and planters elsewhere in the Arkansas delta, see Whayne *A New Plantation South*, 55–59.

64. "Memorandum on Tenancy in the Southwestern States (Extracts from the Final Report of the United States Industrial Relations, 1916)" NAACP MSS., cited in Waskow, *From Race Riot to Sit-In*, 122.

65. Butts and James "The Underlying Causes," 104.

66. U. S. Bratton, who was a native Arkansan, was forced to leave the state with his family after a series of threats. He joined another son, Guy Bratton, who was practicing law in Detroit, Michigan. U. S. worked for a time as attorney for a labor union, the United Brotherhood of Maintenance-of-Way Employes [sic] and Railway Shop Laborers. During the crisis, while O. S. Bratton was still jailed in Helena, friends advised the senior Bratton to refrain from traveling to Phillips County because he would be "shot down without any ceremony" if he did. His son Guy traveled to Helena to confer with local officials concerning his brother's release, and apparently barely escaped a plot against his life. U. S. Bratton to D. Y. Thomas, September 15,

1921, Thomas Papers. U. S. Bratton later became a member of the team of lawyers appealing the convictions of the men sentenced to death.

67. Gwaltney to Alan D. Williams, January 10, 1963, Francis Gwaltney Papers, Special Collections Division, University of Arkansas Libraries, Fayetteville.

68. See Alan D. Williams [Little, Brown & Company] to John Schaffner [Gwaltney's literary agent at the time], January 4, 1963, Box 17, File 20; and Margaret Cousins [Doubleday & Company, Inc.] to John Schaffner, August 15, 1963, Box 17, File 20, Gwaltney Papers. Cousins's blistering critique of the novel greatly angered Gwaltney, and his friend, Norman Mailer, wrote to caution him against trying to write while angry and to express an interest in seeing the rejected manuscript. Norman Mailer to Francis Irby Gwaltney, December 20, 1963, Gwaltney-Mailer Correspondence, Special Collections Division, University of Arkansas Libraries, Fayetteville. McGraw-Hill also rejected the manuscript; Harold Scharlatt to John Schaffner, December 16, 1963, Box 17, File 20, Gwaltney Papers.

69. He began negotiating with Seger & Warburg in London in 1964. See Schaffner to Gwaltney, March 12, 1964, Box 17, File 20, Gwaltney Papers. According to Gwaltney in a letter to Mailer, by December 1965, the book "has received two bad reviews and a batch of glowing ones. *Punch* and the *Times* were especially nice." Gwaltney to Mailer, November 2, 1965, Gwaltney-Mailer Correspondence.

70. Stu Robinson to Francis Gwaltney, October 8, 1965, Box 17, File 21, Gwaltney Papers.

CHAPTER 3

1. *Arkansas Gazette* (Little Rock), June 14, 1946.

2. For treatments of the GI Revolt, see, for example, Dee Brown, *The American Spa: Hot Springs* (Little Rock: Rose, 1982), 88; T. Harri Baker and Jane Browning, *An Arkansas History for Young People* (Fayetteville: University of Arkansas Press, 1991), 336; Michael B. Dougan, *Arkansas Odyssey: The Saga of Arkansas from Prehistoric Times to Present* (Little Rock: Rose, 1994), 480; Diane D. Blair, *Arkansas Politics and Government: Do the People Rule?* (Lincoln: University of Nebraska Press, 1988), 17, 50.

3. Jim Lester, *A Man for Arkansas: Sid McMath and the Southern Reform Tradition* (Little Rock: Rose, 1976), 19–33; V. O. Key, *Southern Politics in State and Nation* (New York: Knopf, 1949), 201–4.

4. Shirley Abbott, *The Bookmaker's Daughter: A Memory Unbound* (New York: Ticknor and Fields, 1991), 206–15.

5. Brown, *American Spa*, 50–60.

6. Inez E. Cline and Fred Mark Palmer, "Belvedere," *The Record: Garland County Historical Society* 33 (1992): 2–5.

7. Lester, *McMath*, 22.

8. Abbott, *Bookmaker's Daughter*, 206–215.

9. Brown, *American Spa*, 87–88.

10. Lester, *McMath*, 22; *Arkansas Gazette*, October 11, 1947.

11. Lester, *McMath*, 22.

12. Key, *Southern Politics in State and Nation*, 593–94.

13. Lester, *McMath*, 22–23.

14. Sid McMath, interview with author, Little Rock, Arkansas, October 16, 1996.

15. McMath, interview.

16. Richard W. Hobbs, "GI Regime," *The Record: Garland County Historical Society* 36 (1995): 129–30

17. Richard Hobbs, telephone interview with author, June 25, 1997.

18. Lester, *McMath*, 23–24.

19. Hot Springs *Sentinel Record*, April 28, 1946.

20. Q. Byrum Hurst, interview with author, Hot Springs, Arkansas, October 17, 1996.

21. *Sentinel Record*, April 28, 1946.

22. *Arkansas Gazette*, April 28, 1946.

23. *Sentinel Record*, June 30, 1946.

24. A contemporary of the GIs, preeminent political scientist V. O. Key, emphasized in 1949 that the broader GI effort in the state was not an attempt to introduce new issues into Arkansas politics but was instead simply an effort to gain honest elections. Key found nothing in the veterans' political doctrines or philosophies that substantiated the charges of radicalism leveled against them by their opponents. Admittedly, free and honest elections in some Arkansas counties would have been a radical change, Key wrote, noting that election fraud in Arkansas was surpassed only by that in Tennessee. Key, *Southern Politics in State and Nation*, 184–203, 443.

25. Hurst, interview; McMath, interview.

26. Hurst, interview; Dallas Herndon, *Annals of Arkansas* (Hopkinsville, KY: Historical Record Association, 1947), 1422–24.

27. McMath, interview.

28. Hurst, interview.

29. McMath, interview.

30. Mark Palmer, interview with author, Hot Springs, Ark., January 29, 1997

31. Hurst, interview.

32. Lester, *McMath*, 26.

33. *Arkansas Gazette*, July 5, 1946.

34. Lester, *McMath*, 28.

35. Abbott, *Bookmaker's Daughter*, 209.

36. *Arkansas Democrat*, July 8, 1946.

37. *Arkansas Democrat*, July 7, 1946.

38. Hobbs, "GI Regime"; Hobbs, interview. Hobbs remembers that campaign workers Birdie Fulton and Walter McLavey were the men robbed by Spears, but the *Arkansas Democrat* identified Livingston and Fulton as the victims.

39. *Arkansas Gazette*, July 10, 1946.

40. *Arkansas Gazette*, July 10–11, 1946; *Arkansas Democrat*, July 9, 1946.

41. Lester, *McMath*, 27–28.

42. *Arkansas Democrat*, July 8, 1946; Lester, *McMath*, 28.

43. *Arkansas Democrat*, July 12, 1946.

44. *Arkansas Democrat.*, July 15, 1946.

45. *Arkansas Gazette*, August 1, 1948.

46. *Arkansas Democrat*, July 30, 1946.

47. *Arkansas Gazette*, August 1, 1946.

48. James Holt, interview with author, Hot Springs, Arkansas, June 12, 1997.

49. Lester, *McMath*, 29.

50. *Arkansas Democrat*, July 31, 1946.

51. *Arkansas Gazette*, August 1, 1946.

52. *Arkansas Gazette*, August 1, 1946.

53. *Arkansas Gazette*, August 1, 1946; November 6, 1946.

54. *Arkansas Gazette*, November 7, 1946.

55. *Arkansas Gazette*, November 6, 1946.

56. *Arkansas Gazette*, November 7, 1946.

57. *Arkansas Gazette*, November 7, 1946.

58. *Arkansas Gazette*, November 6, 1946.

59. *Arkansas Gazette*, April 2, 1947.

60. *Arkansas Gazette*, March 18, 1947.

61. *Arkansas Gazette*, March 18, 1947; Abbott, *Bookmaker's Daughter*, 229.

62. *Sentinel Record*, October 11, 1947; *Arkansas Gazette*, November 12, 1947.

63. *Arkansas Gazette*, November 12, 1947.

64. *Sentinel Record*, November 21, 1948; *Arkansas Gazette*, November 20, 1947.

65. Abbott, *Bookmaker's Daughter*, 216.

66. *Arkansas Gazette*, October 1, 1947.

67. Lester, *McMath*, 37–42.

68. Kelly Bryant, *Historical Report of the Secretary of State: Arkansas* (n.p.: State of Arkansas, 1968), 484.

69. Hobbs, interview; Holt, interview.

70. Hobbs, interview; Hurst, interview. Stories of stuffed ballot boxes and fraudulent poll tax receipts were common in Garland County, as they were in other Arkansas counties, right up to 1965, when the poll tax was removed. Despite rumors, however, there is no proof that any GIs other than Ray Owen were directly involved.

71. Holt, Hurst, McMath, interviews.

72. *Arkansas Gazette*, December 8, 1948.

73. *Sentinel Record*, July 29, 1948.

74. Hurst, interview; Hobbs, interview.

75. Holt, interview; interview by author with retired casino owner who wished to remain unidentified, November 3, 1996. Information provided by this source was corroborated by other sources.

76. *Arkansas Gazette*, January 30, 1948.

77. Hot Springs city jail docket, 1946–1947, Garland County Historical Society. There were no gambling arrests entered after the date of July 5, 1947, in this ledger. No ledgers for later years are available.

78. *Arkansas Gazette*, January 16, 1948.

79. Holt, interview; Hurst, interview; anonymous casino owner, interview.

80. Roy Reed, *Faubus: The Life and Times of an American Prodigal* (Fayetteville: University of Arkansas Press, 1997), 318–19.

81. Hurst, interview.

82. Hurst, interview.

CHAPTER 4

1. The descriptive information in this section is based on two surveys taken in 1968 and 1970, and US Census material. Both surveys were taken in selected precincts according to current demographic and political information. Random samples were then taken in each precinct of registered voters. All surveying was conducted through personal interviews. The 1968 survey was taken in November, immediately after the

general election and contained over 3200 samples; the 1970 survey was taken the month before the November general election and 2500 persons were interviewed.

2. It is highly unusual for more votes to be cast in the race for governor than in the presidential contest. Only 609,593 votes were counted in the Humphrey-Nixon-Wallace election. The reason for the discrepancy was an error in reporting Jefferson County results by the Jefferson County Election Commission. Some 10,000 votes were somewhere omitted in the presidential race.

CHAPTER 5

1. On the 2008 and 2012 presidential elections in Arkansas, see: Jay Barth, Janine A. Parry, and Todd Shields, "Arkansas: He's Not One of (Most of) Us," in *A Paler Shade of Red: The 2008 Presidential Election in the South*, eds. Branwell DuBose Kapeluck, Laurence W. Moreland, and Robert P. Steed, (Fayetteville: University of Arkansas Press, 2009); and Janine A. Parry and Jay Barth, "Arkansas: Another Anti-Obama Aftershock," in *Second Verse, Same as the First: The 2012 Presidential Election in the South*, eds. Scott E. Buchanan and Branwell DuBose Kapeluck, (Fayetteville: University of Arkansas Press, 2014).

2. Frank E. Lockwood, "3 Back Fiorina in a State Less Huckabee's," *Arkansas Democrat-Gazette*, November 17, 2015.

3. Lockwood, "3 Back Fiorina."

4. Erica Sweeney, "Recap: Trump Headlines Reagan Rockefeller Dinner," *Arkansas Money & Politics,* https://goo.gl/65fLkZ (accessed July 2015).

5. Andrew DeMillo, "Arkansas Up for Grabs After Huckabee Exit," *Associated Press*, February 7, 2016.

6. Benjamin Hardy, "Night at the Circus," *Arkansas Times*, February 11, 2016.

7. John Moritz, "Clinton Accuser Paula Jones Attends Little Rock Trump Rally," *Arkansas Democrat-Gazette*, February 5, 2016.

8. Jay Barth, "Arkansas's Moment," *Arkansas Times*, February 25, 2016.

9. "Arkansas Gov. Asa Hutchinson: Donald Trump's `Words Are Frightening,'" *All Things Considered, National Public Radio*, February 24, 2016, https://goo.gl/ Mzz9IB; John Brummett, "All Trumped Up," *Talk Business & Politics*, May/June 2016, 54–61. And the new participants were many . . . more than 630,000 voters participated in that party primary, nearly 100,000 more than any recent Arkansas primary. See Table 1.

10. Arkansas made an earlier bid to increase its significance in the nominating process in 2008, moving its primary from May to February. Participation levels in the state nearly doubled that of previous years. This also proved significant because it separated voters' national partisan preferences from the overwhelming number of local contests in which Republican candidates had not, to date, appeared or were not competitive. The resulting opportunity for voter targeting undoubtedly played a role in the party's growth since that time.

11. For a discussion of turnout patterns in Arkansas primary elections, see Diane D. Blair and Jay Barth, *Arkansas Politics and Government: Do the People Rule?*, Second Edition (Lincoln: University of Nebraska Press, 2005), 104–6.

12. Ara Janak, "Clinton Addresses Arkansas Democrats in NLR," *Arkansas Democrat-Gazette*, July 17, 2015.

13. Brian Fanney, "Clinton Touts State to LR Crowd," *Arkansas Democrat-Gazette,* September 22, 2015.

14. "O'Malley to Speak at Two LR Events," *Arkansas Democrat-Gazette,* December 4, 2015; Brian Fanney, "Candidate O'Malley's College Stop Draws Few," *Arkansas Democrat-Gazette,* December 5, 2015.

15. Arkansas joined several states in a move away from headlining status for Thomas Jefferson and Andrew Jackson, party founders with pasts incommensurate of the party's current values. See Andrew DeMillo, "Arkansas Democrats Dropping Jefferson, Jackson from Dinner," *Associated Press,* May 26, 2016, https://goo.gl/nhX4B3.

16. Steve Brawner, "Clinton: Democrats want more perfect union, while GOP Divisive," *Talk Business and Politics,* July 16, 2016, https://goo.gl/dpPofo.

17. Andrew DeMillo, "Bill Clinton Says Wife Can Bridge Partisan Divide," *Associated Press,* July 16, 2016; Jay Barth, "Bill Clinton Was Right," *Arkansas Times,* November 17, 2016.

18. Frank E. Lockwood, "In LR, Kaine Vows Fight for State in November," *Arkansas Democrat-Gazette,* August 24, 2016.

19. See "Full Text: Bill Clinton's DNC Speech," July 28, 2016, https://goo.gl/05W3tz.

20. Michelle Gorman, "Arkansas Delegates Cheer Two Old Friends, the Clintons, During DNC," *Newsweek,* July 28, 2016, https://goo.gl/mTMONx.

21. Jay Barth, "Hillary in Arkansas," *Arkansas Times,* November 3, 2016.

22. Glenn Kessler, "Fact Checker: The Facts about Hillary Clinton and the Kathy Shelton rape case," *The Washington Post,* October 11 2016, https://goo.gl/orgRuk.

23. Bill Bowden, "Reed Says Laugh Didn't Target Girl," *Arkansas Democrat-Gazette,* October 12, 2016.

24. Frank E. Lockwood, "Hutchinson, Rutledge Rip Clinton in Speeches at GOP Convention," *Arkansas Democrat-Gazette,* July 20, 2016.

25. Frank E. Lockwood, "2 Arkansans Keep Clinton's A-List Supporters Visible, On Message," *Arkansas Democrat-Gazette,* September 28, 2016; Matt Flegenheimer, "Handling Cows by Day, Ever-Growing Clinton Rallies by Night," *New York Times,* October 12, 2016.

26. Jay Barth, "Hillary in Arkansas," *Arkansas Times,* November 3, 2016.

27. Frank E. Lockwood, "State Donations Favored Clinton," *Arkansas Democrat-Gazette,* December 11, 2016.

28. Max Brantley, "Arkansas Poultry Magnate Backs Trump PAC with $2 Million," *Arkansas Blog,* October 16, 2016, https://goo.gl/9oIVob.

29. See David Leip's Election Atlas at https://goo.gl/kUci7Y.

30. Comparative congressional district data available is available here: https://goo.gl/RhHlT8.

31. Diane D. Blair, *Arkansas Politics and Government: Do the People Rule* (Lincoln: University of Nebraska Press, 1988)

32. Barth, Parry, and Shields, "Arkansas: He's Not One of (Most of) Us" ; Parry and Barth, "Arkansas: Another Anti-Obama Aftershock" .

33. Steven Shepard, "Exit polls will skip 22 states this year," *Politico,* November 7, 2016, accessed January 8, 2016, https://goo.gl/FKg5ZQ.

34. See details for the Arkansas Poll at https://goo.gl/SyThN.

35. See the Arkansas Poll, 2016, https://goo.gl/DzpIrN.

36. Allan Smith, "A Senate Candidate Provided a Blueprint for Democrats to Use Donald Trump in Their Attacks," *Business Insider*, May 11, 2016.

CHAPTER 6

1. Lawrence Bobo and Gilliam Franklin Jr., "Race, Socio-political Participation and Black Empowerment," *American Political Science Review* 84 (1990): 377–93; Michael W. Combs, John R. Hibbing, and Susan Welch, "Black Constituents and Congressional Roll Call Votes," *Western Political Quarterly* 37 (1984): 427–34; Arthur B. Levy and Susan Stoudinger, "Sources of Voting Cues for the Congressional Black Caucus," *Journal of Black Studies* 7 (1976): 29–45; Neil Pinney and George Serra, "The Congressional Black Caucus and Vote Cohesion: Placing the Caucus within House Voting Patterns," *Political Research Quarterly* 52 (1999): 583–608; Robert Singh, *The Congressional Black Caucus: Racial Politics in the L.I.S. Congress* (Thousand Oaks, CA: Sage, 1998); Carol M. Swain, *Black Faces, Black Interests: The Representation of African-Americans in Congress* (Cambridge: Harvard University Press, 1993); Katherine Tate, "Black Political Participation In the 1984 and 1988 Presidential Elections," *The American Political Science Review* 85 (1991): 1158–76; Kenny J. Whitby, *The Color of Representation: Congressional Behavior and Black Interests* (Ann Arbor: University of Michigan Press, 1997).

2. Kathleen A. Bratton, "The Effect of Legislative Diversity Agenda Detting: Evidence from Six State Legislatures," *American Politics Research* 30 (2002): 115–42; Kathleen A. Bratton and Kerryl L. Haynie, "Agenda Setting and Legislative Success in State Legislatures: The Effects of Gender and Race," *The Journal of Politics* 61 (1999): 658–79; Charles E. Menifield, "Black Political Life in the Missouri General Assembly," *Journal of Black Studies* 31 (2000): 20–38; Bryron D'Andra Orey, "Black Legislative Politics in Mississippi," *Journal of Black Studies* 30 (2000): 791–814.

3. Diane Blair, *Arkansas Politics and Government: Do the People Rule?* (Lincoln: University of Nebraska Press, 1988), 4.

4. Blair, *Arkansas Politics and Government*, 4.

5. We also included one special session—called in the fall of 1983 to address Gov. Bill Clinton's education reform plan—because of its lasting significance in the state's politics and policy.

6. News articles were inconsistent in the identification of bill (and act) numbers for both chambers. Thus, before examining roll call votes, we first double-checked and/or supplemented the identification of all measures in the *Arkansas Legislative Digest* for each legislative session. Then, we turned to the house and senate journals of the Arkansas General Assembly to record the votes of individual members.

7. A 1973 study by the Voter Education Project, however, reported that Arkansas trailed only Alabama in the number of African Americans elected to public office at all levels (P. Strickland, "State Second in Electing Black Officials," *Arkansas Gazette*, April 3, 1987, 18A). It retained its position, bested only by Mississippi, in the project's 1974 report and the Arkansas Black Political Caucus hosted the second National Black Political Convention that year ("Arkansas Ranks 2d in South in Elected Black Officials," *Arkansas Gazette*, March 4, 1974, 5A; "Blacks Hope LR Sessions Hardworking," *Arkansas Gazette*, March 11, 1974, 7A).

8. "Jewell Defeats Sparks to Win Senate Race," *Arkansas Gazette*, November 8, 1972, 10A.

9. Townsend was nominated in 1969 by Gov. Winthrop Rockefeller to serve on the State Board of Education; the state senate refused to confirm the appointment, however ("Two Blacks, Johnston Win in District Three," *Arkansas Gazette* November 8, 1972, 11A).

10. "Jewell Defeats Sparks to Win Senate Race.

11. Jim Ranchino, "The Arkansan of the '70s: The Good Ole Boy Ain't Whut He Used to Be," *Arkansas Times* 4, no. 1 (September 1977): 40–43.

12. Jeffers v. Clinton 730 F. Supp. 196 (E.D. Ark. 1989).

13. Tony Moser, "Arkansas Case Lies at Heart of Fight Over Redistricting," *Arkansas Democrat-Gazette*, February 20, 1995, 1A.

14. Mark Oswald, "Blacks Must Stand Up for Rights to Achieve Success, Lawyer Says," *Arkansas Gazette*, September 22, 1990, 4A.

15. Elizabeth Caldwell and Rachel O'Neal, "Say Farewells' at Legislature," *Arkansas Democrat-Gazette*, August 25, 1994b, 8A; Noel Oman, "Voter Outrage at Jewell Helped Push Walker Over Top," *Arkansas Democrat Gazette*, May 29, 1994, retrieved December 22, 2002, from http://web.lexis-nexis.com/universe.

16. Seth Blomeley, "Race Emerges as Issue for Democrats Vying in Redrawn LR Senate District," *Arkansas Democrat-Gazette*, May 14, 2002b, 1B.

17. Rachel O'Neal, "Seven Freshman Senators Take Oath," *Arkansas Democrat-Gazette*, January 10, 1995, 5B.

18. Arkansas Legislative Black Caucus, "Official Web Site, History," June 3, 2002, http://www.arklegblackcaucus.org.

19. Arkansas Legislative Black Caucus, "Official Web Site, History."

20. Doug Thompson, "Tax Cuts Not High on List for Legislators This Year," *Arkansas Democrat-Gazette*, January 9, 2001, 1A.

21. Tracy Steele, telephone interview, June 3, 2002.

22. Democratic Party of Arkansas, "Official Web Site, History," June 7, 2002, http://www.arkdems.org.

23. The caucus also sponsors an internship opportunity for undergraduate students during the legislative session and a scholarship program honoring Dr. William Townsend. A US $500 scholarship is awarded to one student from each district represented by a member of the Arkansas Legislative Black Caucus (Arkansas Legislative Black Caucus, "Official Web Site, History.").

24. Seth Blomeley, "Candidate Criticizes Lawmakers," *Arkansas Democrat-Gazette*, April 5, 2002a, 1B.

25. John V. Pennington, "Legislative Black Caucus Meeting Draws Competitors in Senate Race," *Sentinel-Record*, August 3, 2002, 1B.

26. Kern Alexander and James Hale, "Educational Equity, Improving School Finance in Arkansas," Report to the Advisory Committee of the Special School Formula Project of the Joint Interim Committee on Education, Little Rock, General Assembly, 1978.

27. *Dupree v. Alma School District*, 279 Ark. 340, 651 S.W.2d 90 (1983).

28. David Osborne, *Laboratories of Democracy: A New Breed of Governor Creates Models for National Growth* (Boston: Harvard Business School Press, 1990).

29. Long-time observer of Arkansas politics Diane Blair commented that

"Teachers felt like they were being bit by their own dog" when the Clintons backed teacher testing in exchange for the rest of the education reform package (Osborne, *Laboratories of Democracy,* 94).

30. Bob Wells, "Black Caucus Listens to Clinton: Pay Plan, Tax, Tests Opposed," *Arkansas Gazette*, October 2, 1983, 4A.

31. Wells, "Black Caucus Listens to Clinton," 4A.

32. Wells, "Black Caucus Listens to Clinton," 4A.

33. Wells, "Black Caucus Listens to Clinton,"

34. Irma Hunter Brown, telephone interview, June 5, 2002.

35. Michael Arbanas, "Senate Approves 50% Increase in Retirement Pay; Bill Passes 26–8 with No Debate," *Arkansas Gazette*, February 15, 1991b, retrieved May 20, 2002 from http://web.lexis-nexis.com/universe/printdoc.

36. Irma Hunter Brown, telephone interview, June 5, 2002; John Reed, "School Choice Passes Senate After Tie Vote," *Arkansas Gazette*, March 10, 1989, 11A.

37. Lori McElroy, "Education Bills Fly by Panel in Senate," *Arkansas Gazette,* January 31, 1991, retrieved May 20, 2002 from http://web.lexis-nexis.com/universe.

38. McElroy, "Education Bills Fly by Panel in Senate."

39. Ben McGee, telephone interview, May 25, 2002.

40. David Kern and Noel Oman, "With Day Left, Chambers Split on Condom Ban," *Arkansas Democrat,* March 27, 1991, 13A.

41. Democratic Capitol Bureau, "Compromise on Clinics Sends Assembly Home," *Arkansas Democrat*, March 28, 1991, 1A; David F. Kern, "Brownlee Opposes Condom Ban," *Arkansas Democrat*, March 27, 1991, 1E.

42. Democratic Capitol Bureau, "Compromise on Clinics Sends Assembly Home"; S. Morris, "Session Comes to an End," *Arkansas Gazette,* March 28, 1991b, 1A; "Lawsuit Says Bias Corrupted Primaries," *Arkansas Gazette,* May 24, 2002, 15A.

43. Jocelyn Elders, telephone interview, May 24, 2002.

44. Ben McGee, telephone interview, May 25, 2002.

45. Lisa Ferrell, telephone interview, May 29, 2002.

46. Elizabeth Caldwell and Rachel O'Neal, "Bill Cuts Parental Strings on Police Questioning, Would be OK Without Notice," *Arkansas Democrat-Gazette*, August 18, 1994a, 1A.

47. Irma Hunter Brown, telephone interview, June 5, 2002.

48. A.L. May, "Senate has Long, Full Day of Work," *Arkansas Democrat,* March 18, 1977, 12B.

49. Joan Duffy, "House Rejects School Settlement," *Arkansas Democrat,* March 17, 1989a, 1A; Joan Duffy, "68-day Legislative Session Ends," *Arkansas Democrat*, March 18, 1989b, 1A

50. Knight News Service, "School Case Cost May Hit $59 Million," *Arkansas Gazette,* February 9, 1989, 1A.

51. Joan Duffy, "Struggle Looms as Arkansas House Pass Separate Civil Rights Bills," *Commercial Appeal*, February 27, 1993e, A7.

52. Joan Duffy, "Lack of Action on Civil Rights Bill: Leaves Lewellen Measure in Limbo," *Commercial Appeal*, March 10, 1993c, A8.

53. Joan Duffy, "Competing Bills, Lawmakers may Doom Law on Civil Rights," *Commercial Appeal*, March 25, 1993b, A14.

54. Joan Duffy, "Minority Lawmakers Blast Arkansas Rights Bill," *Commercial Appeal*, March 28, 1993d, B1

55. At the April 8 signing ceremony, Walker praised Lewellen for his role in the "tremendous scuffle to get something substantive done." Lewellen stood on the edge of the crowd, opting not to speak though invited, saying only "It was Bill Walker's day," to a reporter covering the event (Joan Duffy, "Civil Right Law Signed to Cap Ark. Legislature," *Commercial Appeal,* 1993a, A1).

56. Ernest Dumas, "Enterprise Zones Aid Firms, not Workers," *Arkansas Gazette,* December 9, 1983.

57. Dumas, "Enterprise Zones," 27A.

58. Irma Hunter Brown, telephone interview, June 5, 2002.

59. Brown, interview.

60. Pam Strickland, "Panel's Approval Moves Sales Tax Closer to Final Test in Full House," *Arkansas Democrat,* April 3, 1987, 1A.

61. "Comments Indicate Job Tough, Not Impossible," *Arkansas Gazette,* March 31, 1987, 9A

62. "Comments Indicate Job Tough, Not Impossible," *Arkansas Gazette* .

63. Grant Tennille, "Necessary Taxes or Highway Robbery? Better Roadways Carry Divisive Price," *Arkansas Democrat-Gazette,* March 20, 1995, 1A.

64. Joe Stumpe, "House Passes Senate Redistricting Plan," *Arkansas Democrat,* March 27, 1991, 1A.

65. Michael Arbanas, "5 Redistricting Plans Discussed in Committee," *Arkansas Gazette,* March 12, 1991a, 3G.

66. Ben McGee, telephone interview, May 25, 2002.

67. Mark Oswald, "New District Plan Issued," *Arkansas Gazette,* March 2, 1991b, 2B; Less overtly, Democrats and many journalists also alleged that Representative McGee's motivations were transparently self-interested: A concentration of black voters into one congressional district would be conducive to his national-level political aspirations (Max Brantley, "GOP District Plan has Two Faces," *Arkansas Gazette,* March 14, 1991, 11; Scott Morris, "House Decides to OK 2 Redistricting Plans," *Arkansas Gazette,* March 22, 1991a, 21; Mark Oswald, "Black House Members, GOP Join Forces," *Arkansas Gazette,* March 13, 1991a, 31A.)

68. Mark Oswald and Scott Morris, "House Accepts Plan for districts," *Arkansas Gazette,* March 27, 1991, 3H.

69. Scott Morris, "12 Blacks Ask to Intervene in Redistricting Suit," *Arkansas Gazette,* June 19, 1991c, 6B.

70. Linda Satter, "Lawsuit Says Bias Corrupted Primaries," *Arkansas Democrat-Gazette,* May 24, 2002, p. 15A.

71. Satter, "Lawsuit Says Bias Corrupted Primaries."

72. C.S. Murphy, "Steele's Style Found Favor with Voters, Pundits Say," *Arkansas Democrat-Gazette,* May 23, 2002, retrieved May 24, 2002, from http://web.lexis-nexis.com/universe.

73. Diane D. Blair, *Arkansas Politics and Government: Do the People rule?* (Lincoln: University of Nebraska Press, 1988), especially chapter 9.

74. The redistricting responsibility was handed off to an interim committee for resolution by 2003.

75. Joceyln Elders, telephone interview, May 24, 2002.

76. Ben McGee, telephone interview, May 25, 2002.

77. McGee, interview.

78. For more on the significance of seniority, see Robert Johnston and Mary

Storey, "The Arkansas Senate: An Overview," *Arkansas Political Science Review* 4 (1983): 69–81.

79. Tracy Steele, telephone interview, June 3, 2002.

80. A similar plan was later that year crafted into a statewide initiative, touted by Gov. Mike Huckabee and adopted by voters at the polls. The appropriations bills necessary for its implementation, however, went right back to the state legislature, at which point the Black Caucus negotiated several key concessions. These included the funding of an Addiction Studies Program at the University of Arkansas, Pine Bluff, a 15% set-aside for minority-targeted prevention and cessation initiatives, and more money to a Minority Health Commission. Ibid.

81. Irma Hunter Brown, telephone interview, June 5, 2002.

82. Lisa Ferrell, telephone interview, May 29, 2002.

83. Tracy Steele, telephone interview, June 3, 2002.

84. Such alliances can, and do, take colorful twists as whites battle for black support in southern states. In Louisiana, for example, conservative lawmakers recently attempted to secure African American support for their cause by arguing that Darwin was a racist, and therefore evolution should be excluded from the state's textbooks (Melinda Deslatte, "Louisiana Lawmakers Say Darwin's Ideology Racist," *Oak Ridger,* May 2, 2001, accessed online, June 1, 2002, http://oakridger.com/stories/050201/stt_0502010060.html).

85. Former Representative Brown (2002) cautioned that the advent of term limits made black members newly dependent on the favor of their white colleagues—instead of the seniority many were finally developing by the close of the 1990s—for their election, or selection, to leadership posts. Whether term limits, and the subsequent loss of seniority as the prevailing criterion for legislative power, serves to advantage or disadvantage the Black Caucus members in the long run remains to be seen.

CHAPTER 7

1. Art English and Linda Goss, "Follow the Leader: Leadership Structure in the Arkansas Senate" paper presentation, Little Rock, Arkansas: Annual Meeting of the Arkansas Political Science Association, 1986.

2. Interviews with members and staff of the Arkansas General Assembly were conducted by Brian Weberg of the National Conference of State Legislatures, and Art English of the University of Arkansas at Little Rock, between November of 2001 and May of 2002. The data collected are part of the National Conference of State Legislatures' Joint Term Limits Project.

3. Bill introductions and adoptions from data compiled by the Bureau of Legislative Research of the Arkansas General Assembly.

4. Data collected from Southwestern Bell Legislative Directories and Legislative Digests from the Secretary of the Senate.

5. Art English and Matthew Warriner, "The Transformation of Political Marginals: Quorum Court Evolution in Arkansas" paper presentation, San Antonio, Texas: Annual Meeting of the Southwestern Political Science Association, 1999).

6. Bill Paschall and Associates, "The Arkansas legislature: A 2001 Retrospective" (Little Rock, Arkansas, nd).

7. Data collected from Southwestern Bell Legislative Directories.

CHAPTER 8

1. V. O. Key Jr., *Southern Politics In State and Nation,* (Knoxville: University of Tennessee Press, 1984), 8. Populism was not restricted to the hill country, but, as Key points out, radical politics had a more marked influence in the thin-soiled uplands than in the planter-controlled delta.

2. Bonnie Pace, interview by author, November 9, 1990, Combs, AR.

3. Pace, interview; Orval E. Faubus, interview by author, June 14, 1988, Conway, AR.

4. *Madison County Record* (AR), March 9, 1933, from the Combs news column by "Jimmie Higgins," Sam Faubus's nom de plume, March 16, 1933, article by Arch Cornett.

5. Orval E. Faubus to author, May 28, 1993.

6. Faubus speech to University of Arkansas Young Democrats, April 30, 1993, Fayetteville.

7. Faubus to author, February 11, 1993.

8. Walt W. Rostow, *The Stages of Economic Growth* (Cambridge: Cambridge University Press, 1963), 18.

9. *Arkansas Recorder,* January, 18, 1957, 8.

10. *Arkansas Recorder,* October 19, 1956, 2.

11. Key, *Southern Politics,* 666.

12. Key, *Southern Politics,* 669. For a discussion of the negative influence of race in shaping the black belt's domination of southern politics, see Chapters 1 and 31.

13. Key, *Southern Politics,* 672.

14. US Bureau of the Census, *Seventeenth Census of the United States, 1950,* Vol. 2: *Characteristics of the Population* (Washington, D.C.: GPO, 1952), pt. 4, 65.

15. Faubus, interview with author, November 29, 1993, Arkansas Educational Television Network, Conway, AR, videocassette.

16. Faubus to John Connally, March 27, 1980, Orval Eugene Faubus Papers, Special Collections, Mullins Library, University of Arkansas, hereafter cited as OEF Papers; Faubus to author, May 27, 1994.

17. Faubus to Harry Dent, January, 10, 1973, OEF Papers,

18. Faubus memorandum to staff, October, 11, 1965; OEF Papers,

19. For various perspectives on southern populism and some of its adherents, see the following: W. Scott Morgan, *History of the Wheel and Alliance and the Impending Revolution* (Fort Scott, KS: J. H. Rice & Sons, 1889); Theodore Saloutos, *Farmer Movements in the South 1865-1933* (Berkeley and Los Angeles: University of California Press, 1960); Francis Butler Simkins, *The Tillman Movement in South Carolina* (Durham: Duke University Press, 1926); C. Vann Woodward, *Tom Watson: Agrarian Rebel* (New York: Oxford University Press, 1938); James Turner, "Understanding the Populists," *The Journal of American History* 67 (September 1980): 354-73; Robert C. McMath, Jr. *Populist Vanguard: A History of the Southern Farmers Alliance* (Chapel Hill: University of North Carolina Press, 1975); John D. Hicks, *The Populist Revolt* (Minneapolis: University of Minnesota Press, 1931); Paul Rogin, "Populism," in *The Intellectuals and McCarthyism* (Cambridge: MIT Press, 1967); Bruce Palmer, *Man Over Money: The Southern Populist Critique of American Capitalism* (Chapel Hill: University of North Carolina Press, 1980); Lawrence Goodwyn, *Democratic Promise: The Populist Moment in America* (New York: Oxford University Press, 1976); and Norman Pollack, *The Populist Mind* (Indianapolis: Bobbs-Merrill, 1967).

20. *Madison County Record*, March 9, 1933.

21. *Madison County Record*, March 16, 1933.

22. For various perspectives on the relative radicalism of southwestern Socialists, see Garin Burbank, *When Farmers Voted Red: The Gospel of Socialism in the Oklahoma Countryside, 1910–1924* (Westport, CT: Greenwood Press, 1976); David A. Shannon, *The Socialist Party of America,* (New York: MacMillan, 1955); James R. Green, *Grass-Roots Socialism: Radical Movements in the Southwest 1894–1943* (Baton Rouge: Louisiana State University Press, 1978); and George Gregory Kiser, "The Socialist Party in Arkansas, 1900–1912," Master's thesis, University of Arkansas, 1980.

23. Shannon, *Socialist Party in America,* 3, 35.

24. Kiser, "Socialist Party in Arkansas," 87–88, 110–11.

25. Shannon, *Socialist Party of America,* 266.

CHAPTER 9

1. *Arkansas Democrat*, April 8, 1968.

2. Taylor Branch, *Parting the Waters: America in the King Years, 1954–63* (New York: Simon and Schuster, 1988), 27–29; Peter Collier and David Horowitz, *The Rockefellers: An American Dynasty* (New York: Holt Rinehart and Winston, 1976), 101.

3. Winthrop Rockefeller to Rodman Rockefeller, May 16, 1969, Winthrop Rockefeller Collection, University of Arkansas at Little Rock Archives and Special Collections, University of Arkansas at Little Rock Library (hereafter cited as WR Papers), Record Group III, Box 571, File 3; *New York Times,* September 26, 1946; April 18, 1947.

4. W. Rockefeller to Robert W. Dowling, president, National Urban League, December 24, 1952, Rockefeller Family Archives, Rockefeller Archive Center, North Tarrytown, New York (hereafter cited as Rockefeller Family Archives), Record Group 2, Office of the Messrs. Rockefeller (OMR), National Urban League, Box 40, Folder III.4; memo, David F. Freeman to Dana S. Creel, 27 April 1960, Rockefeller Family Archives, Record Group II, OMR, National Urban League, Box 41, Folder III.43; Rt. Rev. Msgr. James E. O'Connell, President, Urban League of Greater Little Rock to Winthrop Rockefeller, August 14, 1967, WR Papers, Record Group III, Box 84, File 9; *New York Times,* February 16, June 19, 1956.

5. W. Rockefeller to John D. Rockefeller Jr., September 4, 1936, John D. Rockefeller Jr. to Raymond B. Fosdick, president, Rockefeller Foundation, September 17, 1936, Rockefeller Family Archives, Record Group 2, OMR, Rockefeller Boards, Box 26, Folder 261; W. Rockefeller, "A Letter to My Son," 74–78, unpublished manuscript, WR Papers.

6. Oral history interview conducted by the Rockefeller Archive Center with James Hudson, May 1, 1973, at 30 Rockefeller Plaza, New York, New York, Rockefeller Archive Center, Rockefeller Family Tape; Alvin Moscow, *The Rockefeller Inheritance* (Garden City, NY: Doubleday, 1977), 204; *New York Times,* December 6, 1946.

7. *New York Times,* September 5, 1952; January 2, 1949; December 22, 1948; September 26, 1946; (New York) *Amsterdam News,* January 1, 1949.

8. *Arkansas Gazette,* April 13, 23, 1956.

9. *New York Times,* October 6, 1957; *Arkansas Gazette,* October 5, 1957; Robert Sherrill, *Gothic Politics in the Deep South: Stars of the New Confederacy* (New York: Grossman, 1968), 75.

10. Closing the city's high schools shocked the more moderate citizens of Little Rock into action, and when the schools reopened in 1959, all the high schools were integrated on a limited basis. *Arkansas Gazette,* October 3, 5, 1957; Orval Eugene Faubus, *Down from the Hills Two* (Little Rock: Democrat Printing and Lithographing, 1986), 5; Tony Freyer, *The Little Rock Crisis: A Constitutional Interpretation* (Westport, CT: Greenwood Press, 1984), 148; Harry S. Ashmore, *Arkansas: A History* (New York: W. W. Norton, 1978; reprint, 1984), 152, 155.

11. Belden Associates, "A Study of Voter Opinion in Arkansas October 3– October 10, 1964," WR Papers, Record Group IV, Box 73.

12. "Arkansas Republican Party Platform, 1964," WR Papers, Record Group III, Box 1, File 2; "Meet the Press" transcript, May 3, 1964, WR Papers, Record Group IV, Box 47, File 4.

13. "Meet the Press" transcript, May 3, 1964, WR Papers, Record Group IV, Box 47, File 4; "WR Statement Regarding Federal Guidelines," August 30, 1966, WR Papers, Record Group III, Box 30, File 3; *New York Times,* May 4, 1964.

14. Arkansas Governor's Race, 1966, breakdown of vote by counties, WR Papers, Record Group III, Box 174, File 6; *New York Times,* October 26, November 10, 1966; *Arkansas Gazette,* December 13, 1966; *Arkansas Democrat,* December 18, 1966.

15. *Arkansas Gazette,* March 11, 1967.

16. W. Rockefeller to O'Connell, September 14, 1967, WR Papers, Record Group III, Box 116, File 2.

17. John Ward, *The Arkansas Rockefeller* (Baton Rouge: Louisiana State University Press, 1978), 165.

18. Memo, William T. Kelly, chairman, Governor's Council on Human Resources, to W. Rockefeller, April 29, 1968, WR Papers, Box 52, File 2c; memo, Ozell Sutton to officials, civic leaders, and concerned persons, September 13, 1968; memo, Sutton to mayors, city managers, and chiefs of police, September 13, 1968; newsletter, Governor's Council on Human Resources, December 1968, WR Papers, Record Group III, Box 116, File 2.

19. Memo, Sutton to W. Rockefeller, January 6, 1969; memo, Sutton to mayors, city managers and chiefs of police, September 13, 1968; memo, Sutton to officials, civic leaders and concerned persons, September 13, 1968; newsletter, Governor's Council on Human Resources, December 1968, WR Papers, Record Group III, Box 116, File 2; memo, Sutton to W. Rockefeller, November 19, 1968; memo, Sutton to W. Rockefeller, January 16, 1969; James A. Madison, US Department of Justice, to Sutton, March 5, 1969; press release, Governor's Office, July 10, 1969, WR Papers, Record Group III, Box 88, File 11; *Arkansas Democrat,* June 16, 1968; *Arkansas Gazette,* September 18, 1968.

20. Remarks by Odell Pollard, Republican state chairman, to the Urban League of Greater Little Rock, May 12, 1967; "A Public Progress Report on Advancement of the Negro in State Government," Arkansas Republican State Committee, September 1967, WR Papers, Record Group III, Box 43, File 3; *New York Times,* December 5, 1965; *Arkansas Democrat,* December 18, 1966; May 21, 1967.

21. W. A. Hawkins to W. Rockefeller, January 15, 1968, WR Papers, Record Group III, Box 97, File 1; W. Rockefeller to Lt. Gen. Lewis B. Hershey, Selective Service System, June 19, 1968, WR Papers, Record Group III, Box 492, File 3; Hawkins to Hon. Edward M. Kennedy, November 4, 1969, WR Papers, Record Group III, Box 489, File 3.

22. Hawkins to Truman Altenbaumer, December 6, 1968, WR Papers, Record Group III, Box 233, File 2.

23. *Arkansas Gazette,* December 31, 1970; *Arkansas Democrat,* November 11, 1969; January 30, 1970.

24. *Memphis Commercial Appeal,* April 12, 1968; *Arkansas Gazette,* November 12, 1967; August 30, 1969.

25. United Press International wire copy, WR Papers, Record Group III, Box 326, File 2.

26. Hawkins to W. Rockefeller, January 15, 1968, WR Papers, Record Group III, Box 97, File 1.

27. Alfredo Garcia, civil rights coordinator, to Walter Richter, regional director, Office of Economic Opportunity, Austin, Texas, November 11, 1967; Garcia to Richter, April 29, 1968, WR Papers, Record Group III, Box 323, File 3; *Arkansas Democrat,* February 5, 1967.

28. *Arkansas Gazette,* April 10, 12, 16, 1968; *Arkansas Democrat,* April 10, 11, 1968; Rev. C. B. Knox, Rev. Cecil Cone, and Rev. John H. Corbitt to W. Rockefeller, April 12, 1968, WR Papers, Record Group III, Box 86, File 13.

29. *New York Times,* July 25, 1968.

30. *Arkansas Gazette,* August 30, 1969.

31. George T. Smith to W. Rockefeller, April 8, 1968, Arkansas Republican Party Archives, University of Arkansas at Little Rock Archives and Special Collections, University of Arkansas at Little Rock Library, Series II, Box 1 File 11; Ralph D. Scott, Director, Arkansas State Police, to W. Rockefeller, April 8, 1968, WR Papers, Record Group III, Box 86, File 13; telegram, W. Rockefeller to David Lawrence, *U.S. News and World Report,* April 18, 1968, WR Papers, Record Group III, Box 98, File 2a; Cathy Kunzinger Urwin, *Agenda for Reform: Winthrop Rockefeller as Governor of Arkansas, 1967–71* (Fayetteville: University of Arkansas Press, 1991), 106.

32. State of Arkansas, Executive Proclamation, August 10, 1968, WR Papers, Record Group III, Box 337, File 4; Ralph D. Scott to W. Rockefeller, August 12, 1968, WR Papers, Record Group III, Box 579, File 5; *Arkansas Democrat,* August 10, 15, 1968; *Arkansas Gazette,* August 10, 12, 14, 1968.

33. Patricia Washington McGraw, Grif Stockley, and Nudie E. Williams, "We Speak for Ourselves, 1954 and After," in Tom Baskett Jr., ed., *Persistence of the Spirit: The Black Experience in Arkansas* (Little Rock: Arkansas Endowment for the Humanities, 1986), 40–43; *Arkansas Gazette,* March 21, 22, April 8, 1969.

34. *Arkansas Gazette,* April 8, 1969.

35. *Arkansas Gazette,* June 6, 1969.

36. *Arkansas Gazette,* August 11, 1969.

37. "A Special Meeting in the Governor's Conference Room in Regard to the Racial Situation in Forrest City," transcript, August 6, 1969, WR Papers, Record Group III, Box 328, File 1; telegram, W. Rockefeller to Rev. E. A. Williams, August 5, 1969, WR Papers, Record Group III, Box 98, File 2a.

38. *Arkansas Gazette,* August 20, 1969. The march was cancelled by Brooks and Cooley in September. *Pine Bluff Commercial,* September 16, 1969.

39. Statement by W. Rockefeller, August 18, 1969, WR Papers, Record Group III, Box 116, File 2; telegram, W. Rockefeller to Cato Brooks Jr., August 9, 1969, WR Papers, Record Group III, Box 424; *New York Times,* August 17, 20, 1969; *Arkansas Gazette,* August 14, 17, 20, 1969.

40. Memo, Bob Fisher to W. Rockefeller, September 24, 1969; memo, Fisher to W. Rockefeller, September 9, 1969, WR Papers, Record Group III, Box 86, File 13; memo, Charles Allbright to John Ward, August 19, 1969, WR Papers, Record Group III, Box 116, File 2; Ralph D. Scott to W. Rockefeller, August 18, 1969; memo, Sergeant Jim Wooten to Scott, August 18, 1969, WR Papers, Record Group III, Box 86, File 13; *Arkansas Gazette,* August 14, 1969.

41. Memo, Scott to Lt. Col. Bill Miller, August 19, 1969; Scott to Winthrop Rockefeller, August 19, 1969, WR Papers, Record Group III, Box 86, File 13; *New York Times,* August 22, 1969.

42. State of Emergency Declaration, August 22, 1969, WR Papers, Record Group III, Box 205, File 10; *Arkansas Gazette,* August 20, 22, 25, 1969; *Arkansas Democrat,* August 20, 21, 25, 1969; *Washington Post,* August 23, 1969.

43. *New York Times,* August 29, 30, 1969; State of Arkansas, Executive Department Proclamation, August 27, 1969, WR Papers, Record Group III, Box 207. File 5; *Arkansas Gazette,* August 27, 28, 1969.

44. *Arkansas Gazette,* September 3, 17, 19, 20, October 28, 1969; *Arkansas Democrat,* September 15, 20, 1969; Memphis *Commercial Appeal,* September 18, October 3, 1969.

45. *Arkansas Gazette,* November 30, 1969.

46. Memphis *Commercial Appeal,* September 18, 1969.

47. "Meet the Press" transcript, May 3, 1964, WR Papers, Record Group IV, Box 47, File 4.

48. "WR Statement Regarding Federal Guidelines: Given KTHV," August 30, 1966; memo, Ward to WR, August 27, 1966, WR Papers, Record Group III, Box 30, File 3; memo, Tom Eisele to W. Rockefeller, August 23, 1966, WR Papers, Record Group III, Box 460, File 3.

49. *Arkansas Gazette,* May 29, 22, 1968.

50. Telegram, John W. Walker to W. Rockefeller, May 23, 1968, WR Papers, Record Group III, Box 608; telegram, T. E. Patterson to W. Rockefeller, May 27, 1968, WR Papers, Record Group III, Box 557; *Arkansas Gazette,* June 2, 1968.

51. Telegram, W. Rockefeller to Richard M. Nixon, June 26, 1969, WR Papers, Record Group III, Box 550, File 2; William "Sonny" Walker and Dr. Elijah E. Palnick to W. Rockefeller, July 2, 1969, WR Papers, Record Group III, Box 608; *New York Times,* June 28, 1969; *Arkansas Gazette,* June 28, 1969.

52. *New York Times,* July 4, 1969.

53. Jerris Leonard, assistant attorney general, to Arkansas State Board of Education, April 14, 1970; Leonard to W. Rockefeller, April 14, 1970; W. Rockefeller to Leonard, April 3, 1970, WR Papers, Record Group III, Box 521, File 1.

54. State Board of Education to T. E. Patterson, September 9, 1968, WR Papers, Record Group III, Box 323, File 1.

55. *Arkansas Gazette,* April 4, May 14, June 6, 18, July 28, August 1, 30, October 15, 1970.

56. *New York Times,* October 30, December 14, 1969.

57. *New York Times,* September 18, 1969; Ward, *The Arkansas Rockefeller,* 176.

58. *Arkansas Gazette,* January 24, 1970.

59. Petition to W. Rockefeller, February 5, 1970, WR Papers, Record Group III, Box 83, File 2b; *Arkansas Gazette,* February 5, 1970; Memphis *Commercial Appeal,* February 19, 1970.

60. Memo, Dona Williams to Bob Faulkner and John L. Ward, February 20, 1970, WR Papers, Record Group III, Box 324, File 1.

61. Statement by W. Rockefeller, February 21, 1970, WR Papers, Record Group IV, Box 165, Folder 4.

62. Robert Faulkner, interview by author, February 9, 1988, Little Rock, Arkansas.

63. Memo, Greg Simon to Fisher and Charles Allbright, August 5, 1970, WR Papers, Record Group III, Box 640, File 3; Mid-South Opinion Surveys, April 20, September 13, 1970, WR Papers, Record Group IV, Box 82; *New York Times,* July 28, August 11, 26, September 6, 10, 1970; *Arkansas Gazette,* February 24, September 2, 3, 4, 9, 1970; *Pine Bluff Commercial,* February 24, 1970.

64. Jim Ranchino, *Faubus to Bumpers: Arkansas Votes, 1960–1970* (Arkadelphia, Arkansas: Action Research, 1972), 71.

65. Numan V. Bartley and Hugh D. Graham, *Southern Politics and the Second Reconstruction* (Baltimore: Johns Hopkins University Press, 1975), 122, 149. Numan and Bartley base this figure on the voting returns of predominantly black precincts in Little Rock. Racially mixed precincts were eliminated from their analysis. In *Faubus to Bumpers,* Jim Ranchino asserts that Rockefeller held onto 88 percent of the black vote statewide. But Ranchino does not explain how he arrived at this figure. Rockefeller almost certainly received a higher percentage of the black vote in the delta than he did in Little Rock. The only two counties he carried in 1970 were in the delta. Statewide, the percentage of the black vote carried by Rockefeller probably lies somewhere between the 49 and 88 percent figures. But the statistical analysis necessary to verify this is not available. Numan V. Bartley and Hugh D. Graham, *Southern Elections County and Precinct Data, 1950–1972* (Baton Rouge: Louisiana State University Press, 1978), x, 353; Ranchino, *Faubus to Bumpers,* 72, 74.

66. *Arkansas Gazette,* March 5, 1973; *New York Times,* March 5, 1973.

67. Cal Ledbetter Jr., interview by author, September 15, 1987, Little Rock, Arkansas.

68. *Arkansas Democrat,* September 9, 1969.

69. *Arkansas Democrat,* September 12, 17, 1969.

70. *Arkansas Democrat,* April 11, 1968; *Arkansas Gazette,* April 12, 16, 1968.

71. J. H. Bond, regional director, to W. Rockefeller, December 12, 1968, WR Papers, Record Group III, Box 420, File 1.

72. Report, US Commission on Civil Rights, August 1965, WR Papers, Record Group III, Box 84, File 3.

73. *Arkansas Gazette,* May 25, 1968, September 24, 1967; J. B. Garrett, Superintendent, Arkansas Training School for Girls, to Bob Scott, governor's office, July 29, 1968, WR Papers, Record Group III, Box 334, File 4.

74. *Arkansas Gazette,* September 27, 1967.

CHAPTER 10

1. "The GOP Earthquake," *Washington Post National Weekly Edition,* November 14–20, 1994, 6.

2. See, for example, Diane D. Blair, *Arkansas Politics and Government* (Lincoln: University of Nebraska Press, 1988), 69–87, 264–80.

3. For additional details on Pryor's record as governor see Diane Blair, "David Hampton Pryor," in *The Governors of Arkansas,* ed. Timothy P. Donovan and Willard B. Gatewood, Jr. (Fayetteville: University of Arkansas Press, 1981), 242–47.

4. For additional details on Bumpers' gubernatorial record see Dan Durning, "Dale Leon Bumpers," in *The Governors of Arkansas,* 235–41.

5. For additional details on Senate accomplishments, chairmanships, and voting records see Michael Barone and Grant Ujifusa, *The Almanac of American Politics, 1994* (Washington, D.C.: National Journal, 1993), 59–61; and *Politics in America, 1994,* ed. Phil Duncan (Washington, D.C.: Congressional Quarterly, 1993), 81–87.

6. Mary McGrory, "Is Bumpers the Answer for the Democratic National Committee," *Washington Post,* December 10, 1988; Simon quoted in *Arkansas Gazette,* January 27, 1987, 6A. See also William Greider, "Of Virtue, Quality, and The White House," *Rolling Stone,* March 31, 1983, 9–10; and "Senator Bumpers for President in 1984," *Arkansas Gazette,* December 9, 1982.

7. The most thorough treatment of Clinton's first gubernatorial term is in Phyllis F. Johnston, *Bill Clinton's Public Policy for Arkansas: 1979–80* (Little Rock: August House, 1982). A summary of Clinton's subsequent gubernatorial record and extensive bibliographic guide to additional materials can be found in Diane D. Blair, "William Jefferson Clinton," in *The Governors of Arkansas,* ed. Timothy P. Donovan, Willard B. Gatewood Jr., and Jeannie M. Whayne (Fayetteville: University of Arkansas Press, 1995).

8. *U.S. News and World Report,* December 21, 1987, 52–53.

9. *Newsweek,* July 1, 1991, 27.

10. For this and many similar anti-Arkansas charges by Clinton's opponents in the 1992 contest, see Diane D. Blair, "Arkansas: Ground Zero in the Presidential Race," in *The 1992 Presidential Election in the South,* ed. Robert P. Steed, Laurence W. Moreland, and Tod A. Baker (Westport, CT: Praeger, 1994), 103–18.

11. Analyses of the validity of such charges and counter-charges include Jerry Dean, "Bush Hits Clinton at Home, but Is He on Target?" *Arkansas Democrat-Gazette,* September 17, 1992; David Lauter and James Gerstenzang, "Accuracy of Bush, Clinton Accusations," *Los Angeles Times,* October 11, 1992, A36, A38.

12. On campaign contributions see *Arkansas Democrat-Gazette,* December 29, 1992, B1; Clinton's election night comments in *Arkansas Democrat-Gazette,* November 4, 1992, A15.

13. For Bumpers' and Pryor's legislative success rates see Robert Johnston and Dan Durning, "The Arkansas Governor's Role in the Policy Process, 1955–79," *Arkansas Political Science Journal* 2 (1981): 16–39. Clinton's legislative success rates of 83 percent, 90 percent, and 100 percent documented in *Arkansas Gazette,* May 15, 1983, April 7, 1985, April 1, 1991.

14. A recent example is in Senator Bumpers' commencement address at Arkansas State University, August 5, 1994.

15. Telephone interview with Sen. David Pryor, January 2, 1995. Notes in author's possession. When Pryor's brother took the daughter of Ouachita County's only known Republican, Skidmore Willis, to the movies, Pryor's father brought him home with a reprimand.

16. Excerpts from speech by Sen. Dale Bumpers to US Chamber of Commerce, Washington, D.C., April 3, 1984, in author's possession.

17. Speech by Gov. Bill Clinton to Conference on Early Childhood Issues, Frankfurt, Kentucky, May 11, 1987, in author's possession.

18. Speech by Sen. David Pryor delivered to the Old State House Museum Associates, Little Rock, November 18, 1988, in author's possession.

19. The depth and strength of the progressive, populist Arkansas tradition is described and explained in Roy Reed, "Clinton Country," *New York Times Magazine,* September 6, 1992, 32. See also Blair, *Arkansas Politics and Government,* 93–95, 270–72.

20. Gov. Bill Clinton's Inaugural Address, January 9, 1979, in author's possession.

21. "Remarks Made by Senator David Pryor on Saturday, February 17, 1990, Announcing His Bid for Re-election to the United States Senate," in author's possession.

22. Related by Bumpers to William R. Kincaid on stage at Fayetteville High School commencement, May, 1984, notes in author's possession.

23. See Rex Nelson, "On the Road With David Pryor," *Arkansas Magazine, Arkansas Democrat,* April 26, 1987; "Folksy, Caring Image Major Forces Behind Pryor's Success," *Arkansas Democrat,* February 18, 1990.

24. Blair, *Arkansas Politics and Government,* 269–70.

25. For details on the Arkansas governor's appointive powers see "Arkansas Boards and Commissions, A Fact Sheet" (Little Rock: Arkansas League of Women Voters, 1987); Diane D. Blair, "Gubernatorial Appointment Power: Too Much of a Good Thing?" *State Government* 55 (Summer 1982): 88–91.

26. For additional details see Blair, *Arkansas Politics and Government,* 80–81.

27. On the importance of the Marianna clinic, see "Lee County Clinic Defied Times," *Arkansas Gazette,* September 19, 1991, 1A.

28. "Ex-Republican's Tennessee Link Led to White House," *Arkansas Democrat-Gazette,* November 22, 1994.

29. Number estimated by Henry Woods, Special Projects and Intern Coordinator to Senator Bumpers and Senator Pryor.

30. On the organizational weakness of parties in one-party states, see V. O. Key, Jr., *Southern Politics in State and Nation* (New York: Random House, 1949), 15–18; on the particular "paralysis and disorganization" in Arkansas, see 183–204.

31. In terms of local organizational strength, Arkansas Democrats were ranked 44th in the nation, Republicans 40th, by James L. Gibson, Cornelius P. Potter, John F. Bibby, Robert J. Huckshorn, "Whither the Local Parties?" *American Journal of Political Science* 29 (1985), 152, 154–55.

32. From notes taken by author at event, Kelly's Barn, Fayetteville, Arkansas, October 23, 1993, notes in author's possession.

33. Statement by Sen. Dale Bumpers, Little Rock, Arkansas, April 5, 1983, typescript in author's possession.

34. See "Mr. Clinton Moved the State Forward," *The New York Times,* September 5, 1994.

35. *U.S. Congressional Record,* October 8, 1994, S15002–S15005.

36. John Brummett, *High Wire,* (New York: Hyperion, 1994), 235.

37. For additional details see Anne McMath, *The First Ladies of Arkansas* (Little Rock: August House, 1989), 219–37.

38. McMath, *The First Ladies of Arkansas,* 248–56. See also Rex Nelson, *The Hillary Factor* (New York: Gallen Publishing Group, 1993).

39. See "Clinton, Bumpers had a Scare in Light Plane," *Arkansas Gazette,*

January 10, 1988; John Brummett, "Plane Scare Simply Part of the Job," *Arkansas Gazette,* January 12, 1988.

40. John Brummett, "Republican Newspaper," *Arkansas Times,* November 5, 1992.

CHAPTER 11

1. The authors would like to thank the reviewers, the participants at the 2015 ArkPSA conference, and Dr. Janine Parry for their guidance and support. Of course, any mistakes are those of the authors.

2. Melinda Gann Hall and Chris W. Bonneau,"Mobilizing Interest: The Effects of Money on Citizen Participation in State Supreme Court Elections," *American Journal of Political Science* 52, no.3 (July 2008): 457–70; and Sara C. Benesh, "Understanding Public Confidence in American Courts," *The Journal of Politics* 68, no. 3 (August 2006): 697–707.

3. Jeffrey D. Jackson, "Beyond Quality: First Principles in Judicial Selection and Their Application to a Commission-Based Selection System," *Fordham Urban Law Journal* 34 (2007): 125–61; Thomas R. Phillips, "The Merits of Merit Selection." *Harvard Journal of Law & Public Policy* 32 (2009): 67–96; Michael E. Debow, "The Bench, the Bar, and Everyone Else: Some Questions about State Judicial Selection," *The Missouri Law Review* 74 (2009): 777–81; and Mary L. Volcansek, "Exporting the Missouri Plan: Judicial Appointment Commissions," *Missouri Law Review* 74 (2009): 783–800.

4. Lee Epstein, Jack Knight, and Olga Shvetsova, "Selecting Selection Systems," Eds.. in *Judicial Independence at the Crossroads: An Interdisciplinary Approach,* eds. S. B. Burbank and Barry Friedman (Thousand Oaks, CA: American Academy of Political and Social Science/Sage Publications, 2002) 191–226;and F. Andrew Hanssen, "Learning about Judicial Independence: Institutional Change in the State Courts," *The Journal of Legal Studies* 33, no.2 (June 2004): 431–73.

5. Kay Collett Goss, *The Arkansas State Constitution: A Reference Guide* (Westport, CN: Greenwood Press, 1993).

6. John Moritz, "Opinions vary on picking state justices," *Arkansas Online,* October 16, 2016, http://m.arkansasonline.com/news/2016/oct/16/opinions-vary -on-picking-justices-20161/?latest.

7. Frances Stokes Berry, "Sizing Up State Policy Innovation Research," *Policy Studies Journal* 22 (1994): 442–56; and Frances Stokes Berry, and William D. Berry, "Innovation and Diffusion Models in Policy Research," in *Theories of the Policy Process,* 3rd ed., eds. Paul A. Sabatier and Christopher M. Weible (Boulder, CO: Westview Press, 2014),307–62..

8. Marsha Puro, Peter J. Bergerson, and Steven Puro, "An Analysis of Judicial Diffusion: Adoption of the Missouri Plan in the American States," *Publius* 15, no.4 (Autumn 1985): 85–97.

9. For a thorough discussion on external factors versus internal determinants, see Berry and Berry, "Innovation and Diffusion Models."

10. See Todd Donovan, Daniel A. Smith, Tracy Osborn, and Christopher Z. Mooney, *State and Local Politics: Institutions and Reform.* 4th ed. (Boston: Cengage Learning, 2014), 327–32; and Lee Epstein, Jack Knight, and Olga Shvetsova, "Selecting Selection Systems," in *Judicial Independence at the Crossroads: An Interdisciplinary Approach,* eds. S. B. Burbank and Barry Friedman (Thousand Oaks,

CA: American Academy of Political and Social Science/Sage Publications, 2002); and Paul Pierson, *Politics in Time: History, Institutions, and Social Analysis* (Princeton, NJ: Princeton UP, 2004).

11. See Epstein, Knight, and Shvetsova, *Judicial Independence at the Crossroads.*

12. See Epstein, Knight, and Shvetsova, *Judicial Independence at the Crossroads.*

13. See Epstein, Knight, and Shvetsova, *Judicial Independence at the Crossroads,* 191.

14. Laura Langer, *Judicial Review in State Supreme Courts: A Comparative Study.* (Albany: State University of NY Press, 2002); and Paul Brace, Melinda Gann Hall, and Laura Langer, "Placing State Supreme Courts in State Politics," *State Politics & Policy Quarterly* 1, no.1 (Spring 2002): 81–108.

15. Cal Ledbetter, Jr., Cal "The Constitution of 1836: A New Perspective," *The Arkansas Historical Quarterly* 41, no.3 (Autumn 1982): 215–52.

16. See Langer, *Judicial Review in State Supreme Courts.*

17. Frances Stokes Berry, and William D. Berry, "Innovation and Diffusion Models in Policy Research," en *Theories of the Policy Process,* 3rd ed., eds. Paul A. Sabatier and Christopher M. Weible (Boulder, CO: Westview Press, 2014): 307–62.

18. G. Alan Tarr, *Understanding State Constitutions* (Princeton, NJ: Princeton UP, 1998).

19. See Tarr, *Understanding State Constitutions,* 51.

20. See Tarr, *Understanding State Constitutions,* 95.

21. See Tarr, *Understanding State Constitutions,* 52.

22. Virginia Gray, "Innovation in the States: A Diffusion Study," *American Political Science Review* 67 (1973): 1174–85; and Jack L. Walker, "The Diffusion of Innovations among the American States," *American Political Science Review* 67 (1973): 880–99.

23. See Walker, "The Diffusion of Innovations."

24. Michael Mintrom, and Sandra Vergari, "Policy Networks and Innovation Diffusion: The Case of State Education Reforms," *Journal of Politics* 60 (1998): 126–48.

25. Robert S. Erikson, Gerald C. Wright, and John P. McIver, "Measuring the Public's Ideology Preferences in the 50 States: Survey Responses Versus Roll Call Data." *State Politics & Policy Quarterly* 7 (2007): 141–51; and Paul Brace, Kevin Arceneaux, Martin Johnson, and Stacy Ulbig, "Reply to 'The Measurement and Stability of State Citizen Ideology,'" *State Politics & Policy Quarterly* 7 (2007): 133–40.

26. See Berry and Berry, "Innovation and Diffusion Models.".

27. John Frendreis and Raymond Tatalovich, "'A Hundred Miles of Dry': Religion and the Persistence of Prohibition in the U.S. States," *State Politics & Policy Quarterly* 10 (2010): 302–19; Rodney E. Hero and Caroline J. Tolbert, "A Racial/ Ethnic Diversity Interpretation of Politics and Policy in the States of the U.S.," *American Journal of Political Science* 40 (1996): 851–71; Kim Quaile Hill and Jan E. Leighley, "The Policy Consequences of Class Bias in State Electorates," *American Journal of Political Science* 36 (1992): 351–65; and Elizabeth Rigby and Gerald C. Wright, "Political Parties and Representation of the Poor in the American States," *American Journal of Political Science* 57, no.3 (2013): 552–65.

28. Janine A. Parry, Brian Kisida, and Ronald Langley, "The State of State Polls: Old Challenges, New Opportunities," *State Politics & Policy Quarterly* 8 (2008): 198–216. Of course, even if there were comparable polling data, it seems rather unlikely that judicial selection mechanisms would be a concern of pollsters or citizens. Surprisingly, though, the American Judicature Society does track polling efforts on

this question in individual states. Polling on this question, however, is uneven, and the methodology of the polls is not provided. http://www.judicialselection.us/ judicial_selection/reform_efforts/opinion_polls_surveys.cfm?state=.

29. Robert S. Erikson, Gerald C. Wright, and John P. McIver, *Statehouse Democracy: Public Opinion and Policy in the American States* (Cambridge, MA: Cambridge UP, 1993); and William D. Berry, Evan J. Ringquist, Richard C. Fording, and Russell L. Hanson, "Measuring Citizen and Government Ideology in the American States, 1960–93," *American Journal of Political Science* 42 (January 1998): 327–48.

30. Paul Brace, Kevin Arceneaux, Martin Johnson, and Stacy Ulbig, "Does State Political Ideology Change Over Time?" *Political Research Quarterly* 57 (2004): 529–40; Thomas M. Carsey and Jeffrey J. Harden, "New Measures of Partisanship, Ideology, and Policy Mood in the American States," *State Politics & Policy Quarterly* 10 (2010): 136–56 and Erikson, Wright, and McIver, *Statehouse Democracy.*

31. Chris W. Bonneau, "What Price Justice(s)? Understanding Campaign Spending in State Supreme Court Elections," *State Politics & Policy Quarterly* 5, no.2 (Summer 2005): 107–25; Melinda Gann Hall, "Voting in State Supreme Court Elections: Competition and Context as Democratic Incentives," *The Journal of Politics* 69, no.4 (November 2007): 1147–59; and David Klein and Lawrence Baum, "Ballot Information and Voting Decisions in Judicial Elections," *Political Research Quarterly* 54, no. 4 (December 2001): 709–28.

32. See Tarr, *Understanding State Constitutions* 32–33.

33. Mintrom and Vergari, *Policy Networks and Innovation Diffusion.*

34. See Langer, *Judicial Review in State Supreme Courts.*

35. Jeffrey Stinson, "Battle for State Court Control Intensifies," *Pew Charitable Trusts,* September 17, 2014. http://www.pewtrusts.org/en/research-and-analysis/blogs/ stateline/2014/09/17/battle-for-state-court-control-intensifies.

36. See Langer, *Judicial Review In State Supreme Courts.*

37. See Epstein, Knight, and Shvetsova, *Selecting Selection Systems.*

38. See Tarr, *Understanding State Constitutions.*

39. Quotes from Arkansas' constitutions are taken from Uriah M. Rose, *The Constitution of the State of Arkansas* (Little Rock, AR: Press Printing Co, 1891).

40. See Ledbetter, *The Constitution of 1836.*

41. See Ledbetter, *The Constitution of 1836,* 244.

42. See Ledbetter, *The Constitution of 1836.*

43. See Robert F. Williams, *The Law of American State Constitutions* (New York: Oxford UP, 2010), 290.

44. See Ledbetter, *The Constitution of 1836.*

45. Kermit L. Hall, "Progressive Reform and the Decline of Democratic Accountability: The Popular Election of State Supreme Court Judges, 1850–1920," *American Bar Foundation Research Journal* 9 no. 2 (Spring 1984): 346–47.

46. See Ledbetter, *The Constitution of 1836.*

47. See Ledbetter, *The Constitution of 1836.*

48. See Ledbetter, *The Constitution of 1836.*

49. See Tarr, *Understating State Constitutions.*

50. Cal Ledbetter, Jr., "The Constitution of 1868: Conqueror's Constitution or Constitutional Continuity?" *The Arkansas Historical Quarterly* 44 no. 1 (Spring 1985): 16–41.

51. See Ledbetter, *The Constitution of 1868.*

52. See Ledbetter, *The Constitution of 1868*, 20.

53. The 1868 Constitutional Convention kept meticulous records. Other conventions, by contrast, did not.

54. Arkansas Constitutional Convention, *Debates and Proceedings of the Convention which Assembled at Little Rock, Jan. 7th, 1868 to Form a Constitution for the State of Arkansas*, 1868, 204.

55. L. Scott Stafford, "Post-Civil War Supreme Court," *UALR Law Review* 23 (2001): 355–407.

56. Cortez A. M. Ewing, "Arkansas Reconstruction Impeachments," *The Arkansas Historical Quarterly* 13, no. 2 (Summer 1954): 137–53.

57. James H. Atkinson, "The Adoption of the Constitution of 1874 and the Passing of the Reconstruction Regime," *The Arkansas Historical Quarterly* 5, no. 3 (Autumn 1946): 288–96; Diane D. Blair and Jay Barth, *Arkansas Politics and Government* (Lincoln: Univ. of Nebraska Press, 2005); and Tarr, *Understating State Constitutions.*

58. Marvin Frak Russell, "The Republican Party of Arkansas 1874–1913," PhD diss., University of Arkansas at Fayetteville, 1985, 16.

59. See Tarr, *Understating State Constitutions.*

60. Arkansas Constitutional Revision Study Commission, *Revising the Arkansas Constitution: A Report to the Hon. Winthrop Rockefeller, Governor of Arkansas, and Members of the 66th General Assembly of the State of Arkansas* (Little Rock, AR, 1968), 9.

61. See Arkansas Constitutional Revision Study Commission, *Revising the Arkansas Constitution*, 72.

62. Cal Ledbetter, Jr., "The Proposed Arkansas Constitution of 1980," *The Arkansas Historical Quarterly* 60, no. 1 (2001): 53–74.

63. Raymond Abramson, Letter to supporters, July 20, 1980.

64. See statecourtsguide.com.

65. Cal Ledbetter, Jr., "Proposed Subjects for Limited Constitutional Convention," undated, accessed at the Butler Center, Little Rock, AR, Series II, Box 8, File 4: Constitutional Convention: List of Proposed Articles for Revision, Undated.

66. Seth Anderson, "Examining the Decline in Support for Merit Selection in the States," *Albany Law Review* 67 (2004): 793.

67. For example, in 2000 the voters of Florida overwhelmingly voted rejected a proposed a local option constitutional amendment to change to merit-based selections from nonpartisan elections. In 1987, Ohio voters rejected a switch from judicial elections to merit-based selection.

68. See http://www.judicialselection.us/judicial_selection/reform_efforts/formal _changes_since_inception.cfm?state.

69. Jay Barth, "Arkansas: More Signs of Momentum for Republicanism in Post-'Big Three' Arkansas," *The American Review of Politics* 24 (2003): III-26.

70. John Stroud, Lecture on Amendment 80, University of Arkansas School of Law, Fayetteville, AR, October 2013.

71. See Stroud, Lecture on Amendment 80.

72. See Moritz, *Opinions Vary.*

73. See, e.g., *Williams-Yulee v. Florida Bar*, 135 S. Ct. 1656, 1667 (2015) (holding that Judicial elections can be subjected to greater restrictions, such as campaign finance, than standard political elections cannot due to the fact that a judge is sup-

posed to hold up the highest degree of impartiality, whereas a politician is supposed to respond to the will of the people and their followers).

74. See Williams, *The Law of American State Constitutions*, 290.

75. See Gray, "Innovations In the States"; and Walker, "The Diffusion of Innovations."

76. See Walker, "The Diffusion of Innovations."

CHAPTER 12

1. In re Implementation of Amendment 80: Admin. Plans Pursuant to Admin. Order No. 14, 345 Ark. Adv. app. (June 28, 2001) (per curiam) [hereinafter In re Implementation of Amendment 80].

2. Amendment 80 to the Arkansas Constitution appeared on the 2000 general election ballot as "Referred Amendment 3." It was approved by a vote of 431,137 (57%) for and 323,547 (43%) against. Publisher's Notes, Ark. Const. amend. 80.

3. An elected constitutional convention proposed a new constitution for the state, including a judicial article with provisions very similar to those found in Amendment 80. See State of Arkansas, "Proposed Arkansas Constitution of 1970 with Comments: A Report to the People of the State of Arkansas by the Seventh Arkansas Constitutional Convention," (1970); see also Ronald L. Boyer, "A New Judicial System for Arkansas," 24 Ark. L. Rev. 221 (1970). The proposal was defeated at the 1970 general election.

4. A similar proposal was drafted by a constitutional convention in 1980, submitted to the voters, and defeated. See State of Arkansas, Proposed Arkansas Constitution of 1980 with Comments: A Report to the People of the State of Arkansas by the Seventh Arkansas Constitutional Convention (1980). The Arkansas General Assembly also attempted to place a constitutional amendment on the 1980 general election ballot which would have revised the limitations on jurisdiction and venue of state courts. Prior to the election, the Arkansas Supreme Court struck this proposal from the ballot. See Wells v. Riviere, 269 Ark. 156, 599 S.W.2d 375 (1980).

5. In 1991, the Arkansas Bar Association developed, as a part of its legislative package, a proposed judicial article to the Arkansas Constitution and sought to have the issue referred to a public vote by the general assembly. Senate Joint Resolution 10 of 1991 was one of three amendments referred by the Joint State Agencies and Governmental Affairs Committee for full consideration by the Arkansas House and Senate. The proposal was approved by the senate, but was defeated in the house by one vote.

6. Former Governor Jim Guy Tucker initiated a process in 1995 to draft and submit for voter approval a revised constitution, including a judicial article. A draft was produced and the question was submitted to the voters as whether to call a constitutional convention. Act of Oct. 19, 1995, No. 1, 1995 Ark. Acts 1. The vote failed in a special election in December of 1995.

7. Five items appeared on the 2000 general election ballot. They included constitutional amendments to allow city and county governments to issue short term redevelopment bonds, to adjust real property assessments and provide a property tax credit, to revise the judicial article, and to establish a state lottery and casino gambling. An initiated act on tobacco settlement proceeds also appeared. Only the gambling amendment failed to secure approval by the voter. Arkansas Secretary of

State, "History of Initiatives and Referenda 1938–2000," at http://sosweb.state.ar.us/bi38–00.xls (last visited Mar. 7, 2002).

8. What was obviously a typographical error in the final and official legislation that referred Amendment 80 to the voters resulted in the lack of a specific effective date for the amendment. Section 21 of Amendment 80 provides that the amendment shall become effective on "July, 2001." Ark. Const. amend. 80, § 21. In actions by the supreme court and general assembly to implement the amendment, this omission of a particular date has not been noted and the presumed effective date has been July 1, 2001.

9. See In re Appointment of Special Supreme Court Committee to Be Known as "Amendment 80 Committee," 343 Ark. app. 877 (2000) (per curiam).

10. See In re Appointment of Special Supreme Court Committee to Be Known as "Amendment 80 Committee," 343 Ark. app. 877 (2000) (per curiam). The members are Ronald D. Harrison, Jim L. Julian, Judge Robert J. Gladwin, Judge David B. Bogard, Judge John F. Stroud, Jr., Judge Andree L. Roaf, Justice Annabelle Clinton Imber, Justice Robert L. Brown, and Chief Justice Dub Arnold, Chair. Id.

11. Act of Mar. 19, 2001, No. 914, 2001 Ark. Acts 914 (codified at Ark. Code Ann. § 16–10–136 [LEXIS Supp. 2001]).

12. Act of Mar. 19, 2001, No. 915, 2001 Ark. Acts 915 (repealing Ark. Code Ann. § § 16–16–201 to–1115).

13. Act of Mar. 20, 2001, No. 951, 2001 Ark. Acts 951.

14. Act of Apr. 13, 2001, No. 1582, 2001 Ark. Acts 1582 (codified at Ark. Code Ann. § § 9–27–213, –318, –352, –507 to –508, 510 [LEXIS Supp. 2001]).

15. Act of Apr. 19, 2001, No. 1789, 2001 Ark. Acts 1789 (codified at Ark. Code Ann. § § 7–10–101 to –103, 7–5–205, –704, 7–7103, –401, 14–42–206, 7–5–405, –407 [LEXIS Supp. 2001]).

16. In re Adoption of Admin. Order No. 14, 344 Ark. app. 747 (2001) (per curiam).

17. See In re Implementation of Amendment 80: Amendments to Admin. Orders, 345 Ark. Adv. app. (May 24, 2001) (per curiam).

18. See In re Implementation of Amendment 80: Amendments to Rules of Civil Procedure and Inferior Court Rules, 345 Ark. Adv. app. (May 24, 2001) (per curiam) [hereinafter In re Amendments].

19. In re Ark. Rules of Criminal Procedure 1.5 and 8.2, 345 Ark. Adv. app. (May 17, 2001) (per curiam).

20. In re Implementation of Amendment 80: Amendments to Rules of Appellate Procedure—Civil and Rules of the Supreme Court and Court of Appeals, 345 Ark. Adv. app. (June 7, 2001) (per curiam).

21. In re Arkansas Rules of Civil Procedures and Rules of the Supreme Court and Court of Appeals, 347 Ark. Adv. app. (Jan. 24, 2002) (per curiam).

22. Administrative Order No. 14, para. 4(b), 344 Ark. app. 747, 750 (2001) (per curiam).

23. For an excellent review of the creation and history of Arkansas's chancery courts, see Morton Gitelman, "The Separation of Law and Equity and the Arkansas Chancery Courts: Historical Anomalies and Political Realities," *University of Arkansas Little Rock Law Journal* 17, no. 2 (1995): 215.

24. Administrative Order No. 14, para. 4(b), 344 Ark. app. 747, 750 (2001) (per curiam).

25. In re Implementation of Amendment 80, supra note 1.

26. States that continue to separate law and equity jurisdiction and maintain chancery courts are Delaware, Mississippi, and Tennessee. David Rottman et al., US Dep't of Justice, State Court Organization 342, 361 (1998).

27. Ark. Const. amend. 80, § 19(B)(1).

28. Administrative Order No. 14, para. 1, 344 Ark. app. at 748. Section 6 of Amendment 80 provides as follows: "Subject to the superintending control of the Supreme Court, the Judges of a Circuit Court may divide that Circuit Court into subject matter divisions, and any Circuit Judge within the Circuit may sit in any division." Ark. Const. amend. 80, § 6.

29. Administrative Order No. 14, para. 1, 344 Ark. app. at 747–48.

30. Letter from Bob Tobin, National Center for State Courts, to J. D. Gingerich, Director, Administrative Office of the Courts, Dec. 15, 2000, on file with author.

31. See Administrative Order No. 14, paras. 2, 4(b), 344 Ark. app. at 748–50. After submission of the initial plans in June, 2001, subsequent plans are to be submitted by March 1 of each year following the year in which the judicial election of circuit judges is held. Id. at para. 3, 344 Ark. app. at 749.

32. As a result, the supreme court failed to adopt the National Center for State Court's recommendation of a system of local administrative judges. See Letter from Bob Tobin to J. D. Gingerich, supra note 30. Arkansas joins New York and Wyoming as the only states with no system of administrative judges for the courts of general jurisdiction. See Rottman et al., supra note 26, at 34. In other states, administrative judges are provided a wide range of authority and responsibility. This range includes the assignment of judges, the assignment of cases, the supervision of employees, and the management of the court budget.

33. Administrative Order No. 14, para. 2, 344 Ark. app. at 748–49.

34. Single-judge circuits include the 9-East, 11-East, 18West and 19-East Circuits.

35. The judges in the 6th, 10th, and 11-West Circuits could not reach an agreement at the local level. In each case, more than one proposal was submitted to the supreme court, none of which had the support of all of the judges in the circuit.

36. See In re Implementation of Amendment 80, supra note 1.

37. The Arkansas Supreme Court requested further information from judges in the 21st and 23rd Circuits.

38. Circuits whose plans were initially rejected by the supreme court were the 1st, 13th, 15th, 19-West and 22d Circuits.

39. Arkansas Judiciary, "Circuit Court Administrative Plans," August 8, 2001, http://courts.state.ar.us/ courts/circuitplans.html.

40. Note, however, that cases filed prior to January 1, 2002 that receive a case number under the former version of Administrative Order No. 2 shall maintain their original case numbers. For example, a chancery case that was filed in 2001 and received case number "E-2001I" will continue to use that case number in proceedings that take place after January 1, 2002, even though the case is now being heard in the civil or domestic relations division of circuit court.

41. Administrative Order No. 8, para. 2(c), 345 Ark. Adv. app. (May 24, 2001) (per curiam).

42. Administrative Order No. 8, para. 2(c), 345 Ark. Adv. app. (May 24, 2001) (per curiam).

43. Administrative Order No. 8, para. 2(c), 345 Ark. Adv. app. (May 24, 2001) (per curiam).

44. Administrative Order No. 8, para. 2(c), 345 Ark. Adv. app. (May 24, 2001) (per curiam).

45. See Ark. Const. art. VII, § 19.

46. See Ark. Const. art. VII, § 19. amend. 80.

47. Act of Mar. 21, 2001, No. 997, 2001 Ark. Acts 997 (codified at Ark. Code Ann. § 14–14–502(a)(2)(B) [LEXIS Supp. 2001]).

48. In re Amendments, supra note 18.

49. In re Amendments, supra note 18.

50. See In re Amendments to Admin. Orders Numbers 8 and 14, 346 Ark. Adv. app. (Nov. 1, 2001) (per curiam).

51. Ark. Const. amend. 80, § § 7, 19.

52. Ark. Const. amend. 80, § § 7, 19. § 8.

53. In re Implementation of Amendment 80, supra note 1.

54. See In re Implementation of Amendment 80, supra note 1.

55. See supra note 1.

56. See supra note 1.

57. See supra note 1.

CHAPTER 13

1. John H. Aldrich, Brad Gomez, and John Griffin, "State Party Organizations Study, 1999; State Party Chair Questionnaire," Duke University, 1999.

2. John C. Davis and Drew Kurlowski, "Campaign Inc.: Data From a Field Survey of State Party Organizations," University of Missouri, 2014. Typescript.

3. John C. Davis and Drew Kurlowski, "State Party Organization Survey." University of Missouri, 2013.

4. See Aldrich, Gomez, and Griffin, "State Party Organizations Study, 1999."

5. David A. Dulio and R. Sam Garrett, "Organizational Strength and Campaign Professionalism in State Parties," in *The State of the Parties: The Changing Role of Contemporary American Parties*, eds. John C. Green and Daniel J. Coffey. 5th ed. (Lanham, MD: Rowman and Littlefield, 2007), 199–216.

6. Anthony Downs, *An Economic Theory of Democracy* (New York: Harper and Row, 1957).

7. James Q. Wilson, *Political Organizations* (New York: Basic Books, 1973).

8. Norman H. Nie, Sidney Verba, and John R. Petrocik, *The Changing American Voter* (Cambridge, MA: Harvard University Press, 1979).

9. John F. Bibby, "Political Parties and Federalism: The Republican National Committee" *Publius* 9, no. 1 (1979): 229–36.

10. See Bibby, "Political Parties and Federalism"; Cornelius Cotter and John F. Bibby, "Institutional Development of Parties and the Thesis of Party Decline" *Political Science Quarterly* 95, no. 1 (1980): 1–27; Cornelius Cotter, James L. Gibson, John F. Bibby, and Robert J. Huckshorn, *Party Organizations in American Politics*. (New York: Praeger, 1984); and Robert J. Huckshorn, *Party Leadership in the States* (Amherst: University of Massachusetts Press, 1976).

11. Xandra Kayden and Eddie Mahe, Jr., *The Party Goes On: The Persistence of the Two-Party System in the United States* (New York: Basic Books Inc, 1985).

12. See Cotter, Gibson, Bibby, and Huckshorn, *Party Organizations*.

13. John H. Aldrich, "Southern Parties in State and Nation" *Journal of Politics* 62 (2000):643–70.

14. See Aldrich, Gomez, and Griffin, "State Party Organizations."

15. See Cotter, Gibson, Bibby, and Huckshorn, *Party Organizations.*

16. The state-level data from the Cotter et al. (1984) survey—available from the Interuniversity Consortium for Political Science and Social Research—has been censored for privacy issues. The author's attempts to acquire the state-identifiable results have failed.

17. See Davis, Kurlowski, *Campaign Inc.*; and Aldrich, Gomez, and Griffin, *State Party Organization Study.*

18. On the one hand, broadening the pool of potential respondents within each organization presents the opportunity for a higher response rate. On the other hand, expanding the potential pool of respondents beyond state party chairpersons, exclusively, might introduce bias when comparing the results of this survey to those of Aldrich, Gomez, and Griffin (1999). However, considering both state parties in this analysis were led by different chairpersons in 2013 than in the 1999, the potential for respondent bias could not have been avoided if Davis and Kurlowski (2013) had limited their potential pool of respondents to chairpersons. While it is possible that a party's chairperson and its executive director could give different answers to survey questions, given the objective nature of the questions posed in both surveys, it is assumed that each respondent answered the questions honestly and to the best of his or her knowledge.

19. See Aldrich, Gomez, and Griffin, *State Party Organization Study.*

20. See Davis and Kurlowski, *Campaigns Inc.*

21. See Davis and Kurlowski, *Campaigns Inc.*

22. See Davis and Kurlowski, *Campaigns Inc.*; and Aldrich, Gomez, and Griffin, *State Party Organization Study.*

23. Aldrich, Gomez, and Griffin, *State Party Organization Study.*

24. Aldrich, Gomez, and Griffin, *State Party Organization Study.*

25. See Alan Ehrenhalt, *The United States of Ambition: Politicians, Power, and the Pursuit of Office.* (New York: Times Books, 1991); Linda L. Fowler, and Robert D. McClure, *Political Ambition: Who Decides to Run for Congress.* (New Haven: Yale University Press, 1990); and Gary F. Moncrief, Peverill Squire, and Malcolm E. Jewell, *Who Runs for the Legislature?* (Upper Saddle River, NJ: Prentice Hall, 2001) for literature on groups of citizens and political elites. See Kira Sanbonmatsu, "The Legislative Party and Candidate Recruitment in the American States," *Party Politics* 12 (2006): 233–56 for research on state legislative leaders and James L. Gibson, Cornelius P. Cotter, John F. Bibby, and Robert J. Huckshorn, "Assessing Party Organizational Strength," *American Journal of Political Science* 27 (1983): 193–222 for literature on party recruitment.

26. Thomas A. Kazee and Mary C. Thornberry, "Where's the Party? Congressional Candidate Recruitment and American Party Organizations," *Western Political Quarterly*, 43 (1990): 61–80.

27. Specifically, see page 70 in Paul S. Herrnson and Robert M. Tennant, "Running for Congress Under the Shadow of the Capitol Dome: The Race for Virginia's 8th District," in *Who Runs for Congress? Ambition, Context, and Candidate Emergence*, ed. Thomas A. Kazee (Washington: CQ Press, 1994); and pages 111–12 in Thomas A. Kazee and Susan L. Roberts, "Challenging a 'Safe' Incumbent: Latent Competition in North Carolina's 9th District," in *Who Runs for Congress? Ambition Context, and Candidate Emergence*, ed. Thomas A. Kazee (Washington: CQ Press, 1994).

28. Karl Kurtz, "The Term-Limited States," February 11, 2013. http://www.ncsl

.org/research/about-state-legislatures/chart-of-term-limits-states.aspx (accessed August 25, 2014).

29. Aldrich, Gomez, and Griffin, *State Party Organization Study*.

30. See Davis and Kurlowski, *Campaigns Inc.*

31. See Dulio and Garrett, *Organizational Strength*.

32. Aldrich, Gomez, and Griffin, *State Party Organization Study*.

33. See Davis and Kurlowski, *Campaigns Inc.*

34. The Democratic Party of Arkansas provides a 'Voter File' for candidates and county committees for a fee.

35. See Cotter and Bibby, *Institutional Development*; Huckshorn, Cornelius P. Cotter, John F. Bibby, and James L. Gibson, *The Social Background and Career Patterns of State Party Leaders* Unpublished Manuscript, 1982; and John S. Jackson, III. and Robert A. Hitlin, "The Nationalization of the Democratic Party," *Western Political Quarterly* 34, no. 2 (1981): 270–86.

36. Cornelius Cotter, James L. Gibson, John F. Bibby, and Robert J. Huckshorn, *Party Organizations in American Politics* (New York: Praeger, 1984).

37. William Crotty, *Decision for the Democrats* (Baltimore: Johns Hopkins University Press, 1978).

38. Charles Longley, "Party Reform and Party Nationalization: The Case of the Democrats," in *The Party Symbol: Readings on Political Parties*, ed. William Crotty (San Francisco: W.H. Freeman and Company, 1980).

39. Gary D. Wekkin,"National-State Relations: The Democrats' New Federal Structure" *Political Science Quarterly* 99 (1984): 45–72; Gary D. Wekkin, "Political Parties and Intergovernmental Relations in 1984: The Consequences of Party Renewal for Territorial Constituencies," *Publius: The Journal of Federalism* 15 (1985): 24; and Deil S. Wright, *Understanding Intergovernmental Relations* (Monterey, CA: Brooks/ Cole Publishing, 1982).

40. See Bibby, *Political Parties and Federalism*.

41. Aldrich, Gomez, and Griffin, *State Party Organization Study*.

42. See Davis and Kurlowski, *Campaigns Inc.*

43. Aldrich, Gomez, and Griffin, *State Party Organization Study*.

44. See Bibby, *Political Parties and Federalism*.

45. See Dulio and Garrett, *Organizational Strength*.

46. Aldrich, Gomez, and Griffin, *State Party Organization Study*.

47. The 2013 responses under the category of "candidate support" are used in place of the 1999 study's measures of county support.

48. See Dulio and Garrett, *Organizational Strength*.

49. Aldrich, Gomez, and Griffin, *State Party Organization Study*.

50. Aldrich, Gomez, and Griffin, *State Party Organization Study*; and Davis and Kurlowski, *Campaigns Inc.*

51. Dwaine Marvick, "Party Organizational Personnel and Electoral Democracy in Los Angeles, 1963–1972," in *The Party Symbol: Readings on Political Parties*, ed. William Crotty (San Fransisco: W.H Freeman and Company, 1980), 65.

52. Aldrich, Gomez, and Griffin, *State Party Organization Study*.

53. John F. Bibby, "State Party Organizations: Strengthened and Adapting to Candidate-Centered Politics and Nationalization," In *The Parties Respond: Changes in American Parties and Campaigns*, ed. Sandy L. Maisel (Boulder, CO: Westview Press, 2002); and Sarah M. Morehouse and Malcolm E. Jewell, "The Future of Political

Parties in the States," March 10, 2014, http://www.csg.org/knowledgecenter/docs/BOS2005-PoliticalParties.pdf.

54. Austin Ranney, "Parties in State Politics," In *Politics in the American States*, 3rd. eds. Herbert Jacob and Kenneth N. Vines (Boston: Little Brown, 1976).

55. V. O. Key, Jr., *Southern Politics* (New York: Random House, 1949).

56. John H. Aldrich, "Southern Parties in State and Nation," *Journal of Politics* 62 (2000): 643–70.

57. See Morehouse and Jewell, *The Future of Political Parties*. 1. This now-standard definition of politics is from Harold Lasswell's 1936 book, *Politics: Who Gets What, When, How* (New York: Whittlesey House).

CHAPTER 14

1. This now-standard definition of politics is from Harold Lasswell's 1936 book, *Politics: Who Gets What, When, How (New York: Whittlesey House)*.

2. Aaron Wildavsky, *The Politics of the Budgetary Process* (Boston: Little, Brown and Company, 1964), 5.

3. Ron Snell, "State Experiences with Annual and Biennial Budgeting," National Conference of State Legislatures, 2011, accessed July 29, 2018, at http://www.ncsl.org/documents/fiscal/biennialbudgeting_may2011.pdf

4. See Snell, "State Experiences."

5. National Association of State Budget Officers (NASBO), *Budget Processes in the States*, 2015 accessed June 8, 2017 at https://www.nasbo.org/reports-data/budget-processes-in-the-states.

6. See NASBO, *Budget Processes in the States*.

7. National Conference of State Legislatures (NCSL), *State Budget Procedures*, 2018, accessed September 17, 2018, at http://www.ncsl.org/research/fiscal-policy/state-budget-procedures.aspx.

8. Per email from the state Department of Finance and Administration received August 1, 2018, the luxury tax consists of money from alcohol taxes (17.6% of total), tobacco taxes (62.3%), racing taxes (0.7%), and electronic game of skill fees (19.5%).

9. Information per email from state Department of Finance and Administration.

10. Arkansas Bureau of Legislative Research, *Selected Statistical Financial Data for Arkansas*—"B-Book," Fiscal Services Division, 2018, accessed October 24, 2018, at http://www.arkleg.state.ar.us/bureau/fiscal/Publications/D.%20Various%20Historical%20Data%20for%20State%20Expenditures%20and%20Reciepts%20(B-Book)/2018%20B%20BOOK%20-%20Various%20Selected%20Data.pdf.

11. National Conference of State Legislatures (NCSL), *2013 State and Legislative Partisan Composition*, 2013, accessed September 17, 2018, at http://www.ncsl.org/documents/statevote/legiscontrol_2013.pdf.

12. For a succinct comparison of the nature of state operating and capital budgets, please see Liz Farmer, "What's in Your Capital Budget?" in *Governing*, September 2018, available online at http://www.governing.com/topics/finance/gov-capital-budgets-spending-construction.html.

13. Arkansas Constitution-Amendment 86, 1874, Accessed on October 25, 2018, at http://www.arkleg.state.ar.us/assembly/Summary/ArkansasConstitution1874.pdf.

14. Donald Whistler, *Citizen Legislature: The Arkansas General Assembly.* (Indianapolis: Western Newspaper Publishing Company, 2010).

15. Log Cabin Democrat, "Arkansas Becomes 45th Legislature to Meet Annually," February 10, 2010, accessed May 30, 2018, at http://www.thecabin.net/news/2010–02–07/arkansas-becomes-45th-legislature-to-meet-annually; and J. Weist, "Proposed Constitutional Amendment Would Authorize Annual Legislative Sessions," Arkansas News Bureau, October 27, 2008, accessed March 26, 2018, at http://arkansasnews.com/archive/2008/10/27/News/348702.html.

16. See Weist, *Proposed Constitutional Amendment.*

17. Arkansas Secretary of State, Proposed Constitutional Amendment No.2, accessed March 26, 2018, at https://www.ark.org/elections/index.php?ac:show:contest_statewide=1&elecid=181&contestid=3

18. Joint Budget Committee, Memorandum on Annual Sessions, Arkansas General Assembly, January 15, 2009.

19. Arkansas Department of Finance and Administration, *Instructions for Preparation of the 2017–2019 Biennial Budget Request for State Agencies, Boards, and Commissions, 2016,* accessed January 26, 2018 at https://www.dfa.arkansas.gov/images/uploads/budgetOffice/biennial_budget_instruction_packet.pdf

20. See NASBO, *Budget Processes in the States.*

21. See NASBO, *Budget Processes in the States.*

22. See Arkansas Department of Finance and Administration, *Instructions for Preparation.*

23. The Institutions of Higher Education, Department of Transportation, and Game and Fish Commission submit different budget request forms.

24. See Arkansas Department of Finance and Administration, *Instructions for Preparation.*

25. See NASBO, *Budget Processes in the States.*

26. Arkansas Constitution-Amendment 20, 1874, accessed October 25, 2018, at http://www.arkleg.state.ar.us/assembly/Summary/ArkansasConstitution1874.pdf; and Arkansas Code Annotated 19–1–212; 19–4–201, accessed October 25, 2018, at https://advance.lexis.com/container?config=00JAA3ZTU0NTIzYyozZDEyLTRhYmQtYmRmMS1iMWIxNDgxYWMxZTQKAFBvZENhdGFsb2cubRW4ifTiwi5vLw6cI1uX&crid=2501680d-3deb-470a-8176-67dc8c3c8372.

27. See NASBO, *Budget Processes in the States.*

28. Arkansas Legislative Council, Memorandum on Annual Sessions, December 9, 2008, Arkansas News.com.

29. Arkansas Bureau of Legislative Research, Appropriation and Budget Process-2017, Fiscal Services Division, 2017, accessed September 2, 2017, at http://www.arkleg.state.ar.us/bureau/fiscal/Pages/fiscalpublications.aspx?RootFolder=%2Fbureau%2Ffiscal%2FPublications%2FA%2E%20%20PowerPoints%2C%20Fund%20Types%2C%20Important%20Dates&FolderCTID=0x01200056C8641E695011488F9359B04DEB7359&View={34E8AA0B-60B7-4E32-9D73-417EDBBFD1C6}.

30. See Arkansas Bureau of Legislative Research, *Appropriation and Budget Process.*

31. See NASBO, *Budget Processes in the States.*

32. Council of State Governments, The Book of the States. The Governors—Powers, 2018, accessed October 24, 2018, at http://knowledgecenter.csg.org/kc/content/book-states-2018-chapter-4-state-executive-branch.

33. All agency heads must be present for their agency's budget hearing. However, they cannot be in the committee room for the fiscal analyst's presentation of their

agency. The agency heads are called in from a waiting room if the legislators require additional questioning.

34. See NASBO, *Budget Processes in the States.*

35. See Arkansas Legislative Council, Memorandum on Annual Sessions.

36. Arkansas Department of Finance and Administration-Office of Budget, Funded Budget by Fund Source, 2017, accessed October 11, 2017, at http://www.dfa .arkansas.gov/offices/budget/Documents/fy2017_funded_budget_schedule.pdf.

37. Arkansas adopted a law to require that all bills have a single subject in 1868; the state later replaced that rule with one that required that only each appropriation bill have a single subject, in 1874. Note that Arkansas and Mississippi are the only states in the US that have this rule for appropriation bills. See Michael D. Gilbert, "Single Subject Rules and the Legislative Process," *University of Pittsburgh Law Review* 67 (2006): 803–70.

38. See Arkansas Bureau of Legislative Research, *Appropriation and Budget Process.*

39. See NASBO, *Budget Processes in the States.*

40. National Conference of State Legislatures (NCSL), *Legislative Budget Procedures* (Washington, DC: National Conference of State Legislatures, 1998).

41. Arkansas Constitution, Article 5—Legislative Department, Section 39, 1874, accessed October 25, 2018, at http://www.arkleg.state.ar.us/assembly/Summary/ArkansasConstitution1874.pdf.

42. National Conference of State Legislatures (NCSL), *Supermajority Vote Requirements to Pass the Budget,* 2017, accessed January 31, 2018, at http://www .ncsl.org/research/fiscal-policy/supermajority-vote-requirements-to-pass-the-budget635542510.aspx#1.

43. Encyclopedia of Arkansas, "Amendments 19 and 20," 2014, accessed October 25, 2018, at http://www.encyclopediaofarkansas.net/encyclopedia/entry -detail.aspx?entryID=4161.

44. See NSCL, *Legislative Budget Procedures.*

45. See NCSL, *Supermajority Vote Requirements.*

46. See NASBO, *Budget Processes in the States.*

47. Catherine C. Reese, "The Line-Item Veto in Practice in Ten Southern States," *Public Administration Review* (November/December 1997): 510–16.

48. See Reese, "The Line-Item Veto.".

49. Encyclopedia of Arkansas, "Revenue Stabilization Act," 2015, http://www .encyclopediaofarkansas.net/encyclopedia/entry-detail.aspx?entryID=7840.

50. Meagan M. Jordan, "Arkansas Revenue Stabilization Act: Stabilizing Programmatic Impact Through Prioritized Revenue Distribution," Research Note, *State & Local Government Review* 38, no. 2 (2006): 104–11.

51. See NASBO, *Budget Processes in the States.*

52. See Arkansas Bureau of Legislative Research, *Appropriation and Budget Process.*

53. See Jordan, "Arkansas Revenue Stabilization Act," 109.

54. See Arkansas Bureau of Legislative Research, 2017.

55. See Arkansas Bureau of Legislative Research, 2017.

56. See Arkansas Bureau of Legislative Research, 2017.

57. Christine Vestal, "The Arkansas Approach: How One State Has Avoided Fiscal Disaster," *Stateline,* PEW Trusts, 2011, http://www.pewtrusts.org/en/

research-and-analysis/blogs/stateline/2011/09/20/the-arkansas-approach-how-one
-state-has-avoided-fiscal-disaster.

58. See Jordan, *Arkansas Revenue Stabilization Act*, 109.

59. See Vestal, *The Arkansas Approach*.

60. See NCSL, *Legislative Budget Procedures*.

61. See NCSL, *Supermajority Vote Requirements*.

62. At one time, Arkansas was regarded as the single state that was the hardest-hit by legislative term limits.

63. Tax Foundation, "Tax Cuts Signed in Arkansas," 2017, accessed October 29, 2018, at https://taxfoundation.org/tax-cuts-signed-arkansas/.

64. Wesley Brown, "Legislative Panel Back Governor Hutchinson's Tax Cut Plan, Internet, Sales Tax Proposal," August 7, 2018, *Talk Business*, accessed October 29, 2018, at https://talkbusiness.net/2018/08/legislative-panel-backs-gov-hutchinsons-tax-cut -plan-internet-sales-tax-proposal/

65. US News," Arkansas Unemployment Rate Hits Record Low 3.5 Percent," 2018, accessed October 28, 2018, at https://www.usnews.com/news/best-states/ arkansas/articles/2018–10–20/arkansas-unemployment-rate-hits-record-low-35-percent.

66. National Conference of State Legislatures (NCSL), "The Term-Limited States," 2015, accessed September 19, 2018, at http://www.ncsl.org/research/about -state-legislatures/chart-of-term-limits-states.aspx.

67. Arkansas Constitution-Amendment 73, 1874, accessed October 25, 2018, at http://www.arkleg.state.ar.us/assembly/Summary/ArkansasConstitution1874.pdf.

68. Arkansas Constitution-Amendment 94, 1874, accessed October 25, 2018, at http://www.arkleg.state.ar.us/assembly/Summary/ArkansasConstitution1874.pdf.

CHAPTER 15

1. Major commentaries on the Little Rock crisis include: Tony Freyer, *The Little Rock Crisis: A Constitutional Interpretation* (Westport, CT: Greenwood Press, 1984); Elizabeth Jacoway, *Turn Away Thy Son: Little Rock, the Crisis That Shocked a Nation* (New York: Free Press, 2007); Irving J. Spitzberg, Jr., *Racial Politics in Little Rock, 1954–1964* (New York: Garland Publishing, 1987); John A. Kirk, *Redefining the Color Line: Black Activism in Little Rock, Arkansas, 1940–1970* (Gainesville: University Press of Florida, 2002); Roy Reed, *Faubus: The Life and Times of an American Prodigal* (Fayetteville: University of Arkansas Press, 1997); Corinne Silverman, *The Little Rock Story* (University: University of Alabama Press, 1959).

2. Karen Anderson, *Little Rock: Race and Resistance at Central High School* (Princeton: Princeton University Press, 2010), 100. As Anderson rightly says, what went on inside Central has commonly been treated as "at most, a sidebar to the main story" (p. 275).

3. D. LaRouth S. Perry, "The 1957 Desegregation Crisis of Little Rock, Arkansas: A Meeting of Histories" (PhD diss., Bowling Green State University, 1998), 243–55 (quotations, 252, 245); Sondra Gordy, *Finding the Lost Year: What Happened When Little Rock Closed Its Public Schools* (Fayetteville: University of Arkansas Press, 2009); Sondra Gordy, "Empty Classrooms, Empty Hearts: Little Rock Secondary Teachers, 1958–1959," *Arkansas Historical Quarterly* 56 (Winter 1997): 427–42; Sondra Gordy, "Elizabeth Huckaby and the 'Lost Year,'" *Arkansas Historical Quarterly* 67 (Summer 2008): 141–57.

4. Elizabeth Huckaby, *Crisis at Central High: Little Rock, 1957–58* (Baton Rouge: Louisiana State University Press, 1980), 48, 95–96. The Little Rock Nine were: Ernest Green (a senior); Melba Pattillo, Elizabeth Eckford, Thelma Mothershed, Minnijean Brown, and Terrence Roberts (juniors); and Gloria Ray, Carlotta Walls, and Jefferson Thomas (sophomores).

5. Ralph Brodie and Marvin Schwartz, *Central in Our Lives: Voices from Little Rock Central High School, 1957–59* (Little Rock: Butler Center for Arkansas Studies, 2007), 26.

6. An exception is guidance officer Shirley Stancil in Paul Root, *Learning Together at Last: Memories of the Desegregation of the Arkansas Public School System* (Arkadelphia: Pete Parks Center for Regional Studies, Ouachita Baptist University, 2005), 14–19. The nine faculty who testified during the school board's June 1958 case for a delay in further integration did so in a general way rather than about specific classroom situations; *Aaron v. Cooper*, transcript, June 4–6, 1958, series 2, box 5, files 6 and 7, Virgil T. Blossom Papers, Special Collections, University of Arkansas Libraries, Fayetteville; Tony A. Freyer, *Little Rock on Trial: Cooper v. Aaron and School Desegregation* (Lawrence: University Press of Kansas, 2007), 144–50.

7. Melba Pattillo Beals, *Warriors Don't Cry: A Searing Memoir of the Battle to Integrate Little Rock's Central High* (New York: Pocket Books, 1994).

8. Elizabeth Huckaby diary, May 26, 1958, series 1, box 1, file 1, Elizabeth Paisley Huckaby Papers, Special Collections, University of Arkansas Libraries, Fayetteville [hereafter Huckaby Papers]; Huckaby, *Crisis at Central High*, 210.

9. Henry Hampton and Steve Fayer, eds., *Voices of Freedom: An Oral History of the Civil Rights Movement from the 1950s through the 1980s* (New York: Bantam Books, 1990), 49. While Pattillo does not name her English teacher, Huckaby reports that she was the victim of a pencil throwing incident in Dewberry's classroom; *Crisis at Central High*, 46. Huckaby's schedule for September 1957 shows that Dewberry taught English to the appropriate year level and at the appropriate time to be the person whose classes regularly gave Pattillo grief; Beals, *Warriors Don't Cry*, 111–12, 135–36, 160, 207–8, 256; Terrence Roberts, *Lessons from Little Rock* (Little Rock: Butler Center Books, 2009), 116.

10. *Southern School News*, January 1958, 8; *Arkansas Democrat* (Little Rock), December 15, 1957.

11. Huckaby, *Crisis at Central High*, 41; *Arkansas Democrat*, October 3, 1957; Elizabeth Huckaby, incident report, March 3, 1958 (in possession of Joe Matthews, Little Rock).

12. Phyllis Dillaha, personal communication, March 30, 2010; *Arkansas Democrat*, September 29, 1957.

13. John Chancellor, "Radio and TV Had Their Own Problems in Little Rock," *Quill*, December 1957, 9–10, 20–21; David Halberstam, *The Fifties* (New York: Villard Books, 1993), 680; Gene Roberts and Hank Klibanoff, *The Race Beat: The Press, the Civil Rights Struggle and the Awakening of a Nation* (New York: Knopf, 2006), 143–46, 150–83.

14. J. O. Powell, "Central High School Inside Out: A Study in Disintegration," ch. 9, unpaginated typescript, box 1, files 3–5, Velma and J. O. Powell Collection, Special Collections, University of Arkansas Libraries, Fayetteville; Huckaby, *Crisis at Central High*, 211.

15. Huckaby, *Crisis at Central High*, 163; Powell, police statement, March 6, 1958,

in Powell, "Central High School Inside Out," ch. 8; Jerry Hulett, "Sammy's Story: A Biography of Sammie Dean Parker Hulett," 12, box 1, file 32, Sara Alderman Murphy Papers, Special Collections, University of Arkansas Libraries, Fayetteville; Sara Alderman Murphy, *Breaking the Silence: Little Rock's Women's Emergency Committee to Open Our Schools, 1958–1963*, ed. Patrick C. Murphy II (Fayetteville: University of Arkansas Press, 1997), 53.

    16. Huckaby, *Crisis at Central High*, 108–9, 110; *Arkansas Democrat*, January 21, 1958; *Arkansas Gazette* (Little Rock), September 5, 1957; *New York Times*, December 15, 1957; Daisy Bates, *The Long Shadow of Little Rock* (New York: David McKay, 1962), 123, 131–32; Carlotta Walls LaNier with Lisa Frazier Page, *A Mighty Long Way: My Journey to Justice at Little Rock Central High School* (New York: One World/Ballantine Books, 2009), 105.

    17. Howard Bell, interview with Sondra Gordy, March 13, 1996, 36, Teachers of the Lost Year, Oral Histories, Archives and Special Collections, Torreyson Library, University of Central Arkansas, Conway [all interviews with Gordy cited hereinafter are from this collection]; Anderson, *Little Rock*, 19–20, 37–38; *Arkansas Democrat*, September 19, October 9, December 15, 1957; *Arkansas Gazette*, October 10, 1957.

    18. Robert R. Brown, *Bigger Than Little Rock* (Greenwich, CT: Seabury Press, 1958); Brown was Episcopal bishop of Arkansas and a friend of Central's male vice-principal.

    19. Powell, "Central High School Inside Out," ch. 9; *Arkansas Democrat*, October 16, 1957; Gordy, *Finding the Lost Year*, 19.

    20. *Arkansas Gazette*, September 26, 1957; Huckaby diary, September 24, 1957, February 16, 1958; Huckaby, *Crisis at Central High*, 162, 177, 179; Powell police statement.

    21. Nat Griswold to Harold Fleming, November 29, 1957, box 20, series 1, file 200, Arkansas Council on Human Relations Papers, Special Collections, University of Arkansas Libraries, Fayetteville.

    22. William Ivy, police statement, January 21, 1958, series 14, sub-series 6, box 497, file 11, Orval E. Faubus Papers, Special Collections, University of Arkansas Libraries, Fayetteville; Huckaby, *Crisis at Central High*, 192. A number of teachers were interviewed in response to an Arkansas Legislative Council inquiry into the extent of outside interference in the school situation. The resulting files were originally held by the Criminal Investigation Division of the Arkansas State Police. The few that seem to have survived are scattered across several archives, the largest group in the Faubus Papers. Unless otherwise specified, those cited in this discussion are located in this collection.

    23. Stancil, interview with Gordy, February 27, 1996, 15; Lincoln, interview with Gordy, March 18, 1996, 20; Bell, interview with Gordy, 20. See, also, Gene Hall (coach), interview with Gordy, April 2, 1996, 21.

    24. Ivy police statement; Govie Griffin, police statement, February 7, 1958. As segregationists, Ivy and Griffin might have been more than usually sensitive on a topic that had put them at odds with both their employer and (apparently) a large number of their colleagues.

    25. James Olney, in *The Slave's Narrative*, ed. Charles T. Davis and Henry Louis Gates Jr. (New York: Oxford University Press, 1985); William L. Andrews, *To Tell a Free Story: The First Century of Afro-American Autobiography, 1760–1865* (Urbana: University of Illinois Press, 1986).

    26. Powell, "Central High School Inside Out," ch. 3; Sondra Gordy, "Teachers

of the Lost Year 1958–59: The Little Rock School District" (EdD diss., University of Arkansas at Little Rock, 1996), 12. Distributive education teacher Nyna Keeton, told Gordy she thought Powell was "an angry man" and "a very controversial person"; interview, January 26, 1996, 77.

27. Huckaby, *Crisis at Central High*, 11–12, 53, 117, 139, 145; Brodie and Schwartz, *Central in Our Lives*, 48, 133; LaNier, *Mighty Long Way*, 88; *Arkansas Gazette*, May 10, 1959.

28. *New York Times, Arkansas Democrat*, and *Arkansas Gazette*, September 26, 1957; Beals, *Warriors Don't Cry*, 111–12. Allison Berg, "Trauma and Testimony in Black Women's Civil Rights Memoirs," *Journal of Women's History* 21 (Fall 2009): 93–96. Interestingly, two of the nine have expressed reservations about Beals' reliability; Perry, "1957 Desegregation Crisis of Little Rock, Arkansas," 348. See, also, Anderson, *Little Rock*, 247.

29. Powell, "Central High School Inside Out," ch. 9.

30. Lola Dunnavant, "Steel Helmets under a Summer Sun," *Pulaski County Historical Review* 37 (Summer 1989): 22–35; Lola Dunnavant, "Long Halls Growing Darker: Little Rock Central High, 1958–1959," *Pulaski County Historical Review* 37 (Fall 1989): 46–59.

31. Griffin police statement; Ivy police statement; *Arkansas Democrat*, September 19, 1957.

32. Powell, "Central High Inside Out," chs. 1, 9; Brown, *Bigger Than Little Rock*, 51; Reed, *Faubus*, 184; Brody and Schwartz, *Central in Our Lives*, 48–49, 150; Huckaby, *Crisis at Central High*, 11.

33. Colbert S. Cartwright, "Lesson from Little Rock," *Christian Century*, October 9, 1957, 1194; Brown, *Bigger Than Little Rock*, 48, 51.

34. Keeton interview with Gordy, 21; Stancil interview with Gordy, 16; *Arkansas Gazette*, May 10, 1959; Beth Roy, *Bitters in the Honey: Tales of Hope and Disappointment across Divides of Race and Time* (Fayetteville: University of Arkansas Press, 1999), 233; Jacoway, *Turn Away Thy Son*, 192; *Arkansas Democrat*, March 15, 1958; Anderson, *Little Rock*, 100, 103, 105, 115; Beals, *Warriors Don't Cry*, 109.

35. Spitzberg, *Racial Politics in Little Rock*, 44–45; Huckaby, *Crisis at Central High*, 4, 6–7.

36. Matthews interview, September 13, 1957, box 2, file 1, FBI Little Rock Report, Special Collections, University of Arkansas at Little Rock Libraries.

37. Powell, "Central High School Inside Out," prologue, chs. 3, 5, 7, 9; Roy, *Bitters in the Honey*, 233, 235; Jess Matthews, interview with John Pagan, December 27, 1972, box 2, file 11, Murphy Papers. Interestingly, Pagan comments that "Matthews wasn't an integrationist." According to a Hall High English teacher who had previously worked under him, Matthews was "a good old boy" and "no liberal"; Gordy, "Teachers of the Lost Year 1958–59," 187.

38. Powell, "Central High School Inside Out," chs. 5, 7, 9. Also Jess Matthews, police statement, March 11, 1958, 6 (in possession of Joe Matthews).

39. Huckaby, *Crisis at Central High*, 4, 43, 86, 99, 126, 151, 197. An "outside expert," Dr. Virgil Rogers, dean of education at Syracuse University, told Judge Harry Lemley in June 1958 that "a stronger lead in the principalship would have made a great deal of difference"; *Arkansas Gazette*, June 6, 1958. For an alternative view of Matthews, see Joe Matthews in Roy, *Bitters in the Honey*, 227–28, 231–33; Brodie and Schwartz, *Central in Our Lives*, 12–13, 135–36.

40. The number varies slightly from source to source and even within individual references. Huckaby, for example, notes totals of eighty-nine and ninety in her memoir *Crisis at Central High* (66, 11) and, omitting her substitute Wilma Means, the principal, and Allen Howard (all pictured in the 1958 Central yearbook, *The Pix*), includes eighty-seven names on her schedule for September 1957, series 2, box 2, file 13, Huckaby Papers. At the same time, Central's 1957 "Teacher Directory" lists ninety-one names including three nursery staff but not Means and Howard; series 2, box 2, file 13, Huckaby Papers. Removing the former and substituting the latter gives the same total as Huckaby's schedule, plus the additions indicated. The *Arkansas Gazette*, September 29, 1957, reported a complement of eighty-seven and vice-principal Powell ninety-two; "Central High School Inside Out," ch. 8.

41. Elizabeth Huckaby to Susan Smith (?), 1979, box 10, file 5, Elizabeth Paisley Huckaby Collection, Butler Center for Arkansas Studies, Little Rock.

42. Huckaby, interview with Gordy, December 18, 1995, 21.

43. Only staff identifiable by name are included in these tallies.

44. According to the *Arkansas Gazette*, September 29, 1957, forty-eight (55.2 percent) of Central's staff had postgraduate degrees, thirty-six (41.4 percent) had baccalaureates, and three (3.4 percent) had other qualifications. Fifteen of twenty-seven known moderates had masters degrees (55.6 percent) compared with six of eight segregationists (75.0 percent). Moderates had a median of eleven years of service at large (twenty-nine cases) and a median of two years at Central (thirty cases).

45. Thirty-seven of sixty-seven female staff (55.2 percent) compared with eight of twenty-three males (34.8 percent).

46. Twenty-five of thirty-eight married female staff were known moderates (65.8 percent), and twelve of twenty-nine single female staff (41.4 percent). Among moderates alone, twenty-five of thirty-seven women were married (67.6 percent), and twelve of thirty-seven were single (32.4 percent).

47. Compared with the counselors who formed 5 percent of the total staff but 7.8 percent of the moderates, the seven business teachers (7.8 percent of the total) included one moderate (2.2 percent).

48. Huckaby, *Crisis at Central High*, 11, 115, 184; Bates, *Long Shadow of Little Rock*, 144.

49. Fifteen of nineteen (78.9 percent); Gordy, *Finding the Lost Year*, 140. See, also, Stancil interview with Gordy, 31.

50. Ten cases ranging from no experience to thirty-five years.

51. Lincoln interview with Gordy, 20. Some of that year's educators had in fact been taught by long-serving staff during the 1930s and 1940s; Powell, "Central High School Inside Out," prologue; Hall interview with Gordy, 12.

52. 32.4 percent of moderate women and 45.5 percent of segregationists were single.

53. Huckaby, *Crisis at Central High*, 29–30. Twenty-four of the twenty-six teachers Huckaby lists had identifiable attitudes to integration. At least another three staff members (Naomi Hancock, Micky McGalin, and Wilma Means) had black students as the nine adjusted their enrollments in the course of the year. An unspecified number of physical education instructors also had contact with the nine.

54. Stancil interview with Gordy, 31; Huckaby, *Crisis at Central High*, 30.

55. Staff having black students ranged from twenty-one to sixty-five years of age and from heads of departments to those whose promotion prospects were dim.

Averaging 18.5 years of experience and 13 years at Central with medians of 20.5 years and 11 years respectively, the twenty known cases were more experienced than the identifiable faculty as a whole. The faculty as such averaged 16.6 years of service (thirty-nine cases) and 8.9 years at Central (forty-one cases) with medians of 14 years and 5 years respectively.

56. Huckaby diary, February 14, 18, 1958.

57. *Arkansas Democrat*, May 21, 1959, citing statements made January 21, 1958, as revealed by Ed McKinley, school board president. Edwin Walker was commander of the 101st Airborne Division that had "invaded" Little Rock on September 24, 1957.

58. Lincoln interview with Gordy, 62; Stancil interview with Gordy, 5. On Penton's teaching ability, Huckaby interview with Gordy, 8.

59. Griffin police statement.

60. Stancil interview with Gordy, 31; Barnes, police statement, February 7, 1958.

61. Ivy police statement.

62. Lincoln interview with Gordy, 20. Compare, also, Ivy police statement with LaNier, *Mighty Long Way*, 118–19.

63. Jane Emery Prather to Ralph Brodie, n.d. [April 2010] (in possession of Ralph Brodie, Little Rock).

64. Jerry Dhonau, interview with Ernest Dumas, March 3, 2000, 3–4, *Arkansas Gazette* Project, David and Barbara Pryor Center for Arkansas Oral and Visual History, University of Arkansas Libraries, Fayetteville; *Little Rock Central High School Tiger*, October 31, 1957.

65. Roberts, *Lessons from Little Rock*, 121, 123; LaNier, *Mighty Long Way*, 121–22.

66. Huckaby, *Crisis at Central High*, 108–9, 84, 114; Griffin police statement; Clarence A. Laws, "Nine Courageous Students," *Crisis*, May 1958, 272; Virgil T. Blossom, *It Has Happened Here* (New York: Harper and Brothers, 1959), 159; *Arkansas Democrat*, October 31, 1957.

67. For example, Beals, *Warriors Don't Cry*, 135, 149, 151.

68. Huckaby, *Crisis at Central High*, 52, 90, 99, 132, 143. It was official school policy only to act if examples of harassment could be corroborated by an adult witness; Ibid, 85.

69. LaNier, *Mighty Long Way*, 103; Beals, *Warriors Don't Cry*, 148.

70. Roberts, *Lessons from Little Rock*, 116, 123, 154.

71. Powell, "Central High School Inside Out," chs. 2, 6, 7.

72. Matthews police statement, 5–6.

73. Priscilla Thompson to Ralph Brodie, October 5, 2008 (in possession of Ralph Brodie). Also Huckaby, *Crisis at Central High*, 67; Al Kuettner, *March to the Promised Land: The Civil Rights Files of a White Reporter, 1952–1968* (Sterling VA: Capital Books, 2006), 26. Away from Little Rock at a conference in Grafton, Illinois, Matthews was a little more circumspect; "Off the Record," March 22, 1958, 3, 6, series 2, box 2, file 26, Huckaby Papers.

74. Powell, "Central High School Inside Out," ch. 5.

75. Keeton interview with Gordy, 59.

76. Henry, interview with Gordy, October 25, 1995, 31. Also Hall interview with Gordy, 10–11.

77. Powell, "Central High School Inside Out," ch. 5. The nine participated in normal physical education classes but were not allowed to try out for varsity sports.

78. *Southern School News*, January 1958, 8; *Arkansas Gazette*, November 24, 1957.

79. Bates, *Long Shadow of Little Rock*, 128; Office of the Deputy Chief of Staff for Military Operations, Situation Report: Arkansas, no. 207 (January 31, 1958), White House Office, Office of the Staff Secretary, box 17, Little Rock, vol. 1, Reports (8), Dwight D. Eisenhower Library, Abilene, KS.

80. Ellen Levine, *Freedom's Children: Young Civil Rights Activists Tell Their Own Stories* (New York: G. P. Putnam's Sons, 1993), 46.

81. *USA Today*, August 30, 2007.

82. *Arkansas Gazette*, February 13, 1958; Roberts, *Lessons from Little Rock*, 112–13.

83. Beals, *Warriors Don't Cry*, 112.

84. George M. Cate, *The Good Ground of Central High: Little Rock Central High School and Legendary Coach Wilson Matthews* (Little Rock: Butler Center Books, 2008), 54, 26, 20, 82. Pointedly, Johns' funeral (at which the Tigers acted as pallbearers) was held in Quigley Stadium; Ibid, 75–76.

85. *Arkansas Democrat-Gazette* (Little Rock), May 16, 2002, in Brodie and Schwartz, *Central in Our Lives*, 148.

86. Barry Stollenberger, "Fullerton: More Famous Than Faubus," in *Barry Stollenberger's 1988 Phoenix Metro Football*, 68, in Ralph Brodie (comp.), *Little Rock Central High Tigers 1955–1956–1957* (Little Rock: Ralph Brodie, 2007), n.p.

87. Blossom, *It Has Happened Here*, 158. According to the *New York Post*, September 25, 1957, Blossom "carefully schooled . . . his school's football stars in the example they must set if integration is to succeed." Gordy, *Finding the Lost Year*, 71. Also William G. Cooper, Jr. (school board member), interview with John Luter, December 28, 1970, 23–24, Dwight D. Eisenhower Administration Oral History Project, Columbia University, New York.

88. Beals, *Warriors Don't Cry*, 249–50, 255–57, 263, 271, 278–83. That it is unclear whether Link was inspired by his coach or, as Pattillo Beals suggests, empathy flowing from a special affection for his black nanny or a combination of the two is simply testimony to the complexity of attitudes too easily attributed to a single cause.

89. Little Rock Central High School, *The Pix of '58* (Little Rock: Central High School, 1958). Based on a 25 percent sample from the 1957–1958 Central High student directory, *Dial T for Tiger*, 864 of Central's 1963 students were males (44.0 percent). Of these 160 (18.5 percent) were involved in some sort of protest against the Nine; Graeme Cope, "'Marginal Youngsters' and 'Hoodlums of Both Sexes': Student Segregationists during the Little Rock School Crisis," *Arkansas Historical Quarterly* 68 (Winter 2004): 384. Interestingly, a higher proportion (14.3 percent) of the thirty-five junior varsity players coached by Ralph Holland showed their displeasure at the presence of black students, including one sufficiently prominent to be labelled a leader of the resistance; *Aaron v. Cooper*, transcript, June 3, 1958, 65.

90. Huckaby, *Crisis at Central High*, 141–42; Roberts, *Lessons from Little Rock*, 13–15; Bates, *Long Shadow of Little Rock*, 123, 124, 128; Powell, "Central High School Inside Out," ch. 5; *New York Post Daily Magazine*, October 21, 1957; Hampton and Fayer, *Voices of Freedom*, 48.

91. Huckaby, *Crisis at Central High*, 34; Brodie and Schwartz, *Central in Our Lives*, 149; Jacoway, *Turn Away Thy Son*, 192; *Arkansas Democrat*, September 23, 1957.

92. Roberts, *Lessons from Little Rock*, 120, 123.

93. Huckaby, *Crisis at Central High*, 187, 171; Beals, *Warriors Don't Cry*, 114, 136, 169–71, 186, 188, 208, 186, 190, 205, 208, 212, 254, 257; Booknotes on C-Span: A

Companion Website to C-Span's Sunday author interview series *Booknotes*, Booknotes Transcript, November 27, 1994, 17, www.booknotes.org/transcripts/50014.htm. (accessed June 13, 2000). Beals mistakenly refers to this teacher as Mrs. Pickwick.

94. Scholastic Inc., interview transcripts, Melba Pattillo Beals, 5, teacher .scholastic.com/barrier/hwyf/mpbstory/melchat.htm (accessed June 13, 2000).

95. *Amsterdam News* (New York), September 28, 1957; *New York Herald Tribune*, September 24, 1957; Beals, *Warriors Don't Cry*, 111–12, 135–36, 141, 149, 160, 190–91, 207, 256, 265, 273 (citations from 136, 160, 256).

96. Roberts, *Lessons from Little Rock*, 129; Stancil interview with Gordy, 31; Root, *Learning Together at Last*, 17; Beals, Booknotes on C-Span, 17–18.

97. Huckaby, *Crisis at Central High*, 91. For Melba's perspective on changing from chemistry to the French she soon attempted to abandon for speech: Beals, *Warriors Don't Cry*, 141, 231.

98. LaNier, *Mighty Long Way*, 33, 106, 171, 219; *Arkansas State Press* (Little Rock), May 23, 1958.

99. Bates, *Long Shadow of Little Rock*, 135; Huckaby, *Crisis at Central High*, 72; Beals, *Warriors Don't Cry*, 232; Roberts, *Lessons from Little Rock*, 180.

100. Hampton and Fayer, *Voices of Freedom*, 49.

101. LaNier, *Mighty Long Way*, 88, 104, 121–22.

102. *Arkansas Gazette*, September 16, 1957; Hampton and Fayer, *Voices of Freedom*, 51; Brodie and Schwartz, *Central in Our Lives*, 41–42, 133; Huckaby, *Crisis at Central High*, 202.

103. *New York Post*, September 24, 1957; Hampton and Fayer, *Voices of Freedom*, 51; Brodie and Schwartz, *Central in Our Lives*, 41; Barnes police statement. Perhaps tellingly, Barnes refers to Green as Clarence rather than Ernest. Barnes hints that Green received help from other teachers. He notes that Green always did better on regularly scheduled tests accessible to other faculty than on those sprung without notice.

104. *New York Post Daily Magazine*, October 25, 1957.

105. Elizabeth Jacoway, "Not Anger but Sorrow: Minnijean Brown Trickey Remembers the Little Rock Crisis," *Arkansas Historical Quarterly* 64 (Spring 2005): 13, 19.

106. Huckaby, *Crisis at Central High*, 113–15; Lincoln interview with Gordy, 21.

107. Confidential Bulletin to Teachers, September 23, 1957, in Powell, "Central High School Inside Out," ch. 2.

108. Priscilla Thompson to Ralph Brodie, October 5, 2008. Thompson also suspected the same teacher, again despite her racial sensibilities, arranged for Eckford to sit near her "as a calm individual and not expected to cause trouble."

109. LaNier, *Mighty Long Way*, xiii, 103; Beals, *Warriors Don't Cry*, 191; Roberts, *Lessons from Little Rock*, 129, 116 (original emphasis).

110. LaNier, *Mighty Long Way*, 187–88, 118–19. While LaNier reports that white students "usually" led proceedings, Melba Pattillo did so at least once; Beals, *Warriors Don't Cry*, 198–99. See, also, Larry Taylor (a junior) in Root, *Learning Together at Last*, 27.

111. Stancil, in Root, *Learning Together at Last*, 16–17.

112. *Arkansas Democrat*, October 9, 1957; Blossom, *It Has Happened Here*, 172.

113. *Arkansas Gazette*, May 11, 1959; Brown, *Bigger than Little Rock*, 51.

114. *Arkansas Democrat*, September 10, 1957; *Arkansas Gazette*, June 4, 1958; Dunnavant, "Long Halls Growing Darker," 47; Dunnavant, "Steel Helmets under

a Summer Sky," 33. Also, *Arkansas Democrat*, September 3, 29; October 9, 20;
December 15, 1957; March 15, 1958; *Arkansas Gazette*, September 26; October 30, 1957;
January 19; February 8, 1958; Huckaby, *Crisis at Central High*, 62, 181–82; Powell police
statement.

    115. Huckaby, *Crisis at Central High*, 64, 113–14; Brodie and Schwartz, *Central in
Our Lives*, 32.

    116. Powell police statement.

    117. Henry interview with Gordy, 45.

    118. *Arkansas Gazette*, August 28, 1958; Huckaby, *Crisis at Central High*, 53.

    119. *Arkansas Gazette*, January 29, 1958; Huckaby, *Crisis at Central High*, 115;
Powell, "Central High School Inside Out," ch. 8. Also, Arkansas Council on Human
Relations, Progress Report, Second Quarter, 1957–58, 2, series 1, box 27, file 287,
ACHR Papers. When she returned to Central as a senior in 1959, Carlotta Walls found
that while some of her teachers would still have been happier without her company,
"many . . . seemed to take a more active role in reporting the troublemakers" and "the
grades they gave me were mostly fair"; LaNier, *Mighty Long Way*, 164, 168, 187–88.

    120. Huckaby, *Crisis at Central High*, 29–30; Elizabeth Brandon (English teacher)
in Brodie and Schwartz, *Central in Our Lives*, 96; *USA Today*, August 30, 2007;
Anderson, *Little Rock*, 94–126.

    121. Brodie and Schwartz, *Central in Our Lives*, 84, 133–36.

    122. Joe Matthews, interview with Beth Roy, n.d., 3 (in possession of Joe
Matthews).

    123. Beals, *Warriors Don't Cry*, xx.

    124. Ivy police statement.

    125. Huckaby, *Crisis at Central High*, 30.

    126. Hall interview with Gordy, 21.

CHAPTER 16

    1. On the Civil Rights Act of 1964, see Hugh D. Graham, *The Civil Rights Era:
Origins and Development of National Policy, 1960–1972* (New York: Oxford University
Press, 1990); Robert D. Loevy, *To End All Segregation: The Politics of the Passage of the
Civil Rights Act of 1964* (Lanham, MD: University Press of America, 1990); Robert
Loevy, ed., *The Civil Rights Act of 1964: The Passage of the Law that Ended Racial
Segregation* (Albany: State University of New York Press, 1997); Charles W. Whalen
and Barbara Whalen, *The Longest Debate: A Legislative History of the 1964 Civil Rights
Act* (Cabin John, MD: Seven Locks Press, 1985). On desegregation and the courts, see
Richard Kluger, *Simple Justice: The History of Brown v. Board of Education and Black
America's Struggle for Equality* (New York: Alfred A. Knopf, 1976); Michael Klarman,
From Jim Crow to Civil Rights: The Supreme Court and the Struggle for Racial Equality
(New York: Oxford University Press, 2004).

    2. *Heart of Atlanta Motel, Inc. v. United States*, 379 U.S. 241 (1964); *Katzenbach
v. McClung*, 379 U.S. 94 (1964). See, also, Richard C. Cortner, *Civil Rights and Public
Accommodations: The Heart of Atlanta Motel and McClung Cases* (Lawrence: University
Press of Kansas, 2001).

    3. On Brown and massive resistance, see Numan V. Bartley, *The Rise of Massive
Resistance: Race and Politics in the South during the 1950s* (Baton Rouge: Louisiana State
University Press, 1969); Neil R. McMillen, *The Citizens' Council: Organized Resistance*

to the Second Reconstruction, 1955–1964 (Urbana: University of Illinois Press, 1971); George Lewis, *Massive Resistance: The White Response to the Civil Rights Movement* (London: Hodder and Arnold, 2006).

4. On the generally begrudging acceptance of the Civil Rights Act of 1964, see Taylor Branch, *Pillar of Fire: America in the King Years, 1963–65* (New York: Simon and Schuster, 1998), 388–89.

5. "Compliance with Title II: A Summary of the Field Reports from Southern States," series 1, box 7, folder 64, Arkansas Council on Human Relations Papers (hereinafter ACHR Papers), Special Collections, University of Arkansas Libraries, Fayetteville.

6. "Compliance with Title II: A Summary."

7. Jeff Wiltse, *Contested Waters: A Social History of Swimming Pools in America* (Chapel Hill: University of North Carolina Press, 2007), 156 (quotation).

8. Victoria W. Wolcott, *Race, Riots, and Roller Coasters: The Struggle over Segregated Recreation in America* (Philadelphia: University of Pennsylvania Press, 2012), 121, 164–69.

9. Daisy Bates, *The Long Shadow of Little Rock: A Memoir* (New York: David McKay, 1962), 2.

10. John A. Kirk, *Redefining the Color Line: Black Activism in Little Rock, Arkansas, 1940–1970* (Gainesville: University Press of Florida, 2002), chaps. 2 and 3.

11. Kirk, *Redefining the Color Line*, chap. 5.

12. John A. Kirk, "The Origins of SNCC in Arkansas: Little Rock, Lupper, and the Law," in *Arsnick: The Student Nonviolent Coordinating Committee in Arkansas*, ed. Jennifer Jensen Wallach and John A. Kirk (Fayetteville: University of Arkansas Press, 2011), 3–22.

13. John A. Kirk, "Battle Cry of Freedom: Little Rock, Arkansas, and the Freedom Rides at Fifty," *Arkansas Review* 42 (August 2011): 76–103.

14. *Freeman v. City of Little Rock*, ED Ark., W. Div., #LR-62-C-40.

15. Kirk, "Origins of SNCC in Arkansas," 15.

16. Kirk, *Redefining the Color Line*, chap. 6 (quotation on p. 158).

17. James Reed Eison, "White City," *Pulaski County Historical Review* 59 (Fall 2011): 102–7; Cheryl Griffith Nichols, "The Development of Pulaski Heights," *Pulaski County Historical Review* 30 (Spring 1982): 2–16; Cheryl Griffith Nichols, "Pulaski Heights: Early Suburban Development in Little Rock, Arkansas," *Arkansas Historical Quarterly* 41 (Summer 1982): 129–45.

18. "Pertinent Facts Concerning the Bond Issues for the New Municipal Pool," box 5, folder 11, Leroy Scott City Pool Collection, Butler Center for Arkansas Studies, Arkansas Studies Institute, Little Rock (hereinafter City Pool Collection, ASI); Lynda B. Langford, "The Work Projects Administration in the Pulaski County District," *Pulaski County Historical Review* 35 (Spring 1987): 2–15.

19. Wiltse, *Contested Waters*, chap. 4.

20. "Election on Two Bond Issues Today," *Arkansas Gazette* (Little Rock), August 23, 1940; "Big Majorities Accorded Both of Bond Issues," *Arkansas Gazette*, August 24, 1940; "Bond Issues Approved By Big Vote," *Arkansas Democrat* (Little Rock), August 24, 1940; all clippings in box 5, folder 11, City Pool Collection, ASI.

21. "Fair Park Pool Crowded at Opening," *Arkansas Gazette*, May 29, 1942, clipping in box 1, folder 1, City Pool Collection, ASI. Named the J. Curran Conway Pool after the chair of the Little Rock Recreation Commission (and vice president of

Little Rock's Federal Home Loan Bank), the facility was popularly known by different names. When it first opened, it was billed as Fair Park Pool because of its location in the Fair Park neighborhood. When War Memorial Stadium was built nearby in 1948, it became known as War Memorial Pool. Conway apparently did not object to the alternate names. In fact, a newspaper account noted, "More than modesty prompts him to beg off from the honor. He just can't handle the telephone calls that always follow when his name is connected with the pool in public print. Mothers tell him to send Sonny home, or would he please wade out and look for little Gertrude's bracelet. Some want to know the price of admission; others want to complain about the towels." "It's Not His," *Arkansas Democrat*, September 1952 (no date given), clipping, box 5, folder 12, City Pool Collection, ASI.

　　22. *Plessy v. Ferguson*, 163 U.S. 537 (1896).

　　23. On Gillam Park and its pool, see John A. Kirk, "'A Study in Second-Class Citizenship': Race, Urban Development and Little Rock's Gillam Park, 1934–2004," *Arkansas Historical Quarterly* 64 (Autumn 2005): 262–86. Quotations from *Arkansas State Press* (Little Rock), August 25, 1950, and July 8, 1954.

　　24. Terrance Roberts, *Lessons from Little Rock* (Little Rock: Butler Center Books, 2009), 22. Another of the nine remembers numerous visits to Gillam Park; Carlotta Walls LaNier, *A Mighty Long Way: My Journey to Justice at Little Rock Central High* (New York: One World Ballantine Books, 2009), 30, 38, 63.

　　25. "Little Rock Pool Turns Away Five Negroes," *Arkansas Gazette*, June 28, 1963.

　　26. "City Decides to Sell or Close Pools after Negroes Try Desegregation," *Arkansas Gazette*, June 11, 1964; "Negroes Study Action," *Arkansas Democrat*, June 11, 1964.

　　27. "City Decides to Sell or Close Pools"; "Negroes Study Action."

　　28. "Negro Leaders Plan New Drive On Racial Bars," *Arkansas Gazette*, June 12, 1964.

　　29. "Pool Closing Seen Sunday; Buyer Sought," *Arkansas Democrat*, June 12, 1964.

　　30. "Pool to Open—Then What?," *Arkansas Gazette*, June 13, 1964; "Controversy Muddies Pools," *Arkansas Democrat*, June 13, 1964.

　　31. "Ministers Hit Plan to Close Or Sell Pools," *Arkansas Gazette*, June 14, 1964; "Swim Pool Future Studied," *Arkansas Democrat*, June 14, 1964.

　　32. "Faubus Claims Arkansas Law-abiding," *Arkansas Gazette*, June 15, 1964.

　　33. "Minister's Car Target of Eggs After Protest," *Arkansas Gazette*, June 15, 1964.

　　34. "Two City Pools To Close Today," *Arkansas Gazette*, June 15, 1964.

　　35. "Early Sale Is Predicted As Swim Pool Drained," *Arkansas Democrat*, June 15, 1964.

　　36. "Griswold Criticizes Board for Closing Pools, Says It Will Foster More Intense Crises Later," *Arkansas Gazette*, June 17, 1964.

　　37. "LR Closes Public Pools; Season Tickets Refunded," *Arkansas Gazette*, June 16, 1964.

　　38. "Griswold Criticizes Board for Closing Pools."

　　39. "LR Closes Public Pools."

　　40. "Early Sale Is Predicted As Swim Pool Drained."

　　41. "LR Closes Public Pools."

　　42. "Faubus Doubts Unity on Pools," *Arkansas Gazette*, June 18, 1964.

　　43. "LR Closes Public Pools."

　　44. Sherry Laymon, *Fearless: John L. McClellan, United States Senator* (Mustang,

OK: Tate Publishing, 2011), 256–57; Randall Woods, *Fulbright: A Biography* (New York: Cambridge University Press, 1995), 330–34.

45. "Rights Passage Reaction Varies In Little Rock," *Arkansas Gazette*, June 21, 1964; "State Reaction to Bill Varies," *Arkansas Democrat*, July 3, 1964.

46. "State Reaction to Bill Varies."

47. "Rights Passage Reaction Varies In Little Rock."

48. "State Reaction to Bill Varies."

49. "Bennett Suggests Business As Usual Despite New Law," *Arkansas Democrat*, July 8, 1964; "Ignore New Act, Bennett Advises," *Arkansas Gazette*, July 9, 1964.

50. "Rights Passage Reaction Varies In Little Rock."

51. "State Reaction to Bill Varies."

52. "Rights Passage Reaction Varies In Little Rock."

53. "Fulbright Calls For Obedience Of Rights Law," *Arkansas Gazette*, July 10, 1964.

54. "Rights Passage Reaction Varies In Little Rock."

55. "State Reaction to Bill Varies."

56. "Rights Passage Reaction Varies In Little Rock."

57. "State Reaction to Bill Varies."

58. "State Reaction to Bill Varies."

59. "Arkansas Negroes To Assess Results Of Rights Measure," *Arkansas Democrat*, July 5, 1964.

60. "Post Civil Rights Act Passage Compliance and Non-Compliance, 7/2/64–7/23/64," p. 2, series 1, box 7, folder 64, ACHR Papers; "Rights Bill Opening Causes Little Stir," *Arkansas Democrat*, July 4, 1964; "Efforts to Integrate Partially Successful," *Arkansas Democrat*, July 6, 1964; "Negroes Desegregate Forrest City, Helena, Pine Bluff Facilities," *Arkansas Gazette*, July 8, 1964; "Negroes Eat at Two Cafes In Fort Smith, Admitted To Movie Theater at Malvern," *Arkansas Gazette*, July 9, 1964.

61. "23 Negroes Cited On Riot Charges In Lake Violence," *Arkansas Gazette*, July 7, 1964; "Post Civil Rights Act Passage Compliance and Non-Compliance," 2.

62. "Post Civil Rights Act Passage Compliance and Non-Compliance," 2; "Private Pool Is Proposed," *Arkansas Democrat*, June 18, 1964; "Negroes Desegregate Forrest City, Helena, Pine Bluff Facilities."

63. "Legion Officials Air Pool Purchase," *Arkansas Democrat*, April 13, 1965; "Pool Show Legionnaires Favor Purchase of Pools," *Arkansas Democrat*, April 14, 1965; "Legion May Buy Both Pools, Keep Operation Segregated," *Arkansas Gazette*, April 14, 1965. On Claude Carpenter, see Roy Reed, *Faubus: The Life and Times of an American Prodigal* (Fayetteville: University of Arkansas Press, 1997), 136, 146, 193, 225, 247, 248–49, 311.

64. On the Arkansas State Capitol case, see John A. Kirk, "Capitol Offenses: Desegregating the Seat of Arkansas Government, 1964–1965," *Arkansas Historical Quarterly* 72 (Summer 2013): 95–119.

65. "Bates Says NAACP Opposed to Sale Of City's Swimming Pools to Legion," *Arkansas Gazette*, April 17, 1965.

66. "Legion Post Drops Plans to Acquire Swimming Pools," *Arkansas Democrat*, April 17, 1965; "Committee Plans To Advise Legion Not to Buy Pools," *Arkansas Gazette*, April 18, 1965.

67. "Drive To Get Pools Open Begun," *Arkansas Democrat*, May 21, 1965; "Mail Campaign Begun to Open Swim Facilities," *Arkansas Gazette*, May 21, 1965.

68. "Pressure Rebuilding On City to Reopen Pools," *Arkansas Democrat*, May 22, 1965.

69. "Pool Opening Backed," *Arkansas Democrat*, May 30, 1965; "Open 2 Pools and Integrate As Test, City Director Says," *Arkansas Gazette*, May 30, 1965.

70. Arkansas Project press release, May 31, 1965, and Arkansas Project press release, June 2, 1965, both in box 9, folder 2, Student Nonviolent Coordinating Committee Arkansas Project Records, State Historical Society, Madison, WI.

71. "City Will Reopen Swimming Pools," *Arkansas Democrat*, June 3, 1965; "City Board Votes to Open Pools on Integrated Basis," *Arkansas Gazette*, June 3, 1965.

72. "Gillam Pool Opens, But Crowd Light," *Arkansas Democrat*, June 15, 1965; "Gillam Pool Opened, But Only Negroes Use It," *Arkansas Gazette*, June 15, 1965.

73. "Gillam Pool Opens, But Crowd Light"; "Water Line Break Adds To Swim Pool Problems."

74. "City Pool May Open On Monday," *Arkansas Democrat*, June 17, 1965.

75. "Few Turn Out For Swim Pool Opening," *Arkansas Democrat* June 21, 1965; "Memorial Park Pool Integrated," *Arkansas Democrat*, June 22, 1965; "Memorial Pool Integrated; 22 Negroes Go Swimming," *Arkansas Gazette*, June 22, 1965.

76. "Use of City's Pools Declines 50 Per Cent," *Arkansas Democrat*, August 12, 1965.

77. Wiltse, *Contested Waters*, 182–84 (quotation on pp. 182–83).

78. Little Rock's population in 1960 was 107,813; in 2010 it was 193,524. "Census of Population and Housing," United States Census Bureau, www.census.gov/prod/www/abs/decennial/ (accessed August 23, 2013).

79. "Healthy Crowd of 227 Visits $2.6 Million Fitness Center," *Arkansas Democrat-Gazette* (Little Rock), February 18, 1992; email message to author from Little Rock Parks and Recreation Department, August 20, 2013.

80. *Arkansas Democrat*, June 22, 1952, clipping, box 5, folder 12, City Pool Collection, ASI; email message to author from Little Rock Parks and Recreation Department, August 19, 2013.

81. Email message to author from Little Rock Parks and Recreation Department, August 20, 2013.

82. "History of Southwest Recreation Center Swimming Pool," typescript in the author's possession, courtesy of Little Rock Parks and Recreation Department.

83. "White Flight's Toll," *Arkansas Democrat-Gazette*, March 10, 1992.

84. Kevin M. Kruse, *White Flight: Atlanta and the Making of Modern Conservatism* (Princeton, NJ: Princeton University Press, 2005), 106.

85. "Not By Law But By Choice," *Arkansas Democrat-Gazette*, October 26, 2003.

CHAPTER 17

1. In this sense, "queer" is a technical term used in queer theory and studies. The word, which obviously has several definitions, is here meant as a descriptor, encompassing both those who would claim to be gay and lesbian, as well as those who engage in homosexual sex but would not necessarily label themselves as gay or lesbian. For a useful treatment of the term as employed in gay and lesbian studies, see John Howard, *Men Like That: A Southern Queer History* (Chicago: University of Chicago Press, 1997), xviii-xix.

2. *Cabaret* won several Academy Awards and was hailed by many critics as a cinematic masterpiece. Actor Michael York's depiction of a British man dealing with his

homosexuality is considered the first gay character in mainstream cinema not to be a "sexual pervert" or the stereotypical "sissy."

3. David Bianco, *Gay Essentials* (Los Angeles: Alyson, 1999), 228–30.

4. "Cohabitation Tax, Other Bills Aimed at 'Deviate Acts,'" *Arkansas Gazette* (Little Rock), January 23, 1977, final ed., sec. A: 6.

5. "Cohabitation Tax, Other Bills Aimed at 'Deviate Acts.'" Speaking of cohabitating couples, Tyer declared: "They may have a desire for each other, physically and maybe even spiritually, but they don't want to conform. This country was built on conformity."

6. "Cohabitation Tax, Other Bills Aimed at 'Deviate Acts'"; George Bentley, "New Justice Code Turns the Tables for Novel Ruling," *Arkansas Gazette*, March 26, 1976, final ed., sec A: 16.

7. Bentley, "New Justice Code Turns the Tables for Novel Ruling," 16.

8. Bentley, "New Justice Code Turns the Tables for Novel Ruling," 16.

9. Bentley, "New Justice Code Turns the Tables for Novel Ruling," 16.

10. Bentley, "New Justice Code Turns the Tables for Novel Ruling," 16.

11. Bentley, "New Justice Code Turns the Tables for Novel Ruling," 16.

12. "Jail not Public Place, Charges Dismissed," *Arkansas Gazette,* June 25, 1976, final ed., sec. A: 5.

13. *Carter & Burkhead v. State*, 255 Ark. 255, 500 S.W.2d (1973).

14. Arkansas's first sodomy law mandated a life sentence for whites found guilty. Blacks, whether free or slave, faced a much harsher punishment: death. After the Civil War, the death penalty provision disappeared under mysterious circumstances, having never been debated or acted on by the legislature. George Painter, "The Sensibility of Our Forefathers: The History of Sodomy Laws in the United States" http://www.sodomylaws.org/sensibilities/html. Also see, *Revised Statutes of the State of Arkansas* (Boston: Weeks, Jordan and Co., 1838), page 182, chapter 28.

15. Rafael Guzman, "1976 Criminal Code: General Principles," *Arkansas Law Review* 30 (1976): 111–13. Guzman, a law professor at the University of Arkansas, Fayetteville, served as a member of the Arkansas Criminal Code Revision Commission.

16. David Frum, *How We Got Here: The 70's, the Decade That Brought You Modern Life (For Better or Worse)* (New York: Basic, 2000), 205–6.

17. Guzman, "1976 Criminal Code: General Principles," 111–13. The most notable and recognizable revision came in legal classification. Each felony was placed in one of four classifications: A, B, C, or D. Each misdemeanor was placed in one of three classifications: A, B, or C. For a complete list of revisions as adopted by the legislature, consult the *Arkansas Statutes Annotated*, 41–901–1101 (Criminal Code of 1976).

18. "Cohabitation Tax, Other Bills Aimed at Deviate Acts."

19. "Cohabitation Tax, Other Bills Aimed at Deviate Acts."

20. "Sodomy Bill Amended to Define Restrictions; House Passage Urged," *Arkansas Gazette*, January 26, 1977, final ed., sec. A: 3.

21. "Sodomy Bill Amended to Define Restrictions; House Passage Urged."

22. "Sodomy Bill Amended to Define Restrictions; House Passage Urged."

23. "Sodomy Bill Amended to Define Restrictions; House Passage Urged."

24. "Bill Fails, Would Punish Tenants for No Notice," *Arkansas Gazette*, January 27, 1977, final ed., sec. B: 1.

25. "House Supports Abortion Foes With Voice Vote," *Arkansas Gazette*, February 11, 1977, final ed., sec A: 1. The only representatives to vote against the bill were Jodie Mahony of El Dorado and Henry Wilkins of Pine Bluff; Ted Holder, interview with author, Little Rock, AR, September 23, 2001.

26. "Senate Passes Measures in Drive to Adjourn," *Arkansas Gazette*, March 17, 1977, final ed., sec. A: 21.

27. *The Advocate*, vol. 210, April 1977, 7.

28. "Deadline Nears on Sex Bill Veto; Inquiries Made," *Arkansas Gazette*, March 28, 1977, final ed., sec. B: 6.

29. Ark. Code Ann.§ 5–14–122.

30. Lawrence Yancey, telephone interview with author, January 31, 2002. In an interview, Pryor claimed he had no recollection of signing the sodomy bill into law; he declined to comment beyond that. David Pryor, telephone interview with author, January 31, 2002.

31. Yancey, interview.

32. "Resolution Draws Call from Aide," *Arkansas Gazette*, March 30, 1977, final ed., sec. B: 1.

33. The letter, dated April 10, 1977, was sent directly to Governor Pryor and was signed by the clerk of the executive board, S. D. Hacker. The letter is included in David Pryor's unprocessed gubernatorial papers, Special Collections Division, University of Arkansas Libraries, Fayetteville.

34. Dudley Clendinen and Adam Nagourney, *Out for Good: The Struggle to Build a Gay Rights Movement in America* (New York: Simon and Schuster, 1999), 291–338.

35. Tina Fetner, "Working Anita Bryant: The Impact of Christian Anti-Gay Activism on Lesbian and Gay Movement's Claims," *Social Problems* 48 (2001): 411. The quotation was taken from a direct mail fund-raising letter from Bryant's *Save the Children* organization, which existed from 1977 until 1979. The emphasis is in the original.

36. Clendinen and Nagourney, *Out for Good*, 299.

37. Jim Ranchino, "The Arkansas of the '70s: The Good Ole Boy Ain't Whut He Used to Be," *Arkansas Times*, September 1977, 40.

38. Yancey, interview.

39. Ross Dennis, "We Hold These Truths to be Self Evident . . ." *Lincoln Ledger* (Star City, AR), January 5, 1978, final ed., sec. A: 2; Thomas Roark, "I Want to Clear Things Up" *Lincoln Ledger*, January 12, 1978, final ed., sec. A: 2; Ross Dennis, "An Open Letter to the Readers" *Lincoln Ledger*, January 12, 1978, final ed., sec. A: 1; Doug Smith, "Orange-juice Horseshoe Is Dropped Rapidly" *Arkansas Gazette*, January 19, 1978, final ed., sec. B: 1.

40. Clendinen and Nagourney, *Out for Good*, 329.

41. "She's 'Prolife,' Not 'Antigay,' Singer Asserts," *Arkansas Gazette*, October 22, 1978, final ed., sec. A: 16.

42. *Bowers v. Hardwick*, 478 United States 186 (1986), 6–7.

43. "High Court Upholds Georgia Sodomy Law," *Arkansas Democrat* (Little Rock), July 1, 1986, final ed., sec. A: 1.

44. *Bowers v. Hardwick*, 15–16. Chief Justice Warren Burger, and Justices Lewis F. Powell, William H. Rehnquist, and Sandra Day O'Connor concurred. Justice

Harry Blackmun wrote the dissenting opinion and was joined by Justices William J. Brennan, Thurgood Marshall, and John Paul Stevens.

45. *Bowers v. Hardwick*, 17–18.

46. William Raspberry, "Enforcement of Sodomy Law Difficult," *Arkansas Democrat*, July 8, 1986, final ed., sec. A: 6.

47. "The Sodomy Ruling," *Arkansas Democrat*, July 17, 1986, final ed., sec. A: 10.

48. The riots following a police raid at the Stonewall Inn on June 28, 1969, are considered to be the beginning of the modern gay rights movement. For a detailed account of the riots and their social ramifications, see Martin Duberman, *Stonewall* (New York: Dutton, 1993).

49. By July 2002, Arkansas was one of only six states with sodomy laws applying solely to same-sex behavior. The others were Missouri, Michigan, Kansas, Texas, and Oklahoma. Missouri, when adopting its new criminal code, simply let the sodomy law cross over. The Missouri Supreme Court decided in 1977 that the phrase "crime against nature" was understood by the majority of the population of the state and that the law, which still treated sodomy as felony carrying a life sentence, did not need to be rewritten. *Griffith v. State of Missouri*, 504 S.W. 2nd 324 (1977).

50. The laws were struck down as follows: St. Paul on April 25, 1978; Wichita on May 9, 1978; and Eugene, Oregon, on May 23, 1978; Clendinen and Nagourney, *Out for Good*, 316–19, 327–29.

51. Mark Oswald, "Committee Rejects Sodomy Law Repeal," *Arkansas Gazette*, January 31, 1991, final ed., sec. I: 1, 3; John Hoogester, "Deputies Acting to Remove Gays from Rest Area," *Arkansas Gazette*, February 2, 1991, final ed., sec. B: 1.

52. For a discussion of sodomy laws and their social impact, see John D'Emilio, *Sexual Politics, Sexual Communities: The Making of a Homosexual Minority in the United States, 1940–1970* (Chicago: University of Chicago Press, 1983), 42–44.

53. *Northwest Arkansas Times* (Fayetteville), March 31, 1983.

54. Seth Blomeley, "Seven Sue to Void State Sodomy Law," *Arkansas Democrat-Gazette*, January 29, 1998, final ed., sec. B: 2.

55. *Jegley v. Picado et. al.*, 2002 Ark. LEXIS 401.

56. Traci Shurley, "Justices Strike Down Sodomy Law," *Arkansas Democrat-Gazette*, July 5, 2002, final ed., sec: A: 1.

57. Shurley, "Justices Strike Down Sodomy Law."

CHAPTER 18

1. Martha Solomon, "The Rhetoric of STOP ERA: Fatalistic Reaffirmation," *Southern Speech Communication Journal* 44 (1978): 42–59; Martha Solomon, "The 'Positive Woman's' Journey: A Mythic Analysis of the Rhetoric of STOP ERA," *Quarterly Journal of Speech* 65 (1979): 262–74; Mary Frances Berry, *Why ERA Failed: Politics, Women's Rights, and the Amending Process of the Constitution* (Bloomington: Indiana University Press, 1986); Jane J. Mansbridge, *Why We Lost the ERA* (Chicago: University of Chicago Press, 1986); Mark R. Daniels and Robert E. Darcy, "As Time Goes by: The Arrested Diffusion of the Equal Rights Amendment," *Publius* 15, no. 4 (1985): 51–60.

2. Tracy McKay, *The Equal Rights Amendment in Arkansas: Activism, Fundamentalism, and Traditionalism* (n.p., 1997); Janine A. Parry, "'What Women

Wanted': Arkansas Women's Commissions and the ERA," *Arkansas Historical Quarterly* 59, no. 3 (2000): 265–98; Emily Ward, "The Effects of the Arguments Used by the Anti-ERA Movement on Legislative Results in Arkansas: A Rhetorical Approach," unpublished paper, University of Arkansas, 2006.

3. Mansbridge, *Why We Lost the ERA*.

4. Donald G. Mathews and Jane Sherron Dehart, *Sex, Gender, and the Politics of the ERA* (New York: Oxford University Press, 1990).

5. The political and legal argument that ratification could be accomplished by three additional states voting to ratify and achieving the necessary thirty-eight.

6. Allison L. Held, Sheryl L. Herndon, and Danielle M. Stager, "The Equal Rights Amendment: Why the ERA Remains Legally Viably and Properly before the States," *William and Mary Journal of Women and the Law* 3, no. 1 (1997): 113–36.

7. David C. Huckabee, "Memorandum: Equal Rights Amendment: Ratification Issues" (Washington, DC: Congressional Research Service), March 18, 1996; Thomas H. Neale, "The Proposed Equal Rights Amendment: Contemporary Ratification Issues" (Washington, DC: Congressional Research Service), April 8, 2014.

8. Andy Steiner, "The Future of the Equal Rights Amendment: A New Generation Revives the ERA," *Utne Reader*, January–February 2000.

9. Christine Jordan Sexton, "House Democrats Say 'Equality' Issues Aren't Moving through the Legislature," *Florida Politics*, March 26, 2015; Sean Whaley, "ERA Isn't Nostalgia in Nevada," *Las Vegas Review-Journal*, July 28, 2014; Beth Walton, "WNC Women Call for Passage of Equal Rights Amendment," *Asheville Citizen-Times*, March 5, 2015; Dianne Post and Kaitlin Ford, "It's Time Arizona Recognizes Equal Rights for Women," *Arizona Capitol Times*, January 21, 2016; "Senator Jill Schupp Files Equal Rights Amendment," *Missouri Times*, February 11, 2015; "Va. Senate Clears Equal Rights Amendment," *Falls Church News-Press*, January 27, 2016; Associated Press, "Illinois Senate Approves Equal Rights Amendment," May 22, 2014.

10. Susan Wiles, "Arkansas Groups Hold Rally for ERA," *Arkansas Gazette*, July 1, 1981, 9A; Susan Wiles, "NOW Preparing to Fight to Keep Rights for Women," *Arkansas Gazette*, September 13, 1981, 7A; "White Criticized for Failure to Put ERA on Call for Special Session," *Arkansas Gazette*, November 14, 1981, 6A.

11. Ernest H. Wohlenberg, "Correlates of Equal Rights Amendment Ratification," *Social Science Quarterly* 60, no. 4 (1980): 682.

12. Jerry Cox recorded testimony, https://www.youtube.com/watch?v= GZXn FomU4dU.

13. For the impact of the number of women in legislative bodies generally, see Anne Marie Cammisa and Beth Reingold, "Women in State Legislatures and State Legislative Research: Beyond Sameness and Difference," *State Politics and Policy Quarterly* 4, no.2 (2004): 181–210.

14. Art English and Brian Weberg, *Term Limits in the Arkansas General Assembly: A Citizen Legislature Responds* (Washington, DC: National Conference of State Legislatures, 2005), 19.

15. Berta Seitz, interview by Emily Ward, October 27, 2006.

16. Arkansas 85th General Assembly, Regular Session (2005), SJR 17, Sponsor: Senator Madison, http://www.arkleg.state.ar.us/.

17. Seitz interview.

18. Peggy Jeffries, interview by Emily Ward, November 1, 2006.

19. Dan Craft, "Ratification of Equal Rights Amendment Pushed—Change

to U.S. Constitution First Proposed in 1973," *Morning News of Northwest Arkansas*, March 19, 2005.

20. Laura Kellams, "26 Years Later, Senate to Vote on ERA issue," *Arkansas Democrat-Gazette*, March 27, 2005, 17.

21. Kellams, "26 Years Later."

22. Pam Manard, "ERA Amendment Back Door to Homosexual Agenda," *Arkansas Watch*, March 30, 2005, http://arkansaswatch.blogspot.com/2005/03/era-amendment-back-door-to-homosexual.html.

23. Debbie Pelley, "ERA Amendment Deceptive," *Arkansas Watch*, March 30, 2005, http://arkansaswatch.blogspot.com/2005/03/era-amendment-deceptive.html.

24. Pelley, "ERA Amendment Deceptive."

25. Manard, "ERA Amendment Back Door."

26. Manard, "ERA Amendment Back Door."

27. Seitz interview.

28. Seitz interview.

29. Lindsley Smith, the lead author of this essay, then a member of the Arkansas House of Representatives and the lead House sponsor of the resolution, was present in the Senate Chamber during the debates. These observations are from contemporaneous notes now in the unprocessed Lindsley Smith Papers, Special Collections, Mullins Library, University of Arkansas, Fayetteville; Sue Madison, interview by Emily Ward, November 1, 2006.

30. Opposition of "conservative" women to the Equal Rights Amendment has received significant scholarly attention. See David W. Brady and Kent L. Tedin, "Ladies in Pink: Religion and Political Ideology in the Anti-ERA Movement," *Social Science Quarterly* 56 (1976): 564–75; Iva E. Deutchman and Sandra Prince-Embury, "Political Ideology of Pro and Anti ERA Women," *Women and Politics* 2 (1982): 39–55; Rebecca Klatch, "Women against Feminism," in *A History of Our Time: Readings on Postwar America*, ed. William H. Chafe and Harvard Sitkoff, 259–77 (New York: Oxford University Press, 1999); and Susan E. Marshall, "Ladies against Women: Mobilization Dilemmas of Antifeminist Movements," *Social Problems* 32, no. 4 (1985): 348–62.

31. Madison interview.

32. Rob Moritz, "Elders Urges Women to Fight for Equality," *Southwest Times Record*, August 29, 2005.

33. Lisa Yates, "State Representative Fights to Ratify ERA," *Sentinel Record*, June 8, 2006: 1.

34. Michael Wickline, "On ERA, 1 Gubernatorial Hopeful Says No, 2 Say Yes," *Arkansas Democrat-Gazette*, August 23, 2006, 6.

35. Laura Kellams, "Ratifying ERA Gets Big Support at Capitol," *Arkansas Democrat-Gazette*, January 25, 2007, 11.

36. Adam Wallworth, "Rep. Smith Wants Arkansas to Ratify Equal Rights Amendment," *Northwest Arkansas Times*, January 25, 2007, 1.

37. Doug Thompson, "Governor, Others Rally for ERA—Supporters Say They Have House's Backing," *Morning News of Northwest Arkansas*, January 25, 2007.

38. Kellams, "Ratifying ERA Gets Big Support at Capitol."

39. Kellams, "Ratifying ERA Gets Big Support at Capitol."

40. Laura Kellams, "Beebe, Halter to Join Equal Rights Amendment Rally," *Arkansas Democrat-Gazette*, January 24, 2007.

41. Wallworth, "Rep. Smith Wants Arkansas to Ratify Equal Rights Amendment."

42. Kellams, "Ratifying ERA Gets Big Support at Capitol."

43. Lewis Delavan, "Village Democrats Giddy about Political Fortunes," *Hot Springs Village Voice*, January 31, 2007.

44. Patrick Briney, "Six Reasons to Oppose the ERA," *Arkansas Republican Assembly*, January 27, 2007, http://www.arragopwing.com/eraposition.html.

45. Doug Thompson, "Governor, Others Rally for ERA," *Morning News of Northwest Arkansas*, January 25, 2007; Anne Britton, "Don't Approve Amendment," Letter, *Morning News of Northwest Arkansas*, February 4, 2007.

46. Leo Hauser, "All Deserve Equal Rights," Letter, *Arkansas Democrat-Gazette*, February 7, 2007.

47. John Lyon, "ERA Resolution Defeated in Committee," *Morning News of Northwest Arkansas*, February 8, 2007.

48. Steve Harrelson, "FOR Equal Rights Amendment," *Under the Dome*, February 6, 2007, http://www.steveharrelson.com/blog/2007/02/two-more-special-orders-on-tomorrows.html.

49. Laura Kellams, "After Debate, 10–10 Vote Leaves ERA Stalled in House Panel," *Arkansas Democrat-Gazette*, February 8, 2007, 11.

50. Phyllis Schlafly, "Testimony before the Arkansas House State Agencies Committee," February 7, 2007, http://www.youtube.com/watch?v=oLkcxzy4NXI.

51. Voting no were Rep. David Evans, D-Searcy; Rep. Robert Jeffrey, D-Camden; Rep. Horace Hardwick, R-Bentonville; Rep. Daryl Pace, R-Siloam Springs; Rep. Eric Harris, R-Springdale; Rep. Rick Green, R-Van Buren; Rep. Pam Adcock, D-Little Rock; Rep. Lance Reynolds, D-Quitman; Rep. Buddy Lovell, D-Marked Tree; and Rep. Dan Greenberg, R-Little Rock.

52. Editorial, "A Waste of Time—Legislature Tries to Pass the ERA—25 Years after the Fact," *Northwest Arkansas Times*, February 1, 2007, 4.

53. Editorial, "On a Roll: The Ledge Racks 'em Up," *Arkansas Democrat-Gazette*, February 11, 2007, 98.

54. Mike Masterson, "Teacher Pay Better than Most," *Arkansas Democrat-Gazette*, February 13, 2007, 15.

55. Jake Tidmore, "Content Hits a New Low," Letter, *Arkansas Democrat-Gazette*, April 2, 2007, 13. See also Patty Miller-Marshall, "Many Families Disagree," *Arkansas Democrat-Gazette*, September 3, 2007.

56. Beatryce O. Lewis, "ERA Is Misunderstood," Letter, *Arkansas Democrat-Gazette*, February 26, 2007, 13.

57. Dan Greenberg, "Not Wise for the Constitution," *Arkansas Democrat-Gazette*, March 18, 2007, 101.

58. "A New Push for the Equal Rights Amendment," NPR News and Notes, April 3, 2007. http://www.npr.org/templates/story/story.php?storyId=9311591.

59. Janine A. Parry, "What Would the Equal Rights Amendment Do?—Opponents Are Short on Facts," *Arkansas Democrat-Gazette*, March 18, 2007, 101.

60. James Gately, "ERA Deserves Support in Little Rock," Letter, *Benton County Daily Record*, March 4, 2007, 14.

61. Mara Jarrett, "Reconsider Amendment," Letter, *Arkansas Democrat-Gazette*, February 27, 2007, 13.

62. Adam Wallworth, "Legislators Review '07 Session during Senior Democrats Meeting," *Northwest Arkansas Times*, April 18, 2007, 1.

63. Dustin Tracy, "Following the Session: Local Legislators Reflect on Efforts," *Northwest Arkansas Times*, April 7, 2007, 1.

64. "The Arkansas Poll: Summary Report" (Fayetteville: University of Arkansas, 2007), 6.

65. Editorial, "Survey Says Attitudes Are Changing," *Morning News of Northwest Arkansas*, November 2, 2007.

66. Karin Hill, "Women's Group Stays Involved," *Jonesboro Sun*, December 6, 2008; Doug Thompson, "Sharp Contrast in House 89 Race," *Morning News of Northwest Arkansas*, September 22, 2008.

67. Fran Alexander, "That 'Equality' Thing: Piecemeal Legislation Never Guarantees Legal Security," *Northwest Arkansas Times*, January 26, 2009, 4.

68. Charlie Frago, "Equal Rights Amendment Returns to Legislature," *Arkansas Democrat-Gazette*, February 25, 2009, 8.

69. Michael Wickline, "ERA Resolution Fails in Senate Committee," *Arkansas Democrat-Gazette*, March 4, 2009, 6.

70. Wickline, "ERA Resolution Fails."

71. Trish Hollenbeck, "Lawmakers Share Updates on Recent Legislative Action," *Northwest Arkansas Times*, March 7, 2009, 1.

72. Editorial, "Quitting Time: Is the ERA Something Arkansas Really Wants?" *Northwest Arkansas Times*, March 13, 2009, 4.

73. Scott Shackelford, "ERA Today—Why Can't Our State See Eye to Eye with Equality?" *Northwest Arkansas Times*, March 10, 2009.

74. Brenda Blagg, "Arkansas Should Ratify the ERA," *Morning News of Northwest Arkansas*, March 5, 2009.

75. Berta Seitz, "ERA Is Simply Equality for All Citizens," Letter, *Arkansas Democrat-Gazette*, March 20, 2009, 19.

76. Charlie Frago and Michael R. Wickline, "Beebe Seeks to Save ERA Resolution," *Arkansas Democrat-Gazette*, March 24, 2009, 6.

77. Seth Blomeley, "Beebe Dealt Setbacks on Rights, Energy Bills," *Arkansas Democrat-Gazette*, April 10, 2009, 8.

78. Editorial, "What Lawmakers Left Unfinished," *Benton Courier*, April 19, 2009, 4.

79. Sarah D. Wire, "Parties' Stances Inspire Disputes: Groups Disagree on Platform Goals," *Arkansas Democrat-Gazette*, August 1, 2010, 15.

80. John Lyon, "Arkansas ERA Supporters Plan Rally," *Southwest Times Record*, May 4, 2011.

81. Lyon, "Arkansas ERA Supporters Plan Rally."

82. Lyon, "Arkansas ERA Supporters Plan Rally."

83. Sheryl Flanagin, "Arkansas Behind on Equal Rights," Letter, *Southwest Times Record*, May 6, 2011.

84. Lindsley Smith Papers.

85. Larry Henry, "Candidates Discuss Equal Rights Amendment," *Springdale Morning News*, January 18, 2012, 1.

86. Linda Farrell, "Voting Rights Secured," *Benton County Daily Record*, April 14, 2012, 5.

87. David Sumrell, "It All Started with Vote," Letter, *Arkansas Democrat-Gazette*, Northwest Edition, April 25, 2012, 13.

88. Sherry A. Faubus, "Equality within Reach," Letter, *Arkansas Democrat-Gazette*, May 9, 2012, 17.

89. Bernadette Cahill, "Time to Make Good: Ratifying ERA a Win for State," *Arkansas Democrat-Gazette*, May 26, 2012, 19.

90. Rose Mimms, "Open Up a Grave: Equal Rights Amendment Dead," *Arkansas Democrat-Gazette*, June 25, 2012, 11.

91. Lindsley Smith, "Not Playing Dead—ERA Alive, and Should Be Ratified," *Arkansas Democrat-Gazette*, July 16, 2012, 11.

92. Sarah D. Wire, "Parties, Candidates Do Platform Dance," *Arkansas Democrat-Gazette*, September 2, 2012.

93. Sean Beherec, "Senate Panel Rejects Equal Rights Endorsement," *Arkansas Democrat-Gazette*, April 3, 2013. For the full testimony of the proponents, see https://www.youtube.com/watch?v=D5rKv128qsg.

94. Lindsley Smith, "Testimony FOR the Equal Rights Amendment to the US Constitution," Arkansas, 2013, Senate Committee on State Agencies, Little Rock, https://www.youtube.com/watch?v=D5rKv128qsg.

95. Sean Beherec, "Senate Panel Rejects Equal Rights Endorsement." For the full testimony of the opponents, see https://www.youtube.com/watch?v=GZXnFom U4dU.

96. John Brummett, "Futility, with Side of Possibility," *Arkansas Democrat-Gazette*, April 3, 2013.

97. Roselinda Johnson, "Trying to Stop the Tide," Letter, *Arkansas Democrat-Gazette*, April 20, 2013.

98. Catharine A. MacKinnon, "Unthinking ERA Thinking," *University of Chicago Law Review* 54 (Spring 1987): 759–60.

99. See Jessica Neuwirth, *Equal Means Equal: Why the Time for an Equal Rights Amendment Is Now* (New York: New Press, 2015), 6; and Bill Clinton, *My Life* (New York: Vintage Books, 2005): 338–39.

100. Laura Kellams, "26 Years Later, Senate to Vote on ERA issue," *Arkansas Democrat-Gazette*, March 27, 2005, 17.

101. Michael Wickline, "ERA Resolution Fails in Senate Committee," *Arkansas Democrat-Gazette*, March 4, 2009, 6.

102. Marina Koren, "The Combat Jobs Women Can Now Fight For," *Atlantic*, December 3, 2015, http://www.theatlantic.com/national/archive/2015/12/women-in-the-military/418680/.

103. This objection was proffered by Senator Guy Jones in the 1973 debates during conscription for the Vietnam conflict, and Phyllis Schlafly raised this point in her testimony before the House Committee in 2007. Karoun Demirjian "Are Women Headed for the Draft?" *Washington Post*, April 28, 2016.

104. "Roll Call on Passage of National Defense Authorization Act for Fiscal Year 2017 (S. 2943 As Amended)," June 14, 2016; Selective Service System Office of Public and Intergovernmental Affairs, "Backgrounder: Women and the Draft," December 2015, https://www.sss.gov/Registration/Women-and-Draft/Backgrounder-Women-and-the-Draft.

105. Patrick Briney, "Six Reasons to Oppose the ERA," *Arkansas Republican Assembly*, January 27, 2007, http://www.arragopwing.com/eraposition.html.

106. For the continuity of historical and contemporary concerns about unisex bathrooms, see Neil J. Young, "How the Bathroom Wars Shaped America," *Politico*, May 18, 2016.

107. "U.S. Departments of Justice and Education Release Joint Guidance to Help

Schools Ensure the Civil Rights of Transgender Students," May 13, 2016, https://www.justice.gov/opa/pr/us-departments-justice-and-education-release-joint-guidance-help-schools-ensure-civil-rights.

108. The military services maintain sex-segregated facilities based on gender identity. W. J. Hennigan, "U.S. Military to Allow Transgender Men and Women to Serve Openly," *Los Angeles Times*, June 30, 2016.

109. Michael R. Wickline and Jake Bleed, "Illegal Alien Bill Gets Ax in Senate," *Arkansas Democrat-Gazette*, April 6, 2005, 13.

110. Human Rights Campaign, "Progress in Arkansas," July 8, 2013, http://www.hrc.org/files/assets/resources/AR_PollingMemo_PDF.pdf.

111. *United States v. Windsor*, 133 S. Ct. 2675 (2013); *Wright v. Arkansas* (60CV–2013–2662, Pulaski County Circuit Court, 9 May 2014); *Jernigan v. Crane*, 64 F.Supp.3d 1260 (E. D. Ark., 2014); *Obergefell v. Hodges*, 135 S.Ct. 2071 (2015); and *Smith v. Wright* (CV-14–427, 2015 Ark. 298).

112. The Roper Organization, *The 1985 Virginia Slims American Women's Opinion Poll: A Study* (New York: Roper, 1986), 16; Leslie W. Gladstone, "The Long Road to Equality: What Women Won from the ERA Ratification Effort," in *American Women: A Library of Congress Guide for the Study of Women's History and Culture in the United States* (Washington, DC: Library of Congress, 2001).

113. George Gallup, "63 percent of Americans Favor ERA," *Des Moines Register*, August 9, 1981, 12.

114. Mark R. Daniels, Robert Darcy, and Joseph W. Westphal, "The ERA Won: At Least in the Opinion Polls," *PS: Political Science & Politics* 15, no. 4 (1982): 584. See also Serena Mayeri, A New E.R.A. 116. Ryan Brown, Nathaniel Persily, and Son Ho Kim, "Gender Equality," in *Public Opinion and Constitutional Controversy*, ed. Nathaniel Persily, Jack Citrin, and Patrick J. Egan, 139–61 (New York: Oxford University Press, 2008), 151–54.

115. "Equal Rights Amendment Still Alive," *Lawton* (OK) *Constitution*, October 4, 2001. Daily Kos/SEIU Weekly State of the Nation Poll, April 19, 2012–April 22, 2012, http://www.dailykos.com/weeklypolling/2012/4/19.

116. Carolyn Maloney, "Women's Issues: Equal Rights Amendment," https://maloney.house.gov/issues/womens-issues/equal-rights-ammendment.

117. Jane J. Mansbridge, *Why We Lost the ERA* (Chicago: University of Chicago Press, 1986), 1–5, 42–43.

118. Serena Mayeri, "A New E.R.A. or a New Era? Amendment Advocacy and the Reconstitution of Feminism," *Northwestern University Law Review* 103 (2009): 1223–1302, quote at 1236.

119. Mansbridge, *Why We Lost the ERA*; Judith L. Hudson, "1988 Survey of Books Relating to the Law: V. Gender and Justice," *Michigan Law Review* 86 (1988): 1411–12.

120. Laura Kellams, "26 Years Later, Senate to Vote on ERA issue," 17.

121. Christopher Spencer, "Women's Equal Rights Mean Money, Sponsor Says: Dollars Lost to Potential Business," *Morning News of Northwest Arkansas*, March 20, 2009; Kristina Croslin, "Equality Rejected Again," Letter, *Arkansas Democrat-Gazette*, March 19, 2009, 19.

122. Kimberley Johnson, "Republicans Kill ERA Ratification in Arkansas Senate," Liberals Unite, April 2, 2013, http://samuel-warde.com/2013/04/republicans-kill-arkansas-era-ratification-in-senate-committee/.

123. Lisa Baldez, Lee Epstein, and Andrew D. Martin, "Does the U.S.

Constitution Need an Equal Rights Amendment?" *Journal of Legal Studies* 35 (2006): 244, 272.

124. See, for example, K. Sujata, "ERA? Not Merely Symbolic," *Huffington Post*, June 17, 2015, http://www.huffingtonpost.com/k-sujata/era-not-merely-symbolic _b_7089308.html; and Susan Grigsby, "The 14th Amendment Is Not Enough: We Must Have an Equal Rights Amendment," *Daily Kos*, March 20, 2016, http://www .dailykos.com/story/2016/3/20/1502573/-The-14th-Amendment-is-not-enough-We -must-have-an-Equal-Rights-Amendment.

125. Jessica Ravitz, "The Politics of Feminism: An Unlikely Partnership," CNN, April 16, 2015, http://www.cnn.com/2015/04/09/us/era-womens-movement-unlikely -partners/; Maloney, "Women's Issues: Equal Rights Amendment."

126. "To Pass H.J. Res. 638, the Resolution Extending the Deadline for Ratification of the Proposed Equal Rights Amendment for an Additional Three Years and Three Months," October 6, 1978, https://www.govtrack.us/congress/votes/ 95-1978/s1086; "No One Truly Has Freedom Unless All Do," Remarks of Senator Kaneaster Hodges of Arkansas before the US Senate, October 4, 1978.

127. Janine A. Parry, "'What Women Wanted': Arkansas Women's Commissions and the ERA," *Arkansas Historical Quarterly* 59, no. 3 (2000): 265–98. See also Jocelyn Elise Crowley, "Moving Beyond Tokenism: Ratification of the Equal Rights Amendment and the Election of Women to State Legislatures," *Social Science Quarterly* 87, no. 3 (2006): 519–39.

128. Mansbridge, *Why We Lost the ERA*, 196–97.

129. Johnson, "Republicans Kill ERA Ratification in Arkansas Senate."

130. Mayeri, "A New E.R.A. or a New Era?"

131. Jane Mansbridge, "Whatever Happened to the ERA?" In *Women and the United States Constitution: History, Interpretation, and Practice*, ed. Sibyl A. Schwarzenbach and Patricia Smith, 365–78 (New York: Columbia University Press, 2003), 374.

CHAPTER 19

1. Ernest A. Grant, "Liquor Regulation in America 1619 to 1920," *Congressional Digest* 12, no. 1 (1933): 2–6, 32.

2. Distilled Spirits Council of the United States, Inc., *Summary of State Laws & Regulations Relating to Distilled Spirits,* Thirty-second edition (Washington, DC: Distilled Spirits Council of the United States, Inc., 2002).

3. Eugenia Foedge Toma, "State Liquor Licensing, Implicit Contracting, and Dry/Wet Counties," *Economic Inquiry* 26, no. 3 (1988): 511.

4. H. L. Weinstock, "The Drought of 1944: Craighead County Goes Dry," *The Craighead County Historical Quarterly* 22, no. 4 (1984): 4–7.

5. Kenneth Heard, "Beverage Control Board Denies Eateries a Permit to Serve Alcohol in Jonesboro," *Arkansas Democrat-Gazette*, December 16, 1999, A1.

6. Israel Colon, "County-Level Prohibition and Alcohol-Related Fatal Motor Vehicle Accidents," *Journal of Safety Research* 14, no. 3 (1983): 101–4; David Giacopassi and Russell Winn, "Terminating Prohibition: A Seventeen County Comparison," *American Journal of Criminal Justice* 17, no. 1 (1992): 51–61; R. Todd Jewell and Robert B. Brown, "Alcohol Availability and Alcohol Related Motor Vehicle Accidents," *Applied Economics* 27 (August 1995): 759–65.

7. R. Thomas Dull and David J. Giacopassi, "Dry, Damp, and Wet: Correlates and Presumed Consequences of Local Alcohol Ordinances," *American Journal of Drug and Alcohol Abuse* 14, no. 4 (1988): 499–514; Russell G. Winn and David Giacopassi, "Effects of CountyLevel Alcohol Prohibition on Motor Vehicle Accidents," *Social Science Quarterly* 74, no. 4 (1993): 783–92.

8. Dave Grossman, "Wet vs. Dry Counties," Jonesboro, AR: Killology Research Group, 1997.

9. Robert W. Brown, Todd Jewell, and Jerrell Richer, "Endogenous Alcohol Prohibition and Drunk Driving," *Southern Economic Journal* 62, no. 4 (1996): 1043–53.

10. Colon, "County-Level Prohibition."

11. Winn and Giacopassi, "Terminating Prohibition."

12. Dull and Giacopassi, "Dry, Damp, Wet."

13. Winn and Giacopassi, "Terminating Prohibition."

14. Grossman, "Wet vs. Dry Counties."

15. Brandi Hinkle, "Baptist Group is Opposed to Liquor Permits," *The Jonesboro Sun*, October 12, 1999, Al; Heard, "Beverage Control Board Denies."

16. Grossman, "Wet vs. Dry Counties."

17. Kenneth Sufka, personal communication, September 15, 2000.

18. Other variables considered due to their use in previous studies, but not included here include police per total road miles in a county, urban road miles per square mile in a county, and county road miles per square mile in a county. These three were omitted because they are highly correlated with population density— Pearson's r = .949, .963, and .843 respectively— and present a threat to the equations through multicollinearity. We chose to include population density in the equations because it is a precursor to the other three variables.

19. To assess the soundness of the OLS regression equation as specified, we considered threats of multicollinearity and heteroskedasticity. While there is significant correlation between independent variables, no bivariate correlation coefficient exceeded .8, a level considered highly indicative of multicollinearity (see Michael S. Lewis-Beck, *Applied Regression: An Introduction, #22.* Quantitative Applications in the Social Sciences Series [Thousand Oaks, CA: Sage Publications, 1980], 60).

We ran additional multicollinearity diagnostics with each of the models and considered measures of tolerance, variance inflation factors, eigenvalues, and condition indexes; findings suggest no significant threat to the equations as tested. See Jarija J. Norusis, *SPSS PC+ Base System Users Guide, Version 5.0.* (Chicago, IL: SPSS Inc., 1992); US Census Bureau, Land Area, Population, and Density for States and Counties, prepared by the Population and Housing Programs Division, Bureau of the Census, 1990 (Washington, D.C., 1992), 341–44. Finally, analysis of partial plots for each of the equations was carried out with no indication of heteroskedasticity.

20. Institute for Economic Advancement, Children's Research Center, "Risk Factors for Adolescent Drug and Alcohol Abuse in Arkansas," Risk Factor Data Project (Little Rock: University of Arkansas at Little Rock Institute for Economic Advancement, 1998).

21. Arkansas Crime Information Center, "Narcotic Drug Law: Arrest Data by Contributor (Adult and Juvenile)" (Little Rock: Arkansas Crime Information Center, 1997).

22. Grossman, "Wet vs. Dry Counties."

23. Grossman, "Wet vs. Dry Counties."

24. Grossman, "Wet vs. Dry Counties.".

25. Arkansas Highway and Transportation Department, "Alcohol/Drug Related Crashes, Fatalities and Injuries by County," (Little Rock: Arkansas Highway and Transportation Department, 1997); and Arkansas Highway and Transportation Department, "Arkansas Mileages by County," (Little Rock: Arkansas Highway and Transportation Department, 1999).

26. Winn and Giacopassi, "Terminating Prohibition."

27. Dull and Giacopassi, "Dry, Damp, Wet."

28. Grossman, "Wet vs. Dry Counties."

CHAPTER 20

1. "State Awarded for Welfare-to-Work Success," *Arkansas Democrat-Gazette,* November 3, 2001, 4B; "Welfare-to-Work Efforts Earn $2.8 Million Bonus," *Arkansas Democrat-Gazette,* September 24, 2003, 19.

2. Wendell Primus, "What Next for Welfare Reform?" *The Brookings Review* 19 (2001): 16–19.

3. "Coalition's Practices Scrutinized," *Arkansas Democrat-Gazette,* March 24, 2000, 10B; "Panel Attaches Strings to Funds for Coalitions," *Arkansas Democrat-Gazette,* March 30, 2000, 9B; and "Welfare Coalition Back in Business after Shutdown," *Arkansas Democrat-Gazette,* June 15, 2001: 1B.

4. "State Awarded."

5. Marcia K. Meyers, Norma M. Riccucci, and Irene Lurie. "Achieving Goal Congruence in Complex Environments: The Case of Welfare Reform," *Journal of Public Administration Research and Theory* 11 (2001): 165–201.

6. Stephen E. Condrey, Rex L. Facer, II, and Jack A. Hamilton. "Motivational Climate and Organizational Change: Exploring the Administrative Effects of Welfare Reform." Presented at the Southeastern Conference on Public Administration, Baton Rouge, LA, October 10–13, 2001; Dennis M. Daley, and Michael L. Vasu. "Administrative Capacity and Welfare Reform in North Carolina: Does Administration Matter?" Presented at the Southeastern Conference on Public Administration, Baton Rouge, LA, October 10–13, 2001; Denise Keller and John C. Morris. "Welfare Reform, Mississippi Style: Temporary Assistance for Needy Families and the Search for Accountability," *Public Administration Review* 62 (2002): 92–103; and Meyers, et al., "Achieving Goal Congruence.".

7. Keller and Morris, "Welfare Reform, Mississippi Style."

8. Keller and Morris, "Welfare Reform, Mississippi Style."

9. Keller and Morris, "Welfare Reform, Mississippi Style."

10. Case Management Society of America. *Standards of Practice for Case Management* (Little Rock, AR: CMSA, 2002).

11. *Standards of Practice for Case Management.*

12. Vicki Lens and Daniel Pollack, "Welfare Reform: Back to the Future!" *Administration in Social Work* 23 (2002): 64.

13. Norma M. Riccucci, Marcia K. Meyers, Irene Lurie, and Jun Seop Han, "The Implementation of Welfare Reform Policy: The Role of Public Managers in Front-Line Practices," *Public Administration Review* 64 (2004): 439.

14. Mary Jo Bane and David T. Ellwood, *Welfare Realities: From Rhetoric to Reform* (Cambridge, MA: Harvard University Press, 2004).

15. Thad E. Hall and Laurence J. O'Toole, Jr., "Structures for Policy Implementation: An Analysis of National Legislation," *Administration and Society* 31 (2000): 668.

16. Keller and Morris, "Welfare Reform, Mississippi Style"; and Condrey, et al., "Motivational Climate."

17. Condrey, et al., "Motivational Climate."

18. See for example Richard P. Nathan and Thomas L. Gais, "Early Findings about the Newest New Federalism for Welfare," *Publius* 28 (1998): 95–103; and Jack Tweedie, "From D.C. to Little Rock: Welfare Reform at Mid-Term," *Publius* 30 (Winter 2000): 69–97.

19. Lens and Pollack, "Welfare Reform: Back to the Future!"

20. Meyers, Riccucci, and Lurie, "Achieving Goal Congruence."

21. Keller and Morris, "Welfare Reform, Mississippi Style."

22. Meyers, Riccucci, and Lurie, "Achieving Goal Congruence."

23. Pamela Loprest and Douglas Wissoker, *Employment and Welfare Reform in the National Survey of America's Families* (Washington, D.C.: The Urban Institute, 2002); David Nather, "Welfare Overhaul's Next Wave," *CQ Weekly*, March 17, 2001, 585–90; Tweedie, "From D.C. to Little Rock"; and "Welfare Reform II: A Congress Detached from Reality," *Minneapolis Star Tribune,* September 13, 2003, 24A.

24. Jo Ann J. Ewalt and Edward T. Jennings., Jr., "Administration, Governance, and Policy Tools in Welfare Policy Implementation," *Public Administration Review* 64 (2004): 458.

25. Ewalt and Jennings, "Administration, Governance, and Policy Tools in Welfare Policy Implementation."

26. Evelyn Z. Brodkin, "Inside the Welfare Contract: Discretion and Accountability in State Welfare Administration," *Social Service Review* 71 (March 1997): 1–33;Irene Lurie, and Norma M. Riccucci, "Changing the 'Culture' of Welfare Offices: From Vision to the Front Lines," *Administration and Society* 34 (2003): 653–77.

27. Meyers, Riccucci, and Lurie, "Achieving Goal Congruence."

28. Government Printing Office. *Federal Register* 65 (2000): 7555–7, accessed on May 22, 2007, available online at http:// www.access.gpo.gov/su_docs/fedreg/frcont00.html

29. Barbara Ehrenreich, *Nickel and Dimed: On (Not) Getting By in America* (New York: Henry Holt and Company, 2001).

30. Meyers, Riccucci, and Lurie, "Achieving Goal Congruence."

31. Keller and Morris, "Welfare Reform, Mississippi Style."

32. Robin H. Rogers-Dillon and John David Skrentny, "Administering Success: The Legitimacy Imperative and the Implementation of Welfare Reform," *Social Problems* 46 (1999): 23.

CHAPTER 21

1. *Lake View School District No. 25 v. Tucker*, 92–5318 (Pulaski County Chancery Court Ark. 1994).

2. *Lake View School District No. 25 v. Huckabee*, 2001 92–5318 (Pulaski County Chancery Court Ark. 2001).

3. *Lake View School District No. 25 v. Huckabee*, 91 S.W.3d 472 (Ark. 2002).

4. *Rose v. Council for Better Education, Inc.*, 790 S.W.2d 186 (Ky. 1989).

5. Governor Mike Huckabee, State of the State Address, January 14, 2003, available online at http://www.arkansas.gov/governor/media/releases/press/011403–1. html, retrieved January 9, 2007.

6. Special Masters' Report to the Supreme Court of Arkansas, *Lake View School District No. 25 v. Huckabee*, ___ S.W.3d (Ark. filed Oct 3 2005).

7. *Lake View School District No. 25 v. Huckabee*, S.W.3d (Ark. Dec. 15, 2005).

8. K. Kopotic, S. McKenzie, and G. Ritter, "Comprehensive Analysis of Arkansas Teacher Salaries: State, Region and District," *Office for Education Policy*, 14, no. 1 (2017). Available online at http://www.officeforeducationpolicy.org/downloads/2017/11/teacher_salary_equity_11_30.pdf. retrieved February 2, 2019.

9. I. Morgan, and A. Amerikaner, "Funding Gaps: An Analysis of School Funding Equity Across the US and within Each State," 2018, available at https://edtrust.org/resource/funding-gaps-2018/, retrieved February 2, 2019.

10. Arkansas Comprehensive Testing, Assessment and Accountability Program (ACTAAP) (1999) Ark. Code Ann. § 6–15–401–through 407, 6–15–419 through 422, and 6–15–1003.

11. No Child Left Behind Act of 2001, P.L. 107–110, 20 U.S.C. § 6319 (2002).

12. National Governors Association Center for Best Practices, Council of Chief State School Officers, *Common Core State Standards,* National Governors Association Center for Best Practices, Council of Chief State School Officers, Washington D.C., 2010, retrieved from http://www.corestandards.org/standards-in-your-state/.

13. Andrew Ujifusa, "Arkansas Poised to Drop PARCC's Common-Core Test in Favor of ACT," *Education Week*, June 8, 2015, retrieved from http://blogs.edweek.org/edweek/state_edwatch/2015/06/arkansas_poised_to_drop_parccs_common-core_test_in_favor_of_act.html, retrieved February 2, 2019.

14. Every Student Succeeds Act Arkansas State Plan, September 2017, retrieved from http://www.arkansased.gov/public/userfiles/ESEA/Arkansas_ESSA_Plan_Final_rv_January_30_2018.pdf, retrieved February 2, 2019.

15. Act 696. A.C.A. § 6–15–2101 et. seq.

16. Act 102 of the Second Extraordinary Session of 2003

17. Digital Learning Act of 2013, A.C.A § 6–16–1401 through 1406.

18. Act 187 (2015) A.C.A § 6–16–146

19. E. Swanson, S. McKenzie, and G. Ritter, "Integration in Little Rock, Part 1: Patterns in Enrollment and Characteristics of Student Movers," *Arkansas Education Reports* 13, no. 2 (2016), available online at http://www.officeforeducationpolicy.org/integration-in-little-rock-part-1-patterns-of-enrollment-and-characteristics-of-student-movers/,retrieved February 2, 2019.

20. Achieve, Inc., *Closing the Expectations Gap, 2006,* report released February, 2006, available online at http://www.achieve.org/files/50-statepub-06.pdf,retrieved January 8, 2007.

21. L. Foreman, S. McKenzie, and G. Ritter, "Arkansas Teacher Supply," *Arkansas Education Reports* 16, no. 1 (2018), available online at http://www.officeforeducationpolicy.org/downloads/2018/08/16–1-teacher-supply.pdf, retrieved February 2, 2019.

22. Office for Education Policy, "National Board Certified Teacher Incentive Bonuses: Senate Bill 555," *Office for Education Policy* 14, no. 3 (2017), available online at http://www.officeforeducationpolicy.org/downloads/2017/03/nbct.pdf, retrieved February 2, 2019.

CONTRIBUTORS

JAY BARTH is Distinguished Professor of Politics and Director of Civic Engagement Projects at Hendrix College. He is the co-author (with the late Diane D. Blair) of *Arkansas Politics and Government: Do the People Rule?* (University of Nebraska Press, 2005). His articles have appeared in such journals as *American Politics Research, Political Research Quarterly, Political Psychology, Political Behavior, Women and Politics,* and *State Politics and Policy Quarterly.*

J. R. BAXTER earned a Bachelor of Arts in Political Science as well as a law degree from the School of Law at the University of Arkansas, Fayetteville. He is a practicing attorney.

DIANE D. BLAIR studied and taught political science at the University of Arkansas for more than 30 years. She authored *Arkansas Politics and Government: Do the People Rule* (now in a second edition with Jay Barth) and edited *Silent Hattie Speaks: The Personal Journal of Senator Hattie Caraway*, in addition to authoring and co-authoring dozens of other scholarly works, mainly on the subjects of Arkansas politics and women in politics.

LARRY BRADY is the Research and Court Services Director for the Arkansas Administrative Office of the Courts. He earned a B.A. at the University of Arkansas in 1977 and his law degree from Washington University in 1980. Prior to his service at the AOC he was in private practice in Little Rock.

JEREMY BREWER holds a B.A. in criminology and an M.A. in political science from Arkansas State University. He is currently a security specialist for Honeywell Federal Manufacturing & Technologies, which manages and operates the Kansas City National Security Campus for the US Department of Energy.

GRAEME COPE is an independent scholar living in Melbourne, Australia. Upon his retirement from the faculty at Deakin University, he turned his attention to in-depth examination of the desegregation of Little Rock's public schools. His work has appeared in the *Encyclopedia of Arkansas History & Culture* and in the *Arkansas Historical Quarterly.*

JOHN C. DAVIS is Assistant Professor of Political Science and Director of University Relations at the University of Arkansas at Monticello. His research interests include political parties, legislative behavior, public policy, and state politics. He holds a B.A. and M.A. from the University of Arkansas and a Ph.D. from the University of Missouri.

ART ENGLISH is Professor Emeritus of Political Science at the University of Arkansas at Little Rock. His research has appeared in *Polity, Legislative Studies Quarterly, The American Review of Politics, The MidSouth Journal of Political Science, The Arkansas Political Science Journal, State Legislatures, The National Civic Review,* and *Spectrum.*

J. D. GINGERICH is the Director of the National Judicial Opioid Task Force with the Conference of Chief Justices. Previously, he served as the Director of the Arkansas Administrative Office of the Courts. He received his undergraduate degree from the University of Central Arkansas, his law degree from the University of Arkansas, and a post-graduate degree in international law from the University of Bristol in England. Prior to the AOC he served as chief legal counsel and professor of political science at UCA.

DAVID R. HARDING, JR. is Associate Professor of Political Science in the Department of Political Science at Arkansas State University. His research interests include public policy, public administration, and applied policy/program evaluation. His work has appeared in the *American Review of Public Administration, Public Administration & Management,* and *Politics & Policy,* among others. He has conducted numerous public opinion surveys and program evaluations for a variety of funded projects.

KIM U. HOFFMAN is Associate Professor of Public Administration and Director of Public Administration in the Department of Political Science at the University of Central Arkansas. Her research interests include state and local government budget processes, key budget actors, state and local government revenue systems, and women in bureaucracy. Her work has appeared in *The American Review of Public Administration, Journal of Public Budgeting, Accounting, and Financial Management, State and Local Government Review,* and *Women and Politics,* among others.

JOHN A. KIRK is Distinguished Professor of History and Director of Anderson Institute on Race and Ethnicity at the University of Arkansas at Little Rock. His research focuses on the history of the civil rights movement. In addition to the award-winning *Redefining the Color Line: Black Activism in Little Rock, Arkansas, 1940–1970,* Kirk's publications include *Martin Luther King, Jr.,* Beyond *Little Rock: The Origins and Legacies of the Central High Crisis, Race and Ethnicity in Arkansas: New Perspectives,* and articles in wide variety of outlets.

CAL LEDBETTER was Professor Emeritus (political science) at the University of Arkansas at Little Rock. He served five terms in the Arkansas House of Representatives and was a delegate and a vice-president of the Arkansas Constitutional Convention of 1979–80. His research focused on Arkansas governors and Arkansas constitutions, and he authored articles for the *Arkansas Historical Quarterly*, the *Arkansas Law Review*, *Social Science Journal*, *Arkansas Political Science Journal*, and the *National Civic Review*, as well as a biography of Arkansas Governor George Donaghey: *The Carpenter from Conway*.

SARAH C. MCKENZIE is Executive Director of the Office for Education Policy at the University of Arkansas. She holds a Ph.D. in educational statistics and research methods and an M.A. in early childhood education, and worked previously as Director of Assessment, Research and Accountability for Fayetteville, Arkansas school district.

WILLIAM H. MILLER is Emeritus Professor (public administration) and former director of the DPA program at the University of Illinois at Springfield. His research has focused on political and economic minorities and public policy analysis and has been published in *Public Administration Review, American Review of Public Administration, Public Administration Quarterly, State and Local Government Review, Urban Affairs Review,* and elsewhere.

MARK NABORS earned a master's in public administration and nonprofit studies and a bachelor of arts degree in political science and French from the University of Arkansas, Fayetteville. He completed a master of divinity program at the School of Theology at the University of the South in Sewanee, Tennessee in 2019.

JANINE A. PARRY is professor of political science and director of the Arkansas Poll at the University of Arkansas. Her research on state politics, elections and participation, and gender and politics has appeared in *Political Behavior, State Politics and Policy Quarterly, Social Science Quarterly,* the *Arkansas Historical Quarterly* and other outlets. She also is the coauthor, with Dorothy McBride, of *Women's Rights in the U.S.A.*

PATSY HAWTHORN RAMSEY holds an Ed.D. in higher education curriculum from the University of Arkansas at Little Rock. She served as an instructor in the University of Central Arkansas's department of history, coordinating the social studies education program as well as National History Day in Arkansas. She is retired.

JIM RANCHINO studied and taught political science at Ouachita Baptist University. In addition to his teaching, scholarship and service duties at OBU, he operated a polling and political research firm and served as a regular commentator on Arkansas politics for local, state, and national media.

ROY REED was Professor of Journalism at the University of Arkansas. He also was a reporter at the *Arkansas Gazette* during the Faubus years. He spent most of his newspaper career as a national and foreign correspondent for the *New York Times*. Among his books is *Faubus: The Life and Times of an American Prodigal*.

CATHERINE C. REESE is Professor of Public Administration and Master of Public Administration (MPA) Director in the Department of Political Science at Arkansas State University. Her work has appeared in the *Review of Public Personnel Administration, Public Budgeting & Finance, Public Administration Review,* and *Politics & Policy,* among others. Her research interests include state-level public policy, gender pay equity, state tobacco settlement spending, state budgeting, public human resource administration, and state government finance.

GARY W. RITTTER currently serves as Dean of Education at St. Louis University. Prior to that, he served as the 21st Century Chair in Education Policy in the Department of Education Reform at the University of Arkansas where he directed the Office for Education Policy. His articles on issues such as teacher pay, school accountability, school finance, and racial integration in schools have appeared in *Education Finance and Policy*, the *Review of Educational Research, Education Next*, the *Georgetown Public Policy Review*, the *Journal of Research in Education, Education Week* and elsewhere.

LINDSLEY ARMSTRONG SMITH earned a J.D. from the University of Arkansas, clerked for the Arkansas Court of Appeals and the Eighth Circuit Court of Appeals, and served as Research Assistant Professor of Communication at the UA until retirement. She also was a member of the Arkansas House of Representatives, 2005–2010, and was lead sponsor of the resolutions to ratify the Equal Rights Amendment in 2005, 2007, and 2009 and remains active in the ratification effort.

STEPHEN A. SMITH holds a Ph.D. from Northwestern University and is Emeritus Professor of Communication at the University of Arkansas. As a member of the Arkansas House of Representatives, 1971–1974, he co-sponsored the resolution to ratify the Equal Rights Amendment in 1973, and as a delegate to the Arkansas Constitutional Convention of 1979–1980, he authored language to include "gender" in the equal protection clause of the proposed constitution.

PATRICK A. STEWART is Associate Professor in the Department of Political Science at the University of Arkansas. In addition to his book *Debatable Humor: Laughing Matters on the 2008 Presidential Primary Campaign* (2012), his scholarship has appeared in *Political Psychology, Motivation and Emotion, PS—Political Science & Politics, Presidential Studies Quarterly,* and *Politics and the Life Sciences,* among others.

BROCK THOMPSON holds a doctorate in American studies from Kings College, University of London, in addition to degrees from Hendrix College and the University of Arkansas. His publications examine southern gay and lesbian history, identity politics, and queer theory, and include *The Un-Natural State: Arkansas and the Queer South.* He has served as congressional liaison to the Congressional Research Services of the Library of Congress for the past decade.

CATHY KUNZINGER URWIN is the author of *Agenda for Reform: Winthrop Rockefeller as Governor of Arkansas 1967–1971.* She holds a Ph.D. from the University of Notre Dame and is a former member of the Board of Trustees of the Arkansas Historical Association. She has written most recently for *America in World War II* magazine.

JEANNIE M. WHAYNE is University Professor of History at the University of Arkansas. In addition to numerous articles and essays, she has authored, co-authored, or edited ten books, including *A New Plantation South: Land, Labor, and Federal Favor in Twentieth Century Arkansas* (winner of the Arkansiana Award for best book published in 1996); *Shadows over Sunnyside: An Arkansas Plantation in Transition, 1830–1945;* and *Arkansas Delta: A Land of Paradox,* (winner of the Virginia Ledbetter Prize in Arkansas History).

INDEX